The **Rough Guide** to

The Dodecanese
and the east Aegean islands

written and researched by

Marc Dubin

NEW YORK • LONDON • DELHI

www.roughguides.com

Contents

İstanbul

Kavála

Thássos

Thássos

Alexandhroúpoli

Thessaloníki

Samothráki

Bandırma

Límnos

Gökçeada
(Imbros)

Mýrina

Moúdhros

Vólos

Skiáthos

Ávios
Efstrátios

Alónnisos

Sígri

Ayvalık

Sképelos

Mytilini

Dikili

Skýros

Lésvos

Kými

Psará

Halkídha

Évvia

Hios Town

İzmir

Rafina

Híos

Çeşme

Pireás

Ándhros

Athens

Karlóvassi

Vathý

Kuşadası

Kéa

Tínos

Ikaría

Pythagório

Ermoúpolis

Mýkonos

Foúrni

Sámos
Arkí

Kýthnos

Sýros

Pátmos

Agathoníssi

Sérifos

Páros

Léros

Lipsí

Sífnos

Náxos

Kálymnos

Milos

Síkinos

Amorgós

Kós
Town

Marmaris

S.

Ios

Astypálea

Datça

Folégandhros

Kós

Níssyros

Sými

Anáfi

Tílos

Ródhos
Town

Kýthira

Thíra
(Santorini)

Hálki

Andikýthira

Rhodes

Kárpathos

Dhiafáni

Haniá

Iráklio

Pigádhia

Réthymno

Sitía

Kássos

Áyios
Nikólaos

Crete
(Kríti)

Metres	
1500	
1000	
500	
200	
100	
0	

N

0   100 km

Introduction to the

Dodecanese

and the east Aegean islands

**The Dodecanese archipelago forms the remotest territory
of modern Greece, up to 250 nautical miles from Athens.
All of it is closer to Turkey than the Greek mainland, a fact
not lost on either country; indeed these scattered islands
have only been part of Greece since 1948, representing
the last successful phase of the *Megáli Idhéa*, a century-
long campaign to reclaim historically Greek territories.
Greek nationalists began referring to the islands as the
Dhodhekánisos (Twelve Islands) after 1908, though in fact
there are fourteen major and four minor inhabited isles in
this group, plus nine more, large and small, which make up
the more northerly east Aegean islands, part of Greece since
1912. Numerous military bases and smaller watch-points still
counter the threat (real or imagined) of invasion from Turkey.
Despite high-level civilian rapprochements which have taken
place between Greece and Turkey since 1999, the Greek
armed forces clearly prefer to keep their powder dry.**

These stepping stones en route to the Middle
East or Anatolia have always been fated for **invasion and occupation**: too rich and strategic to
be ignored, but never powerful enough to rule
themselves. Romans, Byzantines, crusading Knights of St John, Genoese,

5

■

Fact file

• Greece is, after Cyprus, the easternmost member of the EU, with a **surface area** of 131,957 square kilometres (50,949 square miles) divided into 51 provinces. No other country, with the obvious exceptions of Indonesia and the Philippines, has so many islands, though they form only about 10 percent of Greece's total territory. The **population** is overwhelmingly **Greek-speaking** and 96 percent are **Greek Orthodox** in religious affiliation; there are notice-able Catholic, Armenian, Sunni Muslim, Jewish and evangeli-cal Christian minorities, plus (mostly on the mainland) pock-ets of Turkish-, Romany- and Macedonian-speakers. Around 370,000 people live in the Dodecanese and east Aegean, nearly half of these in towns of over 5000 people.

• Per "native" total popula-tion of roughly 10.4 million, Greece has the highest propor-tion of immigrants in Europe – estimated at 800,000 to 1.2 million, two-thirds of these Albanian.

• Since 1974 Greece has been a **parliamentary republic**, with the president as head of state, and a 300-seat, single-cham-ber parliament led by a prime minister. PASOK, the (approxi-mately) social-democratic ruling party, governed for 19 of the 23 years since 1981, finally being bested in March 2004 by the centre-right Néa Dhimokratía party. There are also two small communist

Venetians, Ottomans and Italians have for varying periods controlled these islands since the time of Alexander the Great. Whatever the rigours of these occupations, their legacy includes a wonderful blend of architectural styles and cultures: frescoed Byzantine churches and fortified monasteries, castles of the Genoese and Knights of St John, Ottoman mosques and gran-diose Italian Rationalist, Art Deco and mock-oriental buildings. Such **monuments** are often juxtaposed with (or even rest upon) ancient Greek cities and temples that pro-vide the foundation for claims of an enduring Hellenic identity through the centuries; **museums**, particu-larly on Sámos, Rhodes and Límnos, amply document the archeological evidence.

But it was **medieval** Greek peas-ants, fishermen and shepherds, working without an indigenous

The watermill, Ayía Marína, Léros

> **The Dodecanese and east Aegean conform remarkably well to their poster image of purple-shadowed islands and promontories, floating on a cobalt-and-rose horizon.**

ruling class or formal Renaissance to impose models of taste or patronize the arts, who most tangibly contributed to our idea of **Greekness** with their songs and dances, costumes, weaving and vernacular architecture, some unconsciously drawing on ancient antecedents. Much of this has vanished in recent decades under an avalanche of *bouzoúki*-instrumental cassettes, "genuine museum copies" and bawdy postcards at souvenir stalls, but enough remains for visitors to marvel at its combination of form and function. Indeed, only on two islands in this guide – Rhodes and Kós – has local character been largely determined by tourism, and even in these places pockets of traditional life persist.

Most visitors come primarily for hedonistic rather than cultural pursuits: going lightly dressed even on a scooter, swimming in balmy waters at dusk, talking and drinking under the stars until 3am. Such pleasures amply compensate for certain enduring weaknesses in the Greek **tourism** "**product**": don't expect orthopedic mattresses, state-of-the-art plumbing, Cordon Bleu cuisine or obsequious service. Except at a limited number of upmarket facilities, rooms can be box-like, and food at its best is fresh and simply presented.

parties which typically pick up 8–10% of the vote.

• **Tourism** is the country's main foreign-currency earner, with over 10 million visitors from overseas in a good year – but lately more like 5 million. **Shipping**, though also in crisis, is the second-largest enterprise, more or less tied with **agricultural exports**, especially olive oil and olives, citrus, raisins and wine. **Mineral extraction** – in particular, chromium and bauxite – was formerly important but is now in decline, except for marble-quarrying and **cement production**, for which Greece is Europe's largest source. Locally manufactured clothing and household items are aimed at the domestic market, though exports to central Europe are increasing.

• In November 2000, Greece became the first country to have more mobile phones than fixed phones (roughly 6.5 million of the former).

• 97.6 percent of all Greek homes now have a colour television.

• Greeks have dropped from first to fourth worldwide in frequency of sex (Americans are now first), though they are still in second place for the number of sexual partners (behind the French).

• The Greeks are the fattest people in Europe, with 22 percent classed as "overweight" and 15 percent as "clinically obese".

• Inflation dropped from 19.8 percent in the early 1980s to 2.7 percent in 2001, though it's up again slightly since the introduction of the euro.

Yet what impresses most is how, despite the strenuous efforts of developers, arsonists and rubbish-dumpers, the Aegean **environment** has not been utterly destroyed. Seen at the right time of day or year, the Dodecanese and east Aegean conform remarkably well to their poster image of purple-shadowed islands and promontories, floating on a cobalt-and-rose horizon. Island beaches vary from discreet crescents framed by tree-fringed cliffs to deserted, mile-long gifts deposited by small streams and backed by wild dunes, ideal for enacting Crusoe fantasies. But inland there is always civilization, whether tiny cubist villages of the remoter outposts, or burgeoning resorts as cosmopolitan – and brazen – as any in the Mediterranean.

If you're used to the murky waters of the open Mediterranean elsewhere, the **Aegean** will come as a revelation, with forty-foot visibility the norm, and all manner of sea creatures visible, from starfish and octopuses on the bottom to vast schools of fish. The sea here is also a **watersports** paradise: the joys of snorkelling and kayaking are on offer to novices, and some of the best windsurfing areas in the world beckon. Yacht charter, whether bare-boat or skippered, is big business, particularly out of Rhodes and Kálymnos; only the Caribbean can rival the Dodecanese for interest. And

Wayside shrines

Throughout Greece you'll see, by the side of the road, small shrines or *proskynitária* designed to hold a saint's icon, an oil lamp, a few floatable wicks, a box of matches and not much else. Unlike in Latin America, they don't necessarily mark the spot where someone met their end in a motoring accident (though occasionally they do); typically they were erected by one family or even one individual in fulfilment of a vow or *támma* to a particular saint to reciprocate for any favours granted. *Proskynitária* come in various sizes and designs, from spindly, derrick-
like metal constructions to sumptuous, gaily painted models of small cathedrals in marble and plaster which you can practically walk into. Often they indicate the presence of a larger but less convenient (and often locked) church off in the countryside nearby, dedicated to the same saint, and act as a substitute shrine where the devout wayfarer can revere the icon it contains. *Proskynitária* are usually well maintained with fresh supplies of oil – except for the forlorn, abandoned ones on footpaths which are no longer trodden since a new, parallel road was built.

when the sea is too cold or the weather too blustery, many islands offer superb **hiking** on surviving donkey-trails between hill villages, or up the highest summits.

The islanders

To attempt an understanding of the **islanders**, it's useful to realize how recent and traumatic were the events that created the modern Greek state. The east Aegean and the Dodecanese islands remained in **Ottoman or Italian** hands until the early (or even mid-) 1900s; meanwhile, many people from these "unredeemed" territories lived in Asia Minor, Egypt, western Europe, mainland Greece or the northern Balkans. The Balkan Wars of 1912–13, Greece's 1917–18 involvement in World War I, the Greco-Turkish war of 1919–22 and the organized **population exchanges** – essentially regulated ethnic cleansing – which followed each of these conflicts had profound effects. Orthodox refugees from Turkey suddenly made up a noticeable proportion of the east Aegean's inhabitants, and with the forced or voluntary departure of their Levantine merchant class, Muslims and (during World War II) Jews, both these islands and the

9

Boatyards

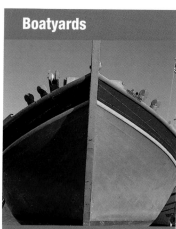

Even in the more touristed island-coastal resorts, a remarkable number of traditional boatyards (*karnáyia*) still survive. As long as there are commissions for wooden fishing boats and tourist *kaïkia*, they will probably continue to do so, though much of the order book these days consists of repairs to existing craft. Small craft are built in the time-honoured way, with the keel and framework assembled first from seasoned pine – which abounds in Greek coastal regions – and then overlaid with planking. You can often spot *karnáyia* from some distance by the bright orange *mínio* or red-lead paint applied to the exposed wood – long illegal in most of the EU but still the preservative of choice in Greece. Equipment can be low-tech, with wooden trellising and launching rollers the rule; serious accidents caused by hulls lurching the wrong way at the wrong time are not unheard of.

Dodecanese lost their multicultural traits. Before the last world war, the Italian occupation of the Dodecanese was characterized by progressively stricter suppression of Greek Orthodox identity, though in general the 1940s hereabouts were not quite so dire as on the mainland.

After World War II, benign neglect was about the best most islands could expect until the late 1960s. Given the chance to **emigrate** to Australia, North America or Africa, many islanders did so, continuing a **depopulation** which ironically had begun as soon as the various archipelagos had been united with the "motherland". This trend was only reversed in the 1970s, as worldwide recession and the advent of retirement age for the original migrants spurred a return home. There are still a few islanders who were born Ottoman subjects before 1912, educated in Italian between 1920 and 1926, lived through fierce battles in 1943 and 1944, left for Australia, Africa or Canada after 1948, and who have returned as pensioners to live out their days in a modern Greek state that's part of the unified EU. Get talking to any of them and you'll have a first-hand idea of how the twentieth century affected the Dodecanese and east Aegean.

The dawn of **mass tourism** in the 1960s arguably saved some islands from complete desolation, though local attitudes towards this deliverance have proven decidedly ambivalent. It galled local pride to become a class of seasonal service personnel (nowadays they are increasingly eastern European), and the encounter between outsiders and villagers has often been **corrosive** to a deeply conservative, rural society. Though younger Greeks have adapted happily at the cash-tills of various resorts, visitors still need to be sensitive in their behaviour. The mind boggles imagining the reaction of black-clad elders to nude bathing, or even scanty apparel, in a country where – despite being increasingly out of step with majority sentiment – the Orthodox Church remains an all-but-established religion and self-appointed guardian of national identity. In the presence of Italian coffee bars, Internet cafés and street-corner ATMs, it's easy to believe that Greece at one stroke became thoroughly European when it joined the EU – until a flock of sheep is paraded along the main street at high noon, or the 1pm ferry shows up at 3pm, if at all.

Where to go

There is no such thing as a "typical" east Aegean or Dodecanese island; each has its distinctive personality, history, architecture, flora – and unique tourist clientele. **Landscapes** vary from lush groves of cypress, pine and olive, to volcanic crags, wind-tormented bare ridges, salt marshes or even year-round streams. Setting aside the scars from a few unfortunate man-made developments, it's difficult to single out an

Ouzeri Ermis, Mytilíni Town, Lésvos

▼ Easter procession, Kárpathos

irredeemably ugly island, and amongst possible destinations there is something for everyone.

The **east Aegean** islands alternate in character: harsh, masculine **Límnos**, **Híos** and **Ikaría**, with their dry climates and stark scenery, bracketing lusher, damper and greener **Sámos** and **Lésvos**, the most important of these islands in antiquity. The latter two are perhaps the best "all-rounders", especially for a two-week holiday, with Sámos offering excellent island-hopping connections if you've arrived on a flight-only arrangement. The **Dodecanese** also display marked topographic and economic contrasts. The dry limestone outcrops of **Kastellórizo**, **Hálki**, **Sými** and **Kálymnos** have always relied on the sea for their livelihoods, and the wealth generated by this maritime culture – especially in the nineteenth century – fostered the growth of their attractive port towns. The first three in particular appeal to a fairly upmarket clientele which values spirit of place over four-star beaches; Kálymnos' "annexe" islet of **Télendhos** offers a car-free alternative to the west-coast resort strip of its larger neighbour. The sprawling, relatively fertile giants **Rhodes** (Ródhos) and **Kós** have had their traditional agricultural economies almost totally displaced by a package-tourism industry attracted by good beaches and nightlife, as well as the most exciting ensembles of historical monuments in the Dodecanese – none better than Ródhos Old Town. **Kárpathos**, marooned between Rhodes and Crete, has some of the most scenic beaches and walking in the Dodecanese; **Tílos**, despite its relative lack of trees, has ample water and more fine beaches and hiking, though the green volcano-island of **Níssyros** is dry. **Léros** shelters softer contours and more amenable terrain than its jagged map outline would suggest, while **Pátmos**, the atmospheric island of Revelation, and **Astypálea** at the fringes of the archipelago, boast architecture and landscapes more appropriate to the Cyclades.

When to go

Most islands and their inhabitants are far more agreeable outside the **busiest period of early July to late August**, when crowds, soaring temperatures and the effects of the infamous *meltémi* detract considerably from enjoyment. The **meltémi** is a cool, fair-weather wind which originates in high-pressure systems over the far north Aegean, gathering momentum as it travels southwards and assuming near-gale magnitude between Híos and Sámos; the lee of the latter (and of the Anatolian landmass) partly shelters the northern Dodecanese, but generally north-facing coasts (especially at Rhodes) bear the full brunt of its howling, which often results in cancelled sea transport.

You won't miss out on warm weather if you come **between late May and mid-June**, or in **September**, when the **sea is warmest** for swimming. During **October** you will likely hit a week's stormy spell, but for most of that month *kalokeráki* or "the little summer of Áyios Dhimítrios", the Greek equivalent of Indian summer, prevails. While autumn choice in nightlife or food can be limited – Greece still eats by season, importing relatively little produce – the light is softer, and going out at midday becomes a pleasure rather than an ordeal. The first migratory **fish** from the Dardanelles also arrive in October, with various species caught until May. As a rule, the further south you go, the longer the tourist season: Lésvos and Sámos, for instance, pretty much shut down by early October, even though their last charters leave at the end of the month, while Rhodes and its closely neighbouring islets see trade well into **November**, when swimming at noon is not unheard of. If you're a fish enthusiast, you

> There is no such thing as a "typical" east Aegean or Dodecanese island; each has its distinctive personality, history, architecture, flora...

The Evil Eye

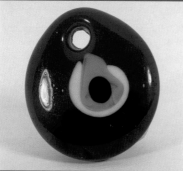

Belief in the Evil Eye (*tó máti*) is pan-Mediterranean and goes at least as far back as Roman times, but nowhere has it hung on so tenaciously as in Greece (and neighbouring coastal Turkey). In a nutshell, whenever something attractive, valuable or unusual – an infant, a new car, a prized animal – becomes suddenly, inexplicably indisposed, it is assumed to be *matisméno* or "eyed". Blue-eyed individuals are thought most capable of casting this spell, always unintentionally or at least unconsciously (unlike *máyia* or wilful black magic). The diagnosis is confirmed by discreet referral to a "wise woman", who is also versed in the proper counter-spell. But prevention is always better than cure, and this involves two main strategies. When admiring something or someone, the admirer – blue-eyed or otherwise – must mock-spit ("*phtoo, phtoo, phtoo!*") to counteract any stirrings of envy which, according to anthropologists, are the root cause of the Eye. And the proud owners or parents will protect the object of admiration in advance with a blue amulet, hung about the baby's/animal's neck or the car's rear-view mirror, or even painted directly onto a boat-bow.

can take advantage of the main netting season while on a winter break in Rhodes.

December to March are the **coldest** and least comfortable months, though glorious **wild flowers** begin to bloom very early: January in the Dodecanese, February in the east Aegean for the same species. The more northerly islands endure the coldest and wettest conditions, with the higher peaks of Sámos, Ikaría, Híos and Lésvos wearing a brief mantle of **snow** around the turn of the year.

As **springtime** proceeds, you simply shift focus further north, remembering that a distance of forty nautical miles may mean the difference between open or still-shut tourist facilities as well as blossoms gone or in bloom. **April** weather is notoriously unreliable, though the air is crystal-clear, the landscape green and colours brilliant – a photographer's dream. **May** is more settled, with an added bonus of the last winter fish and a cornucopia of **spring vegetables**; the south Dodecanesian **sea warms up** comfortably again by mid-May, though around the more northerly islands the water is too cool for prolonged dips. Late May, especially half-term week in the UK, is often very busy; most tourist-related businesses are now properly open, with sea going transport schedules at about eighty percent of peak-season frequencies.

Other factors affecting the timing of a visit have to do with the level of tourism and the related **amenities** provided. Standards, particularly in tavernas, invariably slip under peak-season pressures; the food can be the dreariest representation of Greek cuisine possible – a monotonous sequence of tomato salads, pre-cut Belgian chips and frozen North Sea or California squid, with no fish to speak of. Room rates are at their highest from July to September, and rental cars and bikes booked days ahead. If you can only visit during midsummer, reserve a package well in advance, or plan an oddball itinerary taking in islands with sparse sea going connections or no airport. Between November and April, you have to contend with pared-back ferry schedules (and almost nonexistent hydrofoil or catamaran departures), plus skeletal facilities when you arrive, except on Rhodes, which has significant "winter sun" tourism. You will, however, find fairly adequate services to the most populated islands, and at least one hotel and taverna open in their main town.

Average daily temperatures (°C) and rainfall (cm)

	Jan	Mar	May	July	Sept	Nov
Rhodes						
Av Temp °C	12	14	19	26	26	19
Rainfall cm	14	10	2	0	1	12
Kós						
Av Temp °C	11	13	19	25	23	16
Rainfall cm	17	11	2	0	1	12
Lésvos						
Av Temp °C	9	12	20	26	24	14
Rainfall cm	12	8	3	1	1	11

28

things not to miss

It's not possible to see everything that the Dodecanese and east Aegean islands have to offer in one trip – and we don't suggest you try. What follows is a selective taste of the the region's highlights: outstanding beaches and ancient sites, natural wonders and unique villages. They're arranged in five colour-coded categories, which you can browse through to find the very best things to see and experience. All highlights have a page reference to take you straight into the guide, where you can find out more.

01 Télendhos straits Page **255** • The view across the staits between Massoúri or Myrtiés and the car-free islet of Télendhos is among the most stunning in the Dodecanese.

02 Rhodes, Byzantine frescoes Page
152 • Along with those of nearby Thárri monastery, the late Byzantine frescoes of Kímisis Theotókou church in Asklipió village are the finest in the entire Dodecanese.

| ACTIVITIES | CONSUME | EVENTS | NATURE | SIGHTS |

04 Windsurfing on Rhodes and Kárpathos Page 90 •
A combination of steady winds and ideal topography make these capes a mecca for windsurfers of all abilities

03 Astypálea, Hóra Page
239 • Lovingly preserved houses in this protected settlement sport both Neoclassical iron balconies and the traditional wooden *poúndia*.

05 Híos mastic villages Page 379 •
Strings of sun-drying tomatoes are a common sight during autumn in these architecturally unique villages; shown is Pyrgí.

17

07 Sými's back country Page **210** • The frescoed chapel of Áyios Vassílios, overlooking Lápathos bay, is just one of many possible destinations for walkers on forested Sými.

06 Hokhláki mosaics Page **189** • The art of *hokhláki* or pebble-mosaic work reaches its zenith in the Dodecanese, particularly in the courtyard of Áyios Nikólaos church, Hálki.

08 Lésvos, Skála Eressoú Page **390** • The long, outstanding beach and resort village of Skála Eressoú in the southwest of the island, seen from Vígla hill.

09 **Kárpathos, Kyrá Panayiá beach** Page **173** • This is perhaps the best of many sand-and-pebble beaches hidden along the calmer east coast, reachable by boat, jeep or on foot.

10 **Rhodes, Lindos Acropolis** Page **140** • From the Hellenistic acropolis of Lindos, refortified by the Knights of St John, you look north along the length of Rhodes island.

13 Límnos, Kondiás
Page **435** • The third-largest settlement on Limnos has the typical basalt-built, tile-roof houses of both this volcanic island and neighbouring Lésvos.

11 Ródhos Old Town Page **111**
• The well-preserved medieval walls offer an excellent vantage point over Ródhos Old Town, deservedly a UNESCO Heritage Site; in the foreground is the Ottoman Süleymaniye mosque.

14 Sámos, north coast foothills Page **320** •
Terraced vineyards below Manolátes village present some of the loveliest scenery on the north slope of Sámos.

12 Kós, Brós Thermá thermal springs Page **223** • A soak in these shoreline hot springs is a popular outing, especially on moonlit autumn nights.

15 Kós, Khristós peak Page 228 •

A hike up 846-metre Khristós peak in Kós' Dhíkeos range rewards you with stunning panoramic views; shown is the summit chapel of Metamórfosis.

16 Pátmos, Ayíou Ioánnou Theológou monastery Page 279 •

This monastery in the hóra of Pátmos is an architectural showcase, as well as a bulwark of the Orthodox Church; shown is the courtyard arcade.

17 Lazy fishing ports Page 284 •

Despite recent development, the port of Lipsí remains a relaxing backwater where fishermen still tend their nets.

18 Ikaría, Armenistís Page 335 • Mesakhtí beach is arguably the best beach on Ikaría, with a strong surf guaranteeing action for those with boards.

20 Níssyros, Mandhráki Page 225 • The atmospheric port village of Mandhráki, seen here from its castle of the Knights, sees relatively few overnight visitors.

19 East Aegean islands, distinctive lodging Page 321 • The Aïdhonokastro complex in the village of Valeondadhes, Sámos, is typical of high-quality restoration accommodation on these islands.

21 Níssyros, the volcanic caldera zone Page 229 • No stay on the island would be complete without a visit to its dormant central volcano; shown is Stéfanos crater.

23 Knights' castles Page **267** • The castle above the villages of Pandélli and Plátanos on Léros is one of the best preserved of many erected by the Knights of St John between the thirteenth and sixteenth centuries.

22 Tílos, Ayíou Pandelímona monastery Page **221** • This fortified oasis-monastery in the far west of Tílos is the island's greatest sight – and start-point of some excellent walks.

24 Yachting, the Dodecanese Page **258** • The perfectly protected fjord of Vathýs, on the east coast of Kálymnos, is a popular haven for the many yachts that cruise these islands.

25 Léros, Italian Art Deco monuments

Page **264** • Built during the late 1920s as an Italian naval base, the port of Lakkí on Léros still retains marvellous Art Deco/Rationalist monuments of the era.

27 Kastellórizo harbour

Page **196** • The intimate port-town of Kastellórizo island, with the coastal mountains of Turkey in the background, basks in its reputation as the location for the film *Mediterraneo*.

26 Astypálea mosaics, Tallarás bath Page **244** • The

Byzantine mosaics of these baths at Análipsi are superb; shown here is Time personified.

28 Kárpathos, Ólymbos

village Page **174** • Windswept Ólymbos village in the far north of Kárpathos offers sweeping views along the island's rugged west coast.

Basics

Basics

Getting there

It's close on 2300 miles from the UK or Ireland to any of the Dodecanese or east Aegean islands, so for most north European visitors flying is the only viable option. There are seasonal direct flights to the largest of the islands from several major British airports; flying time is four to four-and-a-half hours, depending on your start point and island destination.

Only two carriers currently fly direct to Greece from North America; there isn't enough traffic on these New York–Athens routes to allow for very cheap fares, so most North Americans travel to a gateway European city, and pick up an onward connecting flight with an associated airline. You may discover that it's cheaper to arrange a final Greece-bound leg of the journey from the UK yourself, in which case your only criterion will be finding a suitable, good-value North America–London flight; such onward flights from the UK are detailed below.

It's fairly easy to track down flights from Australia to Athens, less so from New Zealand. But given most people's travel plans, you might be better off with a Round-the-World (RTW) ticket that includes Greece. If London is your first destination in Europe, and you've picked up a good deal on a flight there, it's probably best to wait until you reach the UK before arranging onward travel to Greece.

Air fares to Greece from Europe and North America depend on the **season**, with the highest in effect from June to August (plus Easter week), when the weather is best; fares drop during the "shoulder" seasons – April/May and September/October – and you'll get the best prices during the low season, November to March (excluding Christmas and New Year weeks, when prices are hiked up and seats are at a premium). Flying at weekends from North America ordinarily adds $50 or so to the round-trip fare; price ranges quoted on pp.33–34 assume midweek travel. Australian and New Zealand fares have their low season from mid-January to the end of February and October/November; high season is mid-May to August, plus

December to mid-January; and shoulder season the rest of the year.

You can often cut costs by going through a **specialist flight agent** – either a consolidator, who buys up blocks of tickets from the airlines and sells them at a discount, or a discount agent, who in addition to dealing with discounted flights may also offer special student and youth fares and a range of other travel-related services such as travel insurance, rail passes, car rentals, tours and the like. Some UK agents specialize in **charter flights**, which may be cheaper than anything available on a scheduled flight, but again departure dates are fixed and cancellation penalties are high. For Greece, you may even find it more cost-effective (especially from the UK) to pick up a **package deal**, with accommodation included, from one of the tour operators listed on pp.32–33.

Don't overlook the possibility of using **Frequent Flyer miles** to reach Athens. From the UK, direct flights on Olympic or BA require 25,000 points, though Hellas Jet (and indirect carriers such as Swiss) only need in the region of 20,000 miles. From North America, most airlines require 70,000 to 80,000 miles. You'll still have to pay all taxes (around £55 from Britain), but a major advantage is that these types of tickets are usually date-changeable for a small fee.

Booking flights online

Many airlines and discount travel websites offer you the opportunity to book your tickets online. **Good deals** can often be found through discount or auction sites, as well as through the airlines' own websites. Even if you don't end up actually buying your ticket online, websites are worth a visit to clue you up on what the prevailing published economy fares are. However, the airlines' own sites tend to give you only a choice between non-changeable/non-refundable fares and full economy ones; for the numerous options in between, you'll have to ring them. The cheapest of the airlines' published fares, all designated by a bewildering "alphabet soup" of capital letters, require a minimum stay of three days away, including a Saturday night, with a typical maximum period of thirty or sixty days, and make you liable to penalties (including total loss of ticket value) if you miss your outbound departure or change your return date. Some airlines also issue "student" tickets to those under 26, often extending the maximum stay to a year. "Senior" or "Golden" fares are also available for those over 60. When exploring a quoted fare on a website, always click the "Rules" link – all conditions will be spelled out in small print.

Some of the general travel sites like Expedia or Travelocity offer substantially discounted "special bargain" fares – the problem with some of these is you don't get to see the scheduling, or the airlines used, until after you've bought the ticket. Any reputable site will have a secure, encrypted facility for making credit card payments – if it doesn't, you're better off not using the site to purchase.

Online booking agents and general travel sites

Ⓦ **www.cheapflights.co.uk** (UK & Ireland), Ⓦ **www.cheapflights.com** (US), Ⓦ **www.cheapflights.ca** (Canada) or Ⓦ **www.cheapflights.com.au** (Australia & New Zealand) Not a booking site itself, but maintains links to the travel agents offering the deals.

Ⓦ **www.cheaptickets.com** Discount flight specialists (US only).

Ⓦ **www.etn.nl/discount.htm** A hub of consolidator and discount agent web links, maintained by the nonprofit European Travel Network.

Ⓦ **www.expedia.co.uk** (UK & Ireland), Ⓦ **www.expedia.com** (US) or Ⓦ **www.expedia.ca** (Canada) Discount air fares, all-airline search engine and daily deals.

Ⓦ **www.geocities.com/thavery2000** An extensive list of airline websites and US toll-free numbers.

Ⓦ **www.kelkoo.co.uk** Useful UK-only price-comparison site, checking several sources of low-cost flights (and other goods and services) according to specific criteria.

Ⓦ **www.lastminute.com** (UK & Ireland), **www.lastminute.com.au** (Australia) or **www.lastminute.co.nz** (New Zealand) Good holiday-package and flight-only deals available at very short notice.

Ⓦ **www.opodo.co.uk** Popular and reliable source of cheap UK air fares. Owned by, and run in conjunction with, nine major European airlines.

Ⓦ **www.orbitz.com** (US only) Comprehensive web travel source, with the usual flight, car rental and hotel deals but also great follow-up customer service.

Ⓦ **www.priceline.co.uk** or **www.priceline.com** Bookings from the UK/US only. Name-your-own-price auction website that can knock around forty percent off standard website fares. You can't choose the airline or flight times (although you do specify dates) and the tickets are nonrefundable, nontransferable and nonchangeable.

Ⓦ **www.skyauction.com** Bookings from the US only. Auctions tickets and travel packages using a "second bid" scheme. The best strategy is to bid the maximum you're willing to pay, since if you win you'll pay just enough to beat the runner-up regardless of your maximum bid.

Ⓦ **www.travelocity.co.uk** (UK & Ireland), Ⓦ **www.travelocity.com** (US) or Ⓦ **www.travelocity.ca** (Canada) Destination guides, hot web fares and deals for car rental, accommodation and lodging as well as fares.

Ⓦ **www.travelselect.com** A subsidiary of lastminute.com (see above) that is useful and fairly easy to use, but without most of the guff and banner adverts of the better-known sites.

Ⓦ **www.travelshop.com.au** Australian website offering discounted flights, packages, insurance and online bookings.

Ⓦ **www.travel.co.nz**. Comprehensive online travel company, with discounted fares.

Ⓦ **www.zuji.com.au** Destination guides, hot fares and great deals for car rental, accommodation and lodging.

Flights from the UK and Ireland

Most of the cheaper flights from Britain and Ireland to Greece are **charters**, which are sold either with a package holiday or (less commonly) as a flight-only option. The flights have fixed and unchangeable outward and return dates, and usually a maximum stay of four weeks.

For longer stays or more flexibility, or if you're travelling out of season (when no charters are available except at Christmas/ New Year), you'll need a **scheduled flight**. As with charters, these vary widely in price, and are again often heavily discounted by agents. Useful advertisements for discounted flights are found in the weekend supplement travel sections of newspapers like *The Independent*, *The Guardian*, *The Observer* and *The Sunday Times*. So far the only **no-frills** airline serving Greece is easyJet; the main advantage in using them is the ability to secure economical **one-way** fares, though Hellas Jet also offers this facility.

You can fly **direct** to the islands of Rhodes, Lésvos, Límnos, Sámos and Kós, though you'll find that the cheapest tickets to Greece tend to be to Athens, or sometimes Thessaloníki. With any flight to Athens or Thessaloníki, you can buy a **domestic connecting flight** on Olympic or Aegean to any island that they currently serve.

Charter flights

Travel agents throughout Britain sell **charter flights** to Greece, which usually operate from late April or early May to late October (Sámos, Kós, Lésvos) or late March to mid-November (Rhodes); late-night departures and early-morning arrivals are common, though you may have a choice of more civilized hours. Even the high-street chains frequently promote "flight-only" deals, or discount all-inclusive holidays, when their parent companies need to offload their seat allocations. The main charter airlines which offer flight-only deals to Greece are Excel, Monarch, Thomas Cook and TUI; you can book tickets for these on the phone or through their websites, though you may find that flight-only offers are rare indeed at peak season. Round-trip purchases are usually mandatory.

Compared to the cost of scheduled flights via Athens, you can pay dearly for the convenience of a direct service to the holiday island of your choice. **Sample return fares** at high season (which includes Easter) range from a reasonable £170–200 (Gatwick to Rhodes or Kós) up to a hefty £260 (Gatwick to Lésvos, Sámos or Límnos), though in low season you can find fares of £130–150 return to most of these spots. To these figures, add £10–20 for departures

from Manchester and Birmingham, and as much as £40 for take-off from Cardiff, Glasgow and Bristol.

The greatest variety of **flight destinations** tends to be from London (Gatwick) and Manchester. In summer, if you book in advance, you should have a choice of all the international east Aegean and Dodecanesian airports. Flying from elsewhere in Britain (Birmingham, Bristol, Cardiff, East Midlands, Luton, Stansted, Glasgow or Newcastle), or looking for last-minute discounts, you'll find options more limited, most commonly to Athens, Rhodes and Kós.

Summer charters operate **from Dublin** to Athens and there are additional services to Rhodes. A high-season charter flight from Dublin to Athens costs upwards of €320 return, while a week's package on Rhodes costs from €650 per person for two weeks.

If you travel to Greece on a charter flight, you may visit another, **non-EU country** (eg Turkey) only as a day-trip; if you stay overnight, you will possibly invalidate your ticket. This rule is justified by the Greek authorities because they subsidize charter airline landing fees, and are therefore reluctant to see tourists spending their money outside Greece. Whether you go along with that rationale or not, there is no way around it, since the Turkish authorities clearly stamp all passports, and the Greeks usually check them. We have, however, had reports of charter-flight-only patrons flying to Kós, happily spending a week in Turkish Bodrum, and then returning without incident, but it would be wise to double-check if the rule is still in effect.

Finally, remember that **reconfirmation** of return charter flights is vital and should be done at least 72 hours before departure. If you've travelled out with a package company, this service will usually be included as part of the rep's duties, but you should not assume that it has been done. Personal visits to the airline's representative office are best, as phone numbers given on ticket wallets are typically engaged.

Scheduled flights

The advantages of **scheduled flights** are that they can be booked up to ten months in advance, have longer ticket validities (from thirty days up to a year), involve fewer of the typical restrictions applicable to charters, and often leave at more sociable hours. However, many of the cheaper, shorter-duration fares do have minimum-stay and/or weekend-stay requirements, and also severe restrictions on date changes or refunds. As with charters, discount fares on scheduled flights are available from most high-street travel agents, as well as from a number of specialist flight and student/youth agencies – though it's always worth contacting the airlines direct, using the telephone numbers and websites below. Most airlines offer per-person discounts of £5–15 for booking return journeys on their website, with e-confirmation and e-ticketing to the fax or email address of your choice. Unlike charters, scheduled tickets don't require reconfirmation for the return leg. As of writing, there are no direct scheduled services to the islands of this guide from Britain or Ireland, though Rhodes in particular is often proposed to receive some in the future.

Scheduled airlines

Aer Lingus UK ☎0845/084 4444, Republic of Ireland ☎0818/365 000, ⓦwww.aerlingus.com.
Air France UK ☎0845/359 1000, Republic of Ireland ☎01/605 0383, ⓦwww.airfrance.com.
bmi ☎0870/607 0555, ⓦwww.flybmi.com.
bmibaby UK ☎0870/264 2229, Republic of Ireland ☎01/435 0011, ⓦwww.bmibaby.com.
British Airways UK ☎0870/850 9850, Republic of Ireland ☎1800/626 747, ⓦwww.ba.com.
easyJet ☎0871/750 0100, ⓦwww.easyjet.com.
Hellas Jet ☎0870/751 7222, ⓦwww.hellas-jet.com.
KLM (Royal Dutch Airlines) ☎0870/507 4074, ⓦwww.klm.com.
Lufthansa UK ☎0845/773 7747, Republic of Ireland ☎01/844 5544, ⓦwww.lufthansa.com.
Maersk Air ☎020/7333 0066, ⓦwww.maersk-air.com.
Olympic Airlines ☎0870/606 0460, ⓦwww.olympicairlines.com.
Ryanair UK ☎0871/246 0000, Republic of Ireland ☎0818 303 030, ⓦwww.ryanair.com.
Swiss UK ☎0845/601 0956, Republic of Ireland ☎1890 200 515, ⓦwww.swiss.com.
The national carrier, **Olympic Airlines**, notorious as the least punctual airline in the skies, offers at least two daily services from London Heathrow to Athens – three (noon,

late afternoon and late evening) in season – as well as up to four weekly evening flights to Athens from Manchester, and five weekly evening departures from London Gatwick to Thessaloníki. **British Airways** still offers two to three daily flights from Heathrow to Athens (most mornings, plus always noon and evening), as well as one morning flight from Gatwick in summer. Both airlines have a range of fares (Olympic is usually slightly more expensive) and, even in July and August, discount flight agents or websites (including BA's own) can come up with deals, valid for sixty days away, for as low as £180 return, including tax, though more realistically you'll pay around £220 return during high season from London, £300 from Manchester. It may be worth avoiding the very lowest fare tiers if you want to be flexible, as no return date changes are allowed on these. In the spring (except around Easter) or autumn, return fares to Athens run at about £160 including taxes, and in winter dip to about £140. As this route is common-rated between these airlines, you'll also be able to book onward connections simultaneously to domestic Greek airports, though discounts on the internal flight will apply only if you're using Olympic on all legs of the journey. Flights from British regional airports route through Heathrow in the first instance, with a supplement applicable (£70–80). Olympic has a code-sharing partnership with bmi, which should ease the pain (and possibly the cost) of connections from Scotland and the north of England in particular.

Olympic and British have both lost business to a pair of relative newcomers, easyJet and Hellas Jet. Potentially the cheapest, no-frills service is provided by **easyJet**, with several flights daily out of Luton and Gatwick to Athens; fares vary from £29 to £189 one way, tax included, with the exact amount depending on the season, how far in advance you book and availability for the particular flight – a last-minute booking for three weeks from the end of August will probably result in a combined return fare of £210, over Christmas/New Year £350. Departures also vary with time of year, but typically there are two daily from Luton, in the early afternoon and late in the evening, and one from Gatwick in the early morning. While there's no on-board meal service (although drinks and snacks are sold), you can change your ticket after booking for a small fee, provided space is available.

The newest airline on the scene is **Hellas Jet**, a subsidiary of Cyprus Airways which began operations in 2003, quickly garnering a reputation for punctuality and competitive fares. It runs a daily late-evening service from Heathrow to Athens, as well as a slightly pricier but very convenient daily late-morning service from Gatwick – though this was suspended in December 2004 and may not be reinstated. Fares range from £100–130 in low season to £210 in high season. It also offers very competitive one-ways, adding up to little more than a round-trip fare for the same dates. Its main disadvantage is that it's the most likely of the airlines on this route to charge for excess baggage – which it does to the tune of about £8 per kilo.

For Irish travellers, year-round scheduled services are operated by **Aer Lingus** and British Airways from both Dublin and Belfast via Heathrow or Manchester to Athens, and by **bmibaby** and Olympic from Dublin via Heathrow. These are pricey, though, compared to charters. Travelling to London and buying a separate ticket when you get there is an alternative if direct flights from Ireland are in short supply, and may sometimes save you a little money, but on the whole it's rarely worth the time and effort. Budget flights to London from Ireland are offered by bmibaby, Aer Lingus and Ryanair.

If cost is an overriding factor, at peak travel seasons you may have little choice but to **go indirectly to Athens**, via intervening European cities. Travel websites will pick the cheapest routes and carriers on the day, but experience has shown that Swiss, Lufthansa, Alitalia and Air France have the most congenial schedules from the UK. All should get you to Athens in time for the last onward flight of the day to the larger islands of this book.

Flight and travel agents in the UK and Republic of Ireland

Avro ☎ 0870/458 2841, ⓦ www.avro.co.uk. Seat-only sales on flights to Rhodes and Kós from most UK airports, on Monarch Airlines; easy-to-use website.

Excel Airways ☎ 0870/998 9898, ⓦ www.excelairways.com. Flight-onlys to almost every major charter-served airport in Greece, mostly from Gatwick and Manchester but often Glasgow, Birmingham and East Midlands; competitive fares, easy-to-use site.

Go Holidays Republic of Ireland ☎ 01/874 4126, ⓦ www.goholidays.ie. City breaks and package tours.

Greece & Cyprus Travel Centre ☎ 0121/355 6955, ⓦ www.greece-cyprus.co.uk. Competent flight consolidator for Olympic and Hellas Jet in particular; a myriad of fares to suit every need, including one-ways.

Independent Aviation Group ☎ 0871/222 3903, ⓦ www.iagflights.com. Charter brokers who periodically offload unsold seats (especially to Rhodes) on a flight-only basis at good rates; website tells you instantly if anything is available.

Joe Walsh Tours Dublin ☎ 01/676 0991, ⓦ www.joewalshtours.ie. General budget fares and holidays agent.

McCarthys Travel Republic of Ireland ☎ 021/427 0127, ⓦ www.mccarthystravel.ie. Established Irish travel agent now part of the Worldchoice chain of travel shops.

North South Travel ☎ 01245/608291, ⓦ www.northsouthtravel.co.uk. Friendly, competitive flight agency, offering discounted fares worldwide – profits are used to support projects in the developing world, especially the promotion of sustainable tourism.

Rosetta Travel Belfast ☎ 028/9064 4996, ⓦ www.rosettatravel.com. Flight and holiday agent, specializing in deals direct from Belfast.

STA Travel ☎ 0870/160 0599, ⓦ www.statravel.co.uk. Worldwide specialists in low-cost flights and tours for students and under-26s.

Thomas Cook ☎ 0870/750 5711, ⓦ www.thomascook.com. Good selection of flight-onlys to Kós, Lésvos, Sámos and Rhodes from a half-dozen UK airports, though difficult to find in this dense site.

Thomson Flights ☎ 0800/000 747, ⓦ www.thomsonflights.com. Limited flight-only deals to Rhodes, Kós, Sámos and Thessaloníki on TUI, its parent-company airline.

Trailfinders UK ☎ 020/7938 3939, ⓦ www.trailfinders.com, Republic of Ireland ☎ 01/677 7888, ⓦ www.trailfinders.ie. One of the best-informed and most efficient agents for independent travellers; branches in all the UK's largest cities, plus Dublin.

Packages and tours

Virtually every British **tour operator** includes Greece in its programme, though with many of the larger, cheap-and-cheerful outfits you'll find choices limited to the established resorts on Rhodes, Kós, and to a lesser extent Lésvos or Sámos. If you buy one of these at a last-minute discount, especially in spring or autumn, you may find it costs little more than a flight – and you can use the accommodation offered as much or as little as you want.

For a more low-key and genuinely "Greek" resort, however, it's better to book your holiday through one of the **specialist agencies** listed below. Most of these are fairly small-scale operations, offering competitively priced packages with flights (unless otherwise stated) and often more traditional village-based accommodation. They also make an effort to offer islands without overdeveloped tourist resorts. Such agencies tend to divide into **two types**: those which, like the major chains, contract a block of accommodation and flight seats (or even their own plane) for a full season, and an increasing number of bespoke agencies that tailor holidays to your needs, making all transport and accommodation arrangements on the spot. These can work out somewhat more expensive, but the quality of flights and lodging is often correspondingly higher.

The **walking** holiday operators listed below either run trekking groups of ten to fifteen people plus an experienced guide, or provide customers with a printed, self-guiding itinerary, and arranged accommodation at the end of each day. Walks tend to be day-long hikes from one or more bases, or point-to-point treks staying in village accommodation en route.

Sailing holidays usually involve small flotillas of four- to eight-berth yachts, taking in different anchorages each night, or are shore-based, with instruction in small-craft handling. All levels of experience are catered for. Prices start at around £420 per person, flights included, in a group of four on a thirty-foot boat for a one-week flotilla. Alternatively, confident sailors can simply arrange to charter a yacht on a bare-boat basis; allow from £900 for a week's hire of a 35-footer with berths for six.

Specialist package operators

Villa or village accommodation

Cachet Travel ☎020/8847 3847, ⓦwww.cachet-travel.co.uk. Unusual range of villas and apartments on Sámos, in the less typical resorts.

Direct Greece ☎0870/516 8683, ⓦwww.direct-greece.co.uk. Moderately priced villas, apartments and restored houses on Rhodes (Líndhos, Péfkos), Hálki and Lésvos (Sígri).

Elysian Holidays ☎01580/766599, ⓦwww.elysianholidays.co.uk. Began as Volissós (Híos) restored-house specialists, now have a wider programme of quality premises on several islands, including Pátmos.

Greek Sun Holidays ☎01732/740317, ⓦwww.greeksun.co.uk. Limited but well-selected accommodation on Kárpathos, Kássos, Rhodes, Sými, Astypálea, Pátmos, Foúrni, Ikaría, Sámos, Híos and Límnos; also tailor-made island-hopping itineraries.

Hidden Greece/Simply Simon ☎020/7839 2553, ⓦwww.hidden-greece.co.uk. Two bespoke agencies, each running for forty-plus years, have joined forces, arranging accommodation on and transport to a score of less-visited islands in the northeast Aegean and Dodecanese; uses Olympic Airlines flights by preference, car rental available. "Tailor made at a package price" is their motto.

Island Wandering ☎01580/860733, ⓦwww.islandwandering.com. Tailor-made island-hopping itineraries on and between Pátmos, Lipsí, Léros, Kálymnos, Astypálea, Kós, Níssyros, Kárpathos, Ikaría and Sámos. Deals range from pre-booked accommodation only (this tends to be on the basic side) to bespoke or off-the-shelf tours, with local ferry or air transfers arrranged.

Laskarina Holidays ☎01444/880380, ⓦwww.laskarina.co.uk. Top-end villas, quality hotels and restored houses on Hálki, Sými, Tilos, Kálymnos, Léros, Lipsí, Pátmos, Ikaría and Sámos; scores consistently high marks for customer service and repeat clientele.

Sunvil Holidays ☎020/8568 4499, ⓦwww.sunvil.co.uk/greece. Durable and consistently high-quality outfit specializing in upmarket hotels and villas across Greece; islands covered in this book are Límnos (unique in the UK), Lésvos, Sámos, Ikaría and Pátmos.

Travel à la Carte ☎01635/863030, ⓦwww.travelalacarte.co.uk. Established Corfu specialist, now branched out to a few quality waterside and rural villas on Hálki and Sými – plus one luxury Sými hotel.

Walking and wildlife holidays

Jonathan's Tours ☎00 33 561046447, ⓦwww.jonathanstours.com. Family-run walking holidays on Lésvos.

Limosa ☎01263/578143, ⓦwww.limosaholidays.co.uk. 1985-established birding specialists with spring and autumn one-week tours to Lésvos, plus a springtime week on Kós.

Marengo Guided Walks ☎01485/532710, ⓦwww.marengowalks.com. Annually-changing programme of easy walks guided by ace botanist Lance Chilton; past one-week offerings have included Sámos, Sými, and northern Lésvos.

Naturetrek ☎01962/733051, ⓦwww.naturetrek .co.uk. Fairly pricey but expertly led one- or two-week natural history tours; past choices have included springtime birds and flora on Sámos.

Ramblers Holidays ☎01707/331133, ⓦwww .ramblersholidays.co.uk. Trying to shed its former fusty image by actively courting a younger clientele; usually offers a two-week "Easter in Sámos" tour, based in Vathý hotels.

Sailing holidays

Nautilus Yachting ☎01732/867445, ⓦwww .nautilus-yachting.co.uk. Bare-boat yacht charter out of Kós, Sámos and Rhodes.

Passion Sailing Cruises ☎00 30 22410 73006, ⓦwww.aegeanpassion.com. French-run, Rhodes-based outfit which offers a bespoke service for skippered cruises, as well as bare-boat charter.

Sportif ☎01273 844919, ⓦwww.sportif-uk.com. Windsurfing packages on Kós, Rhodes and Kárpathos. Instruction clinics in conjunction with nearby accommodation.

Templecraft ☎01273/812333, ⓦwww .templecraft.com. Bare-boat charters out of Rhodes, Kós and Sámos, though in some instances they are repping for local Greek companies.

Travelling with children

Club Med ☎0700/25 82 932, ⓦwww.clubmed .co.uk. Specializes in purpose-built holiday resorts, with kids' clubs, entertainment and sports facilities on-site; has a village on Kós in the Dodecanese.

Mark Warner Holidays ☎0870/770 4227, ⓦwww.markwarner.co.uk. Holiday villages with children's entertainment and childcare provided; has a village on Límnos in the east Aegean.

Special interest holidays

Symi Pilates & Yoga Retreat ☎00 30 22460 71169, ⓦwww.symi-holistic.com. Pilates, yoga and massage-therapy weeks based mainly at a superb remote villa on Nimborió Bay. Morning and evening classes, with the day left free.

Flights from North America

The Greek national airline, Olympic Airlines, flies **direct to Athens** out of New York (JFK), Montréal and Toronto. The airline – and also its domestic competitor, Aegean – can offer reasonably priced add-on flights to the islands of the Dodecanese and east Aegean. Delta is the only North American carrier currently offering any direct service to Athens, though through fares with code-sharing airlines are quoted from Atlanta, Boston, Calgary, Chicago, Dallas/Fort Worth, Los Angeles, Miami, San Francisco, Vancouver, Winnipeg and Washington DC.

Nonstop flights to **Athens** out of **New York-JFK** on Olympic (3–7 weekly) start at around US$600 round-trip in winter, rising to around $1200 in summer for a maximum thirty-day stay. Delta has daily year-round service from New York-JFK to Athens, but at $1000–1200 is rarely the cheapest option except in low season ($550). One-stop high-season options with the likes of Iberia, Swiss, BA or Air France can yield significant savings at just over $1000.

Common-rating (ie price-fixing) agreements between different airlines means that one-stop fares to **Athens** from the **Midwest**, **Deep South** or the **West Coast** don't vary much. From Chicago, the range is $620 low season to $1080 peak season; f rom Houston, it's $650–1120; from San Francisco, you're looking at $700 low, $1280 high season. Such tickets typically involve the use of American Airlines, BA, Delta, United, Air France, Alitalia, Iberia, KLM and Swiss, via their European gateway cities. With little to distinguish itineraries price-wise from any given start point, you might examine the stopover time at their respective European hubs, as these can differ by several hours. You may be better off getting a domestic add-on to New York and heading directly to Athens from there.

As with the US, air fares from **Canada** to **Athens** vary depending on where you start your journey, and whether you take a direct service. Olympic flies out of Toronto, with a stop in Montréal, three times weekly; they're rarely the cheapest option, however. For just over CDN$1300 you might find one-stop service on Delta via New York from Toronto in low season, or about CDN$1500 one-stop on a variety of Europen carriers out of Montréal, climbing to CDN$2100–2600 in summer. From Winnipeg or Vancouver, there are no direct flights; expect to pay

CDN$1900–3150 from Winnipeg during low/high seasons respectively, on two-stop itineraries, and CDN$2400–3300 from Vancouver on a one-stop routing, possibly on Air Canada via Frankfurt.

Scheduled airlines in North America

Air Canada ⓣ1-888/247–2262, ⓦwww.aircanada.com.
Air France ⓣ1-800/237-2747, in Canada ⓣ1-800/667-2747, ⓦwww.airfrance.com.
Alitalia ⓣ1-800/223-5730, Canada ⓣ1-800/361-8336, ⓦwww.alitalia.com.
American Airlines ⓣ1-800/433-7300, ⓦwww.aa.com.
British Airways ⓣ1-800/AIRWAYS, ⓦwww.ba.com.
Continental Airlines domestic ⓣ1-800/523-FARE, international ⓣ1-800/231-0856, ⓦwww.continental.com.
Delta Air Lines domestic ⓣ1-800/221-1212, international ⓣ1-800/241-4141, ⓦwww.delta.com.
Iberia ⓣ1-800/772-4642, ⓦwww.iberia.com.
Lufthansa ⓣ1-800/645-3880, Canada ⓣ1-800/563-5954, ⓦwww.lufthansa.com.
Northwest/KLM domestic ⓣ1-800/225-2525, international ⓣ1-800/447-4747, ⓦwww.nwa.com, ⓦwww.klm.com.
Olympic Airlines ⓣ1-800/223-1226 or 718/896-7393, ⓦwww.olympicairlines.com.
Swiss ⓣ1-877/FLY-SWISS, ⓦwww.swiss.com.
United Airlines domestic ⓣ1-800/241-6522, international ⓣ1-800/538-2929, ⓦwww.united.com.
Virgin Atlantic ⓣ1-800/862-8621, ⓦwww.virgin-atlantic.com.

Discount travel agents

Air Brokers International ⓣ1-800/883-3273 or 415/397-1383, ⓦwww.airbrokers.com. Consolidator and specialist in RTW tickets.
Airtech ⓣ212/219-7000, ⓦwww.airtech.com. Standby seat broker; also deals in consolidator fares.
Educational Travel Center ⓣ1-800/747-5551 or 608/256-5551, ⓦwww.edtrav.com. Low-cost fares worldwide, student/youth discount offers, Eurail passes.
Flightcentre US ⓣ1-866/WORLD-51, ⓦwww.flightcentre.us, Canada ⓣ1-888/WORLD-55, ⓦwww.flightcentre.ca. Rock-bottom fares worldwide.
New Frontiers US ⓣ1-800/677-0720 or 212/986-6006, ⓦwww.newfrontiers.com. Discount firm, specializing in travel from the US to Europe.
STA Travel US ⓣ1-800/329-9537, Canada ⓣ1-888/427-5639, ⓦwww.statravel.com. Worldwide specialists in independent travel; also student IDs, travel insurance, car rental, rail passes, etc.
Student Flights ⓣ1-800/255-8000 or 480/951-1177, ⓦwww.isecard.com/studentflights. Student/youth fares, plus student IDs and European rail and bus passes.
TFI Tours ⓣ1-800/745-8000 or 212/736-1140, ⓦwww.lowestairprice.com. Consolidator with global fares.
Travel Avenue ⓣ1-800/333-3335, ⓦwww.travelavenue.com. Full-service travel agent that offers discounts in the form of rebates.
Travel Cuts US ⓣ1-800/592-CUTS, Canada ⓣ1-888 246-9762, ⓦwww.travelcuts.com. Popular, long-established student travel organization, with worldwide offers.
Travelers Advantage ⓣ1-877/259-2691, ⓦwww.travelersadvantage.com. Discount travel club, with cashback deals and discounted car rental. Membership required ($1 for 3 months' trial).
Travelosophy US ⓣ1-800/332-2687, ⓦwww.itravelosophy.com. Good range of discounted and student fares worldwide.

Specialist package operators

Hellenic Adventures ⓣ1-800/851-6349 or 612/827-0937, ⓦwww.hellenicadventures.com. Small-group (14 max), customized tours, led by an enthusiastic Greek-American. Good information on the website for independent travellers too.
Meander Adventures ⓣ1-888/616-7272, ⓦwww.meanderadventures.com. Sými specialists (principal Shirley Smith is a part-time resident there), with walking programme and lots of villas on offer; also represents Zeus Cruises with its motor yachts accommodating 25 to 140 people.
Valef Yachts ⓣ1-800/223-3845, ⓦwww.valefyachts.com. North American reps for Zeus Cruises' "Aegean Mosaic" tour, a seven-day motor-yacht cruise out of Crete but taking in several Dodecanese; a bit rushed, but affordable at $850–1450 per person (flights extra). Also very expensive bare-boat charter (yachts, mostly 60ft or over); pick your craft from the online brochure.

Flights from Australia and New Zealand

With the huge Greek emigrant community in Australia, it's absolutely staggering that Olympic suspended all through-service to Greece in October 2002 – a measure of its woes (though there are now code-shared services with Gulf Air). Neither are there any direct flights from New Zealand – you'll have to get yourself to Southeast Asia or a North American hub for onward travel. Tickets purchased direct from the airlines tend to be expensive; travel agents or Australia-based websites offer much better deals on fares and have the latest information on limited specials and stopovers.

If Greece is only one stop on a longer journey, you might consider buying a **Round-the-World** (RTW) fare. At present only the more expensive, fifteen-stop "Global Explorer" (roughly A$3400) offered by the One World airline group includes Athens. RTW fares from any point in Australia are usually common-rated, ie the price is the same from whichever Australian airport you commence travel. From New Zealand, allow almost NZ$4000 for the same programme.

For a **simple return fare**, you may have to buy an add-on internal flight to reach the international gateways of **Sydney** or **Melbourne**. Tickets are generally valid for one year; high-season departures can typically be had for A$2300–2500 on such airlines as Emirates, Lufthansa, Singapore Airlines, Thai Airways, Gulf Air or Austrian Airlines plus Lauda Air, for multi-stop itineraries via Southeast Asia, the Middle East and a European hub. A 180-day, two-stop ticket on BA plus Qantas might run A$2300. For $A2270, you could fly eastbound via North America on a combination of United Airlines, Air Canada and Lufthansa. Leaving at low season means fares of A$1547–1736 on Singapore Airlines, Thai Airways, Lufthansa or Qantas plus Royal Jordanian.

From **Auckland**, the usual routes to Athens are either westbound several times weekly via Bangkok, Sydney or Singapore, or eastbound almost daily via Los Angeles with Air New Zealand on the first leg. At high season count on paying NZ$2449–2729 on Singapore Airlines, Emirates, Thai Airways or (for an east-bound itinerary) Air New Zealand plus Lufthansa. During low season prices aren't much different: NZ$2199–2349 for travel on Thai Airways, Emirates or (again going east) Air New Zealand plus Lufthansa.

Scheduled airlines

Aeroflot ☎ 02/9262 2233, @ www.aeroflot.com.au.

Air New Zealand Australia ☎ 13 24 76, @ www.airnz.com.au, New Zealand ☎ 0800/737 000, @ www.airnz.co.nz.
Alitalia Australia ☎ 02/9244 2445, New Zealand ☎ 09/308 3357, @ www.alitalia.com.
British Airways Australia ☎ 1300/767 177, New Zealand ☎ 0800/274 847, @ www.ba.com.
Egyptair Australia ☎ 02/9241 5696, @ www.egyptair.com.eg.
Emirates Australia ☎ 1300/303 777 or 02/9290 9700, New Zealand ☎ 09/377 6004, @ www.emirates.com.
Gulf Air Australia ☎ 02/9244 2199, New Zealand ☎ 09/308 3366, @ www.gulfairco.com.
Lufthansa Australia ☎ 1300/655 727, New Zealand ☎ 0800/945 220, @ www.lufthansa.com.
Qantas Australia ☎ 13 13 13, New Zealand ☎ 0800/808 767 or 09/357 8900, @ www.qantas.com.
Royal Jordanian Australia ☎ 02/9244 2701, New Zealand ☎ 03/365 3910, @ www.rja.com.jo.
Singapore Airlines Australia ☎ 13 10 11, New Zealand ☎ 0800/808 909, @ www.singaporeair.com.
Thai Airways Australia ☎ 1300/651 960, New Zealand ☎ 09/377 3886, @ www.thaiair.com.

Flight and travel agents

Flight Centre Australia ☎ 13 31 33, @ www.flightcentre.com.au, New Zealand ☎ 0800/243 544, @ www.flightcentre.co.nz.
STA Travel Australia ☎ 1300/733 035, New Zealand ☎ 0508/782 872, @ www.statravel.com.
Student Uni Travel Australia ☎ 02/9232 8444, @ www.sut.com.au, New Zealand ☎ 09/379 4224, @ www.sut.co.nz.
Trailfinders Australia ☎ 02/9247 7666, @ www.trailfinders.com.au.

Specialist package operators

Sun Island Tours Australia ☎ 02/9283 3840, @ www.sunislandtours.com.au. An assortment of island-hopping, fly-drives, cruises and guided land-tour options, as well as upscale accommodation on big-name islands such as Rhodes, Kós and Sámos.

Getting there from mainland Greece

Given the limitations of direct flights to the Dodecanese and the east Aegean, many travellers – of necessity those from North America and Australasia – will touch down first at Athens' Eleftherios Venizelos Airport, with a few Brits flying into Thessaloníki or

Kavála as well. From Athens or Thessaloníki you have a choice of making your way to the island of your choice by plane or ferry. Rhodes, Kastellórizo, Kárpathos, Kássos, Kós, Astypálea, Léros, Sámos, Híos, Lésvos and Límnos all have airports served by Olympic Airlines/Olympic Aviation domestic flights from Athens and (usually) Thessaloníki; Aegean flies to Híos, Kós, Lésvos and Rhodes from Athens, and to Rhodes and Lésvos from Thessaloníki.

Flights

Flying out as soon as possible will probably be the most attractive option, especially if you've arrived jet-lagged from another continent. Olympic Airlnes offers a good incentive for using them for the international leg of your trip: a hefty discount on the internal return flight from Athens or Thessaloníki to the selected island. As an example, Athens to Sámos costs about €180 return if purchased within Greece, but as little as €120 equivalent if purchased as part of a continuous, all-Olympic itinerary originating overseas – the same as, or even a bit less than, the cost of a round-trip cabin ticket on an overnight ferry. Making your **onward connection** involves taking the escalator up from the ground-floor arrivals level to the departure concourse with layovers often as short as ninety minutes. If customs rules allow, your luggage should be checked through to your final destination; even if not, you're entitled to the full international 20–23kg **baggage allowance**, not just the puny 15kg Greek domestic one.

Olympic flight frequencies (see "Travel Details" at the end of each island account) from Athens are adequate – three to six daily for the biggest islands – though seats are in heavy demand during peak season. You can have **same-day connections** from the **UK** by using the midday BA or OA flights from Heathrow, or the easyJet/Hellas Jet early- or late-morning flights out of Gatwick. These arrive in Athens in time for the final (April–Oct) evening onward service to Límnos, Híos, Lésvos, Kós and Rhodes on either OA or Aegean; to get to Sámos on the same day, you will have to use either the early-morning BA flight out of Heathrow, the late-morning flight on HellasJet from Gatwick, or an early-morning stopping flight out of Heathrow on Swiss or Lufthansa.

For all the other, smaller islands, your best option is to take an Olympic, Hellas Jet or BA "red-eye" flight out of Heathrow, or easyJet's red-eye from Luton, typically at around 10.30pm, to make a quick connection on the first flight out on the following day – usually sometime between 6am and 9am. EasyJet's early afternoon service from Luton arrives just in time (around 7.30pm) to mesh with the last flights of the night out to Rhodes, Lésvos and Límnos.

Ferries

For those islands without airports, or Athens-bound travellers who prefer to island-hop, the first order of business will be getting to Pireás (Piraeus) or Lávrio, the ports nearest to Athens, and onto a ferry bound for the island of your choice (for routes, see p.54). Boats heading for the east Aegean and Dodecanese usually depart in the late afternoon or early evening. There are just a few morning sailings to the east Aegean, mostly in high season, so if you arrive before dawn you could face a wait of up to twelve hours. Travellers arriving in Thessaloníki or Kavála will find ferry connections to the east Aegean less frequent – typically three or four weekly, even in summer – so check Greek ferry websites (see p.54) before committing to such a flight.

Travelling via Athens and Pireás

If you opt for a cheap flight to **Athens**, you may find yourself with some time on your hands in the Greek capital before the Aegean leg of your journey. This is not necessarily a hardship; the city is, admittedly, no holiday resort, with its concrete architecture and air pollution, but it has modern excitements of its own, as well as some superlative ancient sites. A couple of nights' stopover will allow you to take in the Acropolis, the ancient Agora and some major museums, wander around the old quarter of Pláka and the bazaar area, and sample some of the country's best restaurants and clubs. A morning flight arrival in Athens would allow you enough time for a look at the Acropolis and Pláka, before heading down to the port of **Pireás** (Piraeus) to catch an afternoon or evening ferry.

What follows is a brief guide to city logistics, and some pointers on what to do while you're there. For a fuller account of Athens, see *The Rough Guide to Greece* or *Athens Directions*.

Athens airport

Athens' **Eleftherios Venizelos airport** at Spáta, some 26km east of the city, opened in March 2001, replacing the far more convenient (if tiny) one south of town at Ellinikó. You have to pay for baggage trolleys in arrivals (about €1 in coins, more if you use a card); there are ample banking facilities in the arrivals hall, including several ATMs. The departure concourse shops are decent, and eating opportunities are fairly abundant, though seats are in short supply.

Missing connections at Athens airport is a distinct possibility owing to the airport's poor internal signage and its enormous size (claimed third largest in the world). Mad dashes down nightmarishly endless concourses and up escalators (there are a few well-concealed lifts for luggage trolleys) add further stress.

Printed airport rules stipulate a minimum of 55 minutes between your incoming flight's arrival and onward flight's departure, but some airlines – for example, Olympic – insist on a **minimum leeway** of ninety minutes. Given Olympic's habitual late arrivals, the carrying out of lengthy security checks even for transfer passengers and the fact that all aircraft for domestic flights are parked a very long shuttle-coach-ride away on the runway, prudence would dictate observing this rule when buying fares. Some, but not all, ticketing systems won't let you book an itinerary if the layover is too short. If you miss your onward domestic flight owing to non-observance of this rule, ground staff will likely be unsympathetic, even more so if the two airlines were different.

You may find (if desk staff in your departing country are in a cooperative mood) that you can have your **luggage checked through** to your final domestic destination, even if your international- and domestic-leg airlines are different – there is no legal obstacle to this within the EU/EEA. Do this at the outset as a precaution, and even if your inbound flight is hideously late, you stand a good chance of getting yourself and your carry-on to the end of your itinerary as planned, even if your checked baggage only shows up the next day.

From the airport to Athens or Pireás

Heading into town, you've a choice between bus, metro and taxi. The #E94 express **bus** (every 15–30min 6am–midnight) departs from outside arrivals for metro station Ethnikí Ámyna, from where you continue your journey. Alternatively, take the #E95 express bus (every 25–35min around the clock) all the way to central Sýndagma square, or the #E96 express bus (every 20–40min) to Pireás (Piraeus) port, going via the beach suburbs. All three services cost €2.90 to anywhere en route; for another €3 you can get a one-day travelcard valid on all Athens public transport. Tickets should be bought from a booth beside the stops, or, if this is closed, can be purchased on the bus; make sure you have small change. For a whopping €8 (but €12 for two people, or €16 for three – single trip, *not* a one-day travelcard), you can traipse across to an inconspicuous station, where a light-rail system trundles suprisingly slowly (20min) to the last station of the **metro** proper (Dhoukíssis Plakendías) and then continues to central Athens. Coming *from* Monastiráki, some (but not all) metro-cars go all the way to the airport – read the digital display.

A **taxi** to Athens should cost no more than about €20, to Pireás not more than €23; at most times of the day your driver will find it quicker to imitate the #E96 bus by heading southwest to Vári and Voúla and then north through the southerly beach suburbs en route to Pireás, rather than struggle through traffic in the northern suburbs. This amount should include a €3 airport surcharge and €0.30 for each item of luggage, but make sure the meter is working (fares begin at €0.80, minimum fare €1.60), and is visible from the start – double or even quintuple overcharging of newcomers is not uncommon. When obtaining money at the airport exchange booths, it's best to ask for some small-denomination euro notes and coins – presenting a taxi driver with a €50 note is just inviting a rip-off.

Athens contact numbers for useful domestic/international airlines

Aegean city centre ☏210 33 15 515; airport ☏210 35 30 101.
Air France ☏210 96 01 100; airport ☏210 35 30 380.
Alitalia ☏210 99 48 900; airport ☏210 35 34 284.
British Airways ☏210 89 06 666; airport ☏210 35 30 452.
Delta ☏800 441 29 506 or ☏210 33 11 668; airport ☏210 35 30 116.
easyJet airport only ☏210 35 30 000 or ☏210 35 30 585.
Hellas Jet ☏210 74 57 700 or ☏801 11 53 000; airport ☏210 35 30 815.
Lufthansa ☏210 61 75 200.
Olympic city centre ☏210 96 66 666, countrywide ☏801 11 44 444.
Swiss airport only ☏210 35 37 400.

Accommodation and eating

Finding **accommodation** in Athens poses few problems except during midsummer – though it's always best to phone ahead. For a quick stay, **Pláka**, the oldest quarter of the city, is the obvious area. It spreads southwest of Sýndagma square (Platía Syndágmatos), lies within easy walking distance of the Acropolis, and has lots of outdoor restaurants and cafés. Two of our recommendations, however, lie just south in **Veïkoú/Koukáki** district.

For a good-value pension, try either the *Phaedra* at Herefóndos 16, Pláka (☏210 32 27 795), quiet and recently refurbished, or the welcoming, also recently overhauled *Marble House*, in a quiet alley off Anastasíou Zínni 35, Koukáki (☏210 92 34 058). For marginally more comfort – and rather bumped-up prices – there's *Acropolis House* on Kódrou 6–8, Pláka (☏210 32 22 344) and *Art Gallery Pension* at Erekhthíou 5, Veïkoú (☏210 92 38 376).

Pláka is bursting with touristy **restaurants**, most of them pleasantly situated but representing poor value. Three with both nice sites and good food are *Iy Ipiros*, actually on Platía Ayíou Filíppou in the Monastiráki flea market, and specializing in *mayireftá*; *O Thanasis*, nearby at Mitropóleos 69, known for its dynamite *souvláki* and kebabs; and *Baïraktaris*, around the corner at Platía Monastirakíou 2, with occasional live acoustic music. *Eden*, Liossíou 12, is one of the city's few vegetarian restaurants. In **Koukáki**, *Ouzeri Evvia* at Yeoryíou Olymbíou 8, and *Iy Gardhenia* at Anastasíou Zínni 29

(lunch only), are both good value and close to the recommended accommodation.

Athens: the city and sights

Central Athens is a compact, easily walkable area. Its hub is **Sýndagma square** (Platía Syndágmatos), flanked by the Parliament building, banks, airline offices and the eponymous metro station. Pretty much everything you'll want to see in a fleeting visit – the Acropolis, Pláka, the major museums – lies within twenty to thirty minutes' walk of here. Just east of the square, too, are the **National Gardens** – the nicest spot in town for a siesta, though don't doze off with your valuables strewn about.

Walk south from Sýndagma, along Níkis or Filellínon streets, and then briefly west, and you'll find yourself in Pláka, the surviving area of the nineteenth-century, pre-Independence village. Largely pedestrianized, it's a delightful area just to wander around – and it straddles most approaches to the Acropolis. For a bit of focus to your walk, take in the fourth-century-BC **Monument of Lysikratos**, used as a study by Byron, on Shelley Street, and the Roman-era **Tower of the Winds** (Aéridhes), a bit further west on Dhioyénous. The latter adjoins the **Roman Forum** and the eminently worthwhile **Museum of Greek Popular Musical Instruments** (Tues & Thurs–Sun 10am–2pm, Wed noon–8pm; free). Climb south from the Tower of the Winds and you reach **Anafiótika**, with its whitewashed Cycladic-style cottages (built by labourers from the island of Anáfi) and the eclectic **Kanellopoulou Museum** (Tues–Sun 8.30am–3pm; €2).

Head north from the **Roman Forum** (April–Sept daily 8am–7pm; Oct–March Tues–Sun 8.30am–3pm; €2) along Athinás or Eólou streets, and you come to an equally charcterful part of the city – the **bazaar** area, which shows Athens' most Near Eastern aspect. **Platía Monastirakíou**, home to another metro station, is flanked by an Ottoman mosque (now a museum of ceramic art). This is an annexe of the **Museum of Greek Folk Art** (Tues–Sun 10am–2pm; €2) back on Kydathinéon, which includes some work by Theophilos of Lésvos (see p.404). On Sundays a genuine **flea market** sprawls around Platía Avyssinías, west beyond the lane of tourist shops promoted as the "Athens Flea Market".

Even with just a few hours to spare between flight and ferry, you can take in a visit to the **Acropolis** (daily: April–Sept 8am–7pm; Oct–March 8am–4.30pm; site and museum €12). The complex of temples, rebuilt by Pericles in the "Golden Age" of the fifth century BC, is focused on the famed Parthenon. This, and the smaller Athena Nike and Erechtheion temples, are placed in context by a small museum housing some of the original relief art left behind by Lord Elgin.

If you have more time, make your way down to the **Theatre of Dionysos**, on the south slope (daily: summer 8am–7pm; winter 8.30am–3pm; €2 or joint Acropolis ticket), and/or to the Classical **Agora** (daily: summer 8am–7pm; winter 8.30am–3pm; €4 or joint Acropolis ticket €12), presided over by the Doric **Temple of Hephaestos** (Thissío).

Athens' major museum is the **National Archeological Museum** at Patissíon 28 (summer Mon 12.30–7pm, Tues–Sun 8am–7pm; winter Mon 10.30am–5pm, Tues–Sun 8.30am–2.45pm; €10). Its highlights include Schliemann's Mycenaean treasures, Classical sculpture and, upstairs, the brilliant Minoan frescoes from ancient Thera (Santoríni).

Two other superb museums, very close to each other, are the **Benáki** at Koumbári 1, corner Vassilísis Sofías (Mon, Wed, Fri & Sat 9am–5pm, Thurs 9am–midnight, Sun 9am–3pm; €6, temporary exhibitions €3), a fascinating, personal collection of

ancient, medieval, and folk treasures, and the **Goulandhris Museum of Cycladic and Ancient Greek Art** at Neofýtou Dhouká 4 (Mon & Wed–Fri 10am–4pm, Sat 10am–3pm; €3.50), with its wonderful display of figurines from the Cycladic island civilization of the third millennium BC.

Pireás

Pireás (Piraeus), the port of Athens, is the southwesternmost stop on Line 1 of the **metro** which you can board at Platía Viktorías, Omónia or Monastiráki squares; Line 3 from the airport terminates at Monastiráki. The journey from the centre to the port, within moderate walking distance of many boat-berths, takes about 25 minutes – trains run from 6am to midnight – with a flat fare of €0.60 (€0.70 if you've used Line 2 or Line 3 as well). Otherwise, a **taxi** from the city centre (don't try this at rush hour) will cover the nine-kilometre distance for about €8, including your bags, right to the boat gangplank.

You can buy **ferry and catamaran tickets** from agencies at the harbour in Pireás, or in central Athens (there are several outlets on Lefóros Amalías, which runs south of Sýndagma square). Try to get a ferry that makes a reasonably direct run to your destination. There may be little or no choice to relatively obscure islands such as Astypálea or Foúrni, but ferries to the larger Dodecanese or east Aegean islands can take very different routes – ie "expresses" stopping only at Kós and Rhodes, versus the "milk run" calling at two or three Cyclades plus every intervening Dodecanese before reaching the end of the line.

Other mainland ports

Although Pireás has the widest choice of ferry and catamaran departures, some of the east Aegean islands can be reached more quickly from other ports on the mainland.

Alexandhroúpoli

The third northern port (6hr by bus from Thessaloníki, 20min by taxi from its own airport) has one weekly summer sailing, currently with LANE to Límnos, Lésvos, Híos, Sámos, Kós, Kálymnos and Rhodes.

It's a somewhat unenticing place – you'd really only use it as a jump-off point if coming from Istanbul. If you get stuck, the *Lido* at Paleológou 15 (℡25510 28808) represents by far the best-value budget hotel. A single long-haul **ticket agency**, Kykon Tours at Venizélou 68 (℡25510 25455), handles LANE.

Kavála

The second port of northern Greece (3hr by bus from Thessaloníki, 45min by taxi from its own airport at Khryssoúpoli, 32km northeast) has regular links to **Límnos, Áyios Efstrátios, Lésvos, Híos, Sámos** and **Ikaría**. The city has a line of good tavernas in the old quarter below the castle, but pleasant, affordable hotels are in short supply. In ascending order of comfort and price, try the *Akropolis* (℡2510 223 543) at Venizélou 29, the *Nefeli* (℡2510 227 441) at Erythroú Stavroú 50 or the *Esperia* (℡2510 229 621) at Erythroú Stavroú 42, opposite the archeological museum. Among **ticket agencies**, Nikos Miliadhes, Platía Karaolí Dhimitríou (℡2510 226 147 or 2510 223 421), represents GA, while Yiorgos Zolotas, a few steps further along the quay (℡2510 835 671), handles Saos Ferries.

Lávrio

This small port near Athens (reachable by infrequent "express" bus from the airport, or by regular bus from the Mavromatéon terminal downtown) has far more regular connections than Pireás – typically two to three weekly – to **Áyios Efstrátios, Psará, Sígri** (for western Lésvos) and **Límnos**. It's a bleak place, though, not one to be stuck in unnecessarily, so confirm sailings with the port police on ℡22920 25249. Krialis Travel (℡22920 26040) is the current **ticket agency** for east Aegean boats.

Thessaloníki

The northern capital is a mildly busy alternative port; to reach the harbour area from Macedonia Airport, 15km out, take the #78 bus into town, which passes within a few blocks of the harbour passenger terminal. Alternatively, a taxi won't be much more than €10. Between June and September, there are two weekly services to **Límnos, Lésvos** and **Híos**, less frequently to **Sámos**. Companies serving them are handled by the **ticket agencies** Omikron, Salamínos 4 (℡2310 513 005), and Karacharisis, Koundourióti 8 (℡2310 524 544).

If you have a day in hand, it's worth exploring the Byzantine churches, especially the Áyios Yeóryios Rotonda and tiny Ósios Davíd with their fine mosaics, as well as the Archeological Museum. Hotels are plentiful if mostly uninspiring, noisy and often vastly overpriced; worthwhile exceptions include the *Tourist* on Mitropóleos 21 (℡0310 270 501), the *Nea Mitropolis* at Syngroú 22 (℡2310 525 540), the *Bill* at Syngroú 29, corner Amvrosíou (℡2310 537 666), and the *Orestias Kastorias* at Agnóstou Stratiótou 14 (℡2310 276 517).

Visas and red tape

UK and all other EU nationals (plus those of Norway, Switzerland and Iceland) need only a valid passport or national identity card for entry to Greece; they are no longer stamped in on arrival or out upon departure, and, in theory at least, enjoy the same civil rights as Greek citizens. US, Australian, New Zealand, Canadian and most non-EU Europeans receive mandatory entry and exit stamps in their passports and can stay, as tourists, for ninety days (cumulative) in any six-month period. Such nationals arriving from another EU state not party to the Schengen Agreement may not be stamped in routinely at minor Greek ports, so it's best to make sure this is done in order to avoid unpleasantness on exit. Your passport must be valid for three months after your arrival date.

Unless of Greek descent, visitors from **non-EU** countries are currently not, in practice, being given extensions to tourist visas by the various Aliens' Bureaux in Greece. You must leave not just Greece but the entire Schengen Group – essentially the entire EU as it was before May 2004, minus Britain and Eire, plus Norway and Iceland – and stay out until the maximum-90-days-in-180 rule as set out above is satisfied. If you **overstay** your time and then leave under your own power – ie are not deported – you'll be hit with a huge spot fine upon departure, of €600–1200 depending on the country and how many days you're over-limit, and possibly be banned from re-entering for a period of time; no excuses will be entertained except (just maybe) a doctor's certificate stating you were immobilized in hospital. It cannot be overemphasized just how exigent Greek immigration officials have become on this issue.

By EU law, EU nationals are allowed to stay indefinitely in any EU state (with various exceptions in force concerning employment for the ten new members who joined in May 2004), but to be sure of avoiding any problems, it's best to get a five-year **residence permit** (*ádhia paramonís*) and (if appropriate) a work permit – for both, see "Finding work", p.92. If you're not employed (self- or otherwise), you will be required to prove that you have sufficient resources to support yourself, and health insurance (either UK-based for expats, or locally in Greece). The usual ways to demonstrate solvency are pink, personalized bank **exchange receipts** given whenever you import money by wire or travellers' cheques; confirmation by your home state National Insurance authorities that you are continuing to make contributions towards a public pension scheme; or a Greek **savings account passbook** – the pages of the passbook in particular should be photocopied and given to the police.

Residence/work permits for non-EU nationals can now only be obtained by prior application to a Greek embassy or consulate outside of Greece; you have a much better chance of securing one if you are married to a Greek, or have permanent-resident status in another EU state, but even then you can expect delays, and vetting interviews, once you arrive in Greece.

Greek embassies abroad

Australia 9 Turrana St, Yarralumla, Canberra, ACT 2600 ☏02/6273 3011.
Britain 1a Holland Park, London W11 3TP ☏020/7221 6467, ⓦwww .greekembassy.org.uk.
Canada 80 Maclaren St, Ottawa, ON K2P 0K6 ☏613/238-6271.
Ireland 1 Upper Pembroke St, Dublin 2 ☏01/676 7254.
New Zealand 5–7 Willeston St, Wellington ☏04/473 7775.
USA 2221 Massachusetts Ave NW, Washington, DC 20008 ☏202/939-5800, ⓦwww.greekembassy.org.

Insurance

Even though EU health-care privileges apply in Greece (see opposite for details), you'd do well to take out an **insurance** policy before travelling to cover against theft, loss, illness or injury. Before paying for a whole new policy, however, it's worth checking whether you are already covered: some all-risks homeowners' or renters' insurance policies *may* cover your possessions when overseas, and many private medical schemes (such as BUPA or WPA in the UK) offer coverage extensions for abroad.

In Canada, provincial health plans usually provide partial cover for medical mishaps overseas, while holders of official student/teacher/youth cards in Canada and the US are entitled to meagre accident coverage and hospital in-patient benefits. **Students** will often find that their student health coverage extends during the vacations and for one term beyond the date of last enrolment. Most UK **credit-card issuers** also offer some sort of vacation insurance, which is often automatic if you pay for the holiday with their card. However, it's vital to check just what these policies cover – frequently only death or dismemberment.

After exhausting the possibilities above, you might want to contact a **specialist travel insurance** company, or consider the travel insurance deal offered by Rough Guides (see box). A typical travel insurance policy usually provides cover for the **loss** of baggage, tickets and – up to a certain limit – cash, cards or cheques, as well as **cancellation** or curtailment of your journey. Most of them exclude so-called **dangerous sports** unless an extra premium is paid: in the Greek islands this means motorbiking, windsurfing, sea-kayaking and often sailing, with most visitors engaging in one or the other at some point. Many policies can be chopped and changed to eliminate coverage you don't need – for example, sickness and accident benefits can often be excluded or included at will. If you do take medical coverage, ascertain whether benefits will be paid as treatment proceeds or only after return home, whether there is a **24-hour medical emergency number**, and how much the deductible is (sometimes negotiable). When securing baggage cover, make sure

Rough Guide travel insurance

Rough Guides has teamed up with Columbus Direct to offer you travel insurance that can be tailored to suit your needs.

Readers can choose from many different travel insurance products, including a low-cost backpacker option for long stays; a short-break option for city getaways; a typical holiday package option; and many others. There are also annual multi-trip policies for those who travel regularly, with variable levels of cover available. Different sports and activities (trekking, skiing, etc) can be covered if required on most policies.

Rough Guides travel insurance is available to the residents of 36 different countries with different language options to choose from via our website – ⓦ www.roughguidesinsurance.com – where you can also purchase the insurance.

Alternatively, UK residents should call ⓣ 0800 083 9507, US citizens ⓣ 1-800 749-4922 and Australians ⓣ 1 300 669 999. All other nationalities should call ⓣ +44 870 890 2843.

that the **per-article limit** – typically under £500 in the UK – will cover your most valuable possession. Travel agents and tour operators in the UK are likely to **require travel insurance** when you book a package holiday, though after a change in the UK law in late 1998 they can no longer insist that you buy their own – however, you will be required to sign a declaration saying that you have a policy with a particular company.

If you need to make a **medical claim**, you should keep receipts for medicines and treatment and, in the event you have anything stolen or lost, you must obtain an **official statement** from the police or the airline which lost your bags. In the wake of growing numbers of fraudulent claims, most insurers won't even entertain one unless you have a police report. There is usually also a **time limit** for submitting claims after the end of your journey.

Health

British and other EU nationals are officially entitled to free **medical care** in Greece upon presentation of an E111 form, available from most post offices. In the near future, this and most other E-forms are set to be replaced by a Europe-wide benefits "Smart Card". "Free", however, means admittance only to the lowest grade of state hospital (known as a *yenikó nosokomío*), and does not include nursing care, special tests or the cost of medication. If you need pro-longed medical care, you should make use of private treatment, which – while slightly less expensive than elsewhere in western Europe – is where your travel insurance policy (see opposite) comes in handy. The US, Canada, Australia and New Zealand have no formal health-care agreements with Greece (other than allowing for free emergency trauma treatment).

There are no required **inoculations** for Greece, though it's wise to ensure that you are up to date on tetanus. The **water** is safe pretty much everywhere, though you will come across shortages or brackish supplies on some of the drier and more remote islands. Bottled water is widely available if you're feeling cautious.

Specific hazards

The main health problems experienced by visitors have to do with **overexposure to the sun**, and the odd nasty from the sea. To combat the former, don't spend too long in the sun, cover up limbs, wear a hat, and drink plenty of fluids in the hot months to avoid any danger of **sunstroke**; remember that even hazy sun can burn. As for sea-gear, goggles or a dive mask for swimming and footwear for walking over wet or rough rocks are useful.

Hazards of the deep

In the sea, you may have the bad luck to meet an armada of **jellyfish** (*tsoúkhtres*); they come in various colours and sizes ranging from purple "pizzas" to invis-ible, minute creatures. Various over-the-counter remedies for jellyfish stings are sold in resort pharmacies; baking soda or diluted ammonia also help to lessen the sting. The welts and burning usually subside of their own accord within a few hours; there are no deadly man-of-war species in Greek waters.

Less vicious but much more common are black, spiky **sea urchins** (*ahini*), which infest rocky shorelines; if you step on or graze one, a sewing needle (you can sterilize it by heat from a cigarette lighter) and olive oil are effective for removing spines; if you don't extract them they'll fester. You can take your revenge by eating their roe, which is served as a delicacy in a few seafood restaurants.

Stingrays and skates (Greek names include *platý*, *seláhi*, *vátos* or *trígona*) mainly frequent bays with sandy bottoms where they can camouflage themselves. Though shy, they can give you a nasty lash with their tail if trodden on, so shuffle your feet a bit when entering such water.

When snorkelling in deeper water, you may happen upon a brightly coloured **moray eel** (*smérna*) sliding back and forth out of its rocky lair. Keep a respectful distance – their slightly comical air and clown colours belie an irritable temper and the ability to inflict nasty bites or even to sever fingers.

Sandflies, dogs and mosquitoes

If you are sleeping on or near a **beach**, it's wise to use insect repellent, either lotion or wrist/ankle bands, and/or a tent with a screen to guard against **sandflies**. Their bites are potentially dangerous, as these flies spread leishmaniasis, a parasitic infection characterized by chronic fever, listlessness and weight loss. It's difficult to treat, requiring long courses of medication.

In Greece, the main reservoirs for leishmaniasis are **dogs**. Transmission of the disease to humans by fleas has not been proven, but it's wisest not to befriend strays as they also carry echinococcosis, a debilitating liver fluke. In humans these form nodules and cysts which can only be removed surgically.

Mosquitoes (*kounóupia*) in Greece carry nothing worse than a vicious bite, but they can be infuriating. The widespread solution are the small electrical devices (trade names Vape-Net or Bay-Vap) that vaporize an odourless insecticide tablet; many accommodation proprietors supply them routinely, and if you see them left near your night-table it's a good bet they'll be needed. Insect repellents such as Autan are available from most general stores and kiosks.

Wasps and **hornets** (*sfigónes*, *sfíkes*) are common, particularly during the vintage season (Aug–Oct), when they're attracted by all the fermenting grape-mess. Some mind their own business; others are very aggressive, even dive-bombing swimmers some distance out to sea. One of the best repellent measures (used by tavernas) is coffee grounds set alight.

Creepy-crawlies

Adders (*ohiés*) and **scorpions** (*skorpii*) are found throughout these islands (except Astypálea); both creatures are shy – scorpions in particular are nocturnal – but take care when climbing over dry-stone wall, where snakes like to sun themselves, and don't put hands or feet in places like shoes, where you haven't looked first. Wiggly, fast-moving **centipedes** (*skolópendres*) which look like a rubber toy from Hong Kong should also be treated with respect, as they pack a nasty bite.

The number of annual deaths from **snake-bite** in Europe is very small. Many snakes will bite if threatened, whether venomous or not. If a bite injects venom, then swelling will normally occur within thirty minutes. If this happens, get medical attention; keep the bitten part still; and make sure all body movements are as gentle as possible. If medical attention is not nearby, then bind the limb firmly to slow the blood circulation, but not so tightly as to stop the blood-flow.

Many reptiles, including snakes, can harbour **Salmonella** bacteria, so should be handled cautiously and preferably not at all. This applies particularly to tortoises.

In addition to munching its way through a fair fraction of Greece's surviving pine forests, the **pine processionary caterpillar** – taking its name from the long, nose-to-tail convoys which individuals form at certain points in their life cycle – sports highly irritating hairs, with a poison worse than a scorpion's. If you touch one, or even a tree-trunk they've been on recently, you'll know all about it for a week, and the welts may require antihistamine to heal.

Plants

If you snap a **wild fig** shoot while walking in the countryside, take care not to come in contact with drops of the highly irritant **sap**. The immediate antidote to this alkaloid is a mild acid, like lemon juice or vinegar; left unneutralized, fig "milk" raises welts which take a month to heal. Severe allergic reactions have to be treated with strong steroids, either topical cream (available from pharmacies) or intravenously in hospital casualty wards.

Pharmacies, drugs and contraception

For **minor complaints** it's enough to go to the local **farmakío** (pharmacy). Greek pharmacists are highly trained and dispense a number of medicines which elsewhere could only be prescribed by a doctor. In the larger towns and resorts there'll usually be one who speaks good English. Pharmacies are usually closed evenings and Saturday mornings, but all should have a monthly schedule (in both English and Greek) on their door showing the complete roster of night and weekend duty pharmacists in town.

Greeks are famously hypochondriac, members of one of Europe's champion medicine-guzzling nations, such that pharmacies are veritable Aladdin's caves of **arcane drug and sundry formulas** – just about everything available in North America and northern Europe is here, and then some, at affordable prices. **Homeopathic** and herbal remedies are quite widely available, too, now sold in most larger pharmacies alongside more conventional products.

If you regularly use any form of **prescription drug**, you should bring along a copy of the prescription, together with the generic name of the drug; this will help should you need to replace it, and also avoids possible problems with customs officials. In this regard, it's worth being aware that **codeine is banned** in Greece. If you import any you might find yourself in serious trouble, so check labels carefully; it's the core ingredient of Panadeine, Veganin, Solpadeine, Codis and Empirin-Codeine, to name just a few common compounds.

Hay-fever sufferers should be prepared for the early Greek pollen season, at its height from April to June. Pollen from Aleppo and Calabrian pine in April/May can be particularly noxious. If you are taken by surprise, you'll be able to get tablets at a pharmacy, but best to come prepared.

Contraceptive pills are more readily available every year, but don't count on getting these – or spermicidal jelly/foam – outside of a few large island towns, over the counter at the larger *farmakía*; Greek women tend not to use any sort of birth control systematically, and have an average of four abortions during their adult life. **Condoms**, however, are inexpensive and ubiquitous – just ask for *profylaktiká* (the slangy terms *plastiká* or slightly vulgar *kapótes* are even better understood) at any pharmacy or corner *períptero* (kiosk).

Women's hygiene supplies are sold in pharmacies or in supermarkets near the toilet paper and diapers. Sanitary towels ("Always" brand) are ubiquitous; tampons, known by the trademark catch-all of "Tampax", can be trickier to find in remoter spots, especially on the smaller islands.

Doctors and hospitals

You'll find English-speaking **doctors** in any of the bigger towns or resorts. For an **ambulance**, phone ☎166. In **emergencies** – cuts, broken bones, etc – treatment is given free in **state hospitals** (ask for the *thálamos atihimáton* – casualty ward), though you will only get the most basic level of nursing care. Staff attitudes vary: we've been attended to very satisfactorily on several occasions, but if you're the latest in a series of inebriated foreigners to fall off a hotel balcony in a given resort, your reception may be cavalier at best. Greek families routinely take in food and bedding for relatives, so as a tourist you'll be at a severe disadvantage. Somewhat better are the ordinary state-run **outpatient clinics** (*yiatría*) attached to most public hospitals and also found in rural locales. These operate on a first-come, first-served basis, so go early; usual hours are 8am to noon, though it's sometimes possible to get attended to between 1 and 5pm.

Costs, money and banks

The cost of living in Greece has increased remarkably since it joined the EU and subsequently adopted the euro. The days of renting an island house for a monthly pittance are ancient history, and food prices at corner shops now differ little from those of other EU countries. However, outside the established resorts, travel between and around the islands remains reasonably priced, with the cost of restaurant meals, short-term accommodation and public transport still cheaper than anywhere in northern or western Europe except parts of Portugal and France.

Prices depend on where and when you go. The larger tourist resorts and trendier islands (like Rhodes, Kós, Sými and Pátmos) are more expensive, and costs everywhere increase sharply during July and August, or at Christmas, New Year or Easter. **Students** with an International Student Identity Card (ISIC) or under-26s with an International Youth Travel Card can get discounted (sometimes free) admission at many archeological sites and museums; those **over 60** can rely on site-admission discounts of 25 to 30 percent, as well as similar discounts for transport. These, and other occasional discounts, tend to be more readily available to EU nationals.

Some basic costs

On most islands a **daily per-person budget** of £28/US$54 will get you basic accommodation, breakfast, picnic lunch, a short ferry or bus ride and a simple evening meal, as one of a couple. On £55/$105 a day you could be living quite well, plus sharing the cost of renting a large motorbike or small car.

Inter-island **ferries**, the main unavoidable expense, are reasonably priced, subsidized by the government in an effort to preserve remote island communities. The cheapest cabin for the overnight journey from Athens to Sámos, an eleven-hour trip, costs about €35, a deck-class ticket for the four-hour trip from Rhodes to Kós costs about €10. For €5–8 you can catch a short-hop ferry to the numerous small islands that lie closer to Rhodes, Kós and Sámos, the most likely touchdown points if you're flying to the Dodecanese or east Aegean on a direct charter.

The simplest double **room** generally costs around €25–30 a night, depending on the location and the plumbing arrangements. Bona fide single rooms are rare, and cost about seventy percent of double rates. Organized **campsites** are little more than €4 per person, with similar charges per tent and perhaps 25 percent more for a camper van. With discretion you can camp for free at certain beaches, which are noted in the text.

A basic taverna **meal** with local wine can be had for around €12–15 a head. Add a better bottle of wine, seafood or more careful cooking, and it could be up to €19–23 a head; you'll rarely pay more than that. Sharing seafood, Greek salads and dips is a good way to keep costs down in the better restaurants, and even in the most developed of resorts, with inflated "international" menus, you'll often be able to find a more earthy but decent taverna where the locals eat.

Money

Greece is one of twelve EU countries that changed over to a single currency, the **euro** (€), in February 2002. The fixed conversion rate used was 340.75 drachmas (*dhrakhmés*) to one euro; people still commonly quote prices in drachmas, and many till receipts continue to show the value in both currencies. Rounding up of euro equivalents of drachma prices has prevailed since February 2002, effectively making the country two to three percent more expensive in 2003–4 than in early 2002 even before inflation was taken into account. Greek shopkeepers have not been bothering much with shortfalls of 10 cents or less, whether in their favour (especially) or yours. You will be able to exchange any left-over drachma paper notes until March 2012 at branches of the Bank of Greece.

For the most up-to-date **exchange rates** of your home currency against the euro, consult the very useful currency speculators' website, Ⓦwww.oanda.com.

Euro notes exist in denominations of 5, 10, 20, 50, 100, 200 and 500 euro, and coins in denominations of 1, 2, 5, 10, 20 and 50 cents and 1 and 2 euro. Each country in the euro-zone strikes its own coins (just one face is distinctive), but the other side – and all notes – are uniform throughout Europe. See p.94 for a discussion of counterfeit notes.

Banks and exchange

Greek **banks** are normally open Monday to Thursday 8.30am–2.30pm, and Friday 8.30am–2pm. Always take your passport with you as proof of identity and be prepared for at least one long queue. Outside these times, travel agencies and the largest hotels can often provide this service, albeit with hefty commissions and/or poor rates.

Small-denomination **foreign bank notes** are also extremely useful, and relatively unlikely to be stolen in Greece. A number of authorized brokers for exchanging foreign cash have emerged in major tourist centres such as Rhodes. When changing small amounts, choose those bureaux that charge a flat percentage commission (usually one percent) rather than a high minimum.

In 1998, the Greek **post office** abandoned the business of changing money. You may, however, find that main post offices (in provincial capitals) are the designated receiving points for Western Union Moneygrams (see p.48).

There is no need to **purchase euros** before arrival unless you're coming in at some ungodly hour at one of the remoter land or sea frontier posts. Airport arrival lounges will always have an ATM available for passengers on incoming international flights.

Travellers' cheques

The safest, though most expensive, way to carry money is as **travellers' cheques**.

These can be obtained from banks or from offices of Thomas Cook and American Express; you'll usually pay a commission of between one and two percent, though be aware of any special commission-free deals from your travel agent or your home bank. You can cash the cheques at most Greek banks, though rarely elsewhere. Each travellers' cheque encashment in Greece will incur a minimum commission charge, so you won't want to make too many small-value transactions. For greater amounts, a set percentage will apply. Make sure you keep the purchase agreement and a record of cheque serial numbers safe and separate from the cheques themselves. In the event that cheques are lost or stolen, the issuing company will expect you to report the loss forthwith; most companies claim to replace lost or stolen cheques within 24 hours.

Credit cards and ATMs

Major **credit cards** are not usually accepted by cheaper tavernas or hotels, but they're almost essential for renting cars or for buying Olympic Airlines tickets. Major travel agents may also accept them, but for buying ferry (as opposed to air) tickets a **three percent surcharge** is typically passed on to the consumer. Visa and MasterCard are widely accepted, American Express far less so and Diner's hardly at all.

You can easily use the vast network of Greek **cash machines** (ATMs) by learning the PIN numbers for your debit/credit cards. Larger airports (such as Athens, Kós, Lésvos, Rhodes and Thessaloníki) have at least one of these in the arrivals hall, and almost any town or island with a population of over a thousand (or substantial tourist traffic) also has them. The most common are those of the National Bank/Ethniki Trapeza, the Trapeza Pireos/Bank of Piraeus, and the Emboriki Trapeza, which happily and interchangeably accept Visa, MasterCard, Visa Electron, Plus and Cirrus cards; those of the equally widespread Alfa Trapeza/Alpha Bank also accept American Express cards, though the Agrotiki Bank only takes Cirrus/Plus system- and Visa-affiliated cards.

ATM transactions with **debit cards** linked to a current (checking) account via the Plus/Cirrus/Maestro attract charges of

2.25 percent on the sterling/dollar transaction value, plus a commission fee of 2.65 percent; the "tourist" (not the more favourable "interbank") exchange rate will also be applied. Using **credit cards** at an ATM costs roughly the same – 2 per cent (minimum £2) of the sterling equivalent amount plus a 2.75 per cent "overseas transaction fee", moreover with very high cash-advance interest accruing from the moment the funds are drawn down.

Wiring money

In an emergency, you can arrange to have substantial amounts of **money wired** from your home bank to a bank in Greece. Receiving funds by SWIFT transfer takes a minimum of two, and potentially up to ten, working days. From the UK, a bank charge of 0.03 percent, with a minimum of £17, maximum £35, is typically levied for two-day service; some building societies charge a £20 flat fee irrespective of the amount. If you choose this route, your home bank will need the IBAN (international bank account number) for the account to which funds are being sent, or failing that the bank name and branch code. It's unwise to transfer more than the equivalent of €10,000; above

that limit, as part of measures to combat money-laundering, international terrorism and organized crime, the receiving Greek bank will begin asking awkward questions and impose punitive commissions.

Having money wired from home using one of the **companies** listed below is never convenient – local affiliate offices other than the post office are thin on the ground in Greece – and is even more expensive than using a bank, and should be considered as a last resort. However, unlike with banks, the funds should be available for collection at Amex's, Thomas Cook's or Western Union's local representative office within hours, sometimes minutes, of being sent.

Money-wiring companies

Travelers Express/MoneyGram US ☎1-800/444-3010, Canada ☎1-800/933-3278, UK, Ireland and New Zealand ☎00800/6663 9472, Australia ☎0011800/6663 9472, ⊚www .moneygram.com.
Western Union US and Canada ☎1-800/CALL-CASH, Australia ☎1800/501 500, New Zealand ☎0800/005 253, UK ☎0800/833 833, Republic of Ireland ☎66/947 5603, ⊚www.westernunion .com (customers in the US and Canada can send money online).

Information, maps and websites

The National Tourist Organization of Greece (Ellinikós Organismós Tourismoú, or EOT; GNTO abroad, ⓦ www.gnto.gr) maintains offices in most European capitals, and major cities in Australia and North America (see below for addresses). It publishes an impressive array of free, glossy, regional pamphlets, invariably five to ten years out of date, which are OK for getting an idea of where you want to go, even if the actual text should be taken with a spoonful of salt. Also available from the EOT are a reasonable fold-out map of the country and a number of (equally outdated) brochures on special interests and festivals.

Greek national tourist offices abroad

Australia
51 Pitt St, Sydney NSW 2000 ☎ 02/9241 1663,
ⓔ hto@tpg.com.au.
Canada
91 Scollard St, 2nd Floor, Toronto M5R 1GR, Ontario
☎ 416/968-2220, ⓔ grnto.tor@sympatico.ca.
UK
4 Conduit St, London W1R 0DJ ☎ 020/7734 5997,
ⓔ EOT-greektouristoffice@btinternet.com.
USA
645 Fifth Ave, New York, NY 10022 ☎ 212/421-5777, ⓔ gnto@greektourism.com.

Tourist offices

In the Dodecanese and east Aegean there are official **EOT offices** only in Ródhos Town, Vathý (Sámos) and Mytilíni (Lésvos); elsewhere, specifically on Kós, Híos, Kálymnos, Mólyvos and again Ródhos Town, you'll find **municipal tourist offices**. Staff at either breed of office are happy to provide advice and photocopied sheets on ferry and bus departures, the opening hours for museums and sites, plus occasionally assistance with **accommodation** – though there have been scandals in the provinces concerning certain staff taking backhanders to steer potential clients towards particular outfits. In the absence of any of these, you can visit the **Tourist Police**, essentially a division (often just a single delegate) of the local police. They can sometimes provide you with lists of rooms to let, which they regulate, but they're really where you go if you have a **serious complaint** about a taxi, accommodation or eating establishment.

Maps

No authoritative, authentic maps . . . . Well, isn't that as it should be? Why does anybody need maps? If an individual wants them he's a spy. If a country needs maps it's moribund. A well-mapped country is a dead country. A complete survey is a burial shroud. A life with maps is a tyranny!

That extract from Alan Sillitoe's unjustly forgotten 1971 satire, *Travels in Nihilon*, pretty much sums up the prevailing attitude towards **maps** in Greece, which are an endless source of confusion and often outright misinformation. Each cartographic company seems to have its own peculiar system of transcribing Greek letters into English – and these, as often as not, do not match the semi-official transliterations on the road signs, which again may not match, even in the same region.

The most reliable **general map** of the Dodecanese and east Aegean islands is the GeoCenter map *Greek Islands/Aegean Sea*, which covers all points described in this book at a scale of 1:300,000. It's not perfect, and like all double-sided maps can be cumbersome to use; the single-sided Freytag-Berndt (1:650,000, with index booklet) is a possible alternative. Both of these are widely available in Britain and North America, less easily in Greece (see p.51). Freytag-Berndt also publishes a series of more detailed **regional island maps**, including *Kos – Samos – Ikaria* (1:150,000), *Rhodos* (1:100,000) and *Hios – Lesvos — Lemnos* (1:150,000); these are best bought overseas from specialist outlets.

Maps of **individual islands** are more easily available on the spot and, while some are wildly inaccurate or obsolete, with strange hieroglyphic symbols, others are reliable and up-to-date; we've indicated in the guide where particular maps are worth buying or not. Large-scale products worth keeping an eye out for are those published by Athens-based **Road Editions** (⊛ www.road. gr); based on army topographical maps, they're usually quite accurate but as of writing available for only a few islands covered in this book – Rhodes, Kárpathos/Kássos, Kós, Sámos, Híos and Lésvos. In the UK they can be purchased at the Hellenic Book Service, Stanfords and other good map shops (see opposite for addresses). Two domestic competitors to Road, **Emvelia** (⊛ www.emvelia.gr) and **Anavasi** (⊛ www .mountains.gr/anavasi) have also emerged, but thus far Emvelia has concentrated on the mainland, Crete and major cities, whilst Anavasi specializes in waterproof, rip-proof mountain hiking maps, plus the islands of the Sporades and Cyclades, though they have a good map of Híos. Out in the islands, Road and Anavasi maps can be found in the bookstore chain Newsstand and other independent outlets.

Hiking and topographical maps

Hiking and topographical maps of the east Aegean and Dodecanese islands, including Rhodes, are almost impossible to obtain in Greece; Road and Anavasi products are just a bit too small-scale (1:50,000 and up) to work. The Greek government's equivalent of Ordnance Survey or USGS topographic maps are unavailable indefinitely for "security reasons" owing to continuing tension with Turkey and other Balkan neighbours. Should the rules change, you can try your luck at the Army Geographical Service (*Yeografikí Ypiresía Stratoú*) in Athens at Evelpídhon 4, north of Aréos Park (Mon, Wed & Fri 8am–noon).

At present, the best available hiking maps are those prepared before and during World War II by foreign powers. For the **east Aegean islands** you want those prepared by the British War Office at a scale of 1:50,000, with twenty- or forty-metre contour intervals; while they don't show paths, they depict roads more accurately than many contemporary Greek tourist maps, and also indicate the magnetic declination from true north. All of this series is quite usable except the one for Ikaría, which was evidently hastily produced (the contour lines don't join up correctly).

For the **Dodecanese**, under Italian occupation from 1913 to 1943, the map set published by the Instituto Geografico Militare in Florence from 1927 onwards is your best choice. Sheets for each island have been published at a 1:25,000 scale, with ten-metre contour intervals. Because of that, and their calligraphic lettering, they have a deceptively antiquarian appearance, but are eminently reliable for natural features and village positions, and often show trails remarkably accurately. Difficulties arise principally from the Italianization of all Greek place names, eg Terrarossa for Kokinohóma, so you have to "decode" between two probably unfamiliar languages.

These two series are not commercially available overseas, let alone in Greece, so you'll have to make do with **photocopies** of originals kept by certain large institutions. In the US or Canada, try the map room of a major university library; most will have at least the Italian set, and charge nothing or a nominal fee for copying. In the UK, the only source of both the British and Italian cartography is the map library of the Royal Geographical Society, Kensington Gore, London SW7 2AR (☎020/7591 3050; Mon–Fri 11am–5pm; no mail order service but ☎020/7591 3001 for enquiries). Before you're allowed to make copies (around £1.50 per large A2 sheet), you first have to petition the Directorate of Geographic Information, Military Survey, Block A, Government Buildings, Hook Rise South, Tolworth, Surbiton, Surrey KT6 7NB by letter or fax for permission to use Crown Copyright material (☎020/8335 5338, ☎8335 5387).

Finally, for hiking in particular areas of Sámos, Rhodes, Kálymnos, Kós, Sými and Lésvos, maps-with-guide-booklets published by **Marengo Publications** in England also prove very useful. Stanfords keeps a good stock of these, or order from Marengo direct through ⊛ www.marengowalks.com. The municipality of Níssyros issues a free GPS-compatible topographic map of that island, prepared by two German visitors.

Map outlets

In the UK and Ireland

Stanfords 12–14 Long Acre, London WC2E 9LP ℡ 020/7836 1321, ⓦ www.stanfords.co.uk. Also at 39 Spring Gardens, Manchester ℡ 0161/831 0250, and 29 Corn St, Bristol ℡ 0117/929 9966.
Blackwell's Map Centre 50 Broad St, Oxford OX1 3BQ ℡ 01865/793 550, ⓦ maps.blackwell .co.uk. Branches in Bristol, Cambridge, Cardiff, Leeds, Liverpool, Newcastle, Reading and Sheffield.
The Map Shop 30a Belvoir St, Leicester LE1 6QH ℡ 0116/247 1400, ⓦ www.mapshopleicester .co.uk.
National Map Centre 22–24 Caxton St, London SW1H 0QU ℡ 020/7222 2466, ⓦ www.mapsnmc .co.uk.
National Map Centre Ireland 34 Aungier St, Dublin ℡ 01/476 0471, ⓦ www.mapcentre.ie.
The Travel Bookshop 13–15 Blenheim Crescent, London W11 2EE ℡ 020/7229 5260, ⓦ www .thetravelbookshop.co.uk.
Traveller 55 Grey St, Newcastle-upon-Tyne NE1 6EF ℡ 0191/261 5622, ⓦ www.newtraveller.com.

In the US and Canada

110 North Latitude US ℡ 336/369-4171, ⓦ www.110nlatitude.com.
Book Passage 51 Tamal Vista Blvd, Corte Madera, CA 94925 and in the historic San Francisco Ferry Building ℡ 1-800/999-7909 or 415/927-0960, ⓦ www.bookpassage.com.
Distant Lands 56 S Raymond Ave, Pasadena, CA 91105 ℡ 1-800/310-3220, ⓦ www.distantlands.com.
Globe Corner Bookstore 28 Church St, Cambridge, MA 02138 ℡ 1-800/358-6013, ⓦ www.globecorner.com.
Longitude Books 115 W 30th St #1206, New York, NY 10001 ℡ 1-800/342-2164, ⓦ www .longitudebooks.com.
Map Town 400 5 Ave SW #100, Calgary, AB T2P 0L6 ℡ 1-877/921-6277 or 403/266-2241, ⓦ www.maptown.com.
Travel Bug Bookstore 3065 W Broadway, Vancouver, BCV6K 2G9 ℡ 604/737-1122, ⓦ www .travelbugbooks.ca.
World of Maps 1235 Wellington St, Ottawa, ON K1Y 3A3 ℡ 1-800/214-8524 or 613/724-6776, ⓦ www.worldofmaps.com.

In Australia and New Zealand

Map Centre ⓦ www.mapcentre.co.nz.
Mapland 372 Little Bourke St, Melbourne ℡ 03/9670 4383, ⓦ www.mapland.com.au.
Map Shop 6–10 Peel St, Adelaide ℡ 08/8231 2033, ⓦ www.mapshop.net.au.
Map World 371 Pitt St, Sydney ℡ 02/9261 3601, ⓦ www.mapworld.net.au. Also at 900 Hay St, Perth ℡ 08/9322 5733, Jolimont Centre, Canberra ℡ 02/6230 4097 and 1981 Logan Rd, Brisbane ℡ 07/3349 6633.
Map World 173 Gloucester St, Christchurch ℡ 0800/627 967, ⓦ www.mapworld.co.nz.

Greece on the Internet

Greece is strongly represented on the Internet, with many bilingual English–Greek websites offering information on every conceivable topic. Almost every island will have its own website, though some of these, in bizarre renditions of "Gringlish", are barely readable or packed with turgid, obscure ancient history. Others – mastered by expatriate residents – are fluent enough but rather vague as to specifics, so as to avoid raising local hackles. Moreover, the most-visited spots like Rhodes, Kós or Sámos tend to have the worst (or no current) sites; you generally have better joy with the remoter, lesser-known islands, which are keener to promote themselves. Country-wide and regional sites recommended below are reasonably useful, balanced and literate. To read Greek characters on a website, you might try selecting "Unicode" in "Character Set" under the "View" pull-down menu in Internet Explorer – selecting "Greek" shows accented vowels as a "?" character.

News, views and printed matter

ⓦ www.aegeantimes.net A good digest of current Greece-, Turkey- and Cyprus-related news stories from around the world. You have to log in to post comments – not for the thin-skinned, as debate gets heated.
ⓦ www.athensnews.gr The online edition of the *Athens News*, Greece's longest-running quality English-language newspaper, with the day's top stories.
ⓦ www.ekathimerini.com The online edition of the abridged English translation of *Kathimerini*, one of Greece's most respected dailies. It's fully archived for years back, and has an excellent search facility.
ⓦ www.hellenicbooks.com The website of the UK's premier Greek bookstore. It posts full, opinionated reviews of its stock, offers the possibility of buying online, and has witty descriptions of every island.

Greek culture

ⓦ**www.culture.gr** The Greek Ministry of Culture's website. Good alphabetical gazetteer to monuments, archeological sites and museums; lots of information about the more obscure sites.

ⓦ**www.kemo.gr** The last word on Greece's minority communities, without the usual ranting polemics – many academic but readable papers posted for free download.

ⓦ**www.greekworks.com** US-based e-zine covering Greece- and Greek-related personalities, topics and events. It's $75 a year to register, and little of the content is free, but you get what you pay for in top-flight writing.

Travel in Greece

ⓦ**www.ferries.gr** Maintained by a Cretan travel agency, this site makes a good stab at showing all domestic (and international) ferry schedules, organized by company, though inevitably some information is a couple of months old. Unlike the gtp site (see below), you can make bookings.

ⓦ**www.gtp.gr** The website of Greek Travel Pages, the fat (and expensive) printed manual on every Greek travel agent's desk. Mostly used for its ferry schedules, and completely revamped in 2001, it's still not 100 percent reliable.

ⓦ**www.ktel.org** Bilingual website of the KTEL, or national bus syndicate, which posts – page glitches permitting – fairly reliable schedules. Coverage has increased recently to include larger (but not smaller) islands.

Specific islands

ⓦ**www.astypalaia.com** General all-purpose site detailing island sights, eats and accommodation, though it usually has glitches.

ⓦ**www.chiosnet.gr** Hios municipality's official site; a bit dull, but kept current.

ⓦ**www.island-ikaria.com** Literate, interesting, well organized and fairly current, covering everything from hot springs to festivals.

ⓦ**www.kalymnos-isl.gr** The island's official website, with the English pages edited by expatriate radio journalist and author Faith Warn. Thorough background, plus good travel advice and wide selection of accommodation.

ⓦ**www.kastellorizo.de** Inevitably biased (author Monika is locally married) site giving a limited overview of this tiny islet; slightly ropey English text available.

ⓦ**www.leros.org** A bit of "Gringlish" to contend with, but clearly devised with love, giving a fun, thorough flavour of the island's landscapes, people and traditional architecture.

ⓦ**www.lesvos.com** It's only updated once annually, thus hotel and restaurant recommendations get dated, but still an excellent overview of Lésvos.

ⓦ**www.symivisitor.com** Current news for aficionados (including vital links with Rhodes), plus a range of accommodation, restaurant and beach profiles, presented by the editors of the monthly island newspaper.

Greek weather

ⓦ**http://forecast.uoa.gr** A good one-stop site, maintained by the University of Athens Physics faculty. An eccentric, limited selection of reporting stations, however; for much of Greece you click on a thumbnail image of the entire country which must be enlarged to read conditions at specific places.

ⓦ**www.poseidon.ncmr.gr** A Greek oceanographer's site maintained by the National Centre for Marine Research which profiles Aegean weather meticulously, including groovy graphics of sea currents and surface winds, based on satellite imaging. It's slowish but sophisticated, good for yachties, and reports one topic (rain, temperature, wind speed, etc) at a time.

Getting around

Island-hopping is one of the intrinsic features of a holiday in the Dodecanese or east Aegean, as much a pursuit in itself as a means of transport. The local ferry, catamaran and hydrofoil network is extensive, and few of the 27 inhabited isles featured in this book are difficult to reach. Except for certain routes subsidized until 2007, inter-island plane flights are relatively expensive, but useful if you need to save time or when boat links are inadequate. Both planes and catamarans are steadily edging out less reliable hydrofoils.

For getting around the islands themselves, there are basic bus services, which most tourists choose to supplement at some stage with motorbike or car rental.

Sea transport

Several types of craft ply the islands: **roll-on-roll-off** (ro-ro) barge short-haul ferries, nicknamed *pondófles* or "slippers" in Greek, restricted to the Mastihári (Kós)–Kálymnos run; medium-sized to large **ordinary ferries** (which connect the Dodecanese and east Aegean with each other, the mainland, the Cyclades and Crete); small to large, **high-speed catamarans** (which operate both between certain Dodecanese, and between the east Aegean islands and Pireás); **hydrofoils**, which carry only passengers (confined to Rhodes–Sými and Kós–Sámos via most intervening islands); and local **kaïkia** (small, usually passenger-only boats which do short hops and excursions in season). Costs are very reasonable on the longer journeys, though proportionately more expensive for shorter, inter-island connections.

We've indicated **all sea-going connections** on the maps as well as in "Travel Details" at the end of each island account. Be warned, however, that schedules are notoriously erratic, and must be verified on the spot; the details given are essentially for departures between mid-June and mid-September inclusive. **Out-of-season** services are severely reduced, with many islands served only once or twice a week. However, in spring or autumn those ferries that do operate are often compelled by the transport ministry to call at extra or unusual islands, making possible some interesting connections.

The most reliable, up-to-date information is available from the local **port police** (*limenarhío*), who can be found on or near the harbour of every sizeable island; smaller places may only have a *limenikós stathmós* (marine post), often just a single room with a VHF radio. Their officers rarely speak much English, but they keep complete schedules posted – and, meteorological report in hand, are the final arbiters of whether or not a ship will sail in stormy weather.

Apagorevtikó, or obligatory halt of all seaborne traffic, is applied for weather in excess of force 8 on the Beaufort scale; hydrofoils tend to be confined to port at force 6 or above, with catamarans falling somewhere in between. There are, however, exceptions to this depending on the direction of the wind (southerlies are considered exceptionally dangerous), and port police maintain elaborate charts collating additional factors such as wave height; catamarans, for example, can sail in windier conditions than hydrofoils, but have a poor tolerance for disrupted sea surface. Since the sinking of the *Express Samina* (see box p.56), port police have been erring on the side of caution, though a few can seem to be (and sometimes are) unreasonable and arbitrary. Travellers stuck on a remote island with a flight home to miss often ponder the possibility of chartering a fishing boat to get them to the airport island; the fishermen are entitled to risk their lives at will, and often do sail off in dodgy weather, but they're heavily fined if caught risking passengers' lives, so this is usually a nonstarter.

Most shipping companies produce some sort of **schedule booklet** (rarely available

Mainline ferry companies: principal routes

Blue Star (BS)
Rhodes–Kós–Léros–Pátmos–Sýros–
Pireás
Rhodes–Kós–Mýkonos–Pireás
Rhodes–Kós–Amorgós–Pireás

Gerasimos Agoudimos Ferries (GA)
Rhodes–Kós–Pireás
Rhodes–Kós–Léros–Pátmos–Pireás
Rhodes–Sými–Tílos–Níssyros–Kós–
Kálymnos–Léros–Pátmos–Pireás
Rhodes–Kós–Kálymnos–Astypálea–
Amorgós–Náxos–Pireás
Rhodes–Sými–Kós–Kálymnos–
Léros–Pátmos–Pireás
Vathý–Karlóvassi–Évdhilos or Áyios
Kírykos–Náxos–Páros–Pireás
Vathý–Karlóvassi–Foúrni–Áyios
Kírykos–Náxos–Páros–Pireás
Vathý–Áyios Kírykos–Mýkonos–
Sýros–Pireás
Kavála–Límnos–Lésvos–Híos–Sámos
Vólos–Skiáthos–Skópelos–Límnos–
Lésvos–Híos–Sámos

NB Reverse itineraries are valid in
most cases, but certain ports of call
may be omitted in either direction.

Hellas Flying Dolphins (HF)
Vathý–Karlóvassi–(Foúrni)–Évdhilos–
Mýkonos or Sýros–Pireás
Vathý–Karlóvassi–Évdhilos–Pireás

Ferry company websites

Blue Star ⓦ www.bluestarferries
.com

**Lassithiotikí Anónymi Navtiliakí
Etería (LANE)**
Rhodes–Hálki–Kárpathos (both
ports)–Kássos–Sitía (Crete)–
Áyios Nikólaos (Crete)–Mílos–
Pireás
Rhodes–Kós–Kálymnos–
Sámos–Híos–Lésvos–Límnos–
Alexandhroúpoli
Rhodes–Kastellórizo

Navtiliakí Etería Lésvou (NEL)
Mytilíni–Híos–Pireás
Thessaloníki–Límnos–Lésvos–Híos–
Pireás
Sámos–Híos–Thessaloníki

Saos Ferries (SF)
Lávrio–Áyios Efstrátios–Límnos–
Kavála
Lávrio–Sýros–Tínos–Mýkonos–
Híos–Lésvos–Límnos–Samothráki–
Alexandhroúpoli
Lávrio–Áyios Efstrátios–Límnos–
Samothráki–Alexandhroúpoli
Kavála–Samothráki–Límnos–Áyios
Efstrátios–Lávrio
Lávrio–Psará–Sígri (Lésvos)–Áyios
Efstrátios–Límnos
Kými–Áyios Efstrátios–Límnos–
Kavála

Hellas Ferries ⓦ www.dolphins.gr
NEL ⓦ www.nel.gr

before July) or photocopied sheet particular
to one port. These are rarely adhered to as
the season wears on. Thus there is no all-
inclusive Greek ferry guide booklet akin to
a Thomas Cook rail timetable; for current
schedules, consult the websites on above.

Regular ferries

On most **ferry** routes, your main consideration will be getting a boat that leaves on
the day, and for the island, that you want.
Departures for the more obscure islands, the
so-called *agonés grammés* or subsidized

lines, are famously user-hostile: there may
be no boat for five days, and then suddenly
two appear within two hours of each other,
in the small hours to boot. The Ministry of
Transport, which pays the subsidies for this
behaviour, seems unwilling or unable to
compel more **logical schedules**. However,
when sailing from Rhodes or Kós to the
major Dodecanese islands, you should have
a choice of two – possibly three – sailings,
and may want to bear in mind a few of the
factors below.

Routes taken and the speed of the boats
can vary considerably. The journey from

Rhodes to Pátmos, for instance, can take anything from six hours (Blue Star "speed ferry") to eleven hours (the seven-stop *galatádhiko* or "milk run"). Before buying a ticket it's wise to establish how many stops there will be before your island, and the estimated time of arrival. Many agents act only for one specific boat (they'll blithely tell you that theirs is the only available service), so you may have to ask around to uncover alternatives. Especially in high season, early arrival is critical for getting what may be a very limited stock of accommodation.

Since the *Express Samina* disaster (see box overleaf), a few of the oldest craft have been consigned to the scrap heap or dumped overseas. Though spanking-new **boats** are still a rarity, you will more often than not be surprised to encounter a former English Channel or Scandinavian fjord ferry, rechristened and enjoying a new lease of life in the Aegean.

Regular ferry **tickets** are, in general, best bought on the day of departure, unless you need to reserve a cabin berth or space for a car. Buying tickets in advance will tie you down to a particular craft at a particular time – and innumerable factors can make you regret that. Most obviously there are mechanical breakdowns (frequent) and bad weather, which, particularly off season, can play havoc with the schedules, causing some small boats to remain at anchor and others to alter their routes drastically. (The ticket price is refunded if a boat fails to sail.) There are only three periods of the year – March 23–25, the week before and after Easter, and most of August – when all categories of ferry facility (seat, cabin, car space) need to be booked at least a couple of days in advance. Around the times of elections – whether national, municipal or European – there will also be a crunch for the best cabins, as Greeks are required to return to their home precinct to vote.

Obligatory, personalized advance ticketing, a rule especially enforced since the *Express Samina* disaster, means that you cannot buy your ticket on board; staff at the gangway will bar you from embarking if you don't have a ticket, and in some cases there may not even be a last-minute sales booth at the quayside. **Fares** for each route are set by the transport ministry and should not differ among ships or agencies, though curiously tickets for journeys *towards* Pireás are marginally more expensive than those *from*. There is usually a twenty percent discount on round-trip fares.

The cheapest class of ticket, which you'll be automatically sold unless you specify otherwise, is **deck class**, variously called *tríti* or *gámma*. This gives you the run of most of the boat except for the upper-class restaurant and bar. On the shorter, summer journeys the best place to be, in any case, is on deck – space should be staked out as soon as you get on board. However, most boats seem – with their glaring overhead lights and moulded-plastic bucket seats – expressly designed to frustrate those attempting to sleep on deck. It's well worth the few extra euros for a cabin bunk, especially if you can share with friends (cabins are usually quadruple, occasionally double or triple). Class-consciousness is the rule, so deck-class passengers may find themselves firmly locked out of second-class facilities at night to prevent them from crashing on the plush sofas, and may have to make do with Pullman-type seats. **First-class** cabin facilities usually cost scarcely less than a plane flight and are not terrific value – the main difference between first and second being the presence of a bathroom in the cabin, and a better location. Most cabins, incidentally, are overheated or overchilled, and pretty airless; ask for an *exoterikí* (outer) cabin if you want a porthole (though these are always bolted shut).

Since bookings are now computerized, this should preclude **overbookings**, but occasionally you may be sold a cabin berth at an intermediate port only to find that they are "full" when the boat arrives. Pursers will not refund you the difference between a cabin and third class, palming you off by telling you to take the matter up with the issuing agent. Your first- or second-class fare entitles you to a bunk, and this is clearly stated (in Greek) on the verso of your ticket. Make a scene, if necessary, until you are accommodated – there are often cabins in the bilge, set aside for the crew but generally unused, where you can sleep.

The wreck of the *Express Samina* – and beyond

September 27, 2000 was a sort of Judgment Day for the Greek domestic ferry industry. Around midnight in gale conditions, the *Express Samina*, bound ultimately for Ikaría, Sámos and Lipsí and the oldest ship in the domestic fleet, slammed full speed into the Pórtes rocks outside Páros harbour in the Cyclades, and sank within minutes. The bridge was unstaffed by senior officers, all of whom were elsewhere watching a football match on television. The British and Greek navies, exercising in the area, plus swarms of fishing boats from Páros, together plucked most of the 500-plus aboard from the water, including numerous foreign tourists, but 82 passengers drowned. It was the worst maritime disaster in Greece since the ferry *Iraklion* went down in December 1966, with 226 casualties.

Skipper Vassilis Yiannakis, previously at the helm in the collision and sinking of the *Nireus* (in 1991), and the first mate were quickly remanded in custody to await trial. Once the initial furore died down, the pair seemed on reflection to be easy scapegoats, and at the time of writing no trial date had been set, with prosecutors still unable to decide what charges to file. The boat had formerly been owned by Agapitos Lines, one of several shipping companies swallowed up by Minoan Flying Dolphins in its several-year drive to acquire eighty percent dominance of the Greek passenger-ferry industry – and a near-monopoly on sailings to the Cyclades and the Dodecanese. In this they had been assisted by a previous merchant-marine minister in the PASOK government, who also became a focus of opprobrium, along with Minoan Flying Dolphins' management (one of whom, general manager Pandelis Sfinias, committed suicide on November 30 by jumping from the sixth floor of his Pireás headquarters).

It also emerged that the 34-year-old *Express Samina* was the worst but by no means the only rust bucket in the Greek domestic fleet, well past its scrap-by date. EU regulations normally require ships to be retired after 27 years of service, but Greek shipping interests had wheedled an extension to 35 years from Brussels. With an effective monopoly and regulated fares, there was little incentive (as there is on the Greece–Italy lines) to keep boats up-to-date. Greek newspapers quickly tallied eighteen ferries 29 years old or older. The age of the *Express Samina* was a critical factor in her rapid sinking; newer craft have multiple airtight compartments, so that a single breach in the hull will not be fatal, but the *Express Samina* had just a single compartment, and was effectively doomed the moment the rocks tore a three-metre gash in her side (though the crew having left bulkhead doors open did not help). Most lifesaving equipment, from the ancient, cork-buoyed life jackets to the snail-slow lifeboats, was inadequate or scarcely used at the critical hour. Only

Motorbikes and cars get issued extra tickets, in the latter case four to five times the passenger deck-class fare, depending on size. Car fees are roughly proportionate to distance: for example, Sámos–Ikaría costs €26–30 depending on port and direction, while Sámos–Pireás is about €74. Technically, written permission is required to take rental motorbikes and cars on ferries, though in practice few crew will bother to quiz you on this – in any case, it's almost always cheaper to rent another vehicle at your destination.

Some ferries sell a limited range of **food on board**, though it tends to be overpriced and mediocre. On the short, daytime hops between the various islands of the Dodecanese and east Aegean, it's a good idea to stock up beforehand with your own provisions; the *Dodekanisos Express* and the *Nissos Kalymnos* in particular offer nothing other than biscuits, greasy, cling-wrapped pizzas, coffee and soft drinks.

Hydrofoils and catamarans

Hydrofoils – commonly known as *dhelfínia* (dolphins) – are roughly twice as fast (and

the year before, an inspection engineer had resigned in protest that his verdict on the boat as unseaworthy was being ignored by Minoan.

The government had to be seen to be doing something, and so made a show of granting some minor routes to Minoan's competitors during the weeks following the sinking, and pushed for a thirty-year limit on service time for boats in early 2001 (now in fact the rule). It was in the medium term, however, that the fallout from the disaster had most effect. The oldest members of the domestic fleet were instantly confined to port, pending safety inspections – which several did not pass, leaving a shortfall. Those ships which could be brought into compliance with EU standards were refitted, but clean bills of health were often issued in an arbitrary and biased manner; a loophole in the law allows substandard craft to continue operating if their destination is a non-EU country, if they operate on a chartered rather than scheduled basis, or if they forego government subsidy to operate an unprofitable line.

Investigations of the wreck still proceed at glacial pace, and Minoan Flying Dolphins remains the target of a vast number of civil suits for wrongful death, and also a criminal investigation – not, perhaps, unrelated to the directors' July 2001 decision to rechristen the company Hellas Flying Dolphins. *Express Samina* survivors' claims for compensation for their lost property remain unpaid pending resolution of the wrongful death suits.

In the prevailing climate of protecting profits (and one's legal behind) before service, matters are likely to get worse before they get better. Only a few newly commissioned ferries – such as NEL's high-speed catamarans *Aeolos Express*, *Aeolos Express II* and *Aeolos Kenteris* – have taken to the water since the sinking, but they consistently lose money and their future is in doubt. Terrified of another public relations disaster in the run-up to Greece's hosting of the 2004 Olympics, port police became – and remain – far stricter about confining boats to port in marginal weather conditions, compounding the effect of the bankruptcy (in July 2004) of Rhodes-based DANE lines – only partly compensated for by the good "speed ferry" service provided by Blue Star – and the shrinking of both Kyriakoulis Hydrofoils' and the *Nissos Kalymnos*' territory to the sea between Kós and Sámos.

The only hope of improvement will be after 2005, when cabotage (whereby only Greek-registered lines can provide domestic ferry service) ends, opening competition to the likes of P&O or Fred Olsen. In the meantime, many islands of the Dodecanese and northeast Aegean, left poorly served by the removal of boats and lines, are depending on subsidized peripheral air links provided by Olympic Aviation.

at least twice as expensive) as ordinary ferries. However, they are a useful alternative if you are pushed for time, and their network can also neatly fill gaps in ferry scheduling. Their main drawback (aside from frequent engine breakdowns) is that they were originally designed for cruising on placid Russian or Polish rivers, and are quite literally out of their depth on the open sea; thus they are extremely sensitive to bad weather, and even on a moderate sea are less than ideal for the seasick-prone. Most services don't operate – or are heavily reduced – from early October to late May, and are prone to arbitrary cancellation in any season if not enough passengers turn up. You are generally not allowed to transport scooters or bicycles on hydrofoils.

Because of their need to hug sheltering landmasses, hydrofoils sometimes sail well inside **Turkish territorial waters**, hooting at fishing boats flying the star and crescent. Despite sometimes prickly relations between the two countries, this is specifically allowed, and almost unavoidable anyway on the runs between Rhodes and Kós, or Kós and Léros.

The Nissos Kalymnos

The small, slow but reliable **Nissos Kalymnos** (cars carried) is the most regular lifeline of the northern Dodecanese between Kálymnos and Sámos, inclusive – its "milk run" visits them all a few times weekly between mid-March and mid-January. Recent seasons have seen its range restricted compared to previous years (no more services south of Kálymnos), but especially if the last hydrofoil services in the area pack up, its future should be assured as it was only built in the 1980s. Specimen schedules are likely to be as follows:

Mon, Wed, Fri, Sun: Leaves Kálymnos at 7am, arrives Léros (Lakkí) 8.30–8.45am, Lipsí 9.45–10am, Pátmos 11–11.15am, Arkí noon, Agathoníssi 1–1.15pm, Pythagório (Sámos) 2.30–2.45pm. Return via same islands, with same journey times, departing Pythagório at 3pm, arriving Kálymnos around 10pm.

Tues, Thurs, Sat: Leaves Kálymnos at 7am, arrives Astypálea 10pm; immediate turnaround and arrival back at Kálymnos by 1.30pm.

Two **hydrofoil companies**, Kyriakoulis Maritime and Laoumtzis Flying Dolphins, serve the Dodecanese between mid-May and mid-October, operating out of Sámos and Kós respectively. ANES links Sými and Rhodes all year round, as weather conditions permit. We have excluded companies that only offer charter services to tour agencies, as opposed to scheduled services.

Kyriakoulis Maritime is much reduced from its heyday, down to its last two active craft; even the replacement of obsolete, temperamental Russian Cometa engines with GM Caterpillar ones has not kept them competitive compared to small catamarans. With a slimming down of the fleet has come a simplification of routes. From June through September, a hydrofoil leaves Pythagório, Sámos, at 8am daily, calling at Pátmos, Lipsí, Léros and Kós, returning at 2pm via the same islands, arriving at about 6pm in Pythagório. Twice a week Foúrni and Ikaría (Áyios Kírykos) are included in each direction, with return from Kós at 1.15pm to fit in the extra stops, and on another day Agathoníssi is included. For current routes and schedules, phone ☎22730 25065 (Vathý) or ☎22730 62285 (Pythagório).

Laoumtzis Flying Dolphins, based in Kós, has two craft which are mostly devoted to excursions from late May through October. However, it may be possible to use their services a few days weekly on a scheduled basis to Pátmos or Lipsí. For exact details ring ☎22420 26388.

ANES has at least one daily (two on Wednesday and Friday) link between Rhodes and Sými in each direction, except Sunday. Ring ☎22460 71444, or consult ⓦwww.anes.gr for current schedules.

Catamarans attempt to combine the speed of hydrofoils with the (relative) reliability and vehicle-carrying capacity of conventional ferries. The fact that they are newish, sleek and purpose-built in France or Scandinavia has not prevented numerous breakdowns, since they are constantly playing catch-up to fill in weather-cancelled itineraries and thus miss necessary maintenance. The really big ones also only make a profit during peak season, when they're at least three-quarters full, and odds are that future years will see a reduction in size and thus fuel consumption. **Inside** they are rather soulless: ruthlessly air conditioned, with no deck seating to take the air and the most banal Greek TV blaring at you from numerous aeroplane-type screens – paying a few euro extra for *dhiakikriméni thési* (upper class) gets you a better view and less crowding, but there's no escaping the TV. Cabins are nonexistent and food facilities even more unappetizing than on conventional ferries – after all, you'll be at your destination within six to seven hours, the longest trajectory at present. Car fares are normal, though passenger **tickets** are at least double a comparable ferry journey, ie similar to hydrofoil rates.

Until 2004, two large high-speed catamarans plied the east Aegean: NEL's French-made *Aeolos Express* and *Aeolos Kenteris*, each of which carried a couple of hundred vehicles as well as passengers in a sealed interior. The end of the season saw the *Aeolos Express* disappear, perhaps permanently, to be replaced by Iason Jet's smaller *Superjet* (passengers only). Two smaller catamarans also serve the Dodecanese: the *Dodekanisos Express*, also known as *O Spanos* after the supermarket chain which owns it, and the *Sea Star*. The *Dodekanisos Express*, based on Rhodes, carries four to five cars and a slightly larger number of two-wheelers; it's a sleek, reliable, Norwegian-built craft, with a limited amount of deck space (but no deck chairs). The *Sea Star* (owned by the Tílos municipality) does not carry vehicles, and has proven unreliable to the point of extreme frustration for all involved; it is the wrong craft for the island's needs and will doubtless soon go the way the *Aeolos Express* seems to have gone. The slack *may* be taken up by a second craft, which the *Dodekanisos Express* management is planning to buy for 2005, based on Pátmos. See the box below for specimen routes.

Small ferries, kaïkia and taxi-boats

In season, **kaïkia** (caiques) and **small car ferries** of a few hundred tonnes', displacement sail between adjacent islands and to a few of the more obscure ones. These small boats can be extremely useful and often very pleasant, but are no cheaper than mainline services. In fact, if they're classified as tourist agency charters and not passenger lines controlled by the transport ministry, they tend to be quite expensive, with pressure to buy return fares (one-ways are almost always available).

The more consistent *kaïkia* links are summarized in the "Travel Details" section following each island account, though inevitably departures depend on the whims of local boat-owners, so the only firm information is to be had on the quayside.

Kaïkia and small ferries, despite appearances, have a good safety record; indeed it's the larger car ferries that have most frequently run into trouble. EU regulations being what they are, however, it seems that many of these smaller boats are doomed for trivial reasons, such as not having a second lavatory. Likely to survive are the swarms of **taxi-boats** which are a feature of Sými, Hálki, Pátmos and Astypálea, among other spots; these exist to shuttle clients on set routes to remote beaches or ports which

Catamarans: principal routes

Aeolos Kenteris (May–Oct):
Lésvos–Híos–Pireás (leaves Lésvos 8.30am or 4–5pm)
Thessaloníki–Límnos–Lésvos–Híos–Pireás
Kavála–Limnos–Lésvos–Híos–Pireás

Aeolos Express (May–Oct):
Sámos–Ikaría–Náxos–Páros–Pireás (leaves Sámos early afternoon)

Superjet (June–Oct):
Sámos–Évdhilos–Mýkonos–Tínos–Sýros–Pireás (leaves Sámos at dawn)

Dodekanisos Express (late March to mid-Oct): Rhodes–Kós–Kálymnos–Léros–Pátmos–Lipsí–Léros–Kálymnos–Kós–Rhodes (2–3 weekly)
Rhodes–Sými–Kós–Kálymnos–Leros–Pátmos–Lipsí–Léros–

Kálymnos–Kós–Sými–Rhodes (1 weekly)
Rhodes–Sými–Kós–Kálymnos–Léros–Kálymnos–Kós–Sými–Rhodes (2 weekly)
Rhodes–Kastellórizo–Rhodes (1 weekly)

NB In all cases *Dodekanisos Express* departs Rhodes daily at 8.30am, returning at 6–6.30pm.

Sea Star (early June to early Oct):
Rhodes–Tílos–Níssyros–Tílos–Rhodes (2 weekly, once with extra leg back to Tílos)
Rhodes–Tílos–Rhodes–Tílos–Rhodes (2 weekly)
Rhodes–Hálki–Tílos–Rhodes (1 weekly)
Rhodes–Tílos–Rhodes (1 weekly)
Tílos–Rhodes–Hálki–Tílos–Hálki–Rhodes (1 weekly)

can be only be reached arduously, if at all, overland. Costs on these are generally reasonable, usually per person but occasionally per boat.

Domestic flights

State-run Olympic Airlines and its subsidiary Olympic Aviation at present operate most of the **domestic flights** between the Greek mainland (Athens or Thessaloníki) and the Dodecanese and east Aegean islands, as well as a useful network of radial links between these islands. Privately owned Aegean Airlines has cherry-picked high-volume, high-profit routes such as those between Mytilíni, Kós or Rhodes and Athens. **Tickets** for both airlines are most easily obtained from travel agents (their own high-street outlets are thin on the ground). Aegean sometimes undercuts Olympic pricewise, and always surpasses it servicewise, although flight frequencies can be sparse. This, of course, could change drastically if financially troubled Olympic goes under or is bought up, as is frequently threatened, and a successor offers an inevitably reduced service.

Olympic **schedules** can be picked up at its offices abroad (see "Getting There" sections) or through its branch offices and representatives in Greece, which are maintained in almost every town or island of any size. Aegean's are easiest to get from their desks at major airports. Both airlines publish English-language schedules twice yearly (spring and autumn).

Fares for flights to and between the islands, including the domestic airport tax, work out around three to four times the cost of a ferry journey, but on certain inter-island hauls that are poorly served by boat (Rhodes–Kastellórizo or Kós–Astypálea, for example), you should consider this time well bought. Though tickets on the Rhodes–Kós–Léros–Astypálea run are fairly steeply priced, intervals on the Rhodes–Sámos–Híos–Lésvos–Límnos–Thessaloníki route are a bargain, to be taken advantage of.

Island flights are often full in peak season; if they're an essential part of your plans, it is worth making a **reservation** at least a week or two in advance. If a flight you've set your heart on is full, **waiting lists** exist – and are worth signing onto at the airport check-in

counter; experience has shown that there are almost always one or two no-shows or cancellations. Domestic air tickets are non-refundable, but you can change your flight, space permitting, as late as 24 hours before your original departure.

Incidentally, the only surviving Olympic-run **shuttle buses** between the main town and the airport are on Kós and Kastellórizo; others have long since been axed as a cost-cutting exercise. In two instances (Híos and Rhodes) municipally run services have picked up the slack, but otherwise you're at the mercy of the taxi drivers who congregate outside the arrivals gate.

Like ferries, flights are subject to **cancellation** in bad weather, since many services are on small, 50- or 72-seat ATR turbo-prop planes, or even smaller De Havilland 37-seaters, none of which will fly in strong winds (Force 8–9) or (depending on the destination airport) after dark.

Size restrictions also mean that the fifteen-kilo **baggage weight limit** is occasionally strictly enforced; if, however, you've just arrived from overseas or purchased your ticket outside Greece, you are allowed the standard international limit (20–23kg depending on carrier). All services operated on the domestic network are **non-smoking**.

Contacts for Greek domestic airlines

Aegean Countrywide ☎ 801 11 20 000, ⓦ www
.aegeanair.com.
Olympic Airlines/Aviation Countrywide ☎ 801
11 44 444, ⓦ www.olympicairlines.com.

Island ground transport

Most islands have some kind of bus service, even if it only connects the port with the main town or village, but many visitors prefer to rent a two- or four-wheeler. Even if you just do this for a day, you can get the measure of a small or medium-sized island and work out where you'd like to be based.

Buses

Bus services, grouped in a nationwide syndicate known as the KTEL (Kratikó Tamío Ellinikón Leoforíon), are reliable and frequent between major population centres or resorts. As a rule, departures are amazingly prompt, so be there in plenty of time. For visitors, the main drawback is that – from the remoter villages, at least – schedules are geared to local patterns and often leave punishingly early to shuttle people to school or work in the capital. The **buses** themselves are traditionally two-toned, cream-and-green (except on Rhodes) Mercedes coaches, slowly being supplemented by hi-tech models in other livery, with digital destination panels. Except for Mytilíni Town, which has a dedicated, off-street terminal in a parking lot, central bus stations – even on Rhodes – are little more than a marked (or unmarked) stop at a major intersection or *platía*. Seating is generally first-come, first-served, with some standing allowed, and **tickets** are either dispensed on board by a peripatetic *ispráktoros* or conductor, or beforehand at ticket windows (where present).

Car rental

Car rental in the Dodecanese and east Aegean starts at €280–330 a week in high season for the smallest, A-group vehicle from a one-off outlet or local chain, including unlimited mileage, tax and insurance. Overseas tour operators' and international chains' brochures (particularly on Rhodes) threaten alarming rates of €440 for the same period but, except in August, no rental company expects to fetch that price for a car; even on pricey Rhodes they will settle for €380 or so. Outside peak season, at the smaller local outfits on less touristed islands, you can sometimes get terms of about €35 per day, all-inclusive, with even better rates for three days or more. **Comparison shopping** among agencies in the larger resorts can yield a variation in quotes of up to twenty percent for the same conditions over a four- to seven-day period; the most negotiable variables being whether or not kilometres in excess of one hundred per day (a common hidden catch) are free, or whether there'll be a drop-off charge for picking up at the airport and leaving it in town, or vice versa. Open **jeeps**, an increasingly popular extravagance, begin at about €70 per day, rising to as much as €100 at busy times and places.

Note that brochure prices in Greece never include tax and personal insurance, and sometimes not **collision damage waiver** (CDW). This latter always has an excess of €300–350, which charge you incur for the tiniest scratch or missing mud flap, so it's recommended that you pay a few extra euros a day for "Super Collision Damage Waiver", "Franchise Waiver" or "Liability Waiver Surcharge", as it's variously called, to reduce your risk to zero. Be careful of the hammering that cars get on dirt tracks; tyres, windscreen and the underside of the vehicle are almost always excluded from even supplementary insurance policies. All agencies will want either a **credit card** or a large **cash deposit** up front; minimum age requirements vary from 21 to 23. Driving licences issued by any EU/EEA state (plus Australia) are honoured, but in theory – and, increasingly, in practice – an **International Driving Licence** is required by all other drivers, especially North Americans. This must be arranged before departure, as ELPA (the Greek motoring association) no longer issues IDLs to foreign nationals. You can be arrested and charged for driving without an IDL if you require one.

Car rental agencies

Britain

Avis ℡0870 606 0100, ⊛www.avis.com.
Budget ℡0800 181 181,
⊛www.budget.com.
Hertz ℡0870 844 8844, ⊛www.hertz.com.
National ℡0870 536 5365, ⊛www.nationalcar.co.uk.
Sixt ⊛www.e-sixt.com.
Suncars ℡0870 500 5566, ⊛www.suncars.com.
Thrifty ℡01494/751 600, ⊛www.thrifty.com.
Transhire ℡0870 789 8000, ⊛www.transhire.com.

Ireland

Avis Northern Ireland ℡028/9024 0404, Republic of Ireland ℡01/605 7500, ⊛www.avis.ie.
Budget Republic of Ireland ℡09/0662 7711,
⊛www.budget.ie.
Cosmo Thrifty Northern Ireland ℡028/9445 2565, ⊛www.thrifty.com.
Hertz Republic of Ireland ℡01/676 7476, ⊛www.hertz.ie.
Sixt Republic of Ireland ℡1850/206 088, ⊛www.irishcarrentals.ie.
Thrifty Republic of Ireland ℡1800/515 800, ⊛www.thrifty.ie.

North America

Alamo ☎1-800/462-5266, ⊛www.alamo.com.
Auto Europe US and Canada ☎1-800/223-5555,
⊛www.autoeurope.com.
Avis US ☎1-800/230-4898, Canada
☎1-800/272-5871, ⊛www.avis.com.
Budget US ☎1-800/527-0700, ⊛www.budget.com.
Dollar US ☎1-800/800-3665, ⊛www.dollar.com.
Europe by Car ☎1-800/223-1516, ⊛www
.europebycar.com.
Hertz US ☎1-800/654-3131, Canada ☎1-800/
263-0600, ⊛www.hertz.com.
National ☎1-800/962-7070, ⊛www.nationalcar
.com.
Thrifty ☎1-800/847-4389, ⊛www.thrifty.com.

Australia

Avis ☎13 63 33 or 02/9353 9000, ⊛www.avis
.com.au.
Budget ☎1300/362 848, ⊛www.budget.com.au.
Hertz ☎13 30 39 or 03/9698 2555, ⊛www.hertz
.com.au.
National ☎13 10 45, ⊛www.nationalcar.com.au.
Thrifty ☎1300/367 227, ⊛www.thrifty.com.au.

New Zealand

Apex ☎0800/93 95 97 or 03/379 6897, ⊛www
.apexrentals.co.nz.
Avis ☎09/526 2847 or 0800/655 111, ⊛www
.avis.co.nz.
Budget ☎0800/652-227, ⊛www.budget.co.nz.
Hertz ☎0800/654 321, ⊛www.hertz.co.nz.
National ☎0800/800 115, ⊛www.nationalcar
.co.nz.
Thrifty ☎09/309 0111, ⊛www.thrifty.co.nz.

In peak season only you may get a better
price (and, just possibly, better vehicle
condition) by booking through one of the
overseas booking companies that deal
with local firms, rather than arranging the
rental once you're in Greece. Competitive companies in Britain include Suncars
and Transhire. In the Dodecanese and
east Aegean, Autorent, Budget, EuroHire,
Payless, European, Kosmos, National/
Alamo, Reliable, Eurodollar and Just are
dependable Greek, or smaller international,
chains with branches in many towns. All are
considerably cheaper than the biggest international operators such as Hertz and Avis,
but it is always worthwhile visiting all the
international chains' websites for a quote,
and with a Frequent Flyer discount code
you may well match prices of the discount

booking companies noted above. Specific
local recommendations, mostly based on
author experience, are given in the guide.

In terms of **models**, the more competitive companies tend to offer the Citroën
Saxo, the Fiat Cinquecento/Seisento and
the Suzuki Swift 1000 as A-group cars,
and Opel (Vauxhall) Corsa 1.2, Fiat Uno/
Punto, Peugeot 106, Hyundai Atos, Renault
Clio/Twingo, Toyota Yaris, Hyundai Getz
or Nissan Micra in the B group. Any more
than two adults, with luggage, will generally
require B category, in which the Atos, Yaris
and Clio are the most robust models. The
badly designed, underpowered Suzuki Alto
600 or 800, Fiat Panda 750/900 and Seat
Marbella should be avoided if at all possible as A-group cars, and indeed have been
phased out by the more reputable agencies.
The standard four-wheel-drive option is a
Suzuki jeep (1.3- or 1.6-litre), mostly open-
top – great for bashing down rutted tracks
to remote beaches.

Driving in Greece

Greece has the highest **accident rate**
in Europe after Portugal, and on Lésvos,
Kós or Rhodes – especially along the
stretch between Ródhos Town and Líndhos – it's easy to see why. At the Malóna
bridge, there's a prominent memorial to five
Austrians wiped out in a high-speed wreck
during July 1999. **Driving habits** amongst
both locals and foreigners are atrocious:
overtaking is erratic, tailgating and barging
out heedlessly from side roads are preferred
pastimes, lane markings and turn signals
may as well not exist, and motorbikes hog
the road, or weave from side to side. **Drunk-
driving** is also a major problem; Sunday
afternoons in rural areas are particularly bad,
and for the same reason you should be extra
vigilant if driving late at night at weekends or
holidays. Well-publicized police campaigns
are under way to combat the problem, with
radar guns being deployed against speed-
ers as well.

Matters are made worse by the frequently
perilous **road conditions**: signposting is
absent or badly placed, pavement markings are faded, asphalt can turn into a one-
lane surface or a dirt track without warning on secondary routes, and you're heav-

ily dependent on magnifying mirrors at blind intersections in congested villages. Uphill drivers insist on their **right of way**, as do those first to approach a one-lane bridge; **flashed headlights** usually mean the opposite of what they do in the UK or North America, here signifying that the other driver insists on coming through or overtaking. Even on the so-called motorways of Rhodes and Kós, there is no proper far-right lane for slower traffic, which is expected to straddle the solid white line at the verge and allow rapid traffic to pass.

Parking in the biggest island towns is uniformly a nightmare owing to congestion and high vehicle numbers. **Pay-and-display** systems as in the UK are the rule, and it's not always clear where you obtain tickets from (sometimes a kiosk, sometimes a machine). They're either chits with the expiry time printed on as in the UK, or strip-type, where you pop out the date and starting hour from pre-punched cardboard stock.

Wearing a **seatbelt** is compulsory – you will be fined for non-use at the many checkpoints – as is keeping a first-aid kit in the boot (though some rental companies skimp on this), and children under the age of 10 are not allowed to sit in the front seats. It's illegal to drive away from any kind of accident, and you can be held at a police station for up to 24 hours. If this happens, you have the right to ring your consulate immediately to summon a lawyer; don't make a statement to anyone who doesn't speak, and write, very good English. In practice, once police are informed that there was no personal injury, they rarely come out to investigate.

Tourists with proof of AA/RAC/AAA membership are given free road assistance from ELPA, the Greek equivalent, which runs **breakdown services** on several of the larger islands; in an emergency, ring their road assistance service on ☎10400. Many car rental companies have an agreement with ELPA's equally widespread competitors Hellas Service (☎1057), Interamerican (☎1168) and Express Service (☎1154); however, you will always get a faster response if you dial the local number for the province you're stranded in (ask for these in advance).

Buying fuel

Fuel currently costs €0.70–0.90 per litre for regular unleaded (*amólyvdhi*), super unleaded or super lead-replacement; diesel costs €0.60–0.65 per litre. Lead-replacement fuel for older cars without catalytic converters is called "Neo Super" or "Super 2002", the year leaded fuel was phased out. Most scooters and motorbikes run better on super, even if they nominally take regular.

It is easy to run short of fuel **after dark or at weekends** in both rural and urban Greece; most stations close at 7pm sharp, and nearly as many are shut all day Sunday. One pump per district will always remain open, but interpreting the Greek-only pharmacy-type-rota lists posted at shut stations is another matter. This is not so much of a problem on the major highways of the biggest islands, but it is a factor everywhere else, despite an ever-increasing number of gas pumps. So always fill up, or insist on full rental vehicles at the outset.

Some stations which claim to be open around the clock are in fact **automated-only after hours** – you have to use bill-taking machines, which don't give change. If you fill your tank without having exhausted your credit, punch the button for a receipt and get change the next day during attended hours (assuming you're still in the area). Filling stations run by multinational companies (BP, Mobil, Texaco and Shell) usually take **credit cards**; Greek chains like EKO, Elda, Jetoil, Revoil and Elinoil usually don't, except in the most touristed areas. Shell is the most expensive major chain, BP tends to be much less.

Motorbikes, scooters – and safety

The cult of the **motorcycle** is highly developed in the Greek islands, presided over by a jealous deity apparently requiring regular human sacrifice. **Accidents** among both foreign and local motorbikers are common, with annual fatalities edging into two figures on the busier islands. Some package companies have even taken to warning clients in print against renting motorbikes or scooters (thereby making a bit extra on organized overland excursions), but with a bit of caution and common sense – plus an eye to increasingly enforced traffic regulations – riding a motorbike on an island should be a lot safer than piloting one through London or New York.

Many tourists come to grief on rutted dirt tracks or astride mechanically dodgy machines. In other cases **accidents** are due to attempts to cut corners, in all senses, by riding two-up on an underpowered scooter simply not designed to propel such a load. Don't be tempted by this apparent economy – you won't regret getting two separate scooters, or one powerful 100cc bike to share – and bear in mind, too, that you're likely to be charged an exorbitant sum for any repairs if you do have a wipeout. Also, verify that your travel insurance policy will cover motorbike accidents.

One worthwhile precaution is to wear a **crash helmet** (*krános*); many rental outfits will offer you (an often ill-fitting) one, and some will make you sign a waiver of liability if you refuse it. Helmet-wearing is in fact required by law, with a €78 fine levied for failure to do so; on some smaller islands (eg Léros) the rule is laxly enforced, on others (eg Sámos) random police roadblocks do a brisk commerce in citations, and foreign riders are most definitely not exempt.

Reputable establishments demand a full **motorcycle driving licence** for any engine over 90cc (the law actually applies to anything over 50cc displacement), and you will usually have to leave a passport as security. For smaller models, any driving licence will do, though in fact there are three grades of permit in Greece: 50–125cc, 125–250cc and over 250cc. Failure to carry the correct licence on your person attracts a fine of €86.

Fines of any sort are to be paid within ten working days at the municipal cashier's (*dhimotikó tamío*); proof of payment then needs to be taken to the police station to have the citation cancelled. Nonpayment will be followed by a court date being set, and the Greek authorities – so dilatory in other respects – are amazingly efficient at translating summons into foreign languages and forwarding them to your overseas address. No-shows are automatically convicted, and a conviction will make re-entry to Greece awkward at best.

Small **motor scooters** with automatic transmissions, known in Greek as *papákia* (little ducks) after their characteristic noise, are good transport for all but the hilliest islands. They're available for rent in most main towns or ports, and at the larger resorts, for €13–20. This price range can be bargained down considerably out of peak season, or if you negotiate for a longer period of rental.

Before riding off, make sure you check the bike's **mechanical state**, since many are only cosmetically maintained. By law dealers are supposed to sell or scrap rental bikes every three years, but you often wonder. Bad brakes and worn or oil-fouled spark plugs are the most common defects; dealers often keep the front brake far too loose, with the commendable intention of preventing you going over the handlebars. If you break down it's your responsibility to return the machine, so get the right phone number of the rental agency (not always the obvious one printed on the contract; keep your mobile phone with you too). Better agencies often offer a free retrieval service.

The latest generation of **scooters**, made by Suzuki, Piaggio, Vespa or Peugeot, is practical enough, but thirsty on fuel; make sure there's a kick-start as backups to the battery, since ignition switches commonly fail. The Suzuki Address and its rival the Piaggio Typhoon are popular, fairly reliable models. Bungy cords (a *khtapódaki* or "little octopus" in slang) for tying down bundles are supplied on request, while capacious baskets are also often a feature. The ultra-trendy, low-slung models with fat, small-radius tyres, however, are unstable on anything other than the smoothest, flattest island roads. Especially if you intend to go off-road, always choose traditionally designed bikes with large-radius, nobbly, narrow tyres, if available. Again, if you're going to spend every day of your holiday astride a bike, consider bringing or buying cyclists' or motorcyclists' **gloves**; they'll be hot and silly-looking in midsummer, but you'll look even sillier if you lose all the skin off your hands when you go for a spill. The wounds – hospital staff are wearily familiar with them – take months to heal, and leave huge scars.

In the family of true **motorbikes** (*mihanákia*) with manual transmissions and safer tyres as described above, the long-standing workhorse favourites, in descending order of reliability, are the Honda 50, Yamaha Townmate and Suzuki FB Birdie. Gears are shifted with an easy-to-learn left-foot pedal action, and (very important) they can all be push-started if the starting crank fails. For two riders, the least powerful safe model at nominal extra cost is the Honda Cub 90cc or Yamaha 80 Townmate. Best of all is the attractive Honda Astrea 100 and its rival-brand clones, very powerful but scarcely bigger than older models. If you've the proper licence and off-road experience, dirt bikes of 125cc and up can also be found in most resorts.

Cycling

Cycling on the Greek islands is not so hard going as you might imagine (except in mid-summer), especially on one of the **mountain bikes** that have all but supplanted balloon-tyre boneshakers at rental outlets; rental prices are rarely more than €7 a day. You do, however, need nerves of steel, as roads are generally narrow, with no verges or bike lanes except on Kós, and many Greek drivers consider cyclists as some lower form of life, on a par with the snakes found run over everywhere.

If you have your own mountain or touring bike (the latter not rented in Greece), you might consider bringing it with you. Bikes travel free on most airlines if within your 20–23-kilo international weight allowance, but always arrange this in writing with the airline beforehand to avoid huge charges at check-in. Once in Greece you

should be able to take a bike for free on all ferries. Any small spare parts you might need, however, are best brought along, since specialist bike shops are only found in the main towns of the half-dozen largest islands in this book.

Taxis

Greek **taxis** are among the cheapest in western Europe – so long as you get an honest driver who switches the meter on and doesn't use hi-tech devices to doctor the reading. Use of the meter is mandatory within city or town limits, where Tariff "1" applies, while in rural areas or between midnight and 5am Tariff "2" is in effect. On certain islands, such as Kálymnos and Léros, set rates apply on specific fixed routes for "collective" taxis – these only depart when full. Otherwise, throughout the islands the meter starts at €0.75, though the minimum fare is €1.50; any baggage not actually on your lap is charged at €0.30 apiece. Additionally, there are surcharges of €2 for leaving or entering an airport (except €3 for Athens airport), and €0.80 for entering or leaving a harbour area. If you summon a taxi by phone on spec, there's a €1.50 charge, while a prearranged rendezvous is €2.10 extra; in either case the driver starts running from the moment the driver begins heading towards you. All categories of charges must be set out on a laminated card affixed to the dashboard. For a week or so before and after Orthodox Easter, and Christmas, a *filodhórima* or gratuity of about ten percent is levied. Any or all of these extras will legitimately bump up the basic meter reading of about €8 per ten rural kilometres.

Accommodation

There are huge numbers of beds available for tourists in the Dodecanese and east Aegean islands, so most of the year you can turn up almost anywhere and find a room – if not in a hotel, then in a block of rooms or studios (the standard island accommodation). Only in the major resorts, or during the July–August peak season, or around Easter, are you likely to experience problems. At these times, if you don't have accommodation reserved in advance, you'd be wise to keep well off the main tourist trails, turning up at each new place early in the day and taking whatever is available – you may be able to exchange it for something better later on. However, in the wake of poor occupancy levels during recent seasons, many studios and hotels formerly monopolized by north European package operators are again often available to independent, walk-in travellers.

Out of season, you face a slightly different problem: most private rooms – and campsites – operate only from late April or early May to October, leaving hotels your only option. During winter you may have no choice but to stay in the main towns or ports. There will often be very little life outside these places anyway, with all the seasonal beach bars and restaurants closed. On many smaller islands, you will often find just one hotel – and perhaps one taverna – staying open year-round. Be warned also that any resort or harbour hotels which do operate through the winter are likely to have a certain number of **prostitutes** as long-term guests; licensed prostitution is legal in Greece, and the management reckons this is the most painless way to keep the bills paid.

Old-fashioned, 1970s-vintage rooms in places like northern Kárpathos or Foúrni, very occasionally still without private bath, fall into the ❶ price category. Standard, en-suite rooms without cooking facilities weigh in at ❷; newer, well-equipped rooms and self-catering studios occupy the top half of the ❸ niche, along with the more modest C-class hotels, the better among these edging well into ❹. Category 5 corresponds fairly well to the better-value B-class hotels and the humbler designer inns on islands like Rhodes, Kastellórizo, Híos and Sými, while ❻ tallies with most of B-class and the really state-of-the-art restoration projects. ❼ and ❽ mean A- and L-class, and the sky's the limit here – €400 a night is by no means unheard of these days.

Accommodation prices

Throughout the book we've categorized accommodation according to the following **price codes**, which denote the cheapest available double room in high season. Many hotels, especially those in category ❹ and over, include breakfast in the price; you'll need to check this when booking. During low season, rates can drop by more than fifty percent, especially if you are staying for three or more nights. Exceptions are during the Christmas and Easter weeks, when you'll pay high-season prices. Single rooms, where available, cost around seventy percent of the price of a double.

❶ Up to €25	❺ €71–90
❷ €26–35	❻ €91–120
❸ €36–50	❼ €121–170
❹ €51–70	❽ €171 and up

Prices in any establishment should by law be displayed on the back of the door of your room, or over the reception desk. If you feel you're being overcharged at a place which is officially registered, threaten to report it to the tourist office or police, who will generally adopt your side in such cases. A hotelier is free to offer a room at any amount under the official rate, but it's an offence to charge one euro cent over the permitted price for the **current season**. Depending on location, there are up to three of these: typically October to May (low), June to mid-July, plus late September (mid) and mid-July through August (high). Small amounts over the posted price may be legitimately explained by municipal tax or out-of-date forms. More commonly you will find that you have bargained so well, or arrived so far out of high season, that you are actually paying far less than the maximum prices – which are in any case optimistically pitched for a few high-traffic days in the year.

Hot water

A key variable in both rooms and hotels is the type of **water heating**. Rooftop **solar units** (*iliaká* in Greek), with their nonexistent running costs, are more popular than electric **immersion heaters** (*thermosífona*). Under typical high-season demand, however, solar-powered tanks tend to run out of hot water with the post-beach shower crunch at 6pm, with no more available until the next day. A heater, either as a backup or primary source, is more reliable; proprietors may either jealously guard the **boiler controls** or entrust you with its workings, which involve either a circuit breaker or a rotary switch turned to "I" for fifteen minutes. You should never shower with a *thermosífono* powered up (look for the glow-lamp indicator on the tank) – besides the risk of shock from badly earthed plumbing, it would be fairly easy to empty smaller tanks and burn out the heating element.

Hotels

Hotels in the larger resorts are often contracted out on a seasonal basis by foreign package holiday companies, though there are usually vacancies available (especially in spring or autumn) for walk-in trade. The tourist police set official **categories** for hotels, which range from "De Luxe" down to the rarely encountered "E-class"; all except the top category have to keep within set price limits. The letter system is supposed to be replaced with a star grading system as in other countries, but the process, while already begun, is being resisted; L is five-star, E is no-star, etc. While they last, letter ratings are supposed to correspond to **facilities** available, though in practice categorization often depends on location within a resort, total number of rooms and "influence" with the tourism authorities – there are so-called E-class hotels with under nine rooms which are plusher than nearby C-class outfits. It is mandatory for D-class hotels to have at least some rooms with attached baths; C-class must additionally have a bar or designated breakfast area. The presence of a pool and/or tennis court will attract a B-class rating, while A-category hotels should have at least one restaurant, a bar, conference/business facilities and extensive common areas. Often these, and the L outfits (essentially self-contained complexes), back onto a quasi-private beach.

In terms of **food**, C-class hotels are required only to provide the most rudimentary of continental breakfasts – you may choose not to take, or pay, for it – while B-class and above will usually offer some sort of buffet breakfast including cheese, cold cuts, sausages, yogurt, eggs, and so on. With some outstanding exceptions, noted in the Guide, lunch or supper at hotel-affiliated restaurants will be bland and poor value.

Private rooms

The most common island accommodation is **privately let rooms** – *dhomátia* in Greek. Like hotels, these are regulated and officially divided into three classes (A down to C), according to facilities. These days they are in new, purpose-built, low-rise

The generic Greek hotel room

After travelling around the islands for a while, you'll notice that most hotel and *dhomátia* units are so similar from one end of the archipelago to the other that you'll be able to find your way around any of them blindfolded. Thus we describe the typical room now, once and for all, without wasting undue space in the destination accounts.

The **generic Greek hotel room** is entered via a short corridor, with a closet to one side and the en-suite bath on the other. The sleeping area has coordinated pine furniture, either depressingly dark-stained (1980s vintage) or "natural blonde" (newer units). This will consist of two twin **beds** or (less often) one double bed (*dhipló kreváti*), flanked by one or more **end tables** (*komodhína*). On one of the *komodhína* there might be a telephone, though these are on the wane given the popularity of mobiles. **Televisions** are the Big Thing now, invariably mounted on a bracket high up in the corner, and the remote control will be presented to you at check-in with some ceremony. There will be a single ceiling light fixture, with a two-way switch for turning it off just above the headboard, plus a reading **lamp** over each bed (or half of the double bed), and probably one more over the dressing table. There will seldom be enough **power points/outlets**, sometimes just one in the whole room; if this drives you crazy, invest in a multi-socket adapter (they can be had for under €2 at many shops). The designation "**studio**" usually means the presence of a modular corner unit with steel sink, two electrical hobs, a recessed mini-fridge and basic crockery and pots to whip up spaghetti or eggs.

There will often be a **latticed rack** for resting your baggage, and a small **dressing table** with two drawers, a mirror and a chair. The **closet** will either be freestanding or built-in, of the same wood (more likely veneered MDF) and shade as the rest of the furnishings. Inside will be an assortment of cheap hangers, while in the cupboard above you'll find an extra synthetic-fibre pillow or two and a like number of cheap acrylic extra blankets. The **bed linen** itself will be rough but all-cotton, flat sheets, tucked over a lumpy **mattress** due for replacement. The **walls** will be dazzling white (if recent), probably pinky-beige if from the 1980s, institutional green if older. The **floor** varies, too: hospital-type linoleum in the 1960s-horror relics, mosaic composition (*mosaïkó*) from the 1970s, easy-to-clean white or beige tiles for later vintage. The white-tile, white-wall and blonde-pine

buildings, but a few still have the proprietors living on-site.

License rooms are almost always scrupulously clean, whatever their other amenities (see the box above for the full story). At their **simplest** (now pretty much confined to Ródhos Old Town), you'll get a tiny, almost windowless cell, with a hook on the back of the door in lieu of a closet, and toilet facilities down the hall. At the **fancier** end of the scale, they are modern, fully furnished "studios" with an en-suite bathroom and a fully equipped kitchen. Between these extremes there will be a choice of rooms at various prices – owners will usually show you the most expensive first. Some of the cheap places will also have more expensive rooms with

en-suite facilities – and vice versa, with rare singles often tucked under stairways or in other less desirable corners of the building. Price and quality are not necessarily directly linked, so always ask to see the room before agreeing to take it.

Areas to **look for rooms**, along with specific recommendations, are included in the Guide. As often as not, however, the rooms find you: owners descend on ferry or bus arrivals to fill any space they have, sometimes waving photos of the premises. Many island municipalities have acted, or are moving, to outlaw this practice, owing to widespread bait-and-switch tactics and the pitching of unlicensed rooms. In smaller places you'll often see buildings signposted, sometimes in German (*Zimmer*); the Greek

style is by far the most common, and what we mean by the adjectives "bland", "neutral" or "anodyne". A set of double doors, or possibly a sliding one, will open onto a small **balcony** with some plastic outdoor furniture and a corroded railing that's handy for anchoring clothes lines. The doors themselves will be hidden by a dingy-coloured pair of **acrylic curtains**, which you pull to – there's often no cord or proper runner.

The **bathroom**, tiled to head height, will contain a wall-mounting sink with functional chrome fittings (up to the late 1980s), but a sturdier pedestal model thereafter, or in better outfits. A plastic medicine chest with mirror, or a single shelf scarred by numerous cigarette butts, hovers over the sink. As in Britain, it's illegal to have full-strength power points in the bathroom, so you'll have to plug in hair-dryers at the dressing table (or at an outlet just outside the bathroom door); shavers may be accommodated with a low-amp, dual-voltage point in the light fixture over the mirror. Opposite the toilet, a sign in several languages demands that you throw your used paper in a little plastic **basket or pedal bin**. The **shower** will consist of a flat floor pan and a cheap **chrome flex** attachment, nicknamed a *tiléfono* ("phone"), meant to be perched on a wall bracket. The chrome flex will invariably be unravelling and the rubber liner inside splitting, whereupon the management replaces it with a tough, single-layer "garden hose"-type extension – which can't be suspended from the wall-hook. Whether or not the shower corner has a saggy plastic curtain, you will invariably **flood** the entire room (and any clothes you've been so rash as to bring inside) – thus the little drain in the centre of the floor. During the 1970s there was a craze for **mini-bathtubs**, with a little ledge to sit on; they're more suited to doing laundry than anything else.

The **better, exceptional** rooms – clearly indicated in the accounts – will have some or all of the following: split-level air con/heating, recessed halogen lighting, abundant power points, double glazing, full-sized bathtubs, designer sinks and mirrors, marble or terracotta cladding in the bathroom, a well-sealed shower stall, wooden floors, original wall art, orthopedic mattresses, proper armchairs, wrought-iron bed-frames, pastel-patterned bedspreads or curtains, and an economy switch activated with a key-tab. But for any of this loveliness you should expect to be paying at least category ⑤.

signs to look out for are "ENIKIAZÓMENA DHOMÁTIA" or "ENIKIAZÓNTEH DHOMÁ-TIA". In the more developed island resorts, where package holiday-makers predomi-nate, *dhomátia* owners will often require you to stay for at least three days, or even a week.

It has become standard practice for room proprietors, like hotel staff, to ask to keep your **passport** – ostensibly "for the tourist police", who do require customer particulars – but in reality to prevent you skipping out with an unpaid bill. Some owners may be satisfied with just taking down your details, as is done in hotels, and they'll almost always return the passport once you get to know them, or if you need it for another purpose.

In **winter**, officially from November until early April, private rooms – except in Ródhos Old Town – are closed pretty much across the board to keep the hotels in business. There's no point in traipsing about hoping to find exceptions – most room-owners obey the system very strictly.

Villas and long-term rentals

The easiest – and usually most economical – way to arrange a **villa rental** is through one of the package holiday companies detailed on pp.32–33. They represent some superb places, from fairly simple to luxuri-ous, and costs can be very reasonable, especially if shared between several people. Several of the companies we list will arrange

Eco-friendly tourism

Much has been written lately about the negative **environmental impact** of mass tourism on fragile Mediterranean destinations. As a phenomenon, package travel is here to stay, but following are a few suggestions – endorsed, and in some cases suggested, by readers or the more sensitive package companies – on how to land more lightly in Greece.

Visiting during the spring or autumn **shoulder seasons** eases pressure on oversubscribed water, power and sewage networks, as well as being a good idea for several other reasons (see "When to Go", p.13). Speaking of **water**, try to use the same batch twice – for example, use the rinse water when laundering for soaping up the next batch of clothes. Forego those horrible PVC mineral-**water bottles**, which end up littering every beach and roadside, and bring along a permanent canteen/water bottle; all ferries, hotel bars and restaurants have a tap gushing cold, potable water for serving with *oúzo*, and staff will gladly top up bottles for customers. (Incidentally, many brands of "mineral" water have been repeatedly shown to be fraudulently filled with ordinary tap water.)

Similarly, decline the automatic dispensing of **nylon bags** for every tiny purchase that will fit in a day pack or the palm of your hand – the wind-blown bags invariably end up on the beach, or submerged next to the PVC bottles, where they constitute a hazard to marine life. And last but not least, buy when possible locally produced orange and lemon soda sold in **recyclable glass bottles**, rather than international brands or their local subsidiaries such as Ivi. By doing so, you will keep several people in work at island bottling plants (still operating on Lésvos, Híos, Léros, Kálymnos, Kós and Rhodes) and prevent yet more aluminium cans from joining the plastic on the roadside or in the sea.

"**multi-centre**" stays on two islands over two weeks.

On the islands, a few local travel agents arrange villa rentals, though they are often places the overseas companies gave a miss or couldn't fill. **Out of season**, you can sometimes get a good deal on villa or apartment rental for a month or more by asking around locally, though in these days of EU convergence and the increasing desirability of the islands as year-round residences, "good deal" means anything under €180 per month for a large studio (*garsoniéra*) or €250 for a small one-bedroom flat.

Camping

Officially recognized campsites in the Dodecanese and east Aegean are restricted to Rhodes (one), Kós (one), Léros (one), Astypálea (one), Pátmos (one) and Lésvos (two); see the relevant chapters for full descriptions. Most places cost €4.50 a night per person, slightly less per tent, and €8 per camper van, but at the fanciest sites rates for two people plus a tent can almost add up to the price of a basic room.

Generally, you don't have to worry about leaving tents or other equipment unattended at wardened campsites; the Greeks are one of the most honest nations in Europe.

Camping rough outside authorized campsites is such an established element of Greek travel that few people realize that it's officially illegal. Since 1977 "freelance" camping, as EOT calls it, has actually been forbidden by a law originally enacted to harass gypsies, and regulations are increasingly enforced. Another drawback is the increased prevalence of theft in rural areas, often by marauding bands of refugees from Albania and other north Balkan states. All told, you will feel less vulnerable inside a tent, camper van or even a rock-cave – not that rain is likely during the long Greek summer, but some protection is essential from wind, sun, insects (see p.44) and stray animals raiding your food. You will always need at least a light sleeping bag, since even summer nights get cool and damp at muddy or shady campsites; a foam pad is also recommended for pitching on harder ground.

If you do camp rough, it's vital to exercise sensitivity and discretion. Police crack down on people camping (and especially littering) around popular tourist beaches, particularly when a large community of campers develops. Off the beaten track, however, nobody is very bothered, though it is always best to ask permission locally in the village taverna or café. During high season, when everything – even the authorized campsites – may be full, attitudes towards freelance camping are more relaxed, even in the most touristed places. At such times the best strategy is to find a sympathetic taverna, which in exchange for regular patronage will probably be willing to guard small valuables and let you use their facilities.

Eating and drinking

Greeks spend a lot of time socializing outside their homes, and sharing a meal is one of the chief ways of doing it. The atmosphere is usually relaxed and informal, with pretensions (and expense-account prices) rare outside major resorts on Kós, Pátmos and Rhodes. Greeks are not prodigious drinkers – tippling is traditionally meant to accompany food – though since the mid-1990s a whole range of bars and pubs has sprung up, both in tourist resorts and as pricey music clubs on the outskirts of major towns.

Breakfast, picnic fare and snacks

Greeks don't generally eat **breakfast**, so the only egg-and-bacon kind of places are in resorts where foreigners congregate, or where there are returned North American or Australian Greeks. Such spots can sometimes be fairly good value (€6–8 for the works, maybe even with "French" filter coffee), especially if there's competition. More indigenous alternatives are yogurts at a *galaktopolío* (milk bar), or cheese pies and biscuits from a bakery (see "Snacks", p.72).

Picnic fare

Picnic fare is good, cheap and easily available at bakeries and *manávika* (fruit-and-veg stalls). **Bread**, alas, is often of minimal nutritional value and inedible within a day of purchase. It's worth paying extra at the bakery (*foúrnos* or *psomádhiko*) for *olikís* (wholemeal), *sikalísio* (rye bread), *oktásporo* (eight-grain), or even *enneásporo* (nine-grain), the latter types most commonly baked where large numbers of Germans or Scandinavians are about. When buying **olives**, go for the fat Kalamáta or Ámfissa ones; they're more expensive, but tastier. However, locally gathered olives – especially the slightly shrivelled *throúmbes* or the fully ripened, ground-gathered olives (*hamádhes*) – often have a distinctive nutty flavour, compensating for large kernels. The best **honey** in the islands covered is reckoned to be the pure-thyme variety from Límnos, Foúrni or Astypálea – it's about double the price of honeys from Sámos or Lésvos, where the presence of pine trees and their acrid blossoms makes local honey inferior.

Honey is an ideal topping for the famous local **yogurt** (as opposed to the bland, mass-market stuff of supermarkets). All of the larger island towns have at least one dairy shop where locally produced yogurts are sold in plastic or (better) clay containers of various sizes. Sheep-milk yogurt is richer and sweeter, scarcely requiring honey; cow-milk yogurt is tarter but more widely available. Side by side with these will be *krémes* (custards) and *ryzógala* (rice puddings) in single-serving plastic containers.

Fétta cheese is ubiquitous – sometimes, ironically, imported from Holland or Denmark, though the Greeks are clamping down on this legally, as the French do with non-French "champagne" – and local brands are usually better and not much more expensive. The goat's-milk variety can be very dry and salty, so ask for a taste before buying. If you have access to a fridge, leaving the cheese overnight in a plastic container filled with water will solve both problems, though if left too long like this the cheese simply dissolves. This sampling advice goes for other indigenous cheeses as well, the most palatable of which is the expensive Gruyère-type *graviéra*.

Despite membership of the EU, plus growing personal incomes and exotic tastes, Greece imports very little garden produce from abroad, aside from bananas and a few mangoes or pineapples. **Fruit** in particular is relatively expensive and available only by season, though in the more cosmopolitan spots it is possible to find such things as **avocados** (light-green Fuerte variety from Crete are excellent) for much of the year. Reliable picnic fruits include *yiarmádhes*, a variety of giant **peach** available during August and September; *krystália*, tiny, hard green **pears** that ripen a month or two later and are heavenly; and the *himoniátiko* **melon** (called cassava in North America), which appears at the same time, in its yellow, puckered skin with green flecks. Greece also has a burgeoning **kiwi** industry and, while the first crop in October coincides with the end of the tourist season, availability carries over into the following May. Less portable, but succulent, are the purple Smyrna **figs** (*boúkhnes*), which ripen in August and early September on Sámos, Híos and Ikaría in particular. Salad **vegetables** are more reasonably priced; besides the famous, enormous tomatoes (June–Sept), and the ubiquitous *ambelofásola* (runner beans; July–Sept), there is a bewildering variety of springtime greens, including rocket, dill, enormous spring onions and lettuces. Useful **expressions** for shopping are *éna tétarto* (250g) and *misó kiló* (500g).

Snacks

Traditional **snacks** can be one of the distinctive pleasures of Greek eating, though they are being increasingly edged out by an obsession with Western junk/fast food at nationwide chains such as Goody's (burgers), Everest and Grigoris Mikroyevmata (assorted nibbles), Roma Pizza and Theios Vanias (baked pastries) – somewhat less insipid for being Greek-originated. However, independently produced kebabs (*souvlákia*) are widely available, and in most larger resorts and towns you'll find *yíros* – doner kebab with garnish in thick, doughy *píta* bread that's closer to Indian nan bread. To find the closest outlet for such, ask for a *yirádhiko* or *souvladzídhiko* (*souvláki* and *yíros* bars, respectively).

Other common snacks include *tyrópites* (cheese pies – the best are the *striftés* or the filo-less *kouroú*, if available) and *spanokópites* (spinach pies), which can usually be found at the baker's, as can *kouloúria* (crispy pretzel rings sprinkled with sesame seeds) and *voutímata* (dark biscuits heavy on molasses, cinnamon and butter). Pizza can be very good as well, sold *al metro* (by the piece).

Restaurants

Greek cuisine and **restaurants** are simple and straightforward. There's usually no snobbery about eating out; everyone does it regularly, and it's still reasonable – €11–15 per person for a substantial (non-seafood) meal with a measure of house wine. Even if the cooking is simple, you should expect it to be wholesome; Greeks are fussy about freshness and provenance and do not willingly or knowingly like to eat frozen New Zealand lamb chops, farmed fish or pre-fried chips.

That said, there's a lot of **lazy cooking** about – especially in resorts, where menus are dominated by pizza, spaghetti, chops and "tourist *moussaká*" – a dish heavy with cheap potato slices, and nary a crumb of mince. Sending unacceptable food back is the only potential way to raise the standard of resort dining.

Of late you'll find numbers of what the Greeks call "**koultoúra**" restaurants, often pretentious attempts at Greek *nouvelle*, or updated "traditional", cuisine with speciality wine lists, which tend to be long on airs and graces, and (at €19–28 a head) short on value. The exceptions which succeed have been singled out in the text.

When choosing a restaurant, the best strategy is to go where the Greeks go. And, despite increasing EU labour regulations limiting staff hours, they go late: 2pm to 3.30pm for **lunch**, 9pm to 11pm for **supper**. You can eat earlier, but you're likely to get indifferent service and cuisine if you frequent establishments catering to the tourist schedule. Chic appearance is not a reliable guide to quality; often the more ramshackle, traditional outfits represent the best value. One good omen is the waiter bringing a carafe of refrigerated water, unbidden, rather than pushing you to order bottled stuff.

In busy resort areas, it's wise to keep a wary eye on the **waiters**, who are inclined to urge you into ordering more than you want, then bring things you haven't ordered. Although cash-register receipts are required in all establishments, these are often only for the grand total, and itemized **bills** will often be in totally illegible Greek script. Where prices are printed on menus, you'll be paying the right-hand (higher) of the two columns, inclusive of all taxes and usually **service charge**, although a small extra tip of about ten percent directly to the waiter is hugely appreciated – and usually not expected.

Bread costs extra, but consumption is not obligatory; unless it is assessed as part of the cover charge, you have the right to send it back without paying for it. You'll be considered deviant for refusing it, but so much Greek bread is inedible sawdust that there's little point in paying extra unless you actually want to use it as a scoop for dips. Good restaurant bread is still so remarkable that its existence is noted in establishment listings; at *ouzerís* and *koultoúra* restaurants on Rhodes and Kós, Italian influence has resulted in the emergence of the more appetizing *skordhópsomo* (garlic bread), the local equivalent of bruschetta.

Children are always welcome, day or night, at family tavernas, and Greeks don't mind in the slightest if they play tag between the tables or chase the **cats** running in mendicant packs – which you shouldn't feed, as signs often warn you. They are wild and pretty desperate, and you'll need a doctor's visit and tetanus jab if they whack at a dangled bit of food and claw your hand instead.

Estiatória

There are two basic types of restaurant: the *estiatório* and the taverna. Distinctions between the two are slight, though the former is more commonly found in town centres and tends to have the slightly more complicated casserole dishes known generically as *mayireftá* (literally, "cooked"). With their long hours, old-fashioned-tradesmen's clientele and tiny profit margins, *estiatória* (sometimes known as *inomayiría*) are, sadly, something of a vanishing breed.

An **estiatório** will generally feature a variety of such oven-baked dishes as *moussakás*, *pastítsio*, meat or game stews like *kokinistó* and *stifádho*, *yemistá* (stuffed tomatoes or peppers), the oily vegetable dishes called *ladherá*, and oven-baked meat or fish. Choosing these dishes is usually done by going into the kitchen and pointing at the desired steam trays. For a full rundown of common dishes, see pp.537–542 in Contexts.

Batches are cooked in the morning and then left to stand, which is why *mayireftá* are often lukewarm. Greeks don't mind this (most believe that hot food is bad for you), and dishes like *yemistá* are actually enhanced by being allowed to cool off and stand in their own juice. Similarly, you have to specify if you want your food with little or no oil (*horís ládhi*), but once again you will be considered a little strange since Greeks regard good olive oil as essential to digestion.

Desserts (*epidhórpia* in formal Greek) of the pudding-and-pie variety don't exist at *estiatória*, and yogurt or cheese only occasionally. Fruit, however, is always available in season; watermelon, melon and grapes are the summer standards, and may be offered on the house. Autumn treats worth asking after in more urban restaurants include *kydhóni* or *akhládhi stó foúrno*, baked quince or pear with some sort of syrup or nut topping. Sometimes you may be offered a complimentary slice of sweet semolina halva (*smigdhalísios halvás*).

Tavernas and psistariés

Tavernas range from the glitzy and fashionable to rough-and-ready huts set up under a reed canopy, behind a beach. Really primitive ones have a very limited (often unwritten) menu, but the more established will offer some of the main *mayireftá* dishes mentioned above, as well as the standard taverna fare. This essentially means **mezédhes** (hors d'oeuvres) or **orektiká** (appetizers) and **tís óras** (meat and fish, fried or grilled to order).

Psistariés or grillhouses serve spit-roasted lamb, pork or goat (generically termed *soúvla* or *kondosoúvli*), grilled chicken (*kotópoulo skáras*) or *kokorétsi* (grilled offal roulade). They will usually have a limited selection of *mezédhes*, but no *mayireftá* at all.

Since the idea of courses is foreign to Greek cuisine, starters, main dishes and salads often arrive together unless you request otherwise. The best thing is to order a selection of *mezédhes* and salads to share, in local fashion. Waiters encourage you to take the *horiátiki* **salad** – the so-called Greek salad, including fétta cheese – because it is the most expensive. If you only want tomato, or tomato and cucumber, ask for *domatosaláta* or *angourodomáta*. *Láhano-karóto* (cabbage-carrot) and *maroúli* (lettuce) are the typical winter and spring salads respectively, the latter augmented with onions, dill, olives and maybe rocket.

The most common **mezédhes** are tzatzíki (yogurt, garlic and cucumber dip), *melitzanosaláta* (aubergine/eggplant dip), *kolokythákia tiganitá* (courgette/zucchini slices fried in batter) or *melitzánes tiganités* (aubergine/eggplant slices fried in batter), *yígandes* (white haricot beans in vinaigrette or hot tomato sauce), *tyropitákia* or *spanakópites* (small cheese and spinach pies), *revythókeftedhes* (chickpea patties analogous to falafel) or *pittaroúdhia* (croquettes with a more varied vegetable filling), *piperiá florínes* (red sweet marinated peppers) and *mavromátika* (black-eyed peas).

Among **meats**, *souvláki* (shish kebab) and *brizóles* (chops) are reliable choices. In both cases, pork (*hirinó*) is usually better and cheaper than veal (*moskharísio*). The best *souvláki*, though not often available, is lamb (*arnísio*). At *psistariés*, meaty lamb shoulder chops (*kopsídha*) are more substantial than the scrawny rib chops (usually frozen) called *païdhákia*; roast lamb (*arní psitó*) is often considered *estiatório* fare. *Keftédhes*

Vegetarians

If you are **vegetarian**, you may be in for a hard time, and will often have to assemble a meal from various *mezédhes*. Even the excellent standbys of yogurt with honey, tzatzíki and Greek salad begin to pall after a while, and many of the supposed "vegetable" dishes on the menu are cooked in stock or have pieces of meat added to liven them up. Wholly or largely vegetarian restaurants are slowly on the increase in touristed areas; the Guide highlights them where appropriate.

(breadcrumbed meatballs), *biftékia* (similar, but meatier) and the spicy, homemade sausages called *loukánika* are cheap and good. *Kotópoulo* (chicken), especially grilled, is widely available but typically battery-farmed in Epirus or on Évvia. Other dishes worth trying are stewed (*gídha vrasti*) or baked kid (*katsíki stó foúrno*) – goat in general is a wonderfully healthy meat, typically free-range and undosed with antibiotics or hormones.

As in *estiatória*, traditional tavernas offer fruit rather than sticky **desserts**, though nowadays these are often available, along with coffee, in tavernas frequented by foreigners.

Fish and seafood

Seaside *psarotavérnes* offer **fish**, reckoned by many to be a quintessential part of a Greek holiday experience. For novices, however, ordering can be fraught with peril; see the box opposite, and the species list on p.539, for tips.

Given these considerations, it's often best to set your sights on the **humbler**, seasonally migrating or perennially local species, rather than what you might be familiar with from a UK supermarket fish counter. The cheapest consistently available fish are *gópes* (bogue), *atherína* (sand smelts) and *marídhes* (picarel), eaten head and all, best rolled in salt and sprinkled with lemon juice. Around Rhodes, *yermanós* (leatherback, in Australia) is a good frying fish which

Fish story

Fresh, wild **fish** is becoming increasingly rare and expensive as prices climb and Aegean stocks are depleted. Dodges used by unscrupulous taverna proprietors to get around this problem are legion: selling inferior Egyptian or Moroccan products as "local", at full price; swishing frozen specimens around in the sea to make them look more "lifelike"; and complying minimally with the legal requirement to clearly indicate when fish is frozen or *katapsygméno* (often only by the abbreviation "kat." "k." or just an asterisk on the Greek-language side of the menu).

Unfortunately, from a tourist's point of view, the greatest variety and quantity of fish is on offer outside of summer. **Dragnet trawling** (the *tráta*) is engaged in between October 1 and May 31, with local variations dictated by politics; the season really should end April 30, as most baby fish emerge during May. The latest generation of mechanized trawler or *anemótrata* is extremely destructive to the marine environment, indiscriminately hoovering the sea floor, with one monstrous boat having the impact of a half-dozen old-style wooden craft. During summer, lamp-lure (*pyrofáni*) and trident, stationary drift nets, "doughnut" trap (*kýrtos*) and multi-hook line (*paragádhi*) are the only permitted methods. Fish caught during these warmer months tend to be relatively scrawny and dry-tasting, and are served with a tureen of *ladholémono* (oil and lemon juice) sauce.

Most restaurants use imported and/or frozen fish at this time, or rely on *ikhthyotrofía* (fish farms) for a supply of *tsipoúra* and *lavráki* in particular. These **fish farms**, heavily subsidized by EU grants, are a Big Thing on the smaller Dodecanese such as Agathoníssi, Sými, Hálki, Astypálea and Kálymnos, as well as on most of the east Aegean islands, often serving as significant local employers. But quality products are not their strong point – farmed fish subsist exclusively on a diet of pellet food made from low-grade fish meal or even petroleum by-products, giving them an unmistakable muddy taste. The farms are also something of an environmental disaster, as the parasiticide chemicals used to keep them going are highly toxic.

appears in spring; *gávros* (anchovy) and *sardhélles* (sardines) are late summer treats, at their best in the northeast Aegean. Also in the north Aegean, *pandelís* or *sykiós* (Latin *Corvina nigra*, in French *corb*) is caught in early summer, and is highly esteemed since it's a rock-dweller rather than a bottom-feeder – and therefore a bit pricier than some species. In autumn especially you may encounter *psarósoupa* (fish broth) or *kakaviá* (a bouillabaisse-like stew).

Less esteemed species **cost** about €27–38 per kilo; choicier varieties, such as *barboúni* (red mullet), *tsipoúra* (gilt-head bream), *lavráki* (seabass) or *fangrí* (common bream), will be expensive if wild – €40–50 per kilo, depending on what the market will bear. If the price seems too good to be true, it's almost certainly farmed. Prices are usually quoted by the kilo (less often by the portion), and should not be much more than double the street-market rate. Stand-

ard procedure is to go to the glass-fronted cooler and pick your own specimen, and have it weighed (uncleaned) in your presence. If you are concerned that you may be later overcharged, which sometimes happens, have the amount confirmed on a slip of paper.

Cheaper **seafood** (*thalassiná*) such as *kalamarákia* (fried baby squid) and *okhtapódhi* (octopus) are a summer staple of most seaside tavernas, and occasionally *mýdhia* (mussels), *kydhónia* (warty Venus) and *garídhes* (small prawns) will be on offer at reasonable prices. Keep an eye out, however, for freshness and season; *kydhónia* and a few other species (see p.540) must in fact be eaten alive for safety. The miniature "Sými" shrimps, which are also caught around Hálki and Kastellórizo, would anywhere else just be used for bait, but here are devoured avidly; when less than a day old, they're distinctly sweet-flavoured.

As the more favoured species have become overfished, **unusual seafoods**, formerly the exclusive province of the poor, are figuring more regularly on menus. Ray or skate (variously known as *platý*, *seláhi*, *trígona* or *vátos*) can be fried or steamed and served with *skordhaliá* (garlic dip), and are even dried for decoration. Sea urchins (*ahini*) are also a humble (but increasingly scarce) favourite, being split and emptied for the sake of their (reputedly aphrodisiac) roe, which is eaten raw. Only the reddish ones are gravid; special shears are sold for opening them if you don't fancy a hand full of spines. Many a quiet beach is littered with their halved carapaces, evidence of an instant Greek picnic.

Another peculiar delicacy, frequently available on Rhodes, Kálymnos and several nearby islands, are **foúskes** ("blisters"). These marine invertebrates (*figue de mer* or *violet* in French) live on rocks at depths of 30–40m, and are gathered by sponge-divers for extra income. They're unprepossessing in the extreme – unfortunately, resembling hairy turds – but slice them lengthwise and your opinion will change instantly as you scoop out the liquor and savour the orange and yellow innards, which taste much like oysters and cost about the same. Unfortunately they're commonly pickled in beer bottles of their own liquor mixed with preserving brine, which tends to overpower their delicate intrinsic taste.

Wines

Both *estiatória* and tavernas will usually offer you a choice of bottled **wines**, and many still have their own house variety, kept in barrels, sold in bulk by the quarter-, half- or full litre, and served either in glass flagons or brightly coloured tin "monkey-cups" called *kantária*. Not as many tavernas stock their own wine as once did, but it's always worth asking whether they have wine *varelísio* (**barrelled**) or *hýma* (**in bulk**). You should expect to pay €4.50–7 per litre, with smaller measures priced (more or less) proportionately. Non-resinated wine is almost always more than decent, though even in the islands **retsína** – pine-resinated wine, a slightly acquired taste – is popular, usually imported from the mainland (though Sámos, Rhodes and

Límnos make their own). Retsína is also available straight from the barrel, though the bottled brands Mihali Yeoryiadhi from Thessaloníki, Yeoryios Yeoryiadhi or Cambas from Attica, and Liokri, Villitsa or Malamatina from central Greece (the latter often cut with soda water) are all excellent and likely to be more consistent in quality.

Among the **bottled wines** available **nationwide**, Cambas Attikos, Boutari Lac des Roches and any white from Zítsa are drinkable, inexpensive whites, while Boutari Naoussa and Kourtakis Apelia are decent, mid-range reds. If you want a better but still moderately priced red, go for the Merlot of either Boutari and Tsantali, or Averof Katoï from Epirus.

If you're travelling around **wine-producing islands**, however, you may as well go for **local bottlings**; the best available guide to the emerging Greek domaines and vintners is Nico Manessis' *The Illustrated Greek Wine Book* (see p.526). Almost anything produced on **Límnos** is decent; the Alexandrine muscat is now used for whites, the local *límnio* grape for reds and rosés. **Sámos** is most famous for its fortified (fourteen to fifteen percent alcohol) dessert wines based on the muscat grape, similar to Madeira and still exported in large quantities to France for use as communion wine in church. But the island also has some acceptable premium whites, and some good **rosés**; for example, the pop-top Fokianos label. **Ikaría** produces limited bottlings of red from small domaines in the west of the island, with equally patchy success; Afames is reckoned much better than Nikarya label. Commercial vinting on **Lésvos** has recently been revived by the generally excellent Methymneos winery. On **Rhodes**, Alexandhris products from Émbona are well thought of, as is the Emery label with its Villaré white, and CAIR's dry white "Rodos 2400", though CAIR *retsína* is worth avoiding.

Curiously, island red mass-market wines (except for Rhodes' CAIR Moulin and Emery Cava) are almost uniformly mediocre; in this respect you're better off choosing **reds from the mainland**. Carras from Halkidhikí does the excellent Porto Carras, while Ktima Tselepou offers a very palatable Cabernet–Merlot blend. Antonopoulos

Yerontoklima (Pátra), Ktima Papaïoannou Nemea (Peloponnese) and Tsantali Rapsani (Thessaly) are all superb, velvety reds – and likely to be found only in the better *koultoúra* tavernas or *káves* (**bottle shops**). Antonopoulos, Tselepos (Mantinia domaine) and Papaïoannou also do excellent **mainland whites**, especially the Spyropoulos Orino Mantinia, sometimes found organically produced.

Other **premium micro-wineries** on the mainland whose products have long been fashionable, in both red and white, include the vastly overrated Hatzimihali (central Greece), Athanasiadhi (central Greece), Dhiamandákou (near Náoussa, red and white), Skouras (Argolid) and the two rival Lazaridhi vintners (Dhráma, east Macedonia), especially their superb Merlots. For any of these you can expect to pay €7–11 per bottle in a shop, double that at a taverna.

Last but not least, CAIR on Rhodes makes its very own "**champagne**" ("naturally sparkling wine fermented *en bouteille*", says the label), in both brut and demi-sec versions. It's not Moët & Chandon quality by any means, but at less than €6 per bottle no one's complaining.

Cafés, cake shops and bars

The Greek eating and drinking experience encompasses a variety of other places beyond restaurants. Most importantly, there is the institution of the **kafenío**, found in every town and village in the country. In addition, you'll come across **ouzerís**, **zaharoplastía** (Greek patisseries) and **barákia**.

The kafenío

The **kafenío** (plural, *kafenía*) is the traditional Greek coffee shop or café. Although its main business is "Greek" (generic Middle Eastern) coffee – prepared *skéto* or *pikró* (unsweetened), *métrio* (medium) or *glykó* (sweet) – it also serves spirits such as *oúzo* (see below), brandy (usually Metaxa or Botrys brand, in three grades), beer, the sagebased tea known as *alisfakiá*, juices and soft drinks. Another refreshing drink sold in cafés is *kafés frappé*, iced, jigger-shaken instant coffee with or without milk and sugar

– uniquely Greek despite its French-sounding name. Like Greek coffee, it is always accompanied by a welcome glass of cold water. One quality fizzy soft drink to single out is the Vólos-based Epsa, with its Orangina-like bottles and high juice content.

Usually the only **edibles** available are "spoon sweets" or *glyká koutalioú* (sticky, syrupy preserves of quince, grape, fig, citrus fruit or cherry), and the traditional *ipovrýhio*, a piece of mastic submerged in a glass of water like a submarine – which is what the word means in Greek. Peculiar to Níssyros, but sometimes exported to neighbouring islands, is *soumádha*, concentrated almond syrup similar to Italian *orgeat*; diluted four-to-one with cold water, there's nothing more refreshing on a hot day.

Like tavernas, *kafenía* range from the plastic and sophisticated to the old-fashioned, spit-on-the-floor or mock-retro variety, with marble or brightly painted metal tables and straw-bottomed chairs. An important institution anywhere in Greece, they form the pivot of life in the country villages, especially on Lésvos, Híos and Kós. You get the impression that many men spend most of their waking hours there. Greek women are rarely to be seen in the more traditional places – and foreign women may sometimes feel uneasy or unwelcome in these establishments. Some *kafenía* close at siesta time, but many remain open from early in the morning until late at night. The chief socializing time is 6pm to 8pm, immediately after the siesta. This is the time to take your pre-dinner *oúzo*, as the sun begins to sink and the air cools down.

Oúzo, mezédhes and ouzerís

Oúzo is a simple spirit of up to 48 percent alcohol (see box p.407), distilled from the grape-mash residue left over from wine-making, and then flavoured with herbs such as anise or fennel. There are nearly twenty name brands, with the best island ones reckoned to come from Lésvos and Sámos; inferior ones are either weak (such as the Rhodian Fokiali, at forty percent) or spiked with molasses or grain alcohol to "boost" them.

When you order, you will be served two glasses: one with about 40ml of *oúzo*, and one full of **water** that's tipped into the latter until it turns a milky white. You can drink it straight, but the strong, burning taste is hardly refreshing if you do. It is also common to add **ice cubes** (*pagáki*), a bowl of which will be provided upon request. The next measure up from a glass is a *karafáki* – a deceptively small 200ml vial – which will very rapidly render you legless if you don't alternate tippling with snacks

A much smoother variant of *oúzo* is **soúma**, found chiefly on Rhodes and Sámos, but in theory anywhere grapes are grown. The smoothness is deceptive – two or three glasses of it and you had better not have any other firm plans for the rest of the afternoon.

Until the 1980s, every *oúzo* you ordered was automatically accompanied by a small plate of **mezédhes** on the house: bits of cheese, cucumber, tomato, a few olives, sometimes octopus or even a couple of small fish. Unfortunately, these days "*oúzo mezédhes*" is a separate, more expensive option on a price list. Often, however, they are not featured on any formal menu, but if you order a *karafáki* you will automatically be offered a small selection of snacks.

Though they are confined to select neighbourhoods of the bigger island towns such as Ródhos, and Sými, Kós, Léros, Sámos, Híos and Lésvos, one kind of drinking establishment specializes in *oúzo* and *mezédhes*. This is an **ouzerí** (same in the Greek plural, we've added 's' to the hybrid) and are well worth trying for the marvellous variety of *mezédhes* they serve (though numbers of mediocre tavernas counterfeit the name). At the genuine article, several plates of *mezédhes* plus drinks will effectively substitute for a more involved meal at a taverna (though it usually works out more expensive, if you have a healthy appetite). Faced with an often bewilderingly varied menu, you might opt for the *pikilía* (medley, assortment) available in several sizes, the largest and most expensive one usually heavy on the seafood. At other *ouzerís* the language barrier may be overcome by the waiter wielding an enormous *dhískos* or tray laden with all the current cold offerings – you pick the ones you like the look of, though you'll still have to "blind"-order hot entrées to follow.

Eating at an *ouzerí* is often the best way to get an idea of **regional specialities**, which can be fairly elaborate or incredibly simple. An example of the latter is *krítamo* or rock samphire, mentioned in *King Lear* and offered to the discerning on most of the east Aegean islands. A vitamin- and mineral-rich succulent growing on sea-coast cliffs, it is harvested in June or July by fishermen, pickled in brine, vinegar or wine, and served unadorned, with fish or to jazz up salads.

Sweets, breakfast and Western coffee

Similar to the *kafenío* is the **zaharoplastío**, a cross between café and patisserie, serving coffee, alcohol, yogurt with honey, and sticky cakes.

The better establishments offer an amazing variety of pastries, cream-and-chocolate confections, honey-soaked Greco-Turkish sweets like *baklavás*, *kataïfi* (honey-drenched "shredded wheat"), *galaktoboúreko* (custard pie), and so on.

If you want a stronger slant towards the dairy products and away from the pure sugar, seek out a **galaktopolío**, where you'll often find *ryzógalo* (rice pudding – rather better than the English canned or school-dinner variety), *kréma* (custard) and locally made *yiaoúrti* (yogurt), best if it's *próvio* (from sheep's milk).

Ice cream, sold principally at the *gelaterie* which have swept over Greece of late, can be very good and almost indistinguishable from Italian prototypes. Dhodhoni is the posh local chain, while Häagen-Dazs is also widely available and identical to its north European profile. On Rhodes in particular, the best ice-cream chain, Stani, is in fact run by Rhodian Turks. A scoop (*baláki*) costs €1–1.50; you'll be asked if you want it in a cup (*kypelláki*) or a cone (*honáki*), and whether you want toppings like *santí* (whipped cream) or nuts. By contrast, mass-produced brands like Delta or Evga are pretty average, with the honourable exception of the Skandalo and Nirvana labels.

Both *zaharoplastía* and *galaktopolía* are more family-oriented places than the *kafenío*, and many also serve a basic **continental breakfast** of *méli me voútyro* (honey poured over a pat of butter) or jam (all kinds are called *marmeládha* in Greek; ask for *portokáli* – orange – if you want proper marmalade) with fresh bread or *friganiés* (melba-toast-type slivers). You are also more likely to find approximations of British **tea** here, as obscure Sri Lankan or Madagascan brands of bag, often left to stew in a metal pot.

"Nes"(café) has become the generic term for all instant **coffee**, regardless of brand; it's generally pretty vile, and since the mid-1990s there's been a nationwide reaction against it. Even in the smallest island capital or resort there will be at least one trendy café which does a range of foreign-style coffees – filter, dubbed *filtros* or *gallikós* (French); cappuccino; and espresso – at overseas prices. A more enticing, recent innovation is *freddoccino*, a cappuccino-based alternative to the traditional cold *frappé*. Outside of the largest towns, properly made versions of these drinks will be harder to find and many will come from instant packets.

Bars – and beer

Bars (*barákia* in the plural), once confined to the biggest cities and holiday resorts, are now found all over Greece, especially in pedestrianized areas. They range from clones of Parisian cafés or Spanish *bodegas* to seaside beach-bars, with music or TV running all day. At their most sophisticated, however, they are well-executed **theme venues** in ex-industrial premises or Neoclassical mansions that can hold their own against close equivalents in Spain or London, with Western (currently techno, dub or ambient) soundtracks.

Drinks are invariably more expensive than in a café. Bars are, however, most likely to stock a range of **beers**, mostly foreign labels made locally under licence at just one or two breweries on the central mainland. Genuinely **local brews** include Mythos, a smooth

lager in a green bottle, put out by the Boutari vintners; Veryina, brewed in Komotiní and common on the larger islands; Pils Hellas, a sharp Pilsner; the resurrected Fix, for years until its demise in 1980 Greece's only beer; and 2004 entrant Zorba's(!), decent enough and worth buying for the tacky label alone.

Kronenbourg 1664 and Kaiser are two of the more common quality **foreign-licence** varieties, with the latter available in both light and dark. Bland, inoffensive Amstel and the increasingly rare, yeasty Henninger are the two cheapies; the Dutch themselves claim that Amstel is better than the one available in Holland, and Amstel also makes a very palatable, strong (seven percent) **bock**. Heineken, still referred to as a "*prássini*" by bar and taverna staff after its green bottle, despite the advent of Mythos, is too harshly sharp for many. Since 1993 a tidal wave of even pricier, genuinely imported German beers, such as Bitburger, Fisher and Warsteiner (plus a few British and Belgian ones), has washed over the fancier resorts.

Incidentally, try not to get stuck with the one-third litre cans, vastly more expensive (and more of a rubbish problem) than the **returnable** half-litre **bottles** (see the box on Eco-friendly tourism, p.70). On ferry-boats or in remote locales, you may not have a choice, however.

Mineral water, mostly still, typically comes as half-litre and one-and-a-half-litre plastic bottles. The ubiquitous Loutraki brand is not esteemed by the Greeks themselves, who prefer various brands from Crete and Epirus. In the better tavernas there has been a backlash against plastic bottles – which constitute a tremendous litter problem – and you can now get it in one-litre glass bottles. Souroti is about the only brand of sparkling (*aerioúho*) water.

Communications

Greece's postal system is adequate, especially for outgoing mail. Service provided by OTE (Organismós Tiliepikinoníon tís Elládhos, the telecoms entity) has improved drastically since the 1990s, under the twin threats of privatization and competition from thriving local mobile networks. Mobile phone users are well looked after, with signals in all but the remotest corners of the country. Internet facilities are found in major towns and resorts.

Postal services

Post offices, recognizable by their stylized Hermes-head logo on a blue background, are open Monday to Friday from 7.30am to 2pm. **Airmail letters or postcards** from the islands take three to seven days to reach the rest of Europe, five to twelve days to get to North America, and a bit longer for Australia and New Zealand. Generally, the larger the island (and the planes serving its airport), the quicker the service. Postal rates for up to 20g are a uniform €0.65 to all overseas destinations. For a simple letter or card, a stamp (*grammatósimo*) can also be purchased at an authorized postal agency (usually a stationery store). For a modest fee (about €3) you can shave a day or two off delivery time to any destination by using the **express service** (*katepígonda*). **Registered** (*systiméno*) delivery is also available for a similar amount, but proves quite slow unless coupled with express service. If you are sending large purchases or excess baggage home, **parcels** should and often can only be handled in the main provincial or county capitals. This way, your bundle will be in Athens, and on an international flight, within a day. For non-EU/EEA destinations, always present your box open for inspection, and come prepared with tape, twine and scissors – most post offices will sell cardboard boxes, but nothing to actually close the package. An array of services are available: air parcel (fast and expensive), surface-air lift (a couple of weeks slower but much cheaper), insured, and proof of delivery among others.

Ordinary **postboxes** are bright yellow, express boxes dark red, but it's best to use only those by the door of an actual post office, since days may pass between collections at other street-corner or wall-mounted boxes. If you are confronted by two slots, "ESOTERIKÓ" is for domestic mail, "EXOTERIKÓ" for overseas. Often there are more: one box or slot for mail to Athens and suburbs, one for your local province, one for "other" parts of Greece, and one for overseas; if in doubt, ask someone.

The **poste restante** system is reasonably efficient, especially at the post offices of larger towns. Mail should be clearly addressed and marked "poste restante", with your surname underlined, to the main post office of whichever town you choose. It will be held for a month and you'll need your passport to collect it.

Phones

Making **telephone calls** is relatively straightforward. All land-line exchanges are now digital, and you should have few problems reaching any number from either overseas or within Greece.

Call boxes, poorly maintained and invariably sited at the noisiest street corners, work only with phonecards; these come in three sizes – 1000, 5000 and 10,000 units – and are available from kiosks and newsagents. Not surprisingly, the more expensive cards are the best value in terms of euro per unit. Despite numbers hopefully scribbled on the appropriate tabs, call boxes cannot be rung back; however, green, countertop cardphones kept by many hotels can be rung.

A more economic type of pre-paid calling card, which can also be used on private subscriber lines, is the **Khronokarta**, which comes in three denominations. To use one, dial ☎0808, then at the prompt enter the twelve-digit card number. Charges are about half that of conventional telecards.

Other options for calling include a bare handful of **counter coin-op phones** in bars, *kafenía* and hotel lobbies; these take small euro coins – five-cent, ten-cent, twenty-cent and fifty-cent denominations – and, unlike kerbside phone boxes, can be rung back. Most of them are made in northern Europe and bear instructions in English. You'll probably want to avoid making long-distance calls **from hotel rooms**, as a minimum hundred percent surcharge will be slapped on – we've heard tales of triple and quadruple markups and, since hotels apparently have the legal right to do this, complaining to the tourist police is unlikely to get you anywhere.

For **international** (*exoterikó*) **calls**, it's again best to use kerbside cardphones. **Faxes** are best sent from post offices and some travel agencies – at a price; receiving a fax may also incur a small charge. **Reverse-charge** (*khréosis toú kalouménou* in Greek) or person-to-person calls, as well as **directory enquiries**, can be made from phone boxes or private subscriber phones using the appropriate operator numbers listed in the box below.

Overseas phone calls with a 100-unit card will **cost**, approximately, €0.40 per

Greek phone numbers

During 2002, all Greek phone numbers changed to a system resembling the French one, in which you are obliged to dial all ten numbers of a subscriber, including the former area code (now just a prefix), wherever you may be. All ordinary land lines begin with 2, and all mobiles begin with 6.

minute to all EU countries and much of the rest of central Europe, North America and Australia, versus €0.20 per minute on a private subscriber line. There is no particular cheap rate for overseas calls to these destinations, and dialling countries with problematic phone systems like Russia, Israel or Egypt is rather more. **Within Greece**, undiscounted **rates** are €0.10 per minute on a subscriber line, notably more from a cardphone; a twenty percent discount applies daily from 10pm to 8am, and from 10pm Saturday until 8am Monday.

Mobile phones

Mobile phones are an essential fashion accessory in Greece, which has the highest per-capita usage in Europe outside of Italy – in

Useful phone codes and numbers

Phoning abroad from Greece

Dial the country code (given below) + area code (minus any initial 0) + number
Australia ☏0061
Canada ☏001

Ireland ☏00353
New Zealand ☏0064
UK ☏0044
USA ☏001

Greek phone prefixes

Local call rate ☏801

Toll-free/Freefone ☏800

Useful Greek phone numbers

Ambulance ☏166
Fire brigade, urban ☏199
Forest fire reporting ☏191
Operator ☏132 (Domestic)
Operator ☏139 (International)

Police/Emergency ☏100
Speaking clock ☏141
Tourist police ☏171 (Athens);
☏210 171 (elsewhere)

a population of roughly eleven million, there are claimed to be nearly seven million mobile handsets in use. There are four **networks** at present: Vodafone, TIM, Cosmote and newcomer Q-Telecom. Calling any of them from overseas, you will find that costs are exactly the same as calling a fixed phone – so you needn't worry about ringing them when given as alternative numbers for accommodation – though of course such numbers are pricey when rung locally. **Coverage** country-wide is fairly good, though there are a few "dead" zones on really remote islets. **Pay-as-you-go**, contract-free plans (such as TIM B-Free and Vodafone À La Carte) are heavily promoted in Greece, so if you're going to be around for a while it's well worth obtaining a local SIM card to install in your existing phone (see below); otherwise an outlay of €90 or less will see you to a decent apparatus and your first calling card. This lasts up to a year – even if you use up your talk time you'll still have an incoming number, along with a voice-mail service. Top-up calling cards – starting from denominations of €8–9 depending on the network – are available at all *períptera*.

If you want to use your **home-based mobile abroad**, you'll need to check with your phone provider whether it will work. North American users will only be able to use tri-band rigs in Greece. Any GSM mobile from the UK, Australia or New Zealand should work fine in Greece.

In the UK you'll have to inform your service network before going abroad to get international access ("**roaming**") switched on. You may get charged extra for this depending on the terms of your package. You will also be charged extra for **incoming calls** when abroad, as the people calling you will be paying the usual rate; discount plans are available with many providers to reduce the cost of forwarding the call to you overseas by as much as seventy percent. If you want to **retrieve messages** while you're away, you'll have to ask your provider for a new access number, as your one-stroke "mail" key may not always work abroad.

Experience has shown that the Greek network selected out of the four existing ones for roaming purposes makes little difference in terms of **call charges**: depending on the length of chat, these can equal

£0.70 (plus VAT) per minute, whether to Greek numbers or back to Britain (including voice-mail retrieval). To get round this highway robbery you can buy a Greek-based pay-as-you-go **SIM** upon arrival in the country (roughly €15–20), and substitute it for the UK-based SIM in your phone. UK providers may tell you that this can't be done, but you are legally entitled to the phone-unblock code from the manufacturer after (usually) six months of use. Otherwise, have a phone shop in Greece free up the phone with a simple five-minute computer procedure (they may make a charge).

Email and Internet

Internet cafés are the easiest places to check web-based email accounts (for example, ◉www.yahoo.com and ◉www.hotmail.com) and locations are included throughout the Guide. Rates tend to be about €6 per hour maximum, often less, with half-hour or even ten-minute increments available.

If you are carrying your own **laptop**, you will need about 2m of North American-standard cable (UK cables will *not* work), lightweight and easily purchasable in Greece, with RJ-11 male terminals at each end. The Greek **dial tone** is discontinuous and thus not recognized by most modems – instruct it to "ignore dial tone". Many newer hotel rooms have RJ-11 **sockets**, but some older ones still have their phones hard-wired into the wall. You can often get around this problem with a female–female **adapter**, either RJ-11- or 6P6C-configured, available at better electrical retailers. They weigh and cost next to nothing, so carry both (one is sure to work) for making a splice between your cable and the RJ-11 end of the cable between the wall and phone (which you simply unplug). You will usually have to dial an initial "9" or "0" to get around the hotel's central switchboard for a proper external dial tone.

Compuserve and AOL definitely have **points of presence** in Greece, but more obscure ISPs may also have a reciprocal agreement with Greek-based ISPs like forthnet.gr, otenet.gr and germanosnet.gr, so ask your provider for a list of any available dial-up numbers. **Piggybacking charges** tend to be fairly high, but for a modest number of minutes per day they still work out much less than patronizing an Internet café. **Greek ISPs** are very flexible about subscription periods, offering packages of anything from a month to a year (averaging €10–12 per month for unlimited access, with just a few euro cents per hour surfing charges. So if you're travelling for a while with a laptop, consider signing up; @www .otenet.gr in particular allows you to retrieve mail from any other POP3 account for the price of dialling their nationwide number.

The media

Although the Greek press and airwaves have been relatively free since the fall of the colonels' dictatorship in 1974, nobody would ever propose the Greek media as a paradigm of responsible or objective journalism. Papers are almost uniformly sensational, state-run radio and TV often biased in favour of the ruling party, and private channels imitative of the worst American programming. Most visitors tune all this out, however, seeking solace in the music of private radio stations, or the limited number of English-language publications.

British **newspapers** are fairly widely available in Greece at a cost of €1.75–2.50 for dailies, or €4 for Sunday editions. Out on the islands, you'll find one- to two-day-old copies of *The Times*, *The Telegraph*, *The Independent* and *The Guardian*'s European edition, plus a few of the tabloids, in all the resorts as well as in major towns. American and international alternatives include the turgid *USA Today* and the slightly more readable *International Herald Tribune*, the latter including as a major bonus a free (though somewhat abridged) English translation of the respected Greek daily *Kathimerini* (online at @www.eKathimerini.com; see also below). Among numerous foreign **magazines**, *Time* and *Newsweek* are also widely available.

There are relatively few surviving **locally produced** English-language magazines or papers. Expensive, glossy *Odyssey*, produced every other month by and for wealthy diaspora Greeks, has improved significantly under a new editorial board and has excellent reviews of new books. By far the best of the English-language **newspapers** is the four-colour *Athens News* weekly (every Friday, online at @www.athensnews .gr; €1.80), with good features and Balkan news, plus entertainment and arts listings, available in most resorts.

Before setting out from the **UK**, there are two **Greek-specific periodicals** well worth consulting. One is the *Anglo-Hellenic Review* (£2), published twice yearly by the Anglo-Hellenic League; it has excellent essays by renowned scholars, and good reviews of recently issued books on Greek topics. Obtain it either from the Hellenic Bookservice (see p.526) or The Hellenic Centre, 16/18 Paddington St, London W1M 4AS. The other is the Greek London Embassy's monthly (not Sept) newsletter, *Greece: Background-News-Information*. Though clearly pro-government to the point of verging on propaganda, it's well written (even humorous), giving a lively overview of events in the country over the past few weeks. To register on their mailing list (free), contact them on ⊕020/7727 3071, ⊕7727 8960 or ⊚press office@greekembassy.org.uk.

Greek publications

Many papers have ties (including funding) with specific **political groups**, so their bias tends to decrease the already low quality of Greek dailies. Among these, only the **centrist**

Kathimerini – whose former proprietor Helen Vlahos attained heroic status for her defiance of the junta – approaches the standards of a major European paper of record. *Eleftherotypia*, once a PASOK mouthpiece, now aspires to more independence, and has excellent weekend supplements; *Avriani* has taken its place as the PASOK cheerleading section. *Ta Nea* is a highly popular, MOR tabloid, much loved for its extensive small ads. On the far **Left**, *Avyi* is the Eurocommunist/Synaspismós forum with literary leanings, while *Rizospastis* acts as the organ of the KKE (unreconstructed Communists). *Ethnos* became notorious some years back for receiving covert funding from the KGB to act as a disinformation bulletin. At the other end of the political spectrum, *Apoyevmatini* generally supports the **centre-right** Néa Dhimokratía party, while *Estia's* no-photo format and reactionary politics are both stuck somewhere at the beginning of the twentieth century. The ultra-nationalist, lunatic fringe is staked out by paranoid *Stohos* ("Our Goal: Greater Greece; Our Capital: Constantinople"). With the generally fish-wrap quality of most newspapers, you wouldn't think there'd be room for a designated **gutter press**, but there is: *News Traffic* and *Espresso*.

Among **magazines** that are not merely translations of overseas titles, *Takhydhromos* is the respectable news-and-features weekly; *Ena* is more sensationalist, *Ev* tells the growing yuppie class which exotic vacations, fancy wines and lifestyle accessories they need to burn their cash on, *Klik* is a crass rip-off of Britain's *The Face*, while *To Pondiki* (The Mouse) is a satirical weekly revue in the same vein as Britain's *Private Eye*; its famous covers are spot-on and accessible to anyone with minimal Greek. More specialized niches are occupied by low-circulation titles such as *Adhesmatos Typos* (a slightly rightist, muckraking journal) and *Andi*, an intelligent bi-weekly somewhat in the mould of Britain's *New Statesman and Society*.

Radio

If you have a **radio** on your personal stereo, playing dial roulette can be rewarding. Greek music programmes are always accessible (if variable in quality) and, since abolition of the government's former monopoly of wavelengths, regional stations have mush-

roomed; indeed the airwaves are now positively cluttered as every island town sets up its own studio and transmitter. The two state-run channels are ER1 (a mix of news, talk and popular music) and ER2 (strictly popular music).

On heavily touristed islands like Rhodes, there will usually be at least one station on the FM band (eg Radio International, 102–104.3) trying its luck at English-moderated programming by and for foreigners. The Turkish state radio's Third Channel is also widely (if somewhat unpatriotically) listened to on border islands for its classical, jazz and blues programmes. The **BBC World Service** broadcasts on short wave throughout Greece; 6.18, 9.41, 15.07 and 12.09 MHz are the most common frequencies. However, short-wave services are being phased out in many parts of the world, so consult ⓦ www.bbc.co.uk/worldservice for current frequencies.

Television

Television first appeared in Greece in 1965, but it only became dominant during the 1967–74 junta, with the ruling colonels using it as a means of social control and to purvey anodyne variety revues, sports events and so on. As in many countries, it transformed the Greeks from a nation of live performers and coffee-house habitués to introverted stay-at-homes, which dovetailed nicely with the junta's "family values".

Greece's centralized, government-controlled **TV stations**, ET1, NET and (out of Thessaloníki) ET3, nowadays lag behind private, mostly rather right-wing channels – Antenna, Mega, Star, Alpha, Alter and Makedonia TV – in the ratings. Programming on all stations has evolved little since junta days, tending to be a mix of soaps (especially Italian, Spanish and Latin American), game shows, westerns, B-movies and sports. All foreign films and serials are broadcast in their original language, with Greek subtitles. Most private channels operate around the clock; public stations broadcast from around 5.30am until 3am. Numerous **cable and satellite** channels are received, including CNN, MTV, Filmnet, Euronews (in English), French TV5 and Italian Rai Due. The range available depends on the area (and hotel) you're in.

Opening hours and public holidays

It's impossible to generalize about Greek opening hours, except to say that they change constantly. The traditional timetable starts at a relatively civilized hour, with shops opening between 8.30 and 9am, then runs through until lunchtime, when there is a long break for the hottest part of the day. Most places, except banks and government offices, may then reopen in the mid- to late afternoon. Tourist areas tend to adopt a slightly more northern European timetable, with shops and offices, as well as the most important archeological sites and museums, usually open throughout the day.

Business and shopping hours

Most **government agencies** are open to the public on weekdays from 8am to 2pm. In general, however, you'd be optimistic to show up after 1pm expecting to be served the same day, as queues can be long and key personnel take off early. Private businesses, or anyone providing a service, frequently operate a straight 9am-to-5/6pm schedule. If someone is actually selling something, then they are more likely to follow a split shift as detailed below.

Shopping hours during the hottest months are theoretically Monday, Wednesday and Saturday from approximately 9am to 2.30pm, and Tuesday, Thursday and Friday from 8.30am to 2pm and 6 to 9pm. During the cooler, shorter-day months the morning schedule shifts slightly later, the evening session a half- or even a full hour earlier. But there are so many exceptions to these rules by virtue of holidays and professional idiosyncrasy that you can't count on getting anything done except from Monday to Friday, between 9.30am and 1pm. It's worth noting that **delis** and **butchers** are not allowed to sell fresh meat during summer afternoons (though some flout this rule); similarly **fishmongers** are only open in the morning until they sell out (usually by noon), as are **pharmacies**, which additionally are shut on Saturday (except for the duty pharmacist).

All of the above opening hours will be regularly thrown out of sync by the numerous public holidays and festivals – or nearly as frequent strikes, which can be general or profession-specific. The most important holidays, when almost everything will be closed, are listed below.

Public holidays
January 1
January 6
March 25
First Monday of Lent (variable Feb/March; see below)
Easter weekend (variable April/May; see below)
May 1
Pentecost or Whit Monday (50 days after Easter; see below)
August 15
October 28
December 25 & 26

Variable religious feasts
Lenten Monday
2006	March 6
2007	March 19
2008	March 10

Easter Sunday
2006	April 23
2007	April 8
2008	April 27

Whit Monday
2006	June 12
2007	May 28
2008	June 16

Ancient sites and monasteries

All the major **ancient sites** are now fenced off and, like most **museums**, charge **admission fees** ranging from a token €2 to a stiff €8, with an average fee of around €3. At most of them reductions of 25 to

30 percent apply to senior citizens, and 50 percent to students with proper identification – students from the EU with proper ID will often get in free. In addition, entrance to all state-run sites and museums is **free** to EU nationals on Sundays and public holidays from November to March – non-EU nationals are unlikely to be detected as such unless they go out of their way to advertise the fact.

Opening hours vary from site to site. As far as possible, individual times are quoted in the text, but remember that these change with exasperating frequency, and at smaller sites may be subject to the whim of a local *fýlakas* or site guard. Unless specified, the times quoted are generally summer hours, in effect from around late May to the end of September. Reckon on similar days but later opening and earlier closing in winter. Usually, the **last admission ticket** is typically sold fifteen to twenty minutes before the cited closing time.

Along with your ticket most sites and museums will provide a little colour **folding pamphlet** prepared by the *Tamío Arheolo-yikón Porón* or TAP (Archeological Receipts Fund); they usually include an accurate if potted history and site or gallery plan, and we've found them to be uniformly excellent, in stark contrast to the often miserable labelling of the sites or galleries themselves. Serious students will therefore want to invest in **site guides** or **museum catalogues**, which have often been expertly compiled by the excavating archeologists or curators.

Smaller sites generally close for a long lunch and **siesta** (even where they're not supposed to), as do **monasteries**. The latter are generally open from 9am to 1pm and 5 to 8pm (3.30–6.30pm in winter) for limited visits. Most monasteries impose a fairly strict **dress code** for visitors: no shorts on either sex, with women expected to cover their arms and wear skirts; the necessary wraps are sometimes provided on the spot.

It's free to take **photographs** of open-air sites, though museum photography or the use of tripods or video cameras anywhere requires an extra fee and a written permit. This must be arranged well in advance and in writing with the relevant Department of Antiquities (*Eforía Arheotíton*). For Rhodes and all of the Dodecanese, it's best to fax requests to ℱ22410 31048; for Sámos, to ℱ210 32 51 096; and, for Lésvos, Híos and Límnos, to ℱ22510 20745. It's also worth knowing that Classical Studies students can get a free annual pass to all Greek museums and sites by presenting themselves at the office on the rear corner (Tossítsa/Bouboulí-nas) of the National Archeological Museum in Athens – take documentation, two passport-sized photographs and be prepared to say you're a teacher.

Festivals and cultural events

Many of the big Greek festivals have a religious basis, so they're observed in accordance with the Orthodox calendar. Give or take a few saints, this is similar to the regular Catholic liturgical year, except for Easter, which can fall as many as four (but usually one or two) weeks either side of the Western festival – in 2001 and again in 2004 the two coincided (usually a very rare event).

Easter

Easter is by far the most important festival of the Greek year – infinitely more so than Christmas – and taken much more seriously than it is anywhere in western Europe, aside from Spain. From Wednesday of Holy Week until the following Monday, the state radio and TV networks are given over solely to religious programmes.

The **festival** is an excellent time to be in Greece, both for its beautiful religious ceremonies and for the days of celebration that follow. The remote village of Ólymbos on **Kárpathos** or Pyrgí on **Híos**, and the monastery of Ayíou Ioánnou Theológou on **Pátmos**, are the prime Easter venues among the islands in this guide, but unless you plan well in advance you have no hope of finding accommodation at that time.

The first great public ceremony takes place on **Good Friday** evening as the Descent from the Cross is lamented in church. At dusk the **Epitáfios**, Christ's funeral bier, lavishly decorated with flowers by the women of each parish (in large villages there will be more than one, from each church), leaves the sanctuary and is paraded solemnly through the streets. In many places this is accompanied by the burning of effigies of Judas Iscariot.

Late Saturday evening sees the climax in a majestic *Anástasis* Mass to celebrate Christ's triumphant return. At the stroke of midnight all the lights in every crowded church are extinguished, plunging the congregation into the darkness that envelops Christ as He passes through the underworld. Then there's a faint glimmer of light behind the altar screen before the priest appears, holding aloft a lighted taper and chanting "*Avtó to Fós . . .* " ("This is

the Light of the World"). Stepping down to the level of the parishioners, he touches his flame to the unlit candle of the nearest worshippers, intoning "*Dhévte, lávete Fós*" ("Come, take the Light"). Those at the front of the congregation and on the aisles do the same for their neighbours until the entire church – and the outer courtyard, where it's standing room only for latecomers – is ablaze with burning candles and the miracle reaffirmed.

Even the most committed agnostic is likely to find this moving. The traditional greeting, as fireworks explode around you in the street (and up in the sky at wealthier villages), is "*Khristós Anésti*" ("Christ is risen"), to which the response is "*Alithós Anésti*" ("Truly He is Risen"). In the week up to Easter Sunday you should wish people "*Kaló Páskha*" (Happy Easter); on or after the day, you say "*Khrónia Pollá*" ("Many Happy Returns"). On Kálymnos, there are organized dynamite-tossing contests, and at Vrondádhos on Híos rival parishes fire rockets at each other, with casualties and property damage common in both cases.

Worshippers then take the burning **candles** home; they are said to bring good fortune on the house if they arrive still burning. On reaching the front door it is common practice to make the sign of the cross on the lintel with the flame, leaving a black smudge visible for the rest of the year. The forty-day **Lenten fast** – still observed by the devout and in rural areas – is traditionally broken early on Sunday morning with a meal of *mayerítsa*, a soup made from lamb tripe, rice, dill and lemon. The rest of the lamb will be roasted on spits for Sunday lunch, and festivities often take place through the rest of the day.

The Greek equivalent of **Easter eggs** are hard-boiled eggs (painted red on Holy Thursday), which are baked into twisted, sweet bread-loaves (*tsourékia*) or distributed on Easter Sunday. People rap their eggs against their friends' eggs, and the owner of the last uncracked one is considered lucky.

The festival calendar

Most of the other Greek festivals are in honour of one or another of a multitude of **saints**, the most important of which are detailed below. A village or church bearing a saint's name is a fair guarantee of some observance – sometimes a lively festival right across the town or island, otherwise quiet, local and consisting of little more than a special liturgy and banners adorning the chapel in question. Saints' days are also celebrated as **name days**; if you learn that it's an acquaintance's name day, you wish them "*Khrónia Pollá*" ("Many Years", as in "Many Happy Returns"). Also listed are a few more **secular holidays**, most enjoyable of which are the pre-Lenten carnivals.

In addition to the specific dates mentioned, there are literally scores of **local festivals** (*paniyíria*) celebrating the patron saint of the village church. With hundreds of possible name-saints' days (liturgical calendars list two or three, often arcane, for each day), you're unlikely to travel around Greece for long without stumbling on something.

It is important to remember the concept of the *paramoní*, or **eve of the festival**. Most of the events listed below are celebrated on the night before, so if you show up on the morning of the date given you will very probably have missed any music, dancing or drinking.

January 1

New Year's Day (*Protokhroniá*) in Greece is the feast day of Áyios Vassílios (St Basil), The traditional New Year greeting is "*Kalí Khroniá*".

January 6

Epiphany (*Ayía Theofánia*, or *Fóta* for short), when the *kalikántzari* (hobgoblins) who run riot on earth during the twelve days of Christmas are rebanished to the nether world by various rites of the Church. The most important of these is the blessing of baptismal fonts and all outdoor bodies of water. At seaside locations, the priest traditionally casts a crucifix into the deep, with local youths competing for the privilege of recovering it.

Pre-Lenten carnivals

These – known in Greek as *Apokriá* or *Apokriés* – span three weeks, climaxing during the seventh weekend before Easter. Amongst the islands covered in this guide, Lésvos (Ayiássos) and Kárpathos (Ólymbos) have the most elaborate festivities. *Katharí Dheftéra* (Lenten Monday) of the last carnival week is always seven weeks (48 days, to be precise) before Easter Sunday.

March 25

The feast of the **Annunciation** (*Evangelismós* in Greek) is both a religious and a national holiday, with, on the one hand, military parades and dancing to celebrate the beginning of the revolt against Ottoman rule in 1821, and, on the other, church services to honour the news being given to Mary that she was to become the Mother of Christ. There are major festivities at any locality with a monastery or church named Evangelístria or Evangelismós.

April 23

The feast of **Áyios Yeóryios** (**St George**), the patron of shepherds, is a big rural celebration, with much dancing and feasting at associated shrines and towns. If April 23 falls before Easter, ie during Lent, the festivities are postponed until the Monday after Easter.

May 1

May Day (*Protomayiá*) is the great urban holiday when townspeople traditionally make for the countryside for picnics and return with bunches of wild flowers. Wreaths are hung on their doorways or balconies until they are burnt in bonfires on St John's Eve (June 23). There are also large demonstrations by the Left, claiming the *Ergatikí Protomayiá* (Working-Class First of May) as their own.

May 21

The feast of **Áyios Konstandínos** (St Constantine) and his mother, **Ayía Eléni** (St Helen), the first pro-Orthodox Byzantine rulers. It's widely observed as the name day for two of the more popular Christian names in Greece.

May/June

The **Monday of Áyio Pnévma** (the Holy Spirit, Whit Monday in the UK, Pentecost Monday in the US) marks the descent of the same to the assembled disciples, fifty days after Easter. Usually only a modest liturgy celebrated at rural chapels of the Holy Spirit, gaily decked out with pennants, but this is the major festival day at Pagóndhas, Sámos, with live music on the preceding evening.

June 29–30

The joint feast of **Áyios Pétros and Áyios Pávlos** (saints Peter and Paul), two of the more widely celebrated name days, is on the 29th. Celebrations often run together for the Gathering of (all) the Holy Apostles (Áyii Apóstoli), on the 30th.

July 17

The feast of **Ayía Marína**: a big event in rural areas, as she's an important protector of crops. Ayía Marína village on Kássos will be *en fête*. Between mid-July and mid-September there are religious festivals every few days, especially in rural areas, and, what with these, the summer heat and a mass exodus from the big cities, ordinary business slows or even halts.

July 20

The feast of **Profítis Ilías** (the Prophet Elijah) is widely celebrated at the countless hilltop shrines of Profítis Ilías – nowadays, as on Sámos, with a 4WD trip up to the mountain of the same name with sound systems cranked up and barbecue spits turning on arrival.

July 22

The feast of **Ayía Markélla** (St Marcelle – not the same one as in the Catholic calendar). The major festival of northern Híos.

July 26

The feast of **Ayía Paraskeví**, which is celebrated in parishes or villages bearing that name; for example, on Lésvos and Sámos.

July 27

The feast of **Áyios Pandelímon** (St Pantaleon); liveliest and longest festival at the eponymous monastery on Tílos, with a smaller bash on Agathoníssi.

August 6

Metamórfosis toú Sotíros (Transfiguration of the Saviour) provides another excuse for celebrations, particularly at Khristós Ráhon village on Ikaría, at Plátanos on Léros, and on Psará. On Hálki the date is marked by messy food fights with flour, eggs and squid ink, so beware.

August 15

Apokímisis tís Panayías (Assumption or Dormition of the Blessed Virgin Mary). This is the day when people traditionally return to their home village, and in many places there will be no accommodation available on any terms. Even some Greeks will resort to sleeping in the streets. There are especially major festivities at Ayiássos on Lésvos, at the Panayía Kyrá monastery on Níssyros, at Ólymbos on Kárpathos, at Foúrni port and at several locations on Kálymnos. Curiously, Lipsí celebrates its own Marian festival on the 23rd–24th.

August 29

Apokefálisis toú Prodhrómou (Beheading of John the Baptist). Popular pilgrimages and celebrations at Vrykoúnda on Kárpathos, and the namesake monastery near Kéfalos on Kós.

September 8

Yénisis tís Panayías (Birth of the Virgin Mary) sees special services in churches dedicated to the event. There's also a major pilgrimage of childless women to Tsambíka monastery, Rhodes.

September 14

A last major summer festival, the **Ípsosis toú Stavroú** (Exaltation of the Cross), keenly observed on Hálki, and also Níssyros.

September 24

The feast of **Áyios Ioánnis Theológos** (St John the Divine), observed on Níssyros and Pátmos, where at the saint's monastery there are solemn, beautiful liturgies the night before and early on the morning.

October 26

The feast of **Áyios Dhimítrios** (St Demetrius), another popular name day. In rural areas new wine is traditionally broached on this day, a good excuse for general inebriation.

October 28

Óhi Day, the year's major patriotic shindig – a national holiday with parades, folk dancing and speechifying to commemorate Metaxas's apocryphal one-word reply to Mussolini's 1940 ultimatum: "*Ohi!*"(No!).

November 8

Another popular name day, the feast of the **Archangels Michael and Gabriel** (Mihaíl and Gavriíl, or *tón Taxiárhon*), marked by rites at the numerous churches named after them, particularly at Arhángelos village on Rhodes, Asómati village on Kós, the rural monastery of Taxiárhis on Sými, and the big monastery of Mandamádhos, Lésvos.

December 6

The feast of **Áyios Nikólaos** (St Nicholas), the patron of seafarers, with many chapels dedicated to him.

December 25–26

A much less festive occasion than Greek Easter, **Christmas** (*Khristoúyenna*) is still an important religious feast. In recent years it has acquired all of the commercial trappings of the Western Christmas, with decorations, Christmas trees and gifts. December 26 is not Boxing Day as in England, but the **Sýnaxis tís Panayías** (Gathering of the Virgin's Entourage).

December 31
New Year's Eve (*Paramoní Protokhroniá*), when, as on the other twelve days of Christmas, a few children still go door-to-door singing the traditional *kálanda* (carols), receiving money in return. Adults tend to sit around playing cards, often for money. A special baked loaf, the *vassilópitta*, in which a coin is concealed to bring its finder good luck throughout the year, is cut at midnight.

Cultural festivals and cinema

As well as religious festivals, Greece has a full range of **cultural festivals**, including a few on the more popular islands. The major festivals falling within the scope of this guide are the **Rhodes Festival** (Aug–Oct), the **Ippokrateia** events on **Kós** (July & Aug), the **Sými Festival** (July–Sept) – including events on surrounding islands – and the **Festival of**

Sacred Music on Pátmos (early Sept). as well as the more low-key Manolis Kalomiris and Wine festivals on Sámos (July–Aug) and the Lesviakó Kalokéri/Lesbian Summer on Lésvos.

Greek **cinemas** show a large number of fairly recent American and British movies, always in the **original language**, with Greek subtitles. **Indoor** screenings are highly affordable, currently €6–8 depending on location and plushness of facilities; they shut from mid-May to mid-September unless they have air conditioning. Accordingly in summer numbers of **outdoor** cinemas set up shop; an outdoor movie (marginally cheaper) is worth catching at least once for the experience alone, though it's best to opt for the earlier screening (about 9pm) since the soundtrack on any later show tends to be turned down or even off to avoid complaints from adjacent residences. Summer cinemas are found on Lésvos, Híos, Ikaría, Sámos, Kálymnos, Astypálea, Kós and Rhodes; winter cinemas operate on Límnos, Lésvos, Híos, Sámos, Kálymnos, Kós and Rhodes.

Watersports

The Greek seashore offers endless scope for watersports, with kayaks for rent in most resorts and, less universally, windsurfing and parasailing facilities.

The years since the mid-1980s have seen a massive growth in the popularity of **windsurfing** in Greece. The country's bays and coves are ideal for beginners, and boards can be rented in a score of resorts in this book. Particularly good areas, most with established schools, include the coasts of Sámos (Kokkári), Lésvos (Pétra, Skála Kallonís), Kós (Kamári and Tingáki), Kárpathos (Afiárti region) and Rhodes (Prassoníssi and the west coast). You can almost always find a beginner's course of instruction, and rental rates are very reasonable – about €10 an hour.

Sea kayaks are available in many spots for even less, and of course the necessary skill is very easily mastered. Waterskiing, seen as old-fashioned and passé, has been more or less edged out (especially in youth-orientated resorts) by the delights of "banana" rides, ringo-ing and (most conspicuously) **parasailing** (*parapént* in Greek); rates for the latter start at €18 a go.

A combination of steady winds, appealing seascapes and numerous natural harbours have long made the Greek islands a tremendous place for **sailing**. Holiday companies offer all sorts of packaged and tailor-made

Public beaches, sunbeds and umbrellas

Not many people realize that all **beaches** in Greece are public land; that's understandable, given the extent to which luxury hotels encroach on them, and the sunbeds and umbrellas that carpet entire strands. Greek **law**, however, is very clear that the shore from the winter high-tide mark down to the water must be freely accessible, with a right of way provided around hotels or resorts, and that no permanent structures be built in that zone. Accordingly, you should resist pressure to pay rental for unwanted **sunbeds** or **umbrellas** – particularly the latter, which are often anchored with permanent, illegal concrete lugs buried in the sand. Beaches entirely or relatively free of such obstacles are noted in the guide.

cruises (see p.33 and p.34). Locally, small boats and dinghies are rented out by the day at many resorts. Larger craft can be chartered by the week or longer, either bare-boat or with skipper, from several marinas in the Dodecanese and the east Aegean. Rhodes is by far the busiest, justifiably so given the garland of small, interesting islands less than a day's sail away. Kálymnos is also a major yachting centre, while marinas have been completed at Kós and Sámos. There is relatively little sailing activity north of Sámos owing to the enormous distances of open sea between the east Aegean islands, and the relatively poor anchorage when you finally arrive.

Spring and autumn are the most pleasant and least expensive times; *meltémi* winds make for pretty nauseating sailing between late June and early September, and summer **rates** for the same craft can be three times as high as shoulder-season prices.

Because of the potential for pilfering submerged antiquities, **scuba diving** is severely restricted around the Dodecanese and the east Aegean. Its legal practice is confined among these islands to short stretches of coast off Rhodes, Kálymnos and (best of all) Léros. For an update on the situation – permitted areas are slowly being added since a liberalization in policy was announced by the Ministry of Culture – contact the Union of Greek Diving Centres (☎210 92 29 532 or 210 41 18 909).

Finding work

Since Greece's full accession to the European Union in 1993, any EU citizen has (in theory) the right to work in Greece. In practice, however, there are various bureaucratic hurdles to overcome. Formerly, the most common job for foreigners was teaching English in the numerous private cramming academies (*frondistíria*), but since 1993 severe restrictions have been put on the availability of such positions for non-Greeks, and you will more likely be involved in a commercial or leisure-oriented trade. The influx, since 1990, of between 800,000 and 1.2 million (estimates vary) immigrants from various poor countries has resulted in a surplus of unskilled labour and severely depressed wages for casual work.

Tourism-related work

Work in bars or restaurants, whether waiting, cooking or washing up, is now the exclusive province of men and women from central and eastern Europe, and pretty much the only way you'll end up doing this is if you own the business yourself. The same holds true for windsurfing schools: just about all of the ones listed in the Guide are foreign-owned and -staffed.

Otherwise, the only type of tourism-related work where you've a significant advantage over the new immigrants is that of courier/greeter/group coordinator for a **package holiday company**. All you need is EU nationality and language proficiency compatible with the clientele, though knowledge of Greek is a big plus. English-only speakers are pretty well restricted to places with a significant British package trade, namely Rhodes, Sámos, Kós and Lésvos.

Many such staff are recruited through ads in the tour company's home country, but it's by no means unheard of to be hired on the spot in April or May. A big plus, however you're taken on, is that you're usually guaranteed about six months of steady work, often with use of a car thrown in, and that if things work out you may be re-employed the following season with an explicit contract and better wages.

Documentation for legal employment

If you plan to work professionally for someone else, you first visit the nearest Department of Employment (in Rhodes, on the Street of the Knights, Odhós Ippotón) and collect two forms: one an **employment application**, which you fill in; the other for the formal offer of work by your prospective employer. Once these are vetted, and revenue stamps (*hartósima*, purchased at kiosks) applied, you take them to the Alien's Bureau (Ypiresía Allodhapón) or, in its absence, the central police station, to support your application for a **residence permit** (*ádhia paramonís*). For this, you will also need to bring your passport, several photographs, more *hartósima* and a stable address (not a hotel). Permits are given for terms of five years.

You should allow four to six weeks for all the formalities to be completed; the bottleneck is usually the required **health examination** at the nearest public hospital. There you will be chest-X-rayed for signs of TB, blood-tested for hepatitis B and C, HIV and a couple of other nasties, and have a (farcical) evaluation by a neurologist or psychiatrist for signs of mental disorder; this is all done at a reasonable cost. Once you've assembled all the results, you trot these over yourself to the local public health office, where a periodic (once weekly at best) meeting of its administrative council will vet and endorse these, and issue you with a certificate of approval. Finally you take this to the local police or Alien's Bureau, which should have your permit ready, free of charge other than for a few more *hartósima*, within three to four working days. Renewals are much easier and quicker – you generally skip the health test.

As a **self-employed professional**, you must satisfy the requirements of the Greek state with equivalent qualifications to native Greeks plying the same trade. You should also befriend a good accountant, who will advise you on which of the several varieties of doing business are to your advantage; trading under a corporate name is vastly more expensive tax-wise than doing business as a private person. You will need to sign on with **TEBE**, the Greek National Insurance scheme for self-employed people (analogous to Class 2 National Insurance contributions in the UK). If you are continuing to contribute to a social insurance scheme in a country which has reciprocal agreements with Greece (all EU states do), this must be proved in writing – a tedious and protracted process, involving translation of any resulting documents into Greek (by a lawyer or notary).

You will also have to visit the nearest tax office or *eforía* to be issued a **tax number** (abbreviated "ah-fi-mi" in Greek, similar to a UK Schedule D number) which must be cited in all transactions. To be issued one of these, you need to bring a birth certificate that shows the full unmarried names of *both* your parents. You will be required to prepare receipt and invoice books with your tax number professionally printed on them. The tax office will also determine which rate of **VAT** (the "fi-pi-ah") you should pay for each kind of transaction; VAT returns must be filed every two months, which is where a friendly accountant comes in handy again.

EU nationals who do not wish to work in Greece but still need a residence permit (eg property-owners needing to set up a bank account) will still get a **residence permit** easily, but must present evidence of financial solvency, health insurance and contribution to a state pension scheme.

Undocumented **non-EU nationals** who wish to work in Greece do so surreptitiously, with the ever-present risk of denunciation to the police and instant deportation. Having been forced to accept large numbers of EU citizens looking for jobs in a climate of rising unemployment, Greek immigration authorities are cracking down hard on any suitable targets, be they Albanian, African, Swiss or North American. That old foreigners' standby, teaching English, is now available only to TEFL certificate-holders – preferably Greeks, non-EU nationals of Greek descent, and EU nationals in that order. If you are a non-EU foreign national of Greek descent, you are termed *omoyenís* (returned Greek diaspora member) and in fact have tremendous employment, taxation and residence rights and privileges – you can, for example, open your very own *frondistírio* without any qualifications (something starkly evident in the often abysmal quality of language instruction – and disseminated printed material – in Greece).

Crime and personal safety

As in the past, Greece remains one of Europe's safest countries, with a low crime rate and a deserved reputation for honesty. If you leave a bag or wallet at a café, you'll most likely find it scrupulously looked after, pending your return. Similarly, Greeks are relatively relaxed about leaving possessions unattended on the beach, in rooms or on campsites. The biggest **hazards on beaches**, oddly, are free-ranging goats – who will eat just about anything left accessible – and the wake of passing cruise ships or ferries, which can wash all your possessions out to sea with little or no warning.

Recent years, however, have seen a large increase in **theft** and **crimes against persons** (blamed largely on Albanian and Romanian refugees) at archeological sites, in towns, remote villages and resorts, so it's wise to treat Greece like any other European destination. In particular, there has been a huge rise in pickpocketing on the old section of the **Athens metro** (not the new extension, which is heavily policed).

There are other ways to lose your money – most notably getting stuck with **counterfeit euro notes** (at the moment €100 and €200 ones abound). The currency changeover has proven to be a bonanza for forgers – which has led to the introduction of (useless) electronic bill scanners in many shops. The best tests are done by the naked eye: genuine notes all have a hologram strip or (if over €50) patch at one end, there's a watermark at the other, and a security thread embedded in the middle. If you end up being given a duff note, you'll have to lump it – if you unwittingly try to pass it on, or report it in good faith to the police, you'll still be assumed party to the scam, and face a session of interrogation at the very least.

See p.81 for **emergency phone numbers**.

Police and specific offences

There is a single, nationwide **police force**, the *Elliniki Astynomia*, rather than the division into urban corps and rural gendarmerie normal in most of Europe. Greek cops are gruff at the best of times, frequently unpleasant otherwise, and many have little regard for foreigners. Police practice often falls short of northern European norms, and fit-ups or beatings in custody are not unknown.

You are required to **carry suitable ID** on you at all times (except when in bathing costume) – either a passport or a driving licence.

Otherwise, the most common causes of a brush with authority are nude bathing or sunbathing, public inebriation or lewd behaviour, camping outside an authorized site and taking photographs in forbidden areas.

Nude bathing is tolerated on only a very few beaches (most notably on Rhodes, Sámos, Foúrni, Kós and Lésvos), and is deeply offensive to the more traditional Greeks – exercise considerable sensitivity to local feeling and the kind of place you're in. It is, for example, very bad etiquette to swim or sunbathe nude within sight of a church, of which there are many along the Greek coast. Generally, if a beach has become fairly well established as naturist, or is well secluded, it's highly unlikely that the police are going to come charging in. Where they do get bothered is if they feel nudity is getting too overt on mainstream tourist stretches. Most of the time, the only action will be a warning, but you can theoretically be arrested straight off – facing up to three days in jail and a stiff fine.

Topless (sun)bathing for women is technically legal nationwide, but specific locales often opt out of the "liberation" by posting signs, which should be heeded.

Very similar guidelines apply to **camping rough**, which has been theoretically illegal nationwide since 1977 (see p.70). Even for this you're still unlikely to incur anything more than a warning to move on. The only real risk of arrest is if you are told to clear off and fail to do so. In either of the above cases, even if the police do take any action against you, it's more likely to be a brief spell in their cells than any official prosecution.

The **hours between 3 and 5pm**, the midday *mikró ípno* (siesta), are sacrosanct – one does not make phone calls to strangers or any sort of noise (especially with motorcycles) at this time. **Quiet** is also mandated by law **between midnight and 8am** in residential areas; construction crews are obliged to observe this, and they do so punctiliously, commencing hammering next door to your lodgings at 8.01am (or even 7.59am). There is nothing you can do about this, as they are within their rights.

The well-publicized experience of twelve British plane-spotters who processed slowly through Greek jails and courts in 2001–02 should serve as ample incentive to **take no pictures at all in and around airports or military installations**. The latter are usually well festooned with signs of a bellows camera with a red X through it. "No pictures at all" includes farewell snaps of your loved ones on the runway; most island airports double as air-force bases, and you don't know what the authorities will claim was in your viewfinder.

Any sort of **disrespect** towards the Greek state or Orthodox Church in general, or Greek civil servants in particular, may be construed as offences in the most literal sense, so it's best to keep your comments on how things are working (or not) to yourself. Every year a few foreign louts on Rhodes and Kós find themselves in deep trouble over a drunken indiscretion. This is a society where verbal injuries count, with an appreciable backlog of court cases dealing with the alleged public utterance of *malákas* (wanker).

In the non-verbal field, ripped or soiled clothes and untucked-in shirts are considered nearly as insulting. Don't expect a uniformly civil reception if dressed in **grunge attire**, since Greeks will interpret this in one of two possible ways, neither reflecting well on you. Poverty is an uncomfortably close memory for many, and they may consider that you're making light of hard times. More to the point, the cult of fashion-victim-hood is developed to near-Italian levels in Greece; if you clearly have so little self-respect as to appear slovenly and dishevelled in public, why should any Greek respect you?

Public drunkenness of the sort which fuelled the much-publicized incidents at Faliráki in 2003 (see p.135) has always been held in contempt in Greece, where the inability to hold one's liquor is considered unmanly. Inebriation will be considered an aggravating factor if you're arrested for something else, not an excuse.

Drug offences are treated as major crimes, particularly since there's a substantial local use and addiction problem. The maximum penalty for "causing the use of drugs by someone under 18", for example, is life imprisonment and an astronomical fine. Theory is by no means practice, but foreigners caught in possession of even small amounts of grass do get long jail sentences if there's evidence that they've been supplying the drug to others. Moreover, you could be inside for well over a year awaiting a trial date, with little or no chance of bail being granted.

If you get arrested for any offence, you have a right to contact your **consulate**, who will arrange a lawyer for your defence. Beyond this, there is little they can, or in most cases will, do. There is an honorary British consulate on Rhodes; otherwise the closest diplomatic representation is in Athens.

Directory

ADDRESSES In Greece streets are cited in the genitive case, usually with no tag like "Street" or "Avenue"; the number always follows. Thus something described as 36 Venizelos Avenue in Roman-alphabet letterhead comes out as Venizélou 36, and it's this convention which we've adopted throughout the book. The practice is different with *platía* (square, plaza), which always appears before the name. Postcodes are five-digit, nationwide, and precede the municipality concerned, eg 81100 Mytilíni, on Lésvos.

BARGAINING This isn't a regular feature of touristic life, though you'll find it possible with private rooms and certain hotels out of season. Similarly, you should be able to negotiate discounted rates for vehicle rental, especially for longer periods. Services such as shoe, watch and camera repair don't have iron-clad rates, so use common sense when assessing charges (advance written estimates are not a routine practice).

CHILDREN Children are worshipped and indulged in Greece, sometimes to excess, and present few problems when travelling. As elsewhere in the Mediterranean, they are not segregated from adults at mealtimes, and early on in life are inducted into the typical late-night routine. So you'll see plenty of kids at tavernas, expected to eat (and, up to their capabilities, talk) like adults. Outside of certain all-inclusive resorts, however (see p.33) there are very few amusements specifically for kids.

Most ferry lines and airlines in Greece offer some sort of discount for children, ranging from fifty to a hundred percent depending on their age; hotels and rooms won't charge extra for infants, and levy a modest surcharge for "third" beds, which the child occupies by him/herself. Baby foods and nappies/diapers are ubiquitous and reasonably priced; luxury hotels are more likely to offer some kind of babysitting service than the mid-range, C-class hotels.

DEPARTURE TAX None that isn't included in the ticket price at time of purchase, so you can happily spend your last euro.

DISABLED TRAVELLERS The Greek islands generally are not in the forefront of providing disabled-friendly facilities; wheelchair ramps at pedestrian crossings are rare, pips for the unsighted at same almost nonexistent, and lifts present only in hotels of more than three storeys (but no guarantee of wheelchair-compatible rooms). The outstanding exception is flattish Kós, which, partly because of the Hippocratic medical connection, makes some effort to court disabled travellers; the largest resort hotels on Rhodes will also offer disabled facilities. Elsewhere, we've noted accommodation with these where known.

ELECTRICITY Voltage is 220 volt AC throughout the country. Wall outlets – seldom abundant enough – take double round-pin plugs as in the rest of continental Europe. Three- to two-pin adapters should be purchased beforehand in the UK, as they can be difficult to find in Greece; standard 5-, 6- or 7.5-amp models permit operation of a hairdryer or travel iron. If necessary, you can change the fuse to a higher rating back in the UK; beware, as they're physically smaller than the 13-amp ones popped into all three-prong plugs, and you may have to go to a specialist electrical dealer for them. Unless they're dual voltage, North American appliances will require both a step-down transformer and a plug adapter (the latter easy to find in Greece).

FILM Fuji and Kodak print films are reasonably priced and easy to have processed – you practically trip over "One Hour Foto" shops in some resorts. APS film is also widely sold and processed. Fuji and Ektachrome slide film can be purchased, at more or less UK prices, on the largest islands, but cannot be processed there – exposed rolls will be sent to Athens for handling, so best wait until you return home.

FOOTBALL (Soccer) This is far and away the most popular sport in Greece – both in terms of participating and watching, all the more so since Greece's miraculous victory in the Euro 2004 finals in Portugal over the home side. The most important (and most heavily sponsored) teams are Panathanaïkós and AEK of Athens, Olympiakós of Pireás and PAOK of Thessaloníki; the islands covered in this book have no teams of major standing. If you're interested, matches (usually played on Wednesday nights and Sunday afternoons) are easy enough to catch from September to May.

GAYS Overtly gay behaviour in public remains taboo for men in rural areas, though (if they "behave") foreign same-sex couples will be accorded the standard courtesy as foreigners. There is, however, a sizeable gay contingent in Athens, Thessaloníki and Pátra, plus an appreciable scene on Rhodes (and to a lesser extent on Sámos); we've noted popular cruising beaches and gay-friendly bars where known. Skála Eressoü on Lésvos, the birthplace of Sappho, is (appropriately) an international mecca for lesbians. Homosexuality is legal over the age of 17, and (male) bisexual behaviour common but rarely admitted. Greek men are terrible flirts, but cruising them is a semiotic minefield and definitely at your own risk; "out" gay Greeks are rare, and "out" local lesbians rarer still.

HIKING Greeks are just becoming used to the notion that anyone should want to walk for pleasure, yet if you have the time and stamina it is probably the best way to see many of the Dodecanese and east Aegean islands. This guide includes descriptions of a number of hikes (see p.525 for specialist hiking guides). For essential advice on maps, see p.50.

LAUNDRIES *Plindíria*, as they're known in Greek, are prominent in the main resort towns; sometimes an attended service wash is available for little or no extra charge over the basic cost of €6–7 per wash and dry. Self-catering villas or *dhomátia* will usually be furnished with a drying line and a selection of plastic wash-tubs (*skáfes*) or a bucket (*kouvás*). In hotels, laundering should be done in a more circumspect manner; management can object if you use bathroom washbasins,

or do more than a few socks and undies. It's best to use the flat pans of showers for both washing and hanging to dry.

PERÍPTERA These are street-corner kiosks, or sometimes a hole-in-the-wall shopfront. They sell everything from pens to disposable razors, stationery to soap, sweets to condoms, cigarettes to plastic crucifixes, yogurts to milk-in-cartons – and are often open when nothing else is.

TIME As throughout the EU, Greek summertime begins at 2am on the last Sunday in March, when the clocks go forward one hour, and ends at 2am the last Sunday in October, when they go back. The change is not well publicized, leading scores of visitors to miss planes and ferries every year. Greek time is thus always two hours ahead of Britain. For North America, the difference is seven hours for Eastern Standard Time, ten hours for Pacific Standard Time, with again an extra hour plus or minus for those weeks in April October when one place is on daylight saving and the other isn't. A recorded time message (in distinctly slow Greek, 24hr convention) is available by dialling ☎141.

TOILETS Public ones in towns are usually in parks or squares, often subterranean. Except in areas frequented by tourists (such as Ródhos Town), public toilets tend to be pretty filthy – it's best to use those in restaurants and bars. Remember that throughout Greece you drop toilet paper in the adjacent wastebins, *not* in the bowl.

USEFUL THINGS TO BRING/BUY A high-quality, porcelain-lined canteen or drinking-water bottle; a small alarm clock for early buses and ferries (can be bought locally); a flashlight/torch (power outages on the way back from island tavernas are common); sunscreen of high SPF (25 or above, in better Greek pharmacies); universal flat drain plug (often missing from tubs/sinks); pocket knife (Swiss Army type or similar), with tweezers, mini-screwdriver and other similar accessories (widely sold in Greece at hunting/fishing shops); earplugs for noisy ferries or hotels; and good-quality tea bags if you must have a cuppa.

Guide

Guide

Rhodes

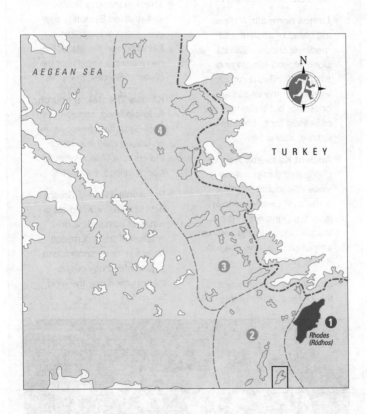

CHAPTER 1 # Highlights

* **Ródhos Old Town** Superbly preserved pebble-mosaic streets and sandstone buildings are inextricably linked with the Knights of St John, who ruled here for over two hundred years. See p.111

* **Lindos acropolis** A pleasing blend of ancient and medieval culture, with its Doric Athena temple and Knights' fortifications; great views over the village and coastline, but try to visit out of season for better atmosphere. See p.140

* **Ancient Kameiros** Having slumbered undiscovered since abandonment, this is the best-preserved town from the Doric era in the islands, with a lovely setting amidst pines above the sea. See p.145

* **Monólithos** The remotest of the Knights' many castles on Rhodes presides over the spectacular forested scenery of Mt Akramýtis, Rhodes' wildest mountain, and the secluded beaches of Foúrni far below. See p.147

* **Thárri monastery** Subtle, well-restored Byzantine frescoes in the oldest religious foundation on the island, hidden away in a forest near the centre of Rhodes. See p.151

* **Kímisis Theotókou church, Asklipió** Vivid, cartoon-like post-Byzantine frescoes are an unexpected surprise in the country church of this sleepy village. See p.152

* **Prassoníssi** One of Greece's best venues for world-class windsurf training; the orientation of the spit means provision for beginners, and a guaranteed day out no matter which way the wind. See p.155

△ Monólithos castle, western Rhodes

Rhodes

t's no accident that **Rhodes** (Ródhos) is, after Crete, the most visited of the Greek islands. Not only is its east coast lined with numerous sandy beaches, but the capital's kernel is a beautiful and remarkably preserved medieval city, a legacy of the crusading Knights of St John who used the island as their main base from 1309 until 1522. Add to this charter-flight arrivals over an eight-month season with three hundred sunny days annually, and you have all the ingredients for touristic success. The only quibble might concern its precise nature: dozens of battery-farm hotels lining the road between the airport and main town hardly bode well for any degree of good taste, nor does the fact that certain guests wear T-shirts inscribed "Sex 90%, Love 1%, Relax 9%, This is Rhodes 100%" or "Ten reasons why a beer is better than a woman/man" without apparent embarrassment. If you're so inclined, you can find this commercialized Rhodes without a guidebook, but those of a more enquiring nature will discover a hilly, intermittently forested interior big enough to get lost in, remote castles and Byzantine churches, pleasant ridges and stream canyons, as well as peaceful villages still living at least partly from agriculture.

Rhodes has an official population of about 110,000, well over half the inhabitants of the entire Dodecanese. As for the transient and foreign population, nearly six thousand permanent expats are joined in a good year by over one million tourists. Of the foreigners, Germans, Brits, Swedes, Italians (especially in August), Finns and Danes predominate, usually in that order; accordingly, smorgasbord, fish fingers and linguini jostle alongside *moussakás* on tourist-taverna menus. Numerous Greeks also frequent the better hotels, as Rhodes is heavily promoted domestically as a chic weekend destination, even in winter; short-break Israelis, too, have appeared of late, drawn by the irresistible lure of a casino and shopping opportunities. All the proceeds of tourism sloshing about have engendered a decadent, mock-Athenian lifestyle, reflected in expensive clothing shops featuring the latest designer glad rags. By way of balance there is also, especially during the cooler months, a lively programme of cinema, Greek-language theatre and other events, courtesy of the local student contingent.

Some mythology and etymology

According to legend, the sun god Helios (then personified separately from Apollo) was away on his daily rounds when Zeus apportioned the world among his fellow Olympian deities. To make amends, he promised Helios any part of the earth that had not yet emerged from the sea. As it happened, Helios had spied the nymph Rodon, daughter of Poseidon and Amphitrite, under the water off Asia Minor; concentrating his rays, he induced her to rise to the surface,

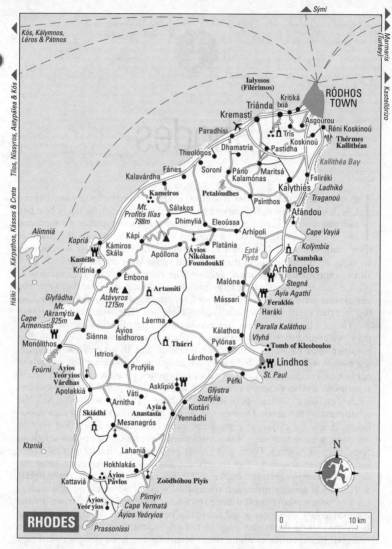

whereupon he married her. In its essentials, this pretty myth deviates little from the Father Sky/Mother Earth prototypes common to many early cultures, though in the case of Rhodes it seems the tale evolved to explain the presence of fossilized seashells up in the Rhodian hills, for indeed the island was thrust up from the sea floor aeons ago by earthquakes and plate tectonics.

The real derivation of the **name** "Rhodes" remains controversial: the tourist board claims that it stems from the ancient Greek word for "rose", though neither the domesticated nor the wild *Cistus* rock species, however abundant now, are native to the island. It is more likely a corruption of *ro(ï)di* or "pomegranate", and ancient coins with a pomegranate on one side and the sun god's head on the other are well documented. A recent, ingenious theory has it that the "rose" is really the hibiscus, which also grows here in profusion, but again is not native.

A brief history

Blessed with an equable climate and strategic position, the island of Rhodes was important from earliest times, despite a paucity of good harbours. The best natural port spawned the ancient town of Lindos, which, together with the other city-states Kameiros and Ialyssos, united in 408 BC to found the new capital of Rhodes at the northern tip of the island. At various moments the cities allied themselves with Alexander, Persians, Athenians or Spartans as prevailing conditions suited, generally escaping retribution for backing the wrong side by a combination of seafaring audacity, sycophancy and burgeoning wealth as a trade centre. Following the **failed siege** of Demetrios Polyorketes in 305 BC (see box on p.106), Rhodes prospered even more, displacing Athens as the major venue for rhetoric and the arts in the east Mediterranean. The ancient town, which lies beneath almost all of the modern town, was initially laid out around 400 BC by early urban planner Hippodamus of Miletus according to a grid layout much in vogue at the time, with planned residential and commercial quarters. Its perimeter walls totalled nearly 15km, enclosing roughly double the area of today's city, and the Hellenistic population exceeded 100,000, a staggering figure for the ancient world.

Decline set in when Rhodes became involved in the **Roman civil wars** late in the first century BC, on the side of Julius Caesar, and Cassius sacked the town. Although Emperor Diocletian (284–305) made it a provincial capital, by late imperial times Rhodes had become a backwater, a status confirmed by numerous barbarian raids during the Byzantine period. The **Byzantines** were compelled to cede the island to the **Genoese**, who in turn (after a three-year resistance) surrendered it in 1309 to the Knights of St John (see box on p.116). The second great siege of Rhodes, during 1522, saw Ottoman **Sultan Süleyman the Magnificent** oust the stubborn Knights, who retreated to Malta; town and island once again lapsed into relative obscurity, though they were heavily colonized and garrisoned until the **Italian seizure** of 1912.

After 1923 and the Treaty of Lausanne, Fascist-ruled Italy selected Rhodes to be the crown jewel of its "Aegean Empire", and lavished great sums on road-building, waterworks, reforestation and the first inklings of a mass tourism industry. More controversially, the Italians engaged in excavation and restoration of archeological sites, as well as indulging their tastes in new civic structures and restoration of medieval monuments. The Greek Orthodox population benefited little from this, on the contrary enduring sustained cultural persecution after 1928 (see "History" in Contexts). In autumn 1943 the Italians capitulated, and certainly the Jews of the Dodecanese must have preferred the relative leniency of their rule to that of the Germans, under whom they suffered almost total annihilation. The British administered the island from mid-1945 until the institution of Greek military rule in April 1947 (prior to the official March 1948 unification with Greece), thus beginning a long-standing love affair between the UK and Rhodes. Only since the early 1990s have the worst memories of Fascist rule begun to fade, as those who directly experienced it pass away, and grudging acknowledgement is finally made of the comprehensive and partly still-usable infrastructure inherited from the Italians.

The first siege of Rhodes

The first great siege of Rhodes in 305 BC, considered the most noteworthy military campaign of ancient times, resulted from power struggles between the generals and deputies of Alexander the Great following his death. Because of their close trade links, Rhodes sided with Egypt, then ruled by Ptolemy. Rival Macedonian general Antigonus ordered Rhodes to attack its ally on his behalf; when the islanders refused, Antigonus, furious at this rebuff, sent his son Demetrios to discipline the defiant Rhodians. Nicknamed "Polyorketes" ("Besieger of Many Cities") and fresh from the capture of Salamis on Cyprus, Demetrios was one of the military geniuses of his day, with intimidating resources to draw upon: 200 warships, nearly as many supporting craft, and 40,000 seasoned infantrymen. Against these forces the Rhodians could muster just 8000 citizen-soldiers, perhaps 2000 Cretan volunteers and Egyptian mercenaries, and 15,000 slaves who were bought up by the municipality and promised their freedom in the event of successful resistance. Additionally, the government guaranteed funerals with full honours for the fallen, plus perpetual subsidy to their surviving relatives. These wise strategies boosted morale, strengthened social cohesion and probably influenced the battle's outcome, as no significant instance of treason was recorded throughout the long siege.

Having blockaded the city with his fleet, Demetrios initially targeted the apparently vulnerable harbour walls, launching projectiles from a pair of ingenious "tortoises": armoured carapaces slung between two ships and protected by booms to repel ramming attacks by the Rhodians. In a daring sortie, these floating weapons were sunk by the Rhodians, whose cause was further helped by the destruction in a storm of a new, land-based siege tower, and the arrival of fresh reinforcements from Ptolemy.

In the light of these reverses, Demetrios changed tactics, devoting his attentions to the landward walls and ordering the construction of the so-called Helepolis or "Overthrower of Cities", the largest siege tower the world had seen. Sheathed in metal and animal hides, it measured 27m on each side at the base, tapering slightly over a nine-storey height, with windows for launching missiles and drawbridges for depositing commandos on top of the walls; over three thousand men were required to arm and move this wheeled, 125-tonne behemoth. In response, the tenacious Rhodians doubled their walls and mounted successful forays to break the Macedonian blockade, while Demetrios' numerous enemies surreptitiously arranged to replenish the city's food supplies. The Helepolis repeatedly damaged the city's fortifications, but the Macedonians failed to gain entry; in one nocturnal raid, the Rhodians almost succeeded in setting the tower alight. Following stalled peace negotiations sponsored by other Hellenic cities, Demetrios opted for a decisive charge on the weakest spot, in conjunction with a general attack along the entire length of the perimeter walls. Some 1500 of his men managed briefly to establish a foothold inside the city, near the theatre, but were surrounded by the Rhodians and cut down almost to a man.

By now the siege had been going on for almost a year, with both sides nearly exhausted; Demetrios' father, Antigonus, and Ptolemy began urging their respective protégés to come to honourable terms, as nobody would gain if the wealthiest city in the Aegean were reduced to rubble. This final truce was in fact prompted by an ingenious act of sabotage: a Rhodian engineer directed a team of sappers to tunnel past the walls and undermine the usual path of the Helepolis, causing it to founder and collapse. Demetrios, finally convinced of the islanders' resolve, confirmed Rhodes as an independent city-state, requiring it only to contribute ships towards Macedonian military expeditions as long as hostilities were not directed against Ptolemy, and to provide one hundred noble hostages as security against any breach of the agreement. He also left all his war machinery with the Rhodians, to play a crucial role in the saga of the Colossus (see box p.124).

Ródhos Town

RÓDHOS TOWN, built around the second-best natural harbour on the island (after Líndhos), is very much the main event on Rhodes, and deservedly so for its exquisite medieval city. Air arrivals miss out on the majestic approach by ferry, usually in the morning light, which shows to advantage a fair amount of the old town's five-kilometre ramparts, their contours softened by gardens and accented by turrets. Once the apotheosis of military architecture, today they are merely a decorative backdrop, dividing the town into two unequal parts: the relatively compact walled quarter, and the sprawling modern neighbourhoods surrounding it on three sides.

The separation of new town from old dates from the Ottoman occupation; the Greeks, forbidden to reside in the walled city built by the Knights of St John, founded several suburb villages or **marásia** in the environs. The churches of Áyios Ioánnis, Áyii Anáryiri, Ayía Anastasía, Mitrópolis and Áyios Yeóryios were initially established due south of the Turkish cemeteries which grew up outside the walls, while Neohóri (alias "Niohóri") – synonymous with the sharp promontory to the northwest – was settled last. Since the Italian era they have all merged into one cement-laced conurbation, but the above-named churches still exist, as do the narrow lanes and older houses immediately around them. Even with this filling-in of previously empty spaces, modern Ródhos Town is still far smaller in both dimensions and population than its Hellenistic precursor.

Tourism is predominant in much of the old town and throughout the Neohóri district west of Mandhráki yacht harbour, where the few buildings that aren't hotels serve as souvenir shops, bars and car rental or travel agencies – easily sixty to seventy in each category. Locals mostly live south and southwest of the walled city, in the older parishes, with students from one of the main campuses of the University of the Aegean supplementing the permanent population of about 50,000.

Arrival, information and transport

The **airport**, expanded for the second time in 2004, but still barely coping with high-season traffic, lies 14km southwest of town, at the north outskirts of Paradhísi village. Any public **city bus** coming from Paradhísi, Theológos, Kalavárdha or Sálakos will stop up on the road opposite the northerly car park entrance (look for the wood-and-perspex shelter and signposting, hidden under vegetation opposite the little chapel), and onward services to the New Market in Ródhos Town run fairly frequently from 6am to almost midnight (see "Travel Details" on p.158 for outbound services). The bus fare to town is currently €1.50, versus €13–14 for **taxis**, the latter figure (including bag and airport supplements) increasing to well over €20 between midnight and 5am; standard fares to the most popular resort destinations are displayed on a placard outside the terminal. Those flying in at an unsociable hour might consider arranging **car rental** in advance of their trip, though at slow times you may be able to get something affordable on arrival from the chains (Alamo/National, Avis, Budget, Drive, Europcar, Hertz, Holiday and Sixt), which have booths at the airport.

All international and inter-island **ferries** drop anchor on the east quay of the middle one of Rhodes' three ports, the so-called commercial harbour, more properly known as **Kolóna**; the *Dodekanisos Express* **catamaran** uses the west quay of the same bay. Local boats to Sými, plus east-coast excursion boats, currently use the south quay of Mandhráki yacht harbour, while **hydrofoils** and the *Sea Star* catamaran dock at the west quay.

Information and maps

Between the east-coast bus stop and the Mandhráki taxi rank there's a fairly useless **municipal tourist office** (theoretically June–Sept Mon–Sat 8am–9.30pm, Sun 9am–3pm; ☎22410 35945), while 200m up Papágou, on the corner of Makaríou, is the more helpful and reliably open **EOT office** (Mon–Fri 8.30am–3pm; ☎22410 44335, ⓦwww.ando.gr/eot), with full information on bus and ferry timetables, archeological sites and the like. Situated behind the EOT, the multilingual **tourist police** (24hr; ☎22410 27423) deal with serious service-related complaints; officers wear a badge or flag indicating languages spoken.

The free island **maps** supplied by tourist offices or car rental firms are as good as any you can buy, with the exception of the excellent 1:100,000 one produced by Road Editions (about €5), which use topographic maps as sources; all others are based on the work of the same Athenian cartographer, Tsopelas. Maps of Ródhos Town, however, are another matter; accept no substitute for the A-to-Z-type mini-atlas "Map of Rhodes Town", which includes an overview poster-map, or "Rhodes, Map of the Old Town", another art-format map of the medieval city that's nonetheless the most accurate available. Both were prepared in 1994 by longtime resident Mario Camerini, and updated again in 1998, though copies are becoming difficult to find (try Triton Holidays; see p.132).

Local buses

KTEL **buses** for all points along the east coast (except for Koskinoú and Kallithéa) leave from, and arrive at, a terminal on Papágou, just above Platía Rimínis, aka "Sound and Light Square"; they're typically ochre and cream (as opposed to the usual Greek green and cream), though a number of sleek, turquoise-and-blue, air-conditioned vehicles have begun appearing. Identically coloured coaches run by RODA depart for the west coast (plus Koskinoú and Kallithéa) from a stop just around the corner on Avérof, under the pavement arcades of the so-called New Market. RODA also runs relatively infrequent city routes from the same terminal, with both services severely reduced on Saturday and Sunday. Tickets for the long-distance RODA buses are sold on board, and those for the numbered city routes (€0.90) both on board or from special kiosks, in either case subsequently cancelled in the bus.

Taxis and parking

Taxi ranks are numerous and shown on the town maps with a circled "T"; the cars themselves are either slate-coloured or midnight blue with white tops, rather than the typical Hellenic grey. Even by the standards of Greek tourist resorts, Rhodian **taxi drivers** can be a source of grief for the inexperienced. Resist their initial gambits to deposit you at inconveniently remote beach-strip hotels, which pay kickbacks to the drivers, and also treat with scepticism any reports that particular hotels or pensions in the old town are "full", "dirty", "closed", "burnt down", etc. If you are luggage-laden, drivers are supposedly obliged by law to take you to the door of your chosen accommodation, even if it is in the old town, which is otherwise off limits to non-residents' vehicles. Most, however, refuse to do so, especially between Easter and October, and only extra tipping will secure an attitude adjustment – otherwise resign yourself to being left outside one of the medieval gates. Once installed at your lodgings, always use the services of "tame" taxi drivers arranged for you by your proprietor. **Problems** with Rhodian taxis are so rife that the EOT office has seen fit to print and distribute a sheet with legal fares on one side and on the other a minuscule incident complaint form to send to the Division of Transport and Communications. You may get more satisfaction if you go to the in-town tourist police (address opposite), who are supposed to investigate such incidents.

As noted above, all vehicular **traffic** is banned within the medieval walls, except for residents' cars and scooters; this law is strictly enforced most of the year by either a warden, or a swivel-bar or chain, or both, at each gate. **Parking** within any reasonable distance of the old town is a challenge, and the closest you're likely to get is along Filellínon, between the Ayíou Athanasíou and Koskinoú gates. At night, there may also be space along the walls facing Kolóna harbour, or just inside on Platía Sýmis. Neohóri, the northern extension of the new town, is a nightmare, though surprisingly you can sometimes find an unmetered parking spot along Aktí Miaoúli (the western esplanade of Neohóri), near the Casino and Villa Cleobolus, or around Ekató Hour-madhiés/"100 Palms" (officially Platía Gavriél Harítou). Elsewhere, most spots are subject during business hours (Mon–Sat 9am–2.30pm & 5–9pm) to pay-and-display schemes – either short-term tickets (€0.60 for 30min) or, more commonly, long-term spaces (*makrís dhiarhías* in Greek) with reload-able cards. If you don't see a ticket machine for hourly windscreen chits and blue kerbside markings, or a "P Free/*Eléfthero*" notice (and white stripes), don't park there – the traffic police are very industrious, and fines cost in the region of €65.

Accommodation

Inexpensive pensions abound in the **old town** and are found almost entirely in the area defined by Omírou on the south, Sokrátous on the north, Perik-léous on the east and Ippodhámou on the west. If you're arriving without a reservation in peak season or late at night, you might consider accepting the offers of proprietors meeting the ferries and change base next day if neces-sary – and it usually is, as many of the unlicensed "rooms" touted turn out to have facilities (and hygiene standards) little changed since the age of the Knights. Establishments recommended overleaf are those most likely to have firm beds, consistent hot water, relatively restrained decor, nocturnal calm and no cockroaches.

The **new town** offers modern, purpose-built hotels, with just a few of the better ones open in winter, as well as a limited number of pensions installed in former Italian villas or traditional vernacular houses. Hotels omitted here tend to be block-booked by package operators, and many are plagued by after-hours noise from the dozens of bars lining nearby streets.

The old town

Andreas Omírou 28d ☎ 22410 34156, ⓦ www
.hotelandreas.com. Perennially popular (reservations
needed) and under the dynamic management of
Belgian-American Constance Rivemal, this is one of
the more imaginative old-house restoration
pensions, thoroughly refurbished in 2003 with
Constance's decades as a fashion designer much
in evidence. En-suite rooms in a variety of formats,
including triples/quads, and a spectacular penthouse
(❻). Terrace-bar with sweeping views, for excellent
breakfasts and evening drinks; two-night minimum
stay, credit cards accepted, indeed vital for advance
booking. Open late March to end Oct. ❹–❺
Apollo Tourist House Omírou 28c ☎ 22410
32003, ⓦ www.apollo-touristhouse.com. Just five
wood-floor-and-ceiling, centrally heated, en-suite
rooms thoroughly overhauled in 2004 by Spanish-
Dutch-Chilean owner Humberto; the self-catering
kitchen makes it good for longer stays. Open most
of the year. ❸
Isole Evdhóxou 75 ☎ 22410 20682, ⓦ www
.hotelisole.com. Simple but salubrious rooms with
Hellenic-blue decor in a converted Ottoman house,
run by a welcoming, multilingual Italian couple.
Pleasant breakfast area at reception (breakfast
included in price), superb roof terrace. Normally
open March to mid-Nov, winter by appointment. ❸
standard rooms, ❹ tower suite.
La Luna Menándhrou 21 ☎ & ⓕ 22410 25856.
Clean, wood-trimmed if plain (no en suites)
pension in another converted old Turkish house,
complete with still-functioning *hamam* (Turkish
bath) on the top floor. Garden bar for breakfast, by
the citrus and banana trees. Open year-round. ❸
Marco Polo Mansion Ayíou Fanouríou 42 ☎ &
ⓕ 22410 25562, ⓦ www.marcopolomansion.web
.com. Superb conversion of an old Turkish mansion,
again with *hamam* on site, but here all rooms are
en suite, unique and exquisitely furnished with
antiques from the nearby eponymous gallery, plus
cotton pillows and handmade mattresses. Large
buffet breakfasts included and provided by Spyros
and Efi in the garden snack-bar. Five-day minimum
stay, reservations and credit card deposit

mandatory; March–Nov, but some rooms open in
winter by arrangement. ❻–❼
Niki's Sofokléous 39 ☎ 22410 25115, ⓦ www
.nikishotel.gr. Some of these plain, tile-floored
rooms can be on the small side, but all are en
suite, most have air con, and upper-storey ones
have fine views (including three with balconies).
There's a washing machine, two communal
terraces (one on the roof) and friendly, very helpful
management to round things off. Someone will wait
up for late-night arrivals; credit cards accepted. ❸
S. Nikolis Ippodhámou 61 ☎ 22410 34561,
ⓦ www.s-nikolis.gr. A variety of restoration
premises in the west of the old town. Hotel/honey-
moon-suite rates (❼) include rooftop-served breakfast, TV and air con; Sotiris and Marianne's self-
catering apartments (❺–❻) are among the finest
restoration results in the old town, and interconnect
to accommodate groups/families. Booking essential,
and accepted only with credit card number or pre-
posted travellers' cheques. Open April–Nov; closed
otherwise, except by special arrangement.
Spot Perikléous 21 ☎ & ⓕ 22410 34737,
ⓔ spothot@otenet.gr Another old town hotel under a
new generation of management, this modern building has cheerfully painted en-suite rooms of varying
formats, with textiles on the walls, fridges and air
con, representing superb value (and including unlimited buffet breakfast). Also Internet facilities, rear
patio, free luggage storage. Open March–Nov. ❹
Via-Via Lysipoú 2, alley off Pythagóra ☎ &
ⓕ 22410 77027, wwww.hotel-via-via.com. Efficiently and congenially run boutique hotel; most
one- to four-person rooms are en suite but two
share a bath; about half have air con. All are simply
but tastefully furnished, with ongoing improvements. Self-catering kitchen, roof terrace for breakfast with an eyeful of the Ibrahim Pasha Mosque
opposite. Three grades of breakfast offered, from
continental to full brunch. Open all year. ❹–❺
Youth hostel Eryíou 12 ☎ 22410 30491. Non-
YHA-affiliated hostel offering three- to five-bunk
dorms (€9) and doubles (❶) in a courtyarded
house with kitchen facilities.

The new town

Anastasia 28-Oktovríou 46, Neohóri ☎ 22410
28007, ⓦ www.anastasia-hotel.com. A pension
with high-ceilinged en-suite rooms housed in an
interwar building; garden bar. ❸
Casa Antica Amarándou 8 ☎ 22410 26206.
Double and quad studios in a made-over

150-year-old house with clean, white-tile decor,
courtyard, roof terrace. Close to some of the better
Neohóri tavernas. ❹
Esperia Yeoryíou Gríva 7, Neohóri ☎ 22410
23941, ⓦ www.esperia-hotels.gr. Well-priced,
well-run B-class hotel with pool, in a quiet location

overlooking a little tree-studded plaza. Small- to medium-sized salubrious and tasteful rooms with showers. Open all year. ❹

Ibiscus/Iviskos Nissýrou 17 ☎ 22410 44213, ⓦ www.helios.gr/hotels/ibiscus. Can't quite match the facilities or cachet of its neighbour, the *Mediterranean* (see below), but also beachfront and well managed, and it's easier to secure a vacancy here. Marble-floored, leather-upholstered common areas, updated rooms. April–Oct. ❻ standard, ❼ suites

Mediterranean Kó 35 ☎ 22410 24661, ⓦ www .mediterranean.gr. Beachfront hotel (own loungers on the sand) in a superb location; nominally A-class, but less expensive than you'd think, especially if booked through Triton Holidays (see p.132). The street-level snack-bar/café is very popular around the clock with non-residents as well. ❻ standard, ❽ suites

New Village Inn Konstandopédhos 10 ☎ 22410 34937, ⓕ 22410 30733, ⓔ newvillageinn@rho .forthnet.gr. Whitewashed, somewhat grotto-like en-suite rooms arranged around a small courtyard; they're "refreshed" yearly, with air con for some units. Friendly Greek and American management;

singles available at a good rate. Open most of the year. ❹

Plaza Ieroú Lóhou 7, Neohóri ☎ 22410 22501, ⓕ 22410 22544, ⓦ www.rhodes-plaza.com. One of the best A-class hotels within Rhodes' city limits, in the heart of Neohóri. Pool, sauna, Jacuzzi, English buffet breakfast, heating/air con. Open all year, offering sweeping low-season discounts off published rates, particularly between Nov and April. ❻

Rodos Park Riga Fereoú 12 ☎ 22410 24612, ⓦ www.rodos-park.gr. Far and away the top standard within the city limits at this half-room, half-suite hotel aimed at the business traveller with its conference facilities, several restaurants, open-air pool and fully equipped gym and sauna. Suites in particular are palatial, and can be linked to a standard double for families. Open all year. ❼ standard room, ❽ suite.

Spartalis Nikoláou Plastíra 2, Neohóri ☎ 22410 24371, ⓕ 22410 20406. Reliable, 1970s-vintage C-class, with east-side rooms overlooking a play-ground-park that's peaceful after dark, most others glimpsing the sea. Medium-sized en-suite rooms, constantly being upgraded. ❹

The old town

Simply to catalogue the principal monuments and attractions cannot do full justice to the infinitely rewarding **old town**. There's ample gratification to be derived merely from slipping through the eleven surviving gates and strolling the streets, under flying archways built for earthquake resistance, past warm-toned sandstone and limestone walls painted ochre and blue, and over *hokhláki* (pebble) pavements, arranged into coloured mosaics in certain courtyards. Getting lost in the maze of alleys is part of the experience, but if you'd rather not, look out for the accurate map–placards posted at strategic junctions.

As a walled medieval city, Rhodes invites favourable comparison with Jerusalem, Dubrovnik, Carcassonne or Ávila; both the European Heritage Commission and UNESCO agree, having designated it a World Heritage Site. All structural alterations are (in theory) strictly controlled by the archeological service, but this doesn't prevent the old town – really just a very large village – from being vibrant ("noisy" in plain English), dirty and/or bombed out in parts, and from having an emphatically "lived-in" feel away from the tourist zones. In these, the tacky souvenir displays and aggressive touting, especially around the intersection of Ippodhámou and Orféos, can be quite overwhelming; the portrait artists quietly plying their trade under the plane trees along Orféos itself are rather less objectionable.

The town today is effectively a legacy of the Knights of St John, who frequently adhered to Hippodamus' grid-plan: Pythagóra, Omírou, Sokrátous and Ayíou Fanouríou are among the most important streets and follow exactly their ancient predecessors. Sokrátous in particular is now the "Via Turista", whose multiple fur and jewellery stores swarm with tourists, but it's as well to remember that this has been the main commercial street of the city since

RÓDHOS OLD TOWN

RESTAURANTS

L'Auberge Bistrot	14
Fotis Melathron	2
Hatzikelis	7
Kasbah	3
Lagamis	10
Marco Polo Café	6
O Meraklis	4
Mikes	E
Myrovolos	1
Nektar & Ambrosia	9
Sea Star	11

BARS & LIVE MUSIC

Baduz Loutra	8
Kafé Besara	9
Mandala	13
Mango Bar	12
Resalto	5
Iy Rogmi tou Khronou	8

ACCOMMODATION

Andreas	J
Apollo	I
Isole	B
La Luna	A
Marco Polo Mansion	G
Niki's	H
S. Nikolis	F
Spot	C
Via-Via	D

KEY

Moat

Southern limit of Kollákio

Last Minute Ticket Booth

Customs & Passport Control

Port Police

Map labels:

Akándia

Promitheos

Cavo D'oro Hotel

Moat Entry

Akandia Gate

Bastion of Italy (Carreto Bastion)

Hospitaller Hospice

Panayía Tou Bourgou

Old Jewish Quarter

Synagogue

Ayia Ekaterini Gate

Services to Turkey

Mylon (or Jews') Gate

Kolóna (Commercial Harbour)

Dodekanisos Express

fishing boats

Byzantine Museum

Tower of Naillac

Áyios Pávlos Tower

Eleftherias Gate

Arsenal Gate

Inn of Auvergne

Arnaldo Gate

Inn of England

Marine Gate

Kastellania

Ibrahim Pasha Mosque

Rejep Pasha Mosque

Koskinou Gate (Kókkini Pylí)

Folk Dance Theatre

Áyios Fanoúrios

Red Light District

Moat Entry

Ayiou Athanasíou Gate

Hamam

Ottoman Library

Clocktower

Moat Entry

Ayios Andonios Gate

D'Amboise Gate

Palace of the Grand Masters

Sound & Light

Moat Exit

Aphrodite Temple

Museum of Modern Greek Art

Decorative Arts Collection

French Chapel

Inn of Provence

Inn of Spain

Villaragut Mansion

Süleymaniye Mosque

Archeological Museum

Inn of France

Áyios Yeóryios Bastion

Tower of Spain

RIGA FEREOU

ROMANOU MELODHOU

Hellenistic times. Foundations of ancient buildings, often well below the present ground level, are on view everywhere. The Ottomans added little to the urban fabric other than a bare handful of purpose-built mosques, minarets and the graceful clocktower just south of the Palace of the Grand Masters. Though not of intrinsic strategic importance, the old city suffered heavy bomb damage at the hands of the Allies from 1943 to 1945 owing to German military installations in the adjacent commercial harbour, and the easternmost district – the former Jewish quarter – is still pretty dilapidated over six decades later.

The Palace of the Grand Masters

The Byzantines first built the Kollákio (Collachium), or fort-within-a-fort, which lies in the northern sector of the city's originally fourteenth-century ramparts, and is dominated by the **Palace of the Grand Masters** (summer Mon 12.30–8pm, Tues–Sun 8am–8pm; winter Tues–Sun 8.30am–3pm; €6). Almost completely destroyed by a lightning-sparked gunpowder magazine explosion in 1856 (which also levelled much of the town and killed over eight hundred people), it was hastily reconstructed by the Italians between 1937 and 1939 as a summer home for Mussolini and Victor Emmanuel III ("King of Italy and Albania, Emperor of Ethiopia"), neither of whom ever visited Rhodes.

The building's exterior is based largely on medieval engravings and accounts and comes reasonably close to the original. Inside, free rein was given to Fascist delusions of grandeur, with ponderous period furnishings rivalling many a European palace. A monumental marble staircase leads up to rooms paved with

△ Italian-restored turrets, Palace of the Grand Masters, Rhodes Old Town

Hellenistic mosaics from Kós; while one may deplore their plundering, they have certainly fared better here than if they had remained in the open air. The best panels, all on the upper floor, which you tour clockwise, are of a nymph riding a sea monster, and the *Nine Muses of Kos*.

Though much has been made of its vulgarity (for example, in Lawrence Durrell's *Reflections on a Marine Venus*), the palace interior is in fact fairly restrained by the norms of 1930s dictatorships. However, during maintenance work in 1994, evidence of the Italians' cavalier attitude to history and of outright vandalism was uncovered: Hellenistic and Ottoman artefacts were found discarded under rubble used to fill hollows and then bricked or tiled over; considerable artistic licence was taken with the ground floor, which had actually survived the 1856 explosion; and the site topography was altered to make the Palace more imposing. Moreover, the materials and techniques employed by the Italians are not destined to last anywhere near as long as the original ones; much of the masonry is cladding rather than structural, with the wall-cores consisting of low-quality, reinforced concrete, whose iron mesh is causing tremendous problems owing to corrosion and expansion.

"Rhodes from the 4th Century until the Turkish Conquest" and "Ancient Rhodes, 2400 Years"

Housed in lower floors of the Palace, **"Rhodes from the 4th Century until the Turkish Conquest"** (Mon same as upper floors; Tues, Thurs & Sat 8am–7.30pm; Wed, Fri & Sun closed) and "**Ancient Rhodes, 2400 Years**" (Mon same as upper floors; Wed, Fri & Sun 8am–7.30pm; Tues, Thurs & Sat closed), are far and away the best-presented and best-interpreted museums on Rhodes. The medieval collection highlights the enduring importance of Christian Rhodes as a trade centre, with exotic merchandise placing the island in a trans-Mediterranean context. Superimposed illuminated colour overlays on one exhibit show how Ródhos Town has shrunk since ancient times to the compact ensemble of today. The Knights are represented with a display covering their sugar-refining industry and a gravestone of a Grand Master; precious manuscripts and books precede a wing of post-Byzantine icons, moved here permanently from Panayía Kástrou (see p.116). A snack-bar, well placed at the far end of the exhibits, provides seating looking out onto the Palace courtyard.

From the snack-bar, cross the courtyard to reach the entrance to "Ancient Rhodes, 2400 Years", which occupies the ground floor and basement vaults of the north wing. This outstanding, well-labelled collection completely eclipses the "official" archeological museum in terms of explaining the everyday life of the ancient city, by arranging the exhibits thematically (beauty aids, toys, cookware, worship, burial customs, etc). Highlights include votive offerings from ancient cult shrines; a Hellenistic floor mosaic of a comedic mask; a rare, triple-faced household idol of Hecate, goddess of the occult arts; a lead casket from an early Roman grave; a gold-leaf wreath from a Hellenistic one; and a Dali-esque mound of "failed" clay amphorae, deformed and discarded during firing.

The city walls

On Tuesday and Saturday afternoons there's a one-hour tour of the **city walls** (starts 2.45pm; separate €6 admission), beginning from a gate next to the Palace and traversing the western and southern reaches as far as the Koskinoú Gate. The tour is the only permitted access to the walls, and worth the expense for unique views of an exotic skyline punctuated with minarets, palm trees and the brooding mass of the Palace. Peering down into seldom-traversed alleys and overgrown gardens, you fully appreciate just how villagey and – since the World War II bombardments – occasionally crumbled the old town really is. The limestone fortifications, at certain points over 12m thick, date in their present form almost entirely from extensive refurbishment following the siege of 1480 (disregarding modern repairs); the various gates and bastions divided the curtain walls into eight sections, one for each of the Order's "Tongues" or nationalities.

Their masonry had become pretty bedraggled from exposure to six centuries of salt air, so the stonework was refurbished in the late 1990s with EU funding. At the same time much of the **moat** was landscaped with lawns and shrubbery, and is open for free walking tours (unrestricted access from several points), shown on the old-town map on p.112.

The "Street of the Knights"

The Gothic "**Street of the Knights**" (Ippotón) leads due east from Platía Kleovoúlou in front of the Palace. Once the main thoroughfare of the Kollákio, it was heavily restored by the Italians, who stripped the facades of their wooden, Ottoman balconies and repaired extensive 1856 blast damage. The **Inns** lining it housed most of the Knights of St John (see box on p.116), according to linguistic/ethnic affiliation – those for England and Auvergne are one block away on Apelloú and Platía Aryirokástrou respectively – and their ground floors served as stables for the Knights' horses. Today the Inns (not generally open to the public) contain government offices and foreign consulates or cultural institutions vaguely appropriate to their past. Although commercialization is forbidden on this thoroughfare, the whole effect is predictably sterile and stagey (indeed, nearby streets were used in the filming of *Pascali's Island* in the late 1980s, based on the Barry Unsworth novel and starring Ben Kingsley). The only hint of life, about halfway up on the south side, is a gated garden where a medieval fountain, surrounded by cannonballs, gurgles – a startling sound amidst the absolute silence prevailing here at night. This is the courtyard of the fifteenth-century **Villaragut Mansion**, restored in 2002 and sporadically open to the public: you're allowed upstairs to see carved wood ceilings and latticework. Directly opposite stands the most ornate of the Inns, that of France, embellished with the coats of arms of several Grand Masters.

The Archeological Museum

At the very foot of Ippotón, the Knights' Hospital has been refurbished as the **Archeological Museum** (summer Tues–Sun 8am–7pm; winter Tues–Sun 8.30am–3pm; €3), though the building, with its arches and echoing halls, rather overshadows the contents. The currently unused ground floor is set to contain more exhibits in the future; as it stands, the collection consists largely of painted pottery dating from the ninth through the fifth centuries BC from various sites, enlivened at one point by Bronze Age grave jewellery from Ialyssos. On the ground floor, occupying a corner of the building, is a small, separate gallery containing enormous *pithoi* (urns), some with intricate reliefs, from ancient Ialyssos and Kameiros. Somewhat more accessible is the Hellenistic statue gallery, located behind the second-storey sculpture garden, where visitors pose for photos with some not-very-naturalistic sculptures of a porpoise-head, lion and sea serpent. In a rear corner stands *Aphrodite Thalassia* or *Aidoumene*, the so-called "Marine Venus" beloved of Lawrence Durrell, lent a rather sinister aspect by her sea-dissolved face; in the adjacent wing crouches a friendlier *Aphrodite Bathing*, or, more precisely, wringing out her tresses.

The Knights of St John and the Second Siege of Rhodes

The Order of the Knights Hospitallers of St John was established in late eleventh-century Jerusalem as a nursing order tending sick Christian pilgrims. But since its original charter involved protecting as well as ministering to Christians, not a great conceptual leap was involved in the Order becoming more militant after the First Crusade. The Knights were compelled to leave Palestine in 1291 after losing their principal strongholds to the Saracens and a competing chivalric Order, the Knights Templar.

Cyprus proved unsatisfactory as a new home, so the Hospitallers migrated further west to Rhodes in June 1306, which they captured from the Genoese after a three-year war. Once in possession, the Knights began modifying and contracting the relatively flimsy Byzantine town fortifications; adequate funds were ensured when their rivals the Templars were suppressed in 1312 and most of their European assets made over to the Hospitallers by Pope Clement. Despite their origins, the Knights became a seafaring Order, aggrandizing themselves with frequent raids on non-Christian shipping. A huge fleet was fitted out for this purpose, its flagship the *Grand Carrack*, an eight-decked galley equipped for six months of continuous sailing by hundreds of men.

There were three classes of membership in the Order, each sworn to quasi-monastic vows of chastity, poverty and obedience that were honoured more often than not. Fully fledged Knights, never numbering more than 650, were recruited only among the nobility, while brothers, who served as soldiers or nurses, could be commoners. Chaplains were assigned to each of the seven, later eight, nationalities or "Tongues": France, Auvergne, Provence, Italy, Spain, Germany and England. Each Tongue was headed by a prior and the priors chose from among them a Grand Master or general prefect, elected for life, though in theory subject to a council of the priors. Of the nineteen Grand Masters fourteen were French, a reflection of the three Francophone contingents, and the fact that French (with Latin) was one of the two official languages of the Order. During the fourteenth century, Spain managed to divide her contingent into the "Tongues" (and inns) of Aragon and Castile, in a ploy to increase Spanish-speaking influence.

After the fall of Constantinople in 1453, the Knights were the only significant obstacle to further Ottoman expansion in the Aegean, as well as a continuing nuisance to their shipping. Although Rhodes withstood three brief Ottoman sieges

---

Opposite are fine, slightly later works of the Rhodian sculpture academy, such as Hygea feeding her familiar serpent and Asklepios leaning on his staff, while in a more central gallery the best of various fifth-century-BC grave steles from Kameiros is that donated by Kriti for her mother Timarista.

The Decorative Arts and Byzantine museums

Near the Archeological Museum, on Platía Aryirokástrou, with its Byzantine fountain from Arnítha village, is the **Decorative Arts Collection** (Tues–Sun 8.30am–3pm; €2), gleaned from old houses across the Dodecanese. There's not much in the way of explanation, but the fine Iznik and Kütahya ceramics, costumes, embroidery and folk pottery are fairly self-explanatory. The most compelling artefacts are carved cupboard doors and chest lids, some painted in naïve style with mythological or historical episodes.

Across the way stands the **Byzantine Museum** (Tues–Sun 8.30am–3pm; €2), housed in the old cathedral of the Knights, who adapted the Byzantine

in 1440, 1444 and 1480, Grand Masters Pierre d'Aubusson and Aimerie d'Amboise decided to embark on a fortification programme to resist any technological advance in Ottoman artillery.

In the early summer of 1522, Sultan Süleyman the Magnificent, determined to stamp out the Knights' piracy, landed on Rhodes with a force of 100,000. For six months the Knights and their auxiliaries, outnumbered thirty to one, resisted until the Ottomans were ready, like Demetrios before them, to concede defeat. But a traitor among the Knights, piqued at not being elected Grand Master, sent word to the Sultan that the garrison was at the end of its tether and could withstand only a few more concerted attacks. The consequent Turkish offensives in October and November ensured victory, following which Süleyman granted unusually magnanimous terms: the 180 surviving Knights were allowed to take all their movable property and ships with them on New Year's Day, 1523 as well as any civilians who preferred not to live under Muslim rule.

For seven years the Knights searched for a new base in the Mediterranean, before settling on Malta, where they successfully repulsed another, four-month Ottoman attack in 1565, and provided three galleys for the defeat of the Ottomans at Lepanto six years later. However, the English "Tongue" had been dissolved in 1534 by Henry VIII, and subsequently the Knights proved to be an anachronism: large, unified states of the sixteenth century could commission and outfit armadas far more efficiently, and the opening of trade routes to the New World and the Far East lessened the importance of controlling Mediterranean trade. The French branch of the Order was dissolved during the Revolution, and its assets confiscated in 1792; Napoleon met little resistance in 1798 when he annexed Malta in a minor diversion en route to Egypt, and dispersed the remaining Knights, apparently for good.

The English "Tongue" was revived in 1831 and reorganized as the St John Ambulance Brigade in 1888. The oldest visible traces of the Order in London's Clerkenwell district are the medieval gate on St John's Lane, all that survives of the twelfth-century priory where English Knights were recruited, and frescoes from the later church facing St John's Square, with a Maltese cross visible outside. In July 1995, today's worldwide Order – also active in Sweden, the Netherlands, Germany and Italy – held its annual four-day convention on Rhodes, with gala events centred (of course) on the Palace of the Grand Masters.

shrine of Panayía Kástrou for their own needs. Numerous medieval icons and frescoes lifted from crumbling, insecure chapels on Rhodes and Hálki, as well as photos of art still *in situ*, constitute the exhibits. Despite transfers of some of the best items to the Palace of the Grand Masters, this museum is still well worth a visit; highlights of the permanent collection include a complete cycle from the domes and squinches of Thárri monastery (see p.151) dating from 1624, lifted in 1967 to reveal much older work beneath, and frescoes from Áyios Zaharías at Finíki, Hálki, and from the spandrels of Panayía Kástrou itself. In the north courtyard, with its geometric mosaic panels, a barred stairway leads down to the original Byzantine *ayíasma* or sacred well, built over shortly after the Knights seized the island.

Ottoman Rhodes

If you head south from the Palace of the Grand Masters, it's hard to miss the most conspicuous Turkish monument in Rhodes, the rust-coloured **Süley-maniye Mosque**. Rebuilt in the nineteenth century on foundations three hundred years older, it's currently closed and under scaffolding, like most local

Ottoman monuments, though soon should emerge from a lengthy refit in all its candy-striped glory. The old town is in fact well sown with mosques and *mescids* (the Islamic equivalent of a chapel), many of them converted from Byzantine shrines after the 1522 conquest, when the Christians were expelled from the medieval precinct. Among these, the **Ibrahim Pasha Mosque** (1531), in the old bazaar quarter off Sofokléous, retains an ornate portico, while on Platía Dhoriéos, the **Rejep Pasha Mosque**, close to collapse until ongoing consolidation work began at the millennium, was built in 1588 from fragments of earlier churches.

The Ibrahim Pasha Mosque is still occasionally used by the sizeable Turkish-speaking minority here (see box opposite), and received a spanking new minaret in 2002; this aside, physical evidence of the four-hundred-year-long Ottoman tenure in Rhodes has been neglected and closed to the public, with neither the funds nor the political initiative to repair even those mosques reconsecrated for Christian use since 1912. The Süleymaniye Mosque's minaret was declared unsafe in 1989 and pulled down, with replacement work only recently undertaken.

However, during 1998 six small **Byzantine churches** in the old town – Ayía Paraskeví, Ayía Ekateríni, Áyios Athanásios, Áyios Ioánnis and two named Ayía Triádha – were refurbished, and they are very occasionally open for visits during unpredictable hours (Tues–Sun; free). One church that is typically open, and hasn't had the accretions of recent centuries removed, is unprepossessing but vividly frescoed **Áyios Fanoúrios**, near the south end of the eponymous street. Fanoúrios is a rather popular saint, much resorted to now as in the past by both Rhodian Greeks and Turks for retrieving lost objects (and persons) – or winning the affections of hitherto oblivious lovers. Custom dictates that if you get what (or whom) you were seeking, you must bake a cake, have it consecrated by the priest at Áyios Fanoúrios and distribute it to your neighbours.

Directly opposite the Sülemaniye Mosque stands the **Ottoman** (or **Hafiz Ahmet Ağa**) **library** (Mon–Sat 9.30am–4pm; tip custodian if they're around), dating from 1794 and endowed with a rich collection of early medieval manuscripts and Korans. Two specimens from the fifteenth century, jointly worth about £400,000, went missing in 1990, but were found at a London auctioneer's and returned in 1994 with appropriate ceremony.

Northwest of the Süleymaniye looms the Baroque **clocktower** erected by Ahmet Fetih Pasha in 1857, now home to a steeply priced café-bar near the top (hefty admission charge to climb to observation terrace).

The hamam (Dhimotiká Loutrá)

The Ottomans' most enduring civic contribution is the imposing **hamam** or Turkish baths, marked as the *Dhimotiká Loutrá* ("Municipal Baths"), on Platía Aríonos up in the southwest corner of the old town (men Mon, Wed & Fri 11am–6pm; women Tues & Thurs 11am–6pm, Sat 8am–6pm). Originally constructed in 1558, they were renovated by the builder of the adjacent Mustafa Pasha Mosque in 1765, badly damaged during World War II and restored afterwards.

In their prime, the Rhodes baths were considered among the most elegant in the Aegean, and are now – under the management of a Scandinavian woman – the last working ones in Greece outside of Thrace. They are capable of holding about two hundred people at any given time, and supposedly consume a tonne of olive wood daily in the process of heating the water, which courses through pipes under the floor as well as out of the "hot" taps. There were formerly separate facilities for each sex, but currently only the grander central section, with its lofty dome pierced by star-shaped skylights, is being used; the actual washing facilities are tucked into smaller, marble-lined rooms off the main hall. The clientele consists principally of old-town Greeks, who use the *hamam* as a social occasion, supplemented by a smattering of tourists and local Turks.

Unlike *hamam*s in Turkey, no towels or sundries are included in the admission price, so bring everything you need; you'll be assigned a free locker for your clothes. Beyond the weighted doors is the cool room, from which you proceed to the steam room, directly above the heating pipes. Massages may be available, performed on the stone platform that's the focus of any *hamam*. In the bathing rooms you sluice yourself down by dipping a bowl into the stone font. In another contrast to Anatolian practice, bathers (both men and women) strut around stark naked. And although the baths are cleaned scrupulously at closing time, don't be too surprised if you glimpse the odd cockroach – their name in Turkish, after all, means "*hamam*-bug".

The old Jewish quarter

The local Turks are still scattered fairly evenly through the old town, but the other Rhodian minority – the Jewish community – were always quite compactly settled. Beyond the tiled centrepiece fountain in Platía Ippokrátous, where broad steps lead up to the Kastellania or medieval traders' tribunal and stock exchange, Aristotélous leads to the **Platía tón Evréon Martýron** (Square of the Jewish Martyrs), renamed in memory of local Jewry who were almost totally exterminated in 1944.

Of the four **synagogues** that once stood in Ródhos Town, the only survivor is **Kahal Kadosh Shalom**, on Simíou, 100m to the south (three doorways

The Turks of Rhodes

The **Turkish community** of Rhodes dates from 1522, when an Ottoman garrison and civil servants took control of the island, settling principally in and around the main town. They were supplemented between 1898 and 1913 by Cretan Muslims fleeing intercommunal troubles on their native island. These Cretan refugees founded the now-dilapidated suburb of Kritiká, not far from the airport.

Some old-town Turks can still trace their ancestry to the sixteenth-century conquest, and will proudly tell you that they have every right to be considered native Rhodians. Such a stance fails to impress the Greek authorities, and their bureaucratic treatment tends to function, as in western Thrace on the mainland, as a barometer of the current state of relations between Greece and Turkey. The decades after 1948 saw a sharp decline in the local Turkish population from about 6500 to under 2000; the 1974 war in Cyprus made the position of Rhodian Turks untenable, and at that time many of the wealthier Muslims sold their property, both in the old town and at Líndhos, at knockdown prices.

Since 1997, however, and a landmark European Court of Human Rights decision, Rhodian Turks who have taken long absences in Turkey, Australia or elsewhere cannot be stripped of Greek nationality and can return freely, and the local population has stabilized at about 2500. Although it's still possible to spot Turkish names on the marquees of various sandalmakers, kebab stalls, jewellers and *kafenía*, local "Muslim Hellenes" (their official designation) generally maintain a low public profile, gravitating towards service trades such as delivery, auto repair, ironwork, wholesale catering, confectionery and a few restaurants in the new town, where they're less likely to come into contact with outsiders.

The Jews of Rhodes

As in much of the rest of Greece, **Jews** had dwelt in Rhodes since at least the second century BC, and during the Ottoman era were permitted – unlike the Orthodox Greeks – to live inside the walled city, in the easternmost quarter allotted them by the conquerors. Neither did the local Jews suffer especially under the Italians, who actively favoured them as a counter to Greek nationalism until the mid-1930s; their population even recovered from medieval vicissitudes to around four thousand by the 1920s.

Thereafter, the *Rodesli* (as Rhodian Jews and their descendants call themselves) began to emigrate in large numbers, travelling on Italian passports to what was then the Belgian Congo, Rhodesia, Egypt, South America and the US (especially the Deep South and the Pacific Northwest). By the time restrictive anti-Semitic laws were promulgated and enforced by the ardently Fascist Governor Cesare Maria de Vecchi in 1938–39, and hostilities commenced between Italy and the Allies shortly after, some two thousand had managed to flee overseas, thus avoiding the fate of the 1973 Rhodian and about 120 Koan Jews deported to Auschwitz by the Nazis in July 1944.

Of these, just 161 (plus fifty or so with Turkish nationality, who were saved by the Turkish consul in Rhodes) survived, while today there are fewer than in Ródhos Town, mostly elderly Jews from Vólos and Lárissa on the mainland who resettled here in the early 1960s on the orders of Greece's head rabbi so that a living Jewish presence would remain on the island. The caretaker, Loukia Modhiano, is an exception, a Rhodian woman who survived Auschwitz and – like so many of her generation – speaks Greek, Ladino (the language historically spoken by Sephardic Jews in the Balkans and Turkey), Italian and French, but little English. The community is too tiny to support a rabbi (the last one left Rhodes in 1936), so one comes annually from Israel to conduct Yom Kippur services.

past Dhosiádhou 16 – look for the Stars of David if a sign's not up; daily 10am–5pm). This ornate structure features a beautiful *votsalotó* floor and eight arcaded columns supporting the roof. Rarely used for religious services, it's maintained essentially as a memorial to the Jews of Rhodes and Kós deported to Auschwitz; plaques commemorating the dead are mostly in French, the preferred language of educated Jews in the east Aegean at the beginning of the twentieth century. There are more such memorials in the Jewish section of the city cemetery behind Zéfyros beach (see p.127).

At the rear of the synagogue, a one-room **museum**, well labelled in English, was set up in 1997 by Aron Hasson, a Los Angeles attorney of *Rodesli* descent (see box above). It functions primarily as a resource centre and meeting point for diaspora *Rodesli* – who can be seen photographing photos of ancestors, and copying documents – but is also of general interest for its photos of diaspora life in such far-flung spots as Alabama and Buenos Aires, plus events in local Jewish history.

The new town

Nobody comes to Rhodes especially to admire Italian town planning and public architecture, but it's difficult to avoid noticing some of the choicer examples of Rationalist, faux-medieval, orientalized or out-and-out Art Deco buildings scattered about Neohóri. Prominent among these are the

△ Platía Ippokrátous, Rhodes Old Town

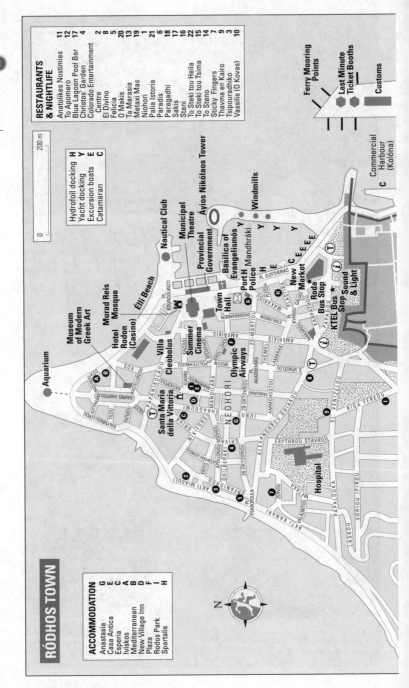

RÓDHOS TOWN

ACCOMMODATION

Anastasia	G
Casa Antica	E
Esperia	C
Iviskos	A
Mediterranean	B
New Village Inn	D
Plaza	F
Rodos Park	I
Spartalis	H

RESTAURANTS & NIGHTLIFE

Anatolikes Nostimies	11
To Apomero	12
Blue Lagoon Pool Bar	17
Christos' Garden	4
Colorado Entertainment Centre	2
El Divino	8
Felicia	5
O Makis	20
Ta Marasia	13
Metaxi Mas	19
Niohori	1
Palia Istoria	21
Paradis	6
Paragadhi	18
Sakis	17
Stani	16
To Steki tou Heila	22
To Steki tou Tsima	15
To Steno	14
Sticky Fingers	7
Thavma en Kairo	9
Tsipouradhiko	3
Vassilis (O Kovas)	10

0   200 m

Hydrofoil docking   H
Yacht docking   Y
Excursion boats   E
Catamaran   C

Ferry Mooring Points

Last Minute Ticket Booths

Customs

122

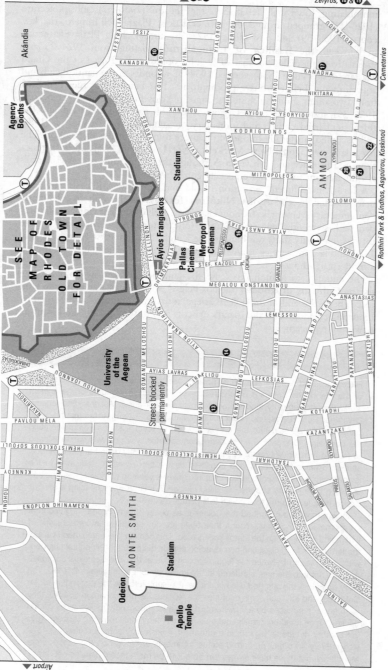

intimidating town hall (1936–39), the theatre (1936–37) and prefecture (1926–27) grouped around the former Fascist Piazza dell'Impero; the law courts (1938–39) and post office (1927–28) further along Platía Eleftherías; in between, the **Basilica of Evangelismós** (dating from 1924–25 and speculatively modelled on that of St John opposite the Palace of the Grand Masters, destroyed in 1856); and the 1934–35 rotondas of the nautical club and aquarium on their respective promontories. The Franciscan order benefited from two other modern churches: angular Áyios Frangískos (San Francesco; 1936–39), just outside of the Ayíou Athanasíou gate and still used, and the fine orientalized church and monastery of Santa Maria della Vittoria (1924; still occupied), ironically in one of the more touristy corners of Neohóri. The irregularly heptagonal **New Market** or *Néa Agorá* from 1925 still (just) functions as a produce and fish vendor's, though the shops, cafés and *souvláki* stalls within are touristy and not especially good value.

A less-than-complete separation of old and new towns is most obviously demonstrated by the **Áyios Nikólaos fortress** at the end of relentlessly contemporary Mandhráki harbour's east jetty, itself of ancient vintage and studded with sixteenth-century windmills (one restored to working order). The fortress (currently shut) was built by the Knights after the first Turkish siege of 1480, and last saw service as a World War II gun emplacement; it now supports a modern lighthouse.

The entrance to Mandhráki is also the sentimental favourite candidate-site for the **Colossus of Rhodes** (see box below), an ancient statue of Apollo built to celebrate the end of the 305 BC siege; today, two columns surmounted by bronze deer, adopted as the island's mascots (see on box p.126), are less overpowering replacements.

The Colossus of Rhodes

Reproduced ad nauseam on maps, posters, tea towels and T-shirts as the symbol of the island, the Colossus of Rhodes, one of the Seven Wonders of the ancient world, has not actually stood intact for over two millennia. According to legend, Demetrios Polyorketes, upon conceding defeat in 305 BC, suggested that his siege paraphernalia be sold and the proceeds used to erect a statue commemorating the campaign. Originally, the Peloponnesian sculptor Lysippos was commissioned to fashion a massive Chariot of the Sun, but subsequently gave the job to a local student, Khares of Lindos, who chose to cast a bronze effigy dedicated to the island's patron deity, Apollo Helios. This took twelve years to complete, near the end of which time Khares supposedly killed himself in shame upon noticing a serious design flaw, leaving the final phase to a certain Lakhes.

Ancient travellers described the Colossus as being 35m high and weighing in at an estimated 125 tonnes, though their texts are coy on the all-important issue of where and in what pose the statue was placed. This has not prevented medieval and modern artists from depicting him standing astride the mouth of Mandhráki harbour with ships sailing between his legs. Our only clue is that the Colossus collapsed on land, not into the sea, sundered at the knees by an earthquake in 227 BC. The story goes that the sun god, via his oracle at Delphi, forbade the restoration of the Colossus, and for nearly nine centuries the remains lay untouched. In 654 AD, they were finally purchased by a Jew from Edessa and supposedly hauled away on the backs of nine hundred camels (debunkers say ninety), only to return (according to yet another debatable legend) in the form of Turkish cannonballs during the 1522 siege. Every so often, purported statue fragments are found on the seabed near Mandhráki, but these have always turned out to be more recent metallic debris.

Museum of Modern Greek Art

Installed during 2002 in the Nestorídhio Mélathro (Mansion) on Ekatón Hourmadhiés square, the **Museum of Modern Greek Art** (Tues–Sat 8am–2pm & 6–9pm; €3) houses one of the most important collections of twentieth-century Greek painting and sculpture. All of the famous names are represented, including Theophilos Hatzimihaïl (see p.405), Ioannis Tsarouhis and Hatzikyriakos-Ghikas, and there are some pleasant surprises from lesser-known figures. What used to be the main, cramped home of the museum, on Platía Sými 2 in the old town, is now the **annexe** (same hours, shared ticket), devoted to maps and prints, medieval vedutte, and special exhibits. Both premises have excellent gift shops.

The Aquarium

At the northernmost point of the island, an Italian-built Art Deco **Aquarium** (daily 9am–8.30pm; €3.50), officially the "Hydrobiological Institute", displays a subterranean maze of seawater tanks containing live specimens of Rhodian sealife. The biggest crowd-pleasers are green turtles, enormous groupers and wicked-looking moray eels; if nothing else, a dusk or rainy-day visit should settle arguments as to what the English equivalents are of the Greek fish offered in tavernas (see also box on p.539). Upstairs you'll find a less enthralling collection of half-rotten taxidermic specimens, including sharks, seals and even a whale.

Murad Reis Mosque, Villa Cleobolus and Casino

Between the aquarium and the similarly curvilinear Nautical Club, but much closer to the latter, stands the **Murad Reis Mosque**, which, in a departure from the usual pattern of official indifference, was fitted with a new minaret during the early 1990s by the Greek Archeological Service. Next to this is the tomb of the eponymous admiral, who died during the 1522 siege, and between them the *votsalotó* courtyard of the caretakers' ramshackle dwelling. To the west extends a eucalyptus-shaded cemetery, the oldest and one of the largest Muslim graveyards on the island, containing several rather battered *türbes* (freestanding domed tombs) of Ottoman worthies and also one belonging to a Shah of Persia. On the far side, a plaque affixed to the **Villa Cleobolus (Kleovoulos)** commemorates Lawrence Durrell's residence here from spring 1945 to spring 1947; after years of neglect the cottage – hardly a villa – was refurbished in 2004 as home for the Dodecanesian Literature and Arts Club.

Just a few paces northwest of this, the 1927-completed Albergo delle Rose (*Hotel Rodon*) was refurbished after decades of abandonment and pressed into service in 1999 as the **Casino of Rhodes**, Greece's third largest. After an extremely rocky start – it did not turn a profit for a year or so, and the Russian Mafia figure managing it used the premises as a front for drug dealing – it is now under more stable stewardship. Unusually, locals are allowed to patronize it, parting with large sums of money in the process, beginning with the €15 admission (open Mon–Thurs 3pm–6am, Fri noon–Mon 6am continuously, minimum age 23, ID required).

Beaches

Complete with sunbeds, parasols and showers (standing room only for late-comers), **Élli** beach is the most sheltered of the mediocre, coarse-sand beaches which, under different names, fringe Neohóri to the north; the westerly, wind-buffeted beaches are better haunts for windsurfers and paragliders than for swimmers and sunbathers.

Other options for taking a dip around the new town are limited: you'll see families, and backpackers awaiting a ship, digging their toes in the sand at Kolóna, or even going for a paddle. But the most hygienic and sheltered option is south-east-facing **Zéfyros** beach, broad and sandy, with a number of tavernas behind it, well placed for lunch (see p.129). There's no bus service, and it's a hefty 25-minute walk from the southerly gates of the old town, so your best option is to take a scooter or a taxi. There are sunbeds at the northeast end, and showers, but a reef to cross getting into the sea with some suspicious green algae on it – though we're assured by regulars that the water is actually clean enough.

Monte Smith: Hellenistic Rhodes

About 2km southwest of Mandhráki, the sparse, unenclosed remains of the Hellenistic acropolis perch atop **Monte Smith**. Formerly Áyios Stéfanos, this hill was rather bizarrely renamed after the British admiral Sydney Smith, who used it as a watchpoint during the Napoleonic Wars. Dating from the third and second centuries BC, the ruins include a restored, garishly marble-clad *odeion* to one side of the more subdued, 200-metre stadium, a peaceful, tree-flanked spot. Above the *odeion* loom the four re-erected columns and pediment of the **temple to Apollo Pythios**; visits are most rewarding at sunset, when both temple and town are shown to advantage, with Turkey and Sými visible on the horizon.

Infrequent #5 city buses run from the New Market if you're not keen on the walk, though from the Ayíou Athanasíou gate of the old town it's not much more than fifteen minutes on foot. Other conspicuously signposted reminders of the ancient city are the foundations of an **Aphrodite temple** in the old town's Platía Sýmis; gauging the distance between there and the acropolis gives you a fair idea of ancient Rhodes' vast extent.

Rodhíni Park

Monte Smith is popular enough with joggers and strollers, but for summer shade and greenery the best spot is probably **Rodhíni park** (free admission),

The deer of Rhodes

The miniature **deer** found on Rhodes, *Dama dama*, are not actually indigenous to the island. They were first introduced in ancient times at the behest of the Delphic oracle in response to islanders' entreaties as to how best to quell an eruption of snakes. Accounts differ as to how the reptiles were dispatched: the deer either repelled them with the odour of their urine, or impaled the serpents on their antlers. The deer themselves subsequently died out and had to be reintroduced by the Knights; the Italians did likewise, after the deer were hunted almost to local extinction during Ottoman rule.

For some years, many specimens lived in the dry moat between the inner and outer walls of the old town. However, eight were killed by feral dogs in 1994, prompting a debate on the future of those remaining. A proposal to release them into the wild south of the island was vetoed for fear of poachers; instead some thirty deer were housed in a pen at Rodhíni park, prior to their transfer to a much larger enclosure near the Ptolemaic tombs – and the donation of some to the municipality of Mýrina, Límnos.

nearly 2km south of town on the road to Líndhos, and served by city bus route #3. This wooded area, known as Zimboúli in Ottoman times, lines either bank of a natural ravine spanned by an aqueduct of indeterminate age. The ravine's watercourse is fed by natural springs and is home to ducks, carp and peacocks.

Hellenistic rock-cut **tombs** at the south end of the park, rather dubiously attributed to the Ptolemies, constitute a final possible attraction. A signposted 700-metre access road winds through a man-made rock tunnel, crosses the top of the ravine, and skirts a football pitch; on the south side of this, beside a subterranean pumping station, stands a hollowed-out natural monolith, constituting the tombs in question (permanently locked).

The cemeteries

The vast **municipal cemeteries** at Korakónero, just inland from Zéfyros beach, might not immediately stand out as a hot tourist destination, but if you have any interest in Rhodes' recent past, they prove strangely compelling. For one thing, this is one of the very few remaining spots in the Balkans – certainly the only one in Greece – where the dead of four faiths lie in proximity, albeit separated by high walls. The easterly **Greek Orthodox section** is, of course, the largest and holds the fewest surprises. The small **Catholic section** (always open) is not only the last home of various north European expatriates, but also demonstrates that – contrary to received wisdom – a fair number of Italians elected to accept Greek nationality and stay on after the 1948 unification with Greece, and that a few native Greeks had succumbed to temptation and renounced the Orthodox faith. There's also a massive Italian mausoleum at the rear of this area, covering the years 1912–41, and another French one commemorating the victims of the cruiser *Indien*, sunk near Kastellórizo in 1915. The **Jewish section** (Mon–Fri 8am–1pm) – shown erroneously transposed with the Muslim one on virtually all maps – has, for reasons made clear on p.120, seen little activity since 1944, and is full of memorials in French to those who were deported. Immediately opposite its gate, across the busy road, is a small **Allied War graves** plot (unenclosed) with 142 burials from 1941 to 1946, some moved here from inconvenient sites on other Dodecanese islands; as ever, there's admirable documentation and a guest register to sign by the gate. Just south of the Jewish section, the "**Muslim" section** (ie Turkish, usually open) is the most heavily used and best maintained of the three minority cemeteries – perhaps indicating that the government does not blatantly interfere with the activities of the Rhodian *vakuf* or Islamic benevolent foundation.

Eating and drinking

Finding good-value **tavernas** in and around Ródhos Town is a challenge, though by no means an insurmountable one. The place is large enough that certain economies of scale apply: tradespeople and students have to eat somewhere, and if you're setting your sights a couple of notches higher, it's possible to find carefully prepared, even exotic, meals at not overly inflated prices. Neohóri fare tends to be more Western and snacky, while restaurants in neighbourhoods south of the old city offer a serious Greek feed. As a general rule, the more you escape the crowds and the further south you go, the better value you'll find.

Cafés and bakeries

Bekir Karakuzu Sokrátous 76. Bags of atmosphere in the last traditional Turkish *kafenío* in the old town, now run by Bekir's son Ali. Oriental-fantasy interior with an ornate *votsalotó* floor; yogurt, *loukoúmi*, *alisfakiá* tea and coffees on the expensive side, but you are effectively paying admission to an informal museum. Open 11am–midnight.

Glykohora Ethnárhi Makaríou 4, 25-Martiou. Just a few tables often packed with lawyers on break from the nearby courts, but some of the best and cheapest coffees in town, plus Western cakes and filo-based pastries.

Kringlan Swedish Bakery Íonos Dhragoúmi 14, Neohóri. The stress is on brioches, pizzas, cakes, sandwiches and rich filter coffee. Closed Sun eve.

Ömer Omírou, near cnr Pythagóra, old town. Turkish bakery selling wholegrain bread and fine cakes.

Stani Ayías Anastasías 28, cnr Paleón Patrón Yermanoú, south of the Koskinoú Gate. Most central outlet of a small chain of Rhodian Turkish confectioners, scooping out two dozen flavours of the best ice cream on the island, publicity for rival *Mikes'* notwithstanding.

Restaurants

The old town

L'Auberge Bistrot Praxitélous 21 ☎22410 34292, ⊛www.bistrorhodes.com. Popular, genuine Lyonnais-run bistro with excellent Frenchified food: allow €21 per person for three hefty courses, maybe €17 for three appetizers plus dessert if you're not of a meaty disposition. Wine (extra) from a well-selected Greek list; jazz soundtrack included. Summer seating in the courtyard of this restored medieval inn – inside under the arches during cooler months. Open late March–late Dec for supper daily except Mon; reservations suggested.

Fotis Melathron alley off Apelloú and Sokrátous ☎22410 24272. Housed in a converted Turkish mansion, this is considered the top *koultoúra* restaurant in the old town. Sample fare: *dolmádhes*, well-presented salads, squash flowers, crayfish nuggets, sweetbreads. The upstairs "snugs" are excellent for private parties of four to eight. Reserve in peak season; budget at least €75 for two with wine.

Hatzikelis Solomoú Alhadhéf 9, just in from the Panayía Gate beyond the bombed-out shell of Santa Maria del Borgo church ☎22410 27215. Ignore the "tourist special" sandwich board and go à la carte with offferings such as rocket and parmesan salad, good wild fish (order in advance, the properietor's brother has a boat) and great stuffed eggplant, at reasonable prices. Open most of the year; best in winter, when local diners predominate at this former Jewish girls' school (find the Hebrew inscription inside).

Kasbah Plátonos 4–8. Somewhat overpriced, but Rhodes' only quasi-Moroccan eatery, offering couscous and tajines, salads, Middle Eastern *orektiká* and very good desserts. If you're light eaters,

two can get out the door for about €35. Supper only Tues–Sun, open March–Nov.

Laganis Solomoú Alhadéf 16. Low-key taverna on a quiet corner that's best for *mezédhes*: *khtapodokeftédhes* (octopus croquettes), sausages, stuffed mussels and so on. Average-sized portions, average prices for Rhodes.

Marco Polo Café Ayíou Fanouríou 42. What started out as the breakfast venue of the eponymous hotel (see p.110) has become, under the ebullient Efi Dede's stewardship, the sleeper of the old town. Excellent generic Mediterranean fare – mostly vegetables, salads and seafood – with good wines (husband Spyros is a fanatic) and desserts made on the premises.

O Meraklis Aristotélous 30. One of the last Rhodian rough edges not yet filed smooth, this *pátsatzídhiko* (tripe-soup kitchen) trotter caters for a pre-dawn clientele of post-club lads, Turkish shopkeepers, gangsters, nightclub singers and travellers just stumbled off a late-arriving ferry. Great free entertainment, including famously rude staff, and the soup's good, too: the traditional Greek working man's breakfast and hangover cure. Open 2–9am only.

Mikes (pronounced "mee-kess", a Kalymnian name) nameless alley behind Sokrátous 17. Inexpensive (for Rhodes, anyway) hole-in-the-wall, serving absolutely nothing but grilled fish, salads and wine.

Myrovolos Láhitos 13 ☎22410 38693. Meals at this popular spot (groups should reserve) are a cross between *koultoúra* taverna fare and a conventional *ouzerí*, on the rich and spicy side: wild mushrooms with rocket and cheese, *psaronéfri*, mussels in fennel sauce. Allow €23 each with (decent) house wine. Lovely indoor seating on several levels, or tables in courtyard (best in summer).

Nektar & Ambrosia Sofokléous 9 ☎ 22410 30363. Small portions of French/Italian/generic Mediterranean fusion cuisine don't come cheap (allow €18–20), but they make an excellent light summer meal. Run by Texan-Australian Besara Harris, one of the old town's characters, who sometimes stages theme nights (such as Madagascan supper) for which booking is mandatory.

The new town

Anatolikes Nostimies Kapodhistríou 60, Minhanouryía district, behind Akándia port. The name means "Anatolian Delicacies" and that's what's on offer at this Rhodian Turkish-run grill: Turkish/Middle Eastern dips and starters, plus sixteen variations of kebab. Not much atmosphere, even after a recent overhaul, but friendly and reasonable; post-prandial hubble-bubble provided on request. Open 11am–midnight.

To Apomero Kolokotróni 5, Mihanouryía district. Rough little dive which got mildly spruced up in 2004, basically a workmen's *kafenío* run by two women, serving good and cheap food: fried fish, chops, a few *mezédhes* and salads, washed down by the usual refreshments and accompanied by taped folk/*laïká* music. Sit outside opposite industrial scenery (the Emery distillery) for a sea breeze and even a sea view.

Felicia Aktí Miaoúli 4–6, just off Platía Psaropoúlou. Genuine, reasonably priced Italian trattoria specializing in pasta and wood-oven pizza; congenial decor, a few sea-view tables outside in a windproof conservatory. Supper only.

Psistaria O Makis Dhendhrinoú 69, Ámmos district. Every conceivable cut of roast beast here, including *kokorétsi* (offal kebab) and *kefalákia* (sheep's head, if you dare); considered by some to be better value for money than *Palia Istoria* across the way (see below). Takeaway too.

Ta Marasia Ayíou Ioánnou 155, just off eponymous *platía*. ☎ 22410 34529. Currently the most daring *ouzerí* in the town limits, operating out of a 1923-vintage house. The food's excellent, if not always very traditional (grilled oyster mushrooms; red cabbage, yogurt-and-nut salad), though there are more usual seafood platters like urchins and *rengosaláta*. Don't over-order, as portions tend to be generous. Groups should reserve.

Metaxi Mas Klavdhíou Pépper 116, Zéfyros beach. No sign or menu in English – look for the elevated boat – at this seafood *ouzerí*, the

Sea Star (aka *Pizanias*) Sofokléous 24, cnr of the square ☎ 22410 22117. In 2003, old Kyriakos Pizanias went to the Big Grill in the Sky, but his successors have maintained quality at this three-decades-old institution. Not only fresh scaly fish – staff show you the pink gills – but shellfish like *kydhónia* (cockles) and *petalídhia* (limpets), grilled octopus and squid. With two bottles of quality wine, starters and loads of seafood, four can eat here for a third less than elsewhere in the old town. Reservations suggested.

first of several to open here, purveying various exotic titbits (*foúskes*, *kydhónia*, etc). Count on €40 per couple with booze, slightly cheaper per person in a group – but still 25 percent less than in the old town. Mon–Sat lunch & dinner, Sun lunch only.

Niohori Ioánni Kazoúli 29, Neohóri, by the Franciscan monastery. Also known as "Kiki's" after the jolly proprietress, this homey, inexpensive local serves lunch and supper; best for grills, sourced from their own butcher/farm.

Palia Istoria Mitropóleos 108, cnr Dhendhrínou, Ámmos district ☎ 22410 32421. Reckoned one of the best *koultoúra* tavernas in town, but predictably expensive for such dishes as cauliflower *yiovétsi*, peppered testicles, celery hearts in egg-lemon sauce and scallops with mushrooms and artichokes, washed down by a hundred-strong wine list. Mon–Sat dinner only; reservations essential in season.

Paragadhi cnr Klavdhíou Pépper and Avstralías, Zéfyros. 2004-opened and very good seafood/fish restaurant (as opposed to *ouzerí*), with fair portions and prices. Their *risótto thalassinoú* is excellent if not puristically authentic. Closed Sun pm & Mon noon.

Sakis Kanadhá 95, cnr Apostólou Papaïoánnou. An old favourite in a new location, with pleasant patio and indoor seating, equally popular with Rhodians and savvy expats. Famed for excellent seafood (try their limpets), meat (Cypriot *seftaliés*) and starters; inexpensive by Rhodian standards. Open for supper daily, also Sun lunch, all year.

To Steki tou Heila Hatziangélou, cnr Episkópi Kyriniás, near Zéfyros. Very popular seafood *ouzerí* which arguably just pips the next listing for quality at similar prices, though the street's noisy. Rocket and onion salad, Sými shrimps, squid, marinated sardines, *fáva*, cockles (check price of last). Open daily, supper only.

To Steki tou Tsima Peloponnísou 22, around cnr from *Stani* (see p.128). Reasonable seafood *ouzerí*, with the stress on aficionados' shellfish titbits (*foúskes, spiniálo*) and small unfarmed fish – always ask about off-menu specials. No airs or graces (except proper table nappery), just patently fresh materials. Open daily, supper only.

To Steno Ayíon Anaryíron 29, 400m southwest of the old town. As the name ("narrow" in Greek) implies, this is a small, welcoming taverna, with outdoor seating in the warmer months. The menu encompasses sausages, chickpea soup, *pitaroúdhia* or courgette croquettes, stuffed zucchini blossoms and fried little fish; "discovery" has meant it's a bit oilier and pricier than it once was, but still worth the trek out.

Thavma en Kairo Eleftheriou Venizelou 16–18 ☎ 22410 39805, ⊛ www.restaurantwonder.com. Andreas, the Norwegian founder of Neohóri's *7.5 Wonder*, has upped sticks and chefs, and migrated to this elegant Belle Époque mansion overlooking parkland. He's repeated his fusion of Asian, Mediterranean and Scandinavian cuisine to good effect, though it (and the four-star wine list) will set you back a minimum of €32 per person. Supper only.

Tsipouradhiko Aktí Miaoúli 20. All the meat and seafood *ouzerí/tsipourádhiko* standards in deceptively small but rich platters – six will feed two people – at competitve prices considering the unobstructed sea view. Run by nice folk from mainland Thessaly, who make their own *tsípouro*. Open daily noon–3am or so.

Vassilis (O Kovas) Kolokotróni 66, 80m east of Kanadhá, Mihanouryía. Sympathetic, very inexpensive workers' and students' canteen with a daily-changing menu of *mayireftá* to choose from: maybe goat stew with celery, *fáva*, baked *biftékia* and big salads, washed down with decent bulk wine. Busiest at lunch, when they run out of the best dishes by 2.30pm or so; also opens at night, with meat on the grill. Vine-shaded conservatory seating between the auto-repair shops.

Nightlife and entertainment

The old town formerly had a well-deserved reputation for being tomb-silent at night, but this has changed drastically since the late 1990s. An entire alley (Miltiádhou) off Apelloú has been given over to loud music **bars and clubs**, extending into Plátonos and Platía Dhamayítou, and frequented almost exclusively by Greeks; their names and proprietors change yearly, but the locations remain the same. Another, somewhat-lower-decibel nucleus of activity is around Platía Ariónos. These are alternatives to the estimated hundred-odd foreigner-patronized bars and clubs in Neohóri (well down from double that in the early 1990s), where theme nights, drinks-with-cover and various other gimmicks predominate. They are found mostly along the streets and alleys bounded by Alexándhrou Dhiákou, Orfanídhou (aka "Skandi Street", after the latter-day Vikings), Lohagoú Fanouráki and Nikifórou Mandhilará.

Sedate by comparison, Ministry-of-Culture-approved folk dances (June 15–Oct 1 Mon, Wed & Fri 9.20pm; €12) are presented with live accompaniment by the **Nelly Dimoglou Company**, performed in the landscaped "Old Town Theatre" off Andhroníkou, near Platía Ariónos. As these things go, they're amongst the best of their kind, but it's perhaps wise to remember the caveat of the late Hellenophile Kevin Andrews: "for the tourist [there are] the official folk-dances, the open-air productions – carefully resurrected, costumed in a way that we shall never again see in any village, flawlessly executed and dead as mutton. Folk do their dancing when drunk or otherwise exalted, or when they feel the earth moving upward through their bodies."

More of a technological extravaganza is the **Sound and Light** show, spot-lighting sections of the city walls, staged in a garden just off Platía Rimíni.

There's English-language narration nightly except Sunday, with screening time varying from 8.15pm to 10.15pm (€6).

Thanks to a large contingent from the local university, there are year-round **cinemas** in the new town showing first-run fare indoors or open air according to season and air-conditioning capabilities. Choose from among the summer-only Rodon outdoor cinema by the Municipal Theatre, next to the town hall in Neohóri; the Metropol multiplex, at the corner of Venetokléon and Výronos, southeast of the old town opposite the stadium; and the nearby Pallas multiplex on Dhimokratías.

Bars and music venues

The old town

Baduz Loutra Platía Ariónos. Shares the same crowd as *Iy Rogmi tou Khronou* next door, and hosts live jazz some nights.

Kafé Besara Sofokléous 11-13. Congenial breakfast café/low-key boozer run by Besara Harris (of *Nektar & Ambrosia* next door), with interesting mixed clientele and live, acoustic Greek music some nights Oct–May.

Mandala Sofokléous 38. Part Swedish-run, enduringly popular snack-café/garden bar; the generic Med-lite salads and pasta dishes are incidental to good beer, the crowd, and live Greek acoustic music Sat evenings. Open all year 2pm–3am; in winter there's a cosy interior with fireplace.

Mango Bar Platía Dhoriéos 3. Piped music and a variety of drinks at this durable bar on an otherwise quiet plaza; also a good source of breakfast after 8am, served under a plane tree.

Resalto Plátonos 6, opposite the mosque. Live Greek *rebétika* and *laïkó* sounds, rather cheaper and more acoustic than nearby rival *Café Chantant*. Typically open Thurs–Sat night; free entry but pricey drinks.

Iy Rogmi tou Khronou Platía Ariónos. Taped music (not house or techno) at a reasonable level and a congenial crowd make this established bar worth a look.

The new town

Blue Lagoon Pool Bar 25-Martíou 2, Neohóri. One of the better theme bars, in this case a "desert island" with palm trees, waterfalls, live turtles and parrots, a shipwrecked galleon – and taped music. Open March–Oct 8.30am–3am.

Christos' Garden/To Dhiporto Dhilberáki 59. This combination art gallery/bar/café occupies a carefully restored old house and courtyard with pebble-mosaic floors throughout. Incongruously classy for the area.

Colorado Entertainment Centre Orfanídhou 57, Ⓦ www.coloradoclub.gr. Triple venue: "Colorado Live" with live in-house band (rock covers), "Studio Fame" with taped sounds and club, plus chill-out "Heaven" R&B bar upstairs.

El Divino Alexándhrou Dhiákou 5. Very classy, Greek-frequented "music bar", affiliated with a namesake on Ibiza, offering garden seating and the usual range of coffees and alcohol. Open June–Oct noon until late.

Paradis 25-Martíou 2. Frequent theme nights and live acts Sat & Sun; cool off in the adjacent, affiliated *Blue Lagoon* (see above). Open 10pm until dawn.

Sticky Fingers Anthoúla Zérvou 6, ☎ 22410 35744. Long-lived music club with reasonably priced drinks; live rock several nights weekly from 10.30pm onwards; off season, Fri & Sat only. Typical admission €12.

Listings

Airlines, domestic Aegean, Ethelondón Dhodhekanisíon 20 ☎ 22410 24400; Olympic, Ieroú Lóhou 9 ☎ 22410 24571.

Airport information Call ☎ 22410 83214 or 2410 82300 for the latest on (often delayed) flight arrivals and departures.

Bookshops Best is Bibliopolis at Stelíou Kotiádhia 14, between the university and Rodhíni, with books in several foreign languages. Newsstand, Grigoríou Lambráki 23, Neohóri, has a limited stock of English-language material, as does To Dhendhro, Himáras 14, near the university.

Car rental Posted prices at non-international chains are fairly standard at €45–55 per day in high season, but can be bargained down to about €25–35 a day, all-inclusive, outside peak season and/or for long periods. Especially recommended is Drive, who change their cars every 12–18 months; they have several premises across the island, including on Avstralías 2, Akándia port ✆ 22410 32202, at the airport ✆ 22410 81011 and the Grand Hotel in town ✆ 22410 26284. Other flexible outfits, all in the new town, include Just/Ansa, Mandhilará 70 ✆ 22410 31811; Kosmos, Papaloúka 31 ✆ 22410 74374; Orion, Yeoryíou Léondos 38 ✆ 22410 22137; and Payless, Íonos Dhragoúmi 29 ✆ 22410 26586. Major chains include Alamo/National, Iraklídhon 41, Ixía ✆ 22410 91117; Avis, Theodhoráki 3, Neohóri ✆ 22410 24990 and airport ✆ 22410 82896; and Hertz at Yeoryíou Gríva 16, Neohóri ✆ 22410 21819 and the airport ✆ 22410 82902.

Consulates UK, Pávlou Melá 3 ✆ 22410 27247; Ireland, Amerikís 111 ✆ 22410 22461; Netherlands, Alexándhrou Dhiákou 25 ✆ 22410 31571. All other English-speaking nationals are represented only in Athens.

Exchange No fewer than eight conventional bank branches are grouped within sight of Platía Kýprou in Neohóri, plus there are various exchange bureaux keeping long hours. There are also several ATMs, either attached to banks or freestanding, in the old town around the main museums.

Ferry agents Blue Star, Amerikís 111 ✆ 22410 22461; Dodhekanisos Navtiliaki, Avstralías 3, by Shell station ✆ 22410 70590, for the Dodekanisos Express catamaran; Inspiration, Aktí Sakhtoúri 4, base of main ferry dock ✆ 22410 24294, for most GA boats to Dodecanese and Cyclades; Tsagaris next door at no. 5, ✆ 22410 28597, handles other GA craft, Blue Star, LANE and the Greek catamaran to Turkey; LANE, Alexándhrou Dhiákou 38 ✆ 22410 33607; Sea Star catamaran, Tárpon Spríngs 14 ✆ 22410 78052 or booth at Mandhráki; ANES, for all Sými catamarans/hydrofoils, Avstralías 88 ✆ 22410 37769. Weekly tourist office departure-schedule handouts are deeply unreliable; authoritative sailing information is available at the limenarhío ✆ 22410 22220 or 22410 28666 on Mandhráki esplanade near the post office.

Internet cafés The most central and competitive of several are Cosmonet, west side of Platía tón Evréon Martýron, and Mango Bar (see "Nightlife" overleaf).

Laundries Central, Erythroú 61, Neohóri; House of Laundry, Erythroú Stavroú 2, Neohóri; Wash & Go, Plátonos 33, old town.

Motorbike rental Low-displacement scooters won't get you very far on Rhodes; sturdier Yamaha 125s, suitable for two people, start at about €22 a day. Recommended outlets in Neohóri include Margaritis, Ioánni Kazoúli 23, with a wide range of late models up to 500cc, plus mountain bikes; Kiriakos, Apodhímon Amerikís 16 (✆ 22410 36047), which will deliver to the old town and take you back once you've finished; or (to roll out in style) Rent a Harley at 28-Oktovríou 80 ✆ 22410 74295 – classic models for two riders start at over €100 per day; for one, about €65.

Post office Main branch with outgoing mail and poste restante on Platía Eleftherías, Mandhráki; mobile office on Orféos, in the old town (service occasionally suspended).

Scuba diving Waterhoppers ✆ & ⒻAX 22410 38146 and Trident ✆ 22410 29160 tout for business nightly at Mandhráki quay; however, days out are expensive – €47 for boat transfer and one dive, €25 for second dive. See box on p.134 for the full story.

Street market Biggest and best for local produce and herbs is on the esplanade just north of the cemeteries, every Wed & Sat 7.30am–2.30pm.

Travel agencies In Neohóri, conveniently located Triton Holidays at Plastíra 9 ✆ 22410 21690, ✉ info@tritondmc.gr is an excellent one-stop option for all local travel arrangements, including car rental, catamaran, ferry and air tickets, plus the catamaran to Turkey. They also have a network of accommodation across the Dodecanese (including Rhodes Town), and can book you an entire itinerary with overnights at attractive rates. Also in Neohóri, Visa Travel Club at Grigóri Lambráki 54 ✆ 22410 33 282, ⓦ www .visatravelclub.gr are worth contacting for overseas charter seats.

Yacht charter French-run Passion Sailing Cruises at Ayíou Fanouríou 65 ✆ 22410 73006, ⓦ www .aegeanpassion.com arranges both bare-boat charter and completely crewed cruises. Yann and Servan have years in the business and their enthusiasm is palpable. Low-season prices (recommended for more comfort at sea) are typically €2100/week bare-boat, €3300/week skippered, for a five-cabin yacht, rising to €3100/week and €4300/week respectively in high season.

Around the island

While it's conceivable to spend an entire vacation within the confines of Rhodes Town, that would certainly be inadvisable. The enormous, diamond-shaped island offers ample scope for a week or so of excursions, and if you're not on an all-inclusive, one-centre package it's recommended that you change your overnight base at least once, given that distances are considerable, despite ongoing road-improvement programmes.

With more consistently wet winters and perennially rich soil, Rhodes could easily feed itself (and export the surplus) if mass tourism were not such a lucrative distraction; the island could also keep its population inebriated indefinitely, with ten million litres of wine produced annually. Unhappily, much of the scenery inland – predominantly arid, scrubby sand-hills in the east and south – has been made that much bleaker by fire-scorched areas extending from Profítis Ilías in the centre to Mesanagrós in the far south.

With the exception of the coast between Líndhos and Yennádhi, tourist facilities are still concentrated in the upper half of Rhodes. What the Italians began, the 1967–74 junta continued, monstrous hotels on the northwest coast between the town and airport being their contribution to posterity. Only during the late 1970s did attention shift to the naturally better-endowed east coast. The process continues slowly as bank loans and official permits allow, with facilities spreading towards the southern tip of the island.

The east coast

Heading down the **east coast** from the capital, you have to go some distance before you escape the crowds from beach hotels at Réni **Koskinoú** and all along Kallithéa Bay, their numbers swollen by visitors on boat tours out of Mandhráki, on scooters or on rental cars. However, once past the excesses of **Faliráki** there is surprisingly little development on this side of the island until you reach **Kálathos** and **Líndhos**, and a fair number of beaches, most of them sandier and more sheltered than anything on the west coast. Incidentally, they face the open Mediterranean, not the windier Aegean, which means that the water tends to be warmer and (usually) cleaner.

Koskinoú

KOSKINOÚ, 7km from Ródhos Town, is famous for the ornate doorways and flower-filled *votsalotó* courtyards of its well-preserved traditional houses. The last bus back, however, is at 9.30pm, so if you've no car you'll have to take a taxi at least one way if you've come out to dine at one of several **tavernas** here, at their best after dark. Doyenne of these is *O Yiannis* in the heart of the old quarter at Vassiléos Yeoryíou toú Dheftérou 23, signed in Greek only. To find it approaching from the coast (rather than inland) road, leave your car or scooter at the eastern square, by the church with the wedding-cake belfry, and take the lane adjacent, heading west. With recently expanded seating into a small courtyard opposite, its stock in trade is abundant *mezédhes* with a Middle Eastern flair, washed down by Émbona wine or *oúzo*; it's very reasonable for Rhodes, and claims to be open daily for dinner all year round.

Thérmes Kallithéas and its beaches

Nostalgia buffs might care to look in at the long-abandoned spa of **Thérmes Kallithéas** (unrestricted access), in a palm grove 3km south of Réni Koskinoú. This is accessible via a signposted side road down through pines, which veers off as soon as the hotels lining Kallithéa Bay pop into sight. If visiting by bus, be sure *not* to get onto a vehicle serving soundalike Kalythiés – this is an inland village reached by an entirely different road.

The present-day spa complex is a prize example of orientalized Art Deco dating from 1928–29, the work of a young Pietro Lombardi, who in his old age designed the European Parliament building in Strasbourg. A pair of swooping staircases, a frequent venue in the past for movie and advertising shots, bracket a six-pillared cupola over a now dried-up pool. The hot springs here were celebrated in antiquity, since Hippocrates of Kós recommended them; whether they have ceased flowing from a natural process or just neglect is unclear. An EU-funded restoration project, begun in 1999, has slowed to snail's pace (if that), with demolition currently more evident than reconstruction, and no date set for completion.

Immediately southeast are several signposted coves, each named after the lunchtime **tavernas** just inland from large patches of sand with sunbeds; the catch is you must cross through or over evocative rock formations to get to the water – wooden boardwalks and ladders are helpfully provided. Each cove/taverna has its loyal partisans; southerly *Nikos* and *Tassos* are the most obvious and popular, but northernmost *Oasis* (supper also June–Aug) fills last and has the nod quality-wise – expect to pay about €23 for a big portion of *yermanós*, beans, roast *fétta* and beer. Off around the headland about 300m to the left as you face the sea is a discreet **nude-gay sunbathing zone** on the rocks.

Faliráki

FALIRÁKI (Ⓦ www.FalirakiBeach.com), at the south end of Kallithéa Bay, has since the early 1990s acquired considerable notoriety as the youth-dominated

---

Scuba diving on Rhodes

The cupola of Thérmes Kallithéas overlooks a small concrete lido giving onto a sandy-bottomed cove, the usual venue for local **scuba diving** programmes. Competing outfitters (see Ródhos Town "Listings", p.132) run daily dive trips here in season, departing Mandhráki at about 9.15am, arriving an hour later, and heading back by 4pm. On offer are a shallow-water, guided "try dive" for the inexperienced, or two deeper dives for those previously certified – count on nearly €70 for a two-dive day, including boat transfer. The more advanced dive, to a depth of just over 12m, explores a cave and tunnel system on the north side of the bay.

As these dives tend to be short and shallow, and the day long, there could easily be scope for a third dive, but scuba instructors confess that two plunges just about exhaust the legal territory of exploration – the confines of this little bay are the sole permitted dive area around Rhodes until further notice. Out of season, at some risk to all concerned, advanced dives at a remote offshore wreck are undertaken by special arrangement.

Snacks (not included) are available on the dive boat or at one of the tavernas noted above, but it's best to bring some food and drink of your own. Diving tends to finish by 2.30pm, but you're more or less stuck here waiting for the boat back as there's no bus service down to Kallithéa spa.

"boozing and bonking" capital of the Dodecanese. Nicknames bestowed on the place by an overwhelmingly British and German clientele have included "Fairly Rocky" or "Feely-Fucky", the latter reflecting the main interest of those in attendance. This unsavoury reputation was emphasized by a string of rapes either side of the millennium and, in August 2003, the fatal stabbing of one British youth and the arrest of several others on charges of public lewdness. It was the inevitable outgrowth of a culture of pub crawls organized by tour reps, many of whom were also arrested and charged for taking kickbacks from bar owners. The British press indulged in an orgy of self-flagellation about "ugly Britons", while local authorities made pious noises about cleaning up the resort, with the alleged malefactors subject to (by the standards of any country, let alone Greece) extraordinarily speedy justice *pour encourager les autres*. The clampdown seems to have exceeded the Rhodian police force's wildest dreams: Faliráki spent most of 2004 as a ghost town, and the party seems to be well and truly over, for now at least.

By day the place still offers the full complement of activities mandatory for such a playpen: bungy-jumping, "sky-surfing", and every imaginable waterborne contraption. So-called "Faliráki North" – with its monstrous hotels and stone-clad, Baroquely kitsch shopping malls – is smarter and more family-orientated. The southern part of the developed strip (where the original fishing village was) is frowsier, while there's also a fair amount of development on the inland side of the busy highway. In slight mitigation, central Faliráki is predominantly low-rise and still fairly low-density, leaving plenty of low-lying ground in which the local mosquitoes breed. There's even a nudist beach at the far south end of it all, in secluded coves beyond a headland. From around here a signposted trail leads to "Anthony Quinn" beach (see below), about forty minutes' walk away.

Practicalities

Given such a self-explanatory, home-from-home environment, specific recommendations for accommodation or restaurants are generally pretty futile. If you decide to take advantage of all the creature comforts by staying here, you may as well be hung for a sheep as a lamb, and splash out at mid-beachfront **hotels** like the *Esperides* (☎22410 85543, ℻85079, ⓦwww.esperia-hotels.gr; ❻), an affiliate of the *Esperia* in Ródhos Town, with particularly good facilities for children, or the nearby *Apollo Beach Hotel* (☎22410 85513, ⓦwww.helios.gr/hotels/apollo-beach; ❼), with lush gardens and recently upgraded bathrooms.

When it comes to eating out, most establishments are predictably plastic, offering either "real English" or faux-ethnic fare; you're here for the **all-day-and-night-life**, not the food. A classic place to start, going from early morning onwards, is *Chaplin's* at the beach, with memorabilia of the Little Tramp and multiple TV screens; after dark the action moves further inland to proper dance venues like *Q Club* and *Frequency*, two of those most likely to survive on "Club Street" running parallel to the Rhodes–Líndhos highway. On the same avenue, *Kelly's Irish Pub* and *The Tartan Arms* are also long-lived but can get a bit rough in the small hours, with punch-ups, muggings (and the odd stabbing or mooning) outside not unknown.

Ladhikó and Afándou

Cape Ladhikó closes off Faliráki to the south; its almost-landlocked, north-facing cove, proclaimed as "**Anthony Queen**" (sic) on certain excursion boat marquees, was a location for the 1961 film *The Guns of Navarone*, and the late Quinn supposedly bought coastal property here. Up close it proves to be harshly pebbly if scenic, with sunbathers staking out odd patches on rock monoliths and availing themselves of a single, limited-fare *kantína* on the clifftop by the car park. Nearly as crowded (even off season) and as scenic, the small, sand and gravel cove of **Ladhikó** to the south has a full-menu fish **taverna**; both bays offer fair to good snorkelling.

South of Ladhikó headland extends the sweeping pebble and sand expanse of **Afándou Bay**, the most undeveloped large beach on the east coast, with just a few stretches of sunbeds and umbrellas. Inland spreads an eighteen-hole **golf course**, the only one in the Greek islands aside from Corfu's, and beyond the coast highway lies Afándou ("the Invisible") village, unobjectionable if not especially memorable. Spare a moment, heading down the main access road to mid-bay, for the atmospheric sixteenth-century **church of Panayía Katho-likí**, paved with a *votsalotó* floor throughout and incorporating fragments of a much older basilica. This ancient monument is currently in poor condition, though very fine frescoes are slowly being cleaned of accumulated mould and soot (votive candles are the main culprit in fresco deterioration). Immediately opposite is a creditable **taverna**, especially good for meat: *Estiatorio Katholiki* (supper Mon–Sat).

The most interesting bit is the far north end of Afándou Bay immediately south of the Ladhikó headland, known as **Traganoú** beach (and signposted as such from the main highway). Beyond the army officers' R&R post of Erimókastro, which overlooks the protected gravel-pebble cove here, are the Traganospília, a trio of **caves** with both land and sea entrance, and freshwater seeps which make the sea cooler than you'd expect. Showers, sunbeds and snacks are offered by a single *kantína*.

Overall, Afándou Bay gets sandier as you head south along it, with umbrellas, sunbeds and showers at intervals, and a largely local patronage. Near the end of the frontage road, you'll find a good **fish restaurant**, *Reni Avantis* (closed Dec), set back from the beach amongst tamarisks; it's resolutely simple, and not cheap for all that, but highly regarded by the islanders for reliable freshness and preparation. Just beyond here, the ominous-looking radio-mast farm belonging to the Voice of America (and others) bars you from going any further; to reach Kolýmbia you must detour through a maze of paved inland lanes.

Kolýmbia and Eptá Piyés

Some 5km south of Afándou on the main highway, the dilapidated church of San Benedetto is your first hint of **KOLÝMBIA**, developed in 1936–38 as a model agricultural scheme by the Italians to house colonists. Identical villa-farmhouses with outsized chimneys and exterior ovens – now much done over by post-1948 occupants – dot the coastal plain to the north of the three-kilometre side road. This avenue, lined with numerous uninspiring hotels and rows of eucalyptus planted by Italians to drain the marshes here, runs east arrow-straight to **Cape Vayiá**. Frankly, the eucalyptus trees lend the place most of its character; otherwise it's a fairly tatty resort, made all the more so by successive vacant, boarded-up commercial premises decimated by a run of poor tourist seasons. Upon reaching the sea, a left fork quickly ends at the edge of Afándou beach, with sweeping views north to Ladhikó point; bearing right at this T-junction takes you past a small, rocky cove with a fish **taverna** (*Tò Limanaki*) to the more picturesque and protected south beach at the base of Tsambíka promontory (see opposite), dominated by the *Golden Odyssey* hotel. The best beachfront **hotels** here are *Irene Palace* (☎22410 56202, ⓦwww.irenepalace.gr;

⑤) and the *Kolymbia Beach* (☎ 22410 56311, ⓦ www.helios.gr/hotels/kolymbia-beach; ⑤), both with well-tended gardens extending down to the sea.

Eptá Piyés

Heading inland from Kolýmbia junction on the main highway, it's a four-kilometre walk or drive to **Eptá Piyés** (Seven Springs), a densely forested oasis with a tiny dam created by the Italians to irrigate their Kolýmbia colony. Refreshments are provided by a rather characterless snack-bar, formerly the oldest (1948) full-service taverna on the island until a disastrous 2001 refit.

A trail and a rather claustrophobic Italian **aqueduct-tunnel** both lead from the vicinity of the springs, with their geese, ducks and shrieking peacocks, to the reservoir. The 186-metre tunnel is strictly one way, with just a single widened passing point and air vent about halfway through – not for claustrophobes. The reservoir at the far end is more of a deep pond, with no prohibitions (as yet) against diving in.

Tsambíka: monastery and beach

The enormous, Gibraltar-like mass of **Tsambíka**, 26km south of Ródhos Town, is actually the eroded flank of a once-much-larger mountain. From the highway, a steep, 1500-metre-long, cement-paved side road terminates at a small car park and taverna, from which 297 concrete steps lead up to the summit monastery of **Panayía Tsambíka** (300m elevation), offering unrivalled views along some 50 km of coastline. It's unremarkable except for the happier consequences of the September 8 festival, when barren women make the climb – sometimes on their hands and knees – to pay homage to an eleventh-century icon and then ingest a small piece of the wick from one of the shrine's lamps. Any children born afterwards are called Tsambikos or Tsambika, names that are particular to the Dodecanese – and common enough to confound sceptics. At any time of the year the little chapel is crammed full of waxen and metal *támmata* (ex votos) in the shape of infants, left by those desirous of offspring – and the wall is festooned with snaps of the resulting toddlers.

From the top you survey Kolýmbia just to the north, and shallow **Tsambíka Bay** on the south side of the headland; of all Rhodian beaches, this warms up earliest in the spring, and teems all summer with watersports enthusiasts and people sheltering under their rental umbrellas. The entire area is owned by the Orthodox Church and thus protected from any development other than the paving of the two-kilometre road (no bus service) down to the bay, and a single, permanent taverna to complement the seven *kantína* caravans (and like number of "watersports") which between them stake out most of the bay.

Much the best **taverna** in the area is *Panorama Tsambikas*, one of a cluster on the climbing grade of the main highway south of the beach turning. The patri-arch mans the grill, turning out good if pricey fish and meat; it's very popular on weekend afternoons with Rhodians. The same family keeps **studios** across the road (☎ 693 72 32 010; ②).

Arhángelos and Stegná

More facilities can be found at **ARHÁNGELOS**, a large inland village 29km from Ródhos Town whose inhabitants perennially figure in island jokes as dim yokels. The place is overlooked by a crumbling fifteenth-century castle, and was formerly home to a much-touted crafts tradition, though only one high-boot cobbler and one potter survive. The courtyard of the main church, with an enormous *votsalotó* surface dating back to 1845, is the only remarkable sight. Though you might explore the warren of alleys between the main road and the citadel, Arhángelos is now firmly caught up in German package tourism, with a full quota of "mini-markets" and jewellery stores, as well as a **bank** and **post office** amongst the commercial life of the single main thoroughfare.

Stegná, three rather steep kilometres by road below Arhángelos, is the closest **beach**, with lots of German-pitched **rooms** beginning to outnumber the summer cottages for locals that straggle along for a kilometre or so to a minuscule fishing anchorage and the most Greek of the local **tavernas** under some trees, *To Periyiali*. The road-fringed beach is sand and gravel but punctuated with rock outcrops; *Ouzeri Pitropos* partway along also gets some islander clientele.

Haráki, Ayía Agáthi and Kálathos

A more convenient overnight base on this stretch of coast is **HARÁKI**, the pleasant, if undistinguished, two-street fishing port of inland Malóna village, overlooked by the stubby ruins of Feraklós castle. Originally a Byzantine fortress, this served as the Knights' initial toehold on Rhodes in 1306, later as a POW compound, and was the last of their strongholds to fall to the Ottomans. **Accommodation** here consists of about twenty self-catering studio outfits overlooking the pedestrianized esplanade; quieter establishments likely to have on-spec vacancies include *Savvas* (T22440 51287; ❸), towards the castle, *Joanna Studios* (T22440 51031; ❸), on the front, or *Yeoryia* (T22440 51170; ❸), at the south end of things near the *Argo Restaurant*. This fish specialist in an Italian-era building is the most upscale choice here; amongst other **tavernas**, Greeks tuck into fish at *Maria's*, while *Makkaroni* (sic) is an Italian-run pizza and pasta specialist.

There's swimming off the reasonable town beach if you don't mind an audience from the row of waterfront cafés and tavernas, but most people head north to the secluded **Ayía Agáthi** beach. Contrary to expectations, this cannot be accessed from the castle road: you have to backtrack 700m out of the village to a separate, signposted dirt side road, and then proceed another 800m to the short but broad sandy bay, full of hermit crabs, overlooked by the chapel of Ayía Agáthi on the far (north) hillside. The beach here is no secret by any means – there are three *kantínas*, wall-to-wall sunbeds and watersports on offer – but more permanent development seems to have come a cropper, with numerous unfinished and abandoned building sites on the adjacent hillsides.

Kálathos, the next inland settlement beyond Mássari, has little intrinsic character – merely being a roadside collection of services and bland eateries aimed at the growing number of foreign villa-owners in the area – but the nearby beach of **Paralía Kaláthou** is another matter. Even in peak season you should find a spot to yourself along this four-kilometre extent of pristine sand and gravel, with clean water offshore and the usual smattering of wooden boardwalks, brollies and strategically placed showers on shore.

Líndhos

LÍNDHOS, the island's number two tourist attraction, erupts from barren limestone surroundings 12km south of Haráki. Like Ródhos Town, its charm is heavily undermined by commercialism and crowds of up to half a million visitors in a "good" year. At midday dozens of coaches park nose-to-tail on the narrow southerly access road, with even more on the drives down to the beach. Back in the village itself, those few vernacular houses not snapped up by package operators have, since the 1960s, been bought up and refurbished by wealthy British – including the likes of the late newspaper astrologist Patric Walker, Pink Floyd stars David Gilmour and Roger Waters – plus numerous Italians. The old *agorá* or serpentine high street presents a mass of fairly indistinguishable bars, crêperies, mediocre restaurants and travel agents. Although high-rise hotels have been prohibited inside the municipal boundaries, it's still a relentlessly mercenary theme park, hot and airless from June to August, and quite ghostly in winter since the village has scarcely any life apart from tourism. Local Greeks have long since converted or sold off their homes for tourist purposes and moved to nearby Péfki, appearing only by day to milk the cash cow of tourism.

However, all is not gloom and doom, as recent developments have forced Líndhos to partially reinvent itself. Several tour companies cut back their presence in the late 1990s, and as a result the resort has moved marginally more upmarket. Partly empty aeroplanes also mean that Líndhos is currently a good spot to snag tickets back to the UK; availability is often posted in travel agency windows (see p.143). And if you arrive before or after peak season (or peak

Rhodian village houses

Vernacular rural houses on Rhodes, and to a great extent those on the nearby islands of Tílos, Hálki, Níssyros and Kós, share certain basic characteristics. These are due to the matrilineal system of inheritance, still common in the Dodecanese, whereby the eldest daughter traditionally got the family house upon marriage. The father was also obliged to build similar houses for any younger girls; this made it inadvisable to build costly, involved structures when so many might be required.

In its simplest form, the surviving **Rhodian village house** interior is a single, undivided, one-storey rectangle or *monóhoro*, built of stone and earth, usually with a corner fireplace indicated from outside by a beaked chimney. Opposite the fireplace, along the rear wall, is a raised sleeping platform or *soufás*, with storage cupboards underneath and an embroidered curtain or *spervéri* around it. This longer wall is usually devoted to racks displaying the celebrated Rhodian collections of decorative plates, both imported and locally made. Depending on room size, the space is often divided either widthwise or lengthwise by a soaring arch; this helps support a flat roof, traditionally made of Anatolian cedar beams resting on the wall tops. The gaps in between are filled with successive layers of wild olive or oleander shoots, calamus reeds, seaweed and, finally, hard-packed special earths called *aspropília* or *patélia*, with the walls extending up to form a low surrounding parapet or *koumoúla*.

In wealthier villages, such as Koskinoú and Lahaniá, the basic *monóhoro* unit, often used only on formal occasions, is found at the rear of an elongated, enclosed courtyard. Auxiliary buildings, such as kitchens, ovens, stables, olive presses and (built much later) toilets, flank the courtyard, which is paved in pebble mosaic (*votsalotó* or *hokhláki*) and entered via a *pyliónas* or ornate doorway. Líndhos represents the most elaborate development of this trend, with considerable money and effort expended on the *votsalotó* (often present inside the rooms as well), high, carved ceilings with painted planks as well as shrub branches or reed canes, and exceptionally ornate *pyliónes* adorned with braided relief work reflecting Frankish or Arab influences. Directly above the *pyliónes* can often be found the so-called "captain's room", from which the master of the house used to watch activity at the north harbour, or scan the horizon for pirates. Though of course such elaborate houses are no longer being built, locals cherish their pebble-courts, which need periodic maintenance – and there are still enough of them around to keep a number of mosaic craftsmen in regular employment.

hours – before 10am, after 4pm), when the pebble-paved streets between the immaculately whitewashed houses are relatively empty of people and donkeys shuttling up to the acropolis, you can still appreciate the beautiful, atmospheric setting of Líndhos.

The post-Byzantine **Panayía church** is covered inside with well-preserved eighteenth-century frescoes. The most imposing fifteenth- to eighteenth-century **captains' residences** (see box p.139) are built around *votsalotó* courtyards, their monumental doorways or *pyliónes* often fringed by intricate stonework, with the number of braids or cables supposedly corresponding to the number of ships owned. Several are open to the public, most notably the **Papakonstandis Mansion**, which is the most elaborate, and now home to an unofficial museum.

The acropolis – and its history

On the 115-metre bluff looming above Líndhos, reached via cypress-shaded rampways, the **acropolis** (summer Mon 12.30–6.40pm, Tues–Sun 8am–6.40pm; rest of year Tues–Sun 8.30am–3pm; €6) represents a surprisingly felicitous blend of ancient and medieval culture, though the Knights of St John destroyed a considerable quantity of the surviving Hellenistic structures by quarrying them for use in fortification. Danish scholars were the first to excavate sympathetically here, from 1902 until 1913; subsequent Italian work here was (as in Ródhos Town) slipshod, introducing lots of destructive iron-work, and the ongoing Greek-run restoration programme is set to run until at least 2008.

Once through the tower-gate and associated structures built by the Knights, you ascend two flights of monumental steps separated by the photogenic colonnade of a **Hellenistic stoa** before reaching a high platform with the rudiments of a propylaia, or monumental gate, and the far more substantial **Doric Temple** of Athena Lindia, assiduously restored since the early 1980s but still under scaffolding indefinitely. The unusual southwest-to-northeast orientation was dictated by the limited triangular area of flat ground on the summit, here tapering to its apex. Visiting sites as close as possible to dawn or dusk is always good advice, and here even more so for the sake of sweeping views: north to Tsambíka and Fáraklos, south to the gaunt cliffs hemming in St Paul's Bay.

Before the founding of ancient Rodos in 408 BC, Lindos, with its 16,000 inhabitants, was the most important settlement on the island, thanks to its natural defences – the acropolis is a sheer drop on all sides except the north-erly approach – and the two excellent harbours nestling beneath the cliffs. The surrounding craggy countryside was as infertile then as it is now (though there was – and is – excellent spring water, collectible on the fig-tree square), and the population was forced to look to the sea for a living, with an enormous fleet trading as far as present-day Spain; the local tradition of boat-building contin-ued well into the nineteenth century. As if in corroboration, a fifth-century BC (some say Hellenistic) relief of a trireme clings to the rock face, on the left at the base of the stairs leading up to the castle gate.

Though the ancient city of Lindos and its original temple date from at least 1100 BC, the first stone temple was erected by the tyrant Kleoboulos in the sixth century BC and replaced by the present structure after a 342 BC fire. The word "tyrant" had not then assumed its modern, pejorative overtones; Kleoboulos was actually revered as one of the Seven Sages of antiquity, and to him was attributed the Delphic inscription MHΔEN AΓAN ("Nothing in Excess", usually mistranslated as "Moderation in All Things"). The only other

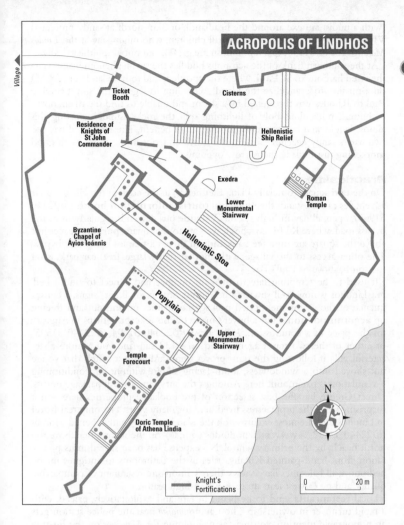

easily found trace of the ancient town is a tiny **theatre** at the south end of the modern village, on the way to the northerly St Paul's beach, carved into the living rock on the southwest slope of the acropolis.

A 45-minute walk east of town, starting from the lane just below *Mavrikos Restaurant*, brings you to the headland and chapel of **Áyios Emilianós**. The latter was originally a round, stone-built tomb, purportedly that of Kleoboulos but actually dating from the first century BC.

Local beaches

Líndhos' principal **north beach**, once the main ancient harbour, is overcrowded in season and possibly less than one hundred percent salubrious until the sewage treatment plant, courtesy of the EU, is completed. Guaranteed cleaner and quieter swimming is to be had one cove beyond at **Pállas** beach (with a nudist annexe around the headland), or 3km north at sandy, protected **Vlyhá** bay, best for families with small children, who might stay at the *Lindos Mare* (☎ 22440 31130, ⊚ www.lindosmare.gr; ❼), laid out amphitheatrically.

At the southern flank of the acropolis huddles the small, phenomenally well-sheltered harbour of **St Paul**, where the apostle is said to have landed in 58 AD on a mission to evangelize the island. According to legend, the ship bringing Paul to Rhodes was threatened by a storm and unable to find the main, north harbour; a miraculous bolt of lightning split the rocks asunder, creating this almost landlocked bay expressly for the saint's benefit. The elongated bay has two partly sandy beaches – one at the north end, one at the south, with good snorkelling just outside the narrow opening.

Practicalities

On the **taxi** square (officially Platía Eleftherías) at the edge of the village, as far as vehicles can go, stands the municipal **tourist information booth** (☎ 22440 31900), open all day in high season. A shuttle bus descends regularly from the bypass road, where KTEL coaches leave you, to the square; **parking** spaces just above the square are on a fee basis, though there's a free lot up on the bypass. The other access to the village, with another (fairly large, free) car park, is on the south, above St Paul's Bay.

It used to be tempting fate to turn up on spec and expect to find a bed, but Líndhos is now well sown with "Room/Studio for Rent" signs, a consequence of those aforementioned package companies pulling out and freeing up **accommodation**. Thus a buyer's market exists (except perhaps in August); for the price of a commission, *Pallas Travel* (☎ 22440 31494, ⓕ 22440 31595) or either of the two travel agents cited on p.132 can find you a more characterful villa if following the signs proves unrewarding. Just watch that you're not shoved into a windowless, south-facing studio without air conditioning – ventilation is paramount here. Amongst the surviving British package outfits, Direct Greece has the best selection of pre-bookable properties here – not surprising since the proprietress lived here for many years. The only real **hotel** in Líndhos, and the most exclusive on the island, is the recently opened *Melenos* (☎ 22440 32222, ⊚ www.melenoslindos.com; ❽), on the second tier above the north beach, by the primary school. No expense has been spared in its preparation, from hand-painted Kütahya tiles in the bathrooms to antiques in the bedrooms; all balconies have views, there's an on-site restaurant of comparable quality, and by ❽ we mean up to €300 in high season.

Local **restaurants** tend to be bland in fare and exploitatively priced, with a rapid turnover in ownership. Though *Arhondiko* near the police station gets an honourable mention, you may as well plump for *Mavrikos* on the fig-tree square, founded in 1933 and in the same family ever since. *Mezédhes* like *manoúri* cheese with basil and pine nuts are accomplished, as are *tour de force* mains like skate terrine with pine nuts and vinegar syrup, cuttlefish in wine sauce or *soupiórizo* (arborio rice with squid ink, onion and black pepper), the Lindhian "national" dish, finishing off with a digestif of red-mulberry-flavoured *soúma*. Dipping into the excellent Greek wine list could add up to €18 a bottle to the typical food charge of €23–28 per person. For **snacks and desserts**, try respectively *Il Forno*, an Italian-run bakery, and *Gelo Blu*, still the best of several *gelaterie* here despite the departure of its Italian founders; it also does excellent baked goods and pies, all of which can be enjoyed in an attractive courtyard. Formal **nightlife** consists of perhaps a half-dozen music bars on the main high street; no point in citing names, as these tend to change every season.

The better of two **Internet cafés** is well-equipped Lindianet, with helpful staff and fast connection; Sheila Markiou's The Link is a unique combination of laundry and secondhand bookshop (Mon–Sat 9am–8pm). Líndhos has one amenity that would be the envy of much larger towns: a **spa** (Mon–Sat 1–9pm), offering the full range of services including all-day packages. Local **car rental** rates can be thirty percent less than in Ródhos Town, though accordingly choice in models may be limited. There are two **banks** with ATMs, as well as a **post office**. Among the more useful **travel agents** are Lindos Suntours (℡22440 31333), offering metered phones (call boxes tend to have huge queues) and charter seats back to the UK, as does Village Holidays (℡22440 31486).

The west coast

Rhodes' **west coast** is the windward flank of the island, so it's damper, more fertile and more forested; windmills, first introduced by the Italians, irrigate crops from the high water table. Most beaches along the often abrupt, cliff-hemmed shoreline are exposed and decidedly rocky, but this hasn't deterred touristic development; as in the east, the first few kilometres of the busy coast road southwest from the capital have been surrendered entirely to industrial tourism. From Neohóri's aquarium down to the airport, the shore is fringed by periodic clusters of 1970s-vintage mega-hotels, though such places as **Triánda** (8km from the city centre), **Kremastí** (12km along) and **Paradhísi** (15km) are still nominally villages, and appear so in their centres.

This was the first part of the island to be favoured by the package operators, and tends to be frequented in summer by a decidedly sedate clientele that often can't be bothered to stir far from the pool. Several local deluxe hotels remain open during the winter, coining a few extra euro from the convention and seminar trade (though not providing anything like full service). But for more enterprising tourists, neither the fierce prevailing winds (beach umbrellas consistently point seaward), the planes buzzing over Paradhísi, nor the giant, exhaust-billowing power plant at Soroní, offer much inducement to pause.

Ixiá and Triánda

If it weren't for Ródhos' town-limits sign, you wouldn't be able to tell when you'd left the capital – on the coast road, at least – and entered **IXIÁ**, where most of the island's deluxe **hotels** cluster. Of these, the *Miramare Wonderland* (℡22410 96251, Ⓦwww.bluegr.com; ❽; open late March–Oct), 5km along, is the most idyllic, consisting of fake-vernacular bungalows in a landscaped setting just behind the beach lawn. They're painted in traditional red, ochre and *louláki* (powder blue), with tasteful mock-antique furnishings and Jacuzzis in some tubs. The complex is so huge that a private mini-railway salvaged from a British mine shunts guests from one end to the other. The on-site, poolside restaurant, *Gulliver*, is unusually good for a hotel and fuses Greek with international notions to good effect.

Among other local **tavernas**, *Ta Kioupia*, 3km inland at Trís hamlet (℡22410 91824 for reservations; closed Sun), attracts a clientele of foreigners and Athenians, particularly well-heeled celebrities, who tend to go into ecstasies over its cuisine (weekly changing, arty *mezédhes*, no fish); however, there's long been a feeling that it's overrated and – at €38 minimum per head set menu – overpriced.

In similarly developed, contiguous **TRIÁNDA**, confusingly (and officially) called Ialyssós (but see below), the beach – harsh shingle – could be better. Windy Triánda hosted some preliminary **windsurfing** training and events for the 2004 Olympics, and has long supported a number of outfitters and schools such as Oxbow (T 22410 91666) and Pro Horizon on the beach.

Ancient Ialyssos and around

At the central junction in Triánda, you can make a detour inland for the five-kilometre ride up to the site of **ancient Ialyssos** (Mon–Sat 8am–6.40pm, Sun 8.30am–2.40pm; €3) on flat-topped, pine-covered Filérimos hill; *Filérimos* means "lover of solitude" and is named after the Byzantine hermits who founded a monastery here in the tenth century. Though only 267m above sea level, this has always been a strategic point; the Knights installed themselves here during their campaign to oust the Genoese, and from its Byzantine castle Süleyman the Magnificent also directed the 1522 siege of Rhodes.

Foundations of third-century-BC **temples to Zeus and Athena**, built atop a far older Phoenician shrine, sprawl just west of the monastery church, while below, further towards the car park, lies the partly subterranean church of **Aï-Yeórgis Hostós**, a simple, barrel-vaulted structure containing fourteenth- and fifteenth-century frescoes. These are unfortunately not as vivid or well preserved as those at Thárri or Asklipió (see p.151 & p.152), but scenes from the life of the Virgin are just discernible on the right (south) vault, while ones from the Christ's Passion, such as the *Scourging and Mocking*, appear opposite. Just southeast of the parking area, a hillside Doric fountain with a columned facade was only revealed by subsidence in 1926 – and is now off limits owing to another landslip, which has covered it again.

Filérimos monastery

Heavily damaged during fighting between Italians and Germans in autumn 1943, the **Filérimos monastery** on view today is for once not just an Italian job, but also the result of postwar restoration by the British and Greeks. Despite the questionable methods of the original 1930s Italian work, the existing structure is beautiful, consisting of an asymmetric chapel built in stages. Behind several rib-vaulted chambers lies a small, low-slung cloister overgrown with bougainvillea, while an early cruciform baptismal font embossed with the Cross of the Knights is sunk in the open space south of the balconied belfry. The northernmost chamber (rear far left as you enter the church) features a tessellated Paleo-Christian mosaic floor, contemporary with the font outside.

As a concession to the Rhodian faithful, the church alone *may* be open after hours, but as the guards make clear you are to light your candles, drop your coins in the box, do reverence to the icon of the Virgin and make a swift exit.

The cross of Filérimos

Southwest of the monastery and archeological zone, a **Via Crucis** (Way of the Cross), its fourteen Stations marked out by copper plaques in the Italian era, leads to an enormous concrete crucifix. This has replaced an original, which the Italians erected in September 1934, and destroyed seven years later to prevent Allied airmen using it for navigation during air raids. Today's cross, built in 1995, is almost identical to the original, standing just under 18m tall with a narrow staircase inside; you're allowed to climb out onto the cross-arms for a supplement to the already amazing view. Illuminated at night, the

crucifix is clearly visible from the island of Sými and – perhaps more perti-
nently – "infidel" Turkey across the straits.

Kremastí, Paradhísi and Theológos

KREMASTÍ, back on the coast and 4km beyond Triánda, is notable for its
gargantuan church, equally enormous barracks and schoolhouse, funded by
expatriate Rhodians in America, and for its festival on August 15–23, one of
the biggest in the Dodecanese, with a street fair, amusement park, and dancing
on the last day.

The airport village of **PARADHÍSI**, literally just outside the terminal, is
often visited when departing flights get delayed. You might even have to – or
want to – **stay** the night, especially if catching a typically early-morning flight
to Kássos or Kastellórizo. Two *dhomátia* places, both within a 500-metre walk of
the airport car park, are *Anastasia* at Alexándhrou Ipsilándou 3 (℡22410 81810;
❷) or *Yiordanis Kladhitis* in the next side street parallel (℡22410 81224; ❷).

The relatively calm village of **THEOLÓGOS**, 6km beyond Paradhísi and
then 1km inland, has a growing beach-resort annexe consisting of a half-dozen
or so **hotels**, best equipped of these being the A-class *Alex Beach* (℡22410
82422, ✉alexb@hol.gr; ❺), at the end of the developed strip and indeed
the southernmost hotel on this coast. The beaches themselves are reasonable,
presumably maintained by the hotels. About the only independent **eatery**
hereabouts is *Mezedhopolio Alliotiko*, between Theológos beach district and the
Soroní power plant.

Ancient Kameiros

Just over 12km southwest of Theológos, the important archeological site of
Kameiros was, together with ancient Lindos and Ialyssos, one of the three
Dorian powers that united late in the fifth century BC to found the powerful
city-state of Rodos. Soon eclipsed by the new capital, Kameiros was abandoned;
only in 1859 was it rediscovered, then completely excavated after 1929.

As a result, it is a particularly well-preserved Doric townscape, doubly worth
visiting for its beautiful, pine-clad hillside location (Tues–Sun: summer 8am–
6.40pm; winter 8.30am–2.40pm; €4). While none of the individual remains
are spectacular, you can pick out the foundations of two small temples, the re-
erected pillars of a Hellenistic house, a late Classical fountain, and the *stoa* of
the upper agora complete with Archaic water cistern. This upper terrace gives
the best overview of the site, much of which is now off limits – pathways tend
to go around rather than through it. Kameiros had no fortifications, nor was
there an acropolis – partly owing to the gentle slope of the site, and also to
the likely settlement here of peaceable Minoans, specifically the half-legendary
prince Althaemenes. Unlike Rodos, Lindos and Ialyssos, Kameiros was primarily a town of farmers and craftsmen, a profile borne out by rich finds now in
the Rhodes archeological museum and the British Museum.

Practicalities

RODA public buses (see "Travel Details", p.158) provide minimal links in
season from Ródhos Town, dumping you at the base of the short but steep
access road. If arriving under your own steam (more likely), park so that
you won't be hemmed in by the phalanxes of tour coaches which inevitably show up later. On the beach below ancient Kameiros there are several
tavernas, very commercialized but ideally placed if you're waiting for one
of the three daily buses back to town. If you're willing to walk 4km east to

KALAVÁRDHA, you'll find departures much more frequent, since besides having its own service this is where the bus routes descending from Sálakos meet the west coast road. Kalavárdha also has the best, sandiest **beach** on the west coast, though this isn't obvious from the highway – a short side road goes there.

Kámiros Skála

There are more restaurants clustered 15km south at **KÁMIROS SKÁLA** (occasionally rendered "Skála Kámiros" or the more pedantically grammatical "Skála Kamírou"). This tiny anchorage is somewhat inexplicably the hapless target of coach tours in search of an "authentic fishing village" – as credit card stickers in the windows of several **tavernas** attest. Best of these is said to be *O Loukas*; otherwise, proceed 400m southwest to off-puttingly named **Paralía Kopriá** ("Manure Beach"), where *Psarotaverna Johnny's* has good non-farmed fish and *orektiká* – it's been "discovered" and is pricier than before, but still worth a stop.

Less heralded is the daily **kaïki to Hálki**, which leaves Monday to Saturday at 2.30pm, weather permitting, and returns early the next morning; on Wednesdays and Sundays day-trips depart at 9am and arrive back at 6pm. The Wednesday services tend to be packed out by package transfers between the two islands (see p.158 for information on return departures). A 1.30pm bus service from Ródhos Town west-side terminal, and a 7.30am departure from Kritinía, are each designed to dovetail with *kaïki* departures/arrivals.

Kritinía: castle and village

A couple of kilometres south of Skála, the local castle, officially signposted as **Kástro Kritinías** but locally known as "Kastéllo", is from afar the most impressive of the Knights' rural strongholds; its access road, though paved from both approaches, is too narrow and steep for tour buses. With only a chapel and a rubbish-filled cistern more or less intact inside, Kástro Kritinías proves close up to be no more than a shell – but a glorious shell, with fine views west to assorted islets and Hálki. You make a "donation" to the intimidating old woman manning the car park booth, in exchange for fizzy drinks, seasonal fruit or flowers if she's in the mood.

KRITINÍA itself, 3km east, is a quiet hillside village of white houses, with a traditional **kafenío** (*Platanos*) and a taverna edging the central sea-view square, below the main church. The name stems from its supposed foundation by emigrants from Crete (*Kríti* in Greek). An interesting **folklore museum** full of rural oddments and costumes stands just north of the village on the main bypass road, housed in a grandiose, purpose-built round structure (unpredictable hours).

Around Mount Akramýtis

Beyond Kritiniá, the main road winds south through dense forest on the lower slopes of **Akramýtis**, Rhodes' second-highest and arguably most beautiful mountain ridge; along with Atávyros peak, just northeast, it has been proposed since 1994 as a nature reserve by the local Association for the Protection of the Environment. Non-walkers can make a road circuit of the mountain by using the dirt track signposted for the rural chapel and festival grounds of Zoödhóhou Piyís – keep going until you emerge on the Monólithos–Foúrni road (see opposite).

Siánna and Glyfádha

SIÁNNA, just east of the 825-metre summit, claims to be the most attractive mountain settlement on the island; the village is less controversially famous for its aromatic pine-and-sage honey and *soúma*, a grape-residue distillate similar to Italian grappa but deceptively smooth. This is produced in most Greek wine-making districts with varying degrees of legality – typically distillation is allowed for just 48 hours per year, in October; on Rhodes its manufacture remains legal owing to an Italian-era licence which continues to be honoured. Bus tours call in at the church on the main square, which contains heavily restored eighteenth-century frescoes. Several **tavernas** on the through road announce themselves (along with their honey and *soúma*) conspicuously.

Despite their touristic inclination, they're probably a better bet for a meal than anything at **Glyfádha**, reached by a twisty, six-kilometre side road heading seaward about 1500m before Siánna. The ride is green and scenic, arrival a thumping anticlimax: a grubby shingle shoreline presided over by a ruined medieval tower, the power company's cables making a dive for their trip to Hálki, and a pair of cheap-and-grumpy, down-at-heel **tavernas** purveying stale seafood – if they're even open.

Monólithos and Foúrni

The tiered, flat-roofed farmhouses of **MONÓLITHOS**, 4km southwest of Siánna at the end of the public bus line, are scant justification for the long trip out here. Food at the four **tavernas** (the most civil and affordable of these being *Christos Corner*) can be indifferent owing to undemanding tour-group trade, but the view over the bay is striking, and you could use the village as a base by staying in advertised **rooms** (❶) or at the *Hotel Thomas* (☎22410 22741 or 22460 61291; ❷), its 2002-refurbished, fair-sized rooms belying a grim exterior. Diversions in the area which make showing up worthwhile include yet another **Knights' castle** 2km west of town (unrestricted access), photogenically perched on a 200-metre-high pinnacle (the "monolith" of the village name) but enclosing even less than Kástro Kritinías.

Some five paved but curvy kilometres below the castle lie assorted sand-and-gravel beaches at **Foúrni**. The 400-metre extent of the main cove by the car park is unadorned except for a handful of loungers belonging to the drinks-and-ice-cream *kantína*. For more privacy, there are good, secluded coves to the right (west), while dedicated naturists can head off to an even more isolated easterly bay. This is accessed by a rough path climbing to a saddle at the base of the headland closing off the main beach, followed by a quasi-cross-country scramble off the ridge into a little stream valley draining to the shore. From there, you can clearly see three east-facing cavities on your right, towards the end of the promontory, under a stubby tower. These may well be the *foúrni* (ovens) of the place name, supposedly **caves** hollowed out by early Christians fleeing persecution. They may in fact have been catacombs, as they're far too conspicuous to have been effective hideouts; in any case they've been Christianized with incised crosses. You can swim to rock-cut steps leading up to them, or reach them more perilously overland via the headland.

The interior

Inland Rhodes is hilly and still mostly wooded, despite the recent depredations of arsonists. You'll need your own vehicle to see its highlights, especially as enjoyment resides principally in getting away from it all; no single site justifies the tremendous expense of a taxi or the inconvenience of trying to make the best of the sparse-to-nonexistent bus schedules.

In retrospect it will probably be the soft-contoured, undulating scenery which stands out, along with the last vestiges of agrarian life in the villages, some barely mustering three-digit populations. Most people under retirement age are away working in the tourist industry, returning only at weekends and during winter. The young that do remain behind stay largely to help with the grape harvest in late summer. If you have time to spare, and a bit of Greek at your command, traditional hospitality in the form of a drink at the *kafenío*, or perhaps more, may still be found.

Petaloúdhes: the "Butterfly Valley"

The only highly publicized tourist "attraction" in the island's interior is **Petaloúdhes** or the "Butterfly Valley" (daily: May–Sept 8.30am–sunset; April & Oct 9am–3pm; admission €3–5 depending on season). Actually a rest-stop for Jersey tiger moths (*Panaxia quadripunctaria*), during July and August it might more accurately be christened the "Valley of the Tour Buses".

In all of Greece, only here and at a similar valley on Páros do these moths come to live out the final phase of their life cycle, attracted for unknown reasons by the oriental sweetgum (*Liquidamber orientalis*) trees that flourish in this steep-sided canyon. Peak arrival time is July to mid-September, when the moths roost in droves on the trees in order to conserve energy for mating; they cannot eat during this stage of their lives, and die soon afterwards. Against the tree trunks, the moths are a well-camouflaged black and yellow, but flash cherry-red overwings in flight. On no account should you clap or shout to scare them into flight, as this causes stress and interferes with their reproduction.

Visiting the valley

Petaloúdhes is reached by a seven-kilometre paved side road bearing inland from the west coast road between Paradhísi and Theológos. Some 2km before Petaloúdhes, the **microwinery** (15,000–20,000 bottles annually) of Anastasia Triandafyllou is well worth a stop for its Athiri whites, muscat rosés and blended reds (daily 9am–7pm); the vineyards just uphill are tended organically.

The canyon itself is divided into two roughly equal sections by a road crossing it, with an admission booth for each – one ticket is valid for both parts. Whether the "butterflies" are abundant or not, it's worth visiting just for the sake of the peaceful valley; the Rhodians certainly think so at weekends, packing out the fairly reasonable **taverna** by the parking area just below the lower section. Seats by the pondside café, just below the upper section of ravine, are also at a premium. An enjoyable trail threads the length of the valley shaded by conifers as well as the sweetgum trees, repeatedly crossing a non-potable stream on rough-hewn wooden bridges. It's a surprisingly brisk 45-minute walk in total; flip-flops or similar footwear won't do.

From the lower taverna, the paved road continues uphill 5km to **PSÍNTHOS** – tucked into a depression in the hills, where the Italians decisively defeated the Turks on May 17, 1912 – which offers a number of **tavernas** suitable for lunch. Generally the best and most reasonable (around €16 a head) of these, at the edge of the village, is the friendly *Piyi Fasouli*, serving excellent grills (goat, *soúvla*, etc) and appetizers as well as a few *mayireftá* of the day, with tables under the plane trees by the namesake spring.

Afterwards, follow signs downstream to visit a nearby aquarium dedicated to captive specimens of *Ladigesocypris ghigii* (**gizáni** in Greek), a rare, now-protected fish of Rhodian mountain streams, about the size of a sand smelt, found only here and at Eleoússa.

Around Profítis Ilías

At an elevation of 798m, Profítis Ilías is Rhodes' third-highest summit, and its most lushly forested. The Italians endowed the area with a number of their typical follies, and several villages in the surrounding foothills also merit brief halts.

From Psínthos, you can proceed 14km southwest via Arhípoli – the road badly deteriorated – to **ELEOÚSSA**, nestled in the shade of the dense forest at the east end of Profítis Ilías' ridge. Originally built (1935–36) by the architects Petrarcho and Bernabiti as the model agricultural village of **Campochiaro**, it can't rank as one of their more inspired efforts. The hilltop square is flanked by the grandiose former summer residence of the Italian governor, now derelict, plus a huge Italian-built church, with intervening arcaded structures now used as a high school and military post. On the outskirts of town, heading west, is an enormous circular pool with a fountain in the middle, now home to more *gizáni* fish. On the northwesterly outskirts, *To Steki* makes a wise, inexpensive **taverna** stop, best for grilled meat and *mezédhes*, with seating under the trees; it's open in winter too, with a fireplace inside.

Head directly west out of Eleoússa, past the circular pool, for 3km and you'll reach the late Byzantine, four-apsed church of **Áyios Nikólaos Foundouklí** (St Nicholas of the Hazelnuts; open all day). Locals descend in force for picnics at weekends at the partly shaded site adjacent, with a fine view north over cultivated valleys; the frescoes inside, dating from the thirteenth to fifteenth centuries, have been blurred by damp and could use a good cleaning, but various scenes from the life of Christ are recognizable.

Continuing west beyond the church along the mostly paved main road brings you finally to **Profítis Ilías** itself, where a pair of 1930-built chalet-hotels, the *Elafos* and the *Elafina* (now used exclusively as children's summer camps), hide in deep woods below the road running just north of the summit; a café/snack-bar across the road is generally open in summer. The **monastery** of Profítis Ilías in the walled compound next to the ex-hotels does not itself exactly hum with traffic except around the day of the annual festival; over the gateway, a relief plaque shows Elijah being fed in the wilderness by a raven.

Local walks and Sálakos

The peak of Profítis Ilías itself is an off-limits military watchpoint, but there's still scope for an hour-long loop-walk on its slopes, using graded and stepped paths originally laid out by the Italians, with fine views north to Sými and Turkey. For a satisfying **ridge walk**, leave vehicles at the westerly sign announcing the "hamlet", and take the track leading up to another pair of Italian-era buildings: the governor's summer villa and a ransacked church. From behind the latter, a stepped trail leads up to the watershed in about fifteen minutes. Turn left or northeast (right dead ends outside the military installation) and proceed until, at the first glimpse of a telecoms installation ahead, the stair-path dips down and left. You continue to follow the ridge, more or less, gradually losing altitude, until you swerve back southwest just before reaching the phone tower, passing a ruined barracks en route to the two follies.

Another popular local walk follows the zigzagging path that begins next to the chapel of Áyios Andónis, below the Profítis Ilías monastery, and descends within 45 minutes to the upper edge of Sálakos village. However, this route is much easier to find going up; the departure point is well signposted near the western edge of town. There's just one critical left fork, about 200m uphill from the point where you leave a cement drive, and faint red paint splodges put you right thereafter; allow an hour going uphill.

The heart and soul of friendly **SÁLAKOS** is a small, pedestrianized roadside *platía*, where an Italian fountain shares space with the tables of several "café-snacks"; the most traditional of these is Mihalis Svourakis' *To Steki* and (for a fuller meal of vegetables and omelette) *Kyria Meni*. During the mid-1990s, the village attempted to capitalize on its Nymph brand of spring water; an old Italian mansion adjoining the bottling plant was revitalized as the *Nymph Hotel Restaurant Café* (℡22460 22206; ❸), though it rarely opens, and you shouldn't count on so much as a coffee here, let alone a room, outside of July or August. The Profitis Ilías area can also be easily approached from Kalavárdha on the west-coast road, via Sálakos.

Around Mount Atávyros

All tracks and roads west across Profitis Ilías converge upon the road up from Kalavárdha bound for **ÉMBONA**, a large and architecturally nondescript village backed up against the north slope of 1215-metre **Mount Atávyros**, roof of the island. Émbona, with its rather meat-oriented tavernas (of which *Panayiotis Bakis* on the outskirts is best, and least likely to be swamped by groups), is more geared to handling tourists than you might expect from its unprepossessing appearance, since it's the venue for summer "Greek nights" and daytime wine-tasting excursions from Ródhos Town.

The village lies at the heart of the island's most important grape-growing and **wine-producing** districts, owing to a combination of granitic soil and cooling sea breezes. CAIR – the vintners' cooperative originally founded by Italians in 1928 – produces a variety of acceptable mid-range wines at its two plants near the capital. However, products of the smaller, family-run Emery winery (℡22460 41208; daily in season 9am–4.30pm) at the village outskirts are much more highly esteemed, as are those of the Alexandhris microwinery in the centre.

To see what Émbona would be like without tourists, carry on clockwise around the mountain past modern, nondescript **Artamíti monastery** (population three or four young monks) – its name a corruption of "Artemis" after a pagan temple in the forests nearby – to less-celebrated **ÁYIOS ISÍDHOROS**. This has as many vines and tavernas as Émbona (all near the central church), a more open feel, and the trailhead for the five-hour return ascent of 1215-metre Atávyros.

This path, beginning at the very northeastern edge of the village, is the safest and easiest way **up the mountain**; sources advocating the steep, cross-country scramble up from Émbona should be disregarded. Look for the wooden placard reading "Arhí Monopatioú" ("Start of Path") at the beginning of a bulldozer track; follow this about 200m to the first hairpin turn, where the trail begins obviously behind a crude, wire-fastened gate in the fence. The route has been consolidated and marked with the occasional red-paint arrow or splodge. Most of the mountain itself is bare, except for some enormous oaks (and a wind-power farm) on the lower slopes, but dense, unburnt forests extend to the east, beyond Artamíti. Your reward for reaching the summit, besides the expected views, are extensive foundations (fenced off but gate open) of an ancient Zeus temple, next to a rather incongruous radar "golf ball" of the Greek Air Force.

Láerma and Thárri monastery

The road from Áyios Isídhoros to Siánna is paved, as is the twelve-kilometre stretch from Lárdhos on the east coast to Láerma, but not the often appalling track that curves for 12km east from Áyios Isídhoros to Láerma, though even the latter is worth enduring if you've any interest at all in Byzantine monuments and Orthodox monasticism.

LÁERMA itself is an attractive inland village with a handful of **tavernas**, including a *psistariá* under two plane trees in the square. But the area's main attraction is **Thárri monastery**, lost in pine forests four well-marked kilometres south. The oldest religious foundation on the island, this was re-established as a community of monks (currently numbering twenty, including some English-speaking ones) in 1990 by the charismatic abbot Amfilohios, educated at Pátmos. Since then he has built up a miniature ecclesiastical empire centred on several repopulated nunneries and monasteries in southern Rhodes, which actively train monks for service in other islands and nations (especially Africa). Somewhat less admirably, the apostolic mission includes the fanatically Orthodox television station ΘAPPI, whose programming consists largely of nationalistic drama series, video footage of monastic churches and interviews with His own Beatitude.

Visitors will find the striking **katholikón** (open daily, all day; smocks provided for the "indecently" attired), consisting of a long nave and short transept surmounted by barrel vaulting, of more immediate interest. Various cleanings during the 1990s restored damp-smudged **frescoes** dating from 1300 to 1450 to their original exquisite glory. Currently the most distinct are those in the transept depicting the Evangelists Mark and Matthew (in the south squinches) plus the Archangel Gabriel engaged in *The Annunciation* (north), while the nave boasts various acts of Christ, including such rarely illustrated scenes as the *Storm on the Sea of Galilee* (north side of vault), *Meeting the Samaritan at the Well* and *Healing the Cripple* (both south).

The monastery, dedicated to the Archangel Michael, supposedly takes the name "Thárri" from its foundation legend. A princess, kidnapped and abandoned here by pirates, was visited in a dream by the Archangel, who promised her eventual deliverance. In gratitude, she vowed to build as many monasteries in his honour as the gold ring cast from her hand travelled in cubits. This she did but, upon being reunited with her parents, the ring was lost in some bushes. Thus "Thárri" is derived from *tharró*, "I think/guess", after the family's futile search for the heirloom, or perhaps from *thárros*, "courage, mettle". In their pique, apparently only this one community was founded.

The far south

South of a line connecting Monólithos and Lárdhos, you could easily begin to think you had strayed onto another island. Gone are most of the multi-star hotels (except for a large concentration around Kiotári), and with them the bulk of the crowds; lacking too are most other tourist facilities and public transport. Only one or two weekday buses (in season) serve the exceptionally depopulated villages here (though Yennádhi has much better service), approaching along the east coast where deserted beaches are backed by sheltering dunes. Seasonal tavernas and daytime beach-bars grace the more popular stretches of sand, but aside from the package resorts of **Lárdhos**, **Péfki** and **Kiotári** there are still few places to stay.

Lárdhos, Stafýlia and Péfki

Beachfront development – both hotels and a new generation of villa projects aimed at foreign owners – mushrooms either side of **LÁRDHOS** village, solidly on the tourist circuit despite an inland position between Láerma and the peninsula culminating in Líndhos. Numerous shops and tavernas flank the central junction where roads head off towards Láerma, Péfki and the south coast. Situated downstream from some of the most fire-ravaged territory on Rhodes, the village endured catastrophic floods during rainy winters following the 1980s blazes.

The beach 2km south of Lárdhos is coarse gravel and dull; you might continue another 3km to **Glýstra** cove, a delightful, 200-metre crescent of dark sand speckled with fine gravel, sunbeds, showers, kayak rental and a snack-bar. It does, however, get packed out in season, with insufficient parking. Just past the turning for Glýstra, another road leads to quieter, straighter **Stafýlia** beach and its two **hotels**, both open April to October. The somewhat basic *Stafýlia* (℡22440 47113, ℱ22440 47310; ❹) is a long, narrow complex whose main asset is a beachfront setting and whose main liability are mosquitoes (insist on a unit with screens). Next door in a well-landscaped plot so extensive that guests have to be ferried about in golf carts, the *Lindian Village* (℡22440 47361, ⓦwww.lindianvillage.gr), completely overhauled in 2004, is bidding to become Rhodes' most exclusive resort. There are three grades of accommodation behind the narrow but protected beach and pool area: standard double bungalows (€350), top-floor junior suites with Jacuzzi deck (€500), and ground-floor suites with private pool and double baths (€650). At those rates, designer furnishings are all state of the art, and there are four in-house restaurants to choose from plus a spa and gym.

Four kilometres east of Lárdhos, on the coastal road to Líndhos, **PÉFKI** (Péfkos on some maps) began life as the garden annexe and overflow for the latter, but is now a fully fledged package resort in its own right, popular with both short- and long-term foreigners who prefer the natural beauty and open vistas to the perceived claustrophobia of Líndhos. The sea is cleaner than at Lárdhos, with a largish main beach as well as small, well-hidden coves which are getting harder to find with all the clifftop development. **Accommodation**, predominantly in villas, is almost totally controlled by package operators; tavernas are bland and unmemorable.

Asklipió and Kiotári

Nine kilometres beyond Lárdhos, a paved side road heads 3.5km inland to **ASKLIPIÓ**, a sleepy village guarded by a crumbling **Knights' castle** and graced by the Byzantine church of **Kímisis Theotókou** (open daily 9am–6pm; €1). The building dates from 1060, with a ground plan nearly identical to Thárri's, except that two subsidiary apses were added during the eighteenth century, supposedly to conceal a secret school in a subterranean crypt.

The **frescoes** in the nave here are in far better condition than those at Thárri, owing to the drier local climate; they are also a bit later, though some sources claim that the final work at Thárri and the earliest here were executed by the same artist, a master from Híos. Their format and subject matter, though common on nearby Cyprus, are rare in Greece: didactic "cartoon strips" which extend completely around the church in some cases, featuring extensive Old Testament stories in addition to the more usual lives of Christ and the Virgin. On the upper right of the vault there's a complete sequence of Genesis episodes, from the *Creation* to the *Expulsion from Eden*; note the comically menacing octopus among the fishes in the panel of the Fifth Day, and Eve subsequently being fashioned from Adam's rib. On the north wall the career of the Prophet Daniel is elucidated, complete with lions' den. A seldom-encountered *Revelation of John the Divine* takes up most of the south transept, while an enormous Archangel Michael dominates the north transept, with sword in right hand and a small soul being carried to judgement in his left. *Votsalotó* flooring decorates both the interior and the vast courtyard.

Two adjacent buildings (formerly the priest's quarters) now house separate **museums** (open same hours): a small exhibit of ecclesiastical treasures (donation requested) and a more compelling folklore gallery in an ex-olive mill crammed with rural oddments and antiquated, belt-driven machinery. Asklipió's other concession to tourism is the **restaurant-bar** *Agapitos* overlooking the central car park and church; they also have a few **rooms** (☎22440 43235; ②) for those not requiring a coastal base.

Kiotári

Just beyond the detour for Asklipió, the beachfront hamlet of **KIOTÁRI** was in fact Asklipió's original site, until Byzantine-era piracy compelled the residents to retreat inland. For years it was virtually unknown to outsiders – in part because it wasn't even shown on most maps – but during the mid-1990s the Orthodox Church elected to sell off its vast landholdings here, and Kotári rapidly became Rhodes' southernmost outpost of (mostly Teutonic and Italian) mass tourism. Luxury mega-hotels sprout uphill from the broad, sandy beach of Kiotári "**North**", but for **rooms** right on the water look no further than the *Paraktio Beach Apartments* (☎22440 47278, ⊛www.Paraktio .com; ④) and the mirror-image *Sea Breeze Apartments* (☎22440 47011, ⊛www .seabreeze-rhodes.com; ③) next door. Both are package-free, air conditioned and built to a high standard; *Paraktio* in particular has a mix of galleried four-person apartments and studios for couples, each with superb view-terraces and adjoining the pleasant adjoining snack-café.

Kiotári "**South**", reached by following the shore frontage road or its own "exit" from the main highway, still just clings to a Stegná-like identity as a summer annexe for locals, who've built simple cottages here. The beach is gravelly but fine for a dip; rock formations and a small offshore reef lend the coast a bit of definition. A half-dozen **tavernas** are scattered along this entire coast. "North" offers *Mourella*, equal parts bar and eatery: go as much for the stylish environment in a raised courtyard, and service, as for the food, which (while creditable) is bumped up in price. *Stefanos*, in Kiotári "South", is more Greek in feel and menu.

Yennádhi and Váti

At **YENNÁDHI**, 4km further south, a dark-sand and gravel beach extends for kilometres in either direction. It's clean and serviceable, with the usual sunbeds, boardwalks, showers and rudimentary watersport gear available, plus three **tavernas** just behind the most central and accessible part of the shoreline, reached by a paved access drive signposted as "Yennádhi Beach". Most popular of these is *Klimis*, though it isn't the same since Klimis and his wife retired, and you're advised to send back the oven chips the current management tries to fob foreigners off with. On summer Sundays, at least one "all day **beach bar**" (such as *Sundance*; 10am–10pm) sets up shop nearby, to the delight of local youth.

The rather drab outskirts of Yennádhi mask the attractive older village core inland, where many houses are being bought up and restored. Various amenities include a **post office**, **car rental**, café-bars and some **accommodation** – pick of this being *Effie's Dreams* at the northern end of things (T 22440 43410, W www .effiesdreams.com; ❸), poised between a fountain fed by a 4000-year-old cave and the resulting oasis. The serviceable studios upstairs all overlook the orchards, and have a loyal repeat clientele; returned Greek-Australians Effie and her brother Phillip also keep a lively bar, **Internet** café and breakfast salon downstairs.

They can also assist in locating the key-keeper for **Ayía Anastasía**, the village cemetery-church 300m northwest through the oasis. Though the present, barrel-vaulted structure dates from the late fifteenth century, it's built on sixth-century foundations – and covered inside with post-Byzantine **frescoes** in a naïve style not seen elsewhere on the island. On the ceiling are scenes from the life of Christ and the young Virgin, and the martyrdom of Anastasia; in the conch of the apse there's a Virgin *Platytera* and *Communion of the Apostles*, while on the west wall's Last Judgment, Jews and Beelzebub are shown together in the River of Fire draining into Hell's Mouth.

From Yennádhi, a good road heads 7km inland, past baby pines slowly greening up a fire-blasted landscape, to the oasis village of **VÁTI**. Here, the better of two **tavernas** is *To Petrino*, also doubling as the central *kafenío*; it's not cheap, and service declined under new management in 2004, but it's still locally esteemed (especially at weekends) for country-style offerings such as spicy *revíthia* soup and roast suckling pig.

Lahaniá and southeast beaches

South of Yennádhi, you'll see more fine if lonely beaches, often marked just by isolated "taverna-rooms" which function in peak season only. Some 10km from Yennádhi, then 2km inland along a side road, invisible from the sea and thus pirate-safe, **LAHANIÁ** village, with its smattering of rooms, is a possible base. Nearly half of the 140 inhabitants are bohemians from the UK and Germany, who since the 1980s have opened craft shops and restored many handsome houses – abandoned after a postwar earthquake – lining the hilly streets in exchange for long-term rent-free occupation. On the main square, strangely sited at the lower, eastern end of the village, *Taverna Platanos* can arrange accommodation and offers reasonable and appetizing **meals** – mains, two starters and a beer for €15 – with seating under the trees between two wonderful fountains, one retaining an Ottoman inscription, and the church of **Áyios Yeóryios** (Sun noon–5pm), whose tiered belfry was pulled down in 2004 (it's to be re-erected). The alternative, up on the village through-road, is the *Akropol Chrissis Taverna*, run by the amiable, bear-like priest Papa Yiorgos, and offering good *mezédhes*; he also rents out **rooms** or even entire **restored houses** (T 22440 46033; ❷–❸).

You can go directly from Lahaniá to **Plimýri**, an attractive, sandy bay backed by dunes, with swimming in the clean, brisk water marred only by strong afternoon winds; the only facility is a single, indifferent **taverna** (*Plimirri Beach*) serving a limited menu. More compelling is the sixteenth-century **church of Zoödhóhou Piyís**, adjacent (interior open May–Oct Sun only noon–5pm), which has ancient Corinthian columns upholding the rib vaulting in its west porch.

Áyios Pávlos, 5km beyond Hokhlakás, is not even a hamlet, merely the current name for the now-derelict Italian model farm complex (built 1936) of San Marco, complete with church and belfry. From here an unmarked, fair-quality dirt road leads southeast 5km to the little monastery of **Áyios Yeóryios**, which lends its name to the local beaches. Heading straight another

1500m brings you to the broadest sandy bay just beyond dunes and low junipers, extending for 2km south of **Cape Yermatá**. Though it's one of the last turtle-nesting sites in the Dodecanese, efforts to protect it came to nought, and building is beginning on the cape. Bearing right at the monastery and continuing 2km on a rougher track – best have a jeep – takes you to a more sheltered fantasy cove, with higher dunes and gently shelving sea.

Kattaviá and Prassoníssi

Shortly beyond Áyios Pávlos the road threads through low stands of windtormented dwarf juniper before entering **KATTAVIÁ**, nearly 90km from the capital, marooned amidst fields of wheat or barley which are the only crops that thrive locally. Several **tavernas**, pricier than you'd expect, preside over the junction, shaded by sycamore figs, that doubles as the village square; the most interesting of these is brightly coloured *Martine's Bakaliko/Mayeriko* (closed Thurs), run by folk from Lahanía, which has vegetarian dishes and homemade desserts. A **filling station** – the first since Kiotári – and a few **rooms/studios** to rent, aimed mostly at windsurfers (read on), complete the list of facilities. Like so many villages in the far south, many of the houses here are seasonally occupied at best, their owners having emigrated to find work in Australia or North America.

From Kattaviá a paved road leads through a frequently used military exercise area to **Prassoníssi**, Rhodes' southernmost extremity and a mecca for European **windsurfers**. The sandspit that tethers Prassoníssi ("Leek Island") and its lighthouse to Rhodes was breached by currents to form a channel in 1996, but enough remains to create flat water on the east side and up to two-metre waves on the west, ideal for different ability levels. Of the two windsurfing centres operating here, Polish-run Prasonisi Center (April–Oct; ☎22440 91044, ⓦwww.windsurfing-rodos.com) is keener and friendlier. They're geared up for one-week packages (from €160 full rental plus €160 for 10hr private instruction), lodged in rooms (☎22440 91030; ④) above the *Lighthouse/Faros Restaurant*, one of two eateries and a half-dozen accommodation outfits here. There aren't enough rooms to go around during peak season, when the scrubby junipers rustle with tents and caravans despite signs forbidding the practice.

Mesanagrós and Skiádhi Monastery

From Lahaniá, an alternative route heads 9km northwest along a narrow but paved road to the picturesque hilltop village of **MESANAGRÓS**. This already existed by the fifth century AD, if the foundations of a ruined basilica at the village outskirts are anything to go by. Within this vast area, amid patches of mosaic flooring, squats a smaller but equally venerable thirteenth-century chapel; any previously existing frescoes are long gone, but there's a *votsalotó* floor and stone barrel arches to admire. You can fetch the key from the nearby *kafenío*, and buy a candle and/or a coffee as a donation.

The monastery of Skiádhi

The onward road to the **monastery of Skiádhi**, 6km distant, is shown incorrectly on most maps. Take the Kattaviá-bound road initially, then after about 2km bear right onto an unsigned dirt track; these last 4km are quite rough, but even the puniest rental car can get through in dry conditions.

Known formally as Panayía Skiadhení, the monastery – despite its undistinguished modern buildings – was originally founded in the thirteenth century to house a miraculous icon of the Virgin. In the fifteenth century a heretic

155

Greek script table

Rodhos (Town/Island)	Ρόδος	ΡΟΔΟΣ
Afándou	Αφάντου	ΑΦΑΝΤΟΥ
Akándia	Ακάντια	ΑΚΑΝΤΙΑ
Akramýtis	Ακραμύτης	ΑΚΡΑΜΥΤΗΣ
Apolakkiá	Απολακκιά	ΑΠΟΛΑΚΚΙΑ
Apóllona	Απόλλωυα	ΑΠΟΛΛΩΝΑ
Arhángelos	Αρχάγγελος	ΑΡΧΑΓΓΕΛΟΣ
Arhípoli	Αρχίπολη	ΑΡΧΙΠΟΛΗ
Arnítha	Αρνίθα	ΑΡΝΙΘΑ
Asgoúrou	Ασγούρου	ΑΣΓΟΥΡΟΥ
Asklipió	Ασκληπιειό	ΑΣΚΛΗΠΙΕΙΟ
Atávyros	Ατάβυρος	ΑΤΤΑΒΥΡΟΣ
Ayía Agáthi	Αγία Αγάθη	ΑΓΙΑ ΑΓΑΘΗ
Áyios Emilianós	Άγιος Αιμιλιανός	ΑΓΙΟΣ ΑΙΜΙΛΙΑΝΟΣ
Áyios Isídhoros	Άγις Ισίδωρος	ΑΓΙΟΣ ΙΣΙΔΩΡΟΣ
Áyios Nikólaos Foundouklí	Άγιος Νικόλαος Φουντουκλή	ΑΓΙΟΣ ΝΙΚΟΛΑΟΣ ΦΟΥΝΤΟΥΚΛΗ
Áyios Pávlos	Άγιος Πάυλος	ΑΓΙΟΣ ΠΑΥΛΟΣ
Áyios Yeóryios Várdhas	Άγιος Γεώργιος Βάρδας	ΑΓΙΟΣ ΓΕΩΡΓΙΟΣ ΒΑΡΔΑΣ
Dhimyliá	Διμυλιά	ΔΙΜΥΛΙΑ
Eleoússa	Ελεούσα	ΕΛΕΟΥΣΑ
Émbona	Έμπωνα	ΕΜΠΩΝΑ
Eptá Piyés	Επτά Πηγές	ΕΠΤΑ ΠΗΓΕΣ
Faliráki	Φακιράκι	ΦΑΛΙΡΑΚΙ
Filérimos	Φικέριμος	ΦΙΛΕΡΙΜΟΣ
Foúrni	Φούρυοι	ΦΟΥΡΝΟΙ
Glyfádha	Γλυφάδα	ΓΛΥΦΑΔΑ
Haráki	Χαράκι	ΧΑΡΑΚΙ
Hokhlakás	Χοχλακάρ	ΧΟΧΛΑΚΑΣ
Ialyssós	Ιαλυσόρ	ΙΑΛΥΣΟΣ
Ixiá	Ιξιά	ΙΞΙΑ
Kalamónas	Καλαμώνας	ΚΑΛΑΜΩΝΑΣ
Kálathos	Κάλαθος	ΚΑΛΑΘΟΣ
Kalavárdha	Καλαβάρδα	ΚΑΛΑΒΑΡΔΑ
Kalythiés	Καλυθιές	ΚΑΛΥΘΙΕΣ
Kameiros	Κάμειρος	ΚΑΜΕΙΡΟΣ
Kámiros Skála	Κάμειρος Σκάλα	ΚΑΜΕΙΡΟΣ ΣΚΑΛΑ
Kápi	Κάπι	ΚΑΠΙ
Kattaviá	Κατταβιά	ΚΑΤΤΑΒΙΑ
Kiotári	Κιοτάρι	ΚΙΟΤΑΡΙ
Kollákio (Collachium)	Κολλάκιο	ΚΟΛΛΑΚΙΟ
Kolóna	Κολόνα	ΚΟΛΟΝΑ

stabbed the painting, allegedly causing blood to flow from the wound in her cheek; the fissure, and suspicious brown stains around it, are still visible. As in all such legends, the offending hand was instantly paralysed.

The immediate surroundings of Skiádhi are rather dreary since a comprehensive fire in 1992, but the views west are stunning. Tiny **Khténia islet** is said to be a petrified pirate ship, transformed into stone by the Virgin in answer to prayers from desperate locals about to experience yet another raid.

Kolýmbia	Κολύμπια	ΚΟΛΥΜΠΙΑ
Koskinoú	Κοσκινού	ΚΟΣΚΙΝΟΥ
Kremastí	Κρεμαστή	ΚΡΕΜΑΣΤΗ
Kritinía	Κρητηνία	ΚΡΗΤΗΝΙΑ
Ladhikó	Λαδικό	ΛΑΔΙΚΟ
Láerma	Λάερμα	ΛΑΕΡΜΑ
Lahaniá	Λαχανιά	ΛΑΧΑΝΙΑ
Lárdhos	Λάρδος	ΛΑΡΔΟΣ
Líndhos	Λίνδος	ΛΙΝΔΟΣ
Malóna	Μαλώνα	ΜΑΛΩΝΑ
Mandhráki	Μανδράκι	ΜΑΝΔΡΑΚΙ
Maritsá	Μαριτσά	ΜΑΡΙΤΣΑ
Mássari	Μάσαρη	ΜΑΣΑΡΗ
Mesanagrós	Μεσαναγρός	ΜΕΣΑΝΑΓΡΟΣ
Monólithos	Μονόλιθος	ΜΟΝΟΛΙΘΟΣ
Mónte Smith	Μόντε Σμίθ	ΜΟΝΤΕ ΣΜΙΘ
Neohóri	Νεοχώρι	ΝΕΟΧΩΡΙ
Paradhísi	Παραδείσι	ΠΑΡΑΔΕΙΣΙ
Pastídha	Παστίδα	ΠΑΣΤΙΔΑ
Péfki	Πεύκοι	ΠΕΥΚΙ
Petaloúdhes	Πεταλούδες	ΠΕΤΑΛΟΥΔΕΣ
Platánia	Πλατάμια	ΠΛΑΤΑΝΙΑ
Plimýri	Πλημμύρι	ΠΛΗΜΜΥΡΙ
Prassoníssi	Πρασονήσι	ΠΡΑΣΟΝΗΣΙ
Profítis Ilías	Προφήτηρ Ηλίας	ΠΡΟΦΗΤΗΣ ΗΛΙΑΣ
Psínthos	Ψίνθος	ΨΙΝΘΟΣ
Pylónas	Πυλώνας	ΠΥΛΩΝΑΣ
Réni Koskinoú	Ρένι Κοσκινού	ΡΕΝΙ ΚΟΣΚΙΝΟΥ
Rodhíni	Ροδίνι	ΡΟΔΙΝΙ
Sálakos	Σάλακος	ΣΑΛΑΚΟΣ
Siánna	Σιάννα	ΣΙΑΝΝΑ
Skiádhi Monastery	Μονή Σκιάδι	ΜΟΝΗ ΣΚΙΑΔΙ
Soroní	Σορωνή	ΣΟΡΩΝΗ
Stafýlia	Σταφύλια	ΣΤΑΦΥΛΙΑ
Stegná	Στεγνά	ΣΤΕΓΝΑ
Thárri Monastery	Μονή Θάρρι	ΜΟΝΗ ΘΑΡΙ
Theológos	Θεολόγος	ΘΕΟΛΟΓΟΣ
Thérmes Kallithéas	Θέρμες Καλλιθέας	ΘΕΡΜΕΣ ΚΑΛΛΙΘΕΑΣ
Triánda	Τριάντα	ΤΡΙΑΝΤΑ
Tsambíka	Τσαμπίκα	ΤΣΑΜΠΙΚΑ
Váti	Βάτι	ΒΑΤΙ
Vlyhá	Βλυχά	ΒΛΥΧΑ
Yennádhi	Γεννάδι	ΓΕΝΝΑΔΙ

The southwest coast and Apolakkiá

West of Kattavía, the paved island loop road emerges onto the deserted, **southwest coast**; Skiádhi can easily be reached from this side too, as the still-dirt road up from here is better signposted than from Mesanagrós. This coast is "deserted" because beaches here are poor and rubbish-strewn, with crashing waves and often a strong undertow; the only amenity is a single taverna about 4km south of Apolakkiá.

The nearest inland village, 7km north of the Skiádhi turning, is nondescript, agricultural **APOLAKKIÁ**, set amid plastic greenhouses and its famous watermelon patches, and also equipped with a few shops and tourist facilities. Several **tavernas** and *kafenía* surround the central junction, where there always seem to be a few stopped motorists perusing maps. Northwest leads to Monólithos, due south back to Kattaviá, while the northeasterly bearing is a paved road cutting quickly back to Yennádhi via Váti – and the evidence of blazes from the late 1980s and early 1990s.

Áyios Yeóryios Várdhas

A few hundred metres along the northeast road to Yennádhi, a signposted paved side road heads north to a new irrigation reservoir that's absent from many maps, but plainly visible from Siánna overhead. The best reason to detour here, however, is to visit the tiny country chapel of **Áyios Yeóryios Várdhas**, arguably the finest remote Byzantine monument on Rhodes. After 3km, with the dam looming overhead, bear left onto a signposted dirt track, veer left again when you see an electricity substation, and then almost immediately right again (following another sign) up a steep turning. After a total 3.8-kilometre journey from the main road, you'll see the shed-like chapel (always open) by the roadside. Its thirteenth- to fourteenth-century frescoes, smudged but wide-eyed and warmly naïve in style, include a fine *Entry to Jerusalem* and *Presentation of the Infant Jesus* on the right (south) wall, a *Panayía Glykofiloússa* (Virgin Kissing the Christ Child) on the left wall, plus what seems to be a personification of Faith, Hope and Charity on the left wall, behind the altar screen.

Travel details

Island transport

Buses

With some exceptions just southeast of Ródhos Town, RODA buses serve points on the west coast, while KTEL buses ply the east coast. The schedules below, keyed to workdays, are sharply reduced at weekends. Fares are usually €1.60–3.70 one way, and never more than €5.60. Journey times vary from 10 to 15 minutes for Koskinoú to almost 2hr for Kattaviá in the far south.

RODA

New Market (Néa Agorá) to: airport (Paradhísi; 25 daily 4.45am–11pm); Émbona (3 daily); Kalavárdha (9 daily 4.45am–9.30pm); Faliráki (26 daily 6.45am–11pm); Kritinía via Kámiros Skála (Mon–Fri 1 daily at 1.30pm, Sat 2 daily at 8am & 2pm); Koskinoú (8 daily 6am–9pm); Monólithos (Mon–Fri 1 daily at 1.30pm, returns following morning); Petaloúdhes (2 daily at 9.30am & 11.30am); Sálakos (5 daily 4.45am–9.30pm); Theológos (14 daily 5.50am–10.40pm).

KTEL

Platía Rimínis (aka "Sound & Light Square") to: Afándou (13 daily 6.45am–9.15pm); Arhángelos (13 daily 6.45am–9.15pm); Haráki (2 daily at 10am & 4.30pm); Kiotári (8 daily 6.45am–7.30pm); Kolýmbia (5 daily 9am–7.30pm); Lárdhos (9 daily 6.45am–7.30pm); Líndhos (14 daily 6.45am–7.30pm); Mássari (4 daily 9am–2.30pm); Péfki (9 daily 6.45am–7.30pm, involves change of bus in Líndhos); Psínthos (2 daily at 2.30pm & 5.30pm); Yennádhi (8 daily 6.45am–7.30pm).

Inter-island transport

Kaïkia and excursion boats

Kámiros Skála to: Hálki (Mon–Sat 1 daily 2.30–2.45pm, Sun 2 daily at 9am & 6pm; 1hr 15min). NB The *kaïkia* each carry several cars (not that you need one on Hálki). Wed & Sun departures may occasionally be fully booked by Hálki package clients and thus unavailable for independent travellers. The boats wait for the arrival of the bus from Ródhos Town, which is usually delayed in traffic.

Mandhráki to: Sými (at least 1 daily at approximately 9am on either *Symi II* or *Panormitis*, usually stopping at Panormítis monastery first; returns about 3.45pm).

NB If these are *ekdhromikó* (excursion sailings) rather than *epivatikó* (scheduled sailings), you are not allowed to bring full luggage onto these craft, and if detected you will be barred from boarding.

Ferries

Rhodes (Kolóna) to: Alexandhroúpoli (1 weekly on LANE; 28hr); Astypálea (1–2 weekly on GA; 9hr); Crete (3–4 weekly on LANE to Áyios Nikolaos & Sitía; 10hr 15min–12hr 45min); Hálki (3–4 weekly on LANE; 2hr); Híos (1 weekly on LANE; 11hr 30min); Kálymnos (5 weekly on GA, 1 on LANE; 5hr 30min–8hr); Kárpathos (3–4 weekly on LANE to Dhiafáni & Pigádhia; 4hr 30min–5hr 30min); Kássos (3–4 weekly on LANE; 6hr 45min); Kastellórizo (1 weekly on LANE or GA; 4–5hr); Kós (5 weekly on GA, 4 on BS, 1 on LANE; 3hr–6hr 30min); Léros (5 weekly on GA, 2 on BS; 4hr 30min–9hr); Lésvos (1 weekly on LANE; 15hr); Límnos (1 weekly on LANE; 21hr 30min); Níssyros (3 weekly on GA; 5hr); Pátmos (5 weekly on GA, 2 weekly on BS; 5hr 45min–9hr 30min); Pireás (5 weekly on GA, 2 weekly on BS; 11hr 30min–20hr); Sámos (1 weekly on LANE; 9hr); Sými (2–3 weekly on GA; 1hr 30min); Tílos (3 weekly on GA; 2hr 30min–4hr).

Catamarans

Four high-speed catamarans or high-speed boats operate out of Rhodes: the *Dodekanisos Express*, also known as *O Spanos* after the supermarket chain which owns it, the *Sea Star*, the *Panormitis* and the *Symi II*.

Rhodes (Mandhráki) to: Hálki (2 weekly, usually Tues & Sat; 1hr 15min); Tílos (at least daily June 15–Oct 1, usually 9am; 1hr 20min); Níssyros (2 weekly, usually Mon & Fri; 6hr including layover on Tílos). Provided by *Sea Star* (unreliable, no cars carried).

Rhodes (Mandhráki) to: Sými (at least daily, typically at 9am or 6.30pm; 50min). *Epivatikó* service provided by *Panormitis* or *Symi II* (no cars carried).

Rhodes (Kolóna) to: Kálymnos (6–7 weekly; 3hr 15min); Kastellórizo (1 weekly June–Oct 15; 2hr 30min); Kós (6–7 weekly; 2hr 30min); Lipsí (3–4 weekly; 4hr 30min–5hr 30min); Pátmos (3–4 weekly; 5hr); Sými (2–3 weekly; 50min). All services provided by *Dodekanisos Express*, departing daily at 8.30am (reliable, carries 4–5 cars and larger number of motorbikes).

Hydrofoil

ANES provides an *epivatikó* hydrofoil service to Sými from Mandhráki west quay at least daily. See Sými "Travel Details", p.213, for a full summary of sailing patterns.

Flights

Rhodes to: Astypália (2–3 weekly; 2hr 10min); Athens (4–5 daily on Olympic, 4–6 daily on Aegean; 1hr); Iráklion, Crete (4–10 weekly on Olympic; 55min); Híos (2 weekly; 55min–1hr 45min); Kárpathos (2–3 daily; 35min); Kássos (1–2 daily; 1hr 15min); Kastellórizo (5 weekly; 40min); Kós (2–3 weekly; 40min); Léros (2–3 weekly; 1hr 25min); Límnos (3–5 weekly; 2hr 15min–3hr 45min); Sámos (2 weekly; 45min); Thessaloníki (6–9 weekly on Olympic, 1–2 daily on Aegean; 1hr 20min–2hr 10min).

International transport

Ródhos Town to: Marmaris, Turkey (up to 2 daily catamarans, May–Oct, departing 8am (Greek) & 4pm (Turkish); 50min–1hr. One-way €46 per passenger including taxes, same-day return €53, open return €71. A Turkish car ferry appears only by request and costs a whopping €230 return for a vehicle. Tsagaris Travel at Aktí Sakhtoúri 5 is the agent for the Greek vessel; Anka Travel at Gallías 13 in Neohóri (☏22410 26835) is the central agent for Turkish vessels. All bookings must be made with passport in hand the day before.

[NB Passenger service to Cyprus and Israel is currently suspended owing to security restrictions.]

2

The southern Dodecanese

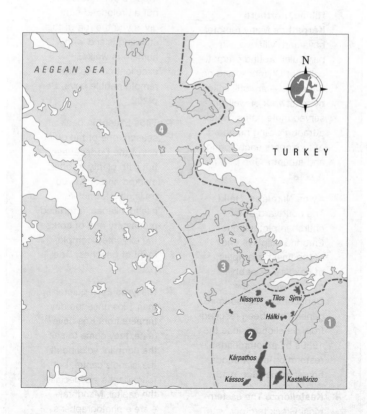

CHAPTER 2 # Highlights

✻ **East coast beaches, Kárpathos** Small, white sand and gravel beaches on the sheltered east coast of Kárpathos approach Caribbean quality with the clarity of their turquoise water. See p.173

✻ **Hiking, northern Kárpathos** Many remoter bays and villages – in particular around dramatically set Ólymbos, and on Saría islet – are still linked by a network of well-preserved mule paths, which attract growing numbers of foreigners each spring and autumn. See p.177 & p.181

✻ **Áyios Nikoláos, Hálki** The courtyard of this church in picturesque Emborió displays one of the finest examples of *hokhláki* or pebble-mosaic work in the Dodecanese; Emborió in general has been rescued from dereliction since the 1980s by a commendable restoration-accommodation scheme. See p.189

✻ **Kastellórizo** The easternmost Greek territory, with an appropriately end-of-the-line feel, quirky Kastellórizo is for self-entertaining pilgrims to the set of *Mediterraneo*, rather than beach buffs. See p.193

✻ **Sými** The officially protected harbour and hillside village teem with trippers during the day, but a prolonged stay gives you the run of this stunning island with numerous walks, excellent cuisine and remote pebble bays. See p.202

✻ **Tílos** Except in peak season, one of the quietest of the Dodecanese, but with plenty to offer: marked and surveyed trails, two attractive inland villages, a fortified monastery and of course the expected complement of beaches. See p.214

✻ **Níssyros** Even quieter than Tílos once the day-trippers from Kós have gone; they come to see the dormant volcano at the island's centre, but four villages – especially the capital, Mandhráki – are a photographer's mecca. See p.224

2

The southern Dodecanese

The seven **southern Dodecanese islands** closest to Rhodes not only offer ideal escapes when the "big island" begins to pall, but constitute worthy destinations in their own right. An increasing number of visitors effectively skip Rhodes, using a flight-only deal to deposit them at Ródhos Town's harbour, where on any given day in season hydrofoils, catamarans or ferries are on hand to whisk them off to these surrounding islands. The three remotest islands are also accessible by daily (or nearly so) domestic flights, so you may not even choose to leave Rhodes airport. If you have the means, and plan well in advance, this is also an excellent and satisfying group to hop by chartered yacht, starting from Mandhráki harbour.

Rhodes' near neighbours present a broad range of landscapes and amenities. Harshly scenic **Kárpathos** is the only really sizeable island of the southern Dodecanese, with direct charter-flight access from Europe (plus useful local flights from Rhodes), magnificent beaches of all compositions, and an area in the far north of ethnological interest. Just next door, melancholy **Kássos** will probably appeal only to misanthropes allergic to other tourists.

The more cheerful duo of **Hálki** and **Sými**, which closely bracket Rhodes to the west and north respectively, are essentially one-town limestone outcrops which, like Kássos, have always been forced to make a living from the sea. Sými is greener, more hikeable, better endowed with pebbly beaches, and more geared up for independent travellers – though its spectacular harbour also makes it the most popular day-trip destination from Rhodes among this selection of islands. The houses of Hálki's port town have been comprehensively restored to provide accommodation for a more gentrified package clientele, who tend not to venture much out of sight of the harbour.

The most remote and depopulated isle of the Dodecanese is **Kastellórizo**, which once represented an extreme example of seafaring resourcefulness spurred by the poverty of onshore resources. Today the island serves as an idiosyncratic haven for a non-packaged, slightly alternative crowd willing to brave the long journey out from Rhodes and an utter lack of beaches.

Bare but relatively well-watered **Tílos**, least maritime of all the Dodecanese, combines (out of season, at least) overwhelming tranquillity and

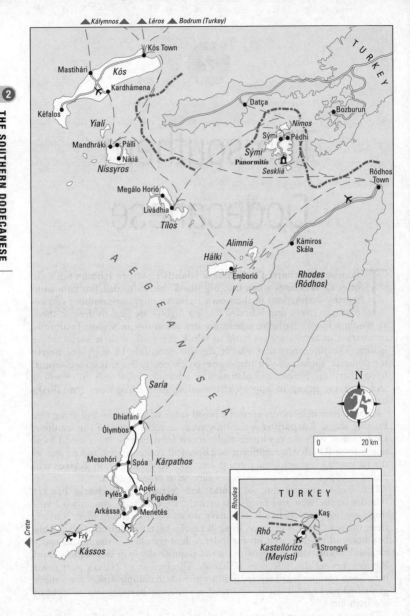

excellent beaches with a growing range of creature comforts, let down only
by problematic access from Rhodes. The round volcano-isle of **Níssyros**,
dry but fertile, receives regular day-excursions from adjacent Kós, but so
far these have scarcely affected the convivial ethos in the main port's many
tavernas; nor have they penetrated the picturesque outlying villages or
hidden coves.

Kárpathos

A long, narrow island stranded between Rhodes and Crete, wild **Kárpathos** has always been something of an underpopulated backwater, although it is physically the third largest of the Dodecanese, fractionally smaller than Kós. A mountainous spine, habitually cloud-capped as it traps moisture-laden west winds, divides the more populous, lower-lying south from an exceptionally rugged north. Despite a magnificent, if windswept, coastline of cliffs and promontories interspersed with little beaches, Kárpathos has surrendered only patchily to tourism. This is owed to lingering stretches of horrid road (though the network is much improved since the mid-1990s); the dearth, save two or three exceptions, of really interesting villages; and the surprisingly high cost of food, which offsets reasonable room prices.

Kárpathos doesn't, moreover, always have the most alluring interior, a fact aggravated by poor water-resource and land management. The central and northern uplands were badly scorched by 1980s forest fires, and by another spate of blazes in 2004 – a far cry from the days when the island's pines were its most prized asset, valuable for shipbuilding. Agriculture plays a slighter role than on any other Greek island of comparable size: while there are in fact good oil-bearing olive groves, luscious May and June apricots, enough livestock to export and some superb bakeries in villages like Óthos and Voládha, the Karpathians are frankly too well off to bother much with farming and rural crafts. Massive emigration to North America and the resulting remittance economy had transformed Kárpathos into one of the wealthiest Greek islands, even before the recent influx of tourists.

Most foreigners come here for a glimpse of the traditional village life that prevails in isolated northern Kárpathos, to hike through the remaining unravaged portions of the interior, and to lounge on numerous superb, secluded **beaches**, among the best in the Aegean. The airport receives several weekly direct charter flights from Scandinavia and Germany (though not, at present, Britain). Since the mid-1990s, package tourism has effectively monopolized Pigádhia and a couple of resorts in the southern half of the island, pushing independent travellers and backpackers into the remote north, where facilities are too basic to interest overseas companies.

Although the Minoans and Mycenaeans established trading posts on the island (then known as Krapathos), Kárpathos' four Classical cities figure little in ancient chronicles. Alone of the major Dodecanese, Kárpathos was held by the Genoese and Venetians after the Byzantine collapse and so has no castle of the crusading Knights of St John, nor indeed any surviving medieval fortresses of consequence. The Ottomans couldn't be bothered to settle or even garrison it; instead they left a single judge or *kadi* in the main town, and made the Greek population responsible for his safety during pirate attacks. Of these there were many, the seas immediately around the island being a favoured haunt.

Getting around the island

For exploring the island as a passenger, there are regular **bus** services to Pylés, via Apéri, Voládha and Óthos, as well as to Ammopí, Menetés, Arkássa, Finíki and (less frequently) to Mesohóri via Paralía Lefkoú; the Pigádhia "station" is at the western edge of town, a block past the post

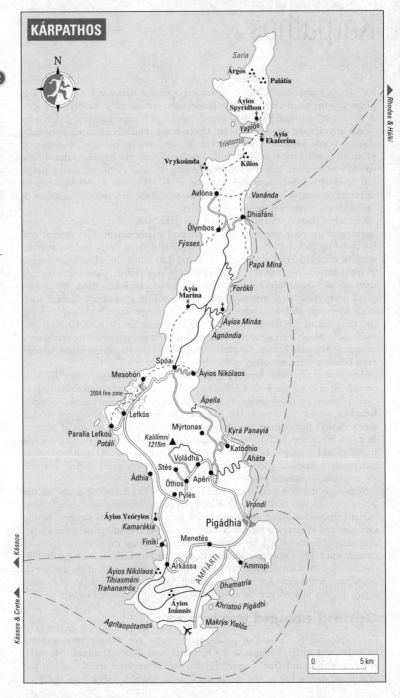

KÁRPATHOS

N

Saría

Árgos
Palátia
Áyios Spyrídhon
Yaplós
Ayía Ekaterína
Tristomo
Vrykoúnda
Kílios
Avlóna
Vanánda
Dhiafáni
Ólymbos
Fýsses
Papá Miná
Forókli
Ayía Marína
Áyios Minás
Agnóndia
Spóa
Mesohóri
Áyios Nikólaos
2004 fire zone
Ápella
Lefkós
Mýrtonas
Kyrá Panayiá
Paralía Lefkoú
Potáli
Kalilímni 1215m
Katódhio
Aháta
Voládha
Stés
Apéri
Ádhia
Óthos
Pylés
Vróndi
Áyios Yeóryios
Kamarákia
Pigádhia
Finíki
Menetés
Ammopí
Arkássa
AMFÍARTI
Dhamatría
Áyios Nikólaos
Tihiasméni
Trahanamós
Khristoú Pigádhi
Áyios Ioánnis
Agrilaopótamos
Makrýs Yialós

Rhodes & Hálki

Kássos

Kássos & Crete

0   5 km

office. Otherwise, rely on set-rate, meterless **taxis** (tables of current fares are posted at strategic points), having a terminal (☎ 22450 22705) in Pigádhia's municipal car park, two blocks inland along Dhimokratías. These aren't too expensive for getting to or from the cheerless **airport** (no snacks or diversions to hand) – 17km distant, sharing a runway with a huge NATO-improved airbase – or to villages on the paved road network, but charge a fortune to go anywhere else.

For getting around under your own steam, **rent cars** from upwards of ten agencies in Pigádhia, though you may have to try every one to find a free vehicle in high season. Rates are well above the norm, though available models and vehicle condition have improved of late. Among the more reputable are Circle (☎ 22450 22690 or 22450 22489), a block from the post office; friendly Avis, at the very north end of town (☎ 22450 22702); Drive (☎ 22450 23873), 2km out behind Vróndi beach; Trust (☎ 22450 81060, ✉ trustgr@yahoo.com), based in Ammopí, which will deliver and collect in Pigádhia; Billy's (☎ 22450 22921 or 697 78 87 875), by the taxi stand; and Hertz, inside Possi Travel (☎ 22450 22235). There are no staffed car rental booths at arrivals in the airport, but Avis and Hertz can deliver cars there upon prior arrangement – which will save €20 in taxi fares.

For **motorbikes**, Moto Carpathos (☎ 22450 22382), 60m uphill from the *dhimarhío*, has the biggest fleet and on-site service. Be warned that the only **fuel** on the island is found at two pairs of filling stations clustered just to the north and south of town, and that tanks on the small bikes are barely big enough to complete a circuit of the south, let alone head up north beyond Spóa – which is, in any case, expressly forbidden by most outfits for both bikes and non-4WD cars. Moreover, locally produced **maps** are among the worst available in the Greek islands, and you won't find anything vastly more detailed or accurate than the one in this book; Road Edition's #201, "Kárpathos-Kasos", is the best of the bunch, but still full of errors. By far the easiest way to reach northern Kárpathos, and some of the more remote east coast beaches, is by **boat** (for details, see box on p.175).

Pigádhia

The island capital of **PIGÁDHIA**, often known simply as Kárpathos, nestles at the south end of extremely scenic **Vróndi Bay**, whose sickle of sand extends 3km northwest. The town itself, curling around the jetty and quay where ferries and excursion boats dock, is as drab as its setting is beautiful; an ever-increasing number of concrete blocks contributes to the air of a vast building site, making the Italian-era port-police and county governmental buildings seem heirlooms by comparison. Although there's absolutely nothing special to see, Pigádhia does offer just about every facility you might need, albeit with a definite package-tourism slant. The name of the main commercial street – Apodhímon Karpathíon ("**Karpathians Overseas**") – speaks volumes about the pivotal role of emigrants and emigration here, and the wealth they've returned with keeps a plethora of sophisticated boutiques and explicitly touristic shops going, with better-than-average stock. Another Pigadhian quirk is the conspicuous community of **Egyptians** here, who have two coffee houses to themselves (but as yet no mosque); numbering several hundred, they all come from the Damietta area, and are locally esteemed as skilled masons, fishermen and carpenters.

Practicalities

Pigádhia now has a **tourism information** bureau, a hexagonal booth on the west quay (Mon–Fri 9am–2pm). Among other essentials, **Olympic Airways** (☏ 22450 22150) is on Platía 5-Oktovríou, at the west end of Apodhímon Karpathíon, but their hours are limited so most people buy tickets from Possi Travel on the waterfront (☏ 22450 22235); Possi is also the main ticket outlet for LANE, the sole **ferry** company serving Kárpathos. The **post office** is a few paces west of Olympic, up Ethnikís Andístasis, while several banks have **ATMs**. Pigádhia's main **Internet** cafés are *Café Galileo* (open all year), two doors down from Olympic on Apodhímon Karpathíon, and *Pot Pourri* (summer only), diagonally across the square from Olympic.

Accommodation

Most ferries are met by people offering **self-catering studios** (better value than conventional rooms), though in response to protests from aggrieved hoteliers they're not actually allowed to tout on the quay itself. Unless you've arranged something in advance, you might consider such offers – the town is small enough that no location will be too inconvenient, though the best places to stay cluster on the hillside above the bus terminal and central car park. The more expensive, luxurious hotels generally lie north, towards and behind Vróndi beach, to either side of the ruined fifth-century basilica of **Ayía Fotiní**, and tend to be wholly occupied by Nordic package groups; independent travellers will have to make do with humbler, in-town facilities as cited below.

Amarillis Studios Slightly downhill and east of *Rose Studios* (see below) ☏ 22450 22375, ℮ johnvolada@in.gr. Not much of a view, but the accommodation comes in enormous, suite-sized units with TV and air con. ❸

Atlantis Opposite the Italian "palace" ☏ 22450 22777, ℮ htlatlantis@yahoo.com. Helpful management, a small pool and hot water guaranteed by a boiler are pluses at this C-class hotel; some packages but walk-ins welcome. B&B ❹

Elias Rooms Just above *Hotel Karpathos* ☏ 22450 22446 or 697 85 87 924, ℮ http://Eliasroooms.tripod.com. Variable, mostly en-suite rooms with a veranda in a converted older house; open mid-May to Sept only. Propietor Elias Hatzigeorgiou is a mine of local info, especially about new worthy restaurants. ❷

Karpathos South end of Dhimokratías, base of stair-street ☏ 22450 22347. Serviceable D-class hotel in a fairly quiet, convenient location;

fair-sized, well-kept 1970s rooms with air con, fridges and TVs. ❸

Paradise Studios Upon an alley, beyond Avis Rent-a-Car ☏ 22450 22949, ℮ www .paradisestudios.gr. Seven simple but practical, good-sized air-con studios in a quiet, aesthetic orchard setting; some packages but walk-ins most welcome; no breakfast available. ❸

Rose Studios On the hillside behind the *Karpathos* ☏ 22450 22284, ℮ rosestudios@hotmail. com. Well-kept if basic rooms with fridge and hotplate, some air con, run by a kind family, long resident in Canada and Zimbabwe. Justifiably popular; must be reserved in advance. ❶

Titania Behind the municipal car park ☏ 22450 22144, ℮ www.titaniakarpathos.gr. Not the most inspired location, but this C-class hotel has largeish rooms, all with balcony (best ones overlook the orchard), TV, air con and fridge; also a pleasant buffet-breakfast salon and bar; claims to be open all year. ❹

Vróndi beach

Pigádhia's magnificent beach, **Vróndi** ("thunder"), takes its name from an attribute of the sea god Poseidon, who was patron of Pigádhia's ancient precursor Potidaion. The beach improves towards its centre, where the tidal zone has the least amount of rock-reef, though the water everywhere is generally clean and warm. Simple **sports** are engaged in, with windsurfing equipment and canoes rented from beachside lean-tos and tables. There are a few independent **restaurants**: right behind the sand at the town end, ever-popular *To Limanaki*, with some locals in attendance, and *Seaside Snack Bar* nearby, both open 10am to 7pm; and *Greenpeace Beach Bar* at the far north end of the sand, also serving snacks through the daylight hours.

Eating, drinking and nightlife

Most of Pigádhia's waterfront **tavernas** are undistinguished – tacky photo-menus and defrosted *yíros*-with-chips reign supreme – and overpriced at Rhodes levels. Locals mutter about high carriage costs for food, but greed and a not-too-discerning package clientele seem more likely reasons. Quality and value tend to improve as you head east towards the ferry dock, with a pair of excellent choices near the end of the strip. *Anna*, run by a colourful family, purveys seafood and generous salads, all carefully prepared despite the chaotic appearance inside. *Iy Orea Karpathos* is the best all-rounder, with palatable local bulk wine, *trahanádhes* soup, spicy sausages, marinated artichokes and great spinach pie – you can, as the locals do, use it as an *ouzerí* and just order *orektiká*. One block inland, the clear winner is *To Ellinikon*, a *mezedhopolío* that caters year-round to a local clientele with hot and cold *orektiká*, meat and good own-made desserts. If *yíros* and chips it must be, then by far the best place for the fresh kind, own-sourced, is *Ovelistirio tis Erasmias*, Dhimokratías corner 28-Oktovríou, opposite the taxi rank.

Kafenio The Life of Angels (June–Sept), in one of the few surviving old buildings next to the church on Apodhímon Karpathíon, gets a mixed crowd of locals and tourists, drawn by twice-weekly impromptu live **music** sessions (not, however, the best on the island); the limited evening menu seems a secondary consideration. The trendier musical **bars** – whose precise identity changes yearly – occupy perennial premises overlooking the bay from perches just below Apodhímon Karpathíon.

A particularly well-developed Karpathian institution are the half-dozen **cafés** along Apodhímon Karpathíon to either side of the fountain, courtesy of returned USA emigrants. They have been spruced up of late, with egg-and-sausage-fry-up odours banished and premium ice creams, sweets and fancy coffee purveyed now.

Southern Kárpathos

The southern extremity of Kárpathos, towards the airport, is flat, extraordinarily desolate and windswept. There are several relatively undeveloped sandy **beaches** on the southeast coast, in the region known as Afiárti (or Amfiárti), some of them dominated by windsurfers who take advantage of the prevailing northwest winds. The most established **surf school** here is Chris and Elke's Pro Center Karpathos (☎22450 91063, ⓦwww.windsurfen-karpathos.com), which as the web address suggests caters mostly to Germanophones, though all are welcome. They have the advantage of three separate bays near the airport to practise: "Luv Spot" for experts (officially **Agrilaopótamos**), 4.4km west of the airport by dirt road, with sandy-beach launch and a scenic backdrop of Kássos, but also hazardous reefs to avoid; "Devil's Bay", just under a kilometre north of the airport, with conditions for intermediate to advanced boarders; and sheltered "Lagune" (officially **Makrýs Yialós**), at the end of the runway, perhaps the least aesthetic – only the Greek Air Force base and landing jets to look at – but this is where beginners are taken.

Non-surfers will be most interested in sheltered, sand-and-gravel **Khristoú Pigádhi** beach, just over 2km north of the airport, with a 500-metre access road, a *kantína* and (just south, reached by clambering over rocks) a nudist annexe. Beyond the headland bounding Khristoú Pigádhi to the north, with a separate 900-metre access drive, stretches **Dhamatría** beach, sandier but more exposed. Here, up the slope, you'll find the peaceful *Hotel Poseidon* (☏ 22450 91066, ⓦ www.hotel-poseidon.gr; B&B ❸), also with a full-service taverna open to all.

Most people go no further in this direction than **Ammopí**, just 7km from Pigádhia. This, together with development at Arkássa and Paralía Lefkoú (see opposite), is the closest thing on Kárpathos to a purpose-built beach resort. Three sand-and-gravel, tree- or cliff-fringed coves are bordered by half a dozen tavernas and increasing numbers of **hotels** and **studios**. Quietest among the latter, not completely dominated by packages, are the highly recommended, well-designed *Vardes Studios* (☏ 22450 81111 or 697 21 52 901, ⓦ www.hotelvardes.com; ❸), with distant sea views and an orchard setting; retractable awnings make the balconies more usable, and breakfast features own-grown fruit and jam. Among **tavernas**, the *Golden Beach* behind the middle cove is acceptable, the only one the locals will be seen in; much-promoted *Amoopi Beach* at the northerly cove is a rank tourist trap.

Heading west from Pigádhia, rather than south along the coast, the road climbs steeply for 9km up to **MENETÉS**, an appealing village with handsome old hilltop houses, a tiny folklore museum and a spectacularly sited church in the precincts of the ancient acropolis. There's also a World War II resistance memorial at the east edge of town by the cemetery, with sweeping views north, and just beyond (almost to the airport road) the best local **taverna**, *Pelagía*, in Kritháres district.

The west coast

Kárpathos' west coast seems far less developed than the east coast, since – with the sterling exception of Paralía Lefkoú – beaches are scanty and exposed, and the shoreline more bleak than dramatic. The local road system isn't too bad, with un-potholed tarmac connecting all points discussed below and even inching across the island's spine as far as Spóa.

Arkássa, Finíki and Ádhia

Beyond Menetés, the road immediately starts its descent to **ARKÁSSA**, lining the slopes of a ravine draining to the west coast, with excellent views across to Kássos en route. A few hundred metres south of where the ravine meets the sea, a signposted cement side road heads towards the whitewashed chapel of **Ayía Sofía**, five minutes' walk away and built on the spot where **Classical and Byzantine Arkessia** stood. Its visible remains consist of several mosaic floors with geometric patterns, one of which runs diagonally under the floor of a half-buried cistern, emerging from the walls on either side. The headland beyond, known as **Paleokástro**, was the site of **Mycenaean Arkessia**; the walk up is again signposted, but scarcely worth it for the sake of a few stretches of polygonal wall and a couple of tumbled columns.

Despite just one good local beach, Arkássa has been intensely developed, with hotels and restaurants sprouting in clusters along the rocky coastline. Most local

accommodation is aimed squarely at the package market, but independent travellers could try for various facilities inland from **Áyios Nikólaos** beach signposted just south, a 200-metre stretch of sand – rare hereabouts. These include the *Seaside Studios* (☏22450 61421; ➍); the higher-standard *Montemar Studios* (☏22450 61394; ➍), almost one-bedroom apartments, though kitchens are rudimentary; and – right behind the beach – the *Glaros* (☏22450 61015, ⓕ22450 61016; ➍), five package-free studios and an attached, full-service **taverna** run by a returned Karpathian-American. Other, mediocre eateries lie north of the ravine in the village centre, though *Family House* on the outskirts is praised for its steaks.

Beyond Áyios Nikólaos, the road dwindles to a dirt track as it passes the remote, sandy beaches of **Tihiasméni** and **Trahanamós** en route to the cape of **Áyios Theódhoros**, over 6km from Arkássa. There's a little monastery here, and an equally diminutive, protected beach a steep scramble down in the southeastern lee of the point, but only misanthropes will reckon it worth the bother. Neither will most relish the rough onward track through a giant wind farm and the dreary, abandoned village of Áyios Ioánnis to Kípos hamlet, at Afiárti.

The tiny fishing port of **FINÍKI**, just 2km north of Arkássa, offers a minuscule beach, regular *kaïki* service to Kássos, several tavernas and a like number of studios. A waterside memorial commemorates the January 1945 journey to Egypt, under sail only, by four brave islanders who went to tell the British high command that the Germans had abandoned Kárpathos the previous month, and would they please stop bombing the island. **Accommodation** includes *Giavasis Studios* (☏22450 61365; ➋), on the road to the jetty, or for more comfort and value the well-designed and -built *Arhontiko Studios* up on the main bypass road (☏22450 61473, ⓕ22450 61054; ➌). Most reliable of the harbourside **tavernas** is *Iy Marina*, open all year and tops for fish; there's another well-loved, cult eatery, *Kostas/Under the Trees*, 800m north under two tamarisks at Áyios Yeóryios monastery above reefy Kamarákia beach. It's open all day until 10pm (book in season ☏697 79 84 791), offering mountainous, fair-priced portions of chops, expertly grilled swordfish and chips made of home-grown courgettes.

Some 7km north of Finíki along the coast road, Karpathian forest resumes at **ÁDHIA** hamlet, giving rise to the name of the *Pine Tree Restaurant*, which serves own-baked bread, lentil soup and octopus *makaronádha* washed down by sweet Óthos wine. There are also six **rooms/studios** adjacent, overlooking the orchard and the sea (☏697 73 69 948, ⓔpinetree_adia@hotmail.com; ➋).

Paralía Lefkoú and Mesohóri

Dense forest continues much of the way to the turning for the resort of **PARALÍA LEFKOÚ**, the beach annexe of inland Lefkós. Unless you rent a car – there are two agencies here now, Lefkos (☏22450 71057) and Drive (☏22450 71415) – it's not a particularly convenient touring base, as buses call infrequently; if you've rented a small motorbike in Pigádhia this is the furthest you can reach and return from without running out of fuel. However, efforts spent getting here will be rewarded with a striking topography of cliffs, hills, islets and sandspits surrounding a triple bay, making this a delightful spot for flopping on the beach. On the spit between two more northerly and progressively wilder bays lie the badly crumbling remains of medieval fortifications; indeed the whole area lies within an archeological protection zone, which acts as a healthy brake on development. The single most impressive monument, well signposted off the northerly access road, is a "**Roman cistern**" (free, unenclosed), actually a catacomb complex with underground cavities and columns.

There are now over two dozen places to **stay**, and perhaps half as many eateries, but package companies have moved in with a vengeance, making it hard to find a room unspoken for between mid-June and September. About the only exception is spartan but en-suite *Sunweek Studios* (☎22450 71025; ❷), on the seaward promontory. You'll have better luck at **Potáli**, a stonier, fourth bay just south of the access road; go here for the excellent, quiet and spacious *Akrogiali Studios* (☎22450 71263, ℉22450 71178; ❸), with balconies overlooking the beach; *Studios Galini* across the ravine (☎22450 71137 or 22450 71368; ❷), simple but overlooking the sea and vegetable gardens; or the smaller *Lefkosia Studios* up on the road (☎22450 71176 or 22450 71148; ❸), which have the plus of the attached *Orama Café*, serving luscious fruit juices and muesli or egg breakfasts. **Tavernas** at the main bay mostly charge well over the odds for limp fare, leaving the kindly *Blue Sea* as the best option, thanks to pizzas, meat-rich *mayireftá* and pancake breakfasts.

Mesohóri and around

Back on the main road, you climb northeast to eventually reaching Spóa (see p.174) overlooking the east coast. But it's well worth detouring along another side road, leading to attractive **MESOHÓRI**. The village tumbles down towards the sea around narrow, stepped alleys, coming to an abrupt halt at the edge of a flat-topped bluff occupied by "Platía" Skopí, dotted with three tiny, ancient chapels and separated from the village proper by a vast oasis of orchards. These are nurtured by the fountain (with the best water on the island) issuing from underneath the mammoth church of **Panayía Vryssianí**, lodged against the mountainside just east and invisible from the car park at the road's end; a special hall adjacent sees celebrations on September 8–9, beginning on the evening of the 7th. On the stair-street leading to the church is an excellent **taverna**, the *Dhramoundana*, remarkably reasonably priced for Kárpathos, and featuring local caper greens, sausages and marinated "sardines" (really a larger, bonier fish, *ménoula*). If you're seized by the urge to **stay**, there are rooms above *Taverna To Steki* (☎22450 22159 or 22450 71349; ❷), near the car park, which hosts walking groups in spring or autumn; the slightly pricey taverna will do dishes to order in the evening.

Mesohóri is – to some extent, was (see below) – a major focus for local **hiking opportunities**. The quickest out-and-back walk, beginning next to Panayía Vryssianí, heads within half an hour to Makrýs Yialós; the walk is satisfying, arrival at the filthy, rocky bay anticlimactic. Well beyond, there's a much sandier, cleaner **beach** at **Ayía Iríni**, accessible only by boat in calm weather; otherwise, locals swim at the little headland of Káfkalos just below Mesohóri. Bearing right at the prominent fork early along the Makrýs Yialós trail takes you to Spóa, from where an onward path descends to Áyios Nikólaos on the east coast.

Red paint-dot waymarking also leads you to the south end of Mesohóri and the path to Paralía Lefkoú, a two-hour walk; coming uphill from Paralía Lefkoú, the trail begins near the mini-market. The road cuts it only in two spots, and the terrain en route is rolling rather than an unmitigated climb. However, in June 2004 one of the worst **fires** in recent years scoured the area between Lefkós and Mesohóri, in all likelihood ruining most of the landscape en route – take local advice before setting out, to avoid disappointment.

Central Kárpathos

The **centre** of Kárpathos supports a quintet of villages blessed with superb hillside settings and ample running water – and a cool climate, even in August. Nearly everyone here has "done time" in North America, then returned home with their nest eggs. New Jersey, Virginia, Maryland and Canadian number plates on huge, imported gas-guzzlers tell you exactly where repatriated islanders struck it rich – in many instances, fabulously so; the area reputedly has the highest per capita income in Greece.

A little above the Finíki–Mesohóri road, **PYLÉS** is perhaps the prettiest of these villages, with views west to Kássos, a few seasonal snack-bars and *kafenía* on the single "high street", and abundant greenery just downhill – fed, as at Mesohóri, by a spring issuing from the foundations of a church. **ÓTHOS** lies just below the second highest summit of the Dodecanese, 1215-metre **Kalí Límni**. The highest (400m) and chilliest settlement on Kárpathos, Óthos is noted for its excellent bread, slender sausages and sweet, tawny-amber wine. Much of this comes from vines at the hamlet of **STÉS**, 2km northwest, with yet another church-spring.

Northeast of Óthos, at the high point of the road, there's a paved side-turning signposted for Kalí Límni ("Beautiful Lake"); after 4.6km, bear left off the pavement (right goes to the air-force relay station) and continue 1km on dirt track to *Iy Kali Kardhia/O Thanassis* **taverna/rooms** (T 697 24 67 688; ❶), the sole local amenity, with a German cult following. Only on this fertile, poplar-studded upland (850m elevation) does a pastoral and agricultural life just hang on, away from beach tourism; reserve a meal or even a bed with Thanassis and make a day of it by **climbing the peak** (3hr). Otherwise, beyond the vineyards at Káto Lastós, only jeeps need apply – the rest of the road circuit around the air-force "golf ball" is rough and steep (if highly scenic), emerging just over 14km from the ridge turning between Voládha and Apéri.

Alternatively, from that summit ridge you can descend on the main road to reach **VOLÁDHA**, endowed with three nocturnal **tavernas** (*Klimataria* comes recommended) and a tiny Venetian citadel. Seven kilometres east of Pylés (and 2km from Voládha) lies **APÉRI**, largest, lowest and wealthiest of the quintet. During the pirate era it served as the island's capital, and is still the seat of the local bishop.

East coast beaches

From Apéri, you can drive 5km east along a recently regraded (but still dirt-surface) road to isolated **Aháta** beach, a 150-metre, pebble bay in a dramatic setting, flanked by pine-tufted, twisted palisades and a rock-islet to snorkel around. There's a freshwater fountain with a memorial plaque to a local fisherman, and a reasonable **taverna** alongside.

North of Apéri, the main road up the east coast is paved all the way to Spóa, passing above beaches still commonly visited by boat excursions from Pigádhia. The first one encountered is **Kyrá Panayiá**, just below **Katódhio** hamlet, reached via a paved, if twisty, side road. There are a surprising number of villas and **rooms** in the ravine behind the 150-metre, fine-gravel bay. Despite the arduous drive in, most accommodation is contracted out to German companies, though you can try your luck at friendly *Akropolis* (T & F 22450 31503; ❸ rooms, ❹ studios), up on the south hillside behind the church, with large if plain, units and an on-site restaurant. In peak season the beach (with a mediocre **taverna** behind) is packed out, understandable given the exceptionally clear, turquoise water sheltered from most summer winds, and rock overhangs at each end providing refuge and shade.

Continuing north along the main road some 10km past Apéri, another 2500-metre-long, dirt side road leads to **Ápella**, the best of the beaches you can reach by road; from below the good-value *Apella Beach Taverna Studios* (📞697 24 23 741; ❸), a brief stair-path drops you onto the 300-metre sand and gravel beach, where shady spots under the pines just behind are at a premium, as is parking at the road's end. There's a second, naturist cove to the southeast; a faint path allows scrambly access over the dividing headland.

From the Ápella turning it's 5km more to a major junction at the watershed of the island, where you encounter a reliable fountain and a cluster of ruined windmills beside the Mesohóri–Spóa asphalt. **SPÓA** itself, high above the shore just east of the island's summit ridge, has a snack-bar (*Folia*) at the end of the southerly village access road, plus the adjacent, more reliably open *Kafenio Akropolis*, which does cheap dishes. Any of these might make a better **meal stop** than **ÁYIOS NIKÓLAOS**, 4km below, a small hamlet with an average beach and a single, overpriced **taverna**, *To Votsalo* (📞22450 71205), which also has more reasonable **studios** (❸). The ruins of a large, if overgrown, early Christian basilica near the fishing port can be explored.

Northern Kárpathos

Although **northern Kárpathos** is connected by a road with Spóa, the initial southerly 8km falls squarely in the "horrid" category as noted above, and taxis charge a whacking €70 per car for a journey up from Pigádhia. The road in fact will never be improved, to protect the lucrative trade in day-trips as described below. So, much the easiest (and most common) way to get up there is by sea, or in a rented jeep. Inter-island ferries call at **Dhiafáni** several times weekly in season, and there are smaller excursion or mail-boats daily from Pigádhia (see box opposite). Excursion boats are met at Dhiafáni by buses for the eight-kilometre trip up to the traditional village of **Ólymbos**, the main attraction in this part of Kárpathos.

Ólymbos and around

High above the west coast, remote **ÓLYMBOS** straddles a long ridge below slopes studded with mostly ruined windmills. The village was originally founded during the eighth century AD as a refuge from the pirates that plagued the shoreline settlements at Vrykoúnda and Saría, the now-uninhabited islet that hovers just north of Kárpathos like a ball balanced on a seal's nose. Over the centuries, Ólymbos evolved a Shangri-la-like **self-sufficiency** necessitated by its extreme isolation; during World War II, for example, famine was not a threat here as elsewhere in the islands, since the locals had abundant flocks and grain. Since then, however, this remoteness has worked against local communities, with massive **depopulation** the result; a daily commute to jobs in Pigádhia is simply not feasible, leaving barely four hundred permanent residents in Ólymbos and Dhiafáni. Besides July and August tourism, stock-raising and subsistence farming are the only activities, with just one or two young fishermen remaining.

The area has long been a mecca for foreign and Greek ethnologists, who treat it as a living museum of peasant dress, crafts, dialect and music that have long since vanished elsewhere in Greece. Like many remote island communities, it is overwhelmingly endogamous, consenting only occasionally to intermarry

Boats to and from northern Kárpathos

Two rival excursion boats are usually moored by the port police in Pigádhia, with inclusive tour-tickets sold on board. At a price of €10–15 (lunch not included) for an all-day tour to Ólymbos, the *Chrisovalandou III* proves more attractive, faster and more stable in heavy seas than the *Arivsovoulos*. Less well publicized is the fact that you can use these boats for a one-way trip between the north and the south of the island, in either direction, for €6–7. Both craft leave Pigádhia at about 8.30am, returning from Dhiafáni at about 4pm; the only morning departures from Dhiafáni which cater for locals who need to go to "town" are three weekly 8am "post boats", which carry just a few passengers, return from Pigádhia at 2pm most days, and also charge €6–7 one way. Any of these craft can, depending on sea conditions, take nearly two hours to travel between Pigádhia and Dhiafáni, so if you can coincide with a regular ferry in either direction, you'll save both money (€3.50 single fare) and time (1hr–1hr 15min journey). Various agents also offer excursions to several isolated east coast beaches which have no (or poor) road access or facilities; enquire as to whether lunch is included, and bring supplies if not.

with emigrants from the island of Níssyros; someone with one grandparent from even the south of Kárpathos is considered an "outsider".

But Ólymbos is inexorably being dragged into the modern era, thanks to the paved road up from Dhiafáni, electricity, and a growing number of tourists; since 1980, the number of day-trippers has increased tenfold to 30,000 annually, to the extent that they often outnumber locals during the day. The tours (and self-drive jeep passengers) have pushed food prices up and quality down, and spontaneous traditions into hiding – or at least they're hard to witness at midday in season, when Ólymbos is little better than an anthropological theme park. It's only women over about 40, and those working in tourist shops, who wear the striking and magnificently colourful traditional dress (though to their credit they do not take it off once the tourist season ends). This garb is in fact worn throughout the north of the island, including Dhiafáni and Avlóna.

After a while you'll notice the dominant role that local **women** play in daily life: tending gardens, carrying goods on their shoulders, or herding goats. Nearly all Ólymbos men emigrate – in particular to the Highlandtown district of Baltimore and Astoria in New York – or work elsewhere on the island, sending money home and returning only on holidays. The long-isolated villagers also speak a unique **dialect**, said to retain traces of its Doric and Phrygian origins; "Ólymbos", for example, is pronounced "Élimbos" locally.

Entering the village, you're obliged to run a gauntlet of tattier-by-the-year **souvenir shops**, from which you can, in high season anyway, expect some persistent if good-natured sales pitches, but beware of Chinese- and Bulgarian-made embroidery touted as "traditional local handicraft". The genuine articles are unfortunately the least portable: carved wooden doors or furniture, and the flamboyantly painted plaster-relief folk art on houses. Plant and animal, mythic and geometric designs are all represented on balustrades, lintels and eaves, though the most popular motif seems to be the double-headed eagle of the Byzantine Paleologos dynasty.

Deceptively modern-looking, the main **Church of the Assumption** sports seventeenth-century fresco fragments, and the altar screen proved to be gold-leafed after a 1993 cleaning. Two working **windmills** just beyond, restored in the mid-1980s, grind wheat and barley during late summer only, more for show than anything else; one is kept under sail whenever tourists are about.

Ólymbos – a mild debunking

The apparent exoticism of **Ólymbos** has prompted numerous sensational write-ups in the past, many of them exaggerated, plagiarized from each other, or simply untrue. Much is made of the local matrilineal property inheritance, with houses passing down from mother to eldest daughter – the so-called *kanakára* – upon her marriage, prompting claims of some rediscovered Amazonian realm. However, this custom is prevalent on several other of the Dodecanese; it was apparently a method of dodging taxation or confiscation dating from Ottoman times, when women weren't systematically counted in censuses. Less known is the fact that an oldest son – the *kanakáris*, literally "favourite son" – also inherits all the real property of his father's line; hence the massive emigration of younger brothers, who have literally no prospects in the village.

For at least some of this mystification, the villagers themselves are partly responsible, not being averse to occasional leg-pulling and succumbing to the natural tendency to tell the gullible and the nosy what they want to hear. Amateur anthropologists on flying visits are particularly easy targets: a reporter for the French edition of *GEO Magazine* was once assured by a certain disgruntled, divorced woman shopkeeper that most local men were either homosexual or impotent. This remark subsequently appeared in print, verbatim, without critique or irony, variously causing consternation and hilarity when the news got back to Ólymbos.

Probably the best way to experience Ólymbos at its most authentic involves turning up at one of the seasonal **festivals**, when traditional music is performed by the men; indeed vast crowds descend on August 15 and at Easter. Few outsiders realize, however, that the winter Carnival is nearly as important folklorically; masquers traipse from house to house, performing in return for hospitality and getting thoroughly drunk through straws (no doffing of masks is allowed).

The order of precedence of **musical instruments** is slightly unusual: the *tsambúna* or bagpipe takes the lead, followed by the *lýra*, or three-string spike fiddle, while the *laoúto*, a relative of the mandolin and principally used for rhythm, defers to both. The *lýra*, with little bells on the curved bow, is unlike the modernized Cretan models, bearing more resemblance to a *politikí* or Pontic *lýra*; for a full description of this and other Dodecanesian music, see p.493 in Contexts.

Under one of the mills is tucked a small, inconspicuous **museum** (sporadic hours; free), with such wooden oddities as a fez rack (from the days when such headgear was worn), infants' sling cradles and a vulture trap, baited with carrion, that looks like an oversized garlic press.

Practicalities

The daytime commercialization of Ólymbos provides a good reason for **staying** overnight (especially out of season), when things are more relaxed. The friendly *Rooms Restaurant Olymbos* (℡22450 51252 or 22450 51009; ❷), near the village entrance, has rooms with baths or unplumbed ones with traditional furnishings, while the *Café-Restaurant Zefiros*, near the centre and run by two young sisters, manages the eight-room, en-suite *Hotel Astro* (℡22450 51421; B&B ❸), with breakfast given in the restaurant. *Hotel Aphrodite* (℡22450 51307; ❷), towards the far edge of the village, offers a like number of en-suite rooms in good condition, with southerly ocean views (but a fair bit of window-rattling from the wind).

There are a few other places to **eat**, though they tend to do greasy, overpriced or microwave-reheated fare; the premier local dish is *makaroúnes*, homemade pasta with onions and cheese. During springtime, *myrgouátana*, a rock-dwelling marine invertebrate (tastier than it sounds), is served up breaded and sautéed as *mezédhes* in Ólymbos *kafenía*, along with *petalídhes* (limpets). Incidentally, there is no bakery in Ólymbos; the village women make their own bread four or five days a week, at one of several rustic communal ovens. If you need some, you could ask your pension or restaurant proprietor.

Hikes from Ólymbos

Ólymbos makes an excellent base from which to do some **hiking**, a big plus being that the slopes between Ólymbos, Avlóna and Dhiafáni have retained much of the island's surviving pine-forest cover. There are a few competing German-language walking guides to Kárpathos, especially the north, but each has defects – especially in mapping – so always put more trust in on-the-spot oral directions. North Karpathian paths were in good shape until the 1996 completion of the deep-water, car-ferry dock at Dhiafáni; now jeep tracks have been bulldozed, the locals drive everywhere, and as far as the trails are concerned it's a case of use them or lose them as they quickly become overgrown and landslid. Most waymarked walks head generally north from Ólymbos, and are of moderate length and difficulty.

Ólymbos to Fýsses
Fairly quickly (if strenuously) reached are the boatsheds and superb, 100-metre sand-and-pebble beach at **Fýsses**, a sharp drop below on the west coast. The path there is deteriorated to nonexistent, with lots of scree, so a stick or walking-pole is useful; begin at the last house of the village, below the school, and allow 35 minutes down (rather less uphill, such is the footing).

Ólymbos to Spóa or Mesohóri
For something more challenging, follow the route from Ólymbos to **Spóa** or **Mesohóri** in the south, a five-hour trek unfortunately made less scenic by a devastating 1983 forest fire (though new trees are now chest-high). The initial two hours or so are on trail, until you meet the Spóa–Ólymbos track; you follow this for a couple of kilometres until adopting another track going west-southwest for the chapel and spring of Ayía Marína, from where an onward trail covers most of the remaining distance to Spóa.

Ólymbos to Dhiafáni
One of the more attractive possibilities, and certainly the easiest, is the hike down to **Dhiafáni**. The path begins just below the two working windmills, well marked with red paint-dots and rock cairns; top up with water at a spring some twenty minutes along. Just under half an hour out of Ólymbos, bear right away from the power lines, briefly down to the stream bed and then up towards the road (the left fork leads to Avlóna; see overleaf), and after ten or so minutes plunge down and left through extensive, unburnt forest, towards the bed of a ravine draining to Dhiafáni. A small stream trickles alongside much of the way, and there's another spring at the one-hour mark; at your approach, snakes slither into hiding and partridges break cover. The entire route takes just under ninety minutes downhill, but unfortunately the final half-hour's approach to Dhiafáni consists mostly of bulldozed riverbed.

Ólymbos to Vrykoúnda
By staying overnight in Ólymbos, you can also tackle the marked trail north to the ruins and beach at **Vrykoúnda**, via the agricultural hamlet of Avlóna;

it's best to take ample food and make a day of it. It's just under ninety minutes to Avlóna, mostly on path (locals claim to do it in 1hr), though you're forced to road-walk ten minutes over the ridge, past the large white church of Áyios Konstandínos; the trail resumes on the descent. There's another brief stretch of road on the final approach to the sizeable hamlet, overlooking a cultivated plain. **AVLÓNA** supports a mere ten permanent inhabitants (though many more in summer), and the father of the *Rooms Olymbos* management has opened an annexe, *Restaurant Avlona* (springtime speciality artichoke hearts with eggs) on the through-road, with four en-suite rooms (℡22450 51046; ❶), an ideal base for committed walkers. Only grain – harvested in May and June – is grown locally, since there isn't enough water for market gardens.

From Avlóna it's just over an hour to "Vroukoúnda", as pronounced in local dialect, using the initially walled-in path, flanked by fig trees, which takes off from the valley-floor track; there may be a sign up, and the way is cairned and red-dotted. The trail, much of it dating from Roman times, describes a moderate but quite long descent to the attractive bay, often over flagstone steps but also loose scree, and becomes markedly steeper towards the end.

Visible traces of **Hellenistic/Roman/Byzantine Brykous** (Vrykoúnda), one of Kárpathos' four ancient city-states, consist of masoned wall courses and rock-cut tombs; the main, waymarked trail continues from the vicinity of a prominent tomb-cut monolith to the festival-grounds and remote **cave-shrine of John the Baptist**, on the left-hand promontory closing off the bay. On August 28–29, this turning is busy with locals en route to the saint's celebrations, but at any time it's worth walking at least partway there for sweeping views back down the west coast.

Scrambling down and right from the tomb-monolith brings you to a long pebble-gravel **beach**, which is serviceable enough, though sometimes tar washes up on it. The best cove is off to the left. Retracing your steps to Avlóna, it's an hour and a quarter from the beach to the fountain at the edge of the hamlet; there's no shade en route except for a single boulder equipped with a cement bench. From Avlóna back to Ólymbos, allow another hour-plus (it's slightly downhill).

Avlóna to Trístomo

Don't be discouraged by the ugly, prominent bulldozer track conspicuously heading northeast out of Avlóna; this has left 95 percent of the old hiking route to the remote fjord of **Trístomo** intact – either beautifully engineered, ancient *kalderími* or waymarked path. It should be said that Trístomo itself is a rather dreary place, with no special attractions or facilities – the walk there is the thing.

Look for the sign in Greek (ΤΡΙΣΤΟΜΟ) at the north edge of the village to get you started correctly; after ten minutes cross the track to pick up the path on the far side, and within five more minutes the old flagstoned way begins in earnest. Just under half an hour along, keep straight, ignoring signed forks right and left and skirting the perimetre dry-stone walling of the **Ahordhéa** agricultural upland here; you'll meet the track again by a concrete wellhead with black PVC pipes exiting it. About 45 minutes out of Avlóna, bear left off the track onto the resumption of the path, climbing to a pass – the highest point of the walk – with walled fig and almond groves. The one-hour mark should see you drop slightly to a well (just potable), with an initial view of Saría island, and then hit the track again, between two more concrete pumping stations. Within ten minutes more the track ends for good in the vicinity of some beehives; continue on the obvious path around a walled garden with a single cypresss. Some ninety minues along, *kalderími* briefly resumes as the way roller-coasters to the first "wow" view-point of Trístomo inlet with its two islets guarding the entrance (thus the name, "Three Mouths"), prominent monastery and cruel illusion of a beach.

Now there's a sharper descent in well-engineered zigzags to the streambed amidst the highest cube-cottages of abandoned **Kílios** hamlet (1hr 45min); proceed to a second ravine, turning left (downstream) – paint-spot waymarks, hitherto mostly blue but some red and yellow, and the path itself all disappear as you approach a salt marsh. Choose your own way around this to reach the filthy, shingly shore, so tempting from afar (around 2hr), and then the little monastery of **Áyii Anáryiri** with its cistern-fed water tap. A path of sorts resumes as you head east along the shore of the windswept inlet, passing almost-submerged **Áyios Nikólaos** chapel, to the lone occupied house of Trístomo hamlet (2hr 30min from Avlóna). There are several other maintained dwellings on the north shore, but three times as many in ruins. Just one elderly, eccentric couple (she refuses to speak to outsiders) live out here permanently and, when they pass on, the place will go the way of Saría. Swimming is complicated by sea urchins (the only comfortable access is at Áyii Anáryiri jetty) and windborne flotsam.

At present there is no safe, easy way to angle back towards Vanánda from Trístomo; you must return the way you came (allow 2hr 45min walking time). The direct Trístomo–Vanánda path has one severely landslid section, below the locale called Xylóskala; the path was destabilized by the quarrying of stone for the new harbour jetty in 1995, and perennial plans to restore the route have so far come to nothing. Currently, the best way to avoid doing the Avlóna–Trístomo stretch twice is to have the Saría excursion *kaíki* (see p.181) drop you at **Ayía Ekateríni**, just fifteen minutes east of Trístomo.

Avlóna to Vanánda

This is perhaps the best walk in northern Kárpathos, and makes possible loops out of Dhiafáni or Ólymbos without using much road or track. Head southeast out of Avlóna, past a water cistern and the last *monastiráki* of Áyios Ioánnis, then adopt a vehicle track for three minutes, before bearing down and right on a narrow path to reach a prominent *kalderími* on the right bank of the valley here. This climbs gently through pines to a small farm with livestock pens, meeting (25min along) an ugly dirt track going down to Dhiafáni. Go left instead almost immediately onto a faint but marked trail, descending sharply northeast towards now-visible **Vanánda** through pines, under which purple orchids sprout in May. On meeting the streambed, the path crosses to the north (true left) bank, where it stays for most of the rest of the way (except for the final minutes when you walk in the streambed itself). Little olive plantations fill terraces, calamus and oleander grow on the banks, and there's even the occasional palm tree for an exotic touch; just overhead, the pines are all bent markedly east, away from the prevailing winds which penetrate even this sheltered valley. It's one hour twenty minutes in total from Avlóna to Vanánda, for more on which see overleaf.

Dhiafáni and around

Although its popularity has grown markedly since the deep-water dock was completed, rooms in **DHIAFÁNI** are still relatively inexpensive, and the pace of life slow, except in August when it's overrun by Italians and Germans. Most of the settlement only dates from the postwar years, so don't expect much in the way of architectural character; there's a general consensus among travellers that a recent building boom has got out of hand, with cement skeletons sprouting everywhere, vying with the forest, which is the place's main attraction.

There are numerous places to stay and eat, several shops, and even a small travel agency, Orfanos Travel (☎22450 51289), which changes money (though there's a freestanding **ATM** on the quay) and sells ferry tickets. In terms of **accommodation**, top of the heap in all senses is hospitable George Niotis' *Hotel Studios Glaros* (☎22450 51501 or 694 79 44 601, ⓦwww.hotelglaros .gr; ❸) up the south slope, with some of its sixteen huge, tiered units having four beds. Worthy alternatives, all 300m on the road west more or less opposite each other, are *The Dolphins/Ta Dhelfínia Studios* (☎22450 51354; ❶) under the eponymous restaurant, pleasant ground-floor units overlooking the garden; *Rooms Anesis* (☎22450 51415; ❶) across the road; and the *Hotel Nikos* (☎22450 51410, ⓔorfanos-hotel@hol.gr; ❸).

As for **tavernas**, best avoid the conspicuous spots on the front which tout aggressively in favour of the following choices. *The Dolphins/Ta Dhelfínia* does very good fish, and vegetables from the garden just below. Vine-shrouded *Iy Aníxi* in a backstreet behind the water does a few simple, cheap *mayireftá* daily, with no touting (and not much English spoken either). Opposite the waterfront fountain, near the ATM, favourite meeting place *Iy Gorgona/L'Angolo*, run by Gigi (Naples) and Gabriella (Genoa) features light dishes, wonderful own-made desserts, proper coffees, and *limoncello* digestif. The small local Egyptian community also gathers here in the evenings to partake of a fragrant hubble-bubble.

Local beaches

The closest beach to Dhiafáni, if not the best, is **Vanánda**, a coarse-pebble bay with a lush oasis just inland, whose powerful springs supply Dhiafáni with water. Here you'll find *Sia keh Araxame* (☎22450 51288; May–Sept), a slogan-bedaubed **campsite/snack-bar** managed by Minas and a young assistant; it is Minas who's posted the signs on the beach forbidding absolutely everything that might degrade the local environment. To reach Vanánda, follow the pleasant path from the primary school (northernmost building in town) through the pines and olives, but don't believe any signs that say "ten minutes" – it's over half an hour away. An ugly, more recent dirt road cuts the path in two spots for a few minutes, but it's not too obtrusive and the trail is still much quicker.

Much better beaches lie south of Dhiafáni; the boat ride in from Pigádhia is an excellent way of spotting likely coves along this coast, and committing their location to memory. The best one within easy walking distance is attractive **Papá Miná**, 100m or so of small-to-medium pebbles, with some tamarisks for shade. It's just under an hour's hike away, the path starting behind the boatyard area just off the ferry-dock road, prosaically next to the oil-changing bay. As with Vanánda, there's also a jeep track to Papá Miná, but the older trail short-cuts it for all except for a five-minute stretch near the harbour, and then for ten minutes about forty minutes along. The trail itself is intrinsically enjoyable, roller-coasting in and out of ravines, mixing sharp grades with level progress through olive groves, but heading counterintuitively inland at times.

With your own jeep (*not* a scooter or saloon car), or by taking a boat excursion, you can reach three other superb beaches below the 19.2km between Spóa and Ólymbos (all but 1km of this is dirt surface). The closest, also with path access from Ólymbos, is 250-metre-long, shingle/gravel **Forókli** (clothing optional), accessed by a bad 5.5-kilometre side-track. Some 7km further towards Spóa, there's the turning for the even worse 3.5-kilometre track down to **Áyios Minás** (bear left at the fork partway along) and **Agnóndia** (bear right), equally pristine. The rewards are commensurate with the hardship; Áyios Minás has 200m of fine pebbles and coarse sand, with pristine water and sea caves to the south. There's a namesake *monastiráki* dedicated to the saint (after whom a quarter of the island population is named) on the north promontory, and a few farmhouses just inland, so you may have to "suit up" at times.

Saría

The now-uninhabited island of **Saría**, with its fine walking traverse, striking gorge and eerie ruins, is the destination for up to two weekly all-day **boat trips** (most reliably on Thurs; enquire at Orfanos Travel; see opposite). Costing about €22 per person, including a decent barbecue lunch, these depart Dhiafáni at around 9.30am and take 45min to reach Yaplós bay at the south end of Saría, with a request stop at Ayía Ekateríni jetty on the north end of Kárpathos, for those walkers wishing to walk one-way Trístomo-Avlóna. The south-to-north walk across Saría is not guided or consistently waymarked, so detailed directions follow.

From where the boat drops you at Yaplós, there's a twenty-minute climb, past **Áyios Spyrídhon**, on the west side of the main ravine forging inland, to a slackening of the grade near a well and the first of several olive plantations. Thread through terraces here, past cottages in good repair, to a pass and chapel of **Áyios Andhréas**, just off the path. Next you pass a house with solar panels to reach the next ridge, of equal height, just under an hour along – the sea is back in view, with the north tip of Saría plainly visible. An hour and a quarter underway, you enter a patch of cliffside pine forest for some welcome shade; leaving the pine grove, you pass under a huge walled cave and (90min along) worm your way over a rock outcrop – high point of the traverse – via a natural stairway. Shortly thereafter, you emerge onto a plateau where the route becomes faint and it's easy to lose the way; the correct path goes down into the top of a ravine draining from a few terraces and house on the left. Just under two hours into the day, the village of Árgos comes into sight; leave the side of the ravine and descend through terraces, skirting an enclosure, to reach (2hr 15min) the bed of another ravine. There's a fork here; going straight up for a few moments detours to **Árgos**, uninhabited since the last elderly resident died in the 1980s. Follow instead a few blue paint splodges into the spectacular narrows of the cliff-flanked ravine, emerging after about ten minutes at the top of a *kalderími* stretch, which gives views of Palátia bay before dropping you down to the chapel of **Ayía Sofía** by the ravine bed, built on Byzantine foundations, with traces of ancient settlement all around. You'll tread the pebbles of the bay underfoot some two and a half hours after quitting Yaplós, but best allow three and a half hours, including photo opportunities, water stops and time for getting lost.

After a well-deserved swim in the delightful bay, make sure to explore the intriguing, so-called **Palátia** on the northerly hillside. These comprise two beehive-domed structures and nine or so barrel-vaulted ones; they're the wrong orientation for chapels and not dug in correctly to be cisterns, so they are most probably grain warehouses, like the vaguely similar buildings on Agathoníssi (see p.314). It's not certain who erected them, or when, though "sixth-century AD Syrian pirates" as bruited locally seems as plausible as any theory.

A large cave near Palátia is the focus of a curious tale, reminiscent of the Homeric legend of Odysseus and the Cyclops. Some two centuries ago, a resident shepherd was repeatedly victimized by pirates who landed and demanded

Greek script table

Kárpathos	Κάρπαθος	ΚΑΡΠΑΘΟΣ
Aháta	Αχάτα	ΑΧΑΤΑ
Ammopí	Αμμοπή	ΑΜΜΟΠΗ
Ápella	Άπελλα	ΑΠΕΛΛΑ
Apéri	Απέρι	ΑΠΕΡΙ
Arkássa	Αρκάσα	ΑΡΚΑΣΑ
Avlóna	Αυλώνα	ΑΥΛΩΝΑ
Ayía Marína	Αγία Μαρίνα	ΑΓΙΑ ΜΑΡΙΝΑ
Áyios Minás	Άγιος Μηνάς	ΑΓΙΟΣ ΜΗΝΑΣ
Áyios Nikólaos	Άγιος Νικόλαος	ΑΓΙΟΣ ΝΙΚΟΛΑΟΣ
Dhiafáni	Διαφάνι	ΔΙΑΦΑΝΙ
Forókli	Φορόκλι	ΦΟΡΟΚΛΙ
Kyrá Panayiá	Κυρά Παναγιά	ΚΥΡΑ ΠΑΝΑΓΙΑ
Lefkós	Λεφκός	ΛΕΦΚΟΣ
Menetés	Μενετές	ΜΕΝΕΤΕΣ
Mesohóri	Μεσοχώρι	ΜΕΣΟΧΩΡΙ
Ólymbos	Όλυμπος	ΟΛΥΜΠΟΣ
Óthos	Όθος	ΟΘΟΣ
Palátia	Παλάτια	ΠΑΛΑΤΙΑ
Paralía Lefkoú	Παραλία Λεφκού	ΠΑΡΑΛΙΑ ΛΕΦΚΟΥ
Pigádhia	Πιγάδια	ΠΗΓΑΔΙΑ
Pylés	Πυλές	ΠΥΛΕΣ
Saría	Σαρία	ΣΑΡΙΑ
Stés	Στές	ΣΤΕΣ
Spóa	Σποα	ΣΠΟΑ
Trístomo	Τρίστομο	ΤΡΙΣΤΟΜΟ
Vanánda	Βανάντα	ΒΑΝΑΝΤΑ
Voládha	Βωλάδα	ΒΩΛΑΔΑ
Vrykoúnda	Βρυκούντα	ΒΥΚΟΥΝΤΑ
Vróndi	Βρόντη	ΒΡΟΝΤΗ

full meals without recompense. One day, the hapless shepherd conceived a plan while stirring milk in a cauldron with an enormous wood ladle. As fifteen or so pirates sat feasting, he blinded them all with a well-aimed arc of scalding milk, then seized their piled-up muskets and did away with the corsairs – and got their beached boat and oars in the bargain.

The return trip from Palátia to Dhiafáni (4pm) takes about an hour and a quarter, including a stop at a deep sea cave where fishing boats (and, it is claimed, World War II patrol boats) could hide in rough weather. Saría and northern Kárpathos are in fact semi-protected environments, with monk seals said to be in residence offshore.

Kárpathos travel details

Island transport

Buses

Dhiafáni to: Ólymbos (2 daily each way, plus tour coaches).

Pigádhia to: Ammopí (6 daily); Apéri (4–6 daily); Arkássa (5 daily); Finíki (5 daily); Mesohóri/Spóa (1 daily Mon–Fri, school term only); Paralía Lefkoú (1 daily Mon, Wed & Sat); Óthos (4 daily); Pylés (4 daily); Voládha (4 daily).

Inter-island transport

Kaïkia

Dhiafáni to: Pigádhia (postbag sailing Mon, Wed & Fri at 8am, returns around 2pm except Fri when boat stays weekend in Pigádhia, returning Sun 5.30pm); Saría (Thurs 10am, to Yaplós, returning 4pm from Palátia).
Finíki to: Kássos (Mon, Wed & Fri at 12.45pm; 1hr).
Pigádhia to: Dhiafáni (at least 1 daily June–Sept; 1hr 30min–1hr 45min).

Ferries

Pigádhia/Dhiafáni to: each other (3–4 weekly on LANE; 1hr); Crete (Sitía/Áyios Nikólaos; 3–4 weekly on LANE; 4hr 15min–7hr 45min); Hálki (3–4 weekly on LANE; 2–3hr); Kássos (3–4 weekly on LANE; 1hr 15min–2hr 15min); Pireás (3 weekly on LANE; 20hr–21hr 15min); Rhodes (3–4 weekly on LANE; 4–5hr).

Flights

Kárpathos to: Athens (3–5 weekly; 1hr 20min); Kássos (9 weekly; 20min); Rhodes (at least 2 daily; 35min).
NB Flights between Kárpathos and Kássos will often fly in winds that prevent ferries from docking, and – taxi fare to the airport aside – don't cost vastly more than a ferry or *kaïki* passage. Given the inconvenient Rhodes–Kárpathos–Kássos ferry links – 4.30am departures from Rhodes are the rule – all local flights are in heavy demand, and although De Havilland 38-seaters have replaced tiny Dornier puddle-jumpers on this route, seats should be booked a week or two in advance in summer.

Kássos

Like Psará in the east Aegean, **Kássos** bravely contributed its large fleet to the Greek revolutionary war effort, and likewise suffered appalling consequences. In late May 1824, an Ottoman army commanded by Ibrahim Pasha of Egypt laid siege to the island; on June 7, aided perhaps by a traitor's tip as to the weak point in Kássos' defences, the invaders descended on the populated north coast plain, slaughtered nearly three-quarters of the 11,000 inhabitants, and put houses, farms and trees to the torch.

Barren and depopulated since then, Kássos attracts few visitors, despite being a regular port of call for large ferries and having reliable air links with Rhodes and Kárpathos. What remains of the population is grouped together in five villages under the shadow of Kárpathos, leaving most of the island deserted. Though the regulation concrete "box-villas" are beginning to sprout even here, ruining architectural homogeneity, there's surprisingly little evidence of the wealth brought to other islands by diaspora Greeks or – since Kássos hasn't much to offer them – by tourists; crumbling houses and disused hillside terraces are poignant reminders of better days.

Kássos is more productive than it appears from the sea, though it's not a fertile island by any stretch of the imagination; as on Psará, wild trees have never taken root again since the holocaust. Sheer gorges slash through lunar terrain, and fenced smallholdings of wind-lashed midget olives provide the only permanent relief. Springtime grain crops briefly soften the usually empty terraces, and livestock manages to get by on a thin covering of thornbush.

Especially after the 1824 events, Kassiots distinguished themselves as skilled pilots (see Contexts, p.505); the rugged, almost harbourless coast here was perhaps the best training ground imaginable. The sailing tradition endures; you might see a *kaïki* fetching the largely Kassiot crew from

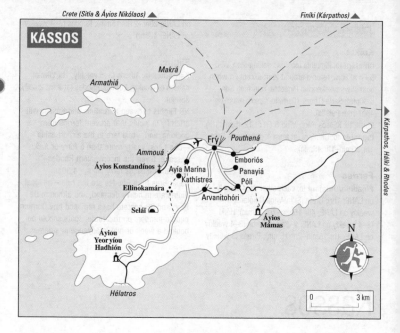

a passing freighter for a three-hour home "furlough". Ironically, in view of Ibrahim Pasha's Egyptian origins, islanders were also instrumental in digging the Suez Canal, and there was for many decades a substantial Kassiot community in Port Said. These days, evidence of emigration to the USA is everywhere: American-logo T-shirts and baseball caps are *de rigueur* in summer, and the conversation of vacationing expatriates is spiked with East Coast Americanisms.

Arrival and other practicalities

Reaching Kássos has been made much easier by the provision of larger aircraft for the daily flights in from Kárpathos and Rhodes, and the completion (by the third contractor to attempt it) of a new **port** at Frý (pronounced "free"), replacing the old, inadequate docking west of Boúka fishing port. The **airport** lies 1km west of Frý, an easy enough fifteen-minute walk (ignore mendacious signs reading "8km"), or a cheap ride in one of the island's two taxis. In July and August, a few boat excursions are offered, plus there's a single **scooter** and quad **rental** outlet, Frangiskos Ikonomou (☎22450 41746 or 697 79 98 676) in central Frý, who claims to operate all year (though machines are assembled and insured only June–Sept). During school holidays, a single white Mercedes van provides a **bus** service, shuffling along an idiosyncratic routing between the inhabited villages, up to six times daily. Otherwise, the only method of exploring the island's remoter corners is by hiking along fairly arduous, shade-less paths and roads. Place-name signposting tends to be in Greek only, and in Kassiot dialect at that – clearly the islanders aren't expecting many non-Kassiot visitors. There's a single stand-alone **bank** ATM at the start of the road to Emboriós, and a **post office** nearby.

Frý and Emboriós

Most of the capital **FRÝ**'s appeal is confined to the immediate environs of the wedge-shaped fishing port of **Boúka**, protected from the sea by the two crab-claws of a breakwater and overlooked by the town cathedral of **Áyios Spirídhon**. On June 7, a memorial service for the victims of the 1824 massacre is held here. Inland, Frý is engagingly unpretentious, even down-at-heel; little attempt has been made to prettify what is essentially a scruffy little town that's quite desolate out of season.

Accommodation can be found at the lone seafront hotel *Anagenissis* (ꔩ 22450 41495, ꔞ www.kassos-island.gr; ❸); despite a 2003 makeover it remains overpriced, with smallish rooms. The manager, Emmanuil Manoussos, also has a few pricier, higher-standard apartments (❹), and runs the all-in-one travel agency just below the hotel (though Olympic has its own premises two doors down). It could be worth getting self-catering digs, as there's no reliable place for breakfast, and the hotel doesn't provide it; **shops** in Frý, including two fruit stalls, are fairly well stocked. During high season a few, better-value **rooms** operate, for example the basic, seaside *Flisvos*, by Elias Koutlakis (ꔩ 22450 41430 or 22450 41284; ❷); 150m east of the new harbour, with a shared kitchen.

Outside of peak season, Frý can support only one full-service **taverna** – *O Mylos*, overlooking the ferry quay and a popular place to wait for the boat. Luckily it's excellent and reasonable, with a good variety of daily-special *mayireftá* and chunky dips at lunch and sometimes fish grills by night. Several **bar-kafenía-ouzerís** perched above Boúka – *Astravi*, *Zantana*, *To Apangio* – are the focus for such nightlife as there is. In the suburb village of **EMBORIÓS**, *Taverna Emborios* matches *O Mylos* in quality (though exceeds it in price), but only operates May to September.

Northern beaches

Frý's town **beach**, if you can call it that, is at **Ammouá** (Ammoudhiá), a thirty-minute walk beyond the airport along the coastal track. This sandy cove, just before the landmark chapel of Áyios Konstandínos, is often caked with seaweed and tar, but persevere five minutes more and you'll find much cleaner pea-gravel coves. The determined can swim off the seventy-metre-long patch of sand at **Emboriós**, and there's a more private pebble stretch off to the right as you face the sea. But having got this far, it's best to continue ten to fifteen minutes along the shore, first along an old track, then on a path past the last house, for a final scramble to the base of the **Pouthená** ravine, where there's another secluded pebble cove. Otherwise, it's worth shelling out for high-season boat excursions to far better beaches on a pair of islets visible to the northwest. **Armathiá** boasts no fewer than five beaches – two small ones on the southeast flank, plus three larger ones on the more exposed northwest shore; **Makrá** has one large sandy cove at its northeast tip. There are no amenities (or shade) on either islet, so bring water, a picnic and some sort of sun protection.

Inland villages and Áï Mámas

Kássos' inland villages cluster at the edges of the agricultural plain just inland from Frý, and are linked to each other by road; all are worth a passing visit, accomplishable by foot in a single day. Larger and more rural than Frý, **AYÍA MARÍNA**, 1500m inland and uphill, is most attractive seen from the south, arrayed above olive groves; one of its two belfried churches is the focus of the island's liveliest festival, on July 17. Some fifteen minutes beyond the hamlet of Kathístres, a further 500m southwest, the cave of **Ellinokamára** is named for the late Classical polygonal wall completely blocking the entrance; its ancient function — perhaps a cult shrine or tomb complex — is uncertain. To reach it, turn south at the two restored windmills in Ayía Marína, then right (west) at the phone-box junction; carry on, straight and down (not level and left) until you see a red-dirt path going up the hillside to a crude, stone-built pastoral hut. Some modern masonry walls enclose the start of this path, but once at the hut (the cave is more or less underneath it) you're compelled to hop a fence to visit — there are no gates. From Ellinokamára another, fainter path — you'll probably need a guide — continues within ninety minutes in the same direction to the larger, more natural cave of **Seláï**, with impressive stalactites in the rear chamber.

Earnest promotion to the contrary, walking opportunities on Kássos are poor — trails are few, not marked and in poor condition, with no shade and few reliable water sources. An exception is the forty-minute path from Arvanitohóri to Póli, which is clearly walled in and enjoyable, short-cutting the road effectively — it starts at the base of the village, where two trees occupy planter wells. **PÓLI**, somewhat impoverished and resolutely agricultural, is the site of a badly deteriorated ancient and medieval acropolis — a few stretches of fortification remain — and marks the start of a dirt road leading southeast to Áyios Mámas, one of two important rural monasteries and signposted in dialect as "Áï Mámas".

To reach **Áï Mámas**, continue on the dirt road started at the far edge of Póli; it's 3km (doable on a scooter) to a window saddle and a landmark, stone-built cottage. It's possible to continue almost another kilometre on a roundabout road system to the monastery, but most will prefer — some 60m past the cottage — to take the second, rough, descending track (not passable to bikes). After about 300m, you'll reach a pumping station, from where a brief final path section brings you to the superbly set *monastiráki*, just visible below on a natural shelf overlooking the sea. Inside, the *katholikón* exemplifies the simplest domed cross-in-square plan, with a fine *votsalotó* floor. The masonry, briefly revealed in 2004 during replastering, suggests a vintage of seventeenth-century, making it the oldest surviving church on Kássos.

Alternatively, from Póli you can descend on walled-in path for the first twenty minutes, then dirt track, to **PANAYIÁ**, famous for its neglected mansions (a few now being renovated) — many of Kássos' wealthiest ship captains hailed from here — and for the second oldest church on the island, eighteenth-century **Panayía toú Yióryi**. The relatively modern, larger church is the venue for the other major island **festival** on August 15. Nearby stands an intriguing Siamese-sextuplet chapel complex, with dedications to six separate saints.

The southwest: Hélatros and Áï Yeóryi

Between Ayía Marína and Arvanitohóri, another paved road veers off southwest from the road linking the two villages; having skirted the narrows of a

Greek script table

Kássos	Κάσος	ΚΑΣΟΣ
Áï Mámas	Άϊ Μάμας	ΑΪ ΜΑΜΑΣ
Áï Yeóryi	Άϊ Γεώργη	ΑΪ ΓΕΩΡΓΗ
Ayía Marína	Αγία Μαρίνα	ΑΓΙΑ ΜΑΡΙΝΑ
Ayíou Yeoryíou	Αγίου Γεωργίου	ΑΓΙΟΥ ΓΕΩΡΓΙΟΥ
Hadhión	Χαδιών	ΧΑΔΙΩΝ
Emboriós	Εμπορειός	ΕΜΠΟΡΕΙΟΣ
Frý	Φρύ	ΦΡΥ
Hélatros	Χέλατρος	ΧΕΛΑΤΡΟΣ
Panayiá	Παναγιέ	ΠΑΝΑΓΙΑ
Póli	Πόλι	ΠΟΛΙ
Pouthená	Πουθενά	ΠΟΥΘΕΝΑ

fearsome gorge, you are unlikely to see another living thing aside from goats, sheep or an occasional Eleonora's falcon. After about an hour, the Mediterranean appears to the south, a dull expanse ruffled only by the occasional ship bound for Cyprus and the Middle East. When you finally reach a fork, adopt the upper, right-hand turning, following phone lines towards the rural monastery of **Ayíou Yeoryíou Hadhión** (signed as "**Áï Yeóryi**"), 12km (3hr on foot) from Frý. This is busiest at its late April festival time – a big new banqueting-hall-with-kitchen was added in 2004 – but during the warmer months there may be a resident caretaker, and there's also cistern water if you need to fill canteens. There are a few guest cells, but it's unlikely you'll be allowed to stay as they're endowed by families for their use or by other Orthodox pilgrims. Since the paving of the road, there's little joy to be had in walking it, certainly not both ways – hire a taxi, rent a vehicle if available, or hitch a lift in at least one direction.

From the monastery it's another 2.5km on dirt track – motorbikes or (probably safer) quads can negotiate all of it – to **Hélatros** (still "Hélathros" on older maps), a lonely cove at the mouth of one of the larger, more forbidding Kassiot canyons. Only the right-hand 80m of this sand-and-pea-gravel beach is really usable, but the water is pristine and – except for the occasional fishing boat or yacht – you'll probably be alone. The lower, left-hand option at the fork is the direct track to Hélatros; this is only 700m shorter but perfectly passable, and makes an interesting variation of the return to town.

Kássos travel details

Inter-island transport

Ferries

Kássos to: Crete (Sitía/Áyios Nikólaos 3–4 weekly on LANE; 2hr 30min–5hr); Dhiafáni, Kárpathos (3–4 weekly on LANE; 2hr 15min); Hálki (3–4 weekly on LANE; 4hr 15min); Pigádhia, Kárpathos (3–4 weekly on LANE; 1hr 15min); Pireás (3 weekly on LANE; 18hr 30min); Rhodes (3–4 weekly on LANE; 6hr 15min).

Kaïki

Kássos to: Finíki, Kárpathos (3 weekly, usually Mon, Wed & Fri at 8am, returns 12.45pm; 45min–1hr).

Flights

Kássos to: Kárpathos (9 weekly; 20min); Rhodes (9 weekly; 1hr 20min).

Hálki

Hálki, a tiny (twenty square kilometres), waterless, limestone speck west of Rhodes, is a fully fledged member of the Dodecanese, though all but about 250 of the former population of six thousand, plus a few hundred from the dependency of Alimniá, emigrated (mostly to Rhodes or to Tarpon Springs, Florida) in response to Italian restrictions on sponge-fishing in 1916. Despite a renaissance through tourism in recent years, the island remains tranquil compared to its big neighbour, albeit with a rather artificial, stage-set atmosphere. This has much to do with foreigners vastly outnumbering native islanders for most of the year; the former tend to be invisible during daylight hours, holed up on the verandas of their pricey package villas. The big event of the day is the arrival of the regular afternoon *kaïki* from Kámiros Skála on Rhodes, since the island has historically been just a bit too remote for the sort of day-trips that plague Sými – though the *Sea Star* catamaran now provides such. Besides people, Hálki is home to about five thousand sheep and goats, plus a sizeable fishing fleet which sends most of its catch to Rhodes – together, the only significant economic activity aside from summer tourism.

The first hint of development came in 1983, when UNESCO designated Hálki as the "isle of peace and friendship" and made it the seat of an annual summer international youth conference. (Tílos was approached first but declined the honour.) As part of the deal, some 150 crumbling island houses were to be restored as accommodation for the delegates and other interested parties, with UNESCO footing most of the bill. As of 1987, just one hotel had been completed; the only tangible sign of "peace and friendship" was an unending stream of UNESCO and Athenian bureaucrats occupying every available bed and staging drunken, musical binges under the rubric of "ecological conferences". Confronted with an apparent scam, the islanders sent UNESCO packing in 1988 and contracted two UK specialist package

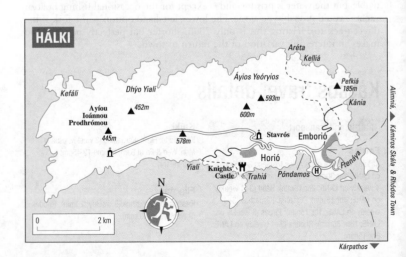

operators to complete restorations and bring in paying guests. Two more tour companies are now present, and most of the ruins have been refurbished (with a few for sale); however, tour clientele was down in 2003–04, and for the first time significant numbers of independent Italian, French and German travellers are appearing.

Emborió

All of the restoration villas are in **EMBORIÓ**, the port and only area of habitation, where the waterfront has been paved with fieldstones, generally prettified and declared off limits to vehicles in season. The skyline is pierced by the tallest freestanding **clocktower** in the Dodecanese, beside the town hall, with each of its four faces permanently stopped – to quote a tour-brochure cliché, time really does stand still here. It's nearly matched in height by the campanile of **Áyios Nikólaos church** below, with its fine *hokhláki* (pebble-mosaic) courtyard.

Accommodation

Most **accommodation** is pretty much block-booked from April to October by the tour companies and occupied by a rather staid, well-mannered, upper-middle class clientele from the British Home Counties. Late June to late September, when the town is often host to consecutive conferences, is pretty well impossible; island-hoppers should scrupulously avoid Hálki at that time unless they have a reservation. Even early or late in the season, independent travellers may be lucky to find anything at all, and if travelling alone should expect to pay the full double rate.

The best place to start your hunt is the *Captain's House* (☎22460 45201; ❷), a wonderful, quiet spot north of the church and three tiers "up". It has the feel of a French country inn, where three en-suite rooms have fridges and you're in close contact with your hosts, Alex (ex-Greek Navy captain) and Christine Sakelaridhes. Owing to its small size, pre-booking is manda-tory, but if they're full they will point you in other likely directions. Frances Mayes, editor of the local bimonthly newspaper *Halki Visitor*, occasionally has a house available, sleeping four (☎22460 45061, ✉francesm@otenet.gr. The taverna at Póndamos beach (see p.191) offers four rather basic, terrazzo-floored, sea-view rooms (☎ & ☎22460 45295; ❸). Finally, the municipally owned *Hotel Halki* (☎22460 45390, ☎22460 45208, ✉depah1@otenet .g; ❹ May–Oct) in the old sponge factory on the south side of the bay, is likely to have a vacancy amongst its 26 rooms; it resumed operations in 2004, and under energetic new management is set for a complete overhaul in 2005–06.

Eating, drinking and entertainment

If lodging in the self-catering villas works out relatively expensive, eating out can be surprisingly reasonable, especially compared to any neighbouring isle. Of the seven full-service **tavernas** on Emborió's waterfront, *Remezzo* is excellent for *mayireftá* and pizzas, *Maria* behind the post office has good grills, *Houvardas* (aka *Asia's*) near the north end of the quay has proven reliable for *mayireftá* and grills over the years, and *Avra* is conscientiously run by Greeks from Georgia in the Caucasus. A similar number of **bars** and **cafés** sit all in a row at mid-quay. *Theodosia's* (aka "The Parrot Bar" after its resident bird), near the base of the jetty, has puddings and homemade ice cream to die for; *Kostas* is an old standby with good breakfast service, while *To Steki* is usually the most musically active, with a sculpted counter outdoors.

More formal entertainment is provided through the **Halki Festival** (late June to mid-Sept), with performances by top Greek musical names like Mario, Eleni Vitali and Eleni Tsaligopoulou.

Other practicalities

Other essential facilities include a **post office** (there's no bank, though an ATM is reportedly arriving in 2005), several shops amply stocked for self-catering, a decent bakery cranking out a range of breads and pies, plus two **travel agencies**: Halki Tours (☎22460 45281), the representative of Laskarina Holidays; and Zifos Tours (☎22460 45028, ✉zifos-travel@rho.forthnet .gr), which handles Direct Greece, Olympic and Travel à la Carte properties, and often has a few studio (◑) vacancies, which they hold back from the UK companies. Both agencies will also **change money** at a pinch – for a two percent commission – and both sell ferry tickets. At the start of the road out of town there's a **gym**, popular with locals and visitors alike; one-offs are welcome, at €10 per day, or you can take out a weekly/fortnightly membership for €30/55.

The interior

Three kilometres inland, 45 minutes' walk west of Emborió, lies the old pirate-proof village of **HORIÓ**, abandoned in the 1950s by its poor shepherd inhabitants. The 1990s laying-down of power lines, and a few restored cottages, suggested that Horió might go the way of Emborió, but the archeological service put its foot down, so deserted it remains. Except during the August 14–15 *paniyíri*, the church is kept securely locked to protect its medieval frescoes; just behind it a clear path climbs for about ten minutes to the dilapidated **castle**, built largely from ancient masonry. Inside this, traces of Byzantine frescoes still cling to an otherwise ruined chapel – in 2003, the archeological authorities cleaned them and left them *in situ*. Across the valley, the little monastery of **Stavrós** is the venue for another festival on September 14.

There's little else to see or do inland, though you can spend three hours (each way) on foot following the paved road across the island from Emborió to the monastery of **Ayíou Ioánnou Prodhrómou**. The caretaker there can put you up in a cell (except around August 28–29, the island's biggest festival), but you'll need to bring supplies. The terrain en route is monotonous, but enhanced by views over half the Dodecanese and Turkey; occasionally an excursion bus or a taxi trundles along to the monastery (there's no scooter rental), sparing you the dull slog (for a better walk, see opposite). The section of road as far as Stavrós is known as "Tarpon Springs Boulevard", its cement pavement originally donated by the expatriate community in Florida to ensure easy Cadillac access to the Stavrós *paniyíri* grounds. The money might have been better spent on a proper sewage system (finally provided in 1996) and salt-free water supply – like most essentials, fresh water has to be brought from Rhodes by tanker, and can run out in peak season.

Island beaches

Póndamos, fifteen minutes' walk west of Emborió, is the only sandy beach on Hálki. Longish (100m) but narrow, its sunbeds are completely packed in summer, though you can escape the crowds for some excellent snorkelling. The main facility is the somewhat pricey *Nick's Pondamos Taverna*, open for lunch daily, plus two or three random evenings weekly. A few minutes' well-signposted path-walk past the *Hotel Halki*, tiny coves of pebbles along the shore known as **Ftenáya** are also heavily subscribed; a dirt track also leads to a decent taverna-bar (*Tou Vangeli*) right above the main cove, with good seafood and *ouzomezédhes* on offer.

Small and pebbly **Yialí**, west of and considerably below Horió, is an hour's hike away from Póndamos, down a jeep track. There's absolutely no shade, and the sea can be rough in this exposed setting. Half an hour's walk north of Emborió lies **Kánia**, with a rocky foreshore but sandy bay-bottom; there's no shade in the morning, and a rather industrial ambience from both the power lines coming in from Rhodes, and the island's only petrol pump off to one side. These four coves lie within easy walking distance but are no great shakes, so it's well worth signing on at Emborió's quay for boat excursions to more remote beaches, difficult or impossible to reach by land. More or less at the centre of Hálki's southern shore, directly below Horió's castle, **Trahiá** (or Trahía) consists of two coves on either side of an isthmus, one or the other providing shelter in any wind. You can in fact (just) reach this overland by rough path from Yialí; the east-facing one is usually much cleaner.

North coast beaches figuring as excursion-boat destinations (weather permitting) include the pretty fjord of **Aréta**, **Áyios Yeóryios** just beyond, and the remote double bay of **Dhýo Yialí**. Of these, Aréta is the most attractive, and the most accessible overland; directions are given below.

Hike to Aréta from Emborió

To do this with extra confidence you'll want to buy the *Chalki, Island of Peace & Friendship* tourist map, based on Italian-era topographical maps; though the path tracings may not always be reliable, with roads bulldozed over them, the contour lines are correct. The following is the most direct of two possible routes to Aréta.

Begin along the cemented track heading to Kánia; above the municipal cisterns, beyond power lines passing overhead, bear left where a power pole stands at the left verge of the road, near a wrecked white car and a small pastoral shed. Go north through a crude gate, then adopt a path which climbs with a fence to your left until reaching a second gate. Once past this, you're in open country, with the trail fairly well grooved into the surface, and marked by occasional cairns. The route skirts a large stone pen, and levels out briefly as it threads between two terraces of stunted olives; this area is called **Petrólakko**, rendered as "Petrolaco" on the Italian map.

Now the path veers briefly northeast and resumes climbing, right under the island's summit-ridge, here punctuated by overhanging caves. Pointing north again, the path slips through a wall and, about an hour out of Emborió, levels out on a vast plateau inclined slightly to the north. Near a second wall, Tílos pops into view, and a few hundred metres off to the left stands a rock outcrop strongly resembling a pimple or a mole. Once through a third and final wall, the path begins to descend, gradually at first and then more sharply as it gets momentarily fainter. It zigzags just past a livestock corral built into the lee of some rock formations; inside the corral is a cistern, with murky water that might do for emergencies. The most obvious nearby canyon draining to the sea is **Kelliá** ("Cellia" on the Italian map) – stay away from that. The again-distinct correct trail, still cairned, heads northwest, then almost west, to cross the top of the gulch leading down to Aréta. You pass through two gates (often propped open), then curl along the top of the left (west) flank of the canyon, dropping to sea level in easy stages; memorize landmarks here carefully, as it's surprisingly easy to get lost on the way back uphill. The final approach to the beach is a steep "ladder-stair" recessed in the rock face, manageable by any fit person; you touch down on the small-pebble strand some ninety minutes from Emborió (allow 15min more if you pause a lot).

Aréta fjord is an impressive place girt by high cliffs where seabirds roost and soar. There's some morning and afternoon shade, but only a brackish well, used by the inquisitive sheep with whom you may share the beach, so it's best to bring plenty of your own water.

Alimniá

One of the more popular trips from Hálki visits the deserted islet of **ALIM-NIÁ** (Alimiá), roughly halfway between Hálki and Rhodes, a favourite swimming and barbecuing venue for both islanders and tour clients. Despite more well-water and greenery, and a better harbour than on Hálki, the village here, overlooked by a couple of palm trees and a Knights' castle, was completely depopulated by the 1960s. It is said that the inhabitants were initially deported during World War II after they confessed to assisting British commandos sent in April 1944 to sabotage the German submarines who used the deep harbour here. The seven commandos themselves were captured by the Nazis, bundled off first to Rhodes, then to Thessaloníki, where six were summarily executed as commandos (not protected by the rules of engagement) rather than regular POWs; Kurt Waldheim allegedly counter-signed their death sentences.

Despite its historical interest, Alimniá is probably not a place you'd want to be stuck for an entire day. Excursions (out at 10am, back at 4pm)

Greek script table

Hálki	Χάλκη	ΧΑΛΚΗ
Alim[n]iá	Αλιμ[ν]ιά	ΑΛΙΜ[Ν]ΙΑ
Aréta	Αρέτα	ΑΡΕΤΑ
Áyios Yeóryios	Άγιος Γεώργιος	ΑΓΙΟΣ ΓΕΩΡΓΙΟΣ
Ayíou Ioánnou	Αγιου Ιοάννου	ΑΓΙΟΥ ΙΟΑΝΝΟΥ
Prodhrómou	Προδρόμου	ΠΡΟΔΡΟΜΟΥ
Dhýo Yialí	Δύο Γιαλοί	ΔΥΟ ΓΙΑΛΟΙ
Emborió	Εμπορειό	ΕΜΠΟΡΕΙΟ
Horió	Χωριό	ΧΩΡΙΟ
Kánia	Κάνια	ΚΑΝΙΑ
Póndamos	Πόνταμος	ΠΟΝΤΑΜΟΣ
Stavrós	Σταυρός	ΣΤΑΥΡΟΣ
Trahiá	Τραχειά	ΤΡΑΧΕΙΑ
Yialí	Γιαλή	ΓΙΑΛΗ

are overpriced at €25–30 depending on passenger numbers, even considering that this includes a light lunch. Matters begin promisingly enough with anchorage in the lee of diminutive Áyios Minás monastery, but then there's a mad scramble from the usual two docked boats for precious spots on the tiny beaches of the bay's south shore. If you go snorkelling in the outer bay beyond Áyios Minás, you can still glimpse outlines of the submarine pens, while the Italian barracks near the mooring point bear the trace lines of bullet holes. The **old village** sits behind a salt marsh at the head of the bay, consisting mostly of derelict shepherds' huts; near the church a grander house which once served as a taverna contains crude paintings of ships and submarines sketched by bored Italian soldiers. Nowadays just one building is inhabited on a seasonal basis, when Alimniá is used by shepherds grazing livestock; otherwise the place sees life only at the festival of St George in late April. The rather battered **castle** is a 45-minute one-way hike away from the anchorage, with poor paths up, though well worth the climb.

Hálki travel details

Inter-island transport

Kaïkia

Hálki to: Kámiros Skála, Rhodes (1 daily on either *Nissos Halki* (5 cars carried) or the *Nikos Express* (3 cars carried); 1hr 30min).

NB Most days at least one of these *kaïkia* leaves Skála at 2.30–2.45pm, returning from Hálki the next morning at 6am. On Sundays, a day-excursion schedule applies, leaving Skála at 9am, returning from Hálki at around 4pm, with another journey back to Halki from Skála at 6pm. Wednesday and Sunday, the typical transfer days for tour clients, can be problematic; enquire as to space availability well in advance if you intend to travel on those days.

Ferries

Hálki to: Kárpathos, both ports (2–3 weekly on LANE; 2hr–3hr 15min); Kássos (2 weekly on LANE; 4hr 30min); Rhodes (2–3 weekly on LANE; 2hr).

Catamaran

2 weekly links with Rhodes and Tilos (40–50min) on the *Sea Star*.

NB On these days (typically Tues & Sat) it is possible to make a day-trip from Rhodes on the catamaran, which leaves Rhodes at 9am and calls at Hálki en route to Tílos. However, on one day you may have to return to Rhodes in the evening by mainline ferry, as the *Sea Star* proceeds directly from Tílos to Rhodes.

Kastellórizo

Kastellórizo's official name, Meyísti ("Biggest"), seems more an act of defiance than a statement of fact. While the largest of a tiny local group of islands, it is actually among the smallest of the Dodecanese, over seventy nautical miles from its nearest Greek neighbour (Rhodes), but hardly more than a nautical mile from the Turkish coast at the narrowest straits. At night its lights are quite outnumbered by those of the Turkish town of Kaş, about four nautical miles across the bay, with whom Kastellórizo has long had excellent relations (indeed Kaş was founded by the islanders during the eighteenth century).

KASTELLÓRIZO (MEYÍSTI)

Áyios Stéfanos   Vathoryáki

MEDITERRANEAN
SEA

Plákes

Psorádhia

Army base   Profítis Ilías

Knights' Castle
Lycian House Tomb
Cemetery

Ayías Triádhos   Horáfia

Paleókastro   Kastellórizo Town   Mandhráki

Power plant   Cape Nýftis

▲ Vígla

AVLÓNIA
Wine press

Ayíou Yeoryíou toú Vounioú   Wine press

Airstrip

Návlakas

Rubbish tip

Perastá (Galázio Spílio)

N

0   1 km

Some history

During the island's heyday (roughly 1860–1910), almost ten thousand people lived here, supported by a fleet of schooners that transported goods – mostly timber – from the then-Greek Orthodox towns of Kalamaki (now Kalkan) and Andifelos (Kaş), on the Anatolian mainland opposite. But the withdrawal of island autonomy after the 1908 "Young Turk" revolution, the Italian seizure of the other Dodecanese in 1912 and an inconclusively inept 1913–15 period of self-rule sent the island into decline. The French, not the Italians, were masters here between 1915 and 1921 when they needed a staging post for the Syrian front, which made Kastellórizo a hapless target for Ottoman artillery on the Anatolian mainland. On January 9, 1917, the British seaplane carrier *Ben-My-Chree*, among the first such craft ever built, was sunk by a well-aimed Turkish shell while at anchor here.

Kastellorizan ship-owners failed to modernize their craft upon the advent of steam power late in the nineteenth century, preferring to sell their fleets to the British for the Dardanelles campaign; the new frontier drawn up between Kastellórizo and republican Turkey, combined with the expulsion of all Anatolian Greeks in 1923, deprived any remaining vessels of their trade. During the 1930s, Kastellórizo enjoyed a brief renaissance when it became a major stopover point for French and British seaplanes en route to Beirut and Haifa respectively, but events at the close of World War II put an end to any hopes of the island's continued viability.

When Italy capitulated to the Allies in the autumn of 1943, Kastellórizo was occupied by nearly 1500 British commandos, most of whom departed of their own accord in November after severe German air raids here and the Allied surrender of Léros – leaving Kastellórizo deserted except for a token force. In July, 1944, a harbour fuel dump caught (or was set on) fire and an adjacent arsenal exploded, taking with it more than half of the two thousand houses on Kastellórizo. Postwar enquiries concluded that, although a small minority of British officers had engaged in some haphazard looting before their departure, it was probably Greeks engaged in pillaging of their own who accidentally or deliberately caused the conflagration. The British government, without admitting guilt, agreed in 1955 to pay compensation for the missing items; however, the settlement was delayed for three decades, and then only the 850 surviving applicants in Athens were considered eligible for compensation – those who had emigrated to Australia and the few who had chosen to stay on the island after 1945 were inexplicably excluded. As a result, the British are not especially popular here.

Even before these wartime events, most of the population had left for Rhodes, Athens, Australia (particularly Perth) and North America; ironically, when the long-sought union of the Dodecanese with Greece occurred in 1948, there were fewer than seven hundred islanders remaining. Today there are just 342 official residents here according to the last census (with only about 250 actually living permanently on Kastellórizo), largely maintained by remittances from the 30,000-plus emigrants and by subsidies from the Greek government, which fears that the island will revert to Turkish sovereignty should their numbers diminish any further. There was in fact an American-sponsored plan promulgated in 1964 whereby, in return for substantial union of Cyprus with Greece, Greece would cede Kastellórizo to Turkey. With so few inhabitants, life is inevitably claustrophobic, especially in winter, when feuds and vendettas are resumed after suspension for the tourist season; nearly fifty children, presumably outcomes of those boring winter nights, keep the joint primary/secondary school thriving.

Yet Kastellórizo may have a future of sorts, thanks to expat "Kassies" who have begun renovating their crumbling homes as retirement or holiday venues. Each summer the population is swelled by returnees of Kassie ancestry, a few of whom celebrate traditional weddings in Horáfia's Áyios Konstandínos cathedral, which incorporates ancient columns pilfered from Patara in Asia Minor. Access to the island has also improved; during the 1980s the government dredged the harbour to accommodate larger ferries and completed an airport for flights to and from Rhodes, now undertaken on 38-seater De Havillands. However, in the wake of the Schengen Treaty, Kastellórizo still isn't an official port of entry, a deficiency – despite the optimistic quayside sign boldly proclaiming "Europe Begins Here" – not exactly helpful to the numerous yachties who drop anchor. Legal niceties scarcely concern the hundreds of desperate Kurds fleeing Turkey, who over the years have landed here, given themselves up and then been sent to refugee camps near Athens.

Perhaps the biggest boost in the island's fortunes, however, was serving as the location for the Italian film *Mediterraneo*, winner of the Oscar for Best Foreign

Film in 1992, which has resulted in substantial numbers of Italian midsummer visitors (though the island in fact gets a broad spectrum of tourists). Most visitors either love the island and stay a week, or crave escape after a day; its detractors dismiss Kastellórizo as a human zoo maintained by the Greek government for the edification of nationalists, while partisans celebrate an atmospheric, barely commercialized outpost of Hellenism.

Kastellórizo Town

The current population is concentrated in the northern town of **KASTEL-LÓRIZO** – supposedly the finest natural harbour between Beirut and Fethiye on the Turkish coast – and the little easterly "suburb" of **Mandhráki**. In summer, it's what the Greeks call a *klouví* (birdcage) – the sort of place where, after two strolls up and down the pedestrianized quay, you'll have a nodding acquaintance with your fellow visitors and all the island's characters – such as the bar-crawling priest Papa Yiorgis, who on occasion has been pitched into the water by rowdy yachties.

Most of the town's surviving mansions are ranged along the waterfront, their tiled roofs, wooden balconies and blue or green shutters on tall, narrow windows having obvious counterparts in the originally Greek-built houses of Kalkan and Kaş across the bay. Recent renovations and new-builds exhibit a variety of taste, including some startling splashes of blue, purple and maroon amongst the more traditional white and cream housefronts. Just one street back, however, many of the properties are still derelict – abandonment having succeeded where 1917 shelling, an earthquake in 1926, 1943 air raids and the 1944 fire failed. Sepia-toned and black-and-white postcards and posters on sale of the town in its prime are poignant evidence of its later decline.

Locations used in the **filming** of *Mediterraneo* have become popular attractions. Locals can point out the blue-fronted house near the *Pension Mediterraneo* which hosted the love scenes, or the neglected but beautiful graveyard beyond Mandhráki, whose small non-Orthodox section contains tenants worthy of the movie scenario: a French-Armenian soldier killed in action nearby in 1917, a young French expat who met his end here in 1974, and Riccardo Lazzeri, Milanese house restorer and island adoptee, who died of a heart attack in 1988.

The fire-blasted hill between the harbour and Mandhráki sports a very ruined, fourteenth-century **castle of the Knights**, once vast but blown up by the Venetians after a successful siege of the Ottoman garrison in 1659, and again in 1788. Reached by steps up from the mosque, the *promáhonas* or outer bulwark once served as the Ottoman governor's quarters and is now home to the local **museum** and its friendly staff (Tues–Sun 7am–2.30pm; free); in the courtyard an old Turkish cistern-fountain still provides potable rainwater after a wet winter. Displays include the old lens from the lighthouse on Strongylí (an islet to the east), plates from a Byzantine shipwreck, seventeenth-century frescoes rescued from the church of Ayíou Nikoláou toú Kástrou, a reconstruction of an ancient basilica on the site of today's gaudy but derelict Ayíou Yeoryíou Santrapé (in Horáfia district between the port and Mandhráki), plus predictable ethnographic mock-ups. Just below and beyond the museum, in the cliff face opposite Psorádhia islet, is tucked Greece's only Lycian, fourth-century BC **house-tomb**; it's well signposted from the shoreline walkway, up some stone steps beside the first wooden lamp standard. House-tombs were the common burial places of Lycian nobles and are scattered all along the Turkish coast opposite.

Accommodation

Despite its 1991 strut in front of the cameras, Kastellórizo is not prepared for – nor, outside high season, does it get – more than a dozen visitors per boat or aeroplane arrival. No package holidays operate here, owing to chronically tenuous links with Rhodes and the scarcity of amenities. **Pensions** installed in the old houses have all been upgraded up to en-suite status, and prices have climbed sharply since the millennium. For such a waterless island, mosquitoes are a surprising nuisance, breeding in abandoned cisterns – thus you need either air con or windows with bug screens.

Pension Asimina Behind the arcaded market ☎22460 49361. Decent, wood-trimmed rooms in a variety of bed formats; fairly quiet considering the location. ❷

Pension Caretta Ask at the souvenir shop behind the arcaded market ☎ & ⑁22460 49028, ⓦwww.kastellorizo.de. Another good budget option a bit inland, with simple but spacious and brightly painted en-suite rooms; they also have a handsomely restored apartment in an old house, suitable for a couple. Rooms ❷, house ❸

Karnayo Apartments Just in from the north-west quay ☎22460 49225, ⑁22460 49266, ⓔkarnayo@otenet.gr. A selection of well-restored, air-conditioned rooms, studios and a family apartment for four in two separate buildings here; currently the best value, and quietest setting, in town. Rooms and studios ❹

Kastellorizo Hotel Apartments A bit north of the preceding, opposite the ferry jetty ☎22460 49044, ⓦwww.kastellorizohotel.gr. 2000-built, air-conditioned, quality-fitted studios and galleried maisonettes, some with sea view; small plunge pool and "private" lido. ❻

Pension Mediterraneo On the northwest quay ☎22460 49007 or 697 36 76 038, ⓦwww .mediterraneopension.org. Waterfront pension, completely overhauled by French architect-proprietress Marie, comprising five standard rooms and two suites. About half the rooms have a sea view, as does the lovely arcaded ground-floor suite, which is worth the extra for the privilege of essentially rolling into the sea from the door. Standard units have fridges, fans and good bathrooms, though no air con. Breakfast at extra cost is available, and the pension operates all year. Room ❹, suite ❻

Eating, drinking and nightlife

Apart from fish, goat meat and various fig-based sweets, plus whatever fresh produce is smuggled over from Kaş Kastellórizo must import staple foodstuffs and also water from Rhodes; taverna prices can consequently be slightly higher than usual, with the further pretext of the island's celebrity status. Incidentally, under no circumstances drink the mains water, which has become contaminated.

The two most conspicuous centre-quay **tavernas** have had a long and pernicious acquaintance with the yachts moored in front – it's best to continue a few steps to *To Mikro Parisi* for affordable, and more likely fresher, seafood and meat grills. Other good quayside choices include *Iy Ipomoni* (dinner only), two doors left from the arcaded market, for simple fish grills; and the inexpensive but savoury *Akrothalassi*, purveying large grills and salads near the west end of the quay, by the church – it's popular at lunch, as they've the only shaded seating. One to recommend inland (still adorned with film posters – it served as the canteen for the *Mediterraneo* film crew) is *Ta Platania* (June to mid-Oct), opposite Áyios Konstandínos in Horáfia, good for daily-changing *mayireftá* (moussaka, green beans) and desserts, often homemade. There are more puddings and good breakfasts at *Zaharoplastio Iy Meyisti*, back on the waterfront.

Nightlife spills out of the half-dozen *barákia* lining the quay, occasionally ending up in the water when tipplers overbalance at their tables. Establishments worth singling out include *Faros* near the mosque, a trendy place with

Trips to (and from) Turkey

Since 1996, it has been possible to arrange a day-trip to Kaş in **Turkey**, on one of several small boats – usually the *Varvara* or the *Ayios Yeoryios* – for the sum of €15 return (€12 one way), perhaps leaving your passport with the port authorities one day before. Monday and Friday, when the islanders go shopping on the mainland, are the most reliable days for a transfer across. These figures do not include a Turkish visa fee, which you will definitely be liable for if you stay overnight (say, Fri–Mon). Turkey-based boats also put in regular appearances, though trippers starting from Kaş are looking at €30 for passage.

What remains moot is whether travellers can use Kastellórizo as a one-way entry or exit point to or from Greece, or take a multi-day return trip. Technically, they can: Kaş is a legal port of exit for Turkey, and the Greek authorities cannot (by pan-European law) deny entry to EU nationals, especially if they arrive on a Greek boat. Problems arise from the fact that Kastellórizo does not yet have a fully functioning customs and immigration office, with the necessary stamps to apply to non-EU passports, nor a computerized Schengen database to keep track of miscreants. If you land at Kastellórizo on a non-EU passport, you may be prevented from travelling onwards for a day or two until your personal details are faxed to Rhodes or even Athens and an approval elicited. The Turkish authorities at Kaş, it must be said, will happily stamp you in or out without bothering to check for any Greek stamps. All this, despite a near-farcical situation whereby Kastellorizans themselves must get everything from haircuts to bread to emergency medical care across the way. It's hard to avoid the suspicion that the delays and foot-dragging in inaugurating the necessary facilities serve mostly to protect the lucrative, overpriced operation run by the Rhodes–Marmaris shuttle operators.

---

a roof terrace and music noise levels kept under control (unlike one of its neighbours); friendly *Mythos* back at centre quay, which also does cheap snacks – good to know about when all the tavernas are booked up in midsummer; and *Kaz-Bar* (late June–Sept) to the right of the market, which also sometimes serves food, typically greens, *tabbouleh*, spring rolls, chicken wings and other light dishes appropriate for summer.

Other practicalities

A single **bank**, with handy ATM, stands on the east quay; the **post office** is on the far side of the bay. The more reliable and competent of the town's two **travel agencies** is Papoutsis (℡22410 70630), which represents all ferries and the catamaran, plus selling Olympic Aviation tickets. In theory an eleven-seater **minibus**, which spent all of 2004 idle owing to lack of registration papers, shuttles between town and airstrip at flight times (fare €1.50); otherwise, passengers are transferred three to four at a time for €5 per person in the lone **taxi**, which makes tedious multiple journeys.

The rest of the island

Kastellórizo's austere hinterland is predominantly bare rock, flecked with stunted vegetation; incredibly, three generations ago much of the countryside was carefully tended, producing wine of some quality and quantity, as it had since antiquity. A rudimentary paved road system links points between

Mandhráki and the airport (and beyond to the rubbish tip), but there are not many specific places to go along it and no scooters to rent (though you'll see plenty of service vans). Additionally, as on many of the lonelier Dodecanese islands, the Greek military presence has been significantly increased on Kastellórizo and its satellites since the Ímia incident (see p.470), with watch points or fully equipped army camps at strategic spots. The island is fringed by sheer karst cliffs, and offers no anchorage except at the main town, Mandhráki, and Návlakas fjord (see overleaf).

Swimming – and Perastá grotto

Swimming options are limited by a total absence of beaches and an abundance of sea urchins and razor-sharp limestone reefs; the safest places near town include a tiny pebble patch (fits three people) below the castle, some rocks – now sullied by concrete dollops – beyond the graveyard and football pitch at **Mandhráki**, or (best of all) a jetty with steps out at **Cape Nýftis**, by the power plant and road's end. Many people just use the handy ladders provided at the hotel/pension lidos on the northwest quay and do laps across the harbour mouth. Once away from the shore and the central port, you're rewarded by clear waters graced by a rich variety of marine life – and great mounds of amphorae shards offshore from the Mandhráki petrol pump, attesting to the quantity of wine exported in ancient times.

Over on the southeast coast, accessible only by a 45-minute boat ride from town (generally departs 9.30am), the grotto of **Perastá** (aka Galázio Spílio) is famous for its stalactites and strange blue light effects; the low entrance, negotiable only by inflatable raft towed behind the main *kaïki*, gives little hint of the enormous chamber within. Splashing about in its depths is magic, though claims of rivalry to Capri's Blue Grotto seem a bit overblown, since the blue tint doesn't reflect well on the walls. There is a second cave, inaccessible to humans, to which resident monk seals retire when disturbed by visitors. Ninety-minute trips (€8–10 each, depending on passenger numbers) visit the cave, or for about double that amount you can take it in as part of a five-hour tour that includes Rhó islet (see p.201). You can also take a boat to **Plákes** on the northerly peninsula, not accessible overland; there's superb swimming off, and sunbathing on, the flat surfaces of this ex-quarry.

Rural monasteries and ruins

During the infernally hot summer months, you're best off imitating the dozens of cats asleep at midday under the café tables. At cooler times of the day or year, you can hike south up the obvious, zigzag stair-path from town, picked out in whitewash, then by trail through the scrub to the monastery of **Ayíou Yeoryíou toú Vouncioú**, reached in just over half an hour. The sixteenth- to eighteenth-century church boasts fine rib vaulting and a carved *témblon*, but its highlight is a crypt, with the frescoed, subterranean chapel of **Áyios Harálambos** off to one side; access is via a narrow, steep passage descending from the church floor – bring a torch and clothes suitable for scrambling. The walled monastery premises are kept locked, so you must first fetch the key from its keeper (who changes from year to year; ask around). From the monastery you can easily continue to Návlakas fjord, partly along a French-built *kalderími*; see p.200 for instructions.

Ancient ruins

An alternative, slightly longer route to Áyios Yeóryios takes in various intriguing antiquities on the way. From *Ta Platania* restaurant, head up the road signposted for "Paleókastro", then bear left onto the first spur driveway; immediately by the "dead end" sign starts a step-path to the region known as **Avlónia**. The worst climb is over after fifteen minutes, where you briefly walk parallel to a high stone wall before reaching a bathtub-like cistern (empty); veer up and right here, away from Avlónia, to find another, larger, clearly ancient **cistern** under two trees, with an elaborate sluice system still keeping it partly full. The nearby path, climbing gently west now, passes a carved-out stone platform in the rock face, and then an odd round structure thought to be a tomb, before swinging south and reaching (just over 30min along) more ancient buildings next to a sixth-century BC *patitíri* or **winepress** – its cavities and sluices among the best preserved of many such presses on the island. Some forty minutes after quitting Horáfia you arrive at Áyios Yeóryios toú Vounioú and, a minute or so further, just east of the old path (*not* the new track), you'll find another winepress of the same design carved into the rock strata.

In the opposite direction out of the port, a fifteen-minute track-walk west leads to the peaceful monastery of **Ayías Triádhos**, perched on the saddle marked by a telecoms tower – and an army strongpoint which has rendered much of the area off limits. The adjacent monastery of Profitis Iliás is military territory, and shouldn't be confused with its neighbour. The signposted onward path to the ancient Doric citadel of **Paleókastro** leaves the cemented track just beyond the monastery; after a twenty-minute walk from Ayía Triádha, your arrival is signalled by masonry from Classical to medieval times, a warren of vaulted chambers, tunnels and cisterns (reputedly a hundred, adapted from ancient sarcophagi, with their lining still intact), plus three maroon-roofed chapels with pebble-mosaic courtyards. The best-preserved section of polygonal wall is just behind the lone olive tree. From any of the heights above town you've tremendous views north over 60km of Anatolian coast and the elephant's-foot-shaped harbour, east to tiny gull-roosts dribbled like batter drops on the griddle of the sea and west to larger islets, including Rhó (see opposite).

Návlakas fjord

From Áyios Yeóryios toú Vounioú, head southwest on an ugly bulldozer track, past several uselessly positioned military bunkers, until, about fifteen minutes along at the high point of the route next to a lone, scraggly olive tree, what remains of the magnificent, French-built cobbled way re-emerges on the left. This now descends south in zigzags past the southeast end of the airport runway, finally dropping ever more sharply to **Návlakas**, a multi-lobed fjord that's a favourite with yachts and fishing boats. The only easy way in overland is on the far left, where the path ends as an inconspicuous ramp, now little better than a mud chute; the French, using local labour, opened this route in early 1917 to facilitate offloading the components of a 120-millimetre gun battery, which eventually succeeded in silencing Ottoman artillery on the mainland. The fjord, uniquely on Kastellórizo, is completely sea-urchin-free, thanks perhaps to cleansing freshwater seeps, which also keep the temperature brisk. The south wall has a sharp drop-off to 25-metre depths near the fjord mouth, providing excellent snorkelling. Allow about half an hour either from or to the monastery.

Greek script table

Kastellórizo

Ayías Triádhos	Αγίας Τριάδος	ΑΓΙΑΣ ΤΡΙΑΔΟΣ
Áyios Yeóryios toú Vounioú	Άγιος Γεώργιος τού Βουνιού	ΑΓΙΟΣ ΓΕΩΡΓΙΟΣ ΤΟΥ ΒΟΥΝΙΟΥ
Áyios Stéfanos	Άγιος Στέφανος	ΑΓΙΟΣ ΣΤΕΦΑΝΟΣ
Mandhráki	Μανδράκι	ΜΑΝΔΡΑΚΙ
Meyísti	Μεγίστι	ΜΕΓΙΣΤΙ
Návlakas	Ναύλακας	ΝΑΥΛΑΚΑΣ
Paleokástro	Παλαιοκάστρο	ΠΑΛΑΙΟΚΑΣΤΡΟ
Perastá	Περαστά	ΠΕΡΑΣΤΑ
Rhó	Ρώ	ΡΩ
Vathoryáki	Βαθορυάκι	ΒΑΘΟΡΥΑΚΙ

Rhó: Lady and islet

Until her death, *Iý Kyrá tís Rhó* (**The Lady of Rhó**), aka Dhespina Akhladhioti (1898?–1982), resolutely hoisted the Greek flag each day on the islet of that name, in defiance of the Turks across the way. In her waning years, an honorary salary, a commemorative postage stamp and television appearances lent her glory and fame, which she revelled in; by most accounts she was a miserly curmudgeon, known to have refused passing sailors emergency rations of fresh water.

Should you take a day-trip out to Rhó, her **tomb** is the first thing you see when you dock at the sandy, northwestern harbour; from here a path heads southeast for 25 minutes to the islet's southerly port, past the sidetrail up to an intact Hellenistic **fortress** on the island's summit. There are no facilities on Rhó – just a few soldiers to prevent Turkish landings or poachings of the hundreds of goats – so bring your own food and water.

Kastellórizo travel details

Inter-island transport

Ferries

Kastellórizo to: Rhodes (2–3 weekly with GA or LANE; 4hr).

NB Kastellórizo has some of the worst ferry connections in the Greek islands; companies who deign to provide this no-profit link do so as a condition for receiving government subsidies. Typically service is only from mid-May to October, leaving the island otherwise dependent on aeroplanes and perhaps one weekly boat.

Catamaran

Kastellórizo to: Rhodes (1 weekly on the *Dodekanisos Express*, May–Oct; 2hr 30min).

Flights

Kastellórizo to: Rhodes (5 weekly; 40min).

International transport

Kaïkia

Kastellórizo to: Kaş, Turkey (2 weekly minimum or by demand, but see box on p.198).

Sými

Sými's most pressing problem, lack of fresh water, is in many ways also its saving grace. As with so many dry, rocky Dodecanese islands, water must be imported at great expense from Rhodes, pending completion of a reservoir in the distant future. Consequently, Sými can't hope to support more than a handful of large hotels; instead, hundreds of people are shipped in daily during the season from its larger neighbour, relieved of their money and sent back. This arrangement suits both the islanders and those visitors lucky enough to stay longer. Many foreigners return regularly, and/or own houses here – indeed since the mid-1980s the most desirable dwellings, ruined or

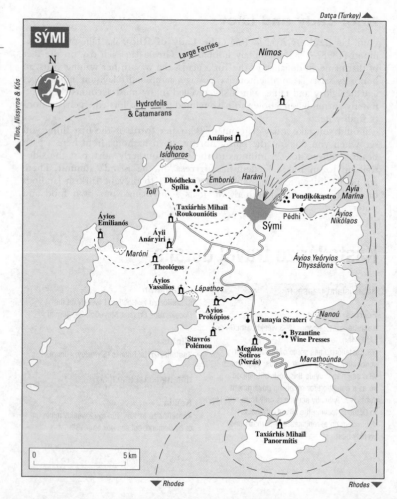

otherwise, have been sold off in such numbers that the island has become the Ídhra of the southeast Aegean. Anything with a view of the water has been, or is being, renovated while the rest remain on sale, at ridiculous prices.

Incredibly, just over a century ago the island was richer and more populous (25,000) than Rhodes, its wealth generated by shipbuilding and sponge-diving, skills nurtured since pre-Classical times. Under the Ottomans, Sými, like many of the Dodecanese, enjoyed considerable autonomy in exchange for a yearly tribute in sponges to the sultan; but the new, Italian-imposed frontier, the 1919–22 Greco-Turkish war, the gradual replacement of the crews by Kalymniots and (after World War II) the advent of synthetic sponges spelt doom for the local economy. Vestiges of past nautical glories remain in the still-active *karnáyia* (boatyards) at Pédhi and Haráni, but today the souvenir-shop sponges come entirely from overseas, and, the recent boom notwithstanding, a significant number of the nineteenth-century mansions still stand roofless and empty.

Once beyond the inhabited areas, you'll find a surprisingly attractive island, and ideal walking country in spring or autumn (rather than midsummer, when temperatures are among the highest in Greece). Sými has managed to retain some of its original forest cover of junipers, valonea oaks and even a few pines; lower on the ground there's a thick herbaceous covering of sage, while late spring sees lavender-blossomed thyme and white-flowered oregano. Another prominent feature of the landscape are dozens of tiny **monasteries** (*monas-tirákia*), most owned by a single family and kept locked except on their patron saint's day – though their cisterns, with a can on a string to fetch water, may be accessible.

Sými Town

SÝMI TOWN, the island's capital and only proper town, consists of two districts: **Yialós**, arrayed around the excellent natural harbour, and **Horió**, which historically led a socially separate existence on the hillside above. The approximately 2500 remaining Symiots are scattered fairly evenly throughout the mixture of surviving Neoclassical and more typical island dwellings; despite the surplus of properties, many outsiders have preferred to build anew rather than restore derelict shells accessible only by donkey or on foot. As on Kastel-lórizo, a wartime blast – this time set off by the retreating Germans – shattered hundreds of houses up in Horió (see p.503). Shortly afterwards, the official German surrender of the Dodecanese to the Allies was signed here on May 8, 1945: a plaque marks the spot at the present-day *Restaurant Les Catherinettes*.

Sými's **port**, an architecturally protected area since the early 1970s, is decep-tively lively between 11am and 3.30pm when the spice-and-sponge stalls and a few jewellery shops throng with Rhodes-based day-trippers, and the several excursion craft disgorging them envelop the north quay with exhaust fumes. But just uphill, away from the water, the more peaceful pace of village life takes over, with livestock and chickens roaming free-range. Two massive stair-paths, the Kalí Stráta and Katarráktes, effectively deter many of the day-trippers and are most dramatic around sunset; massive, owl-haunted ruins along the lower reaches of the Kalí Stráta are lonely and sinister after dark, though these too are now undergoing restoration one by one.

A series of blue arrows through Horió leads you up to the excellent local **museum** (Tues–Sun 8.30am–2.30pm; €2). Housed in a fine old mansion

△ Haráni quay, Sými

at the back of the village, the collection concentrates on Byzantine and medieval Sými, with a gallery of medieval icons and exhibits on frescoes in isolated, locked churches. In addition there are antiquarian maps and the inevitable ethnographic wing of costumed mannequins, embroidery and furniture; a cottage in the garden offers a *sandoúri*, old guns and a rusty Victrola. Nearby, the **Hatziagapitos mansion** has been refurbished as an annexe; it dates from around 1800, but seems much older. Wonderful carved wooden chests are the main exhibits, while above various wall niches are traces of wall-paintings: the eagle of John the Evangelist, and a female figure (perhaps Learning personified) making a gift of a book to a young lad. As you head back to the village centre, it's worth pausing at the nineteenth-century **pharmacy**, with its apothecary jars and wooden drawers labelled for exotic homeopathic and herbal remedies; it still functions (after a fashion), in tandem with the adjacent clinic.

At the very pinnacle of things, a castle of the **Knights of St John** occupies the site of Sými's ancient **acropolis**, and you can glimpse a stretch of Classical polygonal wall on one side, as well as the Grand Master's escutcheon. A dozen churches grace Horió; that of the **Assumption**, inside the fortifications of the acropolis, is a successor to the one blown to bits when the Germans detonated the munitions cache there. One of the bells in the new belfry is the nose cone of a thousand-pound bomb, hung as a memorial. Somehow the islanders have secured permission from the archeological authorities to build another, smaller chapel in stone, on the summit itself.

Arrival, information and getting around

The southerly quay was widened and the berthing offshore dredged in 2002 to accommodate larger boats, but many craft, including all excursion ones (though not the hydrofoil or small catamarans), still insist on docking by the clocktower on the north quay. One of two **catamarans** and a **hydrofoil** run daily to Sými from Mandhráki in Ródhos Town, departing morning and evening on either an *epivatikó* (scheduled service) or more expensive *ekdhromikó* (excursion) basis, but note that you're forbidden from taking large luggage on the latter – and reports indicate this rule is strictly enforced. The few weekly main-line ferry sailings are your cheapest – and slowest – options, and the only one if you've a car.

ANES, the outlet for *Panormitis/Symi II/Aigli* tickets, maintains a booth on the quay and an office in the marketplace lanes (℡22460 71444). GA ferries have no exclusive agency, while the *Dodekanisos Express* catamaran is handled by Symi Tours (℡22460 71307). There's no official tourism bureau, but the island's English-language advertiser-newsletter, *The Symi Visitor* (free; ⓦwww.symivisitor.com), is literate and has current island gossip alongside informative features. The **post office** in the official Italian "palace" is open standard hours; two **banks** both have ATMs.

In deference to the pedestrian clientele, traffic is banned around the harbour except during siesta hours and after midnight, enforced by an automatic barrier by the bus stop on the south quay. During the season this small green **bus** (€0.70 flat fare) shuttles between Yialós and Pédhi via Horió on the hour (returning at the half-hour) until 11pm. There are also six **taxis** (allow €3 Yialós–Horió with baggage), with a rank on the south quay, and two pricey outlets (Nikos Katsaras has the edge, also in Pédhi) for **scooter rental** (minimum €18–22 daily), rates which cunningly just undercut the price of round-the-isle boat excursions. Katsaras also **rents cars** (for a whopping €58–70 daily), though this is a perfect island for boat and walking excursions.

Accommodation

Accommodation for independent travellers is somewhat limited, though the situation isn't nearly so bad as on Hálki; proprietors tend not to meet arriving boats unless arrangements have been made. Studios, rather than simple rooms, predominate, and package operators control most of these, though curiously you may have an easier time finding spots in July/August than during spring/autumn, considered the most pleasant periods here. Despite asphyxiating summer heat, air conditioning and ceiling fans are not universally present – go for north-facing and/or balconied units when possible. If you're planning in advance, the *Symi Visitor* website is worth consulting.

Yialós

Albatros Marketplace ℡22460 71707, ⓦwww.albatrosymi.gr. Partial sea views from this exquisite small hotel; pleasant second-floor breakfast salon, air-con rooms, friendly French co-management can arrange similar-standard lodgings if they're full. ❹

Aliki Haráni quay ℡22460 71665, ⓦwww.simi-hotelaliki.gr. A complete overhaul of an 1895 mansion, and Sými's poshest hotel: tasteful rooms with wood floors and some antique furnishings, plus air con and large bathrooms, though only some have sea views. Standard rooms ❻, suites ❼

Les Catherinettes Above eponymous restaurant, north quay ℡22460 72698, ⓔmarina-epe@rho.forthnet.gr. Creaky but spotless en-suite pension in a historic building with painted ceilings, fridges, fans and sea-view balconies for most rooms. They also offer three studios in Haráni, plus a family apartment. Rooms and studios ❹

Kokona Rear of marketplace, beyond main church ☏ 22460 71549, ℱ 22460 72620. Bland if cheerful tile-and-pine, air-con rooms, some with balcony (and some package presence). Breakfast served outdoors, at base of the church belfry. **❸**

Nireus Next to the clocktower ☏ 22460 72400, ⓦ www.nireus-hotel. Comfortable, balconied sea-view rooms were partly refurbished (with good baths) in 2004; go for these rather than inland-facing units. "Private" lido, on-site restaurant. Standard doubles **❺**, suites **❼** B&B, but much less if booked through Triton Holidays in Rhodes

Niriides Apartments About halfway between Haráni and Emborió bay ☏ 22460 71784, ⓦ wwwniriideshotel.gr. Spacious if plain units, distributed over four hillside buildings, sleep four

and have phone, TV, optional air con. Small beach at the foot of the grade with sun-loungers foreseen in near future, friendly and helpful father-and-son management. **❺**; discount for Internet bookings

Villa Garden Yialós, just up from the basketball courts – no sign, look for the giant arbor vitae ☏ 22460 70024, ⓦ www.symitop5.gr. Variety of studios and apartments, ranging from cool lower-ground-floor "caves" sleeping four, to airier doubles with limited bay views. Phone and mini-kitchen in each, though baths vary; stone-paved common courtyard. Open all year, credit cards accepted, largely package-free. **❺–❻**

Villa Thalassa Far end of the south quay. Contact as for *Hotel Albatros*. Old mansion divided into two air-con studios for couples (**❺**), and three larger apartments (**❻**) accommodating families.

Horió

Fiona At the top of the Kalí Stráta ☏ 02460/72088. Mock-traditional hotel building whose large airy rooms have some double beds and stunning views; breakfast in midair on common balcony. Does not work with package companies. **❹**

Jean Manship c/o *Jean & Tonic Bar* ☏ & ℱ 22460 71819 8pm–1am Greek time. Jean manages four traditional houses in Horió, suitable for 2–6 and with stunning views. **❸–❹**

Symi Visitor Accommodation ☏ 22460 72755, ⓔ symi-vis@otenet.gr. Managed by affable returned Greek-Australian Nikos Halkitis and partner Wendy Wilcox, who offer a variety of restored

houses as double-occupancy studios in prime locations of Horió. Rates range from **❹–❻**; they also have pricier units suitable for four to five persons

Katerina Tsakiris ☏ 22460 71813. Just a handful of rather plain, if en-suite, rooms with separate self-catering kitchen facilities, air con and a grandstand view over the harbour; reservations essential. **❸**

Villa Symeria Up the Kalí Stráta (contact *Albatros Hotel*). Restored Neoclassical view mansion comprising two apartments with either air con or fans, suitable for up to four (downstairs **❼**) and six (upstairs **❽**) persons respectively.

Eating and drinking

You're best off avoiding most **eateries** on the north and west quays of the port, where menus, raw materials, prices and attitudes have been terminally warped by the day-trip trade. Away from these areas, you've a fair range of choice among *kultoúra* tavernas, old-style *mayireftá* places, a few genuine *ouzerís* and even a traditional *kafenío* or two. Indeed Sými has a tradition of hiring good chefs – either native-born or from elsewhere, many trained at the professional tourism school on Rhodes.

Bella Napoli Lane in from south quay, beyond *Vapori* and *Harani* bars. Much-improved Italian eatery with appetizing antipasti, fluffy-crust pizzas, tiramisu to die for in large portions and a decent wine list – though as ever quality will depend on the chef hired for the season.

Dhimitris South quay, on the way out of town. Excellent, family-run seafood-stressing *ouzerí* with exotic items such as *hokhlióalo* (sea snails), *foúskes*, *spinóalo*, pinna-shell flesh and the indigenous miniature shrimps, along with the more

usual plates and lots of vegetarian starters. Tends to close early (2.15pm-ish) at lunchtime if no customers about.

Haritomeni Northeast edge of Horió, about half-way up the hill in kink of the road above Yialós filling station ☏ 22460 71686. Superb *ouzerí* with such fare as pork cheeks, *mydhopílafo* (mussels in rice), artichokes in egg-lemon sauce, stuffed aubergines and snails. Open all year: lovely terrace with views in summer, fireplace interior in winter. Must reserve at peak season.

To **Kantirimi** North side main square, Yialós. A good source of pancake or waffle breakfasts and fruit smoothies under the trees; becomes a snack café/bar later in the day.

O Meraklis Rear of the marketplace. Polite service and fair portions of moderately pricey *mayireftá* and *mezédhes* make this a reliable year-round bet. Sample meal: beans, beets, dips, and roast lamb with potatoes as a tender main course.

Mythos South quay between bus/taxi stop, Yialós. Superb *ouzerí* that's reckoned among the best, and best-value, cooking on the island. There is a menu, but best let chef Stavros hit you with his Frenchified medley which includes salad, seafood starters (squid in basil sauce), *poungí* (seafood parcel in filo), courgette-and-mushroom mould, and homemade desserts. Decent wine list; budget €22 a head before dipping into that. In summer, operations move 150m down the quay to *Aktaion*, a roof-terrace annexe, and *Mythos* becomes a

snack-café open at lunch too; otherwise supper only at the main premises spring and autumn. Credit cards accepted.

Pahos West quay (no sign). The old boys' *kafenío*, in operation since World War II, and still a classic spot for a sundown *oúzo* and people-watching. Pahos himself has retired and can often be found sitting out front as a customer; otherwise it's unchanged.

Yiorgos Near top of Kalí Stráta in Horió. Jolly, much-loved institution maintaining consistent food quality since 1977, with summer seating on a pebble-mosaic courtyard where regular impromptu live music sessions happen. Service can be slip-shod, and portions have gotten smaller and dearer of late, but perennial recipes include feta-stuffed peppers, spinach-rice, chicken in mushroom-wine sauce, artichokes *alá políta* and grilled fish when available. Open random lunchtimes in season, supper all year (indoors in winter).

Nightlife and entertainment

Nightlife continues into the early hours and is somewhat biased towards Yialós, with a number of bars owned by expatriates. Convivial *Jean & Tonic* is the heart and soul of Horió's bar scene, catering to a mixed clientele (visitors and expats until 3am, Greek restaurateurs 3am until dawn) most of the year; *Kafenio Lefteris* is the traditional hangout at the very top of the Kalí Stráta; *Kali Strata*, a few steps below, is a low-key place with unbeatable views, good desserts and excellent, wide-ranging music. Down at Yialós, the *Harani Club* offers a mix of Greek and international music depending on the crowd; in the same alley, *Vapori* was the first outsider-owned bar here (in 1983), and continues the tradition with newspapers draped over chairs, breakfasts and **Internet** access (three terminals). Elsewhere, *Katoi* on the south quay is a no-hassle bar favoured mainly by locals, whilst *The Club* on the *platía* functions between midnight and dawn, and has a pool table.

In terms of more formal **events**, there's a year-round Friday-night **cine-matheque** inside the Petrideio mansion, while the myriad concerts of the July to September **Sými Festival**, which since its mid-1990s inception has become one of Greece's more interesting small summer bashes, with a mix of classical and Greek-popular performances.

Around Sými Town: Pédhi to Emborió

Sými has no long sandy **beaches**, but there are plenty of pebbly stretches in the deep, protected bays which indent the coastline. **PÉDHI**, 1500m below Horió, retains some of its former identity as a fishing hamlet, with enough ground water in the plain behind – the island's largest – to support a few vegetable gardens. The beach is poor, though, and patronage from yachts and the large *Pedhi Beach* hotel (☎22460 71981, ℱ22460 71982; ❹) has consider-ably bumped up prices at the three local beachfront **tavernas**; most reasonable and authentic is fish-and-seafood-strong *Tolis* (no sign), tucked away by the boatyard at the north corner of the bay.

Many will opt for another twenty minutes of walking along a rough but obvious path (sturdy shoes required) along the south shore of almost land-locked Pédhi Bay to **Áyios Nikólaos**. The only all-sand beach on Sými, this offers sheltered swimming, tamarisks for shade, and a mediocre taverna behind its fifty-metre extent. Alternatively, a red-and-blue-paint-splodge-marked path on the north side of the inlet leads from the end of the paved lane beyond the boatyards in just over twenty minutes to **Ayía Marína**, where there's a shingle-and-sunbed lido, plus a fancy, lawn-landscaped taverna. There is also a monastery-capped islet to which you can easily swim. You might vary the return walk to town by using the onward trail through the gate at the far end of the "beach"; it's well waymarked but rough, so allow an hour – some of this cross-country – to emerge at the **Pondikókastro**, a round Hellenistic funerary monument, just before a line of windmills at the east end of Horió.

AroundYialós, ten minutes' walk beyond Haráni and its boatyards, you'll find the tiny **NOS (Navtikós Ómilos Sýmis)** "beach", but there's sun here only until lunchtime – not a bad thing in midsummer; the *kantína* here is now called *Symi Paradise*, but everyone still knows it as "NOS". You can continue along the cement-paved coast road past tiny gravel coves and rock slabs popular with nudists and snorkellers, or cut inland from theYialós square past the former site of the desalination plant, to appealing **Emborió** Bay (sometimes "Nimborió"), with the recommended *Niriides Apartments* (see p.206) on the coastal route in, the recently improved *Metapontis* taverna at one end of the bay, and an artificially strewn sand beach at the other.

Inland from the bay, up a dry ravine and then some steps, a faded Byzantine **mosaic** fragment lies under a protective shelter, next to Siamese-triplet chapels. Much has been obliterated, but you can discern a man leading a camel, a partridge, and a stag in flight from a boar. Beyond a lone pine beside the chapels, a faint trail marked by painted arrows and letters leads 100m further to a slight rise ringed by a collapsing chain-link fence. Inside the enclosure, a hole in the ground gives access to a subterranean complex known locally as **Dhódheka Spília** (Twelve Caves), either catacombs or the crypt of a basilica which once stood here.

Remote bays and monasteries

Plenty of other, more secluded coves are accessible by energetic **walkers** with sturdy footwear. By far the best of two local walking guides is Lance Chilton's *Walks in Symi* (Ⓦ www.marengowalks.com; also stocked at the *Symi Visitor* offices). In any event, most interesting island paths have been admirably marked of late with either cairns or paint splodges.

Otherwise, pay a modest sum (typically €5 return, one ways negotiable) for the **taxi-boats** moored just opposite the main *agorá* street. These operate daily in season, outbound from 10am to noon (though there's the odd "off-peak" service), returning from their destinations between 4pm and 6.30pm depending on the month. It must be said that the tourist bureaux associated with the main package companies tend to push expensive, all-day, multi-stop excursions rather than these simple, DIY itineraries.

The east coast: Nanoú and other bays

You won't necessarily need to use a taxi-boat to get to or from Emborió, Ayía Marína and Áyios Nikólaos, but a boat ride remains the easiest way to reach the southeasterly bays of Marathoúnda and Nanoú, and the only method of getting to the spectacular, cliff-girt fjord of **Áyios Yeóryios Dhyssálona**, which served as a location for the 1961 film *The Guns of Navarone*. Dhyssálona lacks a taverna and lies in shade after 1pm or so, while **Marathoúnda**, though it has a full-service taverna, is unalluringly fringed by coarse, slimy pebbles (and can anyway be reached by motorbike), making **Nanoú** the most popular destination for day-trips. The 200-metre beach there consists of gravel, sand and pebbles, with sunbeds and umbrellas, good snorkelling, a scenic backdrop of rare Symiot pines, and a taverna (squid, chips and salad menu) that's probably the most consistent of Sými's remote eateries.

Hiking to Nanoú

You can reach **Nanoú overland** by a moderately challenging but spectacular three-hour walk from Horió, mostly on path, taking in several of Sými's most interesting rural monasteries en route. As with all island walks, it's best to be equipped with the "Walker's Map of Symi", packaged along with Lance Chilton's *Walks in Symi*.

From the top of the Katarráktes stairway, curl around through the network of village lanes, gaining altitude slightly and turning southwest towards the last, highest houses; paint dots on house corners direct you. Just past the livestock gate at the very western edge of Horió, head up and left at a fork onto a finely engineered *kalderími*. Approaching the asphalt from Horió to island points west and south, you'll find the last 40m of this buried under rubble, necessitating a slippery, steep scramble up to the road. You're obliged to walk on this for about ten minutes along the turning for Panormítis, until you re-adopt it at the first curve; just under half an hour from Horió, you pass Ayía Ekateríni monastery (locked), and then arrive at Panayía Styloú chapel (also shut) after ten more minutes. Here you must leave the *kalderími* (which just goes back up to the road and expires permanently) in favour of a narrower but distinct path, with a few waymarks.

This path initially keeps gloriously high above Áyios Vassílios ravine before slipping over a ridge into a fairly large side canyon draining down to Lápathos and then, just over half an hour from Styloú, entering pine and juniper forest. Some fifteen minutes from the edge of the trees, shun turnings to the right and follow dots left and up to the *monastiráki* of **Áyios Prokópios** (open), which retains some engaging fourteenth- to fifteenth-century frescoes – the *Crucifixion* and *Resurrection* – just right of the door. Ignore bulldozer scrapings in favour of the onward path, starting from the southwest corner of the single outbuilding; it's about twenty minutes from here, up past Panaïdhi monastery (locked) with its two chapels, to the hilltop **Stavrós Polémou** monastery (c. 500m elevation), whose famous views (the earlier in the day, the better) are everything they're cracked up to be. Its courtyard kitchen is usually open, with a chained bucket inside for fetching pure cistern water. Return to Panaïdhi, behind which the onward path, partly cemented over, heads northwest, debouching after twenty minutes on the Panormítis road, just shy of a sign pointing along the side track back to Áyios Prokópios. Turn right (south), and within a couple of minutes you should be abreast the chapel of **Panayía Straterí**, up on a cement terrace studded with a flagpole and a blue-and-rust-coloured belfry, west of the road.

If you've had an early start and have lots of stamina, you might detour fifteen minutes southeast, initially on *kalderími*, to some moderately interesting Byzantine-era **winepresses**, and (just west of the road, opposite the "wine press" sign), the rather more compelling monastery of **Megálos Sotíros** (aka

Nerás), just before the drop down the escarpment to Panormítis, with the best early eighteenth-century frescoes on the island. There's a resident keeper here, so the *katholikón* is usually open, in the middle of the arcaded, pebble-paved courtyard. The frescoes inside, devoted unsurprisingly to the life of the Saviour (*Sotír* in Greek), include a fine *Deposition*, with Joseph of Aramathea holding a winding sheet to receive the dead Christ, and a *Resurrection* with Jesus all but doing a jig on the sepulchre.

But most will be eager to get down to the sea as soon as possible. Immediately opposite Strateri, search bulldozer-tumbled boulders for red-paint arrows and an "X" marking the start of the continuing path; it drops sharply on a scree surface to begin with, then descends more gradually as a corniche trail. This hugs the south flank of a ravine cutting through Sými's thickest forest of junipers and pines, which provide welcome shade. The trail remains distinct throughout, though there are also powder-blue waymarks. It's about forty minutes downhill from the road to a cistern and then a little chapel, just inland from the Nanoú taverna; line these three landmarks up to reverse the itinerary if necessary, which takes less than an hour uphill – better grip offsets the steep grade. With an early enough start from Horió, you should have plenty of time for lunch and a swim at Nanoú before the last taxi-boat of the day back to Yialós.

Áyios Vassílios

No boats serve the scenic gulf of **Áyios Vassílios** on the southwest coast of Sými, so you'll need to make an easy but satisfying hour-and-a-half trek across the island from Horió through patches of natural juniper forest. The path leaves Horió as for the trip to Panayía Strateri (see p.209), climbing gradually within half an hour to the paved road curving out of the village on the Pédhi side; at the second (the first is for Strateri) fork about 25 minutes along, bear left, turn left again when you meet the asphalt and then almost immediately right (south) onto a narrow track, crossing the tree-studded Xissós plateau. Within ten more minutes you pass a few farms and *monastirákia* to reach the last, fenced property on the plateau, to the left of which the true path resumes. Hálki appears on the horizon as the trail descends steadily along the west flank of an imposing gorge; there is little or no possibility of getting lost, and Tílos eventually replaces Hálki in your field of view. A final, slithery couloir leads down to the long, gravel-and-small-pebble beach (40min from track's end) where clothing is optional and the water warm. Perched above the beach, at the top of the final descent, the little **monastery church** of Áyios Vassílios is, unusually, unlocked; it offers a carved wooden *témblon* and tantalizing post-Byzantine frescoes which, if they were ever cleaned properly, would amply reward the trek out here, beach or no.

Áyios Emilianós

The trek to **Áyios Emilianós** at the island's extreme western end takes a minimum two and a half hours one way, depending on your ability and the route chosen. From Yialós, the most direct way begins along the stair-street beginning inland from the plaza, which becomes a *kalderími* by the highest house; from Horió, begin as for Áyios Vassílios and Panayía Strateri (see p.209), but bear right at the aforementioned second fork. Both routes converge on the ridge west of town, near a clump of eucalyptus trees by the paved road. The main path used to continue from the far side of the road directly west to the little convent of Áyii Anáryiri, but a huge army camp now blocks the way and passage is forbidden.

Thus you make a compulsory detour right, trudging along the paved road, to the conspicuous monastery of **Taxiárhis Mihaïl Roukouniótis**, Sými's oldest (daily 9am–2pm & 4–8pm; €0.75 donation to keepers), its gate shaded by an enormous, 300-year-old juniper in a round planter-well. Inside, the church sports lurid eighteenth-century frescoes by local master Gregory and a peculiar ground plan: the current *katholikón* is actually superimposed on a lower, thirteenth-century structure abandoned after being burnt and pillaged by pirates during the 1400s, though a fine fresco of St Lawrence (Áyios Lavréntios) survives behind the altar screen. Resident, trilingual Father Amfilohios will gladly tell you anything else you might wish to know about the place.

From Roukouniótis you head briefly south along a cemented track to **Áyii Anáryiri** (gate open) to pick up the onward trail rudely interrupted by the army base. A gentle saddle marks the high point of the walk, and then the path enters juniper forest. The view west through the trees to Áyios Emilianós from the rural monastery of **Áyios Ioánnis Theológos** is more than alluring, and you can use the bucket-on-a-rope to fish water out of the big cistern behind the church.

For walkers who feel that the intrusion of the Greek military around Roukouniótis – and it is an eyesore – has compromised the landscape, there's another, alternate way to Áyios Ioánnis Theológos, especially worthwhile from Horió. Proceed as if you were going to Áyios Vassílios, but instead of taking the cement drive south across Xissós, take the paved drive beginning a bit further west, bound for Panayía Myrtariótissa, and find the start of a waymarked path amongst the cottages of a pastoral hamlet on the ridge below this little monastery. After half an hour on this trail you reach the "gentle saddle" noted above to join the lower trail, and arrive at Theológos within 25 more minutes.

However you've arrived, bear right at the fork in the path below Theológos and descend gradually to the vicinity of Maróni cove (indifferent swimming) and the church of Áyios Filímonos (cistern water, a quick 45min from Theológos), where the distinct trail becomes a set of concrete steps down to Skoúmissa cove (poor swimming). From here it's line of sight, with an intermittent path at best, for the final twenty-minute distance north to Áyios Emilianós, perched on an islet tethered to the Kefála headland by a wave-lashed causeway. The monastery's courtyard makes an excellent picnic venue, but alas the kitchen and adjoining cell are no longer kept open, so don't plan on staying the night here. The best flotsam-and-sea-urchin-free swimming hereabouts is roughly halfway between Skoúmissa and the monastery, where eel-grass beds just off a patch of clean pebbles give onto deep water.

Returning, budget just under an hour up to Theológos, another half-hour to Áyii Anaryíri, and another thirty minutes past Roukouniótis to the eucalyptus ridge above the army camp. The wide but scandalously crumbling *kalderími* down to Yialós is easy to find in this direction, bringing the total for the west-to-east traverse to about two and a half hours.

Tolí and Áyios Isídhoros

From near the northernmost point of the asphalt road to Taxiárhis Mihaïl Roukouniótis, next to the boundary wall of a cottage, a path heads northwest, only briefly skimming or using track systems, to arrive at the secluded and occasionally garbage-strewn cove of Tolí in 45 minutes; in the final minutes you leave the "main" trail in favour of a spur trail ending near an isolated house and giant tree above the beach. **Tolí** is actually a multiple beach divided by a small headland, with the cleanest and most pebbly bit off to the left as you face the sea. After wet winters a small spring, suitable for emergency purposes, surfaces in the ravine staked by oleanders, descending to the northerly half of the cove. If for any reason Tolí doesn't suit, stay with the high inland path for another fifteen minutes to smaller, north-facing **Áyios Isídhoros**, arguably more scenic with its views to islets, and a shallow, sheltered cove offshore, but likely to be dirty onshore.

Rather than return the way you came, make a loop by heading east to Emborió in just under an hour. The track system on the ridge overlooking Tolí heads northeast towards Áyios Yeóryios Kylindhriótis monastery, but don't go all the way there – below and to the right of the track, a poor trail (very indistinct at first) begins through the ravine draining down to the artificially supplemented beach at Emborió.

Taxiárhis Mihaïl Panormítis

At the southern point of the island looms the huge monastery of **Taxiárhis Mihaïl Panormítis** ("Panormítis" for short), Sými's biggest rural attraction and generally the first port of call for the excursion boats from Rhodes (confirm the itinerary if you wish to proceed direct to Yialós – some craft do). These allow only a quick half-hour tour; if you want more time, you'll have to come by motorbike from Yialós (though the road down from the central escarpment is steep, with nine hairpin bends), or arrange to stay the night in the **xenónas** set (€10 minimum donation) aside for pilgrims. They monopolize it all summer, as Mihaïl has been adopted as the patron of sailors in the Dodecanese (and not a few local men bear this name). The only monk permanently in residence, Archimandrite Gavriïl, lived in Australia for a while and so speaks a little English – certainly enough to chat up single women visitors. He is occasionally assisted by novices from the big monastery on Pátmos, of which the place is a dependency.

Like many of Sými's monasteries, the present Panormítis is of recent (eighteenth-century) vintage and was thoroughly pillaged during the last war, so don't expect too much from the building or its treasures. An appealing pebble-mosaic court surrounds the central *katholikón*, tended by Gavriïl, lit by an improbable number of oil lamps and graced by a fine *témblon*, though the frescoes are recent and mediocre. One of the two small **museums** (€2 fee covers both) contains a strange mix of precious antiques, exotic junk (elephant tusks, stuffed crocodiles and koalas), votive offerings, models of ships named *Taxiárhis* or *Panormítis*, and a chair piled with messages in bottles brought here by Aegean currents – the idea being that if the bottle or toy boat arrived, the sender got their prayer answered. Amenities outside the walls include a small beach, a shop/*kafenío*, a bakery and a **taverna** (*Panormion*) popular with passengers of the many yachts calling in. Near the taverna stands a memorial commemorating three Greeks, including the monastery's abbot, executed in February 1944 by the Germans for aiding British commandos.

Satellite islets

Day boat-trips call at **Nímos**, the satellite islet skirted on different sides by catamarans or ferries approaching Sými from the north, for a beach barbecue and a visit to its monastery; otherwise, Nímos is bare and lonely except for grazing goats. By contrast, **Seskliá**, at the far south end of Sými, has greenery and water, and is also a potential target of boat excursions.

Greek script table

Sými	Σύμη	ΣΥΜΗ
Ayía Marína	Αγία Μαρίνα	ΑΓΙΑ ΜΑΡΙΝΑ
Áyii Anáryiri	Άγιοι Ανάργυροι	ΑΓΙΟΙ ΑΝΑΡΓΥΡΟΙ
Áyios Emilianós	Άγιος Αιμηλιανός	ΑΓΙΟΣ ΑΙΜΗΛΙΑΝΟΣ
Áyios Isídhoros	Άγιος Ισίδωρος	ΑΓΙΟΣ ΙΣΙΔΩΡΟΣ
Áyios Nikólaos	Άγιος Νικόλαος	ΑΓΙΟΣ ΝΙΚΟΛΑΟΣ
Áyios Prokópios	Άγιος Προκόπιος	ΑΓΙΟΣ ΠΡΟΚΟΠΙΟΣ
Áyios Vassílios	Άγιος Βασίλειος	ΑΓΙΟΣ ΒΑΣΙΛΕΙΟΣ
Áyios Yeóryios	Άγιος Γεώργιος	ΑΓΙΟΣ ΓΕΩΡΓΙΟΣ
Dhyssálona	Δυσσάλονα	ΔΥΣΣΑΛΟΝΑ
Emborió	Εμπορειό	ΕΜΠΟΡΕΙΟ
Haráni	Χαράνι	ΧΑΡΑΝΙ
Horió	Χωριό	ΧΩΡΙΟ
Marathoúnda	Μαραθούντα	ΜΑΡΑΘΟΥΝΤΑ
Megálos Sotíros	Μεγάλος Σωτίρος	ΜΕΓΑΛΟΣ ΣΩΤΗΡΟΣ
Mihaïl	Μιχαήλ	ΜΙΧΑΗΛ
Roukouniótis	Ρουκουνιότης	ΡΟΥΚΟΥΝΙΟΤΗΣ
Nanoú	Νανού	ΝΑΝΟΥ
Nímos	Νίμος	ΝΙΜΟΣ
NOS	———	ΝΟΣ
Pédhi	Πέδι	ΠΕΔΙ
Seskliá	Σεσκλιά	ΣΕΣΚΛΙΑ
Stavrós Polémou	Σταυρός Πολέμου	ΣΤΑΥΡΟΣ ΠΟΛΕΜΟΥ
Taxiárhis Mihaïl	Ταξιάρχης Μιχαήλ	ΤΑΞΙΑΡΧΗΣ ΜΙΧΑΗΛ
Panormítis	Πανορμίτης	ΠΑΝΟΡΜΙΤΗΣ
Tolí	Τολή	ΤΟΛΗ
Yialós	Γιαλός	ΓΙΑΛΟΣ

Sými travel details

Inter-island transport

Local catamaran (scheduled – *epivatikó* – services)
Sými to: Rhodes (1–2 daily on the *Symi II* or *Panormitis*, departures at 6–7.30am & 5pm, returns typically 9am & 6.30pm; 55min).
NB No cars are carried on these craft.

Catamaran (*Dodekanisos Express*)
Sými to: Rhodes, Kós, Kálymnos, Léros (2–3 weekly; 3hr 20min max journey); to Lipsí, Pátmos (1 weekly; 4hr 30min max journey).

Ferries
Sými to: Kálymnos (2–3 weekly on GA; 6hr 40min); Kós (2–3 weekly on GA; 5hr 20min); Léros (2–3 weekly on GA; 8hr); Pátmos (2–3 weekly on GA; 9hr 30min); Pireás (2–3 weekly on GA; 17hr 30min); Níssyros (2-3 weekly on GA; 3hr 30min); Rhodes (2–3 weekly on GA; 1hr 40min); Tílos (2–3 weekly on GA; 2hr 15min).

Hydrofoils
Sými to: Rhodes (at least daily on the *Aigli*, variable departures typically 7.30am, 10am or 4pm, returns 9am, 2.30pm or 6.30pm; 55min).

International transport

Sými ranks as an official port of entry to Greece, and in season there are up to 3 weekly *kaïki* (80min) and 1 hydrofoil (40min) services to Turkey (Datça). The hydrofoil, at €30 return including Greek tax (but $12 Turkish tax extra), is cheaper but perhaps not as personable as the *kaïki* trip (€40 plus Turkish tax). These are sold primarily as day-return excursions and are not really the most practical means of travelling one way to Turkey.

Tílos

The small, usually quiet island of **Tílos** is one of the least frequented and (outside of peak season) worst connected of the Dodecanese, though it can (in theory) be visited as a day-trip from Rhodes by catamaran. Why anyone should want to come for just a few hours is unclear: while it's a great place to rest on the beach or go walking, there is nothing very striking at first glance. After a few days, however, you may have stumbled on several of the seven small **castles** of the Knights of St John which stud the crags, or have found some of the inconspicuous medieval **chapels**, often with (locked) frescoed interiors or pebble-mosaic courtyards, clinging to the hillsides.

Tílos shares the physical characteristics of its closest neighbours: limestone mountains resembling those of Hálki, plus volcanic lowlands, pumice beds and red-lava sand as on Níssyros. Though rugged and scrubby on its heights, the island has ample water – from springs, or pumped up from the agricultural plains – and clusters of oak and terebinth near the cultivated areas. The climate is exceptionally salubrious, with relative humidity often well below forty percent. From many points on the island there are startling views across to Kós, Sými, Turkey, Níssyros, Hálki, Rhodes and even (weather permitting) Kárpathos.

Stranded midway between Kós and Rhodes, Tílos has always been a backwater, and among all Dodecanese has the least developed nautical tradition. With ample ground water and rich volcanic soil, the islanders could afford to turn their backs on the sea, and instead made Tílos the

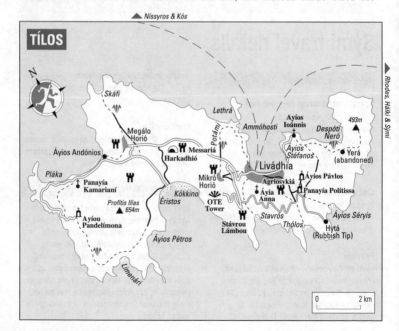

breadbasket of the Dodecanese. Until the 1970s, approaching travellers were greeted by the sight of blond, shimmering fields of grain bowing in the wind; today the hillside terraces languish abandoned, evidence of typical small-island depopulation. Officially, Tílos has about five hundred inhabitants, dwindling to a hundred or so in winter; though, given substantial tax incentives for permanent residence, both these figures are on the increase.

Since the late 1980s, Tílos has arrived touristically in a modest way; there are now well over a thousand guest beds on the island, with several hundred more pending. Laskarina Holidays (see p.33) bookings account for just a fraction of this capacity, and the island principally attracts an independent, disparate return clientele. Recent years, however, have witnessed running three-way battles over the direction of future development among northern European visitors who wish to walk, birdwatch and beachcomb in peace; a more raucous crowd (mainly Italians and Greeks) itching to exercise their dirt bikes, 4WD vehicles and shotguns; and some ambitious locals intent on catering to whichever faction will make the more lucrative bookings. The incumbent mayor has tried to placate the conservationists – Tílos has been a **no-hunting zone** since 1996, with the ban renewed until at least 2006 – plus there's a proposal in the offing for a permanent national wildlife reserve.

Nonetheless, the development boosters are busy reversing the conditions which many visitors historically came to enjoy; besides the "Dodge City" atmosphere of Livádhia (see overleaf), welts of private and publicly funded **jeep tracks** and **paved roads** scar almost every mountain and slope in the east of the island. All is not gloom, however: a 1998-vintage road from the telecom-tower hill, heading southeast along the summit ridge to the rubbish tip, will thankfully not sully the beach at Áyios Séryis, where a fish-farm proposal is suspended indefinitely. A half-dozen critical sections of deteriorating **trail** or **kalderími** have been officially surveyed in preparation for cleaning and consolidation in the distant future, so the number of quality **walking opportunities** may have stabilized. Those visitors who come specifically to hike are assisted by the extremely accurate **map** prepared by Baz "Paris" Ward and sold at local shops – or by certified walking **guides** Iain and Lyn Fulton (☎22460 44128 or 694 60 54 593, @fulton@otenet .gr), who may take you on unusual itineraries not described or mapped in existing literature.

Getting around the island

Tílos' wide main road runs 7km from Livádhia, the port village, to Megálo Horió, the capital and only other significant habitation. A blue-and-white public **bus** links the two, and services are theoretically scheduled to coincide with ferry/catamaran arrivals at the deep-water jetty; at other times the bus makes up to six daily runs along the Livádhia–Éristos stretch. Accommodation proprietors from Éristos, Megálo Horió and the remoter reaches of Livádhia may lay on shuttles to and from the port; there are also two **taxis**, or you can rent a **car** from several outlets in Livádhia, including Drive (☎22460 44173) and Tilos Travel (number as below).

Stefanakis Travel (☎22460 44310) currently has a monopoly on conventional **ferry tickets**; Tilos Travel is arguably the more helpful (☎ & @22460 44294 or 694 65 59 697, @www.tilostravel.co.uk), offering a full accommodation booking service, money exchange, **boat excursions** all season given sufficient passenger numbers, and **scooter rental**. For more active sea-going jaunts with kayaks or windsurfers, contact French-run Tilos Marine at Livádhia beach. The *Sea Star* catamaran has its own office by the church (☎22460 44000). The single **filling station**, keeping odd hours, lies between Livádhia and Megálo Horió.

Livádhia and around

With its hastily paved streets, unfinished building sites in every direction and higgledy-piggledy layout, **LIVÁDHIA** makes a poor introduction to the island, but it remains the far better equipped of the two settlements to deal with tourists, and is closer to the majority of remaining path-hikes. The long pebble beach, which gets more comfortable to sit on near the middle, is merely adequate at the best of times, and the tidal rocks can get slimy with pollution in high summer, when people surreptitiously vent cesspits.

Despite its currently peaceful profile, Livádhia Bay saw a certain amount of action **during World War II**, after the Italian capitulation. The Allies first attempted to take the island from the Germans on 26–27 October 1944, when Greek and British soldiers disembarked from HMS *Sirus*; German reinforcements quickly arrived from Rhodes and reversed the Anglo-Greek gains. In the course of this counterattack, two Greek fighters were killed and subsequently buried where they fell on the west hillside on October 28, a resonant date indeed (see p.457) – their blue-striped white **tombs**, which can be visited, remain a major landmark. On November 5, the HMS *Kimberly* destroyed a German patrol boat near Áyios Stéfanos; with good directions you can still find the **wreck** if you go snorkelling. The bulk of November was spent in inconclusive skirmishes, with the Germans holding on; Tílos finally fell to the Allies when a force of mostly Indian troops, outnumbering the German garrison 4:1, was landed on 27–28 1945.

Accommodation

There are generally enough beds in the various **rooms**, **studios** and **hotels** to go around, but in peak season it's certainly worth phoning ahead (or consulting Tilos Travel's website). The better outfits will provide you with some sort of mosquito control, since much of Livádhia is drained marsh.

Anastasia East about halfway along the bay, behind the *Armenon* taverna ☎22460 44111. A willingness to bargain offsets slightly small rooms; on-site scooter rental. ❷

Anna's Studios On the west hillside above the jetty, a bit north of *Marina's* ☎22460 44334, ℻22460 44342. Immaculate top-choice units built in 2001, priced according to size. ❸–❹

Blue Sky Right above ferry jetty ☎22460 44294. well-appointed, 2002-built, galleried apartments managed by Tilos Travel. ❹

Eleni Beach Hotel About halfway around the bay ☎22460 44062, ℮elenihtl@otenet.gr. Large, airy, white-decor rooms, private beach

facilities, wheelchair access and friendly management, but requires advance booking (especially since six rooms are now allotted to a package company). ❹

Faros Hotel At the extreme northeast end of the bay ☎22460 44068, ℻22460 44029. Widely praised for calm and its hospitable managing family; also has an acceptable restaurant and a tiny private beach. ❸

Hotel Irini 200m inland from mid-beach ☎22410 44293, ⓦwww.tilosholidays.gr. A lushly land-scaped low-rise hotel, with a popular pool, good breakfasts and pleasant lounge making up for somewhat small rooms. The same managment has

the *Studios Ilidi* on the west hillside (④ for 2, ⑤ for 4-person apartments. ③–④
Studios Irinna (aka *Kula's*) ☎ 22460 44366. Well-appointed studios situated inland, within sight of *Joanna's Café* (see below). ②
Kosmos Studios Quiet inland spot, past the cemetery; enquire at Kosmos gift shop ☎ 22460 44164, ⓦ www.tilos-kosmos.com. Four large, white, airy, south-facing apartments for up to three people, equipped with proper kitchen-diners and bedrooms in the cooler rear, mosquito nets and fans. Minimum stay two nights. ③

Marina's Studios Up by the October 1944 graves ☎ 22460 44023. Complex of three buildings; ground-floor units have patio gardens, upper storeys have knockout views; studios are large but basic, with fans only. ③
Pavlos Overlooking the sea near the *Eleni Beach Hotel* ☎ 22460 44011 or 694 24 49 903. Just four small if well-kept rooms, upstairs from a *souvláki* stall; own sunbeds on the beach. ③

Eating, drinking and nightlife

Up to a dozen-plus **tavernas** operate around Livádhia in peak season, of which barely half merit serious consideration. Among the more reliable spots for a no-nonsense feed are *Oasis* on the shore road towards the *Eleni Beach Hotel*, where the Greeks are most likely to go for pizza and grilled meat served in lovely palm-courtyard premises; *To Armenon* (alias *Nikos'*), on the shore road beyond the preceding, an excellent and salubrious beach-taverna-cum-*ouzerí*, with octopus salad, white beans and the like, though it's effectively the Laskarina clubhouse in spring and autumn; and *Mihalis* on the supermarket street with its popular garden tables, but quality varies and it's really best just for fish. For something different to the island norm, go for French-Vietnamese-run *Calypso* on the west hillside (reserve on ☎ 694 72 13 278; supper only), which excels at Creole-colonial dishes like *martiniquois* prawn or cod *acras*, five-flavour Chinese duck, or Vietnamese pork-and-mushroom vermicelli; vanilla custard, exotic rum-based cocktails and a cutting-edge music soundtrack round out the experience, though service can be chaotic when the eldest son – linchpin of the place – is absent.

For **breakfast** (plus evening thin-crust pizzas and homemade desserts), Anglo-Italian *Joanna's Café*, just up from the bakery, is hard to beat, and also features a long list of strong, imaginative cocktails, though there have been some murmurings about jacked-up prices here. *Iy Omonia* – under the Indian fig trees strung with light bulbs, near the post office – is the enduringly popular "traditional" alternative for a sundowner, waiting for a ferry (it's open all afternoon in summer), or breakfast, and also does inexpensive, savoury, generous *mezédhes* (€9 for two plates and a beer). Livelier organized **nightlife** in or near Livádhia is limited to three bars: *Cafe Ino* on the shore for the trendy set, the *Bozi* at the far east end of bay (nightly in summer, weekends otherwise) and a durable music pub in Mikró Horió (see overleaf).

Other practicalities

Near what passes for Livádhia's central junction, there's a **post office**, and a full-service bank with ATM. A **bakery** one street over does decent *píttes*, and several well-stocked "**supermarkets**" stock a range of produce, as do itinerant pick-up trucks, which call regularly from the fertile farms of Éristos. The *Kosmos* gift/souvenir shop opposite *Joanna's Café* has a used-book exchange and offers **Internet** facilities (€3 for 30min).

Walks around Livádhia

Despite ongoing, destructive road-building, there are still enough walks around Livádhia to keep you occupied for a few days. Of the six hiking routes marked out for protection and rehabilitation, four begin in or near the port.

To Lethrá via Ammóhosti

The obvious path on the northwest flank of Livádhia Bay starts at the end of asphalt road opened to serve various hillside studio complexes (though the original start of the route is signposted at the base of the *Calypso Restaurant*). This Italian-built thoroughfare leads within an hour, without complications, except for a brief cross-country stretch through trees at the end, to the pebble bay of **Lethrá**. About two-thirds of the way along, you pass the side-path to the little red-sand beach of **Ammóhosti**, though in all probability at least one party will have beaten you there. Lethrá is cleanest and most usable at its rightmost cove; from the above-noted trees you can trek uphill through the Potámi canyon to Mikró Horió. The full loop Livádhia–Lethrá–Potámi–Mikró Horió–Livádhia (described below) is designated as one of the six routes to be conserved, so should not deteriorate any further.

Mikró Horió and Potámi

From Livádhia, a walk southwest along a trail which short-cuts the road system – part of it is fenced in, but open two gates to follow the course of a pipeline paralleling the path – takes you within 45 minutes up to the ghost village of **MIKRÓ HORIÓ**. Its 1200 inhabitants left for the island's capital during the 1950s owing to water shortages; the name (meaning "Little Village") is rather a misnomer as it was once more populous than Megálo Horió ("Big Village"). The interesting **ruins**, also accessible by dirt road, include threshing cirques strewn with grain millstones. A sprouting of "ΙΔΙΟΚΤΗΣΙΑ..." ("Property of...") signs on the ruins to deter squatters suggests that the owners have woken up to their potential value should power and water be provided, but thus far almost the only intact structures are the castle-guarded church (locked, except for the festival on Aug 15) and an old house which has been restored as a well-publicized, after-midnight **music pub** (July & Aug only). Proportions of Greek and foreign music vary according to tourist numbers, and a shuttle from Livádhia is provided.

From the north end of the village below the castle, a path leads down within twenty minutes to the paved road, meeting it at a double-channelled culvert. Directly below this, the stream-bed here has been ploughed under by a bulldozer track, though a walled-in path going parallel to it allows you to avoid much of this; some fifteen minutes along either, you reach a picturesque, masoned, reliable fountain on the east bank, marked by two poplars – and the end of the track for now. Beyond this point, keep as closely as possible to the bottom of the scenic, steep-sided **Potámi canyon**; do not follow any cairns directing you up and right, as that path merely fizzles out high up on the hillside. By the correct bearing, it's some thirty minutes more down to Lethrá, emerging near the middle of the bay. Going uphill from Lethrá to the spring involves much the same time, as there's some stooping to get through dense vegetation; before June at least, water breaks the surface of the stream-bed in several places.

Eastern loop

This half- to full-day outing, depending on the number of detours off the basic circuit, takes in most of the territory **east of Livádhia**, and remains popular despite a fair amount of jeep track to be trudged. Head off east on the paved road beyond Áyios Stéfanos anchorage, which serves a villa complex, to Áyios Ioánnis church, where the proper trail (again a candidate for rehabilitation) reappears; some fifteen minutes past the church you'll reach a Y-fork. Left leads within half an hour to the abandoned hamlet of **Yerá**, just inland from its eponymous beach (which acts as a very efficient rubbish trap). There's a much cleaner beach just west of the powerful, deliciously potable, shoreline spring of **Despóti tó Neró**, which is reached by a prominent, direct side-path about fifteen minutes past Áyios Ioánnis. From this little beach back to the church, allow 45 minutes.

To execute the loop, bearing right instead at the Y-fork takes you past another spring to the hamlet of Kalámi, where you meet the end of a bulldozed track. You're obliged to follow this west-southwest through a pass in the hills, with the grounds of Panayía Polítissa below on your right and the beach of **Áyios Séryis** to the southeast (no real trail to it, but an easy scramble there). From here it's an easy return northwest, then north down to Livádhia, or you could carry on along the road some 400m to the next prominent saddle, where Thólos cove beckons to the south and Agriosykiá castle looms to the north.

To Thólos via Agriosykiá

Obviously Thólos can be reached directly from Livádhia. The route, with the more recent road avoidable for quite a way by using the old path running in parallel, begins by the cemetery and the chapel of **Áyios Pandelímon** with its Byzantine *votsalotá* court, then curls around under the seemingly impregnable castle of **Agriosykiá**. Once you're up on the saddle (30min out of Livádhia), overlooking the descent to Thólos, a cairned route hairpins back and upwards to the citadel (20min walk). Views are wonderful, especially early in the morning, but there no longer seems to be an easy way into the half-ruined castle itself.

From the saddle, a distinct path – again, surveyed in preparation for refurbishment – leads about five minutes further south, then dwindles to a well-cairned scramble for another twenty minutes down to the popular sandy beach of **Thólos**. The *thólos* or domed structure itself stands on the east side of the bay; what this is – church, tomb or mine works – seems uncertain.

To Stavrós beach

Stavrós is the closest, cleanest, and arguably the most scenic of the south-facing beaches around Livádhia. Take the track between the *Tilos Mare Hotel* and the *Castellania Apartments* and follow this until it becomes a distinct trail at the highest new house of the "village", more or less as shown on the recommended map. The route curls progressively south, passing a dried-up spring (bring plenty of water) to reach the saddle dividing the Livádhia side from the ravine descending to Stavrós. Cairns guide you through the mess created by the road heading east towards the rubbish tip; there may also be "STAVROS" signs pointing vaguely off the upper bend. Soon the path resumes after a fashion, passing under the crumbled walls of **Stavroú Lámbou castle** on the west, and stays on the right bank of the ravine for the final, steepest quarter-hour; again surveyor's marks point the way, and overeager amateur cairning in the bed of the watercourse is best ignored. The **beach** itself, an hour's hike out of Livádhia, turns out to be a hundred-metre crescent of pea-gravel and coarse sand at the head of a cliff-girt inlet; there are sea caves for swimmers to explore on the left, but no shade.

Megálo Horió and around

The rest of Tílos' inhabitants live in or near **MEGÁLO HORIÓ**, and traditionally had very little to do with the Livadhians, with whom they were not on the best terms; this all changed when Livádhia's autonomy was abolished in 1998 and the entire island came under the authority of one municipality. The village's simple, vernacular houses, arranged in tiers, enjoy an enviable perspective over a vast agricultural *kámbos* stretching down to the bay of Éristos. Despite a recent spate of renovations and consequent reduction in derelict dwellings, the village is no metropolis by any standard. But in contrast to "Wild West" Livádhia, it is well planned and "improved", with an anticlockwise one-way traffic system in effect, plus stone paving and landscaping. Monumental interest is provided by the handsome, post-Byzantine parish **church of Taxiárhis**, built on the site of a temple to Apollo and Athena, the **chuch of the Panayía** near the top of the village, both with extensive *votsalotá* courtyards.

Best choices for **accommodation** are the central *Milios Apartments* (☎22460 44204, Ⓕ22460 442665; ❷–❸ depending on size) or *Studios Ta Elefandakia* (☎22460 44213; ❷), set among attractive gardens by the car park. The sole surviving **taverna**, *Kastro*, has reasonable food and a terrace with views, but has proven unwelcoming to outsiders. A couple of souvenir shops have sprung up, as well as several *kafenía* and cafés. There's the traditional locals' **kafenío** by Taxiárhis church and, further up, the Athenian-run *Kafenio Ilakati* (early June–early Sept only; opens 7pm), with cakes and drinks.

The Knights' castle and the Harkadhió cave

Megálo Horió is overlooked by a vast **Knights' castle**, which encloses a sixteenth-century **chapel** with rather battered frescoes. The castle is reached by a stiff, half-hour climb that begins on the lane behind the Ikonomou supermarket, near the village entrance, and threads its way up through a vast jumble of cisterns, house foundations and derelict chapels – testimony to Megálo Horió's much greater ancient and medieval size. A massive gate-tower incorporates Classical masonry, and a block in front of the chapel bearing Greek inscriptions provides additional proof that the *kástro* was built over the ancient acropolis.

From the Knights' castle, two other fortresses are visible across the plain; the easterly one of **Messariá** helpfully marks the location of **Harkadhió cave**, where Pleiocene midget elephant bones were discovered in 1971. Hidden for centuries until exposed by a World War II artillery barrage, the cave is now fenced off while it's being re-excavated, but should eventually be open for visits; meanwhile, a well-signposted paved road leads to the spring just below it, beside which an attractive amphitheatre occasionally hosts summertime events. Bones unearthed thus far have been transferred to a tiny **museum** in Megálo Horió, on the ground floor of the *dhimarhío*; the Greek-labelled displays, which also include the skulls of the Áyios Andónios victims (see opposite), aren't exactly compelling, but you can find the English-speaking warden upstairs (Mon–Fri 8am–2.30pm; free).

Nearby beaches: Skáfi and Éristos

From Megálo Horió you can reach **Skáfi**, the most easily accessible of Tílos' remote beaches; this lies over an hour's walk away along a path that begins below the Ikonomou supermarket and leads directly up the valley to the north. On a scooter you can get there much quicker by taking the first unmarked dirt track on the right past the helipad and following this over the ridge until it stops (the current end point subject to bulldozer doings), with the bay in sight below (and a clump of eucalyptus trees marking the location of a spring, reached by a dead-end path). A trail resumes at track's end, arriving at Skáfi after fifteen minutes' walk. Most of the main bay is goat- or tar-fouled and rocky, but continue five more minutes over the headland on the right to reach a more idyllic pea-gravel cove, with shelter afforded by overhangs.

South of and below Megálo Horió, signs direct you towards the three-kilometre paved side road to long **Éristos** beach, whose sand hue varies from pink to grey depending on the light; it's allegedly the island's best, and indisputably the longest, though summer rubbish piles from campers can be disconcerting, and a reefy zone must be crossed to enter the water. The far southeast end, where the reef is diminshed, is also a designated nudist zone, as are the three secluded, attractive coves at **Kókkino** beyond the headland (path accessible only).

About halfway down the road on the right amongst the orchards is *Taverna-Rooms Tropikana* (☎ 22460 44020; ❶), nothing special in either respect, but the most reliably open all-season venue for a snack near the beach. For more comfort, there's the *Eristos Beach Hotel* (☎ 22460 44024; ❸), recently expanded with a plush annexe (package patrons mainly), pool and restaurant; the original wing of rooms are good value, though the management can be rather erratic.

The far northwest

The main road beyond Megálo Horió hits the coast again at somewhat grim, windswept **Áyios Andónios**, whose principal attraction is a single **taverna**, the *Dhelfíni*, packed at weekend lunches because of its reasonable prices, fresh fish and homemade *melitsanosaláta* (and in spite of often shambolic service). The remoter alternative, *Elpidha*, has fresh, basically presented squid or cuttle-fish, and not much else. A fairly obvious path from the west end of Megálo Horió gets walkers there in twenty minutes. By looking carefully along the exposed, average beach you can find more lava-encased skeletons strung out in a row (see opposite) – human this time, supposedly tide-washed victims of a Nissyrian eruption in 600 BC, and discovered by the same archeologists who found the miniature pachyderms. Other estimates of the age of these relics range from Hellenistic times to the fifteenth century, though most agree that they were "vulcanized" in some way.

There's better, warm-water swimming and afternoon shade from exotic century plants at isolated **Pláka** beach, 2km west of Áyios Andónios. People pitch tents among the olive trees behind, despite a lack of toilet facilities and a brackish well; repeated attempts to transform this area into an official campsite have so far come to nought, though it seems it will be protected as a "nature reserve" from permanent development.

Ayíou Pandelímona monastery and around

The paved road finally ends 8km west of Megálo Horió at the fortified monastery of **Ayíou Pandelímona** (daily: summer 10am–7pm; winter 10am–4pm), founded in the fifteenth century for the sake of its miraculous spring, still the best water on the island. These days the place is not much frequented except for July 25–27, when long cement tables on the terrace below host the island's biggest festival. Its tower-gate and oasis setting nearly two hundred forbidding metres above the west coast are the most memorable features, though the eminently photogenic inner court boasts a *hokhláki* surface, and the church a fine tessellated marble floor. On the walls of the *katholikón*, an early eighteenth-century fresco shows the founder-builder holding a model of the monastery, while behind the ornately carved altar screen, in the conch, hides an unusual, possibly earlier fresco of the Holy Trinity.

A resident caretaker operates a small snack/drinks café on the festival terraces. The public bus shows up here perhaps once or twice daily in season, but to heighten the sense of pilgrimage it's recommended that you arrive on foot from Áyios Andónios. First you've twenty minutes along the shore to the little monastery of **Panayía Kamarianí**, then you go through half-abandoned terraces along the old path to the monastery for 45 minutes to a prominent pass with a stone chapel, and then a final twenty minutes down to the monastery gate (the last five minutes on the road). This route is shown correctly on Baz Ward's map.

An advanced trek: Ayíou Pandelímona to Éristos

Committed and experienced hill-walkers can tackle the challenging path (not on the Baz Ward map) that curls around the southwest flank of Profítis Ilías (651m), Tílos' highest mountain, finishing several hours later at Éristos. This begins, as signposted, beside the monastery; it's a well-surveyed route – one of the six up for revamping – with no real exposure or sharp drops, and extensive surviving stretches of the old *kalderími* still in place. But there's only one spring along the way, rather demoralizing scree at the start, and the wild feel of a remote traverse on a much larger island. In short, novices need not apply, and it's something best done in a group – in 1996, a lone traveller had to be rescued by helicopter.

The initial scree-slides are so bad that they've obliterated the original course of the trail, as shown on the old Italian Ordnance Survey maps; the first 25 minutes of the route are thus forced a bit further inland than you'd expect, with a tough climb past or even over the loose scree, until the grade slackens and you get back onto the proper original path. With the worst over, you spend the next twenty minutes threading through three successive, gentle passes; the second is the highest on this part of the route, and you catch a glimpse of the sea swirling around Tílos' southwesterly cape, far below. An hour along should find you at the top of the first little ravine draining down to Limenári; you can see this bay and the clawlike promontory beyond it, but not (yet) the beach at the head of the gulf. Twenty minutes later you reach the lone spring en route, inside a stone enclosure; the water should be potable from the spout, though there's often a dead goat near (or in) the trough. Continue descending, over some less obvious sections, past a dilapidated chapel to cross the bed of the main ravine descending to **Limenári**, one hour and forty minutes out – before you succumb to the temptation for a detour and swim, remember that you're barely halfway to Éristos.

Now you climb again in earnest, partly along a revetted corniche path, to the southernmost point of the route at a final saddle, two hours and twenty minutes away from the monastery; bear northeast for the more gradual, final descent to your goal. Just under three hours along, the surveyed route debouches onto a track system, where a little sign cheerily (and a

Greek script table

Tílos	Τήλος	ΤΗΛΟΣ
Ammóhosti	Αμμόχωστη	ΑΜΜΟΧΩΣΤΗ
Áyios Ioánnis	Άγιος Ιοάννης	ΑΓΙΟΣ ΙΟΑΝΝΗΣ
Áyios Pétros	Άγιος Πέτρος	ΑΓΙΟΣ ΠΕΤΡΟΣ
Áyios Andónios	Άγιος Αντώνιος	ΑΓΙΟΣ ΑΝΤΩΝΙΟΣ
Áyios Séryis	Άγιος Σέργιος	ΑΓΙΟΣ ΣΕΡΓΗΣ
Éristos	Έριστος	ΕΡΙΣΤΟΣ
Harkadhió	Χαρκαδιό	ΧΑΡΚΑΔΙΟ
Kókkino	Κόκκινο	ΚΟΚΚΙΝΟ
Lethrá	Λεθρά	ΛΕΘΡΑ
Livádhia	Λιβάδια	ΛΙΒΑΔΙΑ
Megálo Horió	Μεγάλο Χωριό	ΜΕΓΑΛΟ ΧΩΡΙΟ
Mikró Horió	Μικρό Χωριό	ΜΙΚΡΟ ΧΩΡΙΟ
Moní Ayíou	Μονή Αγίου	ΜΟΝΗ ΑΓΙΟΥ
Pandelímona	Παντελείμωνα	ΠΑΝΤΕΛΕΙΜΩΝΑ
Panayía	Παναγία	ΠΑΝΑΓΙΑ
Kamarianí	Καμαριανή	ΚΑΜΑΡΙΑΝΗ
Pláka	Πκάλα	ΠΛΑΚΑ
Skáfi	Σκάφη	ΣΚΑΦΗ
Stavrós	Σταυρός	ΣΤΑΥΡΟΣ
Thólos	Θόλος	ΘΟΛΟΣ
Yerá	Γερά	ΓΕΡΑ

bit optimistically) informs those coming in the opposite direction that it's three hours to the monastery. This is your last chance for a private swim, at **Áyios Pétros** bay. The main track system hugs the base of the mountain here; use an obvious side-turning to get down to Éristos, three-and-a-quarter walking hours after leaving Ayíou Pandelímona. However, with rest stops, you'd be prudent to allow four and a half to five hours for the trek.

Tílos travel details

Island transport

Buses
The current bus schedule is posted in Livádhia's central-square-cum-junction; however, it's not to be trusted implicitly, so confirm with the driver.

Inter-island transport

Ferries
Tílos to: Kálymnos (2–3 weekly on GA; 4hr 30min); Kós (3 weekly on GA; 3hr 15min); Léros (3 weekly on GA; 6hr); Níssyros (3 weekly on GA; 1hr 15min); Pátmos (3 weekly on GA; 7hr 15min); Pireás (3 weekly on GA; 17hr); Rhodes (3 weekly on GA; 2hr 30min nonstop, 3hr 45min via Sými); Sými (1 weekly on GA; 2hr).

Catamaran
Tílos' very own *Sea Star* theoretically links Tílos with Rhodes at least once daily from early June to early October; however, it has proven far less reliable than its larger cousin the *Dodekanisos Express*, which no longer calls at Tílos (though efforts are being made to lure it back). Twice weekly (typically Mon & Wed) the run extends to Níssyros, while once or twice weekly (most likely Tues & Sat) the *Sea Star* includes Háki on its route. For its complete (and complex) schedule, see p.59 in Basics.

Níssyros

Volcanic **Níssyros** is noticeably greener than its southern neighbours Tílos and Hálki and, unlike them, has proven attractive and wealthy enough to retain over eight hundred of its population year-round (down, though, from 10,000 in 1900, and 2500 just after World War II). While remittances from abroad (particularly Astoria, New York) are significant, most of the island's income is derived from the offshore islet of Yialí, towards Kós, essentially a vast lump of **pumice** slowly being chipped away by a couple of dozen Nissyrian miners. Rent collected by the municipality from Lava Ltd, the company with the quarry concession for Yialí, has engendered a sort of mini-Kuwait situation – the wealthiest per-capita welfare statelet in Europe, complete with publicly run bakery and pharmacy, plus a well-padded civil service. Under the circumstances, the Nissyrians bother little with agriculture other than keeping cows and pigs; the hillside terraces meticulously carved out for grain and grapes lie fallow, and wine is no longer made here.

The main island's peculiar geology is potentially a source of other benefits: DEI, the Greek power corporation, spent the years between 1988 and 1992 sinking exploratory **geothermal** wells and attempting to convince the islanders of the benefits of cheap electricity. The locals rallied against the project, mindful of DEI's poor track record on Mílos in the Cyclades, which resulted

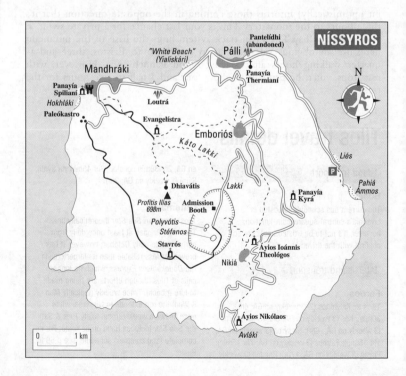

in noxious fumes, industrial litter and land expropriation. Yet in 1991, DEI persuaded the municipality to bulldoze a new road of dubious necessity around the southwest flank of the island, damaging farmland and destroying a beautiful 700-year-old cobbled footpath (to their credit, many islanders now express considerable regret for this act). Metal debris from unsuccessful test bores also did little to endear them to the local populace.

In 1993, a local referendum went massively against the scheme, and DEI, together with its Italian contractor, took the hint and retreated temporarily before returning in 1997 with tempting promises of job offers to locals, and yet another referendum – which again went (narrowly) against. Meanwhile, the desalination plant, still powered (like everything else) by undersea cable from Kós, scarcely provides enough fresh water to spur a massive growth in package tourism; rain cisterns remain important. The relatively few tourists who stay the night, as opposed to the day-trippers from Kós, still find peaceful villages with a minimum of concrete eyesores, and a friendly if rather tight-knit population.

Níssyros also offers good **walking** opportunities through a countryside planted with oak or terebinth, on a network of trails fitfully marked and maintained with EU money; wherever you stroll you'll hear the contented grunting of pigs as they gorge themselves on acorns from the many oak trees. Autumn is a wonderful time, especially when the landscape has perked up after the first rains; the late January almond-blossoming is much reduced owing to an early 1990s blight that devastated the trees, which are now making a slow comeback.

Mandhráki

MANDHRÁKI is the deceptively large port and island capital, with blue patches of sea often visible (and audible) at the end of narrow streets swarming with cats (even by Greek-island standards), and lined with tightly packed houses whose brightly painted wooden balconies and shutters are mandated by law. Except for the tattier fringes near the ferry dock, where multiple souvenir shops and bad tavernas pitched at day-trippers leave a poor first impression, the bulk of the place is cheerful, villagey and indifferent to tourism, arrayed around the community orchard or *kámbos* and overlooked by two ancient fortresses, which protect it somewhat from the prevailing wind.

Into a corner of the nearer of these, the fourteenth-century **Knights' castle**, is wedged the little monastery of **Panayía Spilianí**, built on this spot in accordance with instructions from the Virgin herself, who appeared in a vision to one of the first Christian islanders. The monastery's prestige grew after raiding Saracens failed to discover vast quantities of silver secreted here in the form of a rich collection of Byzantine icons. During 1996–97, the Langadháki area just below was rocked by a series of earthquakes, damaging a score of venerable houses (mostly repaired now); the seismic threat is ever present, quite literally cutting the ground out from under those who erroneously dub the volcano "extinct". A new combination archeological-ethnographical-historical **museum** has been built on the *kámbos* with money partly donated by the Nissyrian founder of the Vitex paint company, and should be ready for visitors by late 2005.

As a defensive bastion, the seventh-century-BC Doric **Paleókastro** (unrestricted access), twenty minutes' well-signposted walk out of Langadháki, is infinitely more impressive than the Knights' castle, and ranks as one of the more underrated ancient sites in Greece. Once restoration scaffolding is removed, you should again be able to clamber up onto the massive, polygonal-block walls, standing mostly to their original height, by means of a broad staircase beside the still-intact gateway.

Accommodation

You'll see a handful of **hotels** on your left as you disembark at the port, convenient (especially for yachties craving a night ashore) but hardly state-of-the-art. Standards in the village itself, all of 400m ahead, are comparable; there's only one establishment on the island that's really above C-class standard, and you get the feeling that the Nissyrians are happy to keep matters that way.

The port

Polyvotis ℡ 22420 31011, 🖷 22420 31204. Municipally run hotel, officially B-class but effectively C-class, which has biggish, neutral-decor rooms with fans and (mostly) knockout sea views. ❷–❸

Romantzo ℡ 22420 31340. Good-value simple but well-kept rooms with fridges and partial sea views. ❶

Three Brothers On the waterfront, opposite the Romantzo ℡ 22420 31344. Not quite as well kept as its rival, but you do have unobstructed sea views in most cases. ❶

Central Mandhráki

Liotridia ℡ 22420 31237, 🖃 liotridia@in.gr. Just four comfortable doubles in a restored olive mill; Níssyros' newest (2003) and plushest accommodation. ❻

Porfyris ℡ 22420 31376, 🖷 22420 31176. Mandhráki's most comfortable hotel; many rooms, all with air con and fridges, overlook the sea and *kámbos*, plus there's breakfast terrace by the large swimming pool. Open May–Sept. ❹

Sunset/Iliovasilema Near the converted windmill ℡ 22420 31159 or 697 21 41 344. Adequate, quiet studios – one of the few places actually on the shore. ❸

Studios Volcano Contacts as for the Romantzo. Fully self-catering units about halfway into town. ❸

Ypapandi In the town proper, ℡ 22420 31485 or visit Taverna Panorama. "Hotel" (really *dhomátia*) that's the main in-town budget option, in a quiet hillside location, but small, very basic and often full. ❶

Eating and drinking

Nissyrian culinary **specialities** include pickled caper greens, honey, *pittiá* (chickpea croquettes), and *soumádha*, an almond-syrup drink widely sold in recycled wine bottles, though it's now made from imported almonds rather than the extinct local bitter almonds, and must be consumed within three months of purchase. When eating out, it's best to give all of the commercialized, shoddy shoreline **tavernas** a miss in favour of more genuine haunts inland. Top of the heap is evening-only, musical *ouzerí Iy Fabrika* (closed Thurs), with indoor/outdoor tables by season and hearty fare from owner Manolis, also the miners' chef on Yialí. Fifty years ago this was a *patitíri* (winepress) and wine shop, and he has returned it to something like its original function. Pricier runners-up include *Panorama*, with bean and mushroom salad or suckling pig on offer, or *Irini* on lively, ficus-shaded Platía Ilikioméni, with more involved *mayireftá* unavailable elsewhere. Finally, little *Taverna Nissiros*, the oldest eatery in town, is always busy despite predictably average grill quality. Focuses of **nightlife** are Platía Ilikioméni, where *Randevou* is the best stocked of the sweet-cafés, and a string of *barákia* on the shore at Lefkándio district, the most popular of these being the *Enallax*.

Other practicalities

The most useful of Mandhráki's four **travel agencies** is Dhiakomihalis (℡22240 31459), which acts as a representative for the *Sea Star* catamaran, rents cars and exchanges money, or Kentris (℡22420 31227), near the town hall, which handles GA ferries, plus Olympic Airways tickets. There's a **post office** at the port and a single **bank** in town, but it has no ATM and levies stiff commissions, as does Dhiakomihalis; a stand-alone ATM at the harbour is unreliable. Also at the base of the jetty is the **bus stop**, with (theoretically) up to five daily departures to the hill villages and six to Páli; otherwise, there are two set-rate **taxis** and two outlets for **scooter rental**, of which John and John (branch also in Páli) provides the best service. Besides Dhiakomihalis, there's also Manos K **car rental** by the single filling station (℡22420 31028).

East of Mandhráki: the coast

Beaches on Níssyros are in even shorter supply than water, so much so that tour agencies here occasionally peddle excursions to a sandy cove on **Áyios Andónios** islet, opposite the mining machinery on **Yialí**. Closer at hand, the 150-metre, black-rock beach of **Hokhláki**, behind the Knights' castle, is accessible by a five-minute stroll along the walkway from the northwest corner of town; the black pebbles here get smaller at the far end, where nudism is tolerated, though the wind picks up in the afternoon.

It's best to head east along the main road, passing the refurbished spa of **Loutrá** (hot mineral-water baths 8–11am only by doctor's referral) and the smallish, partly sheltered **"White Beach"** (properly Yialiskári), 2km along and dwarfed by an ugly, unwelcoming eponymous hotel. The beach name is a bit of a misnomer, as its high percentage of black sand creates a decidedly salt-and-pepper appearance. The Loutrá spa is well worth a stop for its "snack-bar" at the far end of the building; really an **ouzerí** with generous portions of salads, fried appetizers, seafood and meat – though it's become pricey of late, especially the fish.

A kilometre or so further, 4km in total from Mandhráki, the fishing village of **PÁLLI** makes an excellent hangout at lunchtime, when the port fills with trippers, though the yachts that prefer to call here have driven prices up. **Tavernas** are multiplying, but the newer ones have generated reader complaints of price-gouging, so it's best to stick with the two long-term favourites: the less expensive *Ellinis*, with spit-roasted meat by night, grilled fish in season and simple rooms upstairs (℡22420 31453; ❷), or the adjacent *Afroditi* (aka *Nikos & Tsambika*), with big portions of grills and *mayireftá*, Cretan bulk wine and excellent homemade desserts. About the only other **accommodation** is the well-sited *Frantzis Studios* by the bakery (℡22420 31240; ❸), with well-kept units in slightly scruffy grounds. The scooter-rental outlet (branch of John and John's), an excellent bakery cranking out rare brown bread and fine pies (branch in Mandhráki on the fountain *platía*), and modest nightlife east along the quay (try *Captain's House*) also make Pálli worth considering as a base.

A tamarisk-shaded, dark-sand **beach**, kept well groomed, extends east of Pálli to the abandoned Pantelídhi spa, behind which the little grotto-chapel of **Panayía Thermianí** is tucked inside the vaulted remains of a Roman baths complex, now partly open to the sky and with a salt-pool grotto at the rear. To reach Níssyros' best **beaches**, continue in this direction for an hour on foot (or 20min by scooter along the road), past an initially discouraging seaweed- and cowpat-strewn shoreline, to the delightful cove of **Liés,** with a snack-bar, *Oasis*

(July–Aug only). Just beyond here the paved road ends at a car park; in summer, boat trips from Mandhráki call here too. Walking a further fifteen minutes along a dusty pumice trail over the headland brings you to the idyllic, 300-metre expanse of **Pahiá Ámmos**, with grey-pink sand heaped in dunes, limited shade at the far end and a large colony of rough campers and naturists in summer – including the "boho" contingent from the previous night at *Iy Fabrika* – the only time the place is much frequented. Off season it's so secluded, in fact, that smugglers from Turkey have taken to burying drugs on the beach for their Greek cohorts to retrieve, so perhaps don't dig up any suspicious packages.

The interior

The central, dormant **volcano** gives Níssyros its special character and fosters the growth of the abundant vegetation – no stay would be complete without a visit. When excursion boats arrive from Kós, several agency coaches and usually one of the public buses are pressed into service to take customers into the interior. These tours tend to monopolize the crater floor between 11am and 2pm, so if you want solitude use early-morning or late-afternoon scheduled buses to Nikiá (two or three daily continue to the crater floor), a scooter or your own two feet to get there.

Emboriós and Panayiá Kyrá

The road up from Pálli towards the volcano winds first past the virtually abandoned village and crumbled fortress of **EMBORIÓS**, where pigs and free-ranging cattle (a major driving hazard) far outnumber people, though the place is slowly being bought up and restored by Athenians and foreigners. New owners are often surprised to discover natural saunas, heated by volcanic steam, in the basements of their crumbling houses; at the outskirts of the village there's a signposted public **steam bath** in a grotto, its entrance outlined in white paint. The only other "amenity" is a **taverna** on the little square, *To Balkoni tou Emboriou* (lunch & supper early May–late Sept), which has a limited if cheap menu and outdoor tables on the namesake balcony overlooking the volcanic caldera. The enormous mirror inside was shattered by a bullet in a skirmish between the resistance and Germans during the closing days of World War II.

If you're descending **on foot** to Pálli from here, an old *kalderími*, beginning at the sharp bend below the "sauna", offers an attractive short cut of the four-kilometre road. You can also drop south into the volcanic area along another *kalderími* starting behind *To Balkoni tou Emboriou*, indicated from the *platía*; in under half an hour this emerges at the last road-bend below the village, leaving you with another quarter-hour or so to the craters (see opposite).

About halfway between Emboriós and Nikiá, a signposted side road leads down to the island's third major monastery (after Spilianí and Áyios Ioánnis), **Panayiá Kyrá**. Unfortunately, the place is usually locked except around the time of the August 14–15 festival – the island's best – but you can still enjoy the fine setting on fertile terraces overlooking Pahiá Ámmos (to which there is no obvious path down). Over the gate to the courtyard looms a fortification tower; the medieval *katholikón* stands off-centre, on the south side of the compound.

Nikiá and Áyios Ioánnis Theológos

NIKIÁ, the large village on the east side of the volcano's caldera, is (with fifty permanent inhabitants) more of a going concern than Emboriós, and its spectacular situation 14km from Mandhráki offers views out to Tílos as well as across the caldera. There are two places to **drink** (and, modestly, **eat**) here: *Platía* and *Iy Pórta* (summer only, with superior food) on or near the engagingly round *hokhláki* plaza ringed by stone seating, itself called the Pórta and marked out in white paint for the steps of folk dances.

By the bus turnaround area, signs point to the 45-minute trail, initially a stair-path, descending to the crater floor. A few minutes downhill, you can fork right for the brief detour to the eyrie-like monastery of **Áyios Ioánnis Theológos**, with a shady tree and yet another perspective on the volcano. The picnic benches and utility buildings come to life at the annual festival on the evening of September 25.

Incidentally, it is not worth following signs towards **Avláki**, 5km south of Nikiá. This is an abandoned fishing hamlet of about a dozen houses – a few now restored – around the unspectacular monastery of **Áyios Nikólaos**. Its surroundings are dreary and barren, with no beach or easy swimming opportunities, though the old path from Nikiá short-cuts most of the now completely paved road down to a car park. Much-touted hot springs in the shallows, off to the left as you face the sea, are tricky to find and (unlike similar ones at Kós and Ikaría) have scant effect on sea temperature: in short, most will reckon the trip down a waste of time and petrol.

The volcano

To **drive** directly to the volcanic area of **Lákki**, 14km in total from Mandhráki, take the signposted road which veers off to the right just past Emboriós. Whether you approach from this direction or on foot from Nikiá, a sulphurous stench drifts out to meet you as fields and scrub gradually give way to lifeless, caked powder. The sunken main crater of **Stéfanos** is extraordinary, a moonscape of grey, brown and jaundice-yellow; there is another, less visited double crater (dubbed **Polyvótis**) to the west, equally dramatic, with a clear trail leading up to it from the access road. The perimeters of both are pocked with tiny blowholes from which jets of steam puff constantly and around which form little pincushions of pure sulphur crystals.

The whole floor of the larger crater seems to hiss, and standing in the middle you can hear something akin to a huge cauldron bubbling away below you. According to legend, this is the groaning of Polyvotis, a titan crushed here by Poseidon under a huge rock torn from Kós. Hardly less prosaic are the facts of a prehistoric **eruption**, when the volcano apparently blew its top Krakatoa-style; the most recent hiccups, which produced steam, ash and earthquakes, occurred in 1422, 1873, 1888 and 1933, and apparently Polyvótis crater, not the more obvious Stéfanos, was responsible for these.

A small, tree-shaded **snack-bar** in the centre of the wasteland operates whenever tour groups are around. A €1.50 admission is payable at a small booth, flanking the access road just before you get to the café and staffed during most daylight hours.

Island walks

Since the destruction of the old direct trail between the volcano and Mandhráki, pleasant options for **walking** back to town from the interior are limited and can involve a certain amount of asphalt-tramping. That said, there are still quite a number of worthwhile hikes, many of these indicated on Beate and Jürgen Franke's locally available, GPS-drawn topographical map (free from various hotels or the town hall). With the exception of routes beginning from Evangelístra monastery, trailheads are easier to find going downhill – often

△ Unusual round platía at Nikiá, Níssyros

there are crude, handpainted signposts – so the first step will probably be to take a bus or taxi (€10 per car) to Nikiá or Emboriós.

Nikiá to Mandhráki via Stavrós

A few people do still attempt to walk back direct to Mandhráki from Nikiá, a three-hour undertaking. Matters begin well enough along a narrow path exiting the south end of the village, which emerges after 45 minutes at a weather-data station and a rough track linking the caldera with the isolated monastery of **Stavrós**, where a large *xenónas*, or inn, sees tenants only for its September 13–14 festival. You can tramp off west from here through the hills on the jeep track, but it's no comparison to the old *kalderími*, and in season you may have to contend with speeding yobbos on dirt-bikes.

Nikiá to Emboriós

This takes just under ninety minutes, with a short stretch of road-walking towards the end, but presupposes experience on easier walks and good orienteering skills, as the trail has been long abandoned and is not shown on the German-made map. Descend from Nikiá towards the volcano and bear right in the direction of Theológos monastery, but then take the left fork by the wooden gate before reaching it. The path ambles along through neglected terraces on the northeast flank of Lákki, without much altitude change, occasionally obstructed by landslide debris and thick vegetation; you'll eventually emerge after 50–55 minutes by some phone and power lines on the modern Emboriós-Nikiá road, just opposite the drive serving a small army watchpost. Don't bother hunting for a secondary trail parallel to the road, beacause there isn't one; you must asphalt-tramp for about 1km (15min) to the turn-off for Lakkí, where the onward trail continues conspicuously uphill into Emboriós.

The volcano to Mandhráki via Evangelístra

From the admission booth, proceed north along the main crater access road for just over 1km to find the start of a clear, crudely marked path which climbs steeply to a pass, then maintains altitude along the north flank of the small volcanic **Káto Lákki** gulch, and then emerges after ninety minutes at the important monastery of **Evangelístra** with a giant terebinth tree enclosed in a concrete apron just outside. Beyond Evangelístra, you must walk about 1km on the access road – now mostly paved – before the old path kicks in for the final half-hour down to Mandhráki. Look sharp at curves to find the old walled-in path which initially just short-cuts the road, and then for quite a long stretch loops above the port well away from the road, finally curling around to emerge on the fourth terrace above the school.

Evangelístra to Profítis Ilías

Evangelístra – where reports of a pilgrim hostel are decidedly premature – also marks the start of the two-hour, round-trip detour up **Profítis Ilías**; at 698m, the island's summit. From the terebinth-tree roundabout head west about 150m, then left on the start of the rough path. This was cleaned in 1998 and remarked with cairns and white-painted arrows or crosses, so it's hard to get lost. A few minutes before the shrine on the peak, the farm and chapel of **Dhiavátis**, tucked into a small hollow with huge trees, makes a good picnic spot or emergency bivouac.

Evangelístra to Emboriós

Just before arrival at the Evangelístra terebinth tree, coming from the volcano, a paint-splodged path heads right or northeast towards Emboriós, mostly

Greek script table

Níssyros	Νίσυρος	ΝΙΣΥΡΟΣ
Avláki	Αυλάκι	ΑΥΛΑΚΙ
Áyios Andónios	Άγιος Αντώνιος	ΑΓΙΟΣ ΑΝΤΩΝΙΟΣ
Áyios Ioánnis	Άγιος Ιοάννης	ΑΓΙΟΣ ΙΟΑΝΝΗΣ
Theológos	Θεολόος	ΘΕΟΛΟΓΟΣ
Emboriós	Εμπορειό	ΕΜΠΟΡΕΙΟΣ
Evangelístra	Ευαγγελίστρα	ΕΥΑΓΓΕΛΙΣΤΡΑ
Hokhláki	Χοχλάκι	ΧΟΧΛΑΚΙ
(Káto) Lakkí	(Κάτο) Λακκί	(ΚΑΤΟ) ΛΑΚΚΙ
Liés	Λιές	ΛΙΕΣ
Loutrá	Λουτρά	ΛΟΥΤΡΑ
Mandhráki	Μανδράκι	ΜΑΝΔΡΑΚΙ
Nikiá	Νικιά	ΝΙΚΙΑ
Pahiá Ámmos	Παχιά Άμμος	ΠΑΧΙΑ ΑΜΜΟΣ
Pálli	Πάλοι	ΠΑΛΟΙ
Panayiá Kyrá	Παναγία Κυρά	ΠΑΝΑΓΙΑ ΚΥΡΑ
Panayía Thermianí	Παναγια Θερμιανή	ΠΑΝΑΓΙΑ ΘΕΡΜΙΑΝΗ
Stavrós	Σταυρός	ΣΤΑΥΡΟΣ
Yialí	Γιαλί	ΓΙΑΛΙ

along the north flank of Káto Lákki. This route takes 45 minutes and is shown correctly on the German-produced map, though despite haphazard marking and cleaning the trail is still rough or even nonexistent in parts – nonetheless an enjoyable and useful link. You'll enter the village from the top, near the cemetery and small castle; it's marginally easier to find the way in reverse.

Níssyros travel details

Island transport

Buses

Mandhráki to: Emboriós (4–5 daily); Nikiá (4–5 daily); Pálli (5–6 daily). Departures are well spaced (eg 7am, 10am, 1.45pm & 5pm) and at least two uphill trips tend to include the volcano floor.

Inter-island transport

Kaïkia and excursion boats

Níssyros to: Kardhámena, Kós (almost daily in season, 3.30–4pm, or 4–5 weekly to Kós Town at the same time). The unpublicized islanders' "shopping" *kaïki*, the *Chrisoula*, departs Pálli Mon–Sat at 6.30am, Mandhráki 30min later. Unless you're bound for the airport it's not necessarily cheaper to use Kardhámena services when you include the cost (and time) of a bus to Kós Town – €9 to Kardhámena on an excursion boat, versus €11 to Kós. Journey time to Kardhámena 1hr 15min, to Kós Town 2hr 15min.

Ferries

Níssyros to: Kálymnos (2–3 weekly on GA; 3hr); Kós (2–3 weekly on GA; 1hr 40min); Léros (2–3 weekly on GA; 4hr 20min); Pátmos (2–3 weekly on GA; 6hr); Pireás (2–3 weekly on GA; 15–16hr); Rhodes (2–3 weekly on GA; 5hr); Sými (2–3 weekly on GA; 3hr 30min); Tílos (2–3 weekly on GA; 1hr 15min).

Catamaran

Níssyros to: Tílos, Rhodes (2–3 weekly on *Sea Star*, mid-June to Sept only; 2hr to Rhodes).

3

Kós and the northern Dodecanese

CHAPTER 3

Highlights

✳ **Brós Thermá, Kós** After your alpine exertions, relax in these shoreline hot springs which flow into the sea, protected by a boulder ring and mixing to an ideal temperature. See p.249

✳ **Asklepion, Kós** Though little remains standing at this Hellenistic therapeutic spa, the setting – with sweeping views out to Turkey – is magnificent, and the place pregnant with the plain common sense of the Hippocratic method. See p.250

✳ **Dhíkeos range, Kós** The hike up to Khristós peak is increasingly popular; your reward is arguably the most stunning view in all the Dodecanese. See p.254

✳ **Hóra, Astypálea** Astypálea's windswept *hóra*, capped by a beautiful Venetian *kástro*, teeters dramatically above the sea; resembling more a *hóra* of the Cyclades, it is rivalled for beauty only by the Hóra on Pátmos. See p.265

✳ **Análipsi, Astypálea** In and around this resort are some of the most exquisite mosaics in the Dodecanese; on the floor of a Byzantine bathhouse, and at a remoter basilica, you can see zodiacal signs and cavorting dolphins. See p.269

✳ **Kálymnos** The interior of this harshly contoured island offers meaty treks for the well prepared; the capital of Póthia, despite its big-town bustle, is a showcase of Neoclassical architecture; and the view across the Télendhos straits at sunset is unforgettable. See p.271

✳ **Léros** The beaches of this friendly island may not be four-star, but scuba-diving around wrecks, and along submarine walls teeming with sealife, is the best in the Dodecanese. A well-preserved Knights' castle above the trio of villages at the centre of Léros provides onland interest. See p.288

✳ **Pátmos** Atmospheric Hóra is dominated by the fortified, arcaded monastery dedicated to St John the Divine, who wrote the New Testament's Book of Apocalypse on the island. The remoter bays of Pátmos have the best beaches in the northern Dodecanese. See p.298

3

Kós and the northern Dodecanese

C ompared to teeming Rhodes and its often cosy neighbours, **Kós and the northern Dodecanese** fall somewhere in between. Though by no stretch of the imagination unspoilt, sandy **Kós** feels calmer than Rhodes, partly because in roughly one-third the area of Rhodes, with one-quarter of the population, there's perhaps one-sixth as much going on. However, together with Níssyros it forms an *eparhía* (a Greek county), and it's also the transport hub of the region, with the only international airport in this chapter; all packages arranged on its neighbours are of necessity routed through here. If you choose to spend your entire vacation on Kós, you'll find it has the best beaches of these half-dozen isles, ample creature comforts and distractions, plus surprisingly wild scenery on the slopes of the third-highest mountain in the Dodecanese.

The smaller islands fanning out northwest from Kós, except for **Psérimos** – overrun, like Sými, with organized day-trips – lack the intimacy of the southern Dodecanese, though their larger scale means reliable bus services, consistent scooter rentals, and a wider choice of resorts.

Kálymnos, just across the straits from sandy Kós, could hardly be more different: a limestone-core, seafaring island famous for its sponge-gathering tradition. An attempt during the late 1980s to develop a mass-tourism industry at its westerly beaches, and on the peacefully car-free islet of **Télendhos** just opposite, foundered within a few years. **Léros**, a geological continuation immediately northeast of Kálymnos, across an even narrower channel, has long had local tourism inhibited by a sinister (and largely undeserved) institutional reputation, but up close it proves welcoming and varied in its landscapes and townscapes, the latter including some of the best Italian Rationalist buildings in the Dodecanese.

Astypálea and Pátmos, out at the western fringes of this group, are more typical of the adjacent Cyclades archipelago in terms of architecture and general ambience. **Astypálea**, essentially synonymous with its stunningly picturesque *hóra*, is protected from blatant exploitation by problematic access and a skeletal road system, while **Pátmos**, with its imposing medieval monuments and excellent beaches, is not surprisingly the most frequented island in this chapter after Kós.

Lipsí, formerly a backwater dependency east of Pátmos, with a single village and a few beaches, has lately awoken to tourism with a vengeance; by contrast,

▲ Cyclades & Pireás

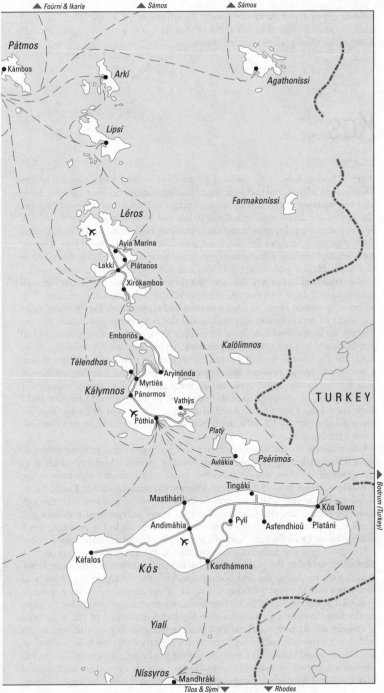

Foúrni & Ikaría ▲   ▲ Sámos   ▲ Sámos

Pátmos

Kámbos

Arkí

Agathoníssi

Lipsí

Farmakoníssi

Léros

Ayía Marína

Lakkí   Plátanos

Xirókambos

Emboriós

Kalólimnos

Télendhos

Aryinónda

Myrtiés

Kálymnos

Pánormos

Vathýs

Póthia

Platý

TURKEY

Avlákia   Psérimos

Bodrum (Turkey)

Tingáki

Mastihári   Kós Town

Andimáhia   Pylí   Asfendhioú   Platáni

Kéfalos   Kós   Kardhámena

Yialí

Níssyros   Mandhráki

Tílos & Sými ▼   ▼ Rhodes

neither depopulated **Arkí** nor lonely **Agathoníssi** off to the north are ever likely to attract more than a handful of visitors at any given time, and accordingly make ideal peak-season hideaways.

Kós

After Rhodes, **Kós** is the second largest and second most popular of the Dodecanese islands, and there are superficial similarities between the two. Here also the harbour is guarded by an imposing castle of the Knights of St John; the streets are lined with grandiose Italian public buildings from the 1930s; and minarets or palm trees punctuate extensive Hellenistic and Roman ruins. Although its hinterland for the most part lacks the wild beauty of Rhodes' interior, acre for acre Kós is among the most fertile of the islands described in this book, blessed with rich, partly volcanic soil and abundant ground water.

Mass **tourism** has largely displaced the former agricultural economy, though transhumance of a sort persists: whereas inland villagers once descended in summer to coastal plains to farm tomatoes and cotton, now the "harvest" takes the form of tourists, who seasonally swell the permanent population of over 28,000. Yet in the lowlands, there are still plenty of tended olive groves, stacked hay bales and grazing cattle, and delicious sheep's-milk yogurt continues to be made locally, though the old tomato cannery in the north of Kós Town is now a restaurant. Alone amongst the largest Dodecanese and east Aegean islands, Kós has no locally made mass-market wine, despite abundant vineyards; the local bottling plant collapsed with huge debts in 1998, so most farmers make their own. Like Tílos further south, Kós never had to earn its living from the sea and consequently has little in the way of a maritime tradition or a contemporary fishing fleet.

Kós' reliance on the tourist industry can push food and lodging prices to near-Rhodian levels, with the strong military presence here only adding to the pressure on these resources; Greek army tanks exercise regularly in the volcanic badlands around the airport. Outside the main town and Kardhámena, however, this is very much a family-holiday isle, where you can turn the kids loose on push-bikes. But Kós doesn't attract many independent travellers and, from early July to early September, unless you've booked a package, you'll usually be lucky to find any sort of room at all without advance reservations.

For these and the following reasons, Kós is the isle travel writers love to hate, often savaging the place without having ventured beyond the main town. It is faulted for being flat and boring – indeed, the centre of the island is so low-lying that the peak of Níssyros can be glimpsed above it from Kálymnos – as well as for its alleged lack of architectural or culinary distinction (except, in the latter instance, for its *krasotýri* – local cheese steeped in red wine until it absorbs the flavour – and candied plum tomatoes). To its credit, one might add that tourism is handled uncharacteristically efficiently on Kós, courtesy of (by Greek-island standards) a well-developed public infrastructure: the city bus service is a marvel, cyclists and the disabled are actively catered for with marked bike lanes and wheelchair ramps, and the proudly signposted biological sewage

KÓS & PSÉRIMOS

Bodrum (Turkey)

Léros

Kálymnos & Léros

Kálymnos

Marathoúnda

Psérimos

Platý

Avláki

Vathý

Grafiótissa

Cape Dhrépano

Limniónas

Áyios Stéfanos

Kamári

Kastrí

Kéfalos

Panayía Palatianí

Astypália

Áyios Theológos

Áyios Ioánnis Thymianós

Zíni 362m

Látra 428m

Aspri Pétra

Cape Krikello

Áyios Ioánnis

Mastihári

Troúlos

Andimáhia

Pláka

Knights' Castle

Kardhámena

Nissyros

Tingáki

Zipári

Marmári

Alykí

ASFENDHIOÚ

Amanioú

Pylí

Lagoúdhi

Harmýlio

Paleó Pylí

Ziá

DHIKEOS

Khristós 846m

Tolári

Evangelístria

Asómatos

Áyios Dhimítrios

Asklepíon

Piatáni (Kermedés)

Ambávris

Áyios Gavriíl

Kós Town

Lámbi

Selvéri

Cape Skandhári

Cape Psalídhi

Brós Thermá

Áyios Fokás

Cape Áyios Fokás

Rhodes

Nissyros, Tilos & Sými

Linopótis

N

0   5 km

plant east of town was completed years ago, with a salutary effect on town beaches – this last partly the result of an unusual continuity in local administration, thanks to an efficient and popular mayor who was re-elected repeatedly from the early 1980s, before moving on to better things as the local MP.

If Kós were half the size and contained the same number of attractions, it would be acclaimed as one of the most interesting Greek islands. But, like an indulgently edited movie, Kós drags a bit in the middle, though there's enough to hold your interest for the one-week duration of the shortest package. Swimming opportunities, for a start, are on the whole excellent – about half of the coastline is fringed by beaches of various sizes, colours and consistencies. But for longer than a week you'd be better off with a multi-centre holiday, taking in one or more of the surrounding islands as well.

Kós Town

Minoan settlers were attracted by the island's only good, natural harbour, opposite ancient Halikarnassos (modern Bodrum), and despite regular and devastating earthquakes throughout its history, **KÓS TOWN** has remained on this site, prospering from seaborne trade. The contemporary city, home to over half of Kós' population, spreads in all directions from the almost landlocked port. Apart from the Knights' castle, the first thing you see arriving by boat, its most compelling attraction lies in the wealth of Hellenistic and Roman remains, many of which were only revealed by the earthquake of 1933 and excavated afterwards by the Italians.

Arrival

Large domestic **ferries**, **catamarans** and all craft from Turkey anchor just outside the harbour at a special jetty by one corner of the castle; **excursion boats** to and from neighbouring islands sail right in and dock all along Aktí Koundouriótou; while domestic **hydrofoils** tie up south of the castle, at their own jetty on Aktí Miaoúli.

The **airport** is 24km west of Kós Town in the centre of the island; an Olympic Airways shuttle bus (€3) meets domestic flights for a transfer to the town terminal at Vassiléos Pávlou 22 (journeys in opposite direction 2hr before flight time). If you arrive on a flight-only deal, you'll have to take a taxi or head towards the giant roundabout outside the airport gate for the KTEL **buses** that pass through here en route between Mastihári, Kardhámena, Kéfalos and Kós Town. The KTEL terminal in Kós Town is merely a series of stops around a triangular park, 400m back from the water, with an information booth adjacent at Kleopátras 7 (tickets sold on the bus).

Information and transport

Driving or pedalling around Kós Town can be complicated, owing to a fairly comprehensive one-way system and a wide-ranging pedestrian-only zone. At the back of the harbour, the round Platía Iróön Polytekhníou – informally known as "Dolphin Square" after its central sculpture – effectively marks one end of the tourist esplanade, Finíkon or "Palm Avenue" the other. For **drivers**, Ippokrátous is the only unrestricted street penetrating the heart of the commercial district from the northeast shore esplanade, while Elefthéríou Venizélou and its continuation, Artemisías, provide the best means of moving

KÓS TOWN

G (200m), Campsite (1500m), Psalídhi, Áyios Fokás & Brós Thermá ▲

RESTAURANTS, CAFÉS & BARS	
Akroyiali	20
Ambavris	18
Apoplous Star	21
Beach Boys	7
Blues Brothers	10
Café Aenaos	11
Central/Kentriko	11
Dell Arte	12
Evdokia	6
Fashion Club	5
Flintstones	2
Four Roses	19
Frangoulis	12
Fresko Gelateria Café	15
Heaven	3
Iy Kanadheza	16
Koakon	17
Law-court café	8
Petrino	13
Pote tin Kyriaki	14
Iy Psaropoula	4
Zio Peppe	9

PLATÍAS	
Ayías Paraskevis	D
Dhiagóras	F
'Dolphin'	A
Eleftherias	C
Kazoúli	B
K. Paleológou	E

ACCOMMODATION	
Afendoulis	F
Alexis	A
Kamelia	C
Martina	D
Moustafa Tselepi	G
Theodhorou Beach	B
Veroniki	

0   200 m

Yacht Marina

ITALIAN QUARTER

Summer Cinema

20 (2 km) & 21 (400 m) ▶

19 (2 km) & 21 ▶

17 ▶

16 ▶

Ferry & Catamaran Dock

Knights' Castle

Ticket Booths & Customs

Hydrofoil Jetty

Hippocrates' Plane Tree

Loggia

Turkish Bath (Hamam Bar)

Agora

Old Synagogue

Pórta toú Fórou

Defterdar

Ferry/Catamaran Terminal

DEAS Terminal

Museum

Winter Cinema

Market

Turkish Fountain

Atik

Hippocrates Park

Port Police

Excursion Boats

Hellenistic Baths

Ancient Stadium

Nymphaion

Western Excavations

Roman Odeion

Catholic Cemetery ▶

Casa Romana

Olympic Airways

KTEL

18 Ambávris & Plataní ▶

Lámbi (2km), 2 & 3 ▲

ITALIAN QUARTER

Villages, Airport & Asklepion ▲

west to east. From the waterfront, Megálou Alexándhrou, or Koraï then Grigoríou toú Pémptou, provide the quickest ways of getting out to the main island trunk road. **Parking** is subject to strict controls (watch for kerbside signs) and fees are payable Monday to Friday, 8am to 9pm; buy hourly scratch-card tickets from kiosks or DEAS, the bus ticket office on the front.

The municipally run **tourist information office** at Vassiléos Yeoryíou 3 (May–Oct Mon–Fri 8am–2.30pm & 5.30–8pm, Sat 8am–2pm; Nov–April no eve hours); ☎22420 28724) is housed in R. Petracco's whimsical Gelsomino Hotel (1928–29). Staff keep stocks of local maps, bus timetables and specimen ferry schedules (which they stress are not to be trusted implicitly).

The main **taxi** stand lies at the east end of Koundouriótou, near Hippocrates' plane tree. The Kós municipality runs its own efficient **local bus** service, DEAS, through the beach suburbs and up to the Asklepion, with a ticket and information office at Aktí Koundouriótou 7. If you're going to make extensive use of them, it's advisable to pre-purchase bulk ticket packets, as fares are more expensive bought on board. There's also a miniature **fake train** hauling folk up from the waterfront to the Asklepion and back (hourly, fare c. €3) during its opening hours only.

Owing to the island's notorious flatness, **bicycle rental** is a very popular option, though there have been complaints about gaps in the bike-lane system which expose cyclists to traffic hazards. Formerly, most islanders got around using this mode of transport too, and the ethos has lingered, despite motor scooters becoming an obligatory fashion accessory for local youth.

Accommodation

If you're just in transit, there's really no viable alternative to staying in Kós Town. But even if you're sticking to the island for some time, the capital and environs makes an excellent touring base: it offers the broadest range of food and nightlife, the majority of the island's car, motorbike and bicycle rental agencies, and is the hub of public transport. Be very wary of the touts who besiege most arriving sea craft – their rooms are apt to be unlicensed, inconveniently remote and of dubious cleanliness, and you'll get little sympathy from the tourist police if things go wrong (which they're apt to).

Most **hotels** are on package operator lists, and relatively expensive; the following establishments are exceptions, amenable to walk-in trade even if they reserve a seasonal block of rooms for package companies. Except where noted, they operate only between April and late October, whilst in July and August absolutely every town bed is booked up weeks in advance. Families looking for a beach-base near Kós Town are best off at calmer, more rural accommodation to either side of Cape Psalídhi.

The relatively pricey but well-appointed **campsite** (☎22420 23910; July–early Sept) also lies 2.5km east towards Cape Psalídhi and can be reached by either the municipal DEAS service or its own minibus (which often meets ferries).

Centre

Afendoulis About 600m east of the ancient agora at Evrypýlou 1 ☎22420 25321, @afendoulishotel@kos.forthnet.gr. Welcoming C-class hotel, where Alexis Zikas, his wife Dionysia and brother Ippokratis do their utmost for guests, ensuring a loyal repeat clientele. Large, cheerful en-suite rooms with fans, most with balconies, air con or fridges on request. The cool, cave-like basement rooms are a haven in summer. No packages; open Easter to end Oct. ③

Alexis Irodhótou 9, corner of Omírou ☏ 22420 25798. Deservedly popular backpacker's pension in an interwar villa overlooking the Hellenistic baths. Rooms are large and parquet-floored though mostly not en suite. There's a self-catering kitchen and garden terrace, and the manager Sonia Zikas is extremely helpful. Usually open late March–early Nov. ❷

Kamelia Artemisías 3 ☏ 22420 28983, ☏ 22420 27391. Another friendly, well-placed, family-run hotel, which the *Afendoulis* refers customers to when full; the rear rooms have an orchard view. Heating available, but lately only open March–Nov. ❸

Maritina Výronos 19, cnr of Venizélou ☏ 22420 23241, ⓦ www.maritina.gr. Large, somewhat overpriced businessmen's hotel in a fairly quiet mid-town location; its main virtue is year-round operation. See above for their better-value annexe, *Maritina Mare*. ❹

Moustafa Tselepi Metsóvou 8 (enquire at Venizélou 35) ☏ 22420 28896. These well-furnished rooms, some with cooking facilities, are a good choice for longer stays. ❷

Veroniki P Tsaldhári 2 ☏ 22420 28122. A 1970s-vintage, no-extras, C-class hotel in a quiet yet convenient location; open all year. ❸

Psalídhi

Maritina Mare Just before Cape Psalídhi, about 4km from town ☏ 22420 24803, ⓦ www.maritina.gr. First impressions suggest a cheap-and-cheerful beach outfit, but the grounds (including pool-bar) are pleasant, the rooms and studios good-sized, plus there's wheelchair access and lifts. Rooms ❸, self-catering ❹

Grecotel Imperial Beyond the cape, next-to-last establishment on strip ☏ 22420 58000, ☏ roomdiv_ki@grecotel.gr. Recently added to this respected chain, this de-luxe resort, including standard hotel rooms plus bungalows set in lush, exotic gardens, incorporates a thalassotherapy centre, conference centre and all conceivable watersports facilities. Half- (or even full) board may be required, but nominal B&B rates ❻ hotel wing, ❽ bungalows

Oceanis Last beachfront hotel, past *Grecotel* ☏ 22420 24641, ⓦ www.oceanis-hotel.gr. Slighty more modest than the preceding, this A-class outfit also offers a mix of standard rooms and villas in a well-landscaped beachfront setting with mini-golf and other sports facilities. Rooms ❻, bungalows ❽

Ramira Beach Psalídhi, 3km from town ☏ 22420 28489 or 22420 22891, ☏ 22420 28489. Well-landscaped mammoth A-class complex, now part of the Mitsis chain, with tennis court, saltwater pool and, unusually this side of the cape, direct access to the beach. Units are both in the main original hotel, and two-storey satellite bungalows. Accommodation on a B&B or half-board basis. Rooms ❻, bungalows ❽

Seagull Apartments Just past Cape Psalídhi, about 6km out of town ☏ 22420 25200 or 22420 22937 for an English-speaker, ☏ 22420 22514. Low-rise, small-scale apartment complex set in a well-landscaped environment with large pool. Units, including two family suites, are a tad on the small side, but are well maintained and well priced. Open May–Oct. ❹

Theodhorou Beach Psalídhi, 1.2km from town centre ☏ 22420 22280, ☏ 22420 23526. Generous-sized rooms with balconies, attractive common areas and gardens, and a small private patch of beach near the marina make this a good choice, especially just before or after a yacht cruise. Friendly management welcomes walk-ins. Price includes buffet breakfast. ❹

The Town

Despite a population of over 16,000, Kós Town feels remarkably uncluttered, thanks to its sprawling, flat layout. Vast areas of open space alternate with a wonderful hotchpotch of archeological zones, surviving Ottoman quarters, and Italian-built mock-vernacular, Rationalist and Art Deco-ish buildings, designed in two phases either side of the earthquake (by Florestano de Fausto, 1926–1929 and R. Petracco/A. Bernabiti, 1934–1939) and incorporating as ever a Foro Italico, the Italian administrative complex next to the castle, and a Casa del Fascio (Fascist Headquarters), with the inevitable speaker's tower for haranguing party rallies gathered on the central square below. The maze-like Ottoman centre notwithstanding, this is mostly a planned town, with the pines and shrubs planted by the Italians now fully matured, especially in the garden suburb extending east of the central street grid, with its model housing mostly attributable to Mario Paolini.

The Knights' castle

For most visitors, the obvious first port of call is the **Knights' Castle** (Tues–Sun 8am–2.30pm; €3), reached by a causeway over its former moat; this has long since been filled in and planted with palms – thus the avenue's Greek name, Finíkon. The original Knights' castle, which stood here from 1314 until 1450, has vanished without trace, replaced by the existing inner castle (1450–78). This in turn nestles within the outer citadel, built to formidable thickness between 1495 and 1514 to withstand new artillery technology following unsuccessful Ottoman sieges in 1457 and 1477.

A fair proportion of ancient Kós, in the form of masonry fragments and tumbled columns, has been incorporated into the walls of both strongholds or, more recently, piled up loose in the southeast forecourt. A bewildering array of escutcheons and coats-of-arms on the various walls and towers will appeal to aficionados of heraldry, as the period of construction spanned the terms of several Grand Masters and local governors. The south corner of the older castle, for example, bears two Grand Masters' escutcheons, best admired from the massive, most technically advanced southwest bastion, identified with Caretto, the Grand Master who finished the job. There are also dozens of cannonballs lying about, few if any fired in anger, since this castle surrendered without resistance in accordance with the terms ending the marathon siege of Rhodes (see p.116). The biggest explosion that ever occurred here was orchestrated for the grand finale of Werner Herzog's first black-and-white feature, *Signs of Life* (1966), in which a low-ranking Wehrmacht officer goes berserk in 1944 and torches an ammunition dump inside the castle.

Hippocrates' plane tree and the Loggia Mosque

Rather sterile steel scaffolding has replaced the ancient pillars that once propped up the sagging branches of **Hippocrates' plane tree**, immediately opposite the causeway leading into the Knights' castle. At seven hundred years of age, this venerable tree has a fair claim to being one of the oldest in Europe, though it's not really elderly enough to have seen the great healer. The trunk has split into four sections, which in any other species would presage imminent demise, but abundant suckers from its roots promise some sort of continuation. Adjacent stand a dried-up hexagonal Turkish pillar fountain, a working one making use of an ancient sarcophagus, and the imposing eighteenth-century mosque of Hassan Pasha, also known as the **Loggia Mosque** after its covered portico on the north side. This three-storey building is locked and still bears the marks of wartime bombardment, especially in the tracery of its upper windows. The ground floor – like that of its near-contemporary, the **Defterdar Mosque** on nearby Platía Eleftherías – is taken up by several shops.

The ancient town

The largest single excavated section of ancient Kós is the **agora**, a sunken zone (unrestricted access) reached via steps from either Ippokrátous or Nafklírou. The latter, a pedestrian street (and nightlife mecca, see p.247), leads away from Platía Eleftherías under the **Pórta toú Fórou**, all that's left of the outer city walls built by the Knights between 1391 and 1396.

What you see is confusing and jumbled owing to successive earthquakes in 142, 469 and 554 AD; the most easily distinguishable items are the foundations of a massive double Aphrodite sanctuary roughly in the centre of the site, some columns of a stoa that once surrounded the so-called Harbour Basilica near the Loggia Mosque, plus two re-erected columns and the architrave of the Roman agora itself, in the far west of the archeological zone.

Another, more comprehensible section of the ancient town, the so-called **western excavations** (unrestricted access), abuts the ancient acropolis which was approximately where Platía Dhiagóras lies today. Intersecting marble-paved **Roman streets** (named Cardo and Decumana), dating from the third century AD, lend definition to this area, as does the **Xystos**, or colonnade, of a covered running track. Inside this the hulking brick ruins of a bath squat alongside the original arch of its furnace room. South of the Xystos stands the restored doorframe of a baptistry belonging to a Christian basilica erected above the baths after 469 AD. The floor of the basilica and of an unidentified building at the northern end of these excavations retain well-preserved fragments of **mosaics**, although the best have been carted off to the Palace of the Grand Masters in Rhodes (see p.113). What remains tends to be under several inches of protective gravel, or – in the case of the famous **Europa mosaic** house, to the north of the east-to-west Decumana street – off limits to visitors, though it, plus others nearby showing gladiators, a boar being speared and sundry gods or muses, can be viewed from a distance. Secreted in a cypress grove just across Grigoríou toú Pémptou is a fourteen-row Roman **odeion**, which at one time hosted musical events associated with the *Asklepieia* festivals (see p.251); it was reclad in rather garish new marble during 1999–2000 and again is a popular concert venue.

The Archeological Museum
The interior of the Italian-built, Rationalist **Archeological Museum**, on Platía Kazoúli (Tues–Sun 8am–2.30pm; €3), is a none-too-subtle propaganda exercise, with a distinct Latin bias in its choice of exhibits. Four rooms containing good, though not superlative, statuary are grouped around a central atrium where a Roman mosaic shows Hippocrates welcoming Asklepios to Kós. The most famous exhibit, a statue thought to portray Hippocrates, is in fact Hellenistic, as is a richly coloured, fragmentary fish mosaic at the rear of the atrium. But most of the other highly regarded works – Hermes seated with a lamb, Artemis hunting, Hygeia offering an egg to Asklepios' serpent, a boxer with his arms bound in rope, statues of wealthy townspeople – are emphatically Roman.

The Ottoman old town: Haluvaziá
Kós heavily promotes its medieval "old town", the former Turkish district of **Haluvaziá**, lining either side of a pedestrianized street running from behind the covered, Art Deco-ish produce market (1934–35) on Platía Eleftherías as far as Platía Dhiagóras and the orphaned minaret overlooking the western archeological zone. This begins life as Iféstou, then becomes Apelloú further on. It was long considered an undesirable area, but while all the rickety townhouses nearby collapsed in the 1933 earthquake, the sturdily built stone dwellings and shops here survived. Today, they are crammed with superfluous tourist boutiques and snack-bars; one of the few genuinely old things here is a dry **Turkish fountain** with an inscription, found where the walkway cobbles cross Venizélou, though it's often obscured by trinket stalls. Another juts out from the wall of the barber shop at the corner of Hristodhoúlou and Passanikoláki, lodged next to the minaret-less but still-functioning **Atik Mosque**, whose name means "Mosque of the Freed Serfs".

Continuing in the same direction, you can make a detour west of Platía Dhiagóras to Nikíta Nissiríou 3, site of the **Anatolia Hamam**. During the Ottoman period this was the mansion of a local pasha, whose descendants emigrated to Izmir in 1950; the small Turkish bath inside (the *hamam* of the name) functioned as the neighbourhood spa until 1970 or so, after which the premises operated sporadically as a brothel before falling into complete disrepair. Since 1992, new leaseholders have restored the original cedar floors and painted ceilings, while making the tiny *hamam* the inner sanctum of an expensive restaurant-bar.

The Casa Romana

The Greeks have apparently attempted to dampen Italian "public relations" by signposting the **Casa Romana** (closed for renovations until end 2005), on Grigoríou toú Pémptou at the rear of town, as "Restored House of Kós, 3rd Century AD". During World War II it was used as an infirmary by the Italians – you can still see faint red crosses painted on the exterior to deter Allied bombers. This building, devastated by the 554 AD earthquake but apparently abandoned long before, was evidently the villa of a wealthy family, and is arrayed around three atria with **tessellated marble or mosaic floors**. The smallest one, by the ticket booth, features panthers attacking a stag; the largest courtyard to the south is flanked by rooms, on opposite sides, showing another panther and a tiger; while the pool of the third atrium is surrounded by dolphins and more fierce felines, plus a damaged nymph riding a horse-headed sea monster, possibly a representation of Poseidon. On your way out, spare a glance for the laundry room in the corner, complete with stone-carved basins.

Eating

Despite an overwhelming first impression of Euro-bland cuisine, it is easy to **eat** well, and even reasonably, in Kós Town. Nearly all the better-value places are a few blocks inland, and scattered fairly evenly across the town grid; you can pretty much write off the waterfront tavernas, which tout aggressively.

Cafés

Café Aenaos Platía Eleftherías, right by the ablutions fountain of the Defterdar Mosque. Join the largely Greek crowd here, and people-watch while you refill your Greek coffee from the traditional *bríki* (copper ewer) used to brew it up.

Central/Kentriko Platía Ayías Paraskevís, behind the municipal produce market. Last survivor of a former handful here, offering American-pancake breakfasts, hot drinks, French toast and fresh juices served under giant Indian fig trees.

Fresko Gelateria Café Cnr Kleopátras and Ioannídhi. Crêpes and waffles in the morning, sticky cakes or decadent homemade ice cream later on, served in a giant "tent" abutting the pavement.

Law-court café Some of the cheapest, and best-brewed, coffees are available (along with cold drinks) under the arches at the rear of the courthouse, a few paces from Hippocrates' plane tree; no sign out, mostly civil-servant clientele.

Restaurants

Central

Dell Arte Hálkonos 3. Slightly pricey, but the best Italian resturant among several contenders: big salads, pasta dishes, wood-oven pizzas, *calzone*. Open April–Nov.

Evdokia (aka **Mummy's Cooking**) Bouboulínas 13. Currently one of the best spots in town for no-nonsense *mayireftá*; hits its stride at lunchtime, when local workers throng the place.

Iy Kanadheza Corner Evrypýlou and Artemisias.

Creditable pizzas as well as grills, to eat in or take away; open all year.

Koakon (aka **Andonis**) Artemisías 56, cnr Manoúsi. The best all-rounder in town, purveying grilled meat and fish, *mezédhes* and a few daily *mayireftá* with equal aplomb; not much atmosphere but always full with locals and visitors, who know a good thing when they see it. Open all year.

Petrino Platía Theológou 1 ☎22420 27251. Kós' best *kultoúra* taverna, and accordingly expensive at €30-plus each for the works, booze extra. You can push the total down a bit by sticking to *orektiká* and the house wine. Extensive garden seating, and indoor salon, allows all-year operation (supper only); large groups should reserve.

Pote tin Kyriaki Pissándhrou 9 ☎22420 27872. Characterful, ten-table *ouzerí* which neither wants nor gets many tourists (Greek-only sign outside). Brief menu in school copybooks that offers excellent value in the basics: *hórta*, *gávros*, *dákos* (Cretan salad), mussels and good bulk wine. Book ahead in peak season with genial proprietors Angelos and Stamatia, and enjoy the company and taped *rebétika* as well as the food. As the name suggests, closed Sun all year, open Thurs–Sat in winter when it moves indoors.

Iy Psaropoula Avérof 17. The least touristy and fairest-priced of several fish tavernas, with indoor and outdoor seating (and a Greek clientele), meaning year-round operation.

Zio Peppe Ríga Feréou 13. Decent fast-food outfit serving excellent pizza by the slice or whole pie, to take away or eat on site.

Suburbs

Akroyiali Yeoryíou Panandhréou, about 2km out on the coast road towards Cape Psalídhi. Grills and competently executed *orektiká* like stuffed peppers or *lahanodolmádhes* without airs or graces, served at outdoor seating overlooking the beach and Turkey. Open May–Oct

Ambavris In the eponymous hamlet, 800m south of the Casa Romana (follow the ruined Ottoman aqueduct by the roadside) ☎22420 25696. Impeccable recipes and fair portions in one of the best tavernas on Kós. Don't order from the rather perfunctory English-only à la carte menu, but take the brief printed hint about the house's seasonally changing "Mezedes": *pinigoúri* (bulgur pilaf), *pikhtí* (brawn), little fish, spicy *loukánika*, stuffed squash flowers and *fáva* are typical – but won't much exceed €19 for six plates, drinks extra. Outdoor seating in the courtyard of this converted farmhouse; booking required for large parties. Open dinner only May–Oct.

Frangoulis Kakó Prinári district. To get there, exit mid-town on Papatheofánous – one street east of Evrypýlou – and keep going about 1500m to the intersection with Aristónos. Well-loved neighbourhood hole in the wall whose outdoor tables are always packed. Grilled meat (and occasionally fish) is its strong point, with a few oven dishes and average bulk wine thrown in. Not superlative cuisine, but decent portions, friendly and very reasonable for Kós – two can easily drink (abstemiously) and eat for €23.

Drinking and nightlife

For loud (120-decibel) **nightlife**, look no further than "Bar Street", officially Nafklírou and Dhiákou, two roughly parallel pedestrian lanes joining Platía Kazoúli and the Loggia Mosque. Every address is a bar, just choose according to the crowd and the (techno) noise level. Near the end, by the main taxi rank, *Hamam Bar* occupies a genuine converted Turkish bath, and is the most reliable establishment for Greek sounds at bearable level; all others tend to change identity every season (if not more often). It is sobering (though not literally) to reflect that in Ottoman and Italian times this was a gritty bazaar quarter, domain of the blacksmiths and socially on a par with Haluvaziá; today it is your eardrums, not your hooves, that will get a hammering after 10pm. Elsewhere, pickings are slim, as the general islands tourism slump has hit Kós bars hardest.

Off "Bar Street"

Beach Boys Dance Bar Kanári 57. Inexpensive drinks, often accompanied by free nibbles, and a tiny dance floor; people spill out onto the pavement.

Blues Brothers Café Aktí Koundouriótou, cnr of Iróon Politekhníou (Dolphin Square). Doyen of the waterfront bars, with rock-and-blues soundtrack, though it doesn't have quite the crowd it did some years ago.

Flintstones Near Faros Taverna at north end of Lámbi beach. Nothing special to look at, but very welcoming and Britophile (the Scottish wife of one of the owners is likely to serve you).

Four Roses Cnr Arseníou and Vassiléos Yeoryíou. One of the longer-lived "dancing bars", attracting a slightly older clientele.

Discos and live venues

Apoplous Star By the *Theodhórou Beach Hotel*, towards Psalídhi. Where most live Greek and foreign acts perform; ☎22420 21916 to reserve.

Fashion Club North side of the port, Kanári 2. The most impressive indoor venue, famous for its light shows.

Heaven 2km northwest of the town centre on Aktí Zouroúdhi, Lámbi. Outdoor, garden venue, so open June–Sept only.

Listings

Airlines, domestic Aegean, airport (☎22420 51654) or most travel agents; Olympic, Vasssiléos Pávlou 22 (☎22420 28331) or at airport (☎22420 51229).

Air tickets Aeolos Travel, central branch at Annétas Laoumtzí 8 (☎22420 26203), is the representative for a number of UK package companies and thus a good source of one-way charter tickets back to Britain.

Banks and exchange No fewer than seven full-service banks in town, plus several more stand-alone ATMs.

Bike and motorbike rental Out of a huge number of establishments, try Moto Drive at Spýrou Ikonómou 9 cnr Makriyiánni, the misnamed Moto Harley at Kanári 42, with a large fleet of well-kept larger motorbikes. To rent a genuine Harley-Davidson, go to their authorized dealership Easy Rider at the edge of town, by the Marmarotó junction (☎22420 29020). Expect to pay €10–15 in high season for a decent scooter, about €4 for a top-end mountain bike, still less for a balloon-tyre pedal bike, with or without gears.

Bookshops Newstand, at Ríga Feréou 2, cnr Platía Kazoúli, or the bookshop inside the Politistiko Polykendro (Cultural Multi-Centre), cnr of Korytsás and Aryirokástrou; both have a sizeable English-language stock.

Car rental Not absolutely essential on smallish, mostly flat Kós unless there's a group of you; rates are €20–35 per day for a basic model, depending on season. Independent local outlets especially recommended for good car condition include Alpha, Bouboulínas 23 (☎22420 22488); Autorent/Helen's, at Vassiléos Pávlou 31 (☎22420 28882 or 694 45 00 062), or in Psalídhi at both the *Ramira* and *Oceanis* hotels; and Autoway, Vassiléos Yeoryíou 22 (☎22420 25326). The major international chains mostly cluster near the yacht marina; these include Alamo-National at Yeoryíou Papandhréou 4 (☎22420 21722), Hertz at Vassiléos Yeoryíou 46 (☎22420 28002), and Sixt at Makriyiánni 64 (☎22420 27380).

Cinemas Municipally supported Orfeas screens

a varied late Sept–May programme in the 1935-vintage, ex-Fascist Party HQ diagonally opposite the Archeological Museum in winter, in summer (June to mid-Sept) in premises on Fenarétis at the east end of Halkónos. Programmes (summer hilariously bilingual, winter Greek-only) are widely available; the play list tends to be fairly current first-run fare. The slightly airless indoor venue also hosts concerts and other special events.

Ferry/catamaran/hydrofoil tickets Many, though not all, ferry and excursion boat agents cluster within 50m of each other at the intersection of Vassiléos Pávlou and the waterfront. Among these, Pulia Tours nearby at no. 3 (☎22420 21130), is the main Laoumtzis Flying Dolphins outlet, while Kyriakoulis hydrofoil tickets are conveniently available from Adris Nissia at no. 2. Useful agents elsewhere include Exas at Andinavárhou Ioanídhi 4 (☎22420 29900), for GA ferries, the *Nissos Kalymnos* and the *Dodekanisos Express*, and the dedicated Blue Star agency on the front near DEAS (☎22420 28914). Stefamar, at Avérof 23 (☎22420 26388), deals strictly with day excursions to neighbouring islands. Failing all these, the passenger terminal on the jetty has dedicated booths for each company, dispensing tickets in the hour before sailing (queues can be long).

Internet cafés *Café del Mare*, Megálou Alexándhrou 4, and *Kimbo* at Mandhilará 22b are the best equipped.

Laundries Happy Wash at Mitropóleos 20; Laundromat Center, Alikarnassoú 124.

Luggage storage Lockers in the passenger terminal building on the quay; €2 per bag per day.

Map Road Editions' 1:60,000 map no. 205. Otherwise, the most accurate locally sold map, for both the island and the town, is that published by Pandelis Vayianos; don't be put off by its 3-D matchbox art.

Scuba outfitters Dive operators are easiest found at their boats, moored along the excursion-craft quay. Note, however, that all diving takes place at a single, authorized area off southern Kálymnos – so nearly three hours is spent getting there and back.

Around Kós Town

All coastal points between Lámbi, to the north of Kós Town, and Áyios Fokás, to the east, are connected by the DEAS bus line; alternatively you can rent a bicycle and take advantage of the designated cycle paths extending as far east as Cape Psalídhi. The closest beaches that answer to the description are at and beyond **LÁMBI**, 3km north towards Cape Skandhári. However, north-facing beaches beyond the point are not among the island's best: narrow, scrappy and closely hemmed by a frontage road. East of Kós Town, the strands extending to and beyond Cape Psalídhi are grey-gravel and uninspiring; however, this hasn't kept almost the entire shoreline, from the tourist information office east almost as far as the campsite, from being parcelled out amongst various umbrella-and-sunbed concessions. Possibly more interesting hereabouts are a few re-erected columns of the fourth-century **basilica of Áyios Gavriïl**, just inland from the road as you clear the edge of the urban grid. Similar beaches, functional at best (except for the excellent, popular strand between the military watchpoint and the *Oceanis* complex), line Cape Áyios Fokás well to the southeast, whose focal point is the purpose-built resort areas at Áyios Fokás, 7km from Kós Town.

The unusual and remote hot springs of **Brós Thermá** emerge from volcanic cliffs 5km beyond Áyios Fokás and, though periodically served by DEAS bus (last service back 6pm), they are most easily reached by rented vehicle; the final kilometre lies along a dirt track heading down and left at a little drinks *kantína* just before the end of the asphalt, where the bus leaves you. The scalding springs issue from a tiny grotto, flowing through a trench to mingle with the sea at comfortable temperatures inside a giant corral of boulders. Winter storms typically disperse the boulder wall, rebuilt every April, so that the pool changes shape from year to year. It's free, and immensely popular with tourists and locals alike, especially late at night during the cooler months. Just adjacent, the long-running *Psarotaverna Therma* does affordable seafood – especially parrotfish, swordfish and tuna – though the rest of the limited menu, comprising sometimes inedible fried *orektiká*, seems strictly incidental.

Platáni

The Greek-Turkish village of **PLATÁNI** lies 2km south of Kós Town, on the road to the Asklepion, and is served by DEAS bus from 8am until late (but last one back around 10pm). Until 1964 it was most commonly known

The Jews of Kós

Jews had lived on Kós since antiquity, but it seems that the Knights of Rhodes exiled the bulk of the Greek-speaking Jewish community to Nice in 1306. Following the Ottoman conquest, Sephardic Jews settled here, their dwindling numbers reinforced early in the 1900s by co-religionists from Izmir in Anatolia.

Despite this long history, there are only two tangible traces of the Jewish community. Just outside Platáni on the road back to the harbour, a **Jewish cemetery** stands in a dark conifer grove, 300m from the Muslim graveyard. Dates on the headstones, inscribed in a mix of Hebrew and Italian, stop ominously after 1940, after which presumably none was allowed the luxury of a natural death at home. The remaining local community of about 120 was transported to Rhodes in summer 1944 by the Nazis, and thence, together with the Rhodian Jews, to Auschwitz for extermination. Just one Koan Jew, who died in the early 1990s, survived the war; in accordance with Jewish communal law, he inherited all the real estate of his deceased co-religionists, which was sold for a tidy sum when mass tourism reached Kós in the 1970s. The former **synagogue**, disused for worship since 1944, is a marvellously orientalized building (1934) back in Kós Town, at Alexándhrou Dhiákou 4, between the ancient agora and the waterfront; it was refurbished in 1991 as a "municipal multipurpose hall".

as Kermedés (*Germe* in Turkish), and the Turkish community had its own primary school, but in the wake of the Cyprus crises of that year, the village was officially renamed and education provided compulsorily in Greek only. Subsequent emigration to Anatolia caused Turkish numbers on the island to drop from around three thousand to less than a thousand; mainly those Turks owning real estate and businesses have stayed.

Platáni's older domestic architecture is strongly reminiscent of styles in rural Crete, from where some of the village's Muslims came between 1898 and 1913; there's even a working Ottoman fountain near the crossroads. This junction is dominated by several excellent, Turkish-run tavernas: *Arap* (summer only), the slightly less touristy *Asklipios* and *Sherif* across the way (ditto) and *Gin's Palace* (all year), each offering Anatolian-style *mezédhes* (fried vegetables with yogurt, *ambelofásola*, *bourekákia*, and so on) and kebabs. Any is better than most eateries in Kós Town, and are best enjoyed in a group, when you can pass the various platters around. Afterwards, the *Zaharoplastio Iy Paradhosi* opposite *Arap* scoops out the best ice cream on the island.

The Asklepion

Native son **Hippocrates** is justly celebrated on Kós; not only does he have a tree, a street, a park, a statue and an international medical institute named after him, but the Hellenistic **Asklepion** (summer Tues–Sun 8am–6.30pm, earlier closure in winter; €3), 4km south of town, one of just three in Greece, is a major tourist attraction. DEAS buses or the miniature train make the trip via Platáni between 8am and 6pm; otherwise you've a 45-minute walk or a shorter (if steepish) cycle ride. There's a small snack-bar near the entrance, or pause for lunch in Platáni en route.

The Asklepion was actually founded just after the death of Hippocrates, but it's safe to assume that the methods used and taught here were his. Both a temple to Asklepios (god of medicine, son of Apollo) and a renowned curative centre, its magnificent setting on three artificial hillside terraces overlooking Anatolia reflects early recognition of the importance of the therapeutic environment. Until recently, two fountains provided the site with a constant supply of clean, fresh water, and extensive stretches of clay piping are still visible, embedded in the ground.

Today, very little remains *above* ground, owing to chronic earthquakes and the Knights' use of the site as a quarry. The lower terrace in fact never had many

---

Hippocrates

Hippocrates (ca.460–370 BC) is generally regarded as the father of scientific medicine, and still influences doctors today through the Hippocratic oath – which probably has nothing to do with him and is in any case much altered from its original form. Hippocrates was definitely born on Kós, probably at Astypálea near present-day Kéfalos, but other details of his life are few and disputed. What seems certain is that he was a great physician who travelled throughout the Classical Greek world, but spent part of his career teaching and practising at the Asklepion on his native island. A vast number of medical writings have been attributed to Hippocrates, only a few of which he could actually have written; *Airs, Waters and Places*, a treatise on the importance of environment on health, is widely thought to be his, but others were probably a compilation from a medical library kept on Kós, which later appeared in Alexandria during the second century BC. This emphasis on good air and water, and the holistic approach of ancient Greek medicine, now seems positively contemporary.

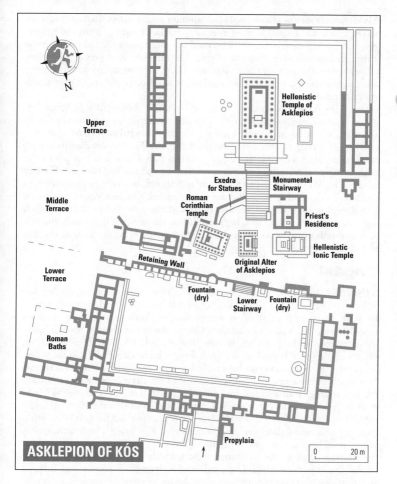

ASKLEPION OF KÓS

0   20 m

structures, being instead the main venue for the observance of the Asklepieia – quadrennial celebrations and athletic or musical competitions in honour of the healing god. Sacrifices to Asklepios were conducted at an **altar**, the oldest structure on the site, whose foundations can still be seen near the middle of the second terrace. Just to its east, the Corinthian columns of a second-century-AD **Roman temple** were partially re-erected by nationalistically minded Italian archeologists. A monumental **staircase** flanked by *exedrae* (display niches) leads from the altar up to the second-century-BC **Doric temple** of Asklepios on the topmost terrace, the last and grandest of a succession of the deity's shrines at this site.

The north coast

Lying well to the southwest of Cape Lámbi, the two neighbouring resorts of **Tingáki** and **Marmári** are separated from each other by a salt marsh called

Alykí, which retains water until autumn after wet winters. Between January and April it's host to hundreds of migratory **birds**, including swans and flamingos, but the half-tame terrapins who used to congregate near the outlet to the warm, shallow sea have disappeared since the millennium – presumed victims of local pesticide spraying for mosquitoes. There's almost always a breeze along this coast, making it a popular destination for windsurfers, who can rent boards at either resort.

Both Tingáki and Marmári are served by KTEL bus from Kós Town, but if you're travelling under your own steam, especially on a two-wheeler of any sort, it's safest and most pleasant to take the **minor road** from the southwest corner of town (follow signs initially for the Vassiliadhis supermarket) as far as Tingáki; this entire route is paved, and involves about the same distance as travelling the main trunk road and marked turn-off. Shortly before Tingáki, in the district known as **Selvéri**, some 5km from town, a dead-end side road goes to the sea in the vicinity of two enormous boats, abandoned in their slips at a disused shipyard; the first really attractive beach out of town in this direction beckons just to the west, with a small sunbed-and-umbrella concession, but only a motorbike or bicycle can span the gap in that direction.

Tingáki

TINGÁKI, the shore annexe of the Asfendhioú villages (see opposite), lies 12km west of Kós Town. It's a busy, somewhat higgledy-piggledy resort popular with Brits, with most of its dozen-plus, medium-sized **hotels** scattered inland among fields and cow pastures. One of the better choices, though heavily subscribed to by packages, is *Hotel Ilios* (☎22420 69411, 🖷22420 69173; ❺), a well-designed bungalow complex about a kilometre back from the water. By far the best local **taverna** here is *Ambeli* (summer daily; winter Fri/Sat eve, Sun lunch), well signposted nearly 3km east of the main beachfront crossroads; the best strategy is to avoid mains and order a pile of starters like *pinigoúri, bekrí mezé* or *yaprákia* (the local *dolmádhes*). Among **car-rental** outfits, Sevi (☎22420 69076) out by the *Zorbas Beach Hotel* can be recommended for good-condition cars, and will even deliver vehicles on request to Kós Town. The **beach** itself is white-sand, long and narrow; it improves, and veers further out of earshot from the frontage road, as you head southwest, with the best patches to either side of the drainage from Alykí. The profiles of Kálymnos, Psérimos and Turkey's Bodrum peninsula on the horizon all make for spectacular scenery, especially at sunset.

Marmári

The traditional coastal annexe of Pylí village (see p.255), **MARMÁRI**, 15km from Kós Town, has a smaller built-up area than Tingáki, and the beach itself is broader, especially to the west, where it forms mini-dunes. A grid of paved rural lanes links the inland portions of Tingáki and Marmári.

If you want to **stay**, you'll have a hard time squeezing in amongst the various tour groups; one worthwhile spot that may have vacancies on spec is the *Esperia* on the main access road down from the island trunk road (☎22420 42010, 🌐www.hotelsperiakos.gr; ❸), with a medium-sized pool in grassy surroundings, overlooked by the better bungalow wings. To really push the boat out, look no further than the nearby *Grecotel Royal Park* (☎22420 41488, 🖂rparkl@otenet.gr; ❽ full board only) at the western edge of matters. Again, the garden-set bungalows closer to the beach are preferable.

For **food**, just inland on the same access road as the *Esperia*, *Apostolis* offers *mezedhákia*, seafood and meat grills at reasonable prices. A perhaps more compelling attraction in the area is the **Salt Lake Riding Centre** (☏694 41 04 446, ✉saltlake.horseriding@freemail.gr; May–Oct), just back from the sea on the west side of the salt marsh. This has fifteen horses and ponies available for rides along the beach or up into the hills; sample rate, including all equipment and open bar, is €45 for the most popular, two-hour sunset coastal ride.

Around Mount Dhíkeos

The main interest of inland Kós resides in the villages on **Mount Dhíkeos** (the ancient Oromedon). This handful of settlements, collectively referred to as **Asfendhioú**, nestles amid the island's only natural forest and remain worth visiting for a glimpse of what Kós looked like before tourism and concrete took hold. They can be reached from the main island trunk road via the extremely curvy side road from Zipári, 8km from Kós Town; a minimally signposted but paved minor road to Lagoúdhi; or the shorter access road to Pylí.

The Asfendhioú villages

The most accessible Asfendhioú village from Kós Town is **EVANGELÍS-TRIA**, up the side road from Zipári, where from behind its namesake parish church extends a neighbourhood of low, whitewashed houses, now two-thirds abandoned in the mad rush down to the coast; the remainder are being bought up and restored by outsiders.

LAGOÚDHI, just west of Evangelístria church, is perhaps livelier, with three **kafenía** (two of these, *Iy Ftohi Kalyva* and *Ioannis Kiaris*, still fairly traditional), a couple of trinket shops, and a hilltop church of its own.

Further up the road from Evangelístria, **ZIÁ**'s spectacular **views and sunsets** make it the hapless target of up to six tour buses per evening, and its daytime tattiness seems to increase by the year as well. A dozen households at most still dwell full-time in the village, but otherwise any building on the main street that isn't a taverna is probably a souvenir shop. Their wares include kitsch throw-rugs in hideous hues and patterns, fortunately unique to the area.

Best of the dozen **tavernas** here, which trade mostly on their position, is the *Olympia*, at the start of the flagstoned walkway up to the church. Since it's the one with the least view, the food has to be good and reasonably priced to make up for this deficiency. Dishes not usually associated with tourist resorts, like chickpeas, bulgur pilaf (*pínigoúri* in Koan dialect), mushroom-based dishes, roe deer and boar from the mainland and dark bread are washed down with sherry-like local red wine from smallholdings. There's a good *pikilía* of *mezédhes* "off-menu", especially at weekends, when a local clientele predominates; it's also open in winter, always a good sign.

East of Ziá the way deteriorates to dirt as it continues to the final pair of Asfendhioú settlements. The first you'll come to is **ASÓMATOS**, home to around thirty villagers plus a handful of foreigners and Athenians renovating houses which steadily come on the market. The place really only comes to life at the November 7–8 festival celebrated around the **church of Arhángelos**, whose spacious courtyard (usually locked) harbours a fine *hokhláki* mosaic.

ÁYIOS DHIMÍTRIOS, 2km beyond Asómati along a fairly rough track, is shown on some maps by its old Ottoman name of Haïhoútes. It was abandoned entirely during the junta years, when the inhabitants went to Zipári or further afield. Today, just one farmer lives here beside the attractive namesake **church**; in the narthex, a small photo display documents a much larger population during the war years, when the village was a centre of resistance against the Germans. Rather than retrace your steps, it's possible to short-cut directly back from Áyios Dhimítrios to the Asklepion, 7km distant (see p.250); bear left and north just outside the hamlet for the first 3.5km on bad track (passable to ordinary cars) before linking up with the paved road descending from the rubbish tip towards the Asklepion.

Up Khristós peak

Ziá is the preferred trailhead for the ascent to the summit of 846-metre **Khristós** peak, the highest point of the Dhíkeos range, and indeed on Kós. Taking something less than half a day, this is within the capabilities of any reasonably fit, properly shod person, and offers what are arguably the best views in the Dodecanese.

From the *Olympia* restaurant (see p.250), head up the paved walkway to the small car park in the upper quarter of the village, then continue south up steps past a few houses. At the top of these stone stairs there's a fountain, the outlet of the famous local Kefalóvrysi spring that keeps Ziá and Evangelístria well watered – and once powered a water mill, now the centrepiece of a tourist shop, near the car park. Top up your water bottle here if it's flowing, as the lone spring further up the mountain is even more unreliable.

Just above this point you follow a narrow track past the *Taverna Kefalovrysi* through a glen, passing the chapel of **Isódhia tís Theotókou** with its vaulted roof, covered porch and bomb nose-cone hung as the bell. Bear right at the junction behind it and head west past the last house in Ziá. A fifteen-minute walk above the restaurant, the chapel of **Áyios Yeóryios** houses frescoes of the patron saint and the Virgin and Child. The rough onward track, now scarcely passable to vehicles, curls gradually south past isolated farm cottages and sheeppens; just above the chapel, a section of path marked by cairns short-cuts a wide bend in the track.

Just over half an hour above the car park by the water mill, you'll reach the true trailhead amid a grove of junipers. The spot is fairly obvious, with the path flanked by red and white paint splodges, possibly also by a sign in Greek Byzantine script ("XRICTOC") and further along by cairns and more paint marks. The distinct trail zigzags eastwards up the mountainside, leaving the juniper forest within twenty minutes and arriving in just over an hour out of Ziá at the ridge leading northeast to the summit. The grade slackens, and several shattered cisterns, once used by shepherds, are visible north of the path. From the point where the ridge is attained, it's another twenty minutes maximum to the summit along the watershed, usually just to its north; the little pillbox-like chapel of the **Metamórfosis toú Sotírou**, visible most of the time from this point on, stands about 40m northeast of the altitude survey marker; there's also a small dugout-shelter nearby, possibly a cistern roofed over in 1996, for staying the night should the need arise – though huge piles of rubbish typically left over from the yearly pilgrimage festival do not make the idea so appealing. Just north, you can ponder the esoteric symbolism of a giant crucifix fashioned from PVC sewer pipes and filled with concrete – clearly Kós has a budding Turner-Prize-calibre artist.

Up on top, Turkey's Knidos Peninsula dominates the view to the southeast; Níssyros, Tílos and Hálki float to the south; Astypálea closes off the horizon on the west; Kálymnos and, on a good day, Léros, are spread out to the north; and the entire west and north portions of Kós are laid out before you.

The south flank of the Dhíkeos range is a sheer drop to the Aegean, and the summit ridge northeast can only be tackled by technical climbers – there are too many knife-edge saddles and arêtes. So the only viable descent is back the way you came, which takes only about ten minutes less than the climb up, owing to the rough surface. Allow two hours thirty minutes minimum walking time for the out-and-back trip from Ziá – three and a half hours inclusive of photo and rest stops.

Pylí: new and old

Further along the main island road from the Asfendhioú turnings is **Linopótis**, a sunken pond fed by a permanent spring, always swarming with ducks and eels. From the junction here, a signposted access road leads left to contemporary **PYLÍ**, which divides into two districts. In the upper neighbourhood, 100m west of the upper square and church, the unpretentious *Taverna Iy Palea Piyi* serves inexpensive but appetizing grills and fried *mezédhes* under a giant Indian fig, in a superb setting overlooking trees, a tankful of carp and frogs, and a giant, sixteenth-century cistern-fountain, the *piyí* of the name. Regrettably, the four carved lion-head reliefs which used to grace this structure were obliterated by municipally employed barbarians in 2004 when new spouts were fitted, and probably won't be restored.

Pylí's other attraction is the so-called **Harmýlio** (Tomb of Harmylos), signposted near the top of the village as "Heroon of Charmylos". This consists of a subterranean vault (alas, fenced off) with twelve niches, probably a Hellenistic family tomb. Immediately above it, traces of an ancient temple foundation have been incorporated into the medieval **chapel** of Stavrós.

Paleó Pylí

Paleó (medieval) **Pylí**, roughly 3km southeast of its modern descendant, was the Byzantine capital of Kós, inhabited from about the tenth century until the Ottoman conquest. Head there via Amanioú (which can offer the German-run Alfa Horse **riding stable**; ☎22420 41908, ⓦwww.alfa-horse.com), keeping straight at the junction where signs point left to Ziá and Lagoúdhi. The road continues up to a wooded canyon, dwindling to a dirt track beside a trough-spring built with local livestock in mind. Some five minutes' walk uphill from the fountain along the dirt track, the remains of a **water mill** sit in the ravine just west.

From opposite the fountain, a stair-path leads within fifteen minutes to a **Byzantine castle** dating from the eleventh century, whose partly intact roof – possibly off limits while restoration proceeds – affords superb views. En route you pass the ruins of the abandoned village, as well as three fourteenth-to fifteenth-century **churches**. That of **Arhángelos**, the first encountered, retains substantial traces of late medieval wall art, particularly numerous scenes from the life of Christ on the vaulted ceiling, including a fine *Betrayal* in the north vault. Outside are the remains of a graceful Latin arcade of a type usually only seen on Rhodes or Cyprus. Rectangular **Áyios Nikólaos**, just south of the route to the citadel, has a *Communion of the Apostles* in the apse, while **Ypapandí**, the largest church and nearest the castle, is almost bare inside but impresses with its barrel vaulting supported by reused Byzantine columns.

Central Kós

Near the **centre of the island**, a pair of giant, adjacent roundabouts by the airport funnel traffic northwest towards Mastihári, northeast back towards town, southwest towards Kéfalos, and southeast to Kardhámena. The fairly dry, desolate countryside hereabouts provides ample ammunition for those who would dismiss Kós as dull or unattractive, and additionally the area is well sown with military installations guarding the airport.

Mastihári

The least developed of the northern shore resorts, three-street-wide **MASTIHÁRI** was a permanent village long before tourist times, as well as the historic summer quarters of Andimáhia. Though shorter than those at Marmári or Tingáki, the local beach extending to the southwest is broader, with less-frequented dunes (and no sunbeds) towards the far end. A kilometre or so east is the secluded beach of **Troúlos**, reached by a narrow, 300-metre dirt track. The fifth-century basilica of **Áyios Ioánnis** lies about 1.5km down the west beach, following the shoreline promenade; it's fairly typical of Kós' numerous early Christian church-foundations, results of Paul's evangelizing of the island, with a row of column bases separating a pair of side-aisles from the nave, a tripartite narthex, and a baptistry tacked onto the north side of the building.

Mastihári, 25km from the capital by the most direct route, is also the **ferry port** for the shortest crossing to Kálymnos; throughout the year there are morning, late-afternoon and late-evening ro-ro sailings, keyed more or less to the arrival times of Olympic flights from Athens – though KTEL buses to or from Kós Town don't (to the delight of taxi drivers) always dovetail well.

Practicalities

Central Mastihári has a much higher proportion of non-block-booked **accommodation** than other coastal resorts on Kós; examples of quieter digs overlooking the west beach include the simple *Hotel Kyma* (T 22420 59045, W http://kyma.kosweb.com; ❸), or the *Hotel Fenareti* (T 22420 59024) further up the grade, with rooms (❷) and studios (❸) in a peaceful garden environment near easy parking. Among **tavernas**, clear winners are *O Makis*, one street inland from the centre of the waterfront, tops for fish and seafood, and *Kali Kardia*, right at the base of the jetty, with excellent *mayireftá*, *mezédhes* and desserts as well as fish; both are well attended by locals.

Andimáhia and Pláka

The workaday village of **ANDIMÁHIA**, 5km southeast of Mastihári, straggles over several of the ridges that extend from here to the far southwestern tip of Kós. The only "sight" and concession to tourism is a much-photographed **windmill** on the main street, the last surviving of more than thirty mills that once dotted the ridges here and at Kéfalos. The museum which used to operate in its interior appears to have closed, but if it has reopened you can climb up to the mast-loft and observe its workings – which incidentally point downwind, not *into* the wind as popularly imagined.

One worthwhile diversion from the main trunk road, immediately west of the airport and Andimáhia, is **Pláka**, a forested ravine with picnic grounds, a spring and a flock of semi-tame peacocks. The unmarked but paved side road leads off from a small white-and-blue-roofed chapel opposite the forest of radio masts in the airport precinct, and its dirt-surface continuation out of the Pláka vale emerges again on the main road, just before Kós' southwestern beaches.

The Knights' castle

East of Andimáhia, an enormous, triangular **Knights' castle** overlooks the islands of Níssyros, Tílos and Hálki. Access is via a marked, 2.8-kilometre side road that begins next to a Greek army barracks 700m northeast of the twin roundabouts, and ends in an informal parking area.

Enormous when seen from afar, the fortifications (unrestricted entry) prove less intimidating close up. Once through the imposing double north gateway, surmounted by the arms of Grand Master Pierre d'Aubusson, you can follow the well-preserved crenellated west parapet. The badly crumbled eastern wall presides over a sharp drop to badlands draining towards Kardhámena (see below). Inside the walls stand **two chapels**: the westerly, dedicated to Áyios Nikólaos, retains a surviving fresco of Áyios Khristóforos (St Christopher) carrying the Christ Child, while the eastern one of Ayía Paraskeví, though devoid of wall painting other than a few fragments above the west door, boasts fine rib vaulting springing from half-columns. The castle was originally built during the fourteenth century as a prison for misbehaving knights, then modified during the 1490s in tandem with the fortification programme at the citadel in Kós Town. Gravel walkways, illumination and a ticket booth were installed in 2001 – and never really used aside from the occasional concert held here.

Kardhámena

KARDHÁMENA, on the southeast coast, 31km from Kós Town, is the island's second-largest package resort after the capital itself, with locals outnumbered in a (nowadays rare) busy season twenty to one by young visitors (mainly Brits), most of them intent on getting as drunk as possible, as cheaply and quickly as possible. Runaway development has banished whatever redeeming qualities it may once have had, reducing the town to a seething, downmarket mass of off-licences, bars (far more numerous than tavernas), trinket shops and excursion agencies. Darts, bingo and karaoke competitions are staged regularly, pubs sport names like *Black Swan* and *Slug and Lettuce* and dispense imported beer on tap, and you can even get fish and chips at British-run stalls.

A hefty sand **beach** stretches to either side of the town, to the east hemmed in by ill-concealed military bunkers and a road as far as **Tolári**, home to the thousand-bedded *Norida Beach Hotel* all-inclusive complex. By forking left before reaching Tolári you'll reach Pylí after 9km – a useful, paved short cut.

Practicalities

Kardhámena is most worth knowing about as a place to catch a **boat to Níssyros**. There are supposedly two daily sailings in season: the morning tourist excursion *kaïki* at either 9am or 9.30am, and another, less expensive, barely publicized one – the *Chrisoula* – at 2.30pm, but in practice the afternoon departure (typically Mon, Wed, Thurs & Fri) can occur any time between 1.30pm and 6.30pm, depending on when the Nissyrians have finished their shopping; Kardhamenans are apt to be reticent about its comings and goings. Arrivals from Níssyros coincide fairly well with bus departures to Kós Town.

In the wake of the prevailing tourism slump, rooms or studios – except perhaps during August – are to be had for the asking. Prices tend to be about a third cheaper than in Kós Town (❷). If you decide – or are compelled – to stay, search out quieter premises west of the riverbed, beyond the *Valinakis Beach Hotel* – not that sleep is a particularly high priority for most holiday-makers here. One name to remember is the simple but en-suite *Milos Pension* (☎22420 91413; ❷), at a fairly calm spot about two-thirds of the way northeast along the waterfront, then a block inland. For more comfort, the nominally B-class *Hotel Rio* (☎22420 91627, ⓕ22420 91895; ❹) can also be recommended.

Eateries here serve predictably mediocre, overpriced fare, and tend to change hands and format every season. The most "Greek" is currently *Avli*, in an old house beside the *Hotel Rio*. Within sight of the *Milos Pension*, a **bakery** (the way signed with red arrows) offers local yogurt, brown bread and filled pies.

Southwestern Kós

The portion of Kós **southwest** of Andimáhia and the airport is the least developed and most thinly populated part of the island, with its permanent inhabitants confined to the lone, bluff-top village of **Kéfalos**. Besides being the area where non-package tourists are most likely to find a vacancy in high season, it also offers the most secluded and scenic beaches on the island, plus a number of minor ancient sites.

South coast beaches

The south-facing **beaches** between the airport and Kéfalos, though shown as separate extents on most tourist maps, form essentially one long stretch at the base of a cliff, interrupted by headlands only between "Paradise" and Áyios Stéfanos. The sections, listed below going from east to west, are given fanciful English names in tourist literature and are mostly provided with sunbeds, at least a rudimentary snack-bar and a jet-ski franchise, though the official Greek place names have returned to signs marking the individual access roads.

"**Magic**", officially Polémi, is the longest, broadest and wildest section, with a full-service taverna above the car park, no jet skis and a nudist zone at the east end. "**Sunny**", officially signed as Psilós Gremmós, the next along and easily walkable from "Magic", has another taverna and jet skis. **Langádhes** is the cleanest and most picturesque, with junipers tumbling off the dunes almost to the shore. "**Paradise**", often dubbed "Bubble Beach" in boat-trip jargon, owing to volcanic gas vents in the tidal zone, is overrated; the sandy area is too small for the hordes descending upon its wall-to-wall sunbeds and two tavernas, while boats attached to the paragliding and banana-ride outfits, plus the inevitable jet skis, buzz constantly offshore. "**Camel**" (Kamíla) is the shortest and loneliest of these strands, flanked by weird rock formations (but no humped beasts) and protected somewhat from crowds by the steep, unpaved dive in past its hillside taverna; the shore here is pure, fine sand, with good snorkelling to either side of the cove.

Limiónas

Just east of the turning for Áyios Stéfanos, a marked, paved side road leaves the main route, bound for **Limiónas** (Limniónas), the only north-facing beach and fishing port in this part of Kós. After 3.5km along the side road, bear right at another narrow but paved road (2.7km). There's just one surviving fish **taverna** here, the rather commercialized *Limionas*. Swimming is actually a secondary consideration, though there are two compact patches of sandy **beach** to either side of a peninsula that ends in an islet now tethered to Kós by a breakwater.

Áyios Stéfanos and Kastrí

Uninterrupted beach resumes at **Áyios Stéfanos** and continues 5km west to Kamári (see below). This area is overshadowed by a huge, 1970s-vintage **Club Med** complex of well-landscaped bungalows around a less attractive main hotel, all refurbished in 2001 and officially renamed as *Karlos Village*. In a reversal of historic policy, you can now get day-use passes for their extensive facilities, or even book overnight stays on the spot (℡22420 71213, ℻22420 72217; ❻, minimum stay in high season four nights). The Club Med has its own sewage treatment plant, which is more than can be said for the haphazard development at Kamári; less commendable is the management's past tendency to imply that both local beaches are private. Other lodging nearby includes the *Alexis Studios* (℡22420 72293; ❹), a small complex of one- and two-storey bungalows overlooking the beach.

The badly marked public access road to the westerly beach begins near the bus stop and cuts through the Club Med grounds, fizzling out just before a peninsula crowned with the exquisite remains of two triple-aisled, sixth-century **basilicas**. Though still the best preserved on the island, these have not been faring well recently; several columns have toppled over since the 1980s. The entire floor, however, is decorated with excellent **mosaics**, most of them under a protective layer of sand. Visible south of the apse, two peacocks perch upon and drink from a goblet; in the north chapel's aisle, next to the baptistry and font, two mosaic ducks can be seen paddling about.

The basilicas overlook the tiny but striking islet of **Kastrí**, sporting a chapel and a distinct volcanic pinnacle. From the sandy cove west of the peninsula it's just a short swim away; in spots, you can even wade across, local water-ski school activity permitting. The sea here warms up early in the year and is shallow enough to stay that way into November. It offers the best snorkelling on an island not otherwise known for it, owing to rock formations cutting across the generally sandy seabed. As at "Paradise", gas bubbles up from the ocean floor.

Kamári

Essentially the shore annexe of Kéfalos, **KAMÁRI** is a sprawling resort of scrappy, unplanned breeze blocks, pitched a few notches above Kardhámena, though here, too, British tour operators used to exert a hammerlock on much of the place. The developed strip, a stream of lower-rise rooms, self-catering studios and tavernas, thins out slightly as you head southwest towards the fishing port; in addition to offering all watersports, particularly windsurfing, in season Kamári may serve as an alternative departure point for Níssyros excursions (up to 5 weekly in season).

Independent **hotels** or **studios** that can be recommended here include *Sydney* (℡22420 71286; ❷) and the adjacent *Maria* (℡22420 71308; ❷), on the seafront west of the junction for the main road up to Kéfalos. *Stamatia*, near the main roundabout, is the oldest and (relatively) most authentic **taverna** hereabouts, with fresh fish often on offer.

Kéfalos

Forty-three kilometres from Kós Town and the end of the line for buses, the inland settlement of **KÉFALOS** squats on a flat-topped hill looking northeast down the length of Kós. As densely packed as Andimáhia is straggly, Kéfalos has little to attract you other than a few shops, the region's only **post office**, a single **bank** with ATM, and a few basic "snak bars" (sic) in the centre. Even the **Knights' castle** here, downhill beside the Kamári-bound road, is rudimentary and unimpressive; the Knights must have thought so, too, abandoning it in 1504. But for better or worse, the village makes a staging point for expeditions south into the rugged peninsula that terminates at dramatically sheer Cape Kríkello.

Cape Kríkello

The first point of interest on a tour of the south peninsula is Byzantine **Panayía Palatianí**, 1km south of Kéfalos; a marked path east from the roadside leads to this chapel, which incorporates generous chunks of an ancient temple. Some 500m beyond, a less obvious sign reading "Palatia" points through fencing down a broader, shady lane to the site of ancient **Astypalia**, the original capital of Kós until abandoned in 366 BC. The most conspicuous remains here are those of a Hellenistic temple with just its foundation-corners intact, and a late Classical amphitheatre with two rows of seats still in place, enjoying a fine prospect over the curve of Kamári Bay – if you ignore the generous sprinkling of litter underfoot.

Immediately past Astypalia, a paved road leaves the ridge road and heads west towards **Áyios Theológos**, 7km from Kéfalos. Besides the namesake chapel, there's a convenient **taverna**, the *Ayios Theologos*, which gets good marks for fish and homemade cheese. Forays along the dirt tracks to either side – a jeep or dirt bike is advisable – will turn up more secluded sandy coves at the base of low cliffs.

The appealing monastery of **Áyios Ioánnis Thymianós** (7km from Kéfalos), reached by following the paved road to its end, is pretty much the end of the line for non-4WD vehicles (jeeps can reach Áyios Mámas, 4km beyond). Set on a natural balcony under two plane trees, the church is locked except during the festival on August 28–29; it's a fine picnic spot at other times, but there's no reliable drinking water.

Áspri Pétra

Just under 2km further along the paved ridge road from the Theológos turning, you can make another detour to the **cave of Áspri Pétra**, inhabited in Neolithic times. Instead of continuing straight towards Áyios Ioánnis Thymianós, bear left onto a dirt track heading east towards a chapel and telecom tower atop Mount Zíni; a downed sign proclaims these attractions, as well as "Áspri Pétra 1.5" on a very rusty upright placard. After 600m, there's another fork, with the left option going up towards a quarry, and the right going down to a jetty serving it. In the "y" of this junction, marked by a red paint dot on a boulder to the left, is a faint dirt track, non-motorable – so leave transport here. Follow this as it dwindles to a path, running more or less parallel to the lower, right-hand road; the path is somewhat overgrown with baby pines and mastic bushes but red dots persist until the vicinity of a distinct, grey limestone outcrop. Here the path splits; adopt the upper, left-hand branch, now marked with green paint blobs and crosses. Just right of this outcrop stands a natural rock arch, in turn marked by a large green cross visible from a distance. The cave – at most 25 minutes' walk from the second junction – is below and left

of this, room-sized and well protected, though quite featureless other than a bit
of rock walling built around the entrance.

Psérimos

Psérimos could be an idyllic – albeit water-starved – little island were it not
so close to Kós and Kálymnos. Throughout the season, both of these larger
neighbours dispatch daily excursion boats, which compete strenuously to dock
at the small harbour village of **Avlákia**. In midsummer, day-trippers blanket the
main sandy beach curving around the bay in front of Avlákia's thirty-odd houses
and huge communal olive grove; even during May or late September you're
guaranteed at least a hundred outsiders daily (versus a permanent population of

Greek script table

Kós	Κώς	ΚΩΣ
Andimáhia	Αντιμάχεια	ΑΝΤΙΜΑΧΕΙΑ
Asfendhioú	Ασφενδιού	ΑΣΦΕΝΔΙΟΥ
Asómatos	Ασώματος	ΑΣΩΜΑΤΟΣ
Áspri Pétra	Άσπρη Πέτρα	ΑΣΠΡΗ ΠΕΤΡΑ
Áyios Dhimítrios	Άγιος Δημήτριος	ΑΓΙΟΣ ΔΗΜΗΤΡΙΟΣ
Áyios Fokás	Άγιος Φωκάς	ΑΓΙΟΣ ΦΩΚΑΣ
Áyios Ioánnis	Άγιος Ιοάννης	ΑΓΙΟΣ ΙΟΑΝΝΗΣ
Thymianós	Θυμιανός	ΘΥΜΙΑΝΟΣ
Áyios Stéfanos	Άγιος Στέφανος	ΑΓΙΟΣ ΣΤΕΦΑΝΟΣ
Áyios Theológos	Άγιος Θεολόγος	ΑΓΙΟΣ ΘΕΟΛΟΓΟΣ
Brós Thermá	Μπρός Θερμά	ΜΠΡΟΣ ΘΕΡΜΑ
Cape Kríkello	Ακρωτήρι Κρίκελο	ΑΚΡΟΤΗΡΙ ΚΡΙΚΕΛΟ
Dhíkeos	Δίκεος	ΔΙΚΕΟΣ
Evangelístria	Ευαγγελίστρια	ΕΥΑΓΓΕΛΙΣΤΡΙΑ
Kamári	Καμάρι	ΚΑΜΑΡΙ
Kardhámena	Καρδάμαινα	ΚΑΡΔΑΜΑΙΝΑ
Kéfalos	Κέφαλος	ΚΕΦΑΛΟΣ
Kermedés	Κερμετές	ΚΕΡΜΕΝΤΕΣ
Khristós	Χριστός	ΧΡΗΣΤΟΣ
Lámbi	Λάμπι	ΛΑΜΠΙ
Langádhes	Λαγκάδες	ΛΑΝΓΑΔΕΣ
Lim(n)iónas	Λιμ(ν)ιώνας	ΛΙΜ(Ν)ΙΩΝΑΣ
Marmári	Μαρμάρι	ΜΑΡΜΑΡΙ
Mastihári	Μαστιχάρι	ΜΑΣΤΙΧΑΡΙ
Pylí	Πυλί	ΠΥΛΙ
Pláka	Πλκα	ΠΛΑΚΑ
Platáni	Πλατάνι	ΠΛΑΤΑΝΙ
Polémi	Πολέμι	ΠΟΛΕΜΙ
Psalídhi	Ψαλίδι	ΨΑΛΙΔΙ
Psilós Gremmós	Ψηλός κρεμός	ΨΗΛΟΣ ΚΡΕΜΟΣ
Tingáki	Τιγκάκι	ΤΙΓΚΑΚΙ
Ziá	Ζιά	ΖΙΑ
Zipári	Ζιπάρι	ΖΙΠΑΡΙ
Psérimos	Ψέριμος	ΨΕΡΙΜΟΣ
Grafiótissa	Γραφιότισσα	ΓΡΑΦΙΟΤΙΣΣΑ
Marathoúnda	Μαραθούντα	ΜΑΡΑΘΟΥΝΤΑ
Vathý	Βαθύ	ΒΑΘΥ

thirty). There are three other, remoter beaches to hide away on during the day: clean **Vathý** (sand and gravel), a well-marked, thirty-minute path-walk east, starting from behind the *Taverna Iy Pserimos*; grubbier, tar-smeared **Marathoúnda** (pebble), a half-hour walk north on the main trans-island track; or the idyllic all-sand beach beside the chapel of **Panayía Grafiótissa** (big festival Aug 14–15), reached by turning west off the Marathoúnda track about twenty minutes along.

Practicalities

Even during the season there won't be too many other overnighters, since there's a limited number of beds available, and your reception at some of the more put-upon snack-bars may become warmer once it's clear that you're **staying**. Pick of the several small pensions is *Tripolitis* (☎22430 23196; ❷), over English-speaking *Nick and Anna's* café-snack bar, or the rooms above *Taverna Manola* on the opposite end of the beach (☎22430 51540; ❷), who also keep the plusher *Studios Kalliston* next door (❸). There's just one small, limited-stock **store**, since most of the island's supplies are brought in daily from Kálymnos. Eating out however, won't break the bank, and there's often fresh fish in the handful of **tavernas**; many of these have contracts with the tour boats, but *Taverna Manola* doesn't, and despite modest appearances proves very adept at *ouzerí* fare and seafood.

Nearly all the **boats** based on Kós and Kálymnos harbour operate triangle tours (approximately €20), which involve departure between 9.30am and 10am, followed by a stop for swimming at either Platý islet or adjacent Psérimos, lunch in Avlákia, or Póthia, or Rína, the ports of Kálymnos (or even on board), and another swimming stop at whichever islet wasn't visited in the morning. If you want to spend the entire day on Psérimos, you're much better off departing Póthia at 9.30am daily on the tiny *Nissos Pserimos*, returning at 4pm (€6 round-trip). The islanders themselves use this boat to visit Kálymnos for shopping and administrative business; with just a bare handful of children, there is no longer a secondary school on the island.

Kós travel details

Island transport

City (DEAS) buses

Kós Town to: Asklepíon (11 daily except Mon 8am–5pm); Áyios Fokás (3 hourly dawn–11pm); Brós Thermá (9 daily 9.45am–5.45pm); Lámbi (roughly every 30min 6.30am–11pm); Platáni (15 daily 8am–10.45pm).

Miniature train

Kós Town to: Asklepion (hourly Mon–Fri 9am–5pm, returns 1hr 15min later; hourly 8.15am–1.15pm Sat & Sun).

Ktel Buses

Kós Town to: Andimáhia, Kardhámena, Kéfalos (6 daily Mon–Sat, 3 daily Sun); Marmári (12 daily Mon–Sat, 7 daily Sun); Mastihári (5 daily Mon–Sat, 3 daily Sun); Pylí (5 daily Mon–Sat, 3 daily Sun); Tingáki (12 daily Mon–Sat, 7 daily Sun); Ziá via Evangelístria (3 daily Mon–Sat).

Inter-island transport

Small ferries

Kardhámena to: Níssyros (4–5 weekly, nominally at 2.30pm, on *Chrisoula*; 1hr). No cars carried.
Mastihári to: Póthia, Kálymnos (3–4 daily most of the year, 9am–10pm, on ANEM – Shipping Company of Mastihári Anonymous; 45min). Departure times are linked to arrivals of Olympic Airways' flight from Athens (☎22420 59027 or ☎22420 59124 for current information). Several cars carried.

Excursion boats

Kardhámena to: Níssyros (at least 1 daily; 1hr).
Kós Town to: Níssyros (4–7 weekly; 1hr 40min); Psérimos (4 weekly; 50min).

NB These departures, meant primarily to serve day-trippers, are also available on a one-way basis, though fares are relatively expensive.

Large ferries

Kós Town to: Alexandhroúpoli (1 weekly on LANE; 21hr); Astypálea (1–2 weekly on GA; 4hr); Kálymnos (7 weekly on GA; 1hr 15min); Léros (9 weekly on BS or GA; 1hr 45min–2hr 30min); Níssyros (1–3 weekly on GA; 1hr 30min); Pátmos (7–9 weekly on BS or GA; 3–4hr); Pireás (7–9 weekly on BS or GA; 10–15hr); Rhodes (11 weekly on BS or GA; 3–5hr); Sámos (1 weekly on LANE; 4hr 30min); Sými (1–2 weekly on GA; 3hr); Tílos (1–3 weekly on GA; 2hr 30min).

Catamaran

The *Dodekanisos Express* links Kós with the following islands at the following frequencies from late March to mid-October: Rhodes (6–7 weekly); Léros (6–7 weekly); Pátmos (6 weekly); Kálymnos, Lipsí (4 weekly); Sými (2–3 weekly). Maximum journey times, including stops, vary from 3hr for Lipsí to 40min for Kálymnos.

Hydrofoils

Kós Town to: Agathoníssi (1 weekly on KR; 3hr 15min); Foúrni (2–3 weekly on KR; 4hr); Ikaría (2–3 weekly on KR; 3hr 30min); Kálymnos (5–7 weekly on KR; 40min); Léros (4–7 weekly on KR; 1hr 30min); Lipsí (4–7 weekly on KR; 2hr); Pátmos (4–7 weekly on KR, 2 weekly direct on LZ; 1hr 30min–2hr 30min); Sámos–Pythagório (4–7 weekly on KR; 3hr 30min–5hr).

Flights

Kós to: Astypálea (2–3 weekly; 1hr 10min); Athens (3 daily on Olympic, 2 daily on Aegean; 50–55min); Léros (2–3 weekly; 25min); Rhodes (2–3 weekly; 40min).

International transport

Kós Town to: Bodrum, Turkey (2–14 weekly; 20–40min). Greek hydrofoils leave almost daily 9–10am, return 4–5pm; €35–40 return, Greek tax inclusive; no cheap day return or one-ways, no Turkish port tax. Identically priced Turkish boat (*Fahri Kaptan*) or hydrofoil departs Bodrum 9am or so, leaves Kós 4.30pm; this provides the only service in winter (Nov–April). Only the Turkish conventional boat (expensively) takes cars.

Astypálea

Geographically, historically and architecturally, **Astypálea** (alias Astropália) would be more at home among the Cyclades – on a clear day you can see Anáfi or Amorgós (to the southwest and northwest respectively) far more easily than any of the other Dodecanese. Astypálea's inhabitants are descendants of medieval colonists from the Cyclades, and the island looks and feels more like the archipelago to the west than its neighbours to the east. Anecdotes relate that Astypálea was mistakenly reassigned to the Ottomans after the Greek Revolution only because the French, English and Russians had such a poor map at the 1830 and 1832 peace conferences.

Despite its evocative butterfly shape, Astypálea does not immediately impress you as especially beautiful. Many beaches along the bleak, heavily indented coastline often have reef underfoot and suffer periodic dumpings of seaweed. The heights, which offer limited walking opportunities, are windswept and covered in thornbrush or dwarf juniper. Yet the herb *alisfakiá*, made into a tea, flourishes too, and hundreds of sheep and goats manage to survive – as opposed to snakes, which are (uniquely in the Aegean) entirely absent; legend claims that migrating cranes ate them all. Lush citrus groves

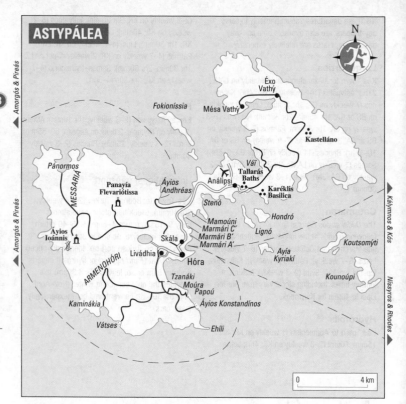

ASTYPÁLEA

N

Éxo
Vathý

Fokioníssia   Mésa Vathý

Kastelláno

Pánormos

MESSARIA

Panayía
Flevariótissa

Ayios
Andhréas

Váï
Tallarás
Baths
Análipsi

Karéklis
Basilica

Stenó

Áyios
Ioánnis

Mamoúni
Marmári C'
Marmári B'
Marmári A'

Hondró

Lignó

ARMENOHÓRI

Skála

Livádhia

Hóra

Ayía
Kyriakí

Koutsomýti

Kounoúpi

Tzanáki
Moúra
Papoú

Áyios Konstandínos

Kaminákia

Vátses

Ehíli

0   4 km

and vegetable patches in the valleys signal the presence of a relatively ample water supply, hoarded in a reservoir above Livádhia.

In antiquity the island's most famous citizen was Kleomedes, a boxer disqualified from an early Olympic Games for causing the death of his opponent. He came home so enraged that he demolished the local school, killing all its pupils. Things have calmed down a bit in the intervening 2500 years, and today Astypálea is renowned mainly for its **honey**, **fish** and **lobsters**; the abundant local catch has only been shipped to Athens since the late 1980s, a reflection of the enduringly poor ferry links in every direction.

These have improved recently with the introduction of extra services towards Pireás via selected Cyclades, and high-season links with Rhodes via a few intervening islets, but outside July and August you still risk being marooned here for a day or two longer than intended; you may need or want to take advantage of the 2003-inaugurated flights to Léros, Kós or Rhodes. Failing this, you'll find yourself adapting pretty quickly to the island's back-of-beyondness; foreign-newspaper delivery is fitful at best, TVs in the café-bars spend – by Greek standards – a fair amount of time switched off, and the locals – including a sizeable contingent of permanent dropouts from Athens – are, if not exactly bone idle, among the most laid-back folk in the islands.

Despite this relative isolation, plenty of people find their way to Astypálea during the short, intense midsummer season (a predictable mid-July to the first September Sunday before school starts), when the 1300 permanent inhabitants are all but overrun by upwards of seven thousand guests a day. Most arrivals are Athens-based Astypaleans, French or Italians, supplemented by large numbers of yachties and foreign owners of restored second homes in the understandably popular Hóra. At such times you won't find a bed without reserving well in advance – camping rough is expressly frowned upon – and the noise and commotion at the densely built port defies belief. There are relatively few English-speakers among the arrivals, especially since Laskarina Holidays deleted the island from their catalogue in 1995, frustrated by chronically unreliable connections to Kós and its airport. Indeed there is no conventional package tourism of any sort, yet passing yachts (and Athenian tastes) ensure the presence of chichi restaurants in the port, poshly stocked bottle shops and a sprinkling of arty souvenir shops that would do London's Covent Garden proud.

Getting around the island

Two **buses** run along the paved road between Hóra, Skala, Livádhia and Analípsi, frequently in July and August from 8am until 11pm, much less regularly out of season. The Análipsi-bound bus usually manages to dovetail well with arriving/departing aeroplanes. There are only two official **taxis** (sample fare, €6 Skála–Airport), far too few to cope in high season when you may have to trudge baggage-laden some distance to your arranged lodgings, adding insult to injury caused by the ungodly arrival times of ferries. Several places rent out **scooters and motorbikes**, the most reliable being Lakis and Manolis (☎22430 61263), with branches below the square in Hóra and at Skála dock; they also rent out a few cars and jeeps, as does Vergoulis (☎22430 61351). The island **map** sold locally is hilariously inaccurate, even by lenient Greek-island standards, though in compensation rural junctions are adequately signposted.

Skála and Hóra

The main harbour of **SKÁLA** or Péra Yialós dates largely from the Italian era; Astypálea was the first Dodecanesian island the Italians occupied in 1912. Most of the settlement between the quay and the line of nine ridgetop windmills is even more recent – and neither terribly attractive nor peaceful in peak season.

Skála's only real bright spot is a small **archeological museum** (June–Sept Mon 10am–1pm & 7–10pm, Tues–Sun 8.30am–2.30pm & 5–11pm; Oct–May Tues–Sun 8am–2pm; free) at the rear of the bay. Into a single, well-lit room are crammed the best local finds spanning all historical eras in chronological order: Late Bronze Age tomb artefacts, a Hellenistic relief of a symposium, a Roman statuette of Aphrodite, marble fragments from early Christian basilicas – and photographs of their mosaics, still left *in situ,* to whet your appetite for cross-country expeditions to find them.

As you climb up beyond the port towards **HÓRA**, the island's official capital and main business district, the neighbourhoods get progressively older and more attractive. Their steep streets are enlivened by the *poúndia,* or colourful wooden balconies-with-staircases of the whitewashed houses, which owe much to the building styles of Mýkonos and Tínos, the origins of the colonists brought to repopulate the island in 1413. Everything culminates in the thirteenth-century **kástro** (Mon–Fri mornings, Sat & Sun shut; free) one of the finest in the Aegean, erected on Byzantine foundations not by the Knights but by the Venetian Quirini clan and subsequently modified by the Ottomans after 1537. Until well into the 1900s, over three hundred people lived inside the *kástro*, but depopulation and a severe 1956 earth-quake combined to leave only a desolate shell today. The fine rib vaulting over the main west gate supports the church of **Evangelístria Kastrianí**, one of two intact here, the other being **Áyios Yeóryios** (both usually locked, though you may be able to climb Kastrianí's belfry for amazing views). In contrast to ongoing renovation activity outside the walls, restoration of any interior dwellings is forbidden, as they're now the property of the Byzantine archeological ephorate. Currently the entire grounds are in the throes of a consolidation and restoration project undertaken by this authority, designed to keep the wind-battered perimeter fortifications from crumbling further.

Accommodation

Skála, and to a lesser extent Hóra, have **accommodation** ranging from spartan, 1970s-vintage rooms to new state-of-the-art studios; proprietors tend not to meet ferries unless arrangements have been made, even if they have vacancies. Owing to high-season harbour noise – particularly the sound of ferries dropping anchor at 3am – you might, if uninterrupted sleep is a priority, prefer accommodation in Hóra. All establishments are open June to September unless otherwise stated. A small, basic **campsite** (℡02430 61338; July & Aug only) operates amongst calamus reeds and tamarisks behind Dhéftero Marmári bay (see p.269), about 4km along the road to Análipsi, but (like much of the island) it can be mosquito-plagued any year after a wet winter.

Skála

Akti Rooms On the east shore of the bay ℡22430 61281 or 22430 61114. Good-value if slightly snug studios, well equipped and maintained, with great views. ❹
Studios Antzela On the hillside above the *Akti Rooms* ℡22430 61561. Pleasant studios also worth trying; vast if unshaded terraces for some units. ❹
Aphrodite Studios On the road up to Hóra ℡22430 61478, ℻22430 61087. Reasonably appointed units with views, if not quite up to the standard of *Akti Rooms*. ❸
Astynea ℡22430 61040, ℻22430 61041.

Standard port hotel, whose en-suite rooms have sea views (plus a certain amount of bustle from tavernas just below and opposite). ❸
Australia Above eponymous restaurant ℡22430 61067, ℻22430 59812. En-suite rooms, refurbished with fans and/or air con in 2003; same management offers more comfortable studios closer to the water. Open most of year. Rooms ❸, studios ❹
Paradisos ℡22430 61224, ℻22430 61450. Elderly but fairly well-kept sea-view port hotel; open all year. ❸

Hóra

Kallihoron Studios Start of road to Livádhia from windmills ℡22430 61934, ⓦwww.astipalea.com.gr. Runner-up in the plushness sweepstakes to the *Kilindra Studios*, these tasteful modern units all have views of Hóra and air con/heating. Open all year. Studios ❺, one-bed apartments ❻
Kilindra Studios Hóra's west slope ℡22430 61966, ⓦwww.astipalea.com.gr. The island's highest-standard and quietest digs are 2000-built, skilfully done mock-traditional units; all luxury amenities including a pool. Units accommodate two to three people (minimum age 14). Open all year. Standard ❻, suite ❽

Kostas Vaïkousis Houses ℡22430 61430 or 697 74 77 800. Atmospheric restored studios and entire houses, which got much-needed overhauls in 2003–4, at three locations near the top of Hóra; enquire at Kostas' antique shop on the quay if you haven't rung in advance. Double occupancy ❺ high, ❸ low season.
Provarma Studios About halfway along the road to Livádhia ℡22430 61096, ℻22430 61228. Remoter and more affordable, these southwest-facing galleried studios with white-tile-and-pine decor have large balconies, but no air con. ❹

Eating and drinking

The restaurant scene is quite distorted seasonally; during August, nearly thirty **tavernas** and beach snack-bars operate across the island, few of them memorable and many concerned primarily with turning a quick profit. Below is a selection of the longer-opening and/or locally oriented restaurants.

Among the more reliable Skála options, *Iy Monaxia* (aka *Viki's* after the proprietress who lived sixteen years in Australia), one block inland from the ferry jetty by the old power plant, has excellent home-style cooking and stays open year-round. The *Astropalia* (closes end Sept), on the hillside above the street up to Hóra, does good – if somewhat pricey – fish and not much else. Best of this lot, with even better seafood, island wine and superbly prepared own-grown vegetable dishes, is homey *Australia* (open all year), just inland from the head of the bay, where Kyria Maria presides over the oldest (est. 1971) and most wholesome taverna in Skála. Behind the *Hotel Paradhisos*, you'll find more careful cooking, polished presentation (and much higher prices) at *Aitherio* and *Maïstrali* (both open into Oct), catering conspicuously to the yacht set; it's pot luck as to which is better any given night. Under the *Hotel Astynea*, the *Dapia Café* is good for full breakfasts, midday crêpes and flavoured teas. Up in Hóra, the only full-service standout is *Barbarosa* (supper all year, lunch also during high season) by the town hall, which gives Greek standards a continental twist.

Nightlife and entertainment

Most **nightlife** happens up in more atmospheric Hóra, where the esplanade between the windmills and the base of the *kástro* hill appears to be one solid café-bar. Among these, favourites include the unsigned *Tou Nikola* (*Iy Myli*) on the corner, with the island's characters installed, and homemade *glyká koutalioú* dished out amidst wonderfully kitsch Greek-royalist decor. This spot, along with much of Hóra, served as the location for *Island*, a truly forgettable 1989 film by Paul Cox, with Irene Pappas lending a bit of star gravitas to what was essentially plotless Indo-Euro-Greek nonsense. *Ayeri Ouzeri*, diagonally opposite, is the trendy alternative, also good for a full-on meal. Relatively subdued **bars**, open peak season only, include long-lived *Kastro Bar*, below the north wall of the castle, classiest and best for conversation-level music, or *Artemis*, also with a terrace. For a livelier time there's *Panorama,* where the island's youth hang out until dawn. More formal **entertainment** means an outdoor cinema (July & Aug only) on the southeast flank of the *kástro*, and a summer **music festival** (late June to early Aug), which attracts a mix of big Athenian names and local amateur acts.

Other practicalities

The **post office** and most shops are located in Hóra, though the island's only **bank**, complete with ATM, is down in Skála by the port police. Near the museum, Astypalea Tours (☎22430 61571) is the main travel agency, representing the *Nissos Kalymnos* and Olympic Airways as well. A **laundry** up in Hóra makes itself well-known to yachties, plus there's a single, well-stocked, long-hours **pharmacy** on the road up from Skála.

The southwest

A twenty-minute walk (or a short bus journey) from Hóra brings you to **LIVÁDHIA**, a fertile valley draining to a popular, good beach, the foundations of a knoll-top **basilica** just to the west, and a generally indifferent collection of restaurants and cafés immediately behind. You can rent a **room or studio** just inland – for example, at *Studios O Manganas* (☏22430 61468; ④), on the frontage road, representing the highest standard here, or *Venetos Studios* (☏22430 61490, ℻22430 61423; ❸; May–Sept), at the base of the westerly hillside, comprising several separate buildings scattered in a pleasant orchard. Among the half-dozen **tavernas**, *To Yerani* in the streambed is about the most consistently open (until Oct) and renowned for its excellent *mayireftá*; they also keep simple rooms adjacent (☏22430 61484; ❷).

Beaches

If the busy, mixed sand-and-gravel beach at Livádhia doesn't suit, continue southwest fifteen minutes on foot to three small pebble coves at **Tzanáki**, packed out with naturists in midsummer. To get there, you can no longer use the old footpath the entire distance – fencing around a mammoth villa-with-swimming-pool blocks the way – but must use the new trail, which plunges straight down from the roadside spot where scooters tend to park. The three coves in question – the first two easy to reach, the third more difficult – huddle at the base of sculpted cliffs, with nose-to-nose views of Hóra.

Beyond the Tzanáki trio, Moúra cove, slimy-rocked and seaweed-strewn, is a complete waste of time; **Papoú**, just beyond, is a rather better eighty-metre fine-gravel strand, but is accessible overland only by a horrifically steep side-track, and then a final path approach to skirt a jealously fenced-off farm.

However, the third bay beyond Tzanáki, **Áyios Konstandínos**, easily reachable by motorbike along 6km of dirt road from Livádhia, is more worth the effort. Here you'll find 200m of partly shaded sand and gravel hemmed in by spring-nurtured orchards, as well as a decent seasonal taverna.

Around Ehíli promontory from Áyios Konstandínos lie two south-facing beaches, Vátses and Kaminákia; both are easiest visited by summer boat excursions (typically 11am departure), which alternate days with outings to the islets of Koutsomýti and Ayía Kyriakí southeast of Astypálea. By land, **Vátses** has the easier dirt track in, only 6km (20min scooter drive) out of Livádhia at the mouth of a fine canyon; it's long (250m) and wild, if often windy, its two headlands framing the view to Anáfi. Vátses is also one of the sandier island beaches, with no dress code when the summer-only *kantína* is shut.

The half-hour drive to **Kaminákia** (8.5km from Livádhia), arguably Astypálea's best and cleanest beach, begins reasonably enough, but once past the farms and rural monastery at Armenohóri the final 2km deteriorates to a bone-jarring, steep descent, best tackled in a four-wheeler, though again there are great views of Anáfi island if you dare take your eyes off the "road". Your reward on arrival is a very sheltered, 150-metre, southeast-facing cove with a sea cave to explore on the left as you face the water. There's a good, stone-clad **taverna** (July–Sept) here, overseeing a handful of sunbeds and offering honest rustic fare (salads and a dish of the day). Excursion boats allow you an hour here, or at Áyios Ioánnis cove (see below), according to passenger consensus.

Áyios Ioánnis monastery and around

A favourite outing in the west of the island is the two-hour walk or half-hour motorbike trip from Hóra to the oasis of **Áyios Ioánnis**, just under 10km distant. Proceed northwest along the signposted, initially paved road beginning from the windmills, passing high above the reservoir, then keep left when a side track goes right towards the remote monastery of **Panayía Flevariótissa**.

Beyond this point the main track (this time ignore a left) curls north at the base of a ridge, where the overflow of two springs may seep across the road. After skirting high above the half-dozen isolated farms in the valley of **Messariá**, you reach a junction with gates across each option. Take the left-hand one, and soon the securely walled orchards of the uninhabited farm-monastery **Áyios Ioánnis** come into view.

From the balcony of the church, Anáfi can be seen on the horizon, and a steep, faint path leads down to the base of a ten-metre **waterfall**; alas, bathing pools at the bottom have silted up, and the cascade itself – apparently tapped for irrigation – is likely to be dry most months. Below, a rather arduous, pathless trek down the canyon ends at a fine, pebbly **beach**, potentially the last stop for southwesterly boat excursions.

The northeast

Northeast of Skála, a series of three bays nestle in the narrow "body" of the "butterfly", known as **Próto** (First), **Dhéftero** (Second) and **Tríto** (Third) **Marmári** (marked as **Marmári A'**, **B'** and **C'** respectively on some maps). The first is home to the local power plant and boatyards; the next one hosts the island's only organized **campsite** (see p.266); while the third, reasonably attractive bay is also the start of a path east to the unfortunately named, but perfectly decent, coves of **Mamoúni** ("Bug" or "Critter" in Greek). Beyond Tríto Marmári, **Stenó** takes its name ("Narrow") from the island's width at this point – a mere hundred metres or so; the middle beach east of the isthmus, with sandy shore and shallows, a few tamarisks and a seasonal *kantína*, is the best.

Análipsi (Maltezána) and beyond

ANÁLIPSI, widely known as Maltezána (after medieval Maltese pirates), is a ten-kilometre bus trip or taxi ride from town. Although the second-largest settlement on Astypálea, there's surprisingly little for outsiders besides a narrow, sea-urchin-speckled **beach** (there are better ones east of the main bay) and a nice view south to some islets. Despite this, blocks of rooms (open only July & Aug) sprout in ranks well back from the sea, spurred by the proximity of the airport, 700m away. By far the best, and most consistently staffed accommodation here is the largest **hotel** on the island, the 48-unit *Maltezana Beach* (℡22430 61558, ⊛www.maltezanabeach.gr; ❺ high, ❸ low season; Easter to late Sept), with large, well-appointed bungalow-rooms in landscaped grounds, a decent restaurant and a pool.

There are about eight independent **tavernas** here, the most reliably open (Feb–Christmas) being *Analipsi* (aka *Ilias and Irini's*, after the managing couple) by the jetty, which doubles as the *kafenío* for the local fishermen and seemingly every passing worker on the island. The fare – fried squid, bean soup, maybe fish soup – is simple but good, though confirm prices and portion size of the often frozen seafood. For more careful preparation, there's *Ovelix* a few hundred metres inland (supper much of the year, lunch also July & Aug), specialists in grilled lobster and scaly fish. Proprietor Panayiotis – bearing a strong resemblance to the cartoon character, hence the name of the restaurant – also offers a few basic rooms upstairs (℡22430 61260; ❷).

Análipsi and its environs boast the best of the island's several Byzantine mosaics, though these are unprotected and shamefully deteriorating. Behind calamus reeds and eucalyptus near the fishing jetty lie the colourful floors of the **early Byzantine Tallarás baths**, with somewhat crude mosaics of zodiacal signs, figures representing the seasons and a central androgynous figure (perhaps Time or Fortune personified), holding the cosmic orb. Beyond the last taverna and club, where the road becomes dirt, signs point seaward towards the **Karéklis basilica**, ten minutes' trail-walk distant; at the edge of geometric floor-mosaics two dolphins can be seen cavorting. En route you pass, on the headland, a memorial obelisk commemorating French sailors who died in the act of scuttling the frigate *Bisson*, trapped by the Ottoman navy here on November 6, 1827, during the Greek War of Independence.

Beyond the turn-off for the mosaic and obelisk, the road hits the sea briefly again at **Vái**, an attractively sandy bay that's unfortunately fully exposed to the prevailing winds and rubbish-laden currents – only a swimming possibility on calm or southerly days.

Many maps show a fully fledged village at **Kastelláno**, reached by a side road about 8km past Maltezána, while other sources fancifully describe an opulent villa for Mussolini here. This was in fact a 1930s Italian military base, a camouflage-painted two-storey barracks plus a bunker, standing barely tall enough to provide shade for sheep and goats, which today are the "garrison".

The motorable dirt track ends 23km from Hóra at Mésa Vathý (invariably and erroneously shown on most maps as Éxo Vathý), a sleepy fishing village with a single **taverna** (*Iy Galíni*) and superb small-craft anchorage in an almost landlocked inlet extending back to a marsh, sporadically home to those snake-eating cranes. Frankly, though, it's not really worth the long, bumpy trip out unless you're a yachtie and, to rub salt in the wound, the fish on the menu is usually frozen (if local). Following several accidents, this is no longer the **backup ferry port** in winter, when Skála is buffeted by the prevailing southerlies; at such times the bleak deep-water quay at **Áyios Andhréas**, just west of Tríto Marmári, is used.

Greek script table

Astypálea	Αστυπάλαια	ΑΣΤΥΠΑΛΑΙΑ
Análipsi	Ανάληψη	ΑΝΑΛΗΨΗ
Armenohóri	Αρμενοχώρι	ΑΡΜΕΝΟΧΩΡΙ
Áyios Andhréas	Άγιος Ανδρέας	ΑΓΙΟΣ ΑΝΔΡΕΑΣ
Áyios Ioánnis	Άγιος Ιοάννης	ΑΓΙΟΣ ΙΟΑΝΝΗΣ
Áyios Konstandínos	Άγιος Κωνσταντίνος	ΑΓΙΟΣ ΚΩΝΣΤΑΝΤΙΝΟΣ
Éxo Vathý	Έξω Βαθύ	ΕΞΩ ΒΑΘΥ
Hóra	Χώρα	ΧΩΡΑ
Kaminákia	Καμινάκια	ΚΑΜΙΝΑΚΙΑ
Karéklis	Καρέκλης	ΚΑΡΕΚΛΗΣ
Maltezána	Μαλτεζάνα	ΜΑΛΤΕΖΑΝΑ
Marmári	Μαρμάρι	ΜΑΡΜΑΡΙ
Mésa Vathý	Μέσα Βαθύ	ΜΕΣΑ ΒΑΘΥ
Papoú	Παπού	ΠΑΠΟΥ
Skála	Σκάλα	ΣΚΑΛΑ
Stenó	Στενό	ΣΤΕΝΟ
Tallarás	Ταλλαράς	ΤΑΛΛΑΡΑΣ
Tzanáki	Τζανάκι	ΤΑΝΑΚΙ
Vái	Βάϊ	ΒΑΪ
Vátses	Βάτσες	ΒΑΤΣΕΣ

Astypálea travel details

Inter-island transport

Ferries

Astypálea to: Amórgos (1–2 weekly on GA; 2hr); Kálymnos (1–2 weekly on GA, 3 weekly on NK; 2hr 30min–3hr 15min); Kós (1–2 weekly on GA; 3hr 15min); Níssyros (1 weekly on GA; 4hr 30min); Pireás (3 weekly on GA; 11hr); Rhodes (1–2 weekly on GA; 4hr); Tílos (1 weekly on GA; 5hr 30min).

Flights

Astypálea to: Athens (4–5 weekly; 1hr 10min); Kós (2–3 weekly; 1hr 10min); Léros (2–3 weekly; 25min); Rhodes (2–3 weekly; 2hr 10min).

Kálymnos

Most of the 17,000-strong population of **Kálymnos** lives in or around the large port of Póthia, a wealthy but not conventionally beautiful town famed for its **sponge industry**. Unfortunately, almost all of the eastern Mediterranean's sponges were devastated by a viral disease in 1986, related to freak warm currents, and only three or four of the fleet of thirty-odd boats – themselves reduced from the 134 active in 1948 – are still in use. In response to this catastrophe (and a smaller repeat outbreak in 1999), the island converted most of its sponge boats for deep-sea fishing, and they now dominate this industry around nearby islands. This has had disastrous effects ecologically, as crews – licensed by the government to use scuba gear in the process – virtually hoover the sea floor of marine life and make themselves unpopular with neighbouring islanders. Warehouses behind the harbour still process and sell sponges all year round – a few of these from reviving deep-water beds near Sicily and Malta, but most now imported from Asia and the Caribbean. There are also dwindling numbers of elderly gentlemen about who rely on two canes, walking frames or (in the case of younger victims) wheelchairs, stark evidence of the havoc wrought by nitrogen embolism ("the bends"), long before divers understood its crippling effects (see box overleaf).

The other response to the decline of sponge-fishing was the establishment of a tourist industry in the late 1980s, mainly confined to one string of beach resorts; but **tourism** proved as unreliable as sponges, and abruptly collapsed just after the millennium. The non-functioning, half-built airport near Árgos village, two decades a-building, and thus the continuing need for tedious transfers from Kós, was the main excuse for a mass pull-out by most package companies. The Kalymnians' solution to this crash in bucket-and-spade holidays has been twofold: selling off redundant hotels and studios as holiday apartments to foreigners, and attempting to establish the island as a world-class **rock-climbing** destination. Their success in this has greatly extended the visiting season; climbers swarm up the cliffs from October to December and again in March and April, and during the annual climbing festival (first week of Oct) you'll be lucky to find a free room or scooter for hire.

Kálymnos essentially consists of two cultivated and inhabited valleys sandwiched between three limestone ridges, harsh in the full glare of noon but magically tinted towards dusk. The **climate**, especially in winter, is alleged to be drier and healthier than that of neighbouring Kós or Léros, since the

Sponges and sponge-diving

Sponges are colonies of microscopic marine organisms which excrete a fibrous skeleton, increasing in size by about thirty percent annually. When alive, they are dark – almost black – in colour, and can be seen throughout the Dodecanese and east Aegean as melon-sized blobs, anchored to rocks in 3–10m of water. However, these are mostly wild sponges, impossible to clean or shape with shears; Kalymnian divers are after the so-called *ímero* or "domesticated" sponges, which are much softer, more pliable, and dwell at greater depths – typically 30–40m.

Before the late nineteenth century, sponge-fishers free-dived for their quarry; weighted with rocks, they descended to the seabed to hand-collect or spear as many sponges as possible on a single breath of air before being hauled to the surface by a safety line. The industrial revolution signalled momentous changes: divers were fitted with heavy, insulated suits – the so-called *skáfandhro* – and breathing apparatus filled by an air-feed line connected to primitive, hand-operated compressors on board the factory boats. They could now attain depths of as great as 70m, but this resulted in the first cases of the "bends", or nitrogen embolism. Divers working at any depth of over 10m and at pressures of several atmospheres would rise too quickly to the surface, so that the dissolved air in their bloodstream bubbled out of solution – with catastrophic results. From the late nineteenth century until well into the twentieth, roughly half of the sponge-divers who left with the fleets in spring never returned in autumn: buried at sea, or in a lonely grave in some remote islet, sometimes while still alive up to his neck so that the hot sand might provide slight relief from the excruciating pain of nitrogen bubbles in the joints.

Not until World War I was the physiological basis of the malady well understood; by then thousands of Kalymnians had died, with many of the "lucky" survivors paralysed, deaf or blind. The *skáfandhro*, despite being the obvious culprit and having been officially banned in many parts of the Mediterranean, returned to improper use until after World War II, wreaking more havoc. The first decompression chambers, and commercial diving schools imparting systematic knowledge of safe diving practices, were only available in Greece from the 1950s on. Now, new technology enabled the seabed to be stripped with ruthless, ever-greater efficiency; the sponge fleets were forced to hunt further and further from home, finally ending up in Egyptian and Libyan territorial waters until the Nasser and Gaddafi regimes imposed punitive duties in 1962 and 1972 respectively.

In its natural form, even the "domestic" sponge is unusable until processed. First the sponges have the smelly organic matter and external membrane thrashed out of them, traditionally by being trodden on the boat deck; next they are tossed in a rotary vat with hot sea water for a day or so, to complete the process. In Póthia you can visit a few workshops (best is the one on the shore road opposite Ayía Iríni, in Vouvális district) where the sponge-vats still spin; in the old days, the divers simply made a "necklace" of their catch and trailed it in the sea behind the boat. A third, optional processing step, that of bleaching the sponges with nitric acid to a pale yellow colour, has been added to accord with modern tastes. But the bleaching process weakens the fibres, so it's best to buy the more durable, natural-brown ones. In line with the risks, and competition from the production of synthetics, natural sponges are not cheap, even on Kálymnos; a good, hand-size bath sponge with a dense network of small holes will cost over €3. The enduring appeal of natural sponges – aside from the mystique of their gathering, and supporting a traditional lifestyle, however harsh – is that they're simply more durable, softer and absorbent than synthetic products, and lend themselves to a wide range of uses, from make-up artistry to canvas-painting to window-washing.

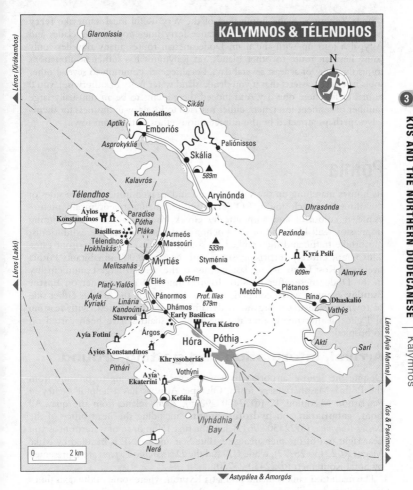

Map labels:
Glaroníssa
Léros (Xirókambos)
KÁLYMNOS & TÉLENDHOS
N
Sikáti
Kolonóstilos
Aptíki
Emboriós
Asprokykliá
Paliónissos
Skália
589m
Kalavrós
Aryinónda
Dhrasónda
Télendhos
Pezónda
Áyios
Konstandínos
Paradise
Pótha
Basilicas
Pláka
Armeós
Kyrá Psilí
Télendhos
Massoúri
609m
Hokhlakás
Myrtiés
533m
Styménia
Almyrés
Melitsahás
Platý-Yialós
Eliés
654m
Metóhi
Plátanos
Léros (Lakkí)
Ayía
Kyriakí
Linária
Pánormos
Prof. Ilías
Rína
Dhaskalió
Kandoúni
Dhámos
679m
Vathýs
Stavroú
Early Basilicas
Ayía Fotiní
Péra Kástro
Árgos
Hóra
Póthia
Áyios Konstandínos
Aktí
Sarí
Léros (Ayía Marína)
Khryssoheriás
Pithári
Ayía
Vothýni
Ekateríni
Kefála
Kós & Psérimos
Vlyhádhia
Bay
Nerá
0   2 km
▼ Astypálea & Amorgós

quick-draining limestone strata, riddled with many caves, doesn't retain as much moisture. The rock does, however, admit seawater, which has tainted Póthia's wells; drinking water must be brought in by tanker truck from the pure bores at Vathý, and there are also potable, public springs at Dhámos, Potamí district of Póthia and Hóra. In the vegetated valleys, mosquitoes can be a problem, so keep chemical or electrical repellents to hand. There are also seasonal plagues of unusually aggressive, brown-and-yellow wasps around Massoúri and Télendhos.

Despite its hostile geology, the island's position and excellent harbours ensured that it was of some importance from ancient times – especially during the **Byzantine era**, as testified to by the presence of more ruined early basilicas here than on any other island in the Dodecanese. Another local Byzantine legacy is the survival of peculiar medieval names (eg Skévos, Sakellários and Mikés for men, Themélina, Petránda and Sevastí for women), found nowhere else in Greece.

Since Kálymnos is the home port of the very useful local namesake **ferry** (see p.288), and also where long-distance ferry lines from the Cyclades and Astypálea join up with the main Dodecanesian routes, many travellers only pause here en route to other islands. Yet Kálymnos has sufficient attractions to justify a stay of at least several days. Local legend, common to several other spots in Greece, asserts that if you drink island water (salty or otherwise), you'll return to live here one day. And indeed there seems to be an unusually large number of resident foreigners, either married to locals or in business for themselves, perhaps attracted by the unpretentious ethos of the main town.

Póthia

Its houses marching up the valley behind and arrayed in tiers up the sides of the mountains enclosing it, **PÓTHIA**, without being stereotypically picturesque, is colourful and authentically Greek. Your first and overwhelming impression will likely be of the phenomenal noise created by exhibitionist motorbike traffic and the cranked-up sound systems of the waterfront cafés. This is not entirely surprising, since with nearly 16,000 inhabitants Póthia overtook Kós Town at the last census as the second-largest municipality in the Dodecanese, after Ródhos Town. Things get even louder on **Easter Sunday** evening, when competing teams stationed on the heights either side of town engage in an organized dynamite-throwing contest, with feasting and general merriment after the inevitable casualties have been carted off to hospital.

Arrival, information and getting around

Despite the "ghost" airport, which will never open owing to pressure from the Póthia–Mastihári ferry mafia, Olympic Airways has a helpful agency at Patriárhou Maxímou 12 (☎22430 29265), 200m inland from the quay. All **boat**, **catamaran** and **hydrofoil agents**, including the head office of the *Nissos Kalymnos* (☎22430 29612), line the first 150m or so of waterfront as you bear right out of the pier-area gate; Blue Star and LANE is handled by Mike Magos (☎22430 28777), while GA and the *Dodekanisos Express* are represented by Sofia Kouremeti (☎22430 23700).

The main **taxi** rank is inland on Platía Kýprou, where some of the taxis function as "taxi-buses" (set route, set rate, may not depart until full); otherwise you sign on with the dispatcher, who calls out your car number when it's ready. Bona fide **buses** in various colours run regularly as far as Aryinónda in the northwest and Vathý in the east, from a stop between the Municipal Nautical and Folklore Museum and the Italian-built municipal "palace", where schedules are helpfully posted. No tickets are sold on board – buy them from the agent in the adjacent mini-market. Except for the line to the main western resorts, services are not terribly frequent, so for any extended explorations you might **rent a motorbike** from one of a handful of outlets; Scooteromania (☎22430 51780 or 697 28 34 628), just back from the front, near where it bends south, can be recommended for bikes in good condition at fair prices, though you might also try Kostas Moto Rental next to the port police (☎22430 50110 or 697 71 93 951). **Car rental** is also available from Auto Market/Drive (numbers as for Scooteromania) and Spiros Kypreos (☎693 79 80 591), though the island's compact enough that only families would need one. Incidentally, the locally sold **map** published by Emmanouil Vallas may look amateurish, but in

△ Trimming sponges for sale, Póthia, Kálymnos

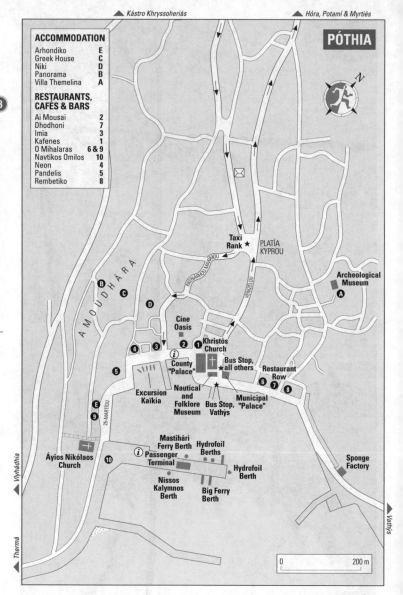

fact is one of the more accurate of Dodecanesian island maps, showing hiking paths more or less correctly.

A minimally helpful municipal **tourist information booth** (sporadic hours; ☎22430 59056) is located at the base of the ferry jetty. The **post office** lies a good 600m inland from Khristós church, above Platía Kýprou; several **banks** on or just behind the waterfront have ATMs.

Accommodation

Accommodation is rarely a problem, since pension proprietors usually meet the ferries (though many of the premises touted are substandard, unlicensed or remote, often all three). The Pothians have so far remained indulgent towards short stays, perhaps realizing that the port won't hold most people's interest for more than a day or two. If you prefer to hunt for yourself, the following establishments are worth contacting in advance.

Arhondiko ☎22430 24051, ℱ22430 24149. Refurbished mansion just a few paces in from the west quay, but fairly quiet. Small-to-medium-sized, somewhat plain rooms have TV, fridge, air con and some harbour-view balconies. ❷

Greek House ☎22430 23752. Pension in Amoudhára district; if necessary ask directions at the Flaskos *souvláki* stand, at the base of the jetty. Run by friendly, voluble Ypapandi Flaskou, whose kitsch rooms are all en suite. Best is the "penthouse", up a terrifying spiral staircase. Cooking facilities available; open most of the year. ❶

Niki ☎22430 28 528 or 693 79 87 403. En-suite pension between Amoudhára and Khristós church, in a fairly quiet spot; run by the friendly management of *Maria's Studios* in Melitsahás (see p.281). ❶

Panorama ☎ & ℱ22430 23138. This well-signposted, well-kept hotel is also in Amoudhára,

high above *Greek House*. Balconied rooms with views, a pleasant breakfast salon, and winter opening by arangement. Rates include breakfast. ❸

Villa Themelina ☎22430 22682, ℱ22430 23920, ℮antoniosantonoglu@yahoo.de. In the quiet Evangelistría district near the archeological museum, this Belle Époque mansion has been converted by Andonis and Themelina into Póthia's most elegant hotel, featuring high-ceilinged, wood-floored, insect-screened rooms, many with balconies and English fireplace surrounds. Behind is a large pool, patio-garden where egg-and-yogurt breakfasts are served, and two modern studio/apartment wings in vernacular style, plus a renovated gardener's cottage. The studios, without air con, can get stuffy, but it's still excellent value. Open all year. Rooms/studios ❸, larger apartments ❹

The Town

Perhaps the most rewarding way to acquaint yourself with Póthia is simply to wander its backstreets, where elegant Neoclassical houses are surrounded by surprisingly large gardens, or craftsmen ply their trade in a genuine workaday bazaar. The Pothians particularly excel in ironwork, and all but the humblest dwellings in the eastern Evangelístria district are adorned by superbly ornate banisters, balcony railings and fanlights. During the Italian occupation, many houses were painted blue and white to irritate the colonial overlords and, though the custom has all but died out, traces of the Greek national colours still appear among more traditional pink, lavender, grey and ochre buildings.

The interior of the eighteenth-century **Khristós** cathedral is noteworthy as a sort of impromptu gallery for Kalymnian painters, while the marble *témblon* is by the great, half-mad Tiniot sculptor Yiannoulis Halepas, who died in 1943. Other public artworks, in the form of bronze statues dotted about the town, are the works of contemporary sculptors Mihalis Kokkinos and his daughter Irini.

The only possibility of a swim in or near Póthia is en route to the defunct spa of Thermá, 2km southwest, at the pebbly cove of **Yéfyra**, at the mouth of a small ravine. At **Thermá** itself, there's just a concrete lido and a rather louche, sporadically open restaurant at one end of the crumbling spa building.

The museums

More formal edification is provided by two local museums. Priority should be given to the **Municipal Nautical and Folklore Museum** (Mon–Fri

8am–1.30pm, Sat & Sun 10am–12.30pm; €2), on the seaward side of Khristós cathedral. Pause first in front of the large foyer photo showing Póthia in the 1880s: no quay, jetty, roads (the Italians reclaimed most of the foreshore) or sumptuous mansions, with most islanders still living up in Hóra. Then it's on to a miscellany of smaller photos – sponge-fishing, shipyards, the Allied liberation of 1945, even a shrine to the crew of a helicopter which crashed during the 1996 Ímia crisis (see p.470). Three-dimensional exhibits include ingenious, dart-shaped nautical-mile logs, dragged off the stern; horribly primitive divers' breathing apparatus, all conducive to the bends; and "cages" designed to keep propellers from cutting air lines, a constant fear. The folkloric hall features the *sandoúri*, *laoúto* and *gáida* beloved of local musicians, plus bread-making equipment and elaborate women's costumes.

The local, somewhat ambitiously titled **Archeological Museum** (closed for renovation), installed in a grand former residence of the Vouvalis family, is sworn by its longtime employees to be thoroughly haunted – not too surprising when you consider the House-of-Usher-esque family details. Nikolaos Vouvalis (1841–1918) made his fortune as the first Greek to export sponges overseas, and then procured a 14-year-old wife who was sent to the Ursulines in France for "finishing". Apparently the marriage was never consummated; Vouvalis's widow kept his corpse embalmed for years in the house, attempting to communicate with him through the aid of a medium summoned from London, until outraged local clergy took the remains away for interment in the crypt of a hillside chapel. Should the mansion ever reopen for guided tours, you're first shown the great man's office, then a room full of Paleolithic and Bronze Age troves from the island's various caves, and finally the upstairs dining room and salon, furnished in utterly over-the-top Second Empire style. A new wing was built in 2002 to house numerous, recent Roman and Byzantine finds, but again is not open at present.

Eating, drinking and nightlife

When **eating out**, the obvious strategy involves following the waterfront northeast past the Italian-built municipal "palace" to a line of fish tavernas and *ouzerí*s, where the local speciality is octopus croquettes, more tender than you'd expect. However, recent years have seen touts multiply, prices climb and quality dip here, such that you're better off altogether avoiding this "restaurant row", except perhaps *Rembetiko*, which has live music on Saturdays. Far and away the best seafood and Kalymnian specialities are found at *Taverna Pandelis*, tucked inconspicuously into a cul-de-sac behind the waterfront *Olympic Hotel*; this features daily, fresh-gathered shellfish like miniature oysters, *foúskes* and *kalógnomes*, plus wild scaly fish at reasonable prices. Excellent wood-fired pizzas are purveyed on the northwest quay, where *Imia* is the better of two rivals, while for an inexpensive (if limited-menu and not always very inspired) pre-ferry meal, *Navtikos Omilos* at the base of the ferry jetty is convenient. The cheap-and-cheerful local characters' *ouzerí* is *Kafenes* opposite the county "palace", where seafood, salads, the odd dip and bulk wine or *oúzo* are consumed to a soundtrack of loud Greek music. Sticky-cake fans will want to attend the traditional *Zaharoplastiki O Mihalaras* (premises near ferry jetty, and on "restaurant row" excellent for *kataïfi*, *baklavás* and *galaktoboúreko*, and worth supporting in the face of inroads made by the local outlet of ice-cream chain *Dhodhoni*.

Most night owls congregate at a half-dozen **cafés** concentrated at the first kink in the harbour quay, opposite the berthing place for the excursion *kaïkia*. Most popular of these is *Neon*, also with three **internet** terminals. Also worth a look-in is *Ai Mousai* ("The Muses"), a tearoom on the waterfront esplanade with a facade of Corinthian columns which, since its inception in 1904, has served as a local Greek culture-club and reading room, except for a decade or two when the Italians appropriated it. The summer **cinema**, Cine Oasis, operates just inland from *Ai Musai*, with a fairly sophisticated play-bill; after a month off from mid-September, it reopens as the winter Cine Splendid. Since the crash in local tourism, however, there are no longer any after-hours music clubs in Póthia.

Hóra and around

From Póthia, the island's main road leads northwest to its main beach resorts. The first place you come to after 1.2km is a castle of the Knights of St John, **Kástro Khryssoheriás** (unrestricted access), in the suburb of Mýli. Huddled inside the whitewashed battlements are some rock-cut Bronze Age tombs and a small monastery, whose usually locked church contains some battered frescoes. The castle's location permits wonderful views southeast over the town to Kós, and north towards Hóra and Péra Kástro.

The island's old capital, **HÓRA** (aka Horió), 1.5km further along the main road, is still a large village of three thousand or so inhabitants; it guards a critical pass in Kalymnian topography, focus of settlement in every era and perhaps the site of the main ancient town. Steep steps ascend from its highest easterly point to the walled precinct of the Byzantine citadel-town **Péra Kástro** (May–Oct daily 10am–2pm; tip to guide), appropriated by the Knights of St John and inhabited until late in the eighteenth century. Inside the imposing gate, the former heaps of rubble – result of a severe 1491 earthquake – are slowly being pieced together; a guided tour by the keeper visits five well-maintained, whitewashed chapels containing late medieval fresco fragments.

The basilicas

Some 200m past the turning for Árgos en route to Dhámos, you can detour left to visit two early Byzantine basilicas which are fairly representative, and the easiest to find, of a vast number on the island. Just as the main highway begins to descend, look for whitewashed steps leading over a stone wall to the immediately visible remains of **Khristós tís Ierousalím basilica**, supposedly built by Byzantine Emperor Arcadius during the late fourth century AD in gratitude for his deliverance from a storm off Kálymnos. The apse is fully preserved (if heavily scaffolded), and sections of marble flooring remain; both liberally incorporate masonry, some with Ancient Greek inscriptions, taken from a Hellenistic sanctuary of Apollo whose foundations lie just south, little else remaining above ground other than tumbled blocks. One field east, reached by a separate path from the road, are the larger, three-aisled but less impressive remains of the **Limniótissa basilica**; the east apse is the best-preserved area, and it would appear to have served as a chapel after the rest of the complex was destroyed during the seventh-century Arab raids.

"Brostá": west coast resorts

From the ridge-top basilicas beyond Hóra, the road dips into the pine- and eucalyptus-shaded valley of Dhámos, site of a Bronze Age settlement, en route

to the consecutive **beach resorts** of Kandoúni, Myrtiés and Massoúri. Islanders refer to these collectively as "*Brostá*" (Forward), the leading side of Kálymnos, as opposed to "*Píso*" (Behind), the Póthia area.

Kandoúni and Platý-Yialós

KANDOÚNI, with some 200m of brown, seaweed-strewn, hard-packed sand,
is effectively the shore annexe of the inland agricultural village of **Pánormos**
(aka Eliés), with lingering trappings of the vanished package-holiday industry
scattered between the two. The clientele has always consisted mostly of local
and other Greek holiday-makers, who keep summer villas here. The area is
unfortunately dominated by an abandoned eyesore of an illegal seven-storey
hotel dating from the junta era, which could benefit from some judiciously
placed dynamite.

Curiously, there is little **accommodation** overlooking the water except for
the package-dominated *Kantouni Beach Apartments* (☎22430 47982, ⓕ22430
47549; ❺). Of a slightly higher standard, just inland and lately rather less full of
tour clients, is the *Kalydna Island Hotel* (☎22430 47880, ⓕ22430 47190; ❻),
with fridges and bathtubs in the above-average-standard units; the best rooms
face the pool-garden. Another good inland choice, well north of Pánormos
in Kamári district on the ridge overlooking Myrtiés, is the family-run, rock
climbers' hangout *Hotel Kamari* (☎22430 47278, ⓔkamari@otenet.gr; ❷;
open all year). Cheerful rooms in the front building have sea views, but there
are no frills, such as a pool or central heating.

LINÁRIA, a smaller cove at the north end of the same bay, has better sand
and is separated from Kandoúni proper by a rock outcrop. Package allotments
permitting, you might **stay** at *Skopellos Studios* (☎22430 47155; ❷), on the
slope below the church. For **eating**, the best option is *Ouzeri Giannis/Ta
Linaria* on the shore, rebuilt after a 2003 landslide, with abundant portions of
grills and seafood. *To Steki tis Fanis*, serving out of an old mansion up on the
hillside, offers local specialities such as *mermizéli* (salad of greens, *kopanistí* and
barley rusks) and ample vegetarian starters, but overall quality suffers from too
many frozen ingredients being used in mains. Further inland on the main highway, just north of the roundabout, the rather gloomy-looking *Taverna Marinos*
is well regarded for its standard *mayireftá* and grills.

For more abundant **sea-view accommodation**, take the side road to
PLATÝ-YIALÓS, where, among a handful of choices for staying on spec,
backpackers' favourite is the multilingual, welcoming Vavoulas family's *Pension
Plati Gialos* (☎ & ⓕ22430 47029, ⓦwww.pension-plati-gialos.de), actually
overlooking Linária, with spacious balconies, mosquito nets and the breakfast
terrace; choose between basic, fan-equipped rooms (❷) or two apartments for
four (❹). Alternatives are *Mary-Popi Studios* (☎22430 47619; ❷), simple but
roomy units at the end of a cul-de-sac – the ground-floor ones are cheapest
and coolest in summer – and *Studios Mousselis* (☎22430 47757; ❸), which
usually has a vacancy, and helpful management. The sandy **beach** itself, though
a bit shorter than Kandoúni, is arguably the best on the island: cleaner than
its southern neighbours, more secluded, and scenically situated opposite Ayía
Kyriakí islet. Those after even more privacy can hunt out tiny, foot-access-only
coves in the direction of Melitsahás. A lone **taverna** (*Kyma*) at the base of the
cliff behind Platý-Yialós will do nicely for simple, inexpensive lunches or a
sunset drink (it closes shortly after).

For a pleasant walk in the area, best towards sunset, take the obvious path
from below the large monastery of Stavroú at Kandoúni to the little monastery

of **Ayía Fotiní** (45min each way), tucked under cliffs towards the westernmost point of the island.

Myrtiés, Massoúri and Armeós

The main road, descending in zigzags, finally meets the sea again 8km from Póthia at **MYRTIÉS**, which shares Kálymnos' dwindling tourist trade with **MASSOÚRI** and **ARMEÓS**, 1km and 2km respectively to the north but reached by an upper bypass road, part of a giant, circular one-way system. The recent implosion of Kalymnian tourism is evident in huge numbers of premises boarded up and/or for sale, with many of their erstwhile proprietors gone to northern Europe to seek work.

Possibly this coast's most appealing feature is its position opposite the evocatively shaped islet of Télendhos (see below), which frames some of the more dramatic sunsets in Greece. It's also possible to go from Myrtiés directly to Léros aboard the daily early-afternoon *kaïki* (see "Travel details", p.288). The **beach** at Myrtiés is narrow, pebbly and cramped by development, though it does improve to nearly the same standard as Platý-Yialós as you approach Massoúri. The closest really good beach to Myrtiés lies 500m south, at **Melitsahás** cove, where *Maria's Studios* (T22430 48135 or 693 79 87 403, Wwww .kalymnos-holidays.com/mariasstudios/; ❷), up at the top of the grade, is one of the few places to **stay** that is not block-booked. The spacious units fit three, the furnishings including small ovens. By far the best local **taverna**, with a partly local clientele, overlooks the fishing anchorage; here *Iy Dhrossia* (aka *Andonis*, open all year) is tops for oysters, lobster and shrimp as well as scaly fish at affordable rates. For cultural stimulation, the basilica of **Áyios Ioánnis Melitsahá** stands just up the hill, above the development; the easiest way there is along a signposted track, starting opposite the *Hotel Kamari*.

As for other **accommodation** in the area, it's now generally a buyer's market, except when the rock climbers are around. Worthy places to try include the *Oasis Hotel*, on the landward side of the road in Massoúri (T22430 47572, Esponga@klm.forthnet.gr; ❸), with large balconies; *Avra Studios* at the far north end of Massoúri (T22430 48511; ❸), on the seaward side of the road, with a small pool; or the *Galini Studios* in Armeós (T22430 47193, Egalinistudios@in.gr; ❸), sea-view, white-tile-and-pine units with a terrace-garden.

Quality choices for **eating out** are by contrast starkly limited; you're best off continuing to Armeós, where friendly *Tsopanakos* (open all year) has fresh meat and cheese from island-grazed goats, for example prepared as *moúri* (goat or lamb baked in a clay pot with rice and chopped liver), along with the usual grills and appetizers.

Scooters and **motorbikes** are available locally from Lakis (T22430 48039), while Avis has a branch in Myrtiés (T22430 47430), doing bikes as well as cars.

Télendhos islet

The trip across the strait to the striking, volcanic **islet of Télendhos** is arguably the best reason to come to Myrtiés; little boats shuttle to and fro constantly throughout the day and late into the night. According to local legend, the mountain of Télendhos is a petrified princess, gazing out to sea after her errant lover; the woman's-head profile is most evident at dusk, before the famous sunsets over the islet and straits. The hardly less pedestrian geological explanation has Télendhos sundered from Kálymnos by a cataclysmic earthquake in 554 AD; extensive traces of a submerged town are said to lie at the bottom of the strait, at a depth of sixteen fathoms.

Home to about fifteen permanent inhabitants, once engaged solely in fishing, Télendhos is car-free and thus blissfully tranquil, though even here increasing numbers of brick-and-concrete constructions are sprouting up, and tourism has arrived in a modest way. As on the main island, early Byzantine ruins are thick on the ground: there's the ruined, three-aisled sixth-century basilica of **Áyios Vassílios** just north of the port, and an even vaster basilica of the same design and vintage, **Ayía Triádha**, excavated only in 1997, at the top of the drop down to Hokhlakás beach (see below). Near Áyios Vassílios, there are also a number of cisterns, early Christian tombs and a baths complex to explore. For the more ambitious, two-hour outing takes in the basilica and ruined, fortified Byzantine village of **Áyios Konstandínos** ninety minutes' uphill hike to the north. Initially, follow the coastal trail for about half an hour past the three small beaches cited below – look for white paint splodges with blue in the middle – before turning sharply left just before another rocky spur descending into the sea. Here the scrambling begins, and it's another thirty minutes up to the chapel. A longer but slightly easier method involves continuing until you intersect the rough path up from the little shore chapel of Aï Yiórgis; this is the way the islanders go up for the annual festival on May 21.

Practicalities

There are about eight places to **eat** and a roughly equal number of **accommodation** options, most (but not all) linked to the tavernas. Establishments that get uniformly positive reviews include *Barba Stathis* taverna en route to Hokhlakás, tops for *mayireftá*; *Pension Studios Rita* (℡22430 47914, ℻22430 47927; ❷), rooms and renovated-house studios managed by the namesake snack-bar/café; *Rinio Studios* (℡22430 23851; ❸) just inland, built in 2002 to a high standard; the simple but en-suite rooms above *Zorba's* (℡22430 48660; ❶), with slightly pricey but excellent fresh squid and goat, or, north beyond Áyios Vassílios, *Plaka* (good for grilled, locally grazed meat) and the Greek-Australian-run *On the Rocks*. This last combines the functions of superbly appointed rooms with double glazing, mosquito nets and so on (℡22430 48260, ⓦwww.telendos.com/otr; ❸), full-service taverna with lovely home-made desserts (though the main courses are rather bland), and a bar that's the heart and soul of local **nightlife**. At one corner of the premises you can visit yet another Byzantine monument, the chapel of **Áyios Harálambos**, occupying a former Byzantine bath. If you want more (relative) luxury on Télendhos, there's just the *Hotel Porto Potha* (℡22430 47321, ℮portopotha@klm.forthnet.gr; ❸), set rather bleakly at the very edge of things, but with a large pool and friendly managing family.

A ten-minute walk west along a well-signposted, improved path, past *Zorba's* and *Barba Stathis*, leads over the ridge to scenic if exposed **Hokhlakás** beach and its double bay, with sunbeds for rent and above-average cleanliness unless the west wind's been up. There's another, sunbed-free cove about ten minutes beyond, towards the rubbish tip. Following instead the coast north from *On the Rocks* brings you to three smaller, more secluded beaches: **Pláka** (with sunbeds), **Pótha** and "**Paradise**" (nudist).

Northern Kálymnos

The nearly sheer cliffs of northern Kálymnos (and Télendhos) are an irresistible magnet for dedicated **big-wall climbers** from Greece, Germany, Austria, Switzerland, France and Britain. If you're in the international climbing fraternity, these formations probably need no introduction; even if not, you can't help but notice the numerous inscribed columns with sketched-out routes from Armeós north. Two specialist shops, one in Massoúri and one in Armeós, sell all the necessary equipment for tackling the palisades. For further information, consult ⓦwww.kalymnos-isl.gr/climb.

Some 5km beyond Massoúri, **ARYINÓNDA** has a clean pebble beach with sunbeds, flanked by a single **rooms** outfit (☎22430 40000; ❶), with a friendly proprietor, and a pair of beach **tavernas**. It is also the trailhead for the spectacular trans-island walk to Vathý (see overleaf). **SKÁLIA**, 3km further, has an eponymous **cave** that's less famous than the one at Kefála (see p.287); ask at the roadside kiosk for a guide, as you won't find it unaided. Also at the kiosk, a steep track descends to the cemetery – and a lovely, protected all-sand **beach** about 70m long.

Just past Skália, a very rough dirt track zigzags east over the ridge some 5km to the popular yacht anchorage of **Paliónissos**, more usually visited by boat excursion from Vathý (see p.328). It's a chore to reach on an ordinary scooter, and many leave these up on the pass by the church and finish the journey on the cairned, blue-paint-dotted trail beginning opposite. However you arrive, there's a ten-minute final walk from the track's end to the coarse-shingle, ninety-metre beach here, threading through the little eponymous hamlet (population five); the only facility is Nikolaos Makarounas' **taverna** *Paradise* (all day school hols, otherwise supper and weekends), something of a cult destination for yachties. **Sikáti** bay, clearly visible to the left (north) of the zigzag road down from the saddle, is sandy but exposed and thus prone to washed-up debris.

The end of the paved road is **EMBORIÓS**, 24km from the port. If the once-daily bus service doesn't suit, there is usually a shuttle boat from Myrtiés at 10am (returning at 4pm). Emboriós offers a gravel-and-sand beach, which improves as you walk west, **accommodation** and a number of **tavernas**, including the long-running *Harry's Paradise*, with attached, air-conditioned garden apartments (☎22430 40061; ❷) in bland white-and-pine decor. The conspicuous tavernas down by the jetty tend to give poor value for money.

One cove beyond Emboriós lies goat-patrolled **Asprokykliá** beach, much the same quality as Emboriós'. A dirt track leads high above the beach to *Barba Nikolas*, which (while looking more like a **bar** than a **taverna**) actually does reasonable meals on its terrace affording striking views south over a landscape of sea, islets and mountains.

Beyond Emboriós there's another cave, **Kolonóstylos**, with column-like formations after which it's named ("Column-Pillar" in Greek), but of more compelling interest for many are the remote beaches in the island's far northwest. Follow the rough dirt track above Asprokykliá to the isthmus by the fish farm, then walk fifteen minutes north on a combination of path and abandoned track to **Aptíki**, a smallish but perfectly formed pea-gravel cove; there are other smaller ones en route in the unlikely event it's overcrowded. There's World War II-vintage debris to see when snorkelling, and perhaps moray eels or skates.

Vathýs fjord and valley

Heading east from Póthia, excursions seem initially unpromising, if not down-right grim; along the first 4km the road passes Póthia's main boatyard, a power plant, three gasworks, two quarries and the local rubbish dump. None of this prepares you for a sudden bend in the road and the dramatic view over Vathýs, a sharp descent below, whose colour provides a startling contrast to the mineral grey and orange elsewhere on Kálymnos. This long, fertile valley, carpeted with orange and tangerine groves, seems a continuation of the cobalt-blue fjord that penetrates the landscape here. A veritable maze of tracks, drives and lanes threads through these orchards, where numerous "For sale" signs suggest that citrus cultivation is no longer as profitable as it was.

Rína

At the little port of **RÍNA**, 8km from Póthia, the modern chapels of Anástasi (south) and Ayía Iríni (north) flanking the head of the fjord sit amidst the ruins of still more Byzantine basilicas – neither very noteworthy but demonstrating the antiquity of settlement here. Near the Anástasi chapel you'll find the best **accommodation** option, the helpful *Rooms Manolis* (☎22430 41300; ❶), simple but en suite and with sweeping views, set in landscaped terraces accessed by a lane behind *The Harbors* taverna; alternatively there's the *Hotel Galini* (☎22430 31241; ❷), overlooking the boatyard. Behind the *Galini*, brack-ish springs feed a pool haunted by huge fish, before draining to the port.

Some of the several **tavernas** are pricier than you'd expect, owing to patron-age from the numerous yachts and excursion boats that call here; the best choice, with shambolic service but good grilled fish, is *The Harbors*, first place on the right at the road's end.

The steep-sided inlet has no beach to speak of; people dive from the lido on the far south side of the quay, where yachts moor. The closest strand, about 3km back towards Póthia, is **Aktí**, a functional pebble beach with sunbeds and a single snack-bar, reached by a steep cement driveway. Boat excursions from Rína visit the stalactite cave of **Dhaskalió**, out by the fjord mouth and inhabited in Neolithic times, as well as the remote northeast-coast beaches of **Almyrés**, **Dhrasónda** and **Pezónda** (this last also reachable overland, see p.286).

Hikes to and from Vathýs valley

For **walkers**, the lush Vathýs valley immediately behind Rína is the focus of two popular hikes which provide a good transect of the island; however, they pass through the valley considerably inland from Rína. Póthia–Vathýs is easy enough and a favourite outing, Aryinónda–Vathýs a bit more challenging; they can of course be linked back-to-back to make a full day's walking, but attention must be paid to choosing your direction of march – and to public transport links at your destination. You also need to carry at least one, preferably two, litres of water per person, and a sunhat, as there's no water or shade away from the valley floor.

Probably the most sensible strategy would be to do the Póthia–Rína leg, break for lunch, and then take a bus or walk as far as Metóhi, where the path from Aryinónda becomes evident. At the latter you would probably have time for a well-deserved swim before catching the late-afternoon bus from Emboriós back to town. If for any reason this was not forthcoming, you'd have to continue 5km further on foot to Armeós to pick up more regular transport.

Póthia to Vathýs valley

The hike from **Póthia to Plátanos** in the Vathýs valley follows the old *kalderími* used in the days before the coastal road existed. Begin behind the old Archeological Museum and *Villa Themelina* hotel, by the church of Ayía Triádha with its prominent wall sundial; red paint splodges guide you through the highest-positioned houses. Climb sharply in zigzags, past the presumed acropolis of ancient Pothaia, until the town slips out of sight and the cobbled way heads off at a more gentle grade into the bare mountains. Kós and Níssyros are spread out behind you and, in autumn, phalanxes of white sea squill provide the only colour. An hour's walk along, you reach the high point of the route, a 350-metre-elevation pass traversed by power lines, from where it's some forty minutes' descent to the edge of Vathýs' cultivated zone. (If you're following the itinerary in reverse, look for a fenced-in grove of young olives just above two water cisterns in a pipeline system, skimmed by power lines; eight stray, elderly olive trees on the hillside above mark the start of the uphill path proper – difficult to find if you're coming in this direction.)

Descending, the path becomes track by the olives and forces you east and even slightly uphill briefly before turning to cement drive by the highest dwellings. Two hours out of Póthia you hit a cement lane on the valley floor in the Ayía Triádha district of Plátanos hamlet; turn right, but collect water if necessary from the sunken potable spring under the namesake plane tree (*plátanos*) across the road. Another half-hour of unavoidable road-walking brings you to Rína, where, if you've started early enough, you should have enough time for lunch before catching an early-afternoon bus back to Póthia.

Aryinónda to Vathýs valley

An itinerary from **Aryinónda to Metóhi** in the Vathýs valley reverses our recommendation, but is slightly easier to follow. Don't believe sources which show the route emerging at Styménia, and be aware that the local authorities have begun bulldozing a road from just behind the beach to somewhere in the Vathýs valley, which may disrupt parts of the trail.

In Aryinónda, the route starts opposite the cistern-spring in the cemented-over car-park and bus-stop area on the inland side of the road. Head southeast, prompted by a red paint-dot on a power pole, to find the start of the true path. Thereafter, occasional blue paint splodges guide you up terraces and briefly into a defile where the path is rough, with scree underfoot. You stay fairly high up the south flank of the ravine here, going east-southeast, except for one point where you dip down to cross the bed of a side-canyon. Half an hour along, you pass an abandoned hamlet graced by a palm tree; at the 45-minute mark, power lines go overhead; and an hour out, where low junipers tuft the landscape, you attain a gentle saddle – probably where the new road will collide with the route. Some fifteen minutes beyond here, you'll have your first views over Pezónda bay; the trail is fainter now, but resist the temptation to descend – paths towards the sea are difficult to nonexistent. The proper way maintains altitude and soon becomes more distinct amidst the vegetation, curling to negotiate the head of a shallow canyon draining to Pezónda.

About thirty minutes from the first saddle, you'll reach a second, more abrupt pass with a cistern (dry) fed by a concrete apron, and your first good views into the Vathýs valley. Ignore paths going straight ahead – this is a rough traverse to the neighbourhood of Kyrá Psilí – and instead begin the descent south down the obvious ravine here towards Metóhi. There are paths on either bank, but (always assuming the new road does not obliterate it) the one along the left (east) side is clearer and, with its patches of well-engineered revetment, appears to have been the main one in the old days. About two hours from Aryinónda, you meet the first, highest buildings of Metóhi, including little Áyios Dhimítrios church, whose courtyard provides some shade but no cistern water. Continue down to the valley-floor road and turn left to reach Rína after another hour (for three walking hours in total); en route you will notice extensive stretches of Hellenistic fortification wall, north of the valley floor.

North of Vathýs: Pezónda and Kyrá Psilí

For hikers who prefer out-and-back itineraries, these make excellent destinations, though you'll benefit from having a scooter or bike at first. From Metóhi in the Vathý valley floor, take two-wheelers up the signed, steep cement track to the visible saddle, where it ends beside a bunker-like chapel with a rain cistern (often containing water). Just beyond, the paths to Pezónda bay (down and left) and Kyrá Psilí monastery (straight and up) are indicated by rustic wooden placards.

For the beach, there's an initial ten-minute drop to a ravine bed; once there bear left (northwest) through a livestock pen, gated at each end. Beyond the pen, don't continue further down the ravine centre – the proper path goes up slightly onto the true right (northeast) bank of the canyon, marked by sporadic cairns. Just under half an hour along, you rejoin the now-narrow streambed, and stay in it for a remaining twenty minutes to the scenic fjord of **Pezónda**. Alas, the fine-gravel beach is apt to be dirty with seaborne litter and tar (the bay opens north) and at summer weekends at least you may not even have the consolation of solitude – some family from town has likely got there first on a boat. Snorkelling in the shallows, you'll see a phenomenal amount of rusty World War II debris: shell casings and tips, a bomb, even a giant mine.

Kyrá Psilí hovers tantalizingly in view for much of the fifty-minute return trip from Pezónda to the wooden placards. From there, it's a maximum half-hour round-trip walk to this fortified monastery and *paniyíri* venue (always open), which only sees use on August 15. There's not much else here other than a series of chapels tucked into grottoes of the overhang in the 609-metre mountain above, the second highest on Kálymnos. Accordingly there are superb views northwest at dusk as far as Ikaría and Mount Kérkis on Sámos, taking in intervening islands like Arkí and Foúrni. Incidentally, the name Kyrá Psilí ("The Tall Lady") has nothing to do with the altitude but is an epithet of the Virgin inherited from her predecessors, Aphrodite and Cybele.

Southwestern Kálymnos

Climbing soutwest out of Póthia towards Áyios Sávvas monastery, the most worthwhile halt is the privately run "**Folklore Museum–Traditional House of Kálymnos**" (daily 9am–9pm; €1.50), a treasure trove of old-time furnishings and costumes. Some 6km southwest of Póthia, the small bay of **Vlyhádhia** is reached via the nondescript village of Vothýni, from which a narrow ravine leads down to the sea. The **beach** here, divided into two separate coves (one sand, one shingle), is too unsecluded and often litter-strewn to justify a special trip, and the bay is frankly sumpy; it's mostly islanders who frequent it and two lacklustre shoreline tavernas, at weekends. Indeed, foreigners seem to be specifically unwelcome here: a bigoted hermit occupies a *monastiráki* at one end of the beach, emblazoned with placards claiming the place for Orthodox Christians and anathematizing the topless heterodox heathens – he has also blotted out all Roman-alphabet road signs in the area.

Only if you're interested in **scuba** is the Vlyhádhia area worth a detour, as it's one of the limited number of legal diving areas in Greece. Stavros Valsamidhes, the local divemaster, has also assembled an impressive **Museum of Submarine Finds** (Mon–Sat 9am–7pm, Sun 10am–2pm; free), which, in addition to masses of sponges and shells, offers a reconstructed ancient wreck with amphorae and World War II debris. Depending on your ability, dives (arrange in advance on ☏ 22430 50662) may visit ancient wrecks *in situ*, as well as seal caves.

Kefála cave and beyond

Póthia-based *kaïkia* make well-publicized excursions to **Kefála cave**, a little to the west of Vlyhádhia. You have to walk thirty minutes from where the boats dock, but the vividly coloured formations are ample reward. The cave was inhabited before recorded history, and later served as a sanctuary of Zeus (who is fancifully identified with a particularly imposing stalagmite in the biggest of six chambers).

The excursion *kaïkia* also usually schedule a stop at **Nerá** islet, out beyond the mouth of Vlyhádhia bay; there's a **monastery** of Timíou Stavroú (festival Sept 14), and a **taverna** that's apt to make a better fist of lunch than anything at Vlyhádhia.

Kefála can lately also be reached via a broad dirt track from the inland monastery of Ayía Ekateríni, itself just west of Vothýni by paved road. From Kefála

Greek script table

Kálymnos	Κάλυμνος	ΚΑΛΥΜΝΟΣ
Ayía Ekateríni	Αγία Αικατερίνη	ΑΓΙΑ ΑΙΚΑΤΕΡΙΝΗ
Aktí	Ακτή	ΑΚΤΗ
Almyrés	Αλμυρές	ΑΛΜΥΡΕΣ
Aptíki	Απτήκι	ΑΠΤΗΚΙ
Aryinónda	Αργυνώντα	ΑΡΓΥΝΩΝΤΑ
Dhaskalió	Δασκαλειό	ΔΑΣΚΑΛΕΙΟ
Dhrasónda	Δρασόντα	ΔΡΑΣΟΝΤΑ
Eliés	Ελιές	ΕΛΙΕΣ
Emboriós	Εμπορειός	ΕΜΠΟΡΕΙΟΣ
Hóra	Χώρα	ΧΩΡΑ
Horió	Χωριό	ΧΩΡΙΟ
Kandoúni	Καντούνι	ΚΑΝΤΟΥΝΙ
Kástro	Κάστρο	ΚΑΣΤΡΟ
Khryssoheriás	Χρυσοχεριάς	ΧΡΥΣΟΧΕΡΙΑΣ
Kefála	Κεφάλα	ΚΕΦΑΛΑ
Kolonóstylos	Κολονόστυλος	ΚΟΛΟΝΟΣΤΥΛΟΣ
Kyrá Psilí	Κυρά Ψηλή	ΚΥΡΑ ΨΗΛΗ
Massoúri	Μασούρι	ΜΑΣΟΥΡΙ
Melitsahás	Μελιτσαχάς	ΜΕΛΙΤΣΑΧΑΣ
Metóhi	Μετόχι	ΜΕΤΟΧΙ
Myrtiés	Μυρτιές	ΜΥΡΤΙΕΣ
Paliónissos	Παλιόνησος	ΠΑΛΙΟΝΗΣΟΣ
Pánormos	Πάνορμος	ΠΑΝΟΡΜΟΣ
Pezónda	Πεζόντα	ΠΕΖΟΝΤΑ
Plátanos	Πλάτανος	ΠΛΑΤΑΝΟΣ
Platý-Yialós	Πλατύ-Γιαλός	ΠΛΑΤΥ-ΓΙΑΛΟΣ
Póthia	Πόθια	ΠΟΘΙΑ
Rína	Ρίνα	ΡΙΝΑ
Skália	Σκάλια	ΣΚΑΛΙΑ
Télendhos	Τέλενδος	ΤΕΛΕΝΔΟΣ
Vathýs	Βαθύς	ΒΑΘΥΣ
Vlyhádhia	Βλυχάδια	ΒΛΥΧΑΔΙΑ
Vothýni	Βοθύνοι	ΒΟΘΥΝΟΙ

it's possible to make an enjoyable trail-trek across the far southwest of the island. First the south-coast path leads past the firmly closed Áyios Andhréas monastery ("*Óhi tourismós stá monastíria*/no tourism in monasteries" says the sign – the work of the Vlyhádhia hermit), before threading high above the sea, through a boulder-field below impressive cliffs. Next you emerge on a spectacular view over Pithári bay and its remote monastery, with an outsize jetty making it resemble some Bond villain's hideout. From here, a short path inland through a narrow gorge takes you up to the more welcoming monastery of Áyios Konstandínos, in the notch overlooking the plateau of Árgos, which you reach some two hours from Ayía Ekateríni.

Kálymnos travel details

Island transport

Buses

Póthia to: Emboriós (1 daily at most in season); Kandoúni (5 daily 10am–3.30pm); Myrtiés–Massoúri–Arméos (15 daily on the hour 7am–10pm); Platý–Yialós (2–4 daily); Vathý (4 daily Mon–Sat, 3 daily Sun); Vlyhádhia (5 daily Mon–Sat, 4 daily Sun).
NB Above frequencies are for the period mid-June to mid-Sept only – in spring or autumn, only the Myrtiés–Massoúri–Arméos line functions, with reduced frequency (around 8 daily).

Inter-island transport

Kaïkia and excursion boats

Póthia to: Psérimos (1 daily; 1hr 15min journey; €6 each way).
Myrtiés to: Xirókambos, Léros (1 daily at 1pm); Télendhos (every 10–30min from dawn till long after dark; €1.50 single).

Small ferries

Kálymnos to: Kós (Mastihári; 3–4 daily, 7am–8pm or 11pm, on ANEM).
NB ANEM ferries to Kós have limited space for vehicles on their craft – book in advance at peak season (☎22430 22909).

Large ferries

Kálymnos to: Agathoníssi (4 weekly on NK; 6hr); Astypálea (2 weekly on GA, 3 weekly on NK; 2hr 30min–3hr 15min); Kós (1 daily on GA; 1hr 15min); Léros (1 daily on GA, 4 weekly on NK; 1hr–1hr 15min); Níssyros (2 weekly on GA; 2hr 45min); Pátmos (1 daily on GA, 4 weekly on NK; 3hr–3hr 30min); Pireás (1 daily on GA; 12hr); Rhodes (1 daily on GA; 5–8hr); Sámos–Pythagório (4 weekly on NK; 7hr 30min); Sými (2 weekly on GA 5hr 30min–6hr 30min); Tílos (2 weekly on GA; 4hr).

NB To simplify the above list, one important sailing has been omitted – the weekly LANE departures, northbound for Sámos, Híos, Lésvos, Mytilíni and Alexandhroúpoli, then southbound a day or so later for Rhodes (long layover there possible), Hálki, Kárpathos, Kássos and Crete.

Catamaran

Kálymnos to: Kós, Léros, Rhodes (6–7 weekly); Lipsí, Pátmos (3–4 weekly); Sými (2–3 weekly).

Hydrofoils

Kálymnos to: Agathoníssi (1 weekly on KR; 5hr 45min); Foúrni (2 weekly on KR; 3hr 15min); Ikaría (2 weekly on KR; 2hr 45min); Kós (5–7 weekly on KR; 45min); Léros (5–7 weekly on KR; 45min); Lipsí (5–7 weekly on KR; 1hr 15min); Pátmos (5–7 weekly on KR; 1hr 45min); Sámos-Pythagório (5–7 weekly on KR; 3hr–4hr 15min).

Léros

Léros is so indented with deep, sheltered anchorages that, between 1923 and 1948, it harboured – in turn – the entire Italian, German, and British

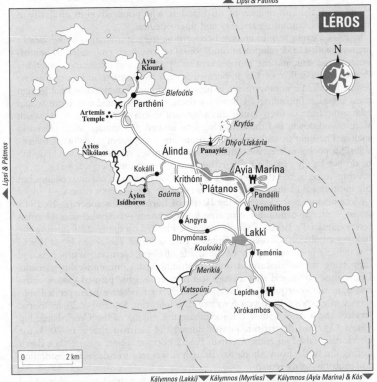

Mediterranean **fleets**. A contemporary echo of this are enormous dry docks and marinas for yachts at Parthéni, Lakkí and Teménia. Unfortunately, many of these magnificent fjords and bays seem to absorb rather than reflect light, and the island's fertile valleys and tufts of hillside greenery can seem scraggy and unkempt when compared to the crisp lines of its more barren neighbours. These characteristics, plus Léros' lack of spectacularly good beaches, meant that until the late 1980s just a few thousand foreigners (mostly Italians who grew up on the island), and not many more Greeks, came to visit each August.

Such a pattern is now history, with German, Dutch, Scandinavian and British package-tour operators alternating by the year in "discovering" Léros and the company of islanders unjaded by mass tourism. Foreign visitor numbers have, however, levelled off or even fallen since the millennium, with change unlikely until and unless the tiny airport is expanded to accommodate jets – at present it only takes fifty-seater ATR-42s.

Until recently Léros didn't strenuously encourage tourism; various **prisons and sanitariums** dominated the Lerian economy from the 1950s onward, directly or indirectly employing about a third of the population of eight thousand. During the junta era, the island hosted a notorious detention centre at Parthéni, and for over four decades several mental hospitals served as warehouses for many of Greece's more intractable psychiatric cases and mentally handicapped children. The island's domestic image problem was compounded by its name, the butt of jokes by off-islanders, who pounced on its similarity to the word *lerá*, connoting rascality and unsavouriness.

In 1989, a major scandal emerged concerning the administration of the various asylums, with EU development funds found to have been embezzled by administrators and staff, and the inmates kept in degrading and inhumane conditions. A subsequent influx of EU inspectors, foreign psychiatrists and extra funding resulted in drastic improvements in patient treatment, though sensational foreign press coverage (including a Channel 4 documentary) ensured that Léros would take some time in overcoming this additional stigma. In 1995 the worst wards were closed down, and the remaining six-hundred-plus inmates were placed in sheltered housing around the island, farming and engaging in other "work internships" for pocket money; the remaining seven hundred carers now haven't enough to do but legally can't be made redundant. Some of the slack was taken up by tourism, some by the 1999 opening of one of Greece's main nursing colleges, but the institutional identity is not nearly as pervasive as you might expect.

More obvious is the legacy of the **Battle of Léros** on November 12–16, 1943, when – after two months of intense bombardment – overwhelming German forces displaced a British division which had landed on the island following the Italian capitulation. Churchill devoted a page or so of *The Second World War* to this debacle in a mini-reprise of the Battle of Crete, German paratroopers and supporting aircraft descended on an outnumbered Commonwealth garrison. Bomb nose cones and shell casings still turn up as gaily painted garden ornaments in the courtyards of churches and tavernas, or have been pressed into service as gateposts. Each year for three days following September 26, memorial services and a naval festival commemorate the sinking of the Greek battleship *Queen Olga* and the British *Intrepid* during the German attack. In 2003, the Greek navy raised an entire German JU-52 troop-transport aircraft, shot down during the battle, from Álinda bay, though it was sent to Athens for restoration and probably won't return.

Unusually for a small island, Léros has abundant ground water, channelled into cisterns at several points (all but one, alas, not currently potable). A giant dam built by the airport proved defective from the start, and has never filled. All this, plus marshy ground staked with eucalyptus trees planted by the Italians, make for a horrendously active mosquito contingent, so come prepared. Some sort of squishy-rubber beach shoes are recommended too, as entry to the sea can often be over foot-bruising rocks.

Léros is sufficiently compact for the energetic to walk around, but there is a reasonably reliable bus service, plus several places renting out motor- and mountain bikes, of which Motoland (outlets in Pandélli, ☎22470 24103, and Álinda, ☎22470 24584) has proven reliable on several occasions. The island is hilly enough to make motorbikes a better bet, though the reasonably fit could manage with just a mountain bike between Álinda and Lakkí.

The south: Lakkí to Xirókambos

All medium-sized and large **ferries** arrive at the main port of **LAKKÍ**, designed from scratch during 1933–38 by R. Petracco and A. Bernabiti as a model town to house 7500 civilian dependents of an adjacent Italian naval base, which accounts for the extraordinary, overdesigned look of the place. Boulevards far too wide for today's paltry amount of traffic are lined with some marvellous Rationalist edifices (see box), including a round-fronted cinema

Italian architecture in the Dodecanese

The three-decade-plus Italian tenure in the Dodecanese left behind a significant architectural heritage, which has only recently begun to be appreciated. Many of these structures were long allowed to deteriorate if not actually abandoned, this neglect apparently a deliberate policy of the Greeks who would just as soon forget the entire Italian legacy, but since the late 1990s maintenance work on the monuments has been fitfully undertaken.

These buildings are often erroneously dubbed "Art Deco"; while some certainly contain elements of that school, they are properly classed as **Rationalist** (or, in the case of Léros, Stream Line Modern). This drew on various post-World-War I architectural, artistic and political trends in vogue across Europe, particularly its immediate predecessor, Novecento (a sort of Neoclassicism), the collectivist ideologies of the time, and the paintings of Giorgio de Chirico. Surviving examples of this design can still be found in places as disparate as Moscow or London (underground stations and blocks of flats), Los Angeles (apartment buildings) and Ethiopia (cinemas), as well as in Italy and Greece.

Italy initially attempted – under the governorship of Mario Lago (1924–36) – to create a hybrid of Rationalist style and local vernacular elements in the Dodecanese, both real and semi-mythical, alluding to a supposed generic "Mediterranean-ness". Every Italian-claimed island had at least one new structure in this "protectorate" style, usually the gendarme station, post office, covered market or governor's mansion, but only on the most populous or strategic islands of Rhodes, Kós, Kálymnos and Léros were plans drawn up for sweeping urban reordering according to the above principles – plus the evolving imperatives of Fascism. During the years cited, the primary architects commissioned to design both the new town-plans of Rhodes, Léros and Kós, plus individual monuments there and on Kálymnos, were Florestano di Fausto, Pietro Lombardi, A. Bernabiti, R. Petracco and Mario Paolini.

The term of office of Cesare Maria de Vecchi (1936–41), second governor of the Dodecanese, was marked by an intensification of Fascist imperial ideology, an increased reference to the Latin heritage of the islands (ie the Romans and their purported successors, the Knights) and the replacement of the "protectorate" style with that of the "conqueror". This involved so-called "purification", the stripping of many public buildings in Rhodes (though not, curiously, in Kós) of their orientalist ornamentation, its replacement with a cladding of porous stone to match medieval buildings in the old town, plus a monumental severity – blending Neoclassicism and modernism – and rigid symmetry to match various institutional buildings (especially Fascist Party headquarters) and public squares across Italy.

(now abandoned), the primary and secondary schools, an underused shopping centre with a round atrium, plus the defunct Leros Palace Hotel. The number of vacant central shopfronts accentuates the air of decline, as most businesses prefer to occupy premises on the outskirts.

Buses don't meet ferries; instead, **taxis** charge set fares to standard destinations (but if you walk a few hundred metres beyond the jetty, you'll get cheaper rates at the official rank). If you want to ride off immediately on a **rented scooter/car**, Kostas Koumoulis (T 22470 22330) on the quay can oblige. Few people stay willingly at the handful of moribund **hotels** in Lakkí, preferring to head straight for Vromólithos, Pandélli or Álinda. If you do get stuck here, the most inspiring choices are the *Miramare* (T 22470 22053, F 22470 22469; ❸), with bay views over a (currently) vacant lot, or the *Katerina* further inland (T 22470 22460, F 22470 23038; ❸), which also keeps studios in Álinda and a shuttle van to get you there. There's also a **post office** inland, and several **banks** offer ATMs. Gribilos (☎22470 24000, branch in Plátanos) is the *Nissos Kalymnos* agent, Leros Travel (☎22470 22154) the GA rep, while Aegean Travel (☎22470 26000) handles Blue Star **ferries**. The best spot to wait for a boat is not the lugubrious jetty **café**, but either *Kafeteria Morano* a bit outside, or *Marina* opposite the yacht anchorage, also the most reliable surviving **taverna**.

Lakkí Bay with its stony shoreline will not appeal to many; the nearest approximation of a beach, still too close to the ferry jetty for most tastes, is sand-and-gravel **Koulóuki**, 500m west, supporting a seasonal taverna and ample trees for shade. You can carry on for a kilometre or so to **Merikiá**, a slight improvement, also with two tavernas. A progressively rougher dirt track continues towards **Katsóuni** bay and its fish-farm; en route, side tracks lead to two pleasant, swimmable coves.

Xirókambos and Lepídha

Nearly 5km from Lakkí in the far south of the island, **XIRÓKAMBOS** is the point of departure for the early-morning *kaïki* to Myrtiés on Kálymnos (it returns in the afternoon). Although billed as a resort, it's essentially a fishing port where people also happen to swim – the poor-to-mediocre beach improves as you head west. Alternatively, there are minuscule, hard-to-reach coves below the coastal track heading southeast. High-standard **accommodation** is available at the *Hotel Efstathia* (☎22470 24099, ⓕ22470 24199; ❹; May–Sept), actually studio apartments with huge, well-furnished doubles as well as family fourplexes, plus a large pool. You've a choice of three **tavernas** at the east end of things, where the road hits the shore.

The village of **LEPÍDHA**, 750m back up the road to Lakkí, also has its own small **castle**; the access road starts 200m north of the campsite (see below). You visit more for simultaneous views over Lakkí and Xirókambos than for the scanty patches of early Christian mosaics in front of the modern chapel within the castle, or ancient masonry foundations behind.

The **campsite** itself, shaded by over two hundred olive trees (☎22470 23372; late May to early Oct), also doubles as headquarters of one of the better **scuba-diving** outfits in the Aegean, Panos Diving Club (☎694 42 38 490, ⓔdivingleros@hotmail.com). They explore Leros' wealth of wrecks from ancient times to World War II, plus natural drop-offs and reefs, in an eight-metre custom dive boat; charges for certified divers vary from €50 for a single dive with rented gear to €450 for a ten-dive package (or a CMAS certification for the unqualified).

Pandélli and Vromólithos

Just less than 3km north of Lakkí, Pandélli and Vromólithos together form the largest resort on the island – and are certainly two of the more attractive and scenic places to stay and eat.

PANDÉLLI is still very much a working port, its modern jetty benefiting local fishermen as well as the increasing numbers of yachts calling here. The shortness of its clean gravel beach is compensated for by a relative abundance of non-package **accommodation**. Where the road down from Plátanos meets the sea, there's *Pension Happiness* (☎22470 23498; ❷), or the newer *Pension Lavyrinthos* directly opposite (☎22470 24165; ❷). For a much higher standard, try the airy, Aussie-run *Niki Studios* (☎22470 25600; ❹) at the base of the road to the castle, with a pool, some air-conditioned units and a package presence. South along the main ridge road from Pandélli to Vromólithos in Spiliá district, *Hotel Rodon* (☎22470 23524; ❸; all year) is an excellent choice, its small but well-kept, mostly balconied rooms belying an official E-class rating; the same welcoming family keeps pricier ground-floor studios (❹), with less of a sea view. Calm here may only be disturbed by wafts of music from *Café del Mar*, on a rock terrace below, facing Vromólithos. The other, long-established **bar** is civilized, English/Danish-run *Savana* (Easter–early Oct), at the far end of Pandélli, with excellent music (you nominate your favourite tracks).

Right next to the *Rodon* is the son's *Mezedhopolio Dimitris*, which stays open most of the year and offers stuffed squash blossoms (in autumn) and chunky Lerian sausages as well as the usual dips – the food's rich, so show up hungry. Back in beachside Pandélli, the soul of the place is the row of waterfront **tavernas**, which come alive after dark. Most are tourist traps, but two to single out for excellence are *Psaropoula* (alias *Apostolis*), open most of the year with a good balance of fresh seafood and *mayireftá*, and the *Kafenio tou Tzouma*, a fishermen's café at the base of the jetty that does excellent seafood *ouzomezédhes* (June–Sept). Even cheaper, and serving food most of the year just inland, is *Tou Mihali* (the sign says *Kafenio "Coffee"*), where expertly fried *gópes*, mixed salads and good wine are scoffed by a largely local crowd for under a tenner.

Vromólithos

VROMÓLITHOS offers the best easily accessible **beach** on the island, carfree and hemmed in by hills studded with massive oaks. The narrow shoreline is gravel and coarse sand, getting better as you head south, and the sea is clean, but (as so often on Léros) you have to cross an uncomfortable reef at most points before reaching deeper water. Two **tavernas** behind the beach trade more on their location than their cuisine (which improves when Greek weekenders are about), but the standard of **accommodation** here is higher than at Pandélli, so Vromólithos tends to be dominated by package companies. Exceptions, which keep at least some beds back for walk-ins, include *Tony's Beach* (☎22470 24743, ⓦwww.tonysbeachstudios.gr; ❹; June to early Oct), spacious studio units set in equally extensive waterside grounds with ample parking, and *Glaros* (☎22470 24358, Ⓕ22470 23683; ❺; May–Oct), more large, stone-floored studios set back and perpendicular to the through-road and beach, with garden views.

Plátanos and Ayía Marína

The Neoclassical and vernacular houses of **PLÁTANOS**, the island capital 1km west of Pandélli, are draped gracefully along a saddle between two hills, one of them crowned by the inevitable Knights' castle. Known locally as the **Kástro** (daily 8am–1pm; also May–Oct Wed, Sat & Sun 3–7pm; €1), this is reached either by a zigzagging road veering off the Pandélli road, or by a more scenic stair-path from the central square; the battlements, and the views from them, are dramatic, especially at sunrise or sunset. The medieval church of **Panayía toú Kástrou,** inside the gate and originally the powder magazine, houses a small **museum** (additional €1), though its carved *témblon* and naïve pulpit are more remarkable than the sparse exhibits, mostly icons and other liturgical items.

The other, and more worthwhile, local exhibit is the **archeological museum** (Tues–Sun 8am–2.30pm; free), well signposted just off the road between Ayía Marína and Plátanos. Although a bit long on photos and maps of sites and rather short on actual artefacts, it does a comprehensive tour of Lerian history, from prehistoric obsidian-tool fragments – proving contact with Mílos and Níssyros islands – to Byzantine votive-mosaic fragments and assorted church masonry, by way of an Attic *lekythos* with a female head in profile, and Roman amphorae.

Plátanos is not really a place to stay or eat, though it's well sown with shops and services. These include Olympic Airways (℡22470 24144), south of the turning for Pandélli, two **banks** with ATMs and the **post office**, down the road towards Ayía Marína. The central **bus** stop (schedules posted) stands opposite the island's main **taxi** rank.

Ayía Marína

Plátanos merges seamlessly with **AYÍA MARÍNA**, 1km north on the shore of a scenic bay, and still graced by a small, Italian-built public market building. If you travel to Léros on any excursion boat, catamaran or hydrofoil, this (not Lakkí) will be your point of arrival unless weather conditions cause a diversion. Helpful Kastis Travel (℡22470 22140) sells tickets for all hydrofoils and catamarans, as well as the recommendable *Barbarossa* excursion *kaïki*; there are also two **bank** ATMs (one freestanding).

Although local **accommodation** is extremely limited – small but clean en-suite rooms, some with sea view, above *Mezedhopolio tou Kapaniri* (℡22470 22750; ❷) are convenient if nothing else – Ayía Marína is, however, one of the best places to **eat** on the island. Start, just west of the police station on the water, with reasonably priced *Kapaniri* itself, best at night, with plenty – bean soup, Cypriot *halloúmi* cheese, *hórta* – for vegetarians, in addition to seafood and draught beer; quality is inconsistent, but they operate all year. Still further west, *Ouzeri Neromylos* (mid-March to late Oct), out by the sea-marooned windmill, indisputably has the most romantic setting on the island (reservations mandatory July & Aug on ℡22470 24894), the best musical soundtrack, and arguably the best food. Host Takis' specialities include *garidhopílafo* (shrimp-rice), superb fresh fish, *kolokythokeftédhes* (courgette patties), and *foúlia* (Egyptian beans with coriander), expertly prepared by his wife and mother-in-law. Central Ayía Marína has an improbable concentration of *zaharoplastía*, as well as lively (for Léros, anyway) **nightlife** provided by various café-bars such as *Enallaktiko* behind the Italian "palace", with a few **Internet** terminals, and cavernous *Apothiki New Face* on the quay; its other *kafenía* are popular places to wait for a hydrofoil or catamaran.

Álinda and nearby beaches

ÁLINDA, 3km northwest of Ayía Marína, ranks as the longest-established resort on Léros, with development just across the road from a long, narrow strip of pea-gravel beach. An **Allied War Graves cemetery**, containing 184 mostly Commonwealth casualties of the November 1943 battle, occupies a walled enclosure near the south end of the beach. Immaculately maintained, and furnished with a guest register and informative booklet inside the gatepost, it serves as a moving counterpoint to the holiday activity outside.

The other principal sight at Álinda is the privately run **Historical and Ethnographic Museum** (May–Sept Tues–Sun 9am–1pm & 6–8pm; €3), housed in the unmistakable castle-like mansion of Paris Bellinis (1871–1957). Most of the top floor is devoted to the Battle of Léros: relics from the sunken *Queen Olga*, a wheel from a Junkers bomber, a stove made from a bomb casing. There's also a rather grisly mock-up clinic (mostly gynecological tools) and assorted rural impedimenta, costumes and antiques. Photos trace the sad decline of many Lerian monuments: a fine market hall in the square of Plátanos was thoughtlessly demolished in 1903, and a soaring medieval aqueduct linking the far hillside with the Kástro was a casualty of the November 1943 battle.

Practicalities

Álinda is the first Lerian area for **accommodation** to open in spring, and (except for Pandélli) the last to shut in autumn. Some of the dozen hotels and studios here are block-booked by package companies, but worthwhile exceptions include the *Hotel Gianna* (T 22470 23153; ❸), with fridge-equipped rooms plus a few studios overlooking the war cemetery, or – set back from mid-beach – the well-kept *Hotel Alinda* (T 22470 23266, F 22470 23383; ❸), with a decent restaurant and sunken Byzantine mosaic out front, plus spacious rooms (some with air con). One definitely to avoid is *Studios Diamantis*, whose unpleasant management touts aggressively from their taxi and gift shop in Ayía Marína. At **Krithóni**, 1.5km south of the cemetery, more comfort is available at the island's top-flight accommodation: *Crithoni's Paradise* (T 22470 25120, F 22470 24680; rooms ❻, suites ❼; all year), a mock-traditional low-rise complex with decent buffet breakfast, on-site travel agency and car/scooter rental, a large pool and all mod cons in the rooms, which do vary in size, and in high season it's best to get one away from the pool. For more character back at Álinda, try the *Arhondiko Angelou* (T 22470 22749 or 694 49 08 182, F 22470 24403; ❹; June–Sept), a restored 1895 mansion set well inland; rooms, with a "French-style" prefab bath in the corner, are a bit creaky, though the orchard setting and outdoor breakfast bar make the place.

Besides the diner at *Hotel Alinda*, worthy **restaurant** options at Álinda include *Finikas* at mid-beach, more than competent, with a few *mayireftá* dishes of the day (baked fish, cauliflower cheese) washed down by Páros bulk wine at waterside seating, or pricier *Osteria da Giusi e Marcello* much further north (supper only; closed early Jan to March), which does pizza, pasta and decadent desserts, accompanied by bulk and bottled Italian wine. As for **nightlife**, a few bars try their luck every season; *Alaloum* seems the most durable.

Dhýo Liskária, Kryfós and Goúrna

At the north end of the main Álinda beach strip, you can follow a signposted lane nearly a kilometre east, past Panayiés chapel, its tiny beach and a cistern, to a well-situated taverna overlooking the partly protected sand-and-gravel bay of **Dhýo Liskária**. From here you can continue to pebbly **Kryfós** cove, 20–25 minutes' hard scramble north on a faint path whose start is marked by paint dots. There's only a cave for shade there, sometimes tar on the shore.

Otherwise, the road towards the north end of the island takes off from Álinda centre; within 1km or so you pass the well-marked turning to **Goúrna**. This is Léros' biggest sandy **beach**, wind-buffeted, hard-packed and gently shelving, with a view west over some islets and a few sunbeds provided by the most reliable taverna. There's another sporadically open taverna 1km south along the paved road which loops back over the hills to Lakkí via the tiny hamlets of Ángyra and Dhrymónas.

A separate road beyond the Goúrna turning leads to **Kokálli**, no great improvement beach-wise, but flanked to one side by the scenic islet of **Áyios Isídhoros**, tethered to the body of Léros by a causeway, its eponymous chapel perched on top.

The far northwest

The hills between Panayiés and Blefoútis are a restricted military zone; explorations on foot or scooter are only advisable west of the main road heading for the north end of the island.

The next turning beyond the one for Kokálli, indicated by a small blue sign (don't continue further to the Toyota dealership), is the start of the rough but motorable track to **Áyios Nikólaos** bay and monastery. The latter is of middling interest, and the single beach here is disappointing, but some walkers find it worthwhile to continue northwest along the rugged coast. Following the track south, then east on a scooter back towards Áyios Isídhoros takes you through country empty except for goat-pens and a giant wind farm on the ridge above. Immediately south of the wind turbines and livestock corrals are a few little secluded coves, much the best along this coast for swimming.

The Artemis "temple", Ayía Kiourá and Blefoútis

Seven kilometres from Álinda along the main route north, a side-track marked with the standard yellow-on-brown sign leads left to the "**Temple**" **of Artemis**, atop a slight rise just west of the airport. In ancient times, Léros was originally sacred to the goddess Parthenos Iokallis, who eventually became syncretized with Artemis, but is still recalled in the place-name Parthéni. All that remains inside a fenced enclosure (gate open) are some jumbled walls, no more than two masonry courses high; as the archeological museum display makes clear, this was an ancient fortress, not a shrine, and the north–south orientation of the ruins is completely wrong for a temple. The real whereabouts of the temple are unknown, but it seems likely that it was somewhere along the shores of the sumpy, reed-fringed bay below – marshes and river-mouths were the usual site of Artemis temples – or perhaps under today's airport runway. Legend asserts that her Lerian sanctuary was inhabited by *meleagrides* or guinea fowl – the grief-stricken sisters of the ancient hunter-hero Meleager, who were metamorphosed thus by Artemis after their brother was killed by the Kalydonian boar.

The onward road skims the shoreline of **Parthéni Bay** before arriving at the eponymous hamlet and Italian-built army base; in its former capacity as a political prison during the junta era, this must have been a dreary place to be detained, and it's still an unpopular posting for conscripts. The camp has, however, left one outstanding cultural legacy: the chapel of **Ayía Kiourá** (always open), reached by a one-kilometre marked access road. During the junta, certain camp inmates decorated this otherwise unremarkable church with striking murals – squarely in the tradition of Diego Rivera's 1930s Leftist art – rather than conventional frescoes. The Orthodox Church has, of course, always abhorred these images – a resident monk obliterated several in the 1980s – but Ayía Kiourá is now a protected monument, with a placard by the door strictly forbidding the plastering over of murals on pain of criminal prosecution. Because several artists were involved, quality varies; most of the scattered panels dwell on the Passion (including the *Agony in Gethsemane*), in a calculated jibe at their jailers. The best murals are a *Dormition of the Virgin* over the central door; a *Deposition* on the north wall, with four women cradling an elongated Christ; and a decidedly heterodox *Last Supper* over the southwest door, where protagonists Judas and Christ stand and stare at you, while the other disciples (some with their head in hands) look on in dismay.

Just over 11km from Plátanos, the paved road ends at **Blefoútis** (often "Plefoútis"), a rather more inspiring sight with its huge, almost landlocked bay backed by greenery-flecked hills. The beach surface and shallows are the Lerian

Greek script table

Léros	Λέρος	ΛΕΡΟΣ
Álinda	Άλυντα	ΑΛΙΝΤΑ
Ayía Kiourá	Αγία Κιουρά	ΑΓΙΑ ΚΙΟΥΡΑ
Ayía Marína	Αγία Μαρίνα	ΑΓΙΑ ΜΑΡΙΝΑ
Ángyra	Άγκυρα	ΑΓΚΥΡΑ
Blefoútis	Μπλεφούτης	ΜΠΛΕΦΟΥΤΙΣ
Dhýo Liskária	Δύο Λισκάρια	ΔΥΟ ΛΙΣΚΑΡΙΑ
Drymón(as)	Δρυμών(ας)	ΔΡΥΜΩΝ(ΑΣ)
Goúrna	Γούρνα	ΓΟΥΡΝΑ
Katsoúni	Κατσούνι	ΚΑΤΣΟΥΝΙ
Kokálli	Κοκάλι	ΚΟΚΑΛΙ
Kouloúki	Κουλούκι	ΚΟΥΛΟΥΚΙ
Krithóni	Κριθώνι	ΚΡΙΘΩΝΙ
Kryfós	Κρυφόρ	ΚΡΥΦΟΣ
Lakkí	Λακκί	ΛΑΚΚΙ
Lepídha	Λεπίδα	ΛΕΠΙΔΑ
Merikiá	Μερικιά	ΜΕΡΙΚΙΑ
Panayiés	Παναγιές	ΠΑΝΑΓΙΕΣ
Pandélli	Παντέλι	ΠΑΝΤΕΛΙ
Parthéni	Παρθένι	ΠΑΡΘΕΝΙ
Plátanos	Πλάτανος	ΠΛΑΤΑΝΟΣ
Vromólithos	Βρομόλιθος	ΒΡΟΜΟΛΙΘΟΣ
Xirókambos	Ξηρόκαμπος	ΞΗΡΟΚΑΜΠΟΣ

norm – watch your toes getting in – but there are tamarisks to shelter under and a decent taverna, *Iy Thea Artemi*, for a *kalamári*-and-chips-type lunch.

Léros travel details

Island transport

Buses
Plátanos to: Parthéni via Álinda in the north, and Xirókambos via Lakkí in the south (4–6 daily).

Inter-island transport

Kaïkia and excursion boats
Léros (Ayía Marína) to: Lipsí (at least 1 daily late May to early Oct).
Léros (Xirókambos) to: Myrtiés, Kálymnos (1 daily 7am May–Oct).

Ferries
Lakkí to: Agathoníssi (4 weekly on NK; 4hr); Arkí (4 weekly on NK; 3hr); Kálymnos (5–6 weekly on GA, 4 weekly on NK; 1hr–1hr 15min); Kós (5–6 weekly on GA; 2hr 30min); Lipsí (4 weekly on NK; 1hr); Níssyros (1 weekly on GA; 4hr); Pátmos (1–2 weekly on BS, 5–6 weekly on GA, 4 on NK; 1hr 15min–1hr 45min); Pireás (7–9 weekly on BS or GA; 8–10hr); Rhodes (2 weekly on BS, 5–6 weekly on GA; 4hr 30min– 5hr 30min); Samos-Pythagório (4 weekly on NK; 5hr 30min); Sými (1–2 weekly on GA; 6hr); Tílos (1–2 weekly on GA; 5hr).

Catamaran
Ayía Marína to: Kálymnos, Kós, Rhodes (6–7 weekly); Pátmos (3–4 weekly); Lipsí (3–4 weekly); Sými (2–3 weekly).

Hydrofoils
Ayía Marína to: Agathoníssi (1 weekly); Foúrni (2 weekly); Ikaría (2 weekly); Kálymnos (4–7 weekly); Kós (4–7 weekly); Lipsí (4–7 weekly); Pátmos (4–7 daily); Sámos-Pythagório (4–7 weekly).
NB All services are on KR.

Flights
Léros to: Astypálea (2–3 weekly; 25min); Athens (6–7 weekly; 55min); Kós (2–3 weekly; 25min); Rhodes (2–3 weekly; 1hr 25min).

Pátmos

Arguably the most beautiful, certainly the best known of the smaller Dodecanese, **Pátmos** has a distinctive, immediately palpable atmosphere. It was in a cave here that St John the Divine (in Greek, *O Theológos* or "The Theologian", one of the most common men's names here) wrote the New Testament's Book of Revelation and unwittingly shaped the island's destiny. The monastery honouring him, founded here in 1088 by the Blessed Khristodhoulos (1021–93), dominates Pátmos both physically – its fortified bulk towering above everything else – and, to a considerable extent, socially. While the monks inside no longer run the island unchallenged as they did for more than six centuries, their influence has nonetheless stopped it going the way of Rhodes or Kós, though Pátmos now has no fewer than four nude-bathing areas, something unthinkable as recently as the early 1990s. Yet the overall tone is confirmed by the annual **Festival of Religious Music**, held during the first two weeks of September in a hillside amphitheatre and featuring performers from Russia, Turkey and the entire Balkans.

Despite vast numbers of visitors and the island's established presence on the cruise-ship, catamaran and yacht circuits, tourism has not been allowed to take over Pátmos completely. Although there are several after-hours clubs around Skála, the port and main town, drunken rowdies are unknown. Package clients only equal independent visitors in certain years, and are pretty much confined to Gríkou and a bare handful of large hotels at Skála and Kámbos. Day-trippers still vastly outnumber overnighters, and Pátmos seems an altogether different place once the last cruise-ship passengers have gone after sunset. Among those staying, no one nationality predominates, lending Pátmos a genuinely cosmopolitan feel unique in the Dodecanese outside of Rhodes.

The steady clientele can be very posh indeed – US ambassador to the UN John Negroponte and the late Aga Khan's extended family (among others) maintain properties here – their residence ensuring the presence of a state-of-the-art wireless Internet system – while the Belgian and (deposed) Greek and ex-Yugoslav royal families are repeat visitors. Away from Skála, tourist development is subdued if not deliberately retarded, thanks to the absence of an airport. On outlying beaches, little has outwardly changed since the early 1980s, though multilingual "For sale" signs on literally every seafront field and farmhouse, plus massive villa developments at coves closer to town, suggest that such days are strictly numbered.

Skála and around

SKÁLA, where most of the island's three thousand people live, seems initially to contradict any solemn, otherworldly image of Pátmos. The waterside, with its ritzy cafés, arty gift boutiques and clientele to match, is a bit too sophisticated for such a small town, and some of the world-weary service personnel can be none too civil at times. During peak season, the quay and commercial district teem by day with trippers and cruise-ship passengers souvenir-hunting or being shepherded onto coaches for the ride up to the monastery. After dark there's still a considerable traffic in well-dressed visitors, mostly on furlough

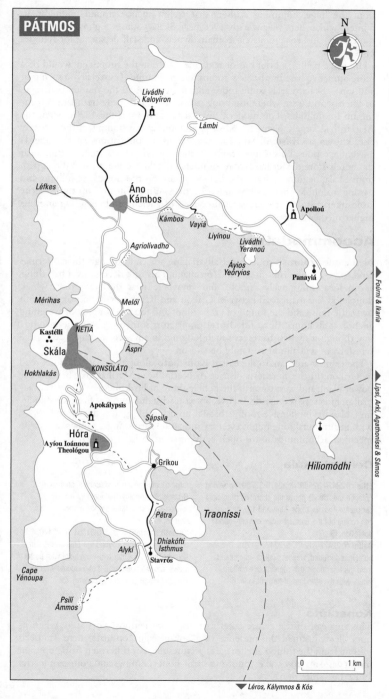

PÁTMOS

N

Livádhi
Kaloyíron

Lámbi

Léfkes

Áno
Kámbos

Kámbos
Vayiá

Apolloú

Agriolívadho

Liyínou
Livádhi
Yeranoú

Áyios
Yeóryios

Panayiá

Mérihas

Melóï

Kastélli
NETIÁ
Skála

Áspri

Hokhlakás

KONSOLÁTO

Apokálypsis

Sápsila

Hóra
Ayíou Ioánnou
Theológou

Gríkou

Hiliomódhi

Pétra

Traoníssi

Dhiakófti
Isthmus

Alykí

Stavrós

Cape
Yénoupa

Psilí
Ámmos

0   1 km

▶ Foúrni & Ikaría

▶ Lipsí, Arkí, Agathoníssi & Sámos

▼ Léros, Kálymnos & Kós

from the huge, humming cruisers that weigh anchor around midnight. In winter (which here means early October), Skála assumes a ghost-town air as most shops and restaurants close, their owners and staff departing for Rhodes or Athens.

Hóra (see p.303), a brief bus or taxi ride south up the mountain, would be a more attractive base but has few rooms. Yet given time – especially in spring or autumn – Skála reveals some more enticing corners in the residential fringes to the east and west, where imposing mansions hem in pedestrian lanes creeping up the hillsides. The modern town dates only from the 1820s, when the Aegean had largely been cleared of pirates, but at the summit of the westerly rise, known as **Kastélli**, you can see extensive foundations of the island's ancient acropolis. This is most easily reached by a dirt-track route starting near the hotels around Mérihas Bay recommended below; there is also a direct path from Skála, beginning from the highest house on the northwest hillside, and passing a double-chapel surrounded by trees. What you find up top – eerily atmospheric at sunset – are several courses of ancient wall enclosing another, higher medieval chapel.

Accommodation

Numerous **"rooms"** touts meet all arriving sea craft, though their offerings tend to be a long walk distant and/or inland. This isn't necessarily a bad thing, as no location is really remote, and anywhere near the waterfront, which doubles as the main road between Gríkou and Kámbos, will be plagued both by traffic noise and the sound of cruise ships and ferries dropping or weighing anchor at all hours. Bona fide **hotel** proprietors sometimes join the quayside fray, though it's wisest to reserve such lodgings in advance, in which case a free transfer van will almost certainly be laid on.

The calmest areas are to the east at **Konsoláto**, along the relatively quiet road to Gríkou; in the northern district of **Netiá**, near Mérihas Bay, beyond the power plant; and west towards the pebble shore of **Hokhlakás**. Pátmos vernacular architecture is quite distinctive, but you wouldn't know it from most lodgings, bland if inoffensive rooms thrown up using EU grants during the 1980s, with institutional (one might even say monastic) furnishings. Unless otherwise specified, accommodation is open early April to early or mid-October.

Central Skála

Effie ☎ 22470 32500, ⓕ 22470 32700. Two-wing hotel on the hillside above the shoreline municipal car park. Anodyne, blond-pine-and-tile, heated/air-con rooms but the unusual virtue of year-round operation. ❹

Galini ☎ 22470 31240, ⓕ 22470 31705. C-class hotel in a secluded, viewless cul-de-sac inland from the ferry dock, this represents excellent value, with the standard of furnishing in the large rooms, most with balconies, approaching B-class; the friendly management usually has a few on-spec vacancies despite a package-tour presence. ❹

Kastelli (Casteli) ☎ 22470 31361, ⓕ 22470 31656. A few paces beyond the *Effie* on the same hillside, this is another two-wing hotel with better views, a small pool, large if plain rooms with air con and fridge, plus ample parking. ❹

Konsoláto

This area east of the centre takes its name from Pátmos' glory days, when its huge fleets justified the presence of a few foreign consulates here. Traffic is minimal and the fishing anchorage is picturesque, but fishermen firing up their motors at 4am may wake you if the small-hours comings and goings of ferries and cruise ships don't.

Blue Bay ☎ 22470 31165, ⓦ www.bluebay.50g
.com. About 150m out of town proper on the Gríkou
road, this is probably the best, quietest choice for
this area, with helpful Australian-Greek management, reasonably furnished sea-view rooms piled
in tiers, plus Skála's most reliable Internet facilities. Credit cards accepted for stays of over two
days. ⑤
Byzance ☎ 22470 31052, ⓦ byzance-hotel
.com. Hotel a few steps inland from fishing
anchorage, with rooms and studios spread over

two buildings – go for the larger units with
balconies. ④
Captain's House ☎ 22470 31793, ⓕ 22470
32277. Somewhat overpriced shoreline hotel
which does, however, offer friendly management,
variably sized rooms with balconies and above-
average furnishings, plus in-house car rental. ⑤
Delfini ☎ 22470 32060, ⓕ 22470 32061. Next
door to the preceding, this somewhat gruffly
managed hotel has plainer balconied rooms and a
pleasant ground-floor terrace-café. ⑤

Netiá

This slightly unglamorous area beyond the yacht anchorage, boatyard and
power plant proves attractive up close and far quieter than town, bar the odd
rumblings from the dynamo.

Asteri Near Mérihas cove ☎ 22470 32465,
ⓔ pasca@otenet.gr. The highest standard in this
area, unimprovably set on a knoll overlooking the
bay, in a well-landscaped environment; guests
have own-produced honey, eggs and tomatoes at
breakfast. 2003-expanded with a large sea-view
lounge and variably sized rooms (including two
with wheelchair access). ③ low, ⑤ high season
Australis ☎ 22470 31576, ⓕ 22470 32284.
1970s-vintage hotel, nominally E-class but en suite,
owned by a returned Greek-Australian family; full
breakfast included in the price and myriad small

kindnesses that guarantee an enthusiastic return
clientele. Affiliated scooter-rental business saves
you traipses into town. There's an apartment
annexe, whose units accommodate 4 people. ④
Pension Sydney ☎ 22470 31689 Just uphill from
preceding, run by the brother of the *Australis* clan,
and where overflow gets referred. Spartan but
adequate balconied rooms with fridge and fan. ③
Villa Knossos ☎ 22470 32189. Managed by the
daughter and son-in-law of the *Australis* clan,
these high-standard, balconied self-catering units
are a bit closer to the road. €44

Hokhlakás

Pebbly **Hokhlakás** bay is most easily reached by following the main commercial pedestrian street inland and southwest ten minutes from the Italian
municipal "palace"; like most of the island's west-facing shore, it's not good for
swimming, but it is dead quiet out here.

Maria In the flatlands, 150m behind the bay
☎ 22470 31201 or 22470 31471, ⓕ 22470 32018.
Air con and big sea-view balconies make up for tiny
bathrooms here; pleasant front garden, breakfast
on request. ⑤
Romeos On south hillside ☎ 22470 31962,
ⓔ romeos@w12.gr. Tiered, B-class bungalow-hotel
with a pool, large common areas, and sizeable
units numerous enough that there's usually a
vacancy despite package patronage, though some

complain of the managing family fighting like cats
and dogs. ⑥
Studios Yvonni On north hillside ☎ 22470 32466
or 22470 33066, ⓦ www.12net.gr/yvonni. Basic
but salubrious 1980s, pine-and-tile, medium-sized
units with fridges, air con and oblique sea views
over a hillside garden. If phones don't answer, call
in at their gift shop next to the *Nissos Kalymnos*
agency. ③

Melóï

Porto Scoutari Hotel ☎ 22470 33123, ⓦ www
.portoscoutari.com. Arguably the premier hotel on
the whole island, this bungalow complex overlooks
Melóï beach from a hillside setting, with vehicle
access from either the main island road or Melóï.

Its enormous standard rooms and suites all have
sea view, TV, phone and air con/heating, as well as
exquisite, mock-antique furnishings and original art.
But what really makes the place is Elina Scoutari's
dedication to her customers' welfare. ⑥–⑧

Eating, drinking and nightlife

Quality **restaurant** options are surprisingly limited in central Skála; despite recent improvements, there are still too many *souvladzídhika* and *yirádhika* joints, sweet shops or cafés, and not enough good-value sit-down places. Aside from the "Central Skála" listings, you're best off heading out of town; this is one island where beach tavernas excel. Another obstacle to dining enjoyment, especially if you're arriving by ferry (and they all dock late), is that Skála eateries tend to take last orders at the very un-Greek early hour of 10.30pm or so, leaving latecomers with the choice of pizza or fast food.

The most reliable **breakfast** venue is the second, smaller *platía* beyond the main shoreline one, where the competent *Dhodhoni* and *Aigaio* patisseries bracket the *Koumanis* bakery which turns out terrific turnovers and Greek pastries. The *Astoria Café*, next to the eponymous travel agency on the quay, is the spot for reasonable ice cream, coffee and unrivalled people-watching.

Central Skála

Cactus On the beach at Hokhlakás. Nouvelle-minceur Italian snacks (don't show up too hungry) accompanied by Italian wines and aperitifs. Supper only May–Sept.

To Hiliomodhi Just off the start of Hóra road, on the left. Durable, inexpensive, seafood-only, *ouzerí* with vegetarian *mezédhes* and delicacies such as limpets (served live), grilled octopus and salted anchovies served at tables on a quiet pedestrian lane, or up on the roof terrace with views of flood-lit Hóra. Open all year for supper only, but best May–Sept when owner Theologos is in the kitchen.

The Old Harbour Opposite the municipal car park and town beach. The chef here moonlights from his day job feeding the monks in Hóra with a meat-rich menu of "continental" specialities. Exceptionally pleasant interior and terrace seating. Supper only May–Sept.

Ostria West end of quay before Emboriki bank. Reliable *ouzerí* that's popular with Greeks, especially off season when the cosy interior comes into its own. Big portions of seafood, smaller and less distinguished *orektiká*. Open all year, and one of the few places taking orders after 11pm.

Pandelis One lane inland behind Astoria Travel. An old-fashioned (if slightly greasy of late) *mayireftá* taverna where a wide-ranging menu makes up for famously dour service. Out of season, likely to be your only lunch option in Skála; open all year.

Veggera Opposite the yacht marina. Reckoned the best all-rounder in town, with a VIP clientele, flawless presentation of French-Mediterranean cooking, and per-head bills of about €37. Open Easter to late Sept; reservations required on ☎22470 32988.

Environs

Aspri Above Áspri cove, 2km north of Skála. All-*mezédhes*-format taverna slightly inland, with indoor seating. Supper only June to early Sept.

Benetos Sápsila cove, 2km southeast of Skála. Since 1998 this has established a reputation as one of the top eateries on the island thanks to its Mediterranean and Pacific Rim fusion dishes, with a stress on seafood. Budget a minimum of €32 for drink and three courses, which may include roast vegetable terrine with balsamic vinegar and raisins, baked fish fillet with risotto and Hubbard squash, pan-seared tuna with sesame crust, or *barboúni* sashimi, topped off with lemon-vodka sorbet. Supper only Tues–Sun, June to early Oct; reservations mandatory on ☎22470 33089, rigid time slots in Aug (from 7.30pm).

Kyma Sea level at Áspri cove. Excellent for seafood, especially lobster and *karavídhes* (cray-fish), and the setting – with floodlights playing on the water and surrounding rock – is magical. Supper only June–Aug.

Melloi (alias **Stefanos**) Melóï beach. Decent, friendly, inexpensive *mayireftá* taverna with good bulk wine that serves food all day. Best at lunch (though it gets coach tours) and open much of the year.

Nightlife

The biggest and longest-lived **café-bar** is the wood-panelled, barn-like *Café Arion* on the waterside, where a mixed clientele sits outside, dances or props up the long bar. Every year, a few other clubs try their luck: among the more consistent are pricey *Isalos*, inland from the Italian "palace", occasionally hosting live music; *Konsolato*, a late-night (midnight till dawn) club on the shore in Konsoláto district; and *Celine*, at the opposite end of the quay, beyond the town beach.

Other practicalities

Almost everything of interest can be found within, or within sight of, the Italian-built municipal "palace"; the **post office** occupies one of its corners, large ferries, catamarans and hydrofoils anchor opposite, while the conspicuous **bus** stop, with a timetable posted, lies in between. There are two **bank ATMs,** as well as two **Internet cafés**: one inside the *Blue Bay Hotel* (€1/10min), the other – *Millennium* (€5/hr) – behind the "palace".

   Motorbike rental outfits (eg Billis ℡22470 32218 and Aris ℡22470 32542) are common, with lowish rates owing to Pátmos' modest size and limited road network. Aris also has **cars** to rent, as does Avis in Netiá (℡22470 33025) and Tassos near the "palace" (℡22470 31753). **Excursion boats** to Psilí Ámmos, Lipsí and Arkí/Maráthi all leave at about 10am from just in front of Astoria Travel (℡22470 31205) and Apollon Travel (℡22470 31324), the two agencies handling **hydrofoil** tickets (Astoria also rents cars). GA Ferries are represented at the back of the central square (℡22470 31217), while the *Nissos Kalymnos* agent has premises (℡22470 32575) in a lane leading off the same *platía*. The *Dodekanisos Express* and Blue Star ferries are represented by Kyriaki Liapi in Konsoláto (℡22470 29303).

The monasteries and Hóra

For most visitors to Pátmos, top of the agenda is likely to be the monastery of Ayíou Ioánnou Theológou (St John), sheltered behind massive defences in the hilltop capital of Hóra. Both this monastery and that of Apokálypsis (see p.304) are on cruise itineraries, becoming hopelessly crowded in the hour or two after ships dock, so keep an eye on the harbour and time your visit accordingly. Both public buses and tour coaches make the climb up here, but the forty-minute walk along a beautiful cobbled path short-cutting the road puts you in a more appropriate frame of mind. To find its start, go through Skála towards Hokhlakás and, once past the telecoms building, bear left onto a narrow street starting opposite an ironmonger's; follow this uphill to its end on the main road – immediately opposite you'll see the start of the cobbles. (There is another narrow, dirt path, easiest to find for the descent, beginning in Hóra just below the school and telecoms antenna.)

   In 1088, the soldier-cleric Ioannis "The Blessed" Khristodhoulos was granted lifetime title to Pátmos by Byzantine Emperor Alexios Komnenos. It had long been Khristodhoulos' ambition to establish a religious community near the site of St John's Revelation, and within three years he and his followers had completed the framework of the monastery now visible, as well as a smaller one around the Grotto of the Revelation. The double threats of piracy and the Selçuk Turks meant that from the outset the main monastery was heavily fortified, with buttresses added later to make its hilltop position virtually impregnable.

   The original imperial grant also included provisions for tax exemption and the right of the monks to engage in sea trade, clauses exploited to the full by the monastery and usually respected by later Ottoman and Venetian rulers. A commercial fleet and extensive landholdings across the Balkans made the

Pátmos has been intimately associated with early Christianity since **John the Evangelist** – later known as John the Divine – was exiled here from Ephesus on the orders of the Roman emperor Domitian, in about 95 AD. While John was on Pátmos, supposedly dwelling in a grotto up the hill from the harbour, an otherworldly voice from a cleft in the ceiling bid him set down in writing what he heard. By the time John was allowed to return home, that disturbing finale to the New Testament, the Book of Revelations (or the Apocalypse), had been disseminated in the form of a pastoral letter to the Seven Churches of Asia Minor.

Revelations, whoever really wrote it, belongs squarely within the Judeo-Christian tradition of apocalyptic books, with titanic battles in heaven and on earth, supernatural visions, plus lurid descriptions of the fates awaiting the saved and the damned following the Last Judgment. As with other, similar books in the Old Testament, Revelations is a product of troubled times, when the religion of the elect – whether Judaism or Christianity – was powerless and thus humiliated in secular terms. Some cosmological justification had to be found for this, so emphasis was laid on the imminence of the Last Days. Of all the chapters of the Bible, Revelations is still among the most amenable to subjective application by fanatics, and was in use as a rhetorical and theological weapon within a century of appearing. Its vivid imagery lent itself easily to depiction in frescoes, adorning the refectories of numerous Byzantine monasteries and the narthexes of Orthodox churches, conveying a salutary message to illiterate medieval parishioners.

In addition to transcribing the Apocalypse, John supposedly wrote his Gospel on Pátmos, and also expended considerable effort combating paganism, most notably in the person of an evil local wizard, Kynops. In an episode related by John's disciple Prohoros, Kynops challenged the saint to a duel of miracles; the magician's stock trick involved retrieving effigies of the deceased from the seabed, so John responded by petrifying Kynops while he was underwater. A buoy near the western edge of Skála harbour today marks a submerged rock that is supposedly the remains of the wizard. All mechanical efforts to remove this marine hazard have failed, and it is claimed that fish caught in the vicinity taste bad. In the far southwest of the island, a foul-smelling volcanic cave has also been identified as a favourite haunt of the magician, whose name lives on as Cape Yénoupa (the modern form of "Kynops").

Forever after in the Orthodox world, heights amidst desolate and especially volcanic topography have become associated with St John, and Pátmos with its eerie landscape of minatory igneous outcrops is an excellent case in point. Other nearby examples include the isle of Níssyros, where one of the saint's monasteries overlooks the volcano's caldera, and Lésvos, where another monastery dedicated to him sits atop an extinct volcano, gazing at basalt-strewn wastelands.

monastic community immensely wealthy, enabling it to steadily augment the library inaugurated by Khristodhoulos, which in its prime contained far more than today's four thousand books and rare manuscripts. During the island's eighteenth-century heyday, local wealth and prestige permitted the foundation of a theological school for training clergy; after a century or so of abandonment, this was restored after World War II and now functions once more.

Monastery of Apokálypsis

Just over halfway up the path, pause at the **monastery of Apokálypsis** ("the Apocalypse"; daily 8am–1.30pm, also Tues, Thurs & Sun 4–6pm; free) built around the grotto where St John heard the voice of God and dictated His words to a disciple, Prohoros – yet again supernaturally, it would seem, since Prohoros apparently lived some centuries after the Evangelist. For many years, a leaflet left for pilgrims pointed out that the "fissure . . . (divides) the rock into three parts, thus serving as a continual reminder of the Trinitarian nature of God" and moreover admonished visitors "to ask yourself whether you are on the side of Christ or of Antichrist". This provocative literature has now vanished, but in the cave wall the presumed nightly resting place of the saint's head is fenced off and outlined in beaten silver.

Monastery of Ayíou Ioánnou Theológou

The grotto compound is merely a foretaste of the **monastery of Ayíou Ioánnou Theológou (St John)** (same hours and admission as Apokálypsis). "Modest" dress is essential, and the monks, fed up with hordes of tourists, can seem brusque, so be discreet. The best time to show up, besides the famous Easter observances, is September 25–26 (Feast of John the Divine) and October 20–21 (Feast of Khristodhoulos), both marked by solemn liturgies and processions of the appropriate icon.

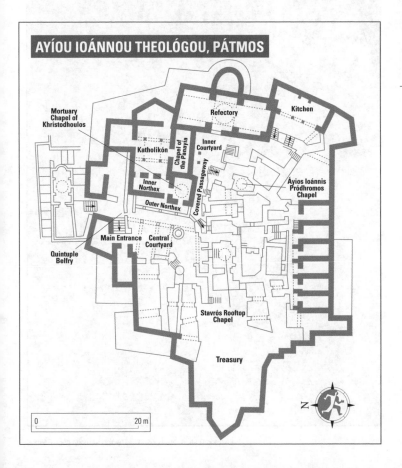

AYÍOU IOÁNNOU THEOLÓGOU, PÁTMOS

Mortuary Chapel of Khristodhoulos

Refectory

Kitchen

Katholikón

Chapel of the Panayía

Inner Courtyard

Inner Northex

Áyios Ioánnis Pródromos Chapel

Outer Northex

Covered Passageway

Main Entrance

Central Courtyard

Quintuple Belfry

Stavrós Rooftop Chapel

Treasury

N

0   20 m

△ East fortification, Ayíou Ioánnou Theológou monastery, Pátmos

A warren of interconnecting courtyards, chapels, stairways, arcades, galleries and roof terraces (the latter regrettably off limits), it offers a rare glimpse of Patmian interior architecture, strongly influenced by the ethos of medieval Crete, owing to the large numbers of Cretans in Khristodhoulos' original working party. Hidden in the walls are fragments of an ancient Artemis temple, which stood here before being admired – and then destroyed – by Khristodhoulos. The narthex of the various chapels to your left as you enter the main courtyard has excellent late medieval **frescoes**, mostly scenes from the life and miracles of Khristodhoulos.

Off to one side, the **treasury** (same hours; separate €6 admission) merits a leisurely visit for its magnificent array of religious treasures, mostly medieval icons of the Cretan School – including St John Damascene wearing what appears to be a *keffiyeh* – and liturgical embroidery of the same era, particularly two satin shrouds threaded with gold for the *epitáfios* or bier of Christ, carried in solemn procession on Good Friday. Among the multiple donations of the pious from across the Orthodox world, with Russia particularly well represented, a filigreed cross of incredible delicacy stands out. Yet pride of place goes to the eleventh-century parchment *khrysóvoulos* (chrysobull) of Emperor Alexios Komnenos, granting the entire island to Khristodhoulos; even earlier are various precious manuscripts and an unusual mosaic icon of St Nicholas.

This tallies just a small fraction of the museum's contents; if you get hooked, the well-stocked gift shop at the end offers a catalogue and high-quality reproductions of favourites. The famous **library** is unfortunately off limits to all except ecclesiastical scholars.

Hóra

The promise of security afforded by Ayíou Ioánnou's stout walls spurred the growth of **HÓRA** immediately outside the fortifications from the late thirteenth century onwards. Despite earthquakes and the Italians' demolition of buildings to create open space, it remains an architecturally homogenous village, with occasionally arcaded, cobbled alleys sheltering dozens of shipowners' mansions, most dating from Pátmos' seventeenth- and eighteenth-century heyday. High, almost windowless walls and monumental wooden doors betray nothing of the opulence within: painted ceilings, *hokhláki* terraces, flagstoned kitchens with carved cistern heads, carved furniture and embroidered bedcurtains.

Inevitably a certain amount of tourist tattiness disfigures the main ramps approaching the monastery gate, but once the crowds are gone the effect is like a more intimate, deserted Líndhos; away from the principal thoroughfares you stumble upon passages rarely disturbed by foot traffic, no wider than one person, lined with ruins or overgrown with night-fragrant *rodhokaliá* bushes. On summer nights, when the monastery ramparts are floodlit to startling effect, it is tempting to nominate Hóra as the most beautiful settlement in the Dodecanese.

Neither should you miss the **view** from Platía Lótza, named after the remnant of an adjacent Venetian loggia. Easiest glimpsed at dawn or dusk, the landmasses to the north – going clockwise – include Ikaría, Thýmena, Foúrni, Sámos with the brooding mass of Mount Kérkis, Arkí, Lipsí and the double-humped Samsun Daĝ (ancient Mount Mycale) in Turkey.

There are over forty "minor" churches and monasteries in and around Hóra, many of them containing beautiful icons and examples of local woodcarving; almost all are locked, to prevent thefts, but someone living nearby will have the key. Among the best are the church of **Dhiasózousa**, the convent of **Zoöd-hóhou Piyís** (daily 9am–1pm & 4–7pm) well southwest of the village, and the convent of **Evangelismoú**, at the edge of village in the same direction (daily 9–11am); follow the wall-arrows.

Practicalities

Among several **tavernas** in Hóra, *Vangelis* on the inner square has a wonderful old jukebox, friendly service and view seating on various levels (plus the square), but alas the cooking is no longer estimable; you'll probably eat better at either *Balkoni* or *Myloi* near the monastery, with views north over the island. Back on the square, *Kafeteria Stoa* is minimally touristy despite its showcase interior, still functioning as the village *kafenío*.

There are, however, hardly any places to **stay** on spec; foreigners here are mostly long-term occupants, who have bought up and restored almost a third of the crumbling mansions since the 1960s. Getting a short-term room can be a pretty thankless task, even in spring or autumn; phone ahead for reservations at *Yeoryia Triandafyllou* (℡ 22470 31963; ❸), en-suite rooms with a communal terrace on the south flank of Hóra. For more comfort, try the *Epavli Apartments* at the east edge of the village, on the ring road near the windmills (℡ 22470 31261, ⓦ www.12net.gr/epavli; ❹–❻), a restored building with superb views towards Lipsí and Léros, high-standard bathrooms and raised bed-platforms.

The rest of the island

Pátmos, as a locally published guide once memorably proclaimed, "is immense for those who know how to wander in space and time". Lesser mortals get around on foot or by scooter and bus. There's still scope for **walking**, though few real paths survive; otherwise the single **bus** offers a surprisingly reliable service between Skála, Hóra, Kámbos and Gríkou.

Southern beaches

After the extraordinary atmosphere and magnificent scenery, **beaches** are Pátmos' main attractions. Heading directly out of Skála from Konsoláto, or descending east from Hóra on a separate road, you arrive at the sandiest part of rather overdeveloped **GRÍKOU** (Gríkos), the main venue for Patmian package tourism – and shut tight as a drum come mid-September. A good **accommodation** option here, open slightly later and only part-dominated by "special interest" groups, is hillside *Hotel Golden Sun* (℡ 22470 32318, ⓦ www .hotel-golden-sun.com; ❺), with most rooms facing the water.

The beach itself, not the island's best, forms a narrow strip of hard-packed sand, giving way to pebbles at **Pétra** beach immediately south, whose far end – beyond the strange volcanic outcrop of Kalikatsoú, honeycombed with caves fashioned by Paleo-Christian hermits – is colonized by nudists. There are several such tiny coves in a row, but only the end ones are easy of access, and then by foot or scooter – no four-wheelers can negotiate the rough onward track to Stavrós.

Pétra's nearside features much the best rural **taverna** on Pátmos, *Ktima Petra* (May–Sept), with brown bread, lush salads, good bulk retsina, carefully cooked *mayireftá*, plus grills after dark. Still later, it becomes a bar with a full cocktails list. En route to Pétra, you pass hillside *Flisvos* (aka *Floros*), now rather eclipsed by nearby *Ktima Petra* but going since the 1960s with a limited choice of inexpensive, savoury *mayireftá*, served on the terrace. They also have basic rooms (**❷**) and fancier apartments (**❹**) – reserve on ☏22470 31380 or ⓕ22470 32094.

A scooter will take you along the paved roads from Hóra as far as the **Dhiakófti** isthmus with its chapel of Stavrós and busy boatyard. From road's end, there's a pleasant, 25-minute trail-walk southwest to **Psilí Ámmos** beach. This is the only pure-sand bay on the island, with shade lent by tamarisks and a good, lunch-only **taverna** that occasionally does roast goat, freshly shot on the surrounding hills. Cliffs and hills to either side create a dramatic backdrop, though the seabed itself shelves gently; by tacit consent, the southern third of the beach is resolutely nudist. In summer Psilí Ámmos can also be reached by taxi-boat, which departs from Skála at about 10am and returns at 4–5pm.

Northern beaches

More good beaches are to be found in the **north of the island**, tucked into the startling eastern shoreline (west-facing bays are uniformly unusable owing to wind and washed-up debris). Most are accessible from side roads off the main route north from Skála, though one or two must be reached on foot in the final moments via stretches of old paths.

Melóï is not only handy – regular taxi-boat service from Skála makes it more so – but quite appealing: there are tamarisks behind the narrow belt of sand, and good snorkelling offshore, as well as a pleasantly set **campsite** (*Stefanos-Flowers*; ☏22470 31821). The first beach beyond Melóï, **Agriolívadho** (Agriolivádhi) has mostly sand at its broad centre, kayak rental and two **tavernas**, the most reliably open (with seafood) being *O Glaros* on the south hillside.

The next beach, **Kámbos**, is popular with Greeks, and the most developed remote resort on the island, with seasonal watersports facilities and two tavernas, though the beach's appeal is diminished somewhat by a rock shelf in the shallows and the road directly behind. There's also an all-day **beach bar**, *Beyond*, its premises once the setting for *The Summer of My Greek Taverna* (see "Books", p.515).

ÁNO KÁMBOS, 600m west and uphill, is the only proper village on Pátmos besides Skála and Hóra, the focus of scattered farms in little oases all around. The road negotiates a cobbled *platía* beside the church and two **tavernas**, the better being the southerly one as you enter the village from the south. From Áno Kámbos, you can detour northwest to **Livádhi Kaloyíron**, a farming valley that lives oblivious of tourism – perhaps because the road in is rough, the beach stony, wave-battered and dirty. The little inland monastery, however, set behind its gardens, is attractive.

East of Kámbos beach, there are several more coves. **Vayiá** (pebbles) and **Livádhi Yeranoú** (sand and gravel) are less visited but arguably more attractive; Yeranoú can offer extensive shade from tamarisks and discreet naturism at the far end, plus a very good, inexpensive namesake **taverna** with something of a cult following, doing simple seafood dishes, *keftédhes*, *hórta* and salads. Just offshore lies the small islet of **Áyios Yeóryios**, which you can easily swim out to, with a little beach to rest up on before the lap back. Between Vayiá and Livádhi Yeranoú, east of the **Liyínou** headland, lie two pebbly coves accessible only by trail from a *kantína* up on the road, the remoter one popular with naturists.

From Kámbos you can also travel north to the bay of **Lámbi**, best for swimming when the prevailing wind is from the south, and renowned for an abundance of multicoloured volcanic pebbles (mixed with gravel and sand).

The Lámbi area has two **tavernas**, open May to October: good-value *Leonidas* up at Koumariá pass overlooking the bay, with lovely terrace seating, massive portions of expertly grilled chops and maybe a dessert on the house; *Lambi* (*Pandelis*) down on the beach has much the same menu, including vegetarian *mezédhes*, but is pipped for quality by its rival.

3

Satellite islets: Lipsí, Arkí, Maráthi and Agathoníssi

Of the various islets to the north and east of Pátmos, **Lipsí** is the largest, most interesting and most visited. The ultra-lonely duo of **Arkí** and **Maráthi** are far less frequented (except during summer) and rather more primitive, while **Agathoníssi** falls somewhere in between as to popularity and size.

Lipsí

Since the early 1990s, **LIPSÍ** has acquired a significant tourist trade: Germans and French in early summer, Italians later on, plus a fair quantity of British package clients (of Laskarina Holidays) from spring to autumn, who occupy most of the better lodgings. All of this (helped along by periodic weekend-supplement features extolling its "undiscovered-ness" and "unspoilt-ness", plus the island's regular appearance on both catamaran and hydrofoil routes, mean that it's unwise to show up in peak season without a reservation (though room proprietors often meet arrivals at other times).

During quieter months, however, Lipsí still makes an idyllic halt, its sleepy pace making plausible a purported link between the island's name and that of **Calypso**, the nymph who legendarily held Odysseus in thrall for several years. Recently, however, Lipsí acquired a definite – and unwanted – association with **Dhekaeftá Noemvríou/17 November**, Greece's (and Europe's) longest-lived terrorist organization (see p.467). In July 2002, the national anti-terrorist squad swooped on the island and apprehended the group's supremo, Alexandhros Yiotopoulos (alias Nikos Ikonomou), in the act of leaving for Sámos, his eventual destination exile in Turkey. He had been living quietly here for seventeen years in a faded-pink hilltop villa, now abandoned and shuttered following his December 2003 conviction on all charges and life sentencing; ironically Yiotopoulos was much liked by the islanders for his generosity and willingness to help with bureaucratic problems.

Lipsí ranks as a dependency of the Monastery of Ayíou Ioánnou Theológou on Pátmos, and is as well sown with blue-domed country chapels as any of the larger Dodecanese. Deep wells provide water for many small, well-tended farms and vineyards (which once produced dark, sweet communion wine for the Vatican), but there is only one flowing spring (in the west), and pastoral appearances are deceptive – four times the relatively impoverished full-time population of about six hundred live overseas (many in Tasmania). Most of those who remained behind (or, increasingly, return as retirees) cluster around the fine harbour, as does the majority of food and lodging.

The port settlement

Despite the construction of a freight-loading dock on the south side of the port, and a breakwater cutting the swell into the fishing anchorage at the east end of the bay, all passenger craft and yachts still anchor at the northwest end

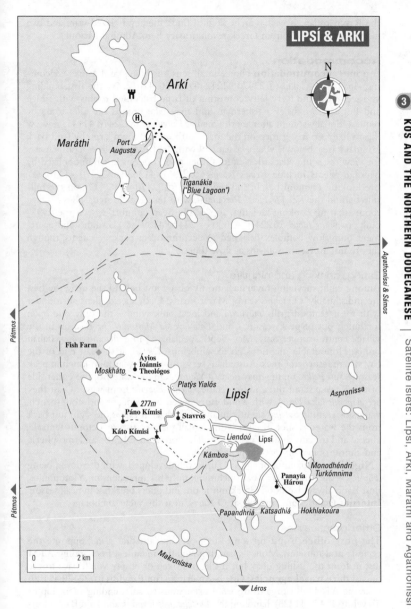

LIPSÍ & ARKI

N

Arkí

Maráthi

Port Augusta

Tiganákia ("Blue Lagoon")

▶ Agathoníssi & Sámos

◀ Pátmos

◀ Pátmos

Fish Farm

Moskháto

† Áyios Ioánnis Theológos

Platýs Yialós

Lipsí

Asproníssa

▲ 277m Páno Kímisi

† Stavrós

Liendoú   Lipsí

Káto Kímisi †

Kámbos

Monodhéndri Turkómnima

Panayía Hárou

Papandhriá Katsadhiá Hokhlakoúra

0   2 km

Makroníssa

▼ Léros

of the quay, a fairly long walk into town (the only significant habitation on Lipsí).

On the attractive square flanking the obvious cathedral of Áyios Ioánnis Theológos, you'll find a hilariously eclectic **ecclesiastical museum** (unpredictable hours, most reliable chance of admission 10am–1pm daily; free) featuring such bottled "relics" as earth collected from Mount Tabor and water from the River Jordan, as well as archeological finds, medieval glazed ware and two faded letters of 1824 from Greek revolutionary hero Admiral Miaoulis.

Accommodation

A prime **accommodation** choice in all senses is Nikos' and Anna's welcoming *Apartments Galini* (☎22470 41212, ℻22470 41012; ❸), the first building you see above the ferry jetty, consisting of large balconied rooms with fridge and hotplate; Nikos is a fisherman and may take groups on *kaïki* tours by request. Equally sought after are the *Studios Kalymnos* (☎22470 41141, ⓦwww .lipsiweb.gr; ❸) in a garden on the road north out of "town", run by Laid Back Holidays (see below), where a garden with barbecue facilities compensates for viewless, somewhat airless units. Other good options not monopolized by package clients include *Rena's Rooms* (☎22470 41363 or 22470 41110; ❸), overlooking Liendoú beach, and the *Glaros* (☎22470 41360; ❷), on the hillside behind the *Kalypso Hotel Restaurant*, with terrazzo-floored 1980s-vintage rooms sharing cooking facilities. Top of the heap comfort-wise is the 1997-built *Aphrodite Hotel* (☎22470 41000 or 22470 41394; ❹), a studio-and-apartment bungalow complex designed to accommodate package clients, though they're not averse to walk-ins at slow times.

Eating, drinking and nightlife

Among eight surviving **tavernas**, mostly on or just behind the quay, the best are indisputably *O Yiannis* (early May to early Oct), an excellent all-rounder with meat/seafood grills, *mayireftá* and local bulk wine – the only one open for lunch out of peak season – and *La Nave da Massimo/The Boat* up in the village centre (supper only; May–Sept), specializing in grills and a few Italian dishes. Honourable mentions go to salubrious *Tholari*, at the east end of the bay, where returned Greek-Australians serve supper all year (plus lunch in peak season), and *Pefkos* on the quay near *O Yiannis*. On the waterfront to either side of the *Kalypso* stand three idiosyncratic *kafenía-ouzerís*; from west to east they are *Asprakis* (aka *Vasso*), with wonderful stacked-bottle decor and stone-bench, waterside seating; *Sofoklis* slightly inland and adjacent *Nikos* (no sign) just back from the water. A shot of *oúzo* with a small plate of fish or octopus tentacle, cheese and tomato shouldn't run to much more than €1.50 – an atmospheric and almost obligatory pre-supper ritual.

    Nightlife at a handful of clubs is fairly well developed, with the doyen being *The Rock*, the "characters'" bar (including, until his apprehension, Yiotopoulos; host Babis always has good Greek music on, and offers breakfast in peak season. **Internet** facilities are available at *O Kavos*, near the yacht anchorage.

Other practicalities

The **post office** is just up some steps on the cathedral *platía*, opposite the ecclesiastical museum. Money-changing facilities include a freestanding **ATM** just in from the fishing quay, but if this is broken or empty you'll have to use one of three **travel agencies**: Greek-American-run Paradisi (☎22470 41120) near the ATM, also organizing *kaïki* excursions to surrounding islets; Lipsos Travel (☎22470 41225), handling the *Dodekanisos Express*; and Laid Back Holidays (☎22470 41141), repping for the hydrofoil and *Nissos Kalymnos*.

Around the island

From May to October, two **minibuses** run all day, departing on the hour, along the route Katsádhia–Harbour–Platýs Yialós, with the town stop near the ATM. Otherwise, there are two **taxis**, and two outfits renting **scooters**:

Shortly before Hokhlakoúra, just right of the road, stands the appealing, sixteenth-century, triple-apsed church of **Panayía toú Hárou** (The Virgin of Death), focus of a miracle, repeated annually since 1943. The church is so named because it once contained an icon of the Virgin cradling the dead Christ, the only such known in the Orthodox world (it is now safely kept in the town cathedral). In gratitude for a favour granted, a parishioner left a sprig of lilies under the glass of the icon; they duly withered, but were found to mysteriously revive only on August 23, the day of the Virgin's reception into Paradise. Each year the island's major festival sees the icon, with rejuvenating flowers, processed with suitable ceremony to its old home and then back to the village square, focus of all-night revelries.

George (℡22470 41340), and the more obvious Markos & Maria (℡22470 41130).

The island's **beaches** are rather scattered, though none is more than an hour's walk (or 20min scooter ride) distant. Closest to town, and sandiest, is **Liendoú**, immediately to the northwest, but many visitors prefer the attractive duo of **Katsadhiá** (sand) and **Papandhriá** (pebbles), adjacent small coves about 2km south of the port by paved road. Right above the sea at Katsadhiá you'll find a musical taverna-café-bar, *Dilaila* (June–Sept), which also runs an informal pine-grove campsite (free but you must buy a meal from them daily). By contrast, **Hokhlakoúra**, on the east coast, consists of occasionally grubby shingle with no facilities; nearby **Turkómnima** offers a 100m or so of tamarisk-shaded sand, but it's mercilessly exposed to the *meltémi* and thus often seaweed-caked. A final ten-minute path scramble from a "parking area" at the end of a rough track gets you to **Monodhéndhri** in the far northeast, poor to mediocre as a beach, but very scenic with its photogenic lone juniper tree and the striking rock islets of Asproníssia offshore. There are far superior coves just to the right, past the gated fence, though they get too much shade after noon; clothing is optional everywhere here.

Some 4km of travel along the paved road leading west from town brings you to **Platýs Yialós**, a small, shallow bay with a single taverna. The boulder-studded, sandy beach here isn't up to much, and the bay is ridiculously shallow and exposed, but the **taverna** (*Kostas*) is quite salubrious and popular for lunch (June–Sept daily; May & Oct Wed, Sat & Sun only), with mountainous salads and grills (sometimes including fish).

A bare handful of surviving paths and narrow tracks provide opportunities for genuine **walks** through the undulating countryside, though the well-signposted road network, surfaced or otherwise, seems to increase each year. One of the better surviving treks heads west to the bay of **Kímisi**, where the religious hermit Filippos, long a cult figure amongst foreign visitors, used to dwell in a tiny monastery just above the shore, next to the single island spring. A particularly ugly road was bulldozed in from the north in 1999 and later paved, disturbing his solitude; Filippos moved to town and died, aged 85, in 2002. To reach the place, bear left onto the faintly waymarked path taking off from the trans-island road at its high point (some 20min above Liendoú). In as much time again you'll reach the chapel-monastery of Stavrós, tracing the north flank of Lipsi's summit ridge; from there you're obliged to follow the new road another twenty minutes to sea level at Káto Kímisi. The beach here is decent, with some masonry "improvements" of obscure purpose just behind; you can detour an extra forty minutes and return up a fieldstoned and walled path to the neatly kept hermitage of **Páno Kímisi**, preserved as it was before Filippos abandoned this for his lower quarters in the early 1980s. From the shore monastery, an obvious path begins threading high above the coast back towards Liendoú, but the trail is faint to barely existent in the middle, so you'll need good hill-walking skills. At rocky **Eléna** beach a broader track resumes towards marginally better **Kámbos** cove, and it's just over an hour from Káto Kímisi to Liendoú, for a total (including side-trip to Páno Kímisi and a swim at Káto) of just over three hours.

Arkí and Maráthi

About two-thirds the size of Lipsí, **Arkí** is considerably more primitive, lacking drinking water, dynamo electricity (there are solar panels), or much in the way of a village centre. Just forty permanent inhabitants eke out a living here, mostly engaged in fishing, though catering for yacht parties attracted by the superb anchorage of Avgoústa ("Port Augusta" on nautical charts) is increasingly important. The island's isolation was considerably eased in 2002–03 with the construction of a helipad and a proper jetty; thus Arkí is now a regular stop on the route of the *Nissos Kalymnos*, whose schedule permits a cheap daytrip from Pátmos (arrival at noon, return at 5pm) if you don't fancy using the pricier, dedicated excursion boats.

Of the three **tavernas** around the harbourside *platía*, the better two – *Nikolas* (☎22470 32477) and *O Trypas* (☎22470 32230) – each control a handful of **rooms** (❷), but avoid August, when Italians and Greeks snap up every vacancy far in advance. *Nikolas* is more food-oriented, with homemade puddings, while *O Trypas* doubles as the happening music pub, courtesy of the owner's enormous collection of CDs and tapes. The next inlet southeast, also used by yachts, offers another eatery, *To Steno*, tops for seafood *mezédhes* like *pínna* and *foúskes* as well as fishy mains.

The only real "sight" is the half-ruined Hellenistic **fortress of Avgoustínis** near the island's summit, its masonry reworked by the Byzantines. You can **swim** at the "Blue Lagoon" of **Tiganákia** at the southeast tip of the island – just follow the obvious dirt track southeast; otherwise all excursions from Lipsí stop there – the only other approximations of beaches on Arkí are the scrappy one just past the jetty, or two patches of sand on the opposite side of the bay, in the shade of two derelict buildings and some trees.

The nearest, tamarisk-shaded, proper sandy beach is just offshore on the islet of **Maráthi**, the only inhabited one of the nine surrounding Arkí, where a pair of **tavernas** cater to day-trippers who come several times a week from Pátmos or Lipsí. *Marathi* (☎22470 31580 or 22470 32759; ❶; open most of year), run engagingly by the habitually barefoot Mihalis Kavouras (who looks like a comic-book pirate), is the more traditional, cosy outfit, with waterside seating, local seafood or Mihalis' own free-range goats on the menu, and simple, adequate rooms upstairs. *Pantelis* (☎22470 32609; ❸; June–Oct) is further inland, at the opposite end of the sand, more commercially minded – and apt to lock the compound's outer gate at 11pm if you go drinking at his rival's bar.

Agathoníssi

The small, steep-sided islet of **Agathoníssi** is still often known by its medieval name Gáïdharo, after its map-outline similarity to a donkey facing east. By contrast its ancient moniker Yetoússa has fallen into disuse; the modern name ("Virtuous-island") was bestowed post-1948 as a tribute to the

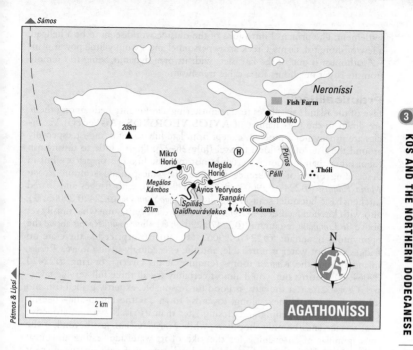

islanders' supposed sterling qualities. Like Lípsi, it was until 1954 formerly owned outright by the monastery on Pátmos, and it seems the locals are descended from a mix of Byzantine political exiles, pirates and agricultural lay workers dependent on the monastery. It's too remote – much closer to Turkey than Pátmos, in fact – for most day-excursions, though some are half-heartedly advertised in Pythagório, Sámos, which (along with Iréon) is where many islanders go to spend the winter and school their children. Intrepid Greeks and Italians (some of whom return annually) form its main clientele, along with a steady trickle of yachts who take advantage of the superbly protected harbour. Even though the *Nissos Kalymnos* (and a weekly hydrofoil) appear regularly, you should count on being marooned here for three days if the wind's up. "Marooned" is perhaps too harsh a word, since Agathoníssi is the perfect venue for what the Greeks call *bánio, mám ke nán'*: a swim, a snack and a nap. The friendly, unspoilt character of the island – no tourist-trinket shops yet, for example, except for a booth on the quay selling T-shirts – hasn't been much affected by a brief spate of villa construction on the hillside, or a slightly increased military garrison whose main task seems to be the apprehension of Kurdish refugees who come ashore here.

There are no springs on Agathoníssi, so rain-catchment basins and cisterns for livestock are ubiquitous, with the village mains system supplemented by water imported from Rhodes. Nevertheless, the island's thirteen-plus square kilometres are greener and more fertile than they appear from the sea; lentisc and carob bushes are interspersed with small oaks and olive trees, while two arable valleys lie to the west of Mikró Horió hamlet – the larger of them known, accurately enough, as Megálos Kámbos (Big Field). Goats, sheep, chickens plus the occasional cow far outnumber the human islanders for whom they provide the main livelihood, but fresh produce is limited to a single shop in the port

315

settlement. The principal intrusions of the outside world seem to be a helipad, a few offshore fish farms, Greek army personnel and a wonky little power plant – Agathoníssi is one of the last islets with its own dynamo, being too remote from its larger neighbours for a cable transfusion.

Practicalities

Five of the island's six places to stay, mustering all of eighty beds among them, are down in the port hamlet of **ÁYIOS YEÓRYIOS (Aï-Yeóryi)**. Vacancies are usually not a problem except from late July to mid-August, especially around the date of the local festival (July 26–27). There's little to distinguish them other than location – certainly not intrinsic luxuries or price – but in descending order of preference they are: the vine-patioed, seafront *Rooms Maria Kamitsi* (℡22470 29003, ℗22470 29004; ❷), with fridges and shared kitchen; basic but quiet seafront *Rooms Theoloyia Yiameou* (℡22470 29005; ❷), also with kitchen facilities; *To Agnandi*, the newest rooms, somewhat noisily set above *To Limanaki* restaurant (℡22470 29019; ❷); the *Seagull Rooms* above the eponymous restaurant (℡22470 29062; ❸), rather overpriced as there are no fridges and hot water is unreliable; and the exceedingly basic *George's Rooms*, inland behind the *Kamitsi* rooms (enquire at his taverna, or ring ℡22470 29064; ❶). **Eating** out, you'll almost certainly try all three full-service tavernas. *George's*, nearest the jetty, is good for reasonable, expertly grilled fish and salads; *To Limanaki*, next along, towards "town", is the cheap-and-cheerful Greeks' hangout, opening and closing later than its rivals, with an attractive roof terrace and the only shop here; while *Seagull/Glaros*, just beyond, is the most popular of an evening for the sake of its waterside seating and meat dishes. **Nightlife**, if you discount the loud, very naff café on the quay, is limited to *Café-Bar Yetoussa* next to the *Seagull*, also a source of good breakfasts and ice creams and going strong since 1990.

Of two inland settlements, the fairly attractive hamlet of **MEGÁLO HORIÓ** can muster just over a hundred people (considerably more than its counterpart Mikró Horió, with eleven inhabitants). Numbers have dropped from several hundred since the last war, but the 146 who've stayed on Agathoníssi seem determined to make a go of it and, in contrast to so many other islands, there are virtually no abandoned or neglected houses here. Just about the entire population turns up in its *platía* for the island festival on the night of July 26–27 (often continuing two days more), which features live music of variable quality.

Megálo Horió **amenities** consist of just two haphazardly stocked shops, the *Estiatorio Irini* (light snacks only) and the *Kafenio Dhekatria Adhelfia*; outside of peak season, one or other of these may be the only place on the island serving food at midday. There is no post office, bank or ATM, here or at the port. A single bakery, on the link road, works mysterious hours; ferry and hydrofoil tickets must be bought in advance at a little booth opposite the *Café-Bar Yetoussa*.

Around the island

Along its south shore, Agathoníssi is nearly as indented as Léros, making it a popular anchorage for yachts in summer. At the heads of various bays lie numerous small, often stony **beaches**, providing adequate, if not brilliant, swimming opportunities – you'll usually find sandy seabed a few paces out. Boat trips to the more remote coves rarely operate, even in peak season, and there's no scooter rental; thus you must reckon on walking there – sometimes on roads but often by faint trail, or even cross-country scrambling.

The closest beach to Áyios Yeóryios is **Spiliás**, a ten-minute stroll southwest along a bulldozed track; this coarse-shingle-and-gravel strand is so named for a small cave at its far end. Despite a lack of fresh water, people camp here. A twelve-minute scramble southwest over the cave headland on faint paths brings you to marginally better **Gaïdhourávlakos** cove, where nudism goes unremarked on its finer-gravel beach, and there's a water cistern for the numerous cattle who leave their pats everywhere. You can enjoyably vary the return to the port by following a trail up the west bank of the ravine feeding the beach (start at the cistern), ending up at another well-and-cistern complex at the south end of Megálos Kámbos, and thence along a broader path to join the track at the plateau's eastern edge (some 40min along), and finally on to Mikró Horió and the port (just under 1hr from Gaïdhourávlakos). The only other swimming cove in the vicinity of the port is **Tsangári**, 25 minutes of cross-country along the shore (around a wire fence at sea level, 5min along) and frankly not worth the effort were it not for **Árama** just before, a fine-pebble nook that just fits two bathers.

The cement-paved road heading east out of Megálo Horió leads within 45 minutes (give or take a few trail short cuts) to **Kathólikó**. There's no real beach here, only a partially ruined fishing hamlet of a half-dozen houses under some tamarisks, with an equal number of fishing boats at anchor. A fish farm, owned by an Athenian supermarket chain, floats just offshore in the lee of **Neroníssi**. A gruesome legend attaches to the area: some years ago a *kaïki* bound for Sámos foundered here, and a woman drowned with her child. The locals buried them in an abandoned lime kiln, without summoning the priest for a proper liturgy; ever since, the woman's ghost is said to be heard screaming after dark, and an otherworldly glow envelops the kiln on moonless nights. Inland to the west are the remains of a Roman dye works, marked by a midden-pile of discarded murex shells.

The closest proper beaches lie twenty minutes' walk south of Kathólikó, along **Póros Bay**, accessible via a cemented drive veering southeast a few minutes before Kathólikó. The sandy beach at the head of the bay has little shade and is often rubbish-strewn. End of the road, an hour's walk from Áyios Yeóryios, is **Thóli**, with good snorkelling and some morning shade, more attractive than previously, now that its fish farm has vanished. The beach of **Pálli** lies on the opposite (west) side of the bay and is arguably the island's best; to reach it, walk eight minutes out of Megálo Horió on the main road, then go down and right opposite the track for the helipad, initially following a pasture wall. It's fifteen minutes more downhill along faint goat-traces to the small, shadeless, but pristine fine-pebble cove.

Thóli cove takes its name from the internal arcades and vaults of a mysterious late Byzantine or early **medieval structure** just inland, by far the most remarkable sight on the island and (almost) unique in the east Aegean – there's a similar building on Farmakoníssi (see below). Neither a public bath nor a manor house, it seems to have had no obvious military use; nor does it appear to be part of a monastery, since no church is associated with it. However, its location at the head of a still-used agricultural valley with two threshing cirques just above, plus the discovery of amphorae in the bay below, suggests that this was a trading post and grain warehouse.

Other, scantier Roman and Byzantine ruins are found on **Farmakoníssi**, an islet south of Agathoníssi which often spurs the curiosity of travellers who glimpse it from hydrofoils. Since the 1996 Ímia crisis, however, it has been taken over by the military and is now off limits to civilians, in particular foreign yachts. Should the ban ever be lifted, the most noteworthy sight here is a series

Greek script table

Pátmos	Πάτμος	ΠΑΤΜΟΣ
Agriolívadho	Αγριολίβαδο	ΑΓΡΙΟΛΙΒΑΔΟ
Apokálypsi	Αποκάλυψγ	ΑΠΟΚΑΛΥΨΗ
(Apocalypse Monastery)		
Ayíou Ioánnou Theológou	Αγίου Ιοάννου	ΑΓΙΟΥ ΙΟΑΝΝΟΥ
(Saint John Monastery)	Θεολόγου	ΘΕΟΛΟΓΟΥ
Gríkou	Γροίκου	ΓΡΟΙΚΟΥ
Hokhlakás	Χοχλακάρ	ΧΟΧΛΑΚΑΣ
Hóra	Χώρα	ΧΩΡΑ
Kámbos	Κάμπος	ΚΑΜΠΟΣ
Lámbi	Λάμποι	ΛΑΜΠΟΙ
Livádhi Yerano	Λειβάδι Γερανού	ΛΕΙΒΑΔΙ ΓΕΡΑΝΟΥ
Melóï	Μελόϊ	ΜΕΛΟΪ
Psilí Ámmos	Ψηλή Άμμος	ΨΙΛΗ ΑΜΜΟΣ
Skála	Σκάλα	ΣΚΑΛΑ
Vayiá	Βαγιά	ΒΑΓΙΑ
Lipsí	Λειψοί	ΛΕΙΨΟΙ
Hokhlakoúra	Χοχλακούρα	ΧΟΧΛΑΚΟΥΡΑ
Liendoú	Λιεντού	ΛΙΕΝΤΟΥ
Katsadhiá	Κατσαδιά	ΚΑΤΣΑΔΙΑ
Kímisi	Κοίμισι	ΚΟΙΜΗΣΗ
Monodhéndhri	Μονοδένδρι	ΜΟΝΟΔΕΝΔΡΙ
Papandhriá	Παπανδριά	ΠΑΠΑΝΔΡΙΑ
Platýs Yialós	Πλατύς Γιαλός	ΠΛΑΤΥΣ ΓΙΑΛΟΣ
Arkí	Αρκιοί	ΑΡΚΟΙ
Avgoústa	Αυγούστα	ΑΥΓΟΥΣΤΑ
Maráthi	Μαράθι	ΜΑΡΑΘΙ
Tiganákia	Τιγανάκια	ΤΗΓΑΝΑΚΙΑ
Agathoníssi	Αγαθονήσί	ΑΓΑΘΟΝΗΣΙ
Áyios Yeóryios	Άγιος Γεώργιος	ΑΓΙΟΣ ΓΕΩΡΓΙΟΣ
Gaïdhourávlakos	Γαΐδουραύλακος	ΓΑΪΔΟΥΡΑΥΛΑΚΟΣ
Katholikó	Καθολικό	ΚΑΘΟΛΙΚΟ
Megálo Horió	Μεγάλο Χωριό	ΜΕΓΑΛΟ ΧΩΡΙΟ
Mikró Horió	Μικρό Χωριό	ΜΙΚΡΟ ΧΩΡΙΟ
Pálli	Πάλοι	ΠΑΛΟΙ
Spiliás	Σπηλιάρ	ΣΠΗΛΙΑΣ
Thóli	Θόλοι	ΘΟΛΟΙ
Tsangári	Τσανγάρι	ΤΣΑΓΓΑΡΙ

of Roman arcades to one side of the little port – supposedly built to house the young Julius Caesar while he was imprisoned here by pirates in 74 BC, but in fact more likely to be ancient food warehouses.

Pátmos, Lipsí, Agathoníssi travel details

Island transport

Buses

Skála (Pátmos) to: Gríkou (6–8 daily); Hóra (11 daily 8am–9pm); Kámbos (4 daily).

Kaïkia

Skála (Pátmos): daily trips to most east coast beaches.

Inter-island transport

Kaïkia and excursion boats

Pátmos to: Arkí (2–5 weekly; 1hr 10min); Lipsí (1 daily; 1hr 20min); Maráthi (almost daily on demand; 1hr).

Lipsí to: Ayía Marína, Léros (5–7 weekly May–Oct); Pátmos (1 daily May–Oct); Arkí/Maráthi (2–3).

Ferries

Pátmos to: Agathoníssi (4 weekly on NK; 2hr); Arkí (4 weekly on NK; 1hr); Kálymnos (4 weekly on NK, 5–6 weekly on GA; 2hr 30min–3hr); Kós (1–2 weekly on BS, 5–6 weekly on GA; 3–4hr); Léros (1–2 weekly on BS, 5–6 weekly on GA, 4 weekly on NK; 1hr–1hr 45min); Lipsí (4 weekly on NK; 1hr); Níssyros (1 weekly on GA; 5hr 30min); Pireás (1–2 weekly on BS, 5–6 weekly on GA; 7–9hr); Rhodes (1–2 weekly on BS, 5–6 weekly on GA; 5hr 30min–7hr); Pythagório-Sámos (4 weekly on NK; 3hr 30min); Sými (1–2 weekly on GA; 7hr); Tílos (1–2 weekly on GA; 6hr 30min).

Lipsí to: Kálymnos (4 weekly on NK; 2hr 15min); Léros (4 weekly on NK; 1hr 15min); Pátmos (4 weekly on NK; 1hr); Pythagório, Pythagório-Sámos (4 weekly on NK; 4hr 30min).

Agathoníssi and Arkí to: each other, Kós, Léros, Lipsí, Pátmos, Pythagório-Sámos (all 4 weekly on NK; sample times Agathoníssi–Pythagório 1hr 30min, Agathoníssi–Pátmos 2hr).

Catamaran

Pátmos to: Léros, Kálymnos, Kós, Rhodes (3–4 weekly); Lipsí (1–2 weekly); Sými (1 weekly, June–Oct).

Lipsí to: Léros, Kálymnos, Kós, Rhodes (3 weekly); Pátmos (2 weekly); Sými (1 weekly, June–Oct).

NB All listed services are on the *Dodekanisos Express*. Another catamaran, the *Iason Superjet*, was introduced once weekly on the route Lipsí–Pátmos–Foúrni–Karlóvassi–Ikaría–Piraeás in late 2004, but it was an emergency replacement for the *Aeolos Express* and may not last.

Hydrofoils

Lipsí and Pátmos to: each other (4–7 weekly); Agathoníssi (1 weekly); Foúrni (2 weekly); Ikaría (2 weekly); Kálymnos (4–7 weekly); Kós (4–7 weekly, plus 1–2 weekly on LZ); Léros (4–7 weekly); Pythagório-Sámos (5–7 weekly).

NB All services are provided by Kyriakoulis Maritime except where indicated.

The East Aegean Islands

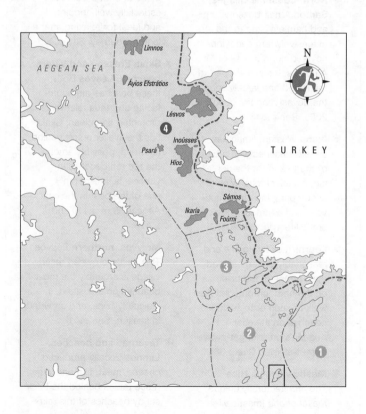

CHAPTER 4 # Highlights

❋ **Vathý, Sámos** Vathý's archeological museum is perhaps the best in the islands of this book; the star is the huge, nearly intact *kouros* from the local shrine of Hera, but the small-objects collection is also fascinating. See p.331

❋ **North-coast hill villages, Sámos** A half-dozen villages and hamlets cling to the extensively terraced, vine-covered north slopes of Mt Ámbelos, the lushest part of the island and largely spared the devastating fire of July 2000. See p.346

❋ **Ikaría** Western Ikaría has superb beaches with a bit of rough surf for the daring, excellent local wine to accompany the many festivals, and a famously idiosyncratic lifestyle. See p.356

❋ **Foúrni** Tuck into a fine and reasonably priced seafood meal at one of the tavernas on the harbourfront, and then walk or scooter to secluded beaches on the east Aegean's premier get-away-from-it-all islet. See p.366

❋ **Mastic villages, Híos** The architecturally unique *mastihohoriá* (mastic villages) were laid out by the Genoese but have a Middle Eastern feel; Pyrgí is enlivened by *xystá*, while Mestá is the best-preserved community. See p.379

❋ **Thermal baths, Lésvos** There are four working Ottoman spas on the island, but those at Loutrá Yéras are especially well appointed and ideal for relaxing after a lengthy journey. See p.406

❋ **Skála Eressoú and Vaterá beaches, Lésvos** Both these beaches are south-facing and thus relatively protected and clean; Skála has the livelier resort behind it. Vaterá, possibly among the top ten beaches in Greece, is indisputably one of the best in the east Aegean. See p.410 and p.416

❋ **Mólyvos, northern Lésvos** This castle-crowned resort village is arguably the most beautiful on the island, if inevitably twee, and crowded in season. See p.418

❋ **Tavernas and beaches, Límnos** Locally produced cheese, meat, fish and wine grace tables behind the thick sandy beaches of this relaxing island. See p.429

The East Aegean Islands

T he five substantial islands and four minor islets scattered off the west Aegean coast of Turkey form a rather arbitrary archipelago. Although there are some passing similarities in architecture and landscape, the strong individual character of each island is far more striking. Despite their proximity to modern Turkey, the members of this "group" (Lésvos excepted) bear few signs of an Ottoman heritage, especially when compared to Rhodes and Kós. There's the occasional mosque, often shorn of its minaret, and some of the domestic architecture betrays obvious influences from Constantinople, Macedonia and further north in the Balkans. But by and large, the enduring Greekness of these islands is testimony to the 3500-year Hellenic presence in Asia Minor just opposite, which only ended in 1923.

This heritage has been regularly referred to by the Greek government in an intermittent propaganda war with Turkey over the sovereignty of these far-flung outposts – as well as the disputed boundary between them and the Turkish mainland. Tensions here have often been worse than in the Dodecanese, aggravated by potential undersea oil deposits in the straits between the islands and the Anatolian mainland. The Turks have also persistently demanded that Límnos, strategically astride the sea lanes to and from the Dardanelles, be demilitarized, but so far Greece has shown few signs of giving in other than to reduce the size of its garrison there.

Ironically, this ongoing conflict has given these long-neglected islands a new lease of life, insomuch as their sudden strategic importance has seen infrastructure improvements to support garrisoning, and given a mild fillip to local economies, engaged in providing goods and services to soldiers, something predating mass tourism. Yet, even in spring 1998, the *Guardian* newspaper published the results of an EU-funded study which showed that, in terms of per-capita income, the "northeast Aegean" still ranked along with Epirus on mainland Greece, Apuglia in Italy and Extremadura in Spain as one of the poorest regions in western Europe. At first, this might seem an incredible or sensational judgement, given the lucrative tourist-takings on Sámos or the shipping-based remittance economy of Híos, but forays off the beaten track through the more backward and depressed corners of Ikaría, Lésvos or Límnos will still uncover early twentieth-century lifestyles which are obviously pulling the average down.

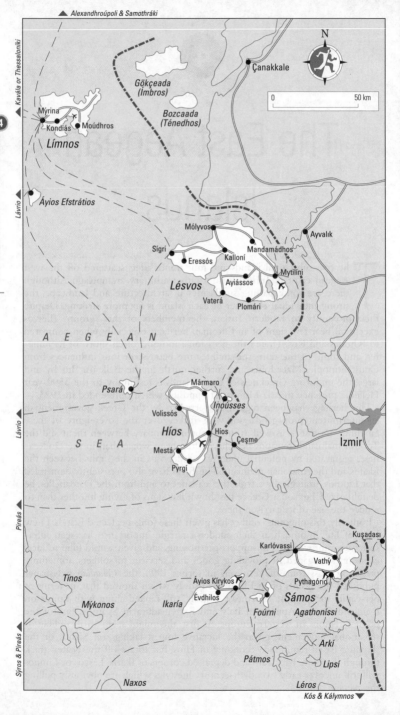

N

0   50 km

Çanakkale

Gökçeada
(Ímbros)

Bozcaada
(Ténedhos)

◀ Kavála or Thessaloníki

Mýrina
Kondiás   Moúdhros

Límnos

◀ Lávrio

Áyios Efstrátios

Ayvalík

Mólyvos

Sígri   Mandamádhos

Eressós   Kalloní

Lésvos   Mytilíni

Ayiássos

Vaterá   Plomári

A   E   G   E   A   N

Psará

Mármaro

Inoússes

Volissós   Híos

Híos   Çeşme

◀ Lávrio

S   E   A

Mestá

Pyrgí

İzmir

◀ Pireás

Kuşadası

Karlóvassi

Vathý

Tínos

Áyios Kírykos   Pythagório

Mýkonos

Évdhilos

Ikaría   Foúrni   Sámos

Agathoníssi

◀ Sýros & Pireás

Arkí

Pátmos   Lipsí

Naxos   Léros

The heavy **military presence** can be disconcerting and, notwithstanding the advent of tourism, large tracts of land remain off limits as military reserves. But as in the Dodecanese, local tour operators do a thriving business shuttling passengers for inflated tariffs between these islands and the **Turkish coast**, with its amazing archeological sites and bustling resorts. Most of the east Aegean's main ports and towns are not the quaint, picturesque spots you may be used to in other parts of Greece, but urbanized bureaucratic, military and commercial centres. In all cases you should suppress an initial impulse to take the next boat out, and delve instead into the worthwhile interiors.

Sámos, immediately north of the Dodecanese, ranks as the most visited island of the group and is still arguably the most verdant and beautiful, even after a devastating July 2000 fire. **Ikaría** to the west remains relatively unspoilt, if a minority taste, with an airport that's too tiny to have much effect on the number of visitors. Nearby **Foúrni** is a haven for determined solitaries (except in Aug), as are Híos' satellites **Psará** and **Inoússes**, neither of the latter with any package-tour facilities. **Híos** itself offers far more cultural interest than any of its southern neighbours, but its natural beauty has been ravaged by wildfires, and the development of tourism has been deliberately retarded. **Lésvos** may not impress initially, though once you grasp its old-fashioned, Anatolian ambience, you may find yourself amongst the substantial number of return visitors. By contrast, almost no foreigners and few Greeks call in at remote **Áyios Efstrátios**, and with good reason. **Límnos**, the northernmost of this group, is much livelier, but its appeal is confined mostly to the area immediately around the attractive port town.

Sámos

Lush, seductive and shaped like a pregnant guppy, **Sámos** seems to swim away from Asia Minor, to which the island was joined until Ice Age cataclysms sundered it from Mount Mykáli (Mycale) on the Turkish mainland. The resulting 1500-to-2500-metre strait is now the narrowest distance between Greece and Turkey in the Aegean, except at Kastellórizo; accordingly military installations bristle on both sides – though, as you ride in from the airport, signs reassuringly announce "Samos unnuclear island" (sic). In its variety of mountainous terrain, beaches and vegetation, Sámos has the feel of a much larger island, and before recent development and wildfires took their toll it was indisputably among the most beautiful in the Aegean; much of value remains, testimony to its ample natural endowments.

There's little tangible evidence of this now, but Sámos was also once the **wealthiest island** in the Aegean. Under the patronage of the local tyrant Polykrates, it became home to a thriving **intellectual community** which included the philosophers Epikouros (Epicurus) and Pythagoras, the astronomer Aristarkhos (Aristarchus) and the bard Aesop. Decline set in as the star of Classical Athens was in the ascendant, though the island's status improved somewhat during early Byzantine times, when Sámos constituted its own *theme* (imperial administrative district).

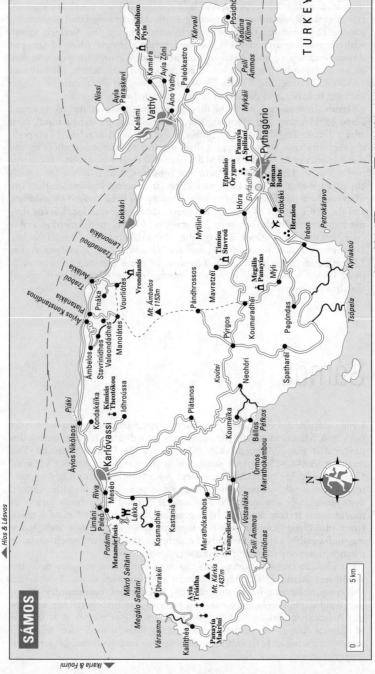

SÁMOS

▲ Kuşadası (Turkey)   ▲ Kuşadası (Turkey)

◀ Hios & Lésvos

▶ Arkí, Lipsí & Agathoníssi

▶ Pátmos & Foúrni

◀ Ikaría & Foúrni

TURKEY

Zoödhóhou
Piyís
Kerveli
Posidhónio
Kamára
Ayía Zóni
Ano Vathý
Kaduna
(Klíma)
Paleókastro
Nissí
Ayía
Paraskeví
Kalámi
Psilí
Ámmos
Vathý
Mykáli
Panayía
Spilianí
Pythagório
Leimonákia
Kokkári
Kérveli
Efpalínio
Órygma
Roman
Baths
Glyfádha
Kondakéïka
Myrtiliní
Timíou
Stavroú
Vrondianís
Vourliótes
Mt. Ámbelos
1153m
Pándhrossos
Mavratzéï
Megális
Panayías
Ýdra
Potokáki
Heraion
Iréon
Tzamadoú
Avlákia
Tzaboú
Platanákia
Ayios Konstandínos
Pnáka
Plátanos
Pýrgos
Koumaradhéï
Mýli
Petrokáravo
Kyriakoú
Ámbelos
Stavinídhes
Valeondádhes
Manolátes
Koútsi
Neohóri
Spatharéï
Pagóndas
Tsópela
Piáki
Kímisis
Theotókou
Idhroússa
Ayios Nikólaos
Karlóvassi
Kouméïka
Bállos
Pérkos
Riva
Meséo
Limáni
Paleó
Lékka
Kastaniá
Marathókambos
Órmos
Marathokámbou
Votsalákia
Potámi
Metamórfosis
Kosmadhéï
Evangelístrias
Psilí Ámmos
Mikró Seïtáni
Dhrakéï
Ayía
Triádha
Mt. Kérkis
1437m
Limniónas
Megálo Seïtáni
Kallithéa
Panayía
Makrini
Vársamo

N

0   5 km

During the 1470s, the Genoese – who controlled Sámos from their base on Híos – evacuated most of the inhabitants, abandoning the island to the mercy of Venetian and Turkish pirates. Following their pillaging and massacring, Sámos remained almost completely **desolate** until 1562, when an Ottoman admiral, Kiliç Ali Pasha, got permission from the sultan to repopulate it with some of the Samians who had fled to Híos with the Genoese, as well as Greek Orthodox settlers recruited from every corner of Greece and Asia Minor. The population was further supplemented after 1923 with an influx of refugees from Anatolia.

The heterogeneous descent of today's islanders largely explains an enduring **identity crisis** and a rather thin topsoil of indigenous culture. Most of the village names are either clan surnames or adjectives indicating origins elsewhere – constant reminders of **refugee descent**. Consequently there is no genuine Samiot music, dance or dress, and little that's original in the way of cuisine and architecture (the latter a blend of styles from northern Greece and the Asia Minor coast). The Samians compensated somewhat for this deracination by struggling fiercely for independence during the 1820s, but despite their accomplishments in sinking a Turkish fleet in the narrow Mycale strait and annihilating a landing army, the Great Powers (Britain, France and Russia) handed the island back to the Ottomans in 1830, with the consolatory proviso that it be **semi-autonomous** and ruled by an appointed Christian prince. This period, referred to as the *Iyimonía* (Hegemony), was marked by a mild renaissance in fortunes, courtesy of the hemp and (especially) tobacco trade. However, union with Greece in 1912, the ravages of a bitter World War II occupation and subsequent mass emigration effectively reversed the recovery until the arrival of tourism during the early 1980s.

Today the Samian economy is increasingly dependent on **package tourism**, with far too much of it in places; the eastern half of the island, and much of the south coast, has almost totally surrendered to the onslaught of holiday-makers, although the more rugged northwestern part has retained most of its undeveloped grandeur. The rather sedate, couples-oriented clientele is overwhelmingly Dutch, Scandinavian, German and Swiss, though lately there are growing numbers of Belgians, Italians, Slovenians, Czechs and – spurred by a favourable BBC radio feature or two and the efforts of such holiday companies as Laskarina and Sunvil – Brits. The absence of an official campsite on such a large island, tame nightlife a world away from that on Rhodes or Kós and phalanxes of self-catering villas hint at the sort of custom expected.

Not coincidentally, the most heavily developed areas have been most afflicted by **repeated wildfires**, none worse than that which burnt for a week in July 2000, ravaging twenty percent of the island's forest and orchards, as well as destroying over ninety dwellings. Even now if you mention Sámos to other Greeks, they say "*Ah, tó nisí poú kaíke*" ('Oh, the island that burnt'), and, taking into account the other quarter of the island area that had been torched piecemeal since 1987, Sámos has indeed lost about half of its original forest cover. Some stands of magnificent black pines survive on the heights, with Calabrian pine lower down, but in the centre and south of the island the devastation is total; brace yourself for broad vistas of ghostly tree trunks or utterly denuded slopes, and pay heed to fire-damage warnings when deciding where to spend a two-week package. The forest, as ever, will be a half-century in returning, and in fact (for other reasons, as well) tourist numbers have never recovered their former levels since the blaze. Volunteer fire-lookouts, complete with trucks, have now sprouted at critical points, but it does seem a case of locking the stable door after the horse has bolted.

Arrival and getting around

Sámos **airport** lies 14km southwest of Vathý and 3km west of Pythagório; a new, enlarged terminal came on-stream in July 2003. By sea, Sámos is the best-connected island in this guide, aside from Rhodes; it has no fewer than three **ferry ports** – Karlóvassi in the west, Vathý and Pythagório in the east. All ferries between Pireás, Sýros, Mýkonos, Páros, Náxos, Ikaría, Foúrni and Sámos call at both Karlóvassi and Vathý. Vathý also receives the weekly LANE and GA sailings between northern Greece and the Dodecanese, via most intervening islands.

Pythagório sees several regular weekly sailings of the local ferry *Nissos Kalymnos*, which plies to and from all of the Dodecanese between Sámos and Kálymnos, and also hosts the last surviving local hydrofoil services, to all the islands down to Kós, plus forays over to Foúrni and southern Ikaría.

The **bus terminals** (no covered stations, just ticket booking offices) in Pythagório and Vathý lie within longish walking distance of their ferry docks; at Karlóvassi, you must usually take a taxi the 3km into town from the port. There is no airport bus service; **taxi** fares to various points are stipulated on prominent placards, and in high season taxis to the airport or docks must be booked several hours (or even a day) in advance.

The KTEL service itself is excellent along the Pythagório–Vathý and Vathý–Kokkári–Karlóvassi corridors, but poor otherwise; you are pretty much expected to **rent a motorbike or car** and, with numerous outlets, it's easy to find a good deal, possibly even in July and August, given the recent drop in tourist numbers. A number of **mountain bikes**, ideal for the island's network of dirt tracks, are also available for rent.

Vathý

Lining the steep northeast shore of a deep bay, beachless **VATHÝ** – often confusingly referred to as "Sámos", like the island – is a busy provincial town which grew from a minor anchorage after 1830, when it replaced Hóra as the island's capital. It's an unlikely, somewhat ungraceful resort, which has seen numerous hotels gone bankrupt or converted to apartments since the late 1990s, and is minimally interesting aside from its excellent museum and old hill quarter.

The provincial authorities are slowly paving and landscaping (after a fashion) a waterfront esplanade beyond the always-full free car park. Between this and the fishing harbour stands the statue of local-boy-made-good Themistoklis Sofoulis, briefly prime minister in 1948–49; fishermen (and women) peddle their catch before 10am at a purpose-built fish stall nearby. The dumping of raw sewage in the bay has ceased, but still nobody in their right mind goes swimming at Vathý; the closest appealing beaches lie a few kilometres away.

Orientation, transport and information

For the moment, all seagoing craft use the traditional jetty as shown on the left of our map, but a new harbour terminal is being prepared at a snail's pace out by the wine co-op; all boats except passenger-only catamarans and excursion craft to Kuşadası are supposed to be shifted out there eventually, but this isn't expected to occur before 2006, and in fact it may only be used as the winter dock.

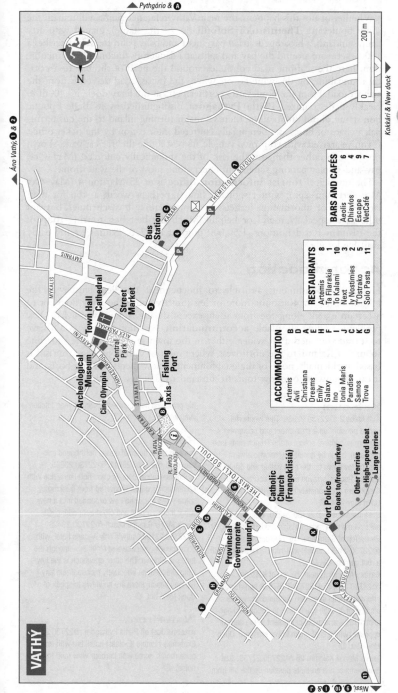

VATHÝ

▲ Pythgório & Ⓐ

▲ Áno Vathý, Ⓘ & ❷

Kokkári & New dock ▶

N

0   200 m

Pythgório

SINHAYS

MYKALIS

Town Hall

Cathedral

Archeological
Museum

Street
Market

Bus
Station

KANARI

THEMISTOKLI SOFOULI

ALEX PASHALII

FATSEVNI

TIMAS NARDU

Central
Park

STAMATI

Cine Olympia

Fishing
Port

Taxis

LARKEN

PLATIA
PYTHAGORIO

PL AYOU
NIKOLAOU

OROFILEI

THEMISTOKLI SOFOULI

KEFALOPOULOU

Catholic
Church
(Frangoklisiá)

Port Police

Boats to/from Turkey

Other Ferries

High-speed Boat

Large Ferries

Laundry

Provincial
Governorate

MANOLI

KATOAMR

AROS

NERHORO

GRAMOU

ENOKFKATOU

▼ Nissi, Ⓘ, Ⓗ, Ⓙ & ❿

ACCOMMODATION

Artemis	B
Avli	D
Christiana	A
Dreams	E
Emily	H
Galaxy	F
Ino	I
Ionia Maris	J
Paradise	C
Samos	K
Trova	G

RESTAURANTS

Artemis	8
Ta Filarakia	1
To Kalami	10
Next	3
Iy Nostimies	2
T'Ostrako	5
Solo Pasta	11

BARS AND CAFÉS

Aeolis	6
Dhiavlos	4
Escape	9
NetCafé	7

Whether or not this happens, the main Vathý reference point will remain the shore boulevard, **Themistoklí Sofoúli** (he of the statue), graced with arty lamp standards, a broad pedestrian pavement and baby palm trees. It describes a 1300-metre arc around the bay and splits at a dangerous uncontrolled junction; from here the seafront road continues around the head of the bay to a critical roundabout by the wine co-op, where the bypass road descends from the airport road. From the boulevard's northern end at the ferry dock, it's 400m to bleakly pedestrianized **Platía Pythagóra**, distinguished by its Belle Époque lion statue; about 800m along there's a major turning inland to the bus terminal, a chaos of buses at a perennially cluttered intersection by the ticket office. If you've arrived with your own vehicle, it's best to use the free car parks shown on the map rather than run the risk of the sporadically enforced (May–Oct) pay-and-display parking scheme in effect along most of the waterfront.

The municipal **tourist information office** is at 25-Martíou 4 (May–Oct Mon–Fri 9am–2pm; winter sporadic hours), perhaps worth a stop for their large stock of information leaflets or comprehensive bus schedules, but not otherwise especially useful or helpful. Much the best touring **map** of the island is Road Editions' 1:50,000 product no. 210, "Samos", fairly easily available locally.

Accommodation

Humbler establishments available to independent travellers cluster in the hillside district of Katsoúni, more or less directly above the ferry dock, or to a certain extent along the front itself; except during August, you'll have few problems finding affordable **accommodation**. For more luxury you'll have to spread your nets a bit wider, either in the town proper or in the shoreline suburb of Kalámi, to the northwest, where most of Vathý's package tourism is based. Incidentally, none of the establishments below meets arriving boats, and it can be unwise to follow touts to substandard facilities.

Katsoúni

Avli Aréos 2 ☎22730 22939. This wonderful period pension, up a stair-street and occupying the former convent school of the French nuns (see opposite), is run by genial Spyros who always has the lowdown on the best eating and drinking venues. Rooms, arrayed around a courtyard (*avlí* in Greek), are appropriately institutional but en suite. Open May–Oct. ❷

Dreams Áreos 9 ☎22730 24350. Well-kept en-suite rooms with fridges at this modern pension. ❷

Emily Top of Grámmou, cnr 11-Noemvríou ☎22730 24691. Small, well-run C-class hotel with a roof garden. ❸–❹

Galaxy Angéou 1, near the top of Katsoúni ☎22730 22665, ℻22730 27679. A surprisingly affordable hotel in garden surroundings with a small pool, though you'll have to dodge package allotments – and avoid being sent to the annexe opposite, which is of much lower standard. Open May–Oct. ❹

Trova Manóli Kalomíri 26 ☎22730 27759. Just five rooms at this en-suite pension up the hill from

the provincial headquarters. Open all year; kitchen available. ❷

Kalámi

Ino Above the hospital on the northbound one-way road ☎22730 23241, ℻22730 23245, ✉ino@samosnet.com. B-class hotel on a rise with commanding views, recovered from bankruptcy some years back and now expanded into a new wing; there's a pool and off-street parking. ❺

Ionia Maris Gangoú beach ☎22730 28428, ℻22730 23108. Vathý's only A-class hotel, with corresponding service and facilities – though the food's a letdown. The other drawback is the low-lying site: despite effectively monopolizing tiny Gangoú beach, there are no views to speak of. Open May–Oct. ❻

Waterfront

Artemis Just off Platía Pythagóra ☎22730 27792. Extremely humble (E-class) hotel, but with en-suite rooms, some with harbour view (and traffic noise). ❷

Samos Themistoklí Sofoúli 11 ℡ 22730 28377, ℻ 22730 28482, 🖳 www.samoshotel.gr. The obvious, C-class behemoth at the base of the ferry dock is a firm favourite as a businessmen's hotel, and isn't so bad for all that. Double glazing against traffic noise, rooftop pool-terrace, popular café out front. Open all year, thus popular with Asian tour groups in winter. ❹

Inland

Christiana Potamáki district ℡ 22730 23084, ℻ 22730 28856. B-class hotel that's the only accommodation in Áno Vathý, where an attractive ravine setting, huge outdoor pool, friendly management and decent rooms offset rather listless breakfasts. In recent seasons, however, it has only worked July and August. ❹

Paradise Kanári 21 ℡ 22730 23911, ℻ 22730 28754. Formerly package-dominated B-class hotel, now more likely to have vacancies on spec, with front rooms overlooking the bus stop; side and rear rooms have views of orchards and its pool. ❹

The Town

A prominent waterfront curiosity near the ferry jetty is the old French **Catholic church**, labelled "Ecclesia Catolica" but universally known as the **Frangoklisiá**; it's only open mid-morning on sporadic weekdays, with an interesting pamphlet available on the fortunes of the Catholic church in Greece. Since 1974, when the last nuns departed Sámos after having schooled the elite for nearly a century, the church has been used at best once weekly, when a priest arrives from Sýros to celebrate mass for interested tourists and the half-dozen or so Samian Catholics. The nun's male compatriots, incidentally, reintroduced the art of systematic wine-making to the island, though the contemporary product must bear little resemblance to the ancient stuff acclaimed by Byron ("Dash down yon cup of Samian wine..."). The local *oúzo* – particularly the Yiokarinis brand – is more highly regarded.

Strolls inland can be more rewarding; you might first visit the expensive, higgledy-piggledy **antiquarian and jewellery shop** of Mihalis Stavrinos, just off the "Lion Square" (Platía Pythagóra), where you can invest in assorted precious baubles or rare engravings. The pedestrianized marketplace just beyond – two-thirds authentic, one-third tourist schlock – and tiers of **Neoclassical houses** on stair-lanes are also of interest. Way up on the through-road in Neápoli, Miltiades Makris' **antique shop**, *Aiones* (one of the best in the islands), is as much museum as store; most of the stock is less portable than Stavrinos', but you're assured of a warm welcome from Miltiades.

The Archeological Museum

If you're pressed for time, the only must in Vathý is the excellent **Archeological Museum** (Tues–Sun 8.30am–2.30pm; €3), set behind the small central park beside the Neoclassical town hall. One of the best provincial collections in Greece is housed in the old Paskhallion building and the modern wing immediately opposite, the latter specially constructed for the star exhibit: a majestic, five-metre-high **kouros**, discovered – like most of the items – at the Heraion sanctuary (see p.340). The opening of this wing was delayed for years, since the roof had to be raised twice as more bits of the statue were found. The *kouros*, the largest freestanding effigy to survive from ancient Greece, was dedicated to Apollo, but found together with a devotional mirror to the Egyptian goddess Mut (syncretized with Hera) from a Nile workshop, one of only two such mirrors discovered in Greece to date.

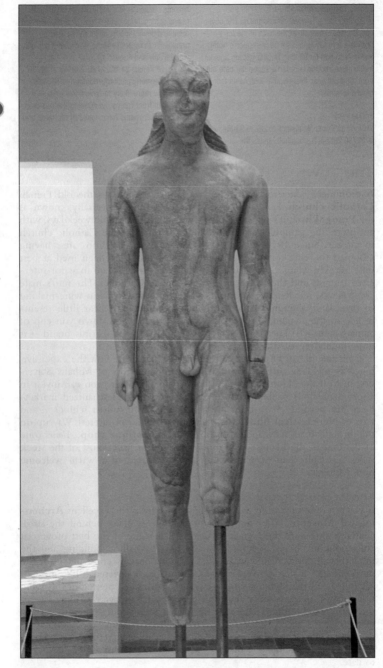

△ Archaic *Kouros*, Archeological Museum, Vathý, Sámos

In the equally compelling collection of small objects in the Paskhallion, more votive offerings of Egyptian design – a hippo, a dancer in Nilotic dress, Horus-as-Falcon, an Osiris figurine – prove trade and pilgrimage links between Sámos and the Nile valley going back to the eighth century BC. The Mesopotamian and Anatolian origins of other artwork confirm the exotic trend at the Heraion, most tellingly in a case full of ivory miniatures: Perseus and Medusa in relief, a kneeling, perfectly formed mini-*kouros* which once adorned a lyre, a pouncing lion, and a *rhyton* or drinking horn terminating in a bull's head. The most famous local artefacts are the dozen or so bronze **griffin-heads**, for which Sámos was the major centre of production in the seventh century BC; mounted on the edge of bronze cauldrons, they were believed to ward off evil spirits. Returned in 2000 from a long sojourn in an Athens basement is an unlabelled **hoard of gold byzants**, imperial coins from the fifth or sixth century AD, found early in the 1980s by a Dutch archeologist wading in the shallows at a remote bay.

Áno Vathý

The best target on foot, a twenty-minute walk south and 150m above sea level, is the atmospheric hill village of **ÁNO VATHÝ**, a nominally protected but increasingly threatened community of tottering, tile-roofed houses being steadily replaced by bad-taste blocks of flats or defaced with aluminium windows and modern flanged tiles. The village's late medieval churches (usually open) are neglected but still worth a look: the tiny chapel of **Ayía Kára**, immediately behind the municipal offices and crèche, boasts a fine *témblon* and naïve frescoes of the Apocalypse, while the quadruple-domed double church of **Aï Yannáki**, in the vale separating the two hillside neighbourhoods of the village, has an intriguing ground plan that compensates for its scandalously deteriorating condition. Few of the eighteenth-century frescoes have survived the damp, but one – a rare and moving one of the dead Christ in His tomb, known as the "Utter Humiliation" in Orthodox iconography – can be found at the rear left of the unlit interior (bring a torch). In the conch of the apse is an equally uncommon depiction of Christ Arkhierévs (Archpriest), flanked by angels. On an aural level, the more used churches offer (for vespers and Sunday mornings) what must be some of the finest bell concerts in the Greek islands. A 1998-constructed **amphitheatre** and gravel esplanade just above make pleasant vantage points to admire Aï Yannáki's profile; the Olympic flame (a plaque marks the spot) stopped here en route to Sydney in 2000.

Eating and drinking

Vathý's **restaurant** profile is not brilliant, but it has improved no end since the millennium. Skip the obvious rip-off merchants between the dock and Platía Pythagóra in favour of these more remote tavernas, most of which operate year-round for the benefit of the locals.

Artemis Kefalopoúlou 4, just north of the ferry jetty. A good all-rounder for a pre-ferry lunch or leisurely supper, with *mezédhes* like *fáva*, *hórta*, *ahiní* and *foúskes* as well as the usual mains. Pleasant indoor/outdoor seating by season.

Ta Filarakia Ayía Matróna, Áno Vathý. The village characters' hangout, with the music (*rebétika* and *kapsoúrika tragoúdhia*) cranked up loud. The food

– typically just a dish or two of the day, plus grills – can be surprisingly good, and cheap.

To Kalami (aka **Triandafyllos**) Kefalopoúlou, about 3km into Kalámi. Despite its location in an unpromisingly touristy enclave, this has a friendly managing family, decent food and occasional musical sessions (spontaneous Saturday performances are apt to be better than Wednesday-night formal "Greek nights"). Open Easter–Oct.

Next Themistoklí Sofoúli 97. Vathý has three or four pizzerias; this is by far the best, also with good salads and pasta dishes, all at reasonable prices. Outdoor – and quite elegant indoor – seating.
Iy Nostimies Áno Vathý, next to the school. Tassos mans the grill while his wife commands the kitchen at this excellent, popular, inexpensive *ouzeri*. Autumn through spring features seafood titbits like shredded steamed skate with *skordhaliá*; summer sees more conventional grilled chops and *koliós* (mackerel). Try also their *bouyiourdí* or pepper-and-cheese hotpot.
T'Ostrako Themistoklís Sofoúlis, next to police station. The name means "the seashell" and this

is Sámos' only dedicated shellfish and seafood restaurant. Portions could be bigger, but quality is high for such delicacies as *yialisterés* (smooth Venus) and *kydhónia* (cockles), both served alive – you are warned. If you can't face their twitching, there are more conventional options like sardines and squid.
Solo Pasta Kefalopoúlou, just before the hospital. Fairly authentic for big portions of exactly the fare described, and patronized by locals. Open May–Sept; go early or late, as the seating area has shrunk owing to building works next door.

Nightlife and entertainment

Vathý **nightlife** revolves around half a dozen waterfront cafés and a roughly equal number of often pretentious clubs, with frequent parties and theme nights aimed at the local clientele – and frequent changes in identity. Early in the evening, the town's *beau monde* have their *mezédhes* and drinks on the ground floor of the *Aeolis Hotel*. Among several **bars and clubs**, *Escape* at Kefalopoúlou 9, north of the jetty (June–Sept), is the most durable of Vathý's more sedate watering holes, with a sea-view terrace, happy hours and outdoor videos, though the hottest till-dawn action is currently at *Hantres*, on Themistokléous Sofoúlis beyond the police station. From early July until early September, Vathý (in repertory with Pythagório) hosts various events of the small **Manolis Kalomiris Festival** – not worth making a detour to attend, but entertaining if you happen to coincide. The last week in August usually sees the **Wine Festival**, with food stalls and a live-music stage for several nights beside the Sofoulis statue. Cine Olympia, inland on Yimnasiárhou Katevéni, is more plushly fitted than many UK/US movie halls, and operates all year with a variable programme of **films**.

Listings

Airlines Olympic, on Kanári, corner of Smýrnis, south of the cathedral ☎22730 27237.
Car rental Among ten or so agencies, three recommendable ones are ranged along Themistoklí Sofoúli: try Aramis/Sixt at no. 7, near the jetty (☎22730 23253); AutoPlan at no. 17 (☎22730 23555); or Hertz next door (☎22730 24771).
Banks and exchange At seven waterfront banks, all with cash machines accepting the usual range of plastic.
Ferry/travel agents The most useful waterfront one for independent travellers is By Ship, with two branches: one at the base of the jetty (☎22730 80445), primarily handling ships and catamarans, and one about 300m southeast (☎22730 25065), with an equal stress on air tickets; between them they sell tickets for most ferry lines as well as for Olympic. The Superjet catamaran has its own agency (☎22730 33605), while NEL's central agency is Nautica (☎22730 25133).

Internet cafés There are two good ones, both on Themistoklí Sofoúli: *Dhiavlos* just around the corner from the KTEL, and *NetCafe* at no. 175, at the south end of the front.
Laundries Lavomatique, at the far north end of the pedestrianized marketplace.
Motor- and mountain-bike rental Vathý is chock-a-block with franchises, which keeps rates reasonable. Aramis, on Kefalopoúlou, north of the jetty, has the largest fleet of bikes and a mechanical support team.
Street market Whether or not you're self-catering, the daily street market or *laïkí agorá*, between the cathedral and OTE headquarters, is one of the largest (and most photogenic) in the islands. Goods on sale include garden produce, honey, wine, dried olives, fish from itinerant pick-up trucks and garden plants.
Taxi rank Beside the National Bank of Greece ☎22730 28404.

Around Vathý: eastern Sámos

In the immediate **environs of Vathý**, all around the eastern end of the island, lie some modest beaches and small hamlets with tavernas, all ideal targets for half-day-trips.

Two kilometres east of and above Vathý spreads the vast inland plateau of Vlamarí, devoted to vineyards and flanked by the hamlets of **Ayía Zóni** and **Kamára** (plus a rapidly growing number of bad-taste modern villas). Ayía Zóni can offer a fortified monastery with an overgrown courtyard, and a rather hopeless **taverna** up at the nearby crossroads; if you need a meal, *O Kriton* in Kamára has the edge, with good salads in particular. From Kamára you can head east on the road to the start of the partly cobbled path which climbs to the ridge-top monastery of **Zoödhóhou Piyís** (open except 2–5pm) for superb views across the end of the island to Turkey.

Heading north out of Vathý, the narrow, tour-bus-clogged street threads through beachless **Kalámi** – formerly the summer retreat of rich Vathy-ots, now home to package hotels – before ending after 7km at the pebbly bay and fishing port of **AYÍA PARASKEVÍ** (aka Nissí), with good, if rather unsecluded, swimming. There are, alas, no longer any reliable facilities here other than a fitfully working **snack-bar**, *Aquarius* (typically July–Sept only), which also has some **rooms** (☎22730 28282; ❸).

Kérveli and Posidhónio

As you head southeast from Vathý along the main island loop road, the triple chapel at **Trís Ekklisíes** marks an important junction, with another fork 100m along the left-hand turning. Bearing left twice takes you through the hilltop village of **PALEÓKASTRO**, where the unassuming-looking *Leonidas* on the square does surprisingly competent snacks. Some 3km beyond this is another junction, with yet another left fork bringing you after 3km to the striking bay of **KÉRVELI**, with a medium-sized gravel beach – often packed out in season – and a quiet valley just inland. Of the two waterside **tavernas**, friendly *Sea and Dolphins* has good *mezédhes* such as egg-based *sgrápa* and pork-based *tigániá*, and *soúma*, the treacherously smooth local firewater, while mains (especially fish) had recovered in quality during 2004. A kilometre back along the access road, *Iy Kryfi Folia* ("The Hidden Nest") is as described: a greenery-shrouded eyrie offering simple but inexpensive and sustaining fare such as *kalamári* rings, lamb chops and roast goat – ring ☎22730 25194 to order your goat. If you want to stay, UK and German package companies tend to get first crack at most **accommodation**, but the B-class *Kerveli Village* hotel (☎22730 23631, ⓔinfo@kerveli.gr; ❻), just above the last road curves descending to the beach, will have vacancies outside peak season and is reckoned one of the best in eastern Sámos, with sympathetic architecture, on-site car rental and a private lido.

Bearing right instead at the junction above Kérveli brings you to the road's end at **POSIDHÓNIO** (still known by its Ottoman name of Mulay-Brahim), whose geese-patrolled gravel beach is rather smaller than Kérveli's. Of the two **tavernas** here, the right-hand *Kerkezos* takes its cooking a bit more seriously – the provincial governors' conference for all Greece has been hosted here – but the seafood, while good, is pricey. Their handful of beach-view self-catering units (☎22730 22267, ⓕ22730 22493; ❹) are usually contracted to UK package companies, but there are plenty of other rooms and studios at Posidhónio. Good ones include the misnamed *Sunset Apartments* (☎22730 28763, ⓕ22730 27011; ❸), which actually face east, and the *Niota* (☎22730 27584; ❸), with partial sea views.

If you decide to base yourself at Posidhónio, it's best to rent wheels elsewhere beforehand; the only other destination within walking distance is the bay of **Klíma**. A paved side road, signposted as "Kaduna", goes there within 2km, but the beach is coarse shingle and the single taverna not worth much consideration.

Mykáli and Psilí Ámmos

The right-hand option at the second junction just beyond Trís Ekklisíes leads to the beaches of Mykáli and Psilí Ámmos, which draw crowds partly by virtue of their views of Mount Mycale (present-day Samsun Daği) in Turkey. The former twice-daily bus service from Vathý out in this direction was suspended in 2004, and may not resume.

Mykáli, a kilometre or so of rather windswept sand and gravel, was developed and fire-scorched in the early 1990s (the two phenomena seem to go together). Winter rains fill a salt marsh just behind, a stopover for migrating flamingos between December and April – several hundred in some years. If you choose to **stay** out here, the *Sirenes Beach Hotel* (℡ 22730 24668, ℻ 22730 25222; ❹), in a garden setting on the inland side of the road, or the *Saint Nikolas* (℡ 22730 25230, ℻ 22730 28522; ❺), on the beach, are the top two B-class choices, though you may find that only the *Villa Barbara* (℡ 22730 25192; ❸), with apartments behind the *Sirenes Beach Hotel*, has vacancies on spec. Far and away the best **eating** on this coast – excellent and well-priced *mayireftá* – is at *Kalypso*, reached by its own dead-end access road off the main Mykáli-bound route.

Psilí Ámmos, further east around the headland, is a sunbed-crowded, sandy cove that's on every local tour operator's signboard. If you show up under your own power, expect to pay for parking. Among several rather commercialized tavernas here, the best is *Psili Ammos*, on the far right as you face the sea, with good seafood or grills, and *Anatoli* down the sand, which hosts live music at weekends. If you swim out to nearby **Vareloúdhi** islet, a logical target, beware of periodically strong west-to-east currents, which sweep through the narrow straits even in the shallows, and the eelgrass beds which complicate the final approach to the islet.

Pythagório and around

Most traffic south of Vathý heads for **PYTHAGÓRIO**, the island's premier resort – jam-packed and rather tacky in peak season. Formerly known as Tigáni ("Frying Pan"), for reasons that become obvious in midsummer, it was renamed in 1955 to honour native ancient mathematician, philosopher and mystic Pythagoras. The sixth-century-BC tyrant Polykrates established his capital here, now the subject of acres of archeological excavations which have forced modern Pythagório to expand northeastward and uphill. The best finds from these digs will be displayed in a new **archeological museum** scheduled to open sometime in 2005 (see map for location). The village core of cobbled lanes and thick-walled mansions abuts a small harbour, which fits almost perfectly into the confines of Polykrates' ancient port and still uses his jetty. Today, however, it's devoted almost entirely to pleasure craft and overpriced cocktail bars.

Sámos' most complete (and 2001-refurbished) castle, the nineteenth-century *pýrgos* (tower-house) of **Lykourgos Logothetis**, overlooks both the town and the shoreline where that local chieftain, together with a certain "Kapetan Stamatis" and Admiral Kanaris, oversaw decisive naval and land victories over the Turks in the summer of 1824. The final battle was won on Transfiguration Day (Aug 6), and accordingly the church inside the castle precinct is dedicated to this festival; for many years a huge overhead banner in Greek announced that "Christ Saved Sámos 6 August 1824". Next to the castle are the easily visible remains of an early Christian basilica, occupying the grounds of a slightly larger Roman villa.

Accommodation

Except perhaps in August, proprietors of the less expensive grades of **accommodation** tend to meet incoming ferries and hydrofoils – unlike in Vathý, there's generally no harm in following them. The friendly **tourist information** booth, on the left up the main thoroughfare Lykoúrgou Logothéti as you face west (daily June–Sept 8am–10pm; ☏22730 62274, ℱ22730 61022), can help with finding rooms. For many visitors Pythagório is just a handy overnight stop before an early hydrofoil south (tickets for hydrofoils, and the *Nissos Kalymnos*, are available from a booth at the base of the jetty).

Nocturnal noise can be a problem in Pythagório, so it's worth heading along Pythagóra to its quiet, seaward end, south of Lykoúrgou Logothéti; here you'll find the modest **pension** *Tsambika* (☏22730 61642; ❷), while a block west *Pension Dora* (T22730 61456; 3) offers higher-standard units occupying an old stone house. Another peaceful area is the hillside north of Platía Irínis, where *Studios Galini* (☏22730 61167; winter ☏21098 42248; ❹) has high-quality self-catering units with ceiling fans, balconies and kind English-speaking management. Not brilliantly located out by the traffic lights – it's convenient only to the airport – but comfortable, good value and friendly is the *Evelin* (☏22730 61124, ℱ22730 61077; ❸), a C-class hotel with a swimming pool, double glazing against noise and on-site motorbike rental.

Eating, drinking and nightlife

Eating out can be frustrating in Pythagório, with value for money and salubrious ingredients often completely alien concepts; tour-company stickers in windows let you know who's been paying backhanders to reps to steer their charges in that direction. Currently the only place the islanders themselves will be caught dead or alive in (especially at weekend afternoons) is also the most atmospherically set: *Varka*, at the base of the jetty. It's fine for seafood and *orektiká* like *fáva*, and you can cause a piscine riot by feeding scraps of their (unusually good) bread to the harbour fish lurking below the seating area. Night owls gather at the *Mythos Club* (international sounds from midnight onwards) on Platía Irínis, or *Labito Club* on Dhespóti Kyrílou; for a quiet afternoon or early-evening drink, head instead for *T'Arsanas* or *Nostos*, adjacent and facing the pebbly beach at the base of the jetty.

Other practicalities

The **bus stop** to get you away is just west of the intersection of Lykoúrgou Logothéti and the road to Vathý; the **taxi** rank is at the harbour end of Lykoúrgou Logothéti. Also on Lykoúrgou Logothéti are two **banks** (both with ATMs) and the **post office**, as well as numerous outlets for car, motorbike and pedal-bike rental. The flattish country to the west of the town is ideal for pedal-bike touring, a popular activity. By contrast, **drivers** are penalized by the closing off of the main street to traffic after 5pm, and all-but-mandatory use of the car park on the hill beside the castle (controlled entrance June–Sept). If you don't want to pay, there's a free car park just below, much used by folk having a dip at the somewhat scrappy town beach.

Around Pythagório: sites and beaches

Aside from the archeologists' potholes, visible remains of ancient Sámos are scattered in a broad zone just beyond the current town limits. Four hundred metres west of Pythagório, just seaward from the main road and signposted as "Thermai", lie the remains of the **Roman baths** (Tues–Sun 8.30am–2.45pm; free): fairly dull, though illuminated at night to good effect.

Considerably more interesting is the **Efpalínio Órygma (Eupalinian Tunnel**; Tues–Sun 8.45am–2.45pm; €1.50), a 1040-metre aqueduct bored through the mountain just north of Pythagório. Designed by one Eupalinos of Mégara, and built by slave labour at the behest of Polykrates, it guaranteed the ancient town a siege-proof water supply, and remained in use until late Byzantine times. To get there on foot, take the well-signposted path heading inland off the shore boulevard just west of town; after fifteen minutes' walk you'll meet the access road, and then it's just five minutes more from here. Visits consist of traversing a hewn rock ledge used to transport the spoil from the water channel far below; there are guard-grilles over the worst drops, lighting for the first 650m, and rather wishful plans to open the entire length of the tunnel in some distant future. Although the work crews started from opposite sides of the mountain, the eight-metre horizontal deviation from true, about halfway along, is remarkably slight, and the vertical error nil: a tribute to the competence of the era's surveyors, and rather better percentage-wise than occurred with the boring of the Channel Tunnel.

You can also climb to the five remaining chunks of the Polykratian **perimeter wall** enclosing the tyrant's hilltop citadel. There's a choice of routes: one leading up from the Glyfádha lagoon, 700m west of Pythagório, past an **ancient watchtower** now isolated from other fortifications; the other approach (easier) leading from the well-signposted monastery of **Panayía Spilianí**, just off the road to the Efpalínion tunnel. The monastery itself, now bereft of nuns and monks, has been insensitively restored and the grounds are crammed with souvenir kiosks, but behind the courtyard, the *raison d'être* of the place is still magnificent: a cool, illuminated, hundred-metre **cave**, at the drippy end of which is a subterranean shrine to the Virgin (open daylight hours; free). It is thought that this was the residence of the ancient oracular priestess Phyto, and a hiding place during the pirate-ridden medieval era.

Potokáki

The main local **beach** stretches for several kilometres west of Pythagório's Logothetis castle, punctuated about halfway along by the end of the airport runway, and the cluster of hotels known as **Potokáki**. The name, which roughly translates as "A Wee Drop to Drink", comes from the informal, shack-like *ouzerí*s which clustered here until the 1960s. If you don't mind the crowds or occasionally being buzzed by low-flying jets (and even lower-flying jet skis), the central zone is equipped with the usual amenities like kayaks and sunbeds. Most of the sand-and-pebble shore here is well groomed, and the water clean, though for more privacy you'll have to head out west towards the end of the road.

Just before the turn-off to the heart of the beach, about 700m from the western edge of Pythagório, sprawls the massive, ultra-luxurious *Doryssa Bay* complex (☎22730 61360, ⓦwww.doryssabay.gr), whose accommodation varies from standard rooms in a brutalist 1970s hotel wing (⑥), right on the beach, to houses

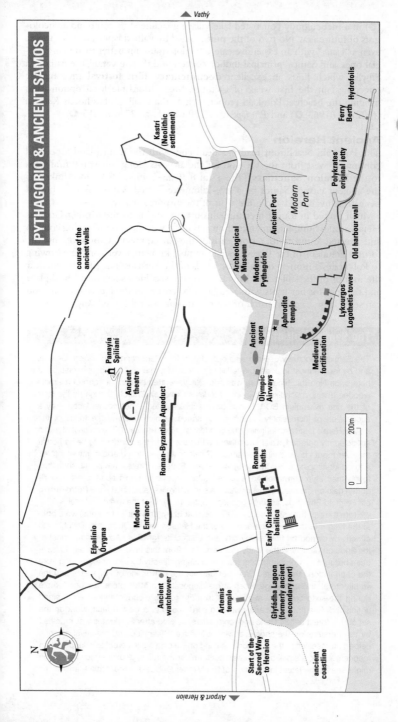

PYTHAGÓRIO & ANCIENT SAMOS

▲ Vathý

course of the ancient walls

Kastrí (Neolithic settlement)

Panayía Spilianí

Ancient theatre

Roman-Byzantine Aqueduct

Efpalínio Órygma

Modern Entrance

Ancient watchtower

Archeological Museum

Modern Pythagório

Ancient Port

Modern Port

Polykrates' original jetty

Ferry Berth   Hydrofoils

Old harbour wall

Aphrodite temple

Ancient agora

Olympic Airways

Lykourgos Logothetis tower

Medieval fortification

Roman baths

Early Christian basilica

Artemis temple

Glyfádha Lagoon (formerly ancient secondary port)

Start of the Sacred Way to Heraion

ancient coastline

▲ Airport & Heraion

N

0   200m

(❽) in a meticulously concocted fake village guaranteed to confound archeologists of future eras. No two of the units, joined by named lanes, are alike; there's even a "*platía*" with an expensive café, a folklore museum better than many official ones, and Sámos' principal indoor concert and theatre venue, the Aithoussa Sibylla, which hosts an excellent **documentary film festival** (free nightly screenings) in the first week of October. More affordable local options, also fringing the beach at Potokáki proper, include the small C-class hotels *Katerina* (☎ 22730 61963; ❹) and *Penelope* (☎ 22730 61601, ℻ 22730 61615; ❹).

Ancient Heraion

The Potokáki beachfront road is a dead end, with the main island loop road continuing west from the turn-off for the airport. Along this you'll find signs to the **Heraion Sanctuary** (Tues–Sun 8.30am–2.45pm; €3), once linked to the ancient city of Sámos by a five-kilometre Sacred Way that's now buried beneath alluvial mud and quite a bit of the airport runway.

Much touted in tourist literature, this massive shrine to the Mother Goddess Hera assumes humbler dimensions on approach, with just one surviving column and assorted foundations. Yet once inside the fenced precinct you can sense the former grandeur of the largest ancient temple known, never completed owing to Polykrates' untimely death at the hands of the Persians. The site chosen, near the mouth of the still-active Ímvrassos stream, was Hera's legendary birthplace and the spot for her trysts with Zeus; in a far corner of the fenced-in zone you can see a large, exposed patch of the paved processional Sacred Way.

The Samian cult of Hera

The Samian sanctuary of **Hera** was one of only four Hera shrines in ancient Greece, and by far the most important; a fertility goddess of some sort had been worshipped here since Neolithic times. Hera was originally venerated here in the form of a simple wooden board, much like the icons of today's Orthodox Church, though by the start of the first millennium BC this had been supplemented – but not replaced – by a succession of increasingly elaborate cult statues, which became the focus of the annual *Heraia* festival celebrating the goddess's union with Zeus. The original idol was still solemnly paraded in a litter of osiers, a tree sacred to the goddess, to be bathed at the river mouth here, during the annual *Tonaia* festivities, which also commemorated a foiled kidnapping of the image by Argive and Etruscan pirates; having stolen it, they found their ship permanently becalmed offshore, and in panic abandoned their ill-gotten gain on the beach. Just offshore, a suggestively shaped islet – the **Petrokáravo** or "Petrified Ship" – is, according to legend, the remains of the thieves' vessel.

From the eighth to sixth century BC, the sanctuary (and ancient Samos) were both at the height of their prestige and allure; the Heraion, unlike Olympia or Delphi, was effectively owned by the nearby city and shared its fortunes. Accordingly, most of the finds on display at the Vathý museum date from this time and are likely to have been brought by worshipful pilgrims approaching directly by sea, or journeying from the capital along the Sacred Way. But despite the patronage of Polykrates and the architectural and artistic geniuses at his disposal, two attempts at a stone temple during the sixth century – successors to more rustic, wooden shrines – remained unfinished. The first collapsed owing to earthquake or a design fault; work on the second, a forest of 134 Doric and Ionic pillars, ceased after Polykrates was crucified by the Persians on the shores of Mount Mycale. Byzantine and medieval masons helped themselves to the cut stone, leaving only a single pillar erect as a landmark to mariners. Later, a small basilica was built amidst the ruins, dedicated to what some might see as the latest incarnation of the Mother Goddess – the Virgin Mary.

Modern Iréon

Adjacent to Heraion is the modern resort of **IRÉON**, a nondescript grid of dusty streets behind a coarse-shingle beach, attracting a slightly younger and more active clientele than Pythagório. Here you'll find more independent **rooms** and a handful of small **hotels** that might have spur-of-the-moment vacancies; for example, *Venetia* (☏22730 95295; ❸) and *Faros* (☏22730 95262; ❸), both within sight of the water. The handful of waterfront **tavernas** may seem tempting, but by far the best eating is a couple blocks inland from the taxi square at *Ankyra*, a super-hygienic, seafood-strong *ouzerí* on a street corner.

Just inland, about 2km along the road to Mýli village, stands the rather squat **Pýrgos Sarakiní** (locked), and a double-naved church (open). Both were built during the mid-fourteenth century by the Genoese: the tower as a warehouse and defence against pirates, the church to be used by Catholic rulers and Orthodox peasants worshipping side by side – a tolerant arrangement seen elsewhere in Greece only on Náxos (and Plátanos, see p.343).

Hóra and Mytiliní

Three kilometres northwest of Pythagório, the island loop road comes to a junction at elongated, hillside **HÓRA**, the island's medieval capital and still a large, noisy village. Among several **tavernas**, *Iy Syntrofia* on the through-road is a tour-coach target and worth avoiding, though its near-neighbour *Iy Synandisi* does a nice line in pizzas and *mezédhes*, as well as grilled meat platters – marred by prefab oven chips, and better at weekends, when *kondosoúvli* and *kokorétsi* are on offer. Food at *O Andonis*, up on the fountain *platía*, doesn't quite match the lovely atmosphere, but it's decent enough.

Heading 4km north from the crossroads takes you through a ravine to **MYTILINÍ**, which initially seems an amorphous, workaday sprawl. A brief exploration, however, reveals a fine main square with some atmospheric *kafenía* and the wintertime **cinema** Rex, down a side street; the summer premises at the north edge of town are great fun, with free *loukoumádhes* served at intermission, decent pizzas to order, and first-run films.

At the southern edge of town, a local worthy initially endowed a **Paleontological & Natural History Museum** (Mon–Sat 9am–2pm, Sun 10.30am–2pm; €2.50) to house bones recovered from a place nearby where Ice Age animals came to die; it has been expanded, with collections on local flora and butterflies, to justify the "Natural History" tag, though it's still not exactly required viewing.

Southern inland villages

Since the circum-island bus passes through or near the villages only a few times weekly, you'll need your own vehicle to explore them all.

Some 4km west of Hóra, an inconspicuous turning leads uphill to the still-functioning monastery of **Timíou Stavroú** (Holy Cross), whose annual festival on September 14 is more an excuse for a tatty open-air market than any music or feasting. One kilometre further on, another detour wends its way to **MAVRATZÉÏ**, which lost 49 houses to the July 2000 fire. It's one of two Samian "pottery villages"; this one specializes in the *Koúpa toú Pythagóra* or "Pythagorean cup", supposedly designed by the sage himself to leak onto the wine drinker's lap if he indulged beyond the "fill" line. More practical wares can be found at three shops in **KOUMARADHÉÏ**, back on the main road, 2km further along.

At Koumaradhéï you can descend a paved road through burnt-off forest to the sixteenth-century monastery of **Megális Panayías** (theoretically daily 9am–noon & 5–7pm), containing sixteenth-century frescoes, alas now very smudged by damp. This route continues to **MÝLI**, a village submerged in citrus groves, also accessible from the Iréon road. Four kilometres above Mýli sprawls **PAGÓNDAS**, a large hillside community with a splendid main square and an unusual communal fountain-house on the south hillside. Though the *platía* restaurants are festooned with tour-op stickers – it's too close to Iréon to have escaped attention – this is also the venue for one of the better Samian festivals, taking place on **Whit Sunday** eve (Ayíou Pnévmatos in Greek), with live music. Pagóndas is also the subject of a scurrilous island legend which holds that the villagers were formerly much given to buggery, and that no lad reached the age of 15 without being "initiated" by his elders.

From here, a paved road curls 9km around the hill to **SPATHARÉÏ**, a rather poky place – more so since the area was devastated by fire in both 1993 and 2000 – but set on a natural balcony offering the best sea views this side of the island. From Spatharéï, the road continues 6km till it joins up with the main road at **PÝRGOS**, a friendly village at the head of a ravine draining southwest, and the centre of Samian honey production. A short distance down the gorge, **Koútsi** is a small roadside oasis of plane trees (supposedly seventeen) shading a gushing spring and an eponymous **taverna** that would make a convenient meal stop were it not so unreliably open. From Koútsi, a popular, waymarked **path** leads down the ravine here – which just escaped the July 2000 blaze – to the village of **Neohóri**, which has minimal facilities.

The southern coast

The rugged, now rather denuded coastline south of the Pagóndas–Pýrgos route conceals a number of largely inaccessible beaches, glimpsed by most visitors for the first and last time from the descending plane bringing them to Sámos. They have been developed in a low-key way, but still host nothing like the crowds of the more obvious beaches – and this is even truer since the 2000 fire ruined most of their backdrops.

Kyriakoú

Furthest east of the more accessible coves, the 250-metre sand-and-gravel beach of **Kyriakoú** lies just 5km southwest of Iréon via a crudely signposted, rough track (jeeps or dirt bikes only). Stavros' "shack" offers grilled snacks, drinks, and a few umbrellas and sunbeds for rent. Though its olive-and-pine hinterland has been incinerated, the water remains pristine, and solitude disturbed only by groups of boat-trippers from Iréon. There is also a slightly longer and less steep but unmarked track in from Pagóndas.

Tsópela

Tsópela, very near the southernmost point of the island, also has marked road access. Matters begin reasonably enough about 4km beyond Pagóndas on the Spatharéï-bound road, but once past the tiny monastery of Evange-listrías the 6.5-kilometre track deteriorates markedly, though you can now just about wrestle an ordinary car through the fire-ravaged landscape. Your reward for persevering is a highly scenic sand-and-gravel bay at the mouth of a gorge, with views towards the satellite islet of Samiopoúla, rock overhangs under which to shelter, and curious freshwater seeps on the seabed. A seasonal **taverna** under the pines just to the east, the only bit of local vegetation saved from the 2000 fire, serves cheaper and better fare (including fish dropped off by passing boats) than you'd expect for such an isolated spot.

Kouméïka, Bállos and Péfkos

The western reaches of this shoreline, which suffered comprehensive fire damage in 1994 but are now recovering well relative to the 2000 blaze zone, are approached via the small village of **KOUMÉÏKA**, which has a massive inscribed marble fountain and a pair of *kafenía* on its plane-tree-shaded square, plus a single snack-bar (*Marabou*) a few paces east. Below extends the long, pebbly bay at **BÁLLOS**, with sand and a cave at the far eastern end where nudism goes unremarked upon. Bállos itself is merely a sleepy collection of summerhouses, several simple places to stay and a few tavernas, all on the shore road. The best **accommodation** for walk-ins is the *Hotel Amfilisos* (℡22730 31669, ℱ22730 31668; ❹), while the finest **dining** is found at seafront *Akrogiali* nearby, with an honourable mention for humbler *Iy Paralia* off to the east.

A separate road from Kouméïka leads to **Péfkos**, at first glance a grubby, narrow beach with no reliable facilities behind. But persevere towards the west, and you'll discover tiny pebble coves tucked in amongst rock overhangs, or a much longer, idyllic strand reached by a track from Péfkos main bay through olive groves – all clothing optional.

Returning towards Kouméïka from Bállos, you'll see a dubious-looking side road just before the village marked "Velanidhiá"; it is in fact completely paved and usable by any vehicle – a very practical short cut if you're travelling towards the beaches beyond Órmos Marathokámbou.

Plátanos

Following the southerly loop road back northeast towards Karlóvassi, it's worth detouring up to **PLÁTANOS**, on the flanks of Mount Karvoúnis; at 520m it's one of the highest villages on the island, with sweeping views west and south. The name comes from the three stout plane trees (*plátanos* in Greek) on its *platía*, which has retained some of the charm utterly lost at Vourliótes (see p.346), and whose spring water in the arcaded fountain-house is immortalized in one of the most popular Samian folk songs; there are also a trio of **tavernas** here – the friendliest being *Sofia* – and a few **rooms** to rent at the outskirts of the village, if you ask around. The only special sight is the thirteenth-century **church of Kímisis Theotókou** (key at house opposite west entrance) in the village centre, double-naved and double-creed like the one at Pýrgos Sarakiní; in this case, however, the Byzantine Nicaean emperors built it, making provision for the spiritual needs of their allies, the Genoese garrison.

Kokkári

Leaving Vathý on the north coastal section of the island loop road, there's little initially to stop for other than the reasonably good beach at **Kédros**, 5km west of town, with an adequate snack-bar and pleasant sand sea-bottom once clear of the pebble shore. Some 12km along you reach **KOKKÁRI**, the third major Samian tourist centre after Pythagório and the capital. It's also the prime source of nostalgia for Sámos regulars; while lower Vathý and Pythagório had little compelling beauty to sacrifice, much has been irrevocably lost here. The town's profile, covering two knolls behind mirror-image headlands known as Dhídhymi or the Twins, remains unaltered, and one or two families still doggedly untangle their fishnets on the quay. But in general its identity has been transformed beyond recognition, with expansion inland (now halted) over vineyards and the fields of shallot onions that gave the place its name. Since the exposed rocky western beach is buffeted by near-constant winds, Kokkári's mostly Germanophone promoters have made a virtue of necessity by developing the place as a successful windsurfing resort.

Practicalities

As at Vathý and Pythagório, a high proportion of Kokkári **accommodation** is block-booked for the season by German and British tour companies. West-beach establishments not completely devoted to package tours include the *Lemos* (☎22730 92250, ☏22730 92334; ❹), near the north end of the strand, and the more modest *Vicky* (☎22730 92231; ❸) nearby. For a guaranteed view of the quiet fishing port, try *Pension Alkyonis* (☎22730 92225; ❸), or *Pension Angela* (☎22730 92052; ❸). For more comfort, the inconspicuously signed *Olympia Beach* on the westerly shore (☎22730 92353; ❹) is a good choice. If you get stuck, seek assistance from the seasonal **EOT** post (☎22730 92217), housed in a Portakabin near the main church.

Most tavernas line the north and west waterfronts, and charge above the norm, though they're steadily losing ground to breakfast, *souvláki/yíros* or cock-tail bars. As of writing, none is worth a special mention – you're probably best off patronizing said *yirádhika*. Most (noisy) drinking bars ring the little square just west of where the concreted stream (with its family of ducks) meets the sea, but there's also the more elaborate, well-established *Cabana* on the west beach, drawing clubbers from across the island.

Other amenities include a stand-alone **bank** ATM on the through-road, a seasonal **post office** in a Portakabin on a lane to seaward, and a long-hours, self-service **laundry** next to that. There are also branches of all the major Vathý travel agents, and a reasonably stocked **bookstore/newsagent**, Lexis. Note that almost everything mentioned in this account is closed between mid-October and mid-April, when scarcely a grocery shop stays open in Kokkári.

West of Kokkári: the north coast

The nearest partly sheltered beaches, aside from the more protected easterly town beach, lie thirty to forty minutes' walk west from Kokkári, all with sunbeds and permanently anchored umbrellas. The first beach, **Lemonákia** (2km along), is a bit too close to the road, though there's a decent taverna here. Just overhead sprawls perhaps the best hotel on Sámos' north coast, the A-class *Arion* (☎22370 92020, ⓦwww.arion-hotel.gr; ❼), a well-designed hotel-wing and bungalow complex on an unburnt patch of hillside.

One kilometre beyond, the graceful crescent of **Tzamadhoú** (rhyming with Coleridge's "Xanadu") figures in virtually every EOT poster of the island. Despite path-only access, it's even more commercialized than

Lemonákia, while the far east end of the beach (saucer-shaped pebbles) has become a well-established nudist/gay/lesbian zone. There's one more pebble bay 7km west, beyond the sleepy, all-Greek resort of Avlákia, called Tzaboú, again with a serviceable snack-bar, but unless you're passing by and want a quick dip this is not worth a special detour as it lies open to the prevailing northwest wind.

Áyios Konstandínos and around

The next spot of any interest along the coast road is **Platanákia**, essentially a handful of tavernas and rooms for rent at a plane-shaded bridge by the turning for Manolátes (see overleaf); best of the **tavernas** is *IyApolavsi*, with a limited daily choice of good *mayireftá*. For **accommodation**, try the *Hotel Iro* (☎22730 94013, ⓕ22730 94610; ❸), or the *Hotel Apartments Agios Konstantinos* (☎22730 94000, ⓕ22730 94002; ❹), both on the road down to the sea.

Platanákia is actually the eastern suburb of **ÁYIOS KONSTANDÍNOS**, 1km distant, a case study in arrested touristic development. The surf-pounded esplanade has been repaved and prettified, but there are no usable beaches within walking distance, so the collection of warm-toned stone buildings (less adulterated than usual by concrete structures) constitutes a peaceful alternative to Kokkári. In addition to modest, 1970s-vintage **rooms**, such as the *Atlantis* (☎22730 94329; ❷) just above the highway, there's a small, well designed bungalow complex with a pool, *Apollonia Bay* (☎22730 94444, ⓕ22730 94090; ❹). **Eating** out, you're spoilt for choice: besides *Iy Apolavsi*, already mentioned, there's *To Kyma* at the east end of the quay (Easter–Sept), possibly the best all-rounder, with good bulk wine, rich *mayireftá* and olive pâté with bread, as well as fish, though for that, *Aeolos* at the far west end of the esplanade (June–Oct) just pips it for quality and choice, served at seaside tables.

Once past "Áyios", as it's known locally, the mountains hem the road in against the sea, and the terrain doesn't relent until near **KONDAKÉIKA**, whose *kafenío*-lined square is worth a visit at dusk for its fabulous sunset views. Afterwards you can descend to its diminutive shore annexe, **ÁYIOS NIKÓLAOS**, for unbeatable fish platters and *mezédhes* at *Iy Psaradhes* (Easter–Oct), with a terrace lapped by the waves; its appearance (deservedly) in so many guides both Greek and foreign means that booking in season is mandatory (☎22730 32489). Though not visible from the upper road, the reasonable pebble-and-sand beach of **Piáki** lies ten minutes' walk east past the last studio units, less dominated by packages than in the past.

Petaloúdha: Kímisis Theotókou church

The next turning inland beyond Áyios Nikólaos, just at the riverbed marking the eastern boundary of Karlóvassi, leads 6km to the little-visited village of Ídhroussa, gateway to the Byzantine **church of Kímisis Theotókou**, the oldest and most artistically noteworthy on Sámos, its extensive frescoes contemporaneous with the bulding (late twelfth or early thirteenth century).

Once in Idhroússa, find the *platía* with a church, plane tree and *kafenío*; continue northeast on the lane out of the plaza, then bear right almost immediately following the sign indicating a parking area. Before this veer left, obeying a Greek-only placard for "Petaloúdha", "Kouroúta" and "Vatía", then go left again at a second sign for "**Petaloúdha**", the name of the forested rural district in which the church is located. An ordinary car can just make it out here, but you'll be more confident with a 4WD vehicle. Drop down to a stream bed, then climb to a pumping station next to a double power column. Leave all transport here and descend south on foot on a rough, steep track, which quickly becomes a path, into a glade of plane trees; first you find a natural amphitheatre used for the yearly festival, and then a bit downhill and west, the whitewashed church itself, domeless and heavily buttressed, with just a tiny slit-window in the apse.

The deceptively simple interior (unlocked), a single barrel-vaulted aisle, is covered with frescoes, many still vivid except on the ceiling, where damp has blurred them. On the north wall are the soldier-saints Demetrios, George and the two Theodores, along with Constantine and Helen, plus a Virgin and Child. The south wall is mostly taken up by prophets reading their texts, as well as a fine Archangel Michael, but the most unusual image lies behind the altar-screen, on the north wall. Here the early bishop Peter of Alexandria is shown in dialogue with a youthful, beardless, dishevelled Christ ("Who has torn your robe?" "The foolish and abominable Arius"). The fresco and exchange made clear to simple parishioners the presumed damage to the Body of Christ done by the Arian heresy of the early fourth century.

Inland from Kokkári: hill villages

Inland between Kokkári and Kondakéïka, an idyllic landscape of pine, cypress and orchards is overawed by dramatic mountains and, except for the slopes below Vrondianís monastery and some streaks of scorched trees reaching the sea between Lemonákia and Tzaboú, the area miraculously escaped the July 2000 fire. Despite ongoing destructive nibblings by bulldozers, a few stretches of the trail system which once comprehensively linked the various **hill villages** remain intact, and you can walk for as long or as little as you like, returning to the main highway to catch a bus home. Failing that, most of the communities can provide a bed at short notice.

Vrondianís, Vourliótes and Pnáka

The monastery of **Vrondianís** (Vrondá), directly above Kokkári, is the oldest on the island, just predating Megális Panayías (see p.342). However, the lovely trail up from Kokkári was completely destroyed in 1998 and the army used the monastery outbuildings as a barracks prior to their severe damage in the 2000 fire, so the place is closed until repairs are completed. **VOURLIÓTES**, 2km north of the monastery, and still accessible by an intact, ninety-minute trail from Kokkári (though the countryside is fire-grim), has beaked chimneys and brightly painted shutters sprouting from its typical tile-roofed houses. Restaurateur greed has ruined the formerly photogenic central square; they have cut down two ancient mulberries and jammed tables into every available corner, so it's best to pass over the **tavernas** here in favour of *Iy Pera Vrysi*, at the village entrance, instead; with its enormous plane tree and glimpses of the sea below, this is a popular weekend venue for Athenian Greeks. Even more appealing is the *Piyi Pnaka* taverna, in the idyllic eponymous hamlet of **PNÁKA**, just off the ascending Vourliótes road.

Manolátes and Valeondádhes

MANOLÁTES, an hour-plus walk uphill from Vourliótes via the deep Kakórrema stream canyon, has been gentrified with trinket shops and a half-dozen **snack-bars** and **tavernas**; of these, *Iy Yeoryidhes* by the central fountain is obvious, but much the best one is *Iy Filia* (lunch only), co-run with *Iy Apolavsi* at Platanákia and occupying a stone-built cottage at the high edge of the village. Here the chef produces a fair selection of quality *mayireftá*, accompanied by wine from the surrounding vineyards – and the biggest 180-degree eyeful on the island.

Iy Filia sits just below the start of the trail up **Mount Ámbelos** (Karvoúnis), at 1153m the island's second-highest summit; the trek, mostly on trail surface, takes five hours round trip. The trail has been cut perilously in three places by a pointless jeep track (which you may be forced to follow) a few minutes along, and there are swaths of fire damage, but overall the scenery, including some surviving 25-metre-tall black pines, is still alluring away from the burn zones.

From Manolátes you can no longer easily continue on foot to Stavrinídhes (see below), the next village, but there is a path to Platanákia on the coast (about a 1hr walk). From Manolátes plunge straight down, partly on a cobbled path, through the shady valley known as "**Aïdhónia**" ("Nightingales", which sing here in May). At a point shortly downhill from where the path hits the valley floor, you'll find the *Hotel Aidonokastro* (℡22730 94686 or 697 46 66 708, ℻22730 94404; ❹; May–Oct), up on the hillside to the west; here kindly, English-speaking Yannis Pamoukis has renovated about half the abandoned hamlet of **VALEONDÁDHES** as a unique cottage-hotel, each former house comprising a pair of two- or four-person units with traditional touches. Package companies have most of the cottages, but Yannis always reserves two or three studios for walk-in customers. The closest alternative accommodation – again with a package allotment most years – is the well-priced and well-managed *Hotel Daphne* (℡22730 94003, ℻22730 94594, ⓦwww.daphne-hotel.gr; ❹), sited a bit more obtrusively on the same slope just a kilometre or so closer to the sea where the valley has opened out, with sweeping views from its pool-terrace.

Stavrinídhes and Ámbelos

Should you manage to fight your way on foot or by bike to **STAVRINÍDHES** through the deplorable mess of bulldozer tracks beyond Manolátes, you'll find that the place has little in the way of tourist facilities and much in the way of recent notoriety. To the infinite chagrin of Sámos' bishop, many local villagers have become **Jehovah's Witnesses**, a pacifist sect abhorred and actively persecuted in Greece, though in the late 1990s they won the right to alternative civilian national service rather than the five years' imprisonment they formerly faced.

Similar conversions have occurred at neighbouring **ÁMBELOS**, more spectacularly perched on a natural balcony above the sea. Its setting has prompted numerous foreigners to buy and renovate houses here, but again there are few specific delights for outsiders other than a few souvenir shops and a decent **taverna** on the square at the village entrance, serving good *mezédhes* (especially out of peak season).

Karlóvassi and the northwest coast

KARLÓVASSI, 31km west of Vathý and the second town of Sámos, is decidedly sleeper and more old-fashioned than the capital, despite having roughly the same population. Though lacking much aesthetic distinction, it's popular as a base from which to take a number of rewarding walks or to explore western Sámos' excellent beaches and a smattering of medieval ruins.

The name, incidentally, despite scant evidence of Ottoman legacy elsewhere on Sámos, appears to be a corruption of *karlova*, Turkish for "snowy plain" – the plain in question being the conspicuous saddle of Mount Kérkis overhead, which is indeed snow-capped in harsh winters.

The town divides into no fewer than five straggly neighbourhoods: **Néo**, well inland, whose untidy growth was spurred by the influx of post-1923 refugees from Asia Minor; **Meséo**, across the usually dry riverbed, tilting appealingly off a knoll and then blending with **Ríva**, the shoreline district; and postcard-worthy **Paleó** (or **Áno**), perched above **Limáni** (or Limín), the small harbour district.

Limáni and Paleó

The port of **LIMÁNI** is a fairly pleasant place with a part-pedestrianized quay and working boatyard at the west end. **Ferry-ticket agencies** are scattered within a short distance of each other on the through-road and at the jetty. Some 400m east of the harbour is the town **beach**, better than you'd expect for the location and very popular in season. Just inland from the shorefront road, still further east, sits Karlóvassi's branch of the **EOS** (Union of Samian Wine-Producers), open for tours of the production line (and a sample glass) during normal weekday working hours.

Most visitors to the area **stay** in or near Limáni, which has a handful of rooms and several overpriced hotels. The **rooms**, all in the inland pedestrian lane behind the through-road, are quieter: try those of Vangelis Feloukatzis (☎22730 33293; ❷). Otherwise the best of the hotels is the comfortable *Samaina Port Hotel* (☎22730 34527, ℗22730 34471; ❺), overlooking the quay, co-managed with the *Samaina Maisonettes* apartments (❻) slightly inland.

Tavernas and bars abound, though the only remarkable quayside one is *Rementzo* (April–Oct), tellingly the locals' hangout, with good fish in season plus *mayireftá*. The local university contingent (a maths and computer science faculty is based here) keeps **nightlife** active; try the cavernous dance hall *Popcorn*, in an old stone warehouse opposite the ferry jetty.

Immediately above Limáni perches the partly hidden hamlet of **Paleó** (no reliable tourist facilities), whose hundred or so houses are draped to either side of a leafy ravine.

Meséo and Ríva

MESÉO, just east, could be an alternative to Limáni as a base, though one of two **hotels** – the *Aspasia* (☎22730 30201, ℗22730 30200) appears to have closed down, leaving just the more basic *Astir* (☎22730 33150, ℗22730 34074; ❸), between the hillside and Ríva. There's far more choice in eating out, with three **tavernas** on the central *platía*, of which the most accomplished is *Dionysos* (all year), with a range of creative dishes, equally pleasant indoor/outdoor tables and a wine list aspiring to Athenian sophistication. Next door, the students patronize the *Para Pende* **bar**. Following the street linking this square to the waterfront, you pass one of the improbably huge turn-of-the-twentieth-century churches, topped with twin belfries and a blue-and-white dome, which dot the coastal plain here. Just at the intersection with the shore road, in the heart of **RÍVA**, you'll find the friendly, good-value, sunset-view *To Kyma ouzerí* (May–Oct), where Ethiopian proprietress

Letekindan Berhane adds a welcome Middle Eastern/East African touch (for example, *alí saláta*, with sun-dried tomatoes, cashews and courgettes) to the broad variety of seafood and vegetarian dishes – most days you'll fight for a table (no reservations taken).

Néo

NÉO has little to recommend it besides a wilderness of derelict stone warehouses and mansions on the east bank of the river mouth, reminders of the extinct leather industry which flourished here during the first half of the twentieth century (the last tannery only closed in the late 1970s). However, if you're staying at Limáni, you'll almost certainly visit one of the several **banks** (all with ATMs), the **post office**, or the **bus stop** on the main lower square. A few, though not all, buses from Vathý continue down to the harbour; ask for details. While waiting for a bus, one of two traditional **kafenía** might interest you: slightly tarted up *O Kleanthis*, on the lower *platía*, or *O Kerketevs*, by the upper square. There are no recommendable eateries, but on the one-way street down to the traffic lights and giant church there are plenty of student café-bars (such as *Toxotis*) and, near the Agricultural Bank, an excellent **cinema**, the Gorgyra, which alternates its play list with the Olympia in Vathý.

Potámi and around

The closest decent **beach** to Karlóvassi beckons at **POTÁMI**, forty minutes' walk via the coast road from Limáni or an hour by a much more scenic, high trail from Paleó, via the minimally interesting grotto-church of Áyios Andónios. This broad arc of sand and pebbles, flecked at one end with tide-lashed rocks (and the strikingly hideous clifftop chapel of Áyios Nikólaos, a junta-supported project of 1971), gets crowded at summer weekends, when seemingly the entire population of Karlóvassi descends here. Near the end of the trail from Paleó stands *To Iliovasilema* (lunch only), a *psistariá* grown complacent on coach tours and recommended only in the absence of anything else; there are also a very few rooms signposted locally, but many folk camp rough (in defiance of prohibition signs) along the lower reaches of the river that gives the beach its name.

A streamside path leads twenty minutes inland, initially past the exquisite eleventh-century church of **Metamórfosis** – the oldest on Sámos, its dome supported on four early Christian columns – to a point where the stream is squeezed between sheer rock walls. Beyond this point, you have to swim and wade 100m further in heart-stoppingly cold water through a series of fern-tufted rock pools (home to harmless freshwater crabs), before reaching a low but vigorous **waterfall**. Since the mid-1990s this enchanting site has become the worst-kept secret of western Sámos, probably worth avoiding in high season, when it's included in the "Jeep Safari" trips of certain tour agencies. An extended trail – initially very steep and guard-railed – loops around the narrows to climb up to some pools above the waterfall, and a rope is fixed at the main, lowest cascade to facilitate abseiling.

Just above the Metamórfosis church, another clear if precipitous path leads up to a small, contemporaneous **Byzantine fortress**. There's little to see inside other than a cistern and a badly crumbled lower curtain wall, but the views out to sea and up the canyon are terrific, enhanced in October by a carpet of pink autumn crocus. Some islanders claim that a secret tunnel links the castle grounds with the church just below.

Along with certain remote islets of the Sporádhes in the North Aegean, and Saria north of Kárpathos, Sámos is one of the last remaining Greek habitats of the Mediterranean **monk seal** (*Monachus monachus*). Within living memory they were a fairly common sight, even inside Vathý Bay, but their numbers throughout the Aegean began to dwindle alarmingly in the 1960s, when steadily reduced fish stocks saw them in increasing competition with humans. Seals can eat nearly their own weight in fish each day and often damage fishnets to get at "ready meals"; aggrieved fishermen have rarely hesitated to kill them, despite their protected status. In addition, the isolated beaches which the seals used to prefer for giving birth have now been invaded by humans, forcing the shy creatures to retire for this purpose to remote sea caves, preferably with a submerged entrance.

Efforts to preserve the severely diminished Samian seal community began in 1979, when the Swiss–English team of Rita Emch and William Johnson, working successively on behalf of Greenpeace and the World Wildlife Fund, attempted to have the area around Megálo Seïtáni declared a natural refuge, with all shoreline construction prohibited. However, the local authorities (in particular, the secret police) were unable to reconcile the pair's countercultural garb and lifestyle with expensive Zodiac rafts and other sophisticated surveillance equipment, concluding that they were obviously in the pay of a foreign power (ie Turkey). After huge ructions amongst various Greek government ministries, Johnson in particular was declared *persona non grata* and expelled in October 1982 – ironically just before an official refuge was designated at Megálo Seïtáni. He got his own back in a tendentious but fascinating book chronicling the whole episode (*The Monk Seal Conspiracy*; see "Books", p.514).

Conservationists have long feared that the local seals had gone for good – they can swim up to 200km a day if necessary – and that the Seïtáni area would be decommissioned as a reserve and officially opened to roads, power lines and hotels; illegal summer cottages already proliferate at Megálo Seïtáni and, despite strictures from the forest service, dirt roads have crept part of the way down from Kosmadhéï and Dhrakéi villages. So it was with considerable excitement that the spring of 1995 featured several sightings of at least three individuals – including a 1.7-metre-long, several-hundred-kilo adult – basking on pebble coves at the opposite end of the island, near Cape Kótsikas between Vathý and Ayía Paraskeví. Why the seals should have begun surfacing so far from their former haunts is unclear; it may be that they have found inadvertent protection from fishermen's pot shots in the regular coastguard patrols mounted to prevent landings of Kurdish refugees from Turkey.

In 2001, a solitary adult was again regularly seen napping on the rocks near the cape, but local fishermen's attitudes remain hostile and, with Samian seal numbers estimated at fewer than five, the local community is finished as a viable breeding population. If you're lucky enough to see a basking seal, you may find that it will tolerate you from a discreet distance, but on no account should it be touched.

The Seïtáni coves

The coast beyond Potámi ranks among the most beautiful and unspoilt on Sámos; this has been an officially designated refuge for monk seals since 1982, though most recent sightings have been at other points of the island (see box above). The dirt track at the west end of Potámi Bay ends after twenty minutes on foot (or five by car), from which you backtrack a hundred metres or so to find the well-cairned start of the side-trail running parallel to the water. After twenty minutes' walk along this you'll arrive at **Mikró Seïtáni**, a small pebble cove guarded by sculpted rock walls, with a cave to shelter in.

Just under an hour's walk from the trailhead, passing through olive terraces, you'll come to **Megálo Seïtáni**, the island's finest beach, at the mouth of the intimidating Kakopérato gorge. You'll have to bring food, water and some sort of shade, though not necessarily a swimsuit – there's no dress code at either of the Seïtáni bays, though nudists are advised to stay away from the summer-cottage end of Megálo. If you don't fancy the walk in, during peak season there are a couple of daily **water-taxi** services from Karlóvassi port (€10 return).

The southwest coast

Heading south out of Karlóvassi on the island loop road, the first place you'd be tempted to stop off at is **Marathókambos**, a pretty, amphitheatrical village overlooking the eponymous gulf; there's a taverna or two, but no short-term accommodation. Most visitors (and islanders) skip Marathókambos by using the 2003-built bypass that drastically shortens the journey to several growing resorts on the coast below.

Órmos Marathokámbou

ÓRMOS MARATHOKÁMBOU, a small harbour 18km from Karlóvassi, has since the late 1990s been pressed into service as a tourist centre, though some of its original character still peeks through in the backstreets. The port has been improved, with *kaïkia* offering day-trips to Foúrni and the nearby islet of Samiopoúla, while the pedestrianized quay has become the focus of attention; a curiosity at its west end is one of the island's two sets of traffic lights, controlling entry to a one-lane alley. An indifferent beach extends immediately to the east of the quay, though this improves markedly the further east you go.

The most established place to **stay** here is the seaview *Hotel Kerkis Bay* (☎22730 37202, ✆22730 37372; ❸); most studios and apartments are contracted to tour companies, but you might try *Studios Avra* (☎22730 37221; ❸) just above the jetty. Among several **tavernas** on the esplanade, best by a nod is *Lekatis*, though portions had shrunk and seafood freshness was variable in 2004. Nearby, Brit-owned *The Mad Pomegranate Tree* is a slightly pricey but tasteful **café-bar** with a good line in piped music.

Votsalákia

For better beaches continue 2km west to **VOTSALÁKIA** (officially dubbed "KÁMBOS"), Sámos' most recently "arrived" resort, which straggles a further 2km behind the island's longest (if not its most beautiful) beach. The place's appeal has been diminished by wall-to-wall rooms, apartments and often rather poor tavernas. But for most tastes Votsalákia is still a considerable improvement on the Pythagório area, and the hulking mass of 1437-metre Mount Kérkis overhead rarely fails to impress.

In terms of on-spec **accommodation**, Emmanouil Dhespotakis (☎22730 31258) seems to control a fair proportion of the beds (❸–❹) available here, with his several premises towards the quieter, more scenic western end of things. In the same area is the highly recommended, spacious *Studios Popi* (☎22730 37071, ✉ad_kia@hotmail.com; ❷), set back from the road and thus quiet. Also in the vicinity is *Loukoullos*, an unusual *koultoúra* taverna overlooking the sea where all fare is prepared in a wooden oven. In the same area is inconspicuously signed *Akroyialia* (aka *Anna's*), which has been going since 1979 and offers more traditional food. Other facilities include branches of nearly all the main Vathý travel agencies (such as By Ship, ☎22730 37100), a phenomenal number of **car** and **motorbike rental** outfits (necessary, as only two daily buses call here) and a **bank** ATM or two, all catering to an overwhelmingly family clientele. Like Kokkári, the place is a ghost town from late October to May.

Psilí Ámmos

If Votsalákia doesn't suit, you can continue 3km further to the 600-metre sandy beach at **Psilí Ámmos** (sometimes Khryssí Ámmos), more aesthetic and not to be confused with its namesake in the southeast corner of the island. The sea shelves gently here – ridiculously so, as you're still only knee-deep a hundred paces out – and cliffs shelter clusters of naturists at the east end. Surprisingly, there is little development; just three small studio complexes in the pines at mid-beach, and two **tavernas** back up on the approach road as you approach.

Mount Kérkis

A limestone/volcanic oddity in a predominantly schist landscape, **Mount Kérkis** (Kerketéfs) – the Aegean's second highest summit after Mount Sáos on Samothráki – attracts legends and speculation as easily as it does the cloud pennants that usually wreathe it. Hermits colonized and sanctified the mountain's many caves in Byzantine times; the *andártes* (resistance guerrillas) controlled it during the last world war; and mariners still regard it with superstitious awe, especially when mysterious lights – presumed to be the spirits of the departed hermits, or the aura of some forgotten holy icon – are glimpsed at night near the cave-mouths.

Climbing the peak

Gazing up from a supine posture on the beach, you may be inspired to go and **climb the peak** of Mount Kérkis. The classic route begins at the west end of the Votsalákia strip, along the bumpy jeep track leading inland towards the convent of **Evangelistrías**. After an initial 45 minutes through fire-damaged olive groves and past charcoal pits (a major industry hereabouts), the proper path begins, more or less following power lines steeply up to the convent. One of several friendly nuns will proffer an *oúzo* in welcome and point you up the sporadically paint-marked trail continuing even more steeply up to the peak.

The views are tremendous, though perhaps less sweepingly comprehensive than you'd expect since the mountain is rather blunt-topped, and the climb itself is humdrum once you're out of the trees. About an hour before the top, there's a chapel with an attached cottage for shelter in emergencies and, just beyond, a welcome spring that's most reliable after a wet winter. Elation at attaining the summit may be tempered somewhat by the knowledge that one of the worst aviation disasters in Greek history occurred here on August 3, 1989, when an aircraft flying out of Thessaloníki slammed into the mist-cloaked peak, with the loss of all 34 aboard; if you look carefully you can still find uncollected debris from the accident. All told, it's a seven-hour outing from Votsalákia and back, not counting rest stops.

Around the mountain

Less ambitious walkers might want to circle the flanks of the mountain, covering part of the way by vehicle and continuing by foot. The road beyond Limniónas to Kallithéa and Dhrakéï, truly end-of-the-world villages with views across to Ikaría, has been paved the entire distance, making it possible to venture out here by car or on an ordinary motorbike. During term time a bus from Karlóvassi via Marathókambos travels to these villages every weekday at around 1.30pm, less frequently in summer (currently Mon & Fri, same time).

From **DHRAKÉÏ**, the end of the line, a ninety-minute route – almost entirely on waymarked path – descends, with one recovering patch of 1994-burnt forest, to Megálo Seïtáni, from where it's an easy two-hour-plus onward walk to Karlóvassi. Note that the return bus from Dhrakéï is at dawn, so if you're doing this itinerary in reverse you'll either have to retrace your steps or stay overnight at one of two unofficial **rooms** establishments. These are controlled by one or other of the four **snack-bar/kafenía** that may tout assiduously for your custom as you walk through – in particular, the priest's wife, Athena Halepi (☎22730 37861; ❷). For an unusual approach to Mount Kérkis via Zastáni peak, ask for help from the local shepherds.

KALLITHÉA, 7km southwest, can offer only a single, simple *psistariá* on the tiny square and no reliable accommodation at present. From Kallithéa you can follow a newer jeep track (starting beside the cemetery) or walk for 45 minutes along an older trail to a spring, rural chapel and plane tree on the west flank of Kérkis. From here it's a half-hour, path-only walk to a pair of **cave-churches**. **Panayía Makriní** stands detached at the mouth of a high, wide but shallow grotto, whose balcony affords terrific views of Sámos' western extremity; inside (bring a flashlight) there are a few fourteenth-century frescoes. A ten-minute scramble overhead will take you to **Ayía Triádha**, whose structure by contrast is largely composed of cave wall. Just adjacent yawns a narrow volcanic cavern; with that handy flashlight you can explore some hundred metres into the mountain, perhaps further on hands and knees and with proper equipment.

After these subterranean exertions, the closest spot for a swim is **Vársamo** (Válsamo) cove, 4km below Kallithéa and reached via a well-signposted dirt road. The beach here consists of wonderful multicoloured volcanic pebbles, and there are two caves to shelter in on one side of the bay, plus a single, very welcoming **rooms/snack-bar** establishment (☎22730 38302; ❷) just inland, run by three generations of women.

Sámos travel details

Island transport

Buses

Pythagório to: Hóra/Mytiliní (4–5 daily Mon–Sat); Iréon (4–5 daily Mon–Sat, 3 daily Sun); Karlóvassi (1 daily Mon, Tues, Wed, Fri); Potokáki (5 daily Mon–Fri, 3 Sat, 4 Sun); Pýrgos (1 daily Mon, Tues, Wed, Fri).

Vathý to: Hóra (6 daily Mon–Fri, 5 Sat); Iréon (4–5 daily Mon–Sat, 3 Sun); Karlóvassi (7 daily Mon–Fri, 4–5 Sat & Sun); Kokkári (11 daily Mon–Fri, 8 Sat, 5 Sun); Mytiliní (4 daily direct, 1 via Pythagório Mon–Sat); Pythagório (13 daily Mon–Fri, 10 Sat, 7 Sun); Tzamadhoú 11 daily Mon–Fri, 8 Sat, 5 Sun); Vourliótes (1 daily, Mon, Wed, Fri).

Karlóvassi to: Dhrakéi (1 daily Mon–Fri Sept–early June, Mon & Fri only mid-June to early Sept); Votsalákia (2 daily Mon–Fri).

NB All frequencies are for the period June–Sept except where noted.

Greek script table

Sámos	Σάμος	ΣΑΜΟΣ
Ámbelos	Άμπελος	ΑΜΠΕΛΟΣ
Áno Vathý	Άνω Βαθύ	ΑΝΟ ΒΑΘΥ
Ayía Paraskeví	Αγία Παρασκευή	ΑΓΙΑ ΠΑΡΑΣΚΕΥΗ
Ayía Zóni	Αγία Ζώνη	ΑΓΙΑ ΖΩΝΗ
Áyios	Άγιος	ΑΓΙΟΣ
Konstandínos	Κωνσταντινος	ΚΩΝΣΤΑΝΤΙΝΟΣ
Bállos	Μπάλλος	ΜΠΑΛΛΟΣ
Dhrakéï	Δρακαίοι	ΔΡΑΚΑΙΟΙ
Evangelistrías	Ευαγγελιστρίας	ΕΥΑΓΓΕΛΙΣΤΡΙΑΣ
Hóra	Χώρα	ΧΩΡΑ
Iréon	Ηραίον	ΗΡΑΙΟΝ
Kalámi	Καλάμι	ΚΑΛΑΜΙ
Kallithéa	Καλλιθέα	ΚΑΛΛΙΘΕΑ
Kamára	Καμάρα	ΚΑΜΑΡΑ
Karlóvassi	Καρλόβασι	ΚΑΡΛΟΒΑΣΙ
Kérkis	Κέρκης	ΚΕΡΚΗΣ
Kérveli	Κέρβελι	ΚΕΡΒΕΛΙ
Kyriako	Κυριακού	ΚΥΡΙΑΚΟΥ
Kokkári	Κοκκάρι	ΚΟΚΚΑΡΙ
Koumaradhéï	Κουμαραδαίοι	ΚΟΥΜΑΡΑΔΑΙΟΙ
Kouméïka	Κουμέϊκα	ΚΟΥΜΕΪΚΑ
Koútsi	Κούτσι	ΚΟΥΤΣΙ
Limniónas	Λιμνιώνας	ΛΙΜΝΙΩΝΑΣ
Manolátes	Μανολάτες	ΜΑΝΟΛΑΤΕΣ
Marathókambos	Μαραθόκαμπος	ΜΑΡΑΘΟΚΑΜΠΟΣ
Mavratzéï	Μαυρατζαίοι	ΜΑΥΡΑΤΖΑΙΟΙ
Megális Panayías	Μεγάλης Παναγίας	ΜΕΓΑΛΗΣ ΠΑΝΑΓΙΑΣ
Mykáli	Μυκάλη	ΜΥΚΑΛΗ
Mytilíni	Μυτιληνιοί	ΜΥΤΙΛΗΝΙΟΙ

Inter-island transport

NB To simplify matters, the once-weekly sailing offered by LANE, northbound from Sámos to Híos, Lésvos, Límnos and Alexandhroúpoli, and southbound to Kálymnos, Kós, Rhodes, Hálki, Kárpathos, Kássos and Crete, has been omitted from the following schedules.

Ferries

Vathý to: Foúrni (2–4 weekly on GA or HF; 2hr 15min); Híos (3 weekly on GA, 1 weekly with NEL; 3hr 30min); Áyios Kírykos, Ikaría (3–4 weekly on GA; 3hr); Évdhilos, Ikaría (3–5 weekly on HF; 3hr 30min); Kavála (2 weekly on GA; 18hr 30min); Lésvos (3 weekly on GA; 7hr); Límnos (1 weekly on GA; 11hr 30min); Pireás (1–2 daily on GA or HF; 12–14hr); Thessaloníki (1 weekly on NEL; 17hr 30min); Vólos (1 weekly on GA; 24hr). **Karlóvassi**: as from Vathý, except no services to the Dodecanese with LANE, or to Vólos with GA.

Pythagório to: Agathoníssi (4 weekly on NK; 1hr 30min); Arkí (4 weekly on NK; 2hr 30min); Kálymnos (4 weekly on NK; 6hr 45min); Léros (4 weekly on NK; 5hr 30min); Lipsí (4 weekly on NK; 4hr 30min); Pátmos (4 weekly on NK; 3hr 30min).

NB See p.58 for a more detailed specimen schedule for the *Nissos Kalymnos*.

Catamarans

NEL's *Aeolos Express* has historically linked Vathý with Pireás from April to October along this route: Vathý–Karlóvassi–Áyios Kírykos or Évdhilos–Náxos–Páros–Pireás.

Total journey time 7hr 30min–10hr, depending on weather conditions. Departure from Vathý typically in the early afternoon, 4–7 weekly.

In September 2004, the *Aeolos Express* was pulled from the route described, and may not return. It was replaced, perhaps temporarily, by the Iason

Neohóri	Νεοχώρι	ΝΕΟΧΩΡΙ
Órmos	Όρμος	ΟΡΜΟΣ
Marathokámbou	Μαραθοκάμπου	ΜΑΡΑΘΟΚΑΜΠΟΥ
Pagóndas	Παγώντας	ΠΑΓΩΝΤΑΣ
Paleókastro	Παλαιόκαστρο	ΠΑΛΑΙΟΚΑΣΤΡΟ
Péfkos	Πέφκος	ΠΕΦΚΟΣ
Petaloudha	Πειαλούδα	ΠΕΤΑΛΟΥΔΑ
Plátanos	Πλάτανος	ΠΛΑΤΑΝΟΣ
Pnáka	Πνάκα	ΠΝΑΚΑ
Pýrgos	Πύργος	ΠΥΡΓΟΣ
Pythagório	Πυθαγόρειο	ΠΥΘΑΓΟΡΕΙΟ
Posidhónio	Ποσειδώνιο	ΠΟΣΕΙΔΩΝΙΟ
Potámi	Ποτάμι	ΠΟΤΑΜΙ
Potokáki	Ποτοκάκι	ΠΟΤΟΚΑΚΙ
Psilí Ámmos	Ψιλή Άμμος	ΨΙΛΗ ΑΜΜΟΣ
Seïtáni	Σεϊτάνι	ΣΕΪΤΑΝΙ
Spatharéï	Σπαθαραίοι	ΣΠΑΘΑΡΑΙΟΙ
Stavrinídhes	Σταυρινήδες	ΣΤΑΥΡΙΝΗΔΕΣ
Timíou Stavroú	Τιμίου Σταυρού	ΤΙΜΙΟΥ ΣΤΑΥΡΟΥ
Tsópela	Τσόπελα	ΤΣΟΠΕΛΑ
Tzabo	Τζαμπού	ΤΖΑΜΠΟΥ
Tzamadho	Τζαμαδού	ΤΖΑΜΑΔΟΥ
Valeondádhes	Βαλεοντάδες	ΒΑΛΕΟΝΤΑΔΕΣ
Vársamo	Βάρσαμο	ΒΑΡΣΑΜΟ
Vathý	Βαθύ	ΒΑΘΥ
Votsalákia	Βοτσαλάκια	ΒΟΤΣΑΛΑΚΙΑ
Vourliótes	Βουρλιότες	ΒΟΥΡΛΙΟΤΕΣ
Vrondianís	Βροντιανής	ΒΡΟΝΤΙΑΝΗΣ
Zoödhóhou Piyís	Ζωοδόχου Πηγής	ΖΩΟΔΟΧΟΥ ΠΗΓΗΣ

Jet *Superjet* (no cars carried), whose route was as follows: Vathý–Karlóvassi–Évdhilos–Mýkonos–Tínos–Sýros–Pireás (3–4 weekly; 7hr–9hr).

Kaïkia and excursion boats

Pythagório to: Pátmos (4–6 weekly June–Sept); Samiopoúla islet (2–3 weekly; June–Sept).
Órmos Marathokámbou to: Foúrni (1–2 weekly in season, by demand).
Karlóvassi to: Foúrni (3 weekly, either Tues/Thurs/Sat or Mon/Wed/Fri, at 1.30pm; 2hr 10min, calling at Khryssomiliá and Thýmena en route).

Hydrofoils

Pythagório to: Agathoníssi (1 weekly; 45min); Foúrni (2 weekly; 1hr); Áyios Kírykos, Ikaría (2 weekly; 1hr 30min); Kálymnos (5–7 weekly; 3hr–4h 15min); Kós (5–7 weekly; 3hr 45min–5hr); Léros (5–7 weekly; 2hr–3hr 30min); Lipsí (5–7 weekly; 1hr 30min–3hr); Pátmos (5–7 weekly; 1hr–2hr 30min).

NB All services are with Kyriakoulis Maritime/Samos Hydrofoils. There is no longer any afternoon service from Pythagório except for a few days of the week in April/May – the *Nissos Kalymnos* has taken up the slack for most midday departures.

Flights

Sámos to: Athens (3–5 daily; 55min); Híos (1 weekly; 25min); Lésvos (2 weekly; 55min–1hr 35min); Límnos (2 weekly; 2hr–2hr 35min); Rhodes (2 weekly; 45min); Thessaloníki (4 weekly; 1hr 20min–3hr 45min).

International ferries

Vathý to Kusadası, Turkey: at least 1 daily, late April to late Oct; otherwise a small Turkish boat only on demand in winter, usually Fri or Sat. Greek boat at 8am, 4–5 weekly (passengers only); afternoon (4.45pm) Turkish boats (usually 2 daily in season). Journey time is 1hr 30min. Rates are

€39 one way, including taxes on both the Greek and Turkish sides, €53 open return; no day-return rate. As of writing the Turkish ferries on this route are not allowed to carry cars between the two countries owing to deficient liability insurance – space for three vehicles if/when this is sorted out. 2–3 times weekly, there are excursions direct from Pythagório to Kus*adası use marks as above. Journey time is 2hr and fares are similar to those from Vathý.

Ikaría

Ikaría, a narrow, windswept landmass between Sámos and Mýkonos, not surprisingly displays geographical characteristics of both the Cyclades and east Aegean. Except for the forested northwest, it's not a strikingly beautiful island, with most of the landscape being scrub-covered granite and schist put to good use as building material. The mostly desolate **south** coast is fringed by steep cliffs, while the **north** shore is less sheer but furrowed by deep canyons which deflect the road system into terrifying hairpin bends, extreme even by Greek-island standards. Nor are there many picturesque villages, since the rural stone-roofed houses are generally scattered so as to be next to their famous apricot orchards, vineyards and fields, with the community store or *kafenío* often resolutely inconspicuous.

Though there's been a slow but steady increase in the quantity and quality of facilities in and around Armenistís, the only resort of consequence, Ikaría overall remains little visited (except by Germans and Greeks) and invariably dismissed by travel writers who usually haven't bothered to show up. Until the mid-1990s, the islanders resisted most attempts to develop Ikaría for conventional tourism, which still splutters along almost exclusively between late June and early September. Though an airport began operating in 1995, with a runway graded across Ikaría's northeast tip to permit approaches in any wind, it wasn't built to accommodate jets – thus there are no direct charters from overseas.

For years, the only significant tourism was generated by a number of **hot springs** on the south coast, some reputed to alleviate rheumatism and arthritis, others to cure infertility. Several, however, have in recent decades become blocked through neglect, and one – "Artemídhos" – was so lethally radioactive that it had to be sealed after World War II. An unnerving dockside sign, "Welcome to the island of radiation" (courtesy of the radon gas in the granitic rock), was replaced late in the 1980s by one proclaiming "Welcome to the island of Ikaros". The island's name supposedly derives from that legendary figure, who fell into the sea just offshore after the wax bindings on his wings melted; as some locals are quick to point out, Ikaría is clearly wing-shaped. (First Test Pilot Icarus has been adopted as the patron of the Greek Air Force – on reflection, a rather inauspicious choice.)

Ikaría, along with Thessaly on the mainland, western Sámos and Lésvos, has traditionally been one of the **Greek Left's strongholds**. This tendency dates from long decades of right-wing domination in Greece, when (as in prior ages) the island was used as a place of exile for political dissidents, particularly Communists; apparently the strategy backfired, as the transportees in their hundreds (including, in 1947, Mikis Theodhorakis) impressed their hosts as the most noble and selfless figures they had encountered, worthy of emulation. At the same time, many Ikarians emigrated to North America and,

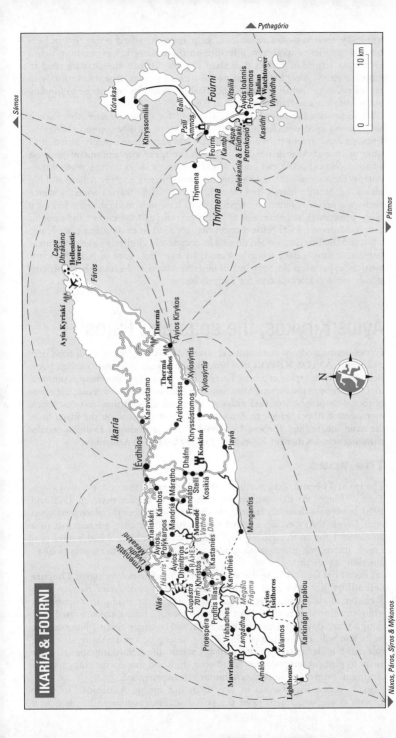

IKARÍA & FOÚRNI

THE EAST AEGEAN ISLANDS | Ikaría

▲ *Pythagório*

Foúrni
Kórakas ▲
Khryssomiliá
Psilí Ámmos
Balí
Vitsiliá
 Áyios Ioánnis
Pródhromos
Italian Watchtower
Ulyhádha
Foúrni
Kámbi
Pelekánia & Elidháki
Petrokopió
Áspa
Kasídhi

◄ *Sámos*

Thýmena
Thýmena

▶ *Pátmos*

Cape Dhrákano
Hellenistic Tower
Fáros
Ayía Kyriakí
Thermá
Ayios Kírykos
Thermá Lefkádhos
Xylosýrtis
Xylosýrtis
Karavóstamo
Aréthoussa
Évdhilos
Khryssóstomos
Dháfni
Koskiná
Playiá
Stélli
Kosíkia
Yialiskári Kámbos
Mandríá Máratho
Frandáto
Áyios
Polýkarpos
Ármenístis
Livádhi Mesakhtí
Áyios
Dhimítrios
RÁHES
Moundé
Vathés
Kastaniés Dam
Manganítis
Nás
Hálaris
Loupástra
70m Khristós
Karydhiés
Proéspera
Profítis Ilías
Megálo Fárma
Áyios Isídhoros
Mavrianoú
Vráhadhes
Langádha
Kálamos
Karkinágri Trapálou
Amálo
Lighthouse

N

◀ *Náxos, Páros, Sýros & Mýkonos*

10 km
0

ironically, their capitalist remittances help keep the island going. It can be a bizarre experience to receive a lecture on the evils of US imperialism delivered by a retiree in perfect Alabaman English. Of late, the Ikarians tend to embrace any vaguely Left-internationalist cause; posters urge you variously to attend rallies on behalf of Turkish political prisoners, or contribute to funding a Zapatista teacher-training school in Chiapas.

These are not the only Ikarian quirks, and for many outsiders the place is an acquired taste, with loathing and enchantment equally common reactions. Even its most ardent partisans admit that the island hasn't nearly as much to offer as its east Aegean neighbours. If you've spent any amount of time on adjacent Sámos, Ikaría can come as either quite a shock or the perfect antidote, as the two islands could hardly be more different socially. Athens and big provincial brother Sámos have historically reacted to Ikaria's contrary stance with long periods of punitive neglect, which have only made the islanders even more profoundly self-sufficient and idiosyncratic, and tolerant of the same in others. Moreover, local pride dictates that approval from outsiders matters not a bit, and the Ikarians – often dressed in decade-old clothes, unlike the Samian fashion victims – until recently seemed to have little idea of what "modern tourists" expect. It is this very lack of obsequiousness, and a studied eccentricity, which some visitors mistake for unfriendliness.

Áyios Kírykos, the spas and Fáros

Ferries between Sámos and Pireás call several days weekly at the south coast port and capital, **ÁYIOS KÍRYKOS**, a nondescript though inoffensive enough place. Because of the spa trade in nearby Thermá, beds are at a premium here in summer, so if you arrive in the evening from Sámos or Pátmos, accept any reasonable offers of rooms, or proposals of **taxi rides** to the north coast; it shouldn't cost much more than €40 per vehicle to Armenistís. A **bus** sets out across the island from the main square (July 15–Sept 15 Mon–Fri only at noon) to Évdhilos, usually changing vehicles there at 1.30pm for the onward trip to Armenistís.

The spas

The spa at **Thermá**, 1km northeast of the harbour by the minor coastal access drive or longer via the main inland route, saw its heyday between 1920 and 1940, but is now distinctly faded. From June to September the place is mobbed with Greek OAPs taking a social-service-subsidized cure, packed five to a hotel room, for up to eighteen days. Only two rather clinical bathhouses, plus a more interesting grotto-sauna (under restoration and due to reopen in 2006) function at present.

A better bet for a soak are the more natural shoreline hot springs at **Thermá Lefkádhos**, just over 2km southwest from the base of Áyios Kírykos jetty. A cluster of eucalyptus trees on the inland side of the road grows opposite a white-on-blue sign reading "Hot Mineral Spring"; follow the indicated path along a fence down to the shore, turn right, and continue about 100m over the rocks. You will see the springs (55–58° C) welling up on the shore, and some volcanic-boulder corrals in the shallows where the lightly sulphurous water mixes to pleasant temperatures. Mind your shins and toes on the slimy rocks; a maximum immersion of twenty minutes is recommended.

Finally, Áyios Kírykos has its very own hot spring, **Asklipioú**. To reach it, walk down some steps from the police station/courthouse building to a pumping station, then continue 150m over rock slabs to a large seaside pool under a rock overhang. The water is clean, non-sulphurous and 35–40° C depending on that day's sea-surge; there's good swimming adjacent. During summer, you may be barred by the attendant of the upper Asklipioú bathhouse (fee) from using the lower springs.

Fáros and around

For more conventional beaches, there's a pebble cove at **Xylosýrtis**, 7km southwest beyond Thérma Lefkádhos, but the largest (2km long) and best one on the south coast is found at **FÁROS** (Fanári), 10km northeast of Áyios Kírykos along a good paved road (which also serves the airport). A considerable colony of summer cottages shelters under tamarisks fringing the mixed sand-and-gravel strand, with a reefy zone to cross before deep water; this rather end-of-the-world place looks across to Foúrni and Thýmena, whose beaches (and landscape) it strongly resembles.

An excellent reason to make the trip out are two inexpensive **fish tavernas**: *Leonidas* (open all year; reserve on ☎22750 32202 in peak season), with grilled or fried seafood plus bulk wine; and the more dour, less popular but qualitywise superior *O Grigoris* next door. Both are better than anything in Áyios itself (see overleaf).

Cape Dhrákano and another spa

From a point just inland on the access road, a rough track leads 2km to the trailhead for the ten-minute walk to **Cape Dhrákano** and its third-century-BC **Hellenistic tower**, originally three storeys high, now shedding masonry but still impressive and emphatically worth the trip out. The round tower, the oldest surviving structure on the island, was part of a much larger, now mostly crumbled fort, which extends halfway to the cape, and its pretty rustic chapel of **Áyios Yeóryios**. Below this to the north, perfectly sheltered in most weathers, is a fantasy-image sand **beach**, with assorted rocks and islets off the cape-tip for decor.

Hot springs aficionados might care to seek out the spa of **Ayía Kyriakí**. Take the road past the airport, then instead of carrying on to the quarry head down to a group of summerhouses on an obvious bay. The old bathhouse on the point is derelict, but facing the sea you'll notice a cement, sea-level enclosure tucked under a rock overhang to the left, just big enough for three adults (or parents and two kids). You may have to scoop out some eelgrass debris brought by the waves, but the water (35–38° C) is lovely.

Accommodation

If you decide to **stay** in Áyios Kírykos, there are a few hotels and pensions, such as the *Isabella* (☎22750 22839; ➋) above the National Bank, or the friendly, spotless, air-con, en-suite *Akti* (☎22750 22694; ➌), on a knoll east of the hydrofoil and kaïki quay, with views of Foúrni from the garden; Marcia (Moskhoula), the helpful and knowledgeable proprietress, spent twenty years in America. Otherwise, directly behind the base of the ferry jetty and two blocks inland, uphill on Artemídhos, there's the well-appointed *Pension Maria-Elena* (☎22750 22835, ℱ22750 22223; ➌), a large modern block in a quiet setting. All in a row above the eastern quay sit the prominently marked *Pension Ikaria* (☎22750 22804; ➋), the studios (☎22750 23400; ➌) above *Taverna Dedalos* and the clean *dhomátia* run by Ioannis Proestos (☎22750 23176; ➋), though these can get noise from several kafenía and snack-bars below.

Eating, drinking and nightlife

Eating out, you've even less choice than in lodging, with *Dedalos* as noted above the only year-round choice. It's best to give the obvious quayside eateries a miss in favour of the grilled dishes served up at the *Estiatorio Tzivaeri* (summer only), just inland from Ioannis Proestos' rooms, or less distinguished *mayireftá* at *Iy Klimataria* (summer only) just around the corner. With transport, it's worth heading out the 7km to Xylosýrtis village, where *Toula's* opposite the church works year-round and purveys homemade *kapnistó* (smoked pork), wild pickled bulbs, ace *tzatzíki* and local lamb chops, let down only by poor-quality commercial wine.

On the gentrified waterfront, *Casino* is the last remaining traditional *kafenío*; for further entertainment there's a **summer cinema**, the Rex, with first-run fare, plus a couple of musical clubs on the shore road west of the jetty-base.

Other practicalities

Hydrofoils and *kaïkia* use the small **east jetty**; large ferries and catamarans dock at the main **west pier**. Several ferry/catamaran/hydrofoil agents – the most useful and comprehensive being Nikos Speis (T 22750 22397) and Lakios (T 22750 22426) – can be coy about giving details of the early-afternoon *kaïki* to Foúrni, whose tickets are only sold on board. Three **banks** with ATMs, a **post office** on the rear road of the one-way loop system, an Olympic Airways office a few steps back from the quay-esplanade (T 22750 22214) and an Internet café (*Ic@rian Sea*) round up the list of essentials. You can **rent motorbikes and cars** here, too, but there will be better selection and better prices in Armenistís.

Évdhilos and around

The twisting, 41-kilometre road from Áyios Kírykos to Évdhilos is one of the steepest and most hair-raising on any Greek island (especially as a taxi passenger), and the long ridge extending the length of Ikaría often wears a coiffure of cloud, even when the rest of the Aegean sky is clear. Karavóstamo, with its tiny, scruffy port, is the first substantial place on the north coast, with a series of three beaches between it and **ÉVDHILOS**. Although this is the island's second town and a regular ferry stop on the Sámos–Pireás line (more or less alternate days; tickets from the Nikos Speis **agency** T 22750 31572), it's rather less equipped to deal with visitors than Áyios Kírykos. There are, however, two C-class **hotels** – the smallish *Evdoxia* on the slope southwest of the harbour (T 22750 31502; ❹), and the low-lying *Atheras* (T 22750 31434, W www.atheras-kerame.gr; ❹), with a small pool – plus a few **rooms**. Among several waterfront **restaurants**, the wood-signed *Coralli* is the most reliable and reasonable option, but for more interesting fare head 1km west of the harbour to **Fýtema** hamlet. Just on the roadside here *To Inomayerio tis Popis* (alias *To Fytema*; May–Sept) has lots of options for vegetarians, excellent local wine, low prices and pleasant terrace seating, though portions are on the small side. A **post office** up towards the *Evdoxia*, a pair of **bank** ATMs, two **car rental** outlets (including Car Mania, T 22750 32983), and two good **beaches** just to the east, are also worth knowing about, though the nearer beach will be blighted in the coming years by a new, much-needed harbour jetty.

Kámbos and inland

KÁMBOS, 1.5km west of Fýtema, boasts a small hilltop museum with finds from nearby **ancient Oinoe**, the island's capital in antiquity; the eleventh-century church of **Ayía Iríni** (locked) lies just below, with the remains of a larger fifth-century Byzantine basilica – including mosaic patches, and columns of the carved-stone *témblon* – serving as the entry courtyard. Lower down still are the sparse ruins of a **Byzantine palace** (just above the road), which was used to house exiled nobles, and, last but not least, a 250-metre-long, excellent sandy **beach** with a drinks *kantína*. Comfortable, en-suite **rooms** (*Dionysos*) are available by asking at the village store run by Vassilis Kambouris (☎22750 31300 or 22750 31688; ❷), who also acts as the unofficial but enthusiastic tourism officer for this part of Ikaría, controlling the keys for both the church and a one-room, village-centre museum of finds from Oinoe. Meals are served at a **taverna** that keeps bizarre 10pm-to-4am hours (see overleaf). More organized **nightlife** consists of the *Petrino* bar above the east end of the beach, with a diet of traditional music at variance with the techno, ambient and dub still all the rage in the rest of Greece.

Kámbos is also one possible jump-off point for visits up into the hamlet-speckled valley inland. **STELLÍ** and **DHÁFNI** are attractive examples of the little oases that sprout on Ikaría, while **FRANDÁTO** has a summer-only café-bar-*ouzerí*, *To Anonymo*.

Évdhilos, however, is the start of another, better-marked route (beginning from the large church), which passes below the Byzantine-Genoese **castle of Koskiná** (Nikariás), just over 15km south. The paved road signposted for Manganítis leads through Kosikiá, just over 9km away, and then for a steeper 2km to a marked side-track, along which you can get a sturdy motorbike or jeep to within a short walk of the tenth-century castle. Perched on a distinctive conical hill, this has an arched gateway and a fine, if bare, vaulted chapel in the middle, incorporating ancient masonry.

Beyond this turning, the road creeps over the island watershed and drops precipitously in hairpins towards the south coast; almost all of this is paved, and with your own vehicle offers an alternative (and far less twisty, 8km shorter) way **back to Áyios Kírykos**, in much the same time as via Karavóstomo. It's an eminently scenic route worth taking once for its own sake, the narrow road threading corniche-like through oaks at the pass, and then olives at Playiá village on the steep southern slope of the island; out to sea the islands of Pátmos and Dhonoússa are generally visible, and on really clear days Náxos and Amorgós as well.

Armenistís and around

Most people carry on to **ARMENISTÍS**, 57km from Áyios Kírykos, and with good reason: this little resort lies below Ikaría's finest (if somewhat diminished) forest, with two enormous, sandy beaches battered by seasonal surf – **Livádhi** and **Mesakhtí** – five and fifteen minutes' walk to the east respectively. The sea between here and Mýkonos is perhaps the windiest patch in the Aegean, making this one of the few spots in Greece with anything resembling a consistent surf in summer. The waves – which attract Athenian surfers, boards on car-tops – are complicated by strong lateral currents (as signs warn), and several annual summer drownings have prompted the institution of that Greek rarity, a lifeguard service.

Mesakhtí is so vast that it has no less than three music-bars-cum-drinks-*kantínas* along its length, and when the sea is calm the paddling's idyllic.

Armenistís itself is spectacularly set, looking northeast along the length of Ikaría toward sun- and moonrise, with Mount Kérkis on Sámos closing off the horizon on a clear day. A dwindling proportion of older, schist-roofed buildings, plus fishing boats hauled up in a sandy cove, lend Armenistís the air of a Cornish fishing village. Despite inexorable growth it remains a manageable place, reminiscent of similar youth-oriented, slightly "alternative" spots in southern Crete, though gentrification (and a strong package presence) has definitely established itself. The long-running, semi-official campsite behind Livádhi beach closed in 2001 – a sign of the times – and hasn't reopened; a few "freelance" tents still sprout in the river-mouth greenery behind Mesakthí, and a few naturists cavort, both practices defying posted signage forbidding them.

Just east of Mesakhtí, the fishing settlement of **Yialiskári** has a handful of tavernas and perhaps half a dozen rooms establishments (look for the signs), with views of a picturesque landmark church on the jetty.

Accommodation

There are easily a score of **rooms** establishments in the Armenistís area, as well as four bona fide **hotels**. Note that many proprietors don't open their units until mid- to late May.

Armena Inn Top of the hill, across the road from Kirki Rooms ℡22750 71320. Spartan, 1980s block which has private parking, enviable seclusion, unobstructed views and cooking facilities in the rooms. ❸

Atsahas Apartments Far east end of Livádhi beach ℡ & ℱ 22750 71226. Cheerful carpeted or tile-floor units with French-windowed balconies offer the best standard and setting outside of the hotels; accordingly it fills even during low season, so book in advance. Open early and late in the year. ❸

Daidalos West edge of Armenistís, start of Nás road ℡22750 71390, ℱ22750 71393. The less impersonal and less package-dominated of two adjacent C-class hotels, with an eyrie-pool, unusually appointed, good-sized rooms and a shady terrace for taking the included buffet breakfast. ❺

Erofili Beach Right at the entrance to "town" ℡22750 71058, ⓦwww.erofili.gr. This 1999-built B-class hotel is considered the best on the island; common areas and furnishings are above average (though rooms are not huge, and a tendency to turn the air con off in mid-Sept, whatever the weather, has been reported). A loyal repeat clientele bobs in a small pool perched dramatically over Livádhi beach. ❻

Kirki Rooms On the town's southeast approach road ℡22750 71254, ℱ22750 71083, or enquire at *Delfini Taverna*. Pine-and-tile-bland but en-suite units, with large private balconies and knockout sea views. Rooms ❷, studios ❸

Messakhti Village Just above Mesakhtí beach ℡22750 71331, ⓦwww.messakti-village.gr. B-class bungalow complex with a larger pool than *Erofili*'s, plus tasteful common areas and large private terraces making up for reportedly listless breakfasts and the slightly minimalist self-catering units suitable for families of three to six. The two tower suites (for up to four) are the best-appointed. ❻

Paskhalia Rooms Shore lane, village centre ℡22750 71302, winter ℡210 24 71 411. Rather plain budget rooms are on the small side, but en suite and good value, with great sea views (except for two); popular, and usually requiring advance booking. ❷

Valeta Apartments (aka *Kostas and Sofias*), next to *Atsahas Apartments* ℡22750 71252. Spacious, high-standard studio units with big balconies, friendly managing family. ❹

Eating, drinking and nightlife

Discounting the sweet shops and *souvláki* stalls (a pair each), there are eight full-service **tavernas** in Armenistís, of which four have a consistently good reputation. *Dhelfini*, its terrace hovering right above the fishing cove, is the cheap-and-cheerful favourite – come early or very late for a table, and a mix of grills or *mayireftá*. *Paskhalia* (aka *Vlahos* after the helpful managing family), below the rooms noted on opposite, feels slightly more commercial, but portions of fish, chops and vegetables are hearty, and it's the most reliable venue for both breakfast and off-season travel. Down on the quay itself, *Symposio* is pricier but worth the extra for creative recipes and rich ingredients reflecting the German co-management and chef. Further afield, the *Atsahas*, attached to the namesake apartments, is pretty good as a beach taverna, with generous portions of slightly oily but vegetarian fare. At the village entrance there's an **Internet** café, *Ic@rian Sea*, and a laundry.

Just east of Mesakthi in the pine-set fishing settlement of **Yialiskári**, there's another cluster of tavernas overlooking the boat-launching slips, of which *Tramountana* and *Kelaris* (aka *Eleftheria Kastania*) are the most popular, the former purveying superb parrotfish fry-ups, the latter doing excellent, reasonable grilled fish and standard *mayireftá*.

Several "music bars", often with live Greek gigs, operate seasonally behind Livádhi and at the quay's north end, and in Yialiskári (eg *Karnayio*), but for most visitors **nightlife** takes the form of extended sessions in the tavernas and cafés overlooking the central anchorage, or the sweet shops (especially *En Plo*) at the village entrance.

Getting around – and away

Nas Travel and Ikaros Travel are the two main ferry and money-changing agencies. There are now at least four **scooter/mountain-bike rental** agencies in Armenistís (eg Glaros, ☎22750 71348); among a like number of **car rental** outlets, Aventura (☎22750 71117) is the most prominent, with a branch in Évdhilos which could facilitate a self-transfer to eastbound ferries at an ungodly hour (they typically pass by at 4am). Indeed, getting away when you need to is the main drawback to staying in Armenistís, since both taxis and buses can be elusive, though predictability has improved slightly over the years. Theoretically, **buses** head for Évdhilos three times daily mid-June to mid-September, fairly well spaced (typically 7.15am, noon & 7pm, returning an hour or so later), the morning and evening services designed to coincide with westbound ferries from Évdhilos; Áyios Kírykos has only one through-service year-round at 7.15am, though this can be full with schoolkids in term time. If you've a boat to catch, it's far easier on the nerves to pre-book a **taxi**: ring Kostas Stroupas (☎22750 41132) or Yiannis Tsantiris (☎22750 41322).

Inland: Ráhes and around

Armenistís is actually the shore annexe of four inland hamlets – Áyios Dhimítrios, Áyios Polýkarpos, Kastaniés and Khristós – collectively known as **RÁHES**. Despite the modern, mostly paved, access roads in through what remains of the pines after mid-1990s fires (trails short-cut them; see p.365), they still retain a certain Shangri-La quality, with mists frequently cloaking the ridges (*ráhes*) of the name, and the older residents speaking a positively Homeric dialect. On an island not short of foibles, **Khristós** (Khristós Rahón, in full) is particularly strange, inasmuch as the adults sleep until 11am or so, shop and snack until about 4pm, then have another nap until 9pm, whereupon they rise and spend the entire night shopping, eating and drinking until almost dawn. In fact most of the villages west of Évdhilos adhere to this schedule, defying central-government efforts to bring them into line with the rest of Greece (though they have been forced to educate their children from 8.30am to 2pm). Not coincidentally, this was one of the main centres of Leftist exile from the 1930s to the 1970s; the irony of daubing "Che", "Lenin" and more elaborate Communist slogans on the rusted chassis of East-bloc Wartburgs and Polskis seems to have escaped the locals.

Near the pedestrianized *agorá* of Khristós, paved in schist and studded with gateways fashioned from the same rock, there's a **post office** and a **hotel-restaurant** (☎22750 71269; ❸); asking around will turn up some unlicensed rooms in the ❶ category. After dark several other eateries operate for example; *Kapilio*, and (in Áyios Dhimítrios) *O Platanos* – which doubles as the favourite Sunday-afternoon *kafenío* – but, in accordance with the above diurnal schedule, lunchtime can offer pretty slim pickings.

The slightly spaced-out demeanours of those serving anywhere hereabouts – and numbers of old boys shambling nonchalantly about in dirty clothes, with their flies unzipped – may be attributable to overindulgence in the excellent home-brewed **wine** which everyone west of Évdhilos seems to make: smoky-hued from the *fokianós* grape, organic, strong but not hangover-inducing, and stored in rather off-putting goatskins. The local festival, with merrymaking and (it is said) controlled substances a-plenty, is August 6, though better ones take place further southwest in the woods at Langádha valley (Aug 14–15) or at Áyios Isídhoros monastery (May 14). The Whit Monday observance at Kastaniés is fairly typical of minor festivals: 11pm until 3am, overdone goat *soúvla* and rough wine on sale, and locals doing freestyle *harsilamás* to a three-man acoustic band.

The **monastery of Moundé**, dating back to the fifteenth century (though the present buildings are 300 years newer), stands 4.5km east of Khristós in a beautiful wooded hollow; take the paved road to Kastaniés hamlet, and continue another couple of kilometres on the dirt road signposted for Frandáto. In summer there will be a warden about, who tends a small **café-snack-bar** (10am–7.30pm; no alcohol served) with courtyard seating, and keeps the keys for the triple-aisled church with its interior arcade. Just west, immediately south of the dirt track, lies the little **reservoir of Vathés**, originally dammed in the 1950s and now a designated wildlife reserve for ducks and migratory birds.

Nás

By tacit consent, Greek or foreign hippies and beachside naturists have been allowed to shift 3km west of Armenistís by paved road to **Nás**, a tree-clogged river canyon ending in a small but deceptively sheltered sand-and-pebble beach. This little bay is almost completely enclosed by weirdly sculpted rock formations, but for the same reasons as at Mesakhtí it's unwise to swim outside the cove's natural limits. The crumbling foundations of the fifth-century temple of **Artemis Tavropoleio** (Patroness of Bulls) overlook the permanent deep pool at the mouth of the river. If you continue inland along this, Ikaría's only year-round watercourse, past colonies of "alternative" types defying no-camping signs, you'll find secluded rock pools for freshwater dips.

Back at the top of the stairs leading down to the beach from the road are six **tavernas**, most of which offer **rooms**. Among these, the *Artemis* (☎22750 71485; ❷ rooms, ❸ studios), a rambling, tiered complex overlooking the river canyon, has newer apartment annexes of high standard, while all units at *Thea* (☎22750 71491; ❸) face the sea; like their counterparts in Armenistís, both places halve their rates out of season. *Thea* has by far the most accomplished cooking, with lots of vegetarian options like *soufikó* (the local stove-top version of *briám*), and works weekends in winter.

The southwest coast

By joining an organized "jeep safari" or renting a sturdy scooter, you can make a tour through several villages at the southwestern tip of the island. **VRAHÁDHES**, with two *kafenía* and a natural-balcony setting, makes a good first or last stop on a tour. A sharp drop below it, the impact of the empty convent of **Mavrianoú** lies mostly in its setting amid gardens overlooking the sea. Nearby **AMÁLO** has two summer-only tavernas; just inland, **Langádha** is not a village but a hidden valley containing an enormous *exohikó kéndro* (rural taverna), used as the venue for the local *paniyíri* on August 14–15, one of the island's biggest.

Walking in western Ikaría

You might well forgo car or scooter rental around Armenistís, as the best of Ikaría lies within a couple of hours' walk from the resort. Beginning in the early 1990s, **walking** between Ráhes and the coast rocketed in popularity, though (as everywhere in Greece) bulldozers and forest fires have reduced the number of attractive possibilities by the year, and additionally on Ikaría paths are poorly marked and used to be jealously guarded as secrets by interested parties in the excursion industry. Since 1998, however, locally produced, accurate if somewhat chatty map-guides are widely available, as well as a good general touring map (sold in the photo shop at Khristós). The black-and-white "Road & Hiking Map of Western Ikaria" (€1.20) shows most asphalt roads, tracks and trails in the west-centre of the island; the more closely focused, colour "Round of Ráhes on Foot" (€3) details a loop hike taking in the best the Ráhes villages have to offer. The route sticks mostly to surviving paths, and is well marked; it's suggested you allow a full day for the circuit, with ample rests, though total walking time won't be more than six hours.

More advanced outings involve descending the Hálaris canyon to Nás, or crossing the island to Manganítis via Ráhes. In either case you'll still need to follow the first portion of the "Round of Ráhes", beginning at the Livádhi road bridge by the *Pleiades Nightclub*, climbing up to Áyios Dhimítrios within eighty minutes and to Khristós within 1hr 45min. From Áyios Dhimítrios, it's possible to descend the Hálaris canyon – initially on a steep hillside trail, later along the riverbed – directly to Nás within an hour and a half. From Khristós there's a well-marked trail leading down in forty minutes to a medieval bridge in the Hálaris canyon, where you can fight your way down the stream bed to Nás (some sharp drops, and pools to bathe in), again within ninety minutes.

The main onward path from the bridge, rather intimidatingly signposted "Proespéra 8km, Langádha 22km, Karkinágri 36km", fizzles out in a track system half an hour uphill, on the shoulder of Mount Loupástra. Thus those wishing to traverse Ikaría are best advised to keep on the "Round of Ráhes" route from Khristós a bit further to Karydhiés, from where a historic path crosses the lunar Ammoudhiá uplands before dropping spectacularly southeast to Managanítis on the south coast, a generous half-day's outing from Armenistís; there's a taverna in Manganítis, plus a few unlicensed rooms for the asking.

Other outings for which you'll appreciate an initial vehicle transfer are the hour-plus hike from Vrahádhes to Langádha, visiting 800-year-old troglodytic stone houses en route, or the descent from Áyios Isídhoros monastery to either Karkinágri or Trapálou on the south coast. The trick would be to combine these by closing the short gap between Langádha and Áyios Isídhoros for a proper half-day hike.

It's a sturdy motorbike that gets all the way to **KARKINÁGRI**, at the base of cliffs near the southern extremity of Ikaría, and a dismal anticlimax. One thing that is likely to bring a smile to your lips, however, is the marked intersection of Leofóros Bakunin and Odhós Lenin – surely the last two such forthrightly Marxist streets remaining in Greece, not to say all of Europe – at the edge of the village. You'll find two sleepy, seasonal **tavernas** and two **rooms** establishments near the jetty. Before the road to Karkinágri was opened (the continuation to Manganítis and Áyios Kírykos has been abandoned at Trapálou, owing to a difficult-to-dynamite rock-face), the village's only easy link with the outside world was by ferry or *kaïki*. There is in fact still a thrice-weekly post-and-shopping boat from Karkinágri (via Manganítis; Mon, Wed & Fri at 7am, returning from Áyios Kírykos at 1pm), an invaluable facility if you've just made a trek across the island ending here.

Satellite islets: Thýmena and Foúrni

The straits between Sámos and Ikaría are speckled with a mini–archipelago of three islets, of which the inhabited ones are Thýmena and Foúrni. More westerly **Thýmena** has one tiny hillside settlement, at which regular *kaïkia* call on their way between Ikaría or Karlóvassi and Foúrni, but there are no tourist facilities or attractions to speak of – save one large beach south of "town" – and day-trips are only possible starting from Foúrni.

Foúrni is home to a huge fishing fleet and one of the more thriving boat-yards in the Aegean. Thanks to these, and the 1989 improvement of the jetty to receive car ferries, its population is stable at about 1600, unlike so many small Greek islands. The islets here were once the lair of Maltese pirates, and indeed many of the islanders have a distinctly North African appearance.

Apart from the remote hamlet of **Khryssomiliá** in the north, where the island's longest (and worst) road goes, most of Foúrni's inhabitants are concentrated in the **port** and **Kambí**, a hamlet just south. The harbour community is larger than it seems from the sea, with the locals' friendliness adding to a general ambience reminiscent of 1970s Greece.

Getting to Foúrni

The islanders' shopping-and-post **kaïki** leaves Foúrni port around 7.30am at least four days weekly (typically Mon, Wed, Fri & Sun) for Ikaría, returning at about 2pm the same day; this is supplemented by three weekly small local ferries from Karlóvassi (departing 1.30pm), one of which – the *Samos Spirit* – takes several cars. These, and the larger car ferries which appear almost daily, are not tourist excursion boats but exist for the benefit of the islanders. The only practical way to visit Foúrni on a day-trip is by using the tourist *kaïki Samos Sky*, which leaves Áyios Kírykos daily in season at 10am, returning from Foúrni at 5pm, or on one of two weekly morning **hydrofoils** out of Pythagório.

Foúrni port practicalities

Touts for some of the fourteen **rooms** establishments meet most incoming craft at the main jetty, but there's nothing stopping you from phoning ahead to reserve space at the more desirable places noted here. About the most popular are the various premises run by Manolis and Patra Markakis (T22750 51268,

22750 51355), immediately to your left as you disembark, which range from simple rooms (**②**, some with balconies), to fourteen superb hilltop apartments, most sleeping up to four, in a tiered complex (**④**). If they're full, head inland to the plain, 1970s-vintage block of *Evtyhia Amoryianou* (☎22750 51364; **①**), whose father Nikos Kondylas meets all boats and is a mine of information about the island; the bright, modern palace of *Andonis Ahladhis* (☎22750 51077; **②**), in the westernmost lane; or *Kosta-Reli*, just back from the little town beach (☎22750 51481; **③**).

There are three full-service waterfront **tavernas**: local favourite *Rementzo*, better known as *Nikos'*, where if you're lucky the local *astakós* or Aegean lobster may be on the menu (except Sept–Jan); shambolically manged *Miltos*, but with good seafood such as the succulent *skathári* (black bream), which thrives in the surrounding waters, and wild (not farmed) *tsipoúra*; or newer contender *Ta Dhelfinakia*, a good all-rounder with more meat dishes and limited seating (book in person in high season).

For breakfast and homemade desserts, repair to the tamarisk terrace at the Markakis family's café-bar, *To Arhondiko tis Kyras Kokonas*, under their inn. There's surprisingly lively **nightlife** at a half-dozen musical clubs and *ouzerís*, often until 5am, particularly at *To Steki tou Skevou* and *Mylos Club*.

The central "high street", fieldstoned and mulberry-shaded, ends well inland at a handsome square with *Kafenio Iy Dhrosia* (doing good sweets) under the first of two giant plane trees. Between them stands a Hellenistic **sarcophagus** that was found in a nearby field, and overhead on the conical hill of Áyios Yeóryios looms the site of the island's nocturnally illuminated **ancient acropolis**. Nearby is a **post office** and a single stand-alone **bank** ATM. Shops (including two bakeries and a pharmacy) are surprisingly numerous and well stocked, so there's no reason to haul in supplies from Foúrni's larger neighbours. Neither is there a need to buy bottled water: the island has plenty of potable stuff from deep well-bores, and there are public fountains at each end of the main street. A more worthwhile purchase is the local **thyme honey**: strongly flavoured, very expensive, and available after any rainy winter – the bakeries sell it. For getting around the island, there are two **taxis** and a single outlet **renting scooters**, Escape (☎22750 51514).

Southern Foúrni: Kambí, Áyios Ioánnis Pródhromos and beaches

A fifteen-minute path-walk south from the port, beginning at the school, skirting the cemetery and then slipping over the ridge with its four restored windmills, brings you to **KAMBÍ**, a scattered community overlooking a pair of sandy, tamarisk-shaded coves which you'll share with hauled-up fishing boats – and, in season, quite a few other visitors, a kayak-rental concession and taxi-boat service to "town". Kambí has two cheap and sustaining **tavernas**: Andreas Sklavos' *Kambi* with tables on the sand, and somewhat more accomplished *O Yiorgos* clinging to the side of a valley inland. If you wish to **stay**, try *Studios Rena* (☎22750 51364, ℉22750 51209; **②**), stacked in three tiers on the north hillside, or *Buzakos Apartments*, up the valley past *O Yiorgos* (☎697 79 45 877; **②**).

A path system starting at Kambí's last house continues south around the headland to other, more secluded bays of varying sizes and beach consistencies, which like Kambí cove are favourite anchorages for passing yachts, but unlike Kambí have substantial summer communities of rough campers and naturists. In order of appearance they are sand-and-pebble **Áspa** (20min along), with a tiny spring seeping from the rocks just before you arrive, **Pelekanía** (5min further) and (5min further still) **Elidháki** – both of these coarse pebble, the latter also with track access. The trail can be slippery and steep in places between Kambí and Áspa; you may prefer to arrive by motorbike as far as Elidháki, or on the taxi-boat service offered from the port.

The track serving Elidháki from the main island ridge-road also has an option for **Petrokopió** (Marmári) cove, so named for its role as a quarry for ancient Ephesus in Asia Minor. The quarry itself with obvious chisel-marks, and abandoned half-worked stones down by shore, proves impressive; the beach, with a seasonal drinks *kantína* at the far end, is made of the same stone.

The ridge-road drops to the hamlet and monastery of **Áyios Yiánnis Pród-hromos**, 8km from the port. There are no facilities whatsoever here except for mineral-tasting spring water in the monastery courtyard. The spring nurtures a tiny oasis, originally planted by a fugitive-hermit from Asia Minor late in the nineteenth century, but the monastery itself is lively only around the dates of the local festival (Aug 28–29).

From the monastery spring, you can follow an obvious path uphill and then down, within fifteen minutes, to secluded **Kasídhi** – there may be some goats and tar, but otherwise it's pristine and deserted. If you're on a scooter you may prefer the sandy, popular double-cove of **Vlyhádha**, with its own 1300-metre access track, or the less crowded, sand-and-fine-gravel bay of **Vitsiliá** on the east coast, again with its own track access beside the Vlyhádha turning. Like most Foúrni beaches, none of these coves has any amenities.

Northern Foúrni: Kryssomiliá and beaches

Heading north from Foúrni harbour via steps, then a trail, you'll find more, slightly sullied **beaches**. **Psilí Ámmos**, in front of a derelict fish-processing plant and equally defunct "music bar" at the end with tamarisks, is superior to **Kálamos**, further along the path, dominated by a military watchpoint; both now have road access and (in the former case) a new jetty.

At the extreme north of the island, remote **KHRYSSOMILIÁ** still lives in a 1960s time warp, engaged mostly in fishing. It's more usually approached by a daily taxi-boat, or the Karlóvassi-based small ferry, as the eighteen-kilometre road in is execrable; only the first 3km out of the port, and the final approach of 2km, are paved. The village, split into the shore district of Ayía Triádha and a hill settlement at the top of a canyon, has a decent beach flanked by better, if less accessible, ones. Two **tavernas** of sorts flank the jetty; equally simple **rooms** – not more than ten – can be arranged on the spot. It should be said, however, that the locals are pretty suspicious of outsiders and not terribly forthcoming, especially outside of high season.

Should you decide to walk back to town, it's a full three-and-a-half-hour hike from Khryssomiliá to the port. The first two hours are a dreary tramp along the shadeless track, before the old *kalderími* reappears just past the hamlet and isthmus of **Ballí** for the final hour-plus up to the monastery of **Panayía**, which overlooks the town from a ridge to the north. The last section of the path, with two decent beaches in the bay of Ballí below Panayía to the north, are the walk's main redeeming features. Taxis are likely to charge well over the odds for the trip, and on an 80cc scooter it's an uncomfortable 75-minute journey riding two-up; not really worth the effort.

Greek script table

Ikaría	Ικαρία	ΙΚΑΡΙΑ
Armenistís	Αρμενιστής	ΑΡΜΕΝΙΣΤΗΣ
Áyios Isídhoros	Άγιος Ισίδωρος	ΑΓΙΟΣ ΙΣΠΔΩΡΟΣ
Áyios Kírykos	Άγιος Κήρυκος	ΑΓΙΟΣ ΚΗΡΥΚΟΣ
Áyios Polýkarpos	Άγιος Πολύκαρπος	ΑΓΙΟΣ ΠΟΛΥΚΑΡΠΟΣ
Dháfni	Δάφνη	ΔΑΦΝΗ
Évdhilos	Εύδηλος	ΕΥΔΗΛΟΣ
Fáros	Φάρος	ΦΑΡΟΣ
Frandáto	Φραντάτο	ΦΡΑΝΤΑΤΟ
Fýtema	Φύτεμα	ΦΥΤΕΜΑ
Kámbos	Κάμπος	ΚΑΜΠΟΣ
Karavóstamo	Καραβόσταμο	ΚΑΡΑΒΟΣΤΑΜΟ
Karkinágri	Καρκινάγρι	ΚΑΡΚΙΝΑΓΡΙ
Kastaniés	Καστανιές	ΚΑΣΤΑΝΙΕΣ
Khristós	Χριστός	ΧΡΙΣΤΟΣ
Khrysóstomos	Χρυσόστομος	ΧΡΥΣΟΣΤΟΜΟΣ
Koskiná	Κοσκινά	ΚΟΣΚΙΝΑ
Langádha	Λαγκάδα	ΛΑΓΚΑΔΑ
Manganítis	Μαγγανίτης	ΜΑΓΓΑΝΙΤΗΣ
Mavrianoú	Μαυριανού	ΜΑΥΡΙΑΝΟΥ
Moundé	Μουντέ	ΜΟΥΝΤΕ
Nás	Νάς	ΝΑΣ
Playiá	Πλαγιά	ΠΛΑΓΙΑ
Ráhes	Ράχες	ΡΑΧΕΣ
Stellí	Στελι	ΣΤΕΛΙ
Thermá	Θερμά	ΘΕΡΜΑ
Thermá Lefkádhos	Θερμά Λευκάδος	ΘΕΡΜΑ ΛΕΥΚΑΔΟΣ
Trapálou	Τραπάλου	ΤΡΑΠΑΛΟΥ
Vathés	Βαθές	ΒΑΘΕΣ
Xylosýrtis	Ξυλοσύρτης	ΞΥΛΟΣΥΡΤΗΣ
Foúrni	Φούρνοι	ΦΟΥΡΝΟΙ
Áyios Yiánnis	Άγιος Ιοάννης	ΑΓΙΟΣ ΓΙΑΝΝΗΣ
Pródhromos	Πρόδρομος	ΠΡΟΔΡΟΜΟΣ
Ballí	Μπαλλοί	ΜΠΑΛΛΟΙ
Elidháki	Ελιδάκι	ΕΛΙΔΑΚΙ
Khryssomiliá	Χρυσομηλιά	ΧΡΥΣΟΜΗΛΙΑ
Kambí	Καμπή	ΚΑΜΠΗ
Kasídhi	Καπίδι	ΚΑΣΙΔΙ
Marmári	Μαρμάρι	ΜΑΡΜΑΡΙ
Pelekanía	Πελεκανία	ΠΕΛΕΚΑΝΙΑ
Petrokopió	Πετροκοπειό	ΠΕΤΡΟΚΟΠΕΙΟ
Psilí Ámmos	Ψιλή Άμμος	ΨΙΛΗ ΑΜΜΟΣ
Thýmena	Θύμαινα	ΘΥΜΑΙΝΑ
Vitsiliá	Βιτσιλιά	ΒΙΤΣΙΛΙΑ
Vlyhádhia	Βλυχάδια	ΒΛΥΧΑΔΙΑ

4

THE EAST AEGEAN ISLANDS | Satellite islets: Thýmena and Foúrni

Ikaría and Foúrni travel details

Island transport

Buses

Armenistís to: Évdhilos (3 daily, well spaced, summer only); Ráhes (2–3 daily, reliable in summer only).

Áyios Kírykos to: Évdhilos (1 daily Mon–Fri, at noon; connects with onward service to Armenistís). NB Departures can be unreliable except from late June to early Sept, and schedule times must always be double-checked.

Inter-island transport

Kaïkia and excursion boats

Foúrni to: Áyios Kírykos, Ikaría (at least 4 mornings weekly, typically Mon, Wed, Fri & Sun); twice weekly via Khryssomiliá; 1hr–1hr 15min); Karló-vassi, Sámos (3 mornings weekly via Thýmena; 4–6 cars taken; 2hr 15min).

Áyios Kírykos to: Foúrni (daily in season, or by demand; 1hr).

Karkinágri/Manganítis to: Áyios Kírykos (3 mornings weekly, typically Mon, Wed & Fri; 2hr).

Ferries

Ikaría (Áyios Kírykos) to: Foúrni (2–3 weekly on GA; 45min); Piréas (4 weekly on GA or HF; 8hr 30min–9hr 30min); Sámos, both northern ports (3–4 weekly on GA).

Ikaría (Évdhilos) to: Foúrni (1 weekly on GA or HF; 2hr); Piréas (6–7 weekly on HF or GA; 7hr 30min–8hr 30min); Sámos, both ports (6–7 weekly on HF or GA; 2hr 30min).

Foúrni to: Áyios Kírykos, Ikaría (2–3 weekly; 45min); Évdhilos, Ikaría (1 weekly on GA or HF; 2hr); Piréas (2–3 weekly on GA or HF; 10hr); Sámos, both northern ports (3–4 weekly GA or HF; 4hr).

Catamaran

NEL's *Aeolos Express* has historically called 4 times weekly at Évdhilos bound for Sámos or Piréas, Vathý, Sámos and Piréas via Náxos and Páros. Alternate days it called at Áyios Kírykos, bound for the same ports. Journey time to Vathý, 1hr 15min–1hr 45min; to Karlóvassi (only from Áyios Kírykos), 1hr.

In September 2004 the *Aeolos Express* was withdrawn from this route – possibly permanently – and replaced (possibly temporarily) by the Iason Jet *Superjet* (no cars carried), which plied daily between Sámos and Piréas via Évdhilos only, plus intervening Cyclades such as Sýros and Mýkonos. Journey times were identical.

Hydrofoils

Foúrni and Ikaría (Áyios Kírykos) to: each other (2 weekly on KR); Pátmos (2 weekly on KR); Kálymnos (2 weekly on KR); Kós (2 weekly on KR); Léros (2 weekly on KR); Pythagório, Sámos (2 weekly on KR). Journey times range from 1hr 10min Foúrni–Pythagório, to 4hr Ikaría–Kós.

Flights

Ikaría to: Athens (3–4 weekly; 50min).

Híos

"Craggy **Híos**", as Homer aptly described his putative birthplace, has a turbulent history and a strong identity. This large island has always been relatively prosperous, in medieval times through the export of mastic **resin** – a trade controlled by Genoese overlords of the Giustiniani dynasty between 1346 and 1566, when they held the island in return for services rendered to the faltering Byzantine Empire, and later by the Ottomans, who dubbed the place *Sakız Adası* (Resin Island).

Under the Genoese, Hiot prowess in **navigation** was exploited by the scores of ships that called in annually; island legend asserts that Christopher Columbus stayed here for two years, studying with local sea captains, prior to his voyages of discovery. Since union with Greece in 1912, this tradition has

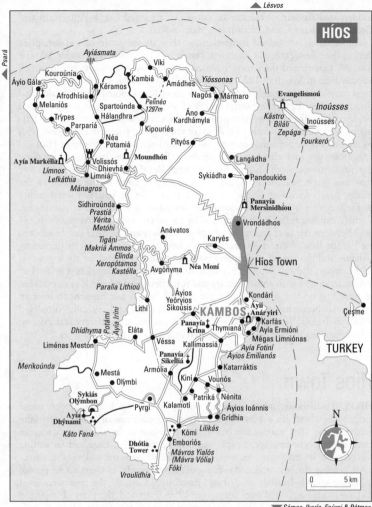

▲ *Lésvos*

◄ *Psará*

Ayiásmata

Kouroúnia
Áyio Gála
Afrodhísia
Melaniós
Kéramos
Trýpes
Spartoúnda
Parpariá
Hálandhra
Víki
Kambiá
Amádhes
Yióssonas
Nagós
Mármaro
Pelinéo 1297m
Áno Kardhámyla
Kipouriés
Néa Potamiá
Pityós
Ayía Markélla
Límnos
Lefkáthia
Volissós
Dhievhá
Limniá
Moundhón
Langádha
Sykiádha
Pandoukiós
Mánagros
Sidhiroúnda
Prastiá
Yérita
Metóhi
Panayía Mersinidhíou
Tigáni
Makriá Ámmos
Elínda
Xeropótamos
Kastélla
Anávatos
Karyés
Vrondádhos
Paralía Lithioú
Néa Moní
Avgónyma
Híos Town
Lithí
Áyios Yeóryios Sikoúsis
Dhídhyma
Potámi
Ayía Iríni
Eláta
KÁMBOS
Panayía Krína
Thymianá
Kondári
Ayii Anáryiri
Karfás
Liménas Mestón
Véssa
Kallimassiá
Ayía Ermióni
Mégas Limniónas
Merikoúnda
Mestá
Panayía Sikelliá
Ayía Fotiní
Áyios Emilianós
Armólia
Kiní
Vounós
Katarráktis
Olýmbi
Sykiás Olýmbon
Pyrgí
Kalamotí
Patriká
Nénita
Áyios Ioánnis
Grídhia
Ayía Dhýnami
Káto Faná
Lilikás
Kómi
Emboriós
Dhótia Tower
Mávros Yialós (Mávra Vólia)
Fóki
Vroulídhia

Evangelismoú
Inoússes
Kástro Biláli
Inoússes
Zepága
Fourkeró

Çeşme

TURKEY

N

0   5 km

▼ *Sámos, Ikaría, Foúrni & Pátmos*

re-emerged in the form of several **shipping dynasties** based here, continuing the pattern of wealth. Participation in the maritime way of life is almost universal, with someone from every family, including women, serving as radio operators or officers in the merchant navy.

The more powerful shipowning dynasts, the local government and the military authorities did not encourage tourism until the late 1980s, when the combined effect of a worldwide shipping crisis and the saturation of other, more obviously "marketable" islands eroded their resistance. Since then, numbers of foreigners have discovered a Híos beyond its rather daunting port capital: fascinating villages, important Byzantine monuments and a respectable, if remote, complement of beaches. While unlikely ever to be dominated by tourism, especially in light of the recent slump, the local scene has a distinctly modernized flavour – courtesy of numerous returned Greek-Americans and Greek-Canadians – and English is widely spoken.

Unfortunately, the island suffered more than its fair share of **catastrophes** during the nineteenth and twentieth centuries. The **Ottomans** under Admiral Kara Ali perpetrated their most infamous, if not their worst, anti-revolutionary atrocity here in March of 1822, massacring 30,000 Hiots and enslaving or exiling even more. In 1881, much of Híos was destroyed by a violent **earthquake**, and throughout the 1980s the natural beauty of the island was severely compromised by devastating **forest fires**, compounding the effect of generations of tree-felling by boat-builders. Nearly two-thirds of the majestic pines are now gone, with patches of woods persisting only in the far northeast and the centre of Híos.

In 1988, the first charters from northern Europe were instituted, signalling potentially momentous changes for the island. But there are still fewer than five thousand guest beds on Híos, the vast majority of them in the capital or the nearby beach resorts of Karfás and Ayía Ermióni. So far, **tourists** seem evenly divided among a babel of nationalities, including a small British contingent. Further expansion has been hampered by the distances and sparse public transport between the port and many of the more interesting villages and beaches as well as the lack of direct international air links from most countries (including Britain), and the refusal of property owners to part with land for the extension of the airport runway – forced expropriation finally saw it lengthened in 2004 to 1900m, enough for all contemporary jets. You often get the feeling, as an outsider, of intruding on the workings of a private club which just happens to have an "open" day. Nonetheless, the provincial authorities have optimistically completed a yacht marina at Vrondádhos, home to many professional seafarers, and existing tourist facilities to date have been pitched at a fairly sophisticated level.

Híos Town

HÍOS, the harbour and main town, will come as a shock after modest island capitals elsewhere; it's a bustling, concrete-laced commercial centre, with little predating the 1881 earthquake. Yet in many ways it is the most satisfactory of east Aegean ports; time spent exploring is rewarded with a large and fascinating marketplace, several museums, some good, authentic tavernas and, on the waterfront, possibly the best-attended evening *vólta* (promenade) in Greece. Old photos show the quay beautifully shaded and paved in red marble; the trees were axed and the marble asphalted over during the 1950s to smooth the rides of imported Cadillacs, but you can still see a few exposed blocks at the water's edge.

Arrival, transport and information

Ferries and *kaïkia* large and small dock at various points as shown on the town map. The **airport** lies 3km south along the coast at Kondári, a €3.50 taxi ride away; otherwise any **city bus** labelled "ΚΟΝΔΑΡΙ ΚΑΡΦΑΣ", departing from the station on the north side of the park, passes the airport gate, opposite which is a conspicuous stop-with-shelter.

The standard green-and-cream **long-distance KTEL buses** leave from a parking area beside their ticket office on the south side of the park, behind the Omirio Cultural Centre. While services to the south of Híos are adequate, those to the centre and northwest of the island are almost nonexistent, and to explore these areas you'll need to rent a powerful motorbike (*not* a 50cc scooter) or a car (see "Listings" for suggestions). Alternatively, you could share a

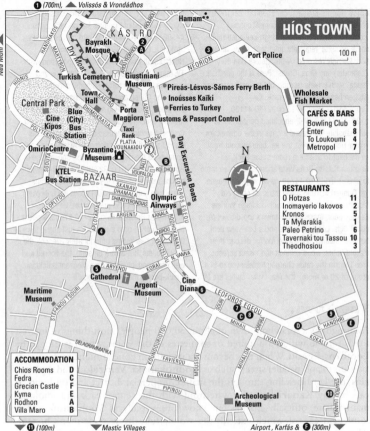

Map labels:

❶ (700m), ▲ Volissós & Vrondádhos

Hamam

KÁSTRO

HÍOS TOWN

Bayraklı Mosque

Port Police

0   100 m

Turkish Cemetery

Giustiniani Museum

Pireás-Lésvos-Sámos Ferry Berth

Inoússes Kaïki

Ferries to Turkey

Customs & Passport Control

Wholesale Fish Market

Néa Moní ◄

Central Park

Town Hall

Porta Maggiora

Cine Kipos

Blue (City) Bus Station

Taxi Rank

PLATIA VOUNAKIOU

CAFÉS & BARS

Bowling Club	9
Enter	8
To Loukoumi	4
Metropol	7

OmirioCentre

Byzantine Museum

KTEL Bus Station

BAZAAR

Day Excursion Boats

Olympic Airways

RESTAURANTS

O Hotzas	11
Inomayerio Iakovos	2
Kronos	5
Ta Mylarakia	1
Paleo Petrino	6
Tavernaki tou Tassou	10
Theodhosiou	3

Maritime Museum

Cathedral

Argenti Museum

Cine Diana

LEOFOROS EGEOU

N

ACCOMMODATION

Chios Rooms	D
Fedra	C
Grecian Castle	F
Kyma	E
Rodhon	A
Villa Maro	B

Archeological Museum

❶ (100m)   ▼ Mastic Villages   Airport, Karfás & ❺ (300m) ▼

taxi from the main rank on Platía Vounakioú – they're bright red on Híos, not grey as in most of Greece. **Parking** is a nightmare in town, even where it's not controlled by a pay-and-display scheme; usually the only spaces to be had are northwest of the Kástro walls, along Hándhakos, or at the extreme south end of the harbour, in the side streets behind the *Hotel Kyma*.

The helpful municipal **tourist office** (May–Sept daily 7am–10pm; Oct–April Mon–Fri 7am–3pm; ☎22710 44389) is at Kanári 18, near the Alpha Bank. The most accurate **maps** of the island available are Road Editions' 1:60,000 product, #211 "Chios", or Anavasi's identical-scale product, both available at Newsstand **bookshop**, at the first "kink" in Leofóros Egéou.

Accommodation

Híos Town has a relative abundance of affordable **accommodation**, rarely completely full, and generally open year-round. Most places line the water-front or the perpendicular alleys and parallel streets behind, and almost all are plagued by traffic noise to some degree – we've focused on the more peaceful establishments.

Chios Rooms Kokáli 1, cnr Egéou ☎ 22710 20198 or 697 28 33 841, ℮ chiosrooms@hotmail .com. Tile- or wood-floored, high-ceilinged rooms, some en suite, relatively quiet for a seafront location; lovingly restored by proprietors Don (New Zealander) and Dina (Greek). Best is the penthouse "suite" with private terrace, but the self-catering kitchen has a common terrace. ❷

Fedra Mihaïl Livanoú 13 ☎ 22710 41130, ℱ 22710 41128. Well-appointed pension in an old mansion, with stone arches in the downstairs winter bar; in summer the bar operates out front, so it's best to ask for a room at the back. ❸

Grecian Castle Bella Vista shore avenue, en route to airport ☎ 22710 44740, ⓦ www.greciancastle .gr. Opened in 1996 using the shell of an old factory, and popular with such package tourists as Híos gets, these are the town's top-drawer (A-class) digs. Lovely grounds and a sea-view pool, but the smallish main-wing rooms, despite their marble floors, wood ceilings and insect screens, aren't worth the rates charged (unless you're in a group of 20 or more); the rear "villa" suites are far

more pleasant. ❻ standard rooms, ❽ suites

Kyma East end of Evyenías Handhrí ☎ 22710 44500, ℱ 22710 44600, ⓦ http://chios.proodos .gr/kyma. En-suite B-class hotel rooms in a Neoclassical mansion or modern extension, with TV, huge terraces on the sea-facing side and Jacuzzis in some rooms, splendid service from Theo and Güher, and big breakfasts really make the place. The old wing saw a critical moment in modern Greek history in September 1922, when Colonel Nikolaos Plastiras commandeered it as his HQ after the Greek defeat in Asia Minor, and announced the deposition of King Constantine I. ❹

Rodhon Platéon 10 ☎ 22710 24335. The owners can be awkward, and the D-class hotel rooms are not en suite, but it's just about the only place inside the *kástro*, and pretty quiet. ❸

Villa Maro Roïdhou 15 ☎ 22710 27003. Modern pension tucked onto a tiny plaza just inland from the water; rear rooms unfortunately overlook the public toilets, but all are en suite, tile-floored and well equipped, plus there's a pleasant breakfast/snack-bar on the ground floor. ❹

The Town

Although it's a sprawling town of about 30,000 people, most things of interest to visitors lie within a hundred or so metres of the water, which is fringed by **Leofóros Egéou**. When this becomes a pedestrian zone at night, traffic circulates on inland parallel streets such as **Rodhokanáki**, **Venizélou** and **Aplotariás**, the last threading through the main commercial district and off limits to cars by day. **Kanári** links the waterfront with the central park and adjoining main square, officially Plastíra but known universally as **Vounakioú**, to the south and east of which extends the wonderfully lively tradesmen's **bazaar**, where you can find everything from parrots to cast-iron woodstoves. Híos must boast more varieties of **bread** than any other island in Greece – corn, wholewheat, multigrain, "dark" and "village" – and most of these are on sale from the bakers in the marketplace. Like its neighbours Sámos and Lésvos, Híos also makes respectable **oúzo**; the best brand is reckoned to be Tetteris.

The museums

Opposite the Vounakioú taxi rank, occupying the nineteenth-century **Mecidiye Tzami** (Mosque), the grandiosely titled "**Byzantine Museum**" (Tues–Sun 8.30am–3pm; free) is little more than an archeological warehouse, with a preponderance of Jewish marble gravestones in the courtyard – plus a few Armenian, Genoese and Turkish ones – testifying to the island's varied population in past centuries. Also on view, in the mosque porch, is the top layer of frescoes (1734 vintage) from Panayía Krína (see p.384).

The actual **archeological museum** is on Mihalón (June–Sept daily 8am–7pm; Oct–May Tues–Sun 8.30am–3pm; €3). The wide-ranging and well-lit collection, arranged both thematically and chronologically from Neolithic to Roman times, demands at least an hour or so of your attention. Highlights include limestone column bases from the Apollo temple at Faná in the shape of lion's claws; numerous statuettes and reliefs of Cybele (the Asiatic goddess was especially honoured here); Archaic faience miniatures from Emborió in the shape of a cat, a hawk and a flautist; terracottas from various eras including a dwarf riding a boar, and figurines (some with articulated limbs) of *hierodouloi* or sacred prostitutes, presumably from an Aphrodite shrine. Most famous of all is an inscribed edict of 332 BC from Alexander the Great, commanding local political changes and setting out relations between himself and the Hiots.

Near the town centre stands the **Argenti Folklore Museum** (Mon–Thurs 8am–2pm, Fri 8am–2pm & 5–7.30pm, Sat 8am–12.30pm; €2), housed on the top floor of the Koraï Library building at Koraï 2 and endowed by a leading Hiot family. Accordingly, there's a rather ponderous gallery of genealogical portraits, showing – if nothing else – the local aristocracy's compulsion to adopt English dress and artistic conventions in every era. The other wing boasts a hall of costumes and embroidery, kitsch figurines in traditional dress, and carved wooden implements. Among multiple replicas of Delacroix's *Massacre at Hios*, instrumental in arousing European sympathy for the Greek cause, are engravings of eighteenth-century islanders as seen by assorted Grand Tourists.

The **Maritime Museum** at Stefánou Tsoúri 20 (Mon–Sat 10am–1pm; free) consists principally of model ships and oil paintings of various craft, Greek and foreign, all rather overshadowed by the mansion containing them. In the foyer is enshrined the knife and glass-globe grenade of Admiral Kanaris, a native of nearby Psará who commanded the Greek fleet during the events of 1822.

The Kástro

Until the 1881 earthquake, the Byzantine-Genoese **Kástro** was completely intact; thereafter developers razed the seaward walls, filled in much of the moat to the south and made a fortune selling off the real estate thus created around present-day Platía Vounakioú. Today the most dramatic entry to the **Kástro** is via the Porta Maggiora behind the town hall, leading to a little square with an equally diminutive Muslim graveyard. The top floor of a medieval mansion just inside the *porta* is home these days to the **Giustiniani Museum** (Tues–Sun 9am–3pm, in summer may close later; €2), housing a satisfying (and periodically changing) collection of unusual icons and mosaics rescued from local churches. Amongst semi-permanent exhibits are masterly fourteenth-century frescoes of Old Testament prophets from the dome of Panayía K* rína (see p.384). Seventy-five Hiot notables were briefly held prisoner in the small dungeon adjacent to the museum before their execution by the Ottomans in 1822.

The old **residential quarter** inside the surviving castle walls, formerly the Muslim and Jewish neighbourhoods, is well worth a wander. Among the wood-and-plaster houses with overhanging second storeys you'll find assorted Ottoman monuments in various states of decay, including a box-like, minaret-less mosque, several inscribed fountains, a ruined *hamam* (Turkish bath) and the small **Muslim cemetery** noted above. This contains, among others, the grave of Kara Ali, villain of the spring 1822 massacres; the rebels had their revenge in June 1822, when a ship under Greek Admiral Kanaris rammed Kara Ali's flagship, blowing it up and killing most of the crew along with the "Butcher Admiral".

Eating

Eating out in Híos Town can be far more pleasurable than the fast-food joints and multiple *barákia* on the waterfront (not to mention US-style pizza parlours inland) would suggest; it is also usually a fair bit cheaper than on neighbouring Sámos or Lésvos.

O Hotzas Yeoryíou Kondhýli 3, cnr Stefánou Tsoúri, off map. Oldest (and arguably best) taverna in town, with chef Ioannis Linos, the fourth generation of his family, presiding. Menu varies seasonally, but expect a mix of vegetarian dishes (*mavromátika*, cauliflower, chunky *fáva*, stuffed red peppers), and *lahanodolmádhes*, sausages, baby fish and *mydhopílafo* (rice and mussels) washed down by own-brand *oúzo* or retsina. Supper only, garden in summer; closed Sun; allow €13 each, with local drink as described.

Inomayerio Iakovos Ayíou Yeoryíou Frouríou 20, Kástro ☎ 22710 23858. A repertoire of fishy dishes, grilled titbits, cheese-based recipes and vegetables, washed down with very good local bulk wine or *oúzo*, has got unevenly executed and pricey of late, but most will still reckon it worth dining here. Atmospheric garden seating in a vine-cloaked ruin opposite, or inside during winter. Closed Sun, and no lunch Sept–June. Budget €17 each; limited seating, so it's best to book.

Kronos Filíppou Aryéndi 2, cnr Aplotariás. The island's best purveyor of homemade ice cream, in business since 1929; limited seating or take away. Open until about midnight.

Ta Mylarakia By three restored windmills in Tambákika district, on the road to Vrondádhos; official address Kaloutá 113 ☎ 22710 40412. A large, well-priced seafood selection, every kind of Hiot *oúzo* and limited waterside seating make reservations advisable in summer. Supper all year, lunch also Oct–April.

Paleo Petrino Egéou 80. Standard, no-nonsense *ouzerí* with such delights as *iliókafto* (sun-dried fish) on the Greek-only menu – mainly patronized by locals. In the cooler months the interior, with 1950s Greek record and film posters, is more pleasant than quayside seating where you often ingest car fumes with your food.

Tavernaki tou Tassou Stávrou Livanoú 8, Bella Vista district. Superb all-rounder with crea-tive salads, better-than-average bean dishes, *dolmádhes*, snails, properly done chips, and a strong line in seafood; a bit pricier than usual, but Tassos' and Tsambika's cooking (with son Dhimitris at the grill) is worth it. Open lunch and supper most of the year, with seaview garden seating during warmer months and heated gazebo in winter.

Theodhosiou Ouzeri Neoríon 33. The oldest, least expensive *ouzerí* on the quay, moved in 2001 to these domed, arcaded premises. A fair number of meat grills for this type of eatery, plus a long list of seafood standards like shrimp-and-onion fry-up. Generally, it's best to avoid fried platters in favour of grilled or boiled ones. Dinner only; closed Sun.

Drinking, nightlife and entertainment

The 1400 or so students at the local technical schools and ecomomics/busi-ness management faculties of the University of the Aegean help keep things lively, especially along the portion of the waterfront between the two "kinks" in Egéou. There were once more than a dozen traditional, high-ceilinged, wood-floored, mirror-walled *kafenía* along the front; now there are none, all replaced by numerous trendy *barákia* more in keeping with the aspirations of younger Hiots. Shooting **pool** is a big thing in town; many bars have several tables.

Bowling Club East end of Egéou. The seven alleys (and to a lesser extent, five pool tables) are very popular with local youth. Open until at least midnight.

Cine Kipos In central park from early June to mid-Sept. Quality/art-house first-run fare, two screenings nightly; watch for flybills around town or enquire at *Pension Fedra*. During winter, the action shifts to Cine Diana, under the eponymous hotel.

Enter Just seaward from the *Fedra* hotel. The best-equipped Internet café with ten or so termi-nals upstairs; a bargain by island standards at about €3.50/hr.

To Loukoumi Alley off Aplotariás 27/c. Old warehouse refitted as a café (8am–2pm), *ouzerí* (8pm–2am) and occasional events venue. Well executed and worth checking out, but closes Sun & May–Oct.

Metropol/Metropolis Egéou. The longest lived and most civilized of a string of music bars on this stretch of the front, always crowded from sunset until the small hours.

Omirio South side of the central park. Cultural centre and events hall with frequently changing exhibitions; foreign musicians often come here after Athens concerts to perform in the large auditorium.

Listings

Banks/exchange At least eight banks, all with ATMs.

Car rental Three independent, non-chain agencies sit in a row on Evyenías Handhrí 5–7, near *Hotel Kyma*; of these, Vassilakis/Reliable Rent a Car (☎22710 29300 or 694 43 34 898), with a branch at Mégas Limniónas (☎22710 31728), is particularly recommended. The Hertz airport booth (☎22710 28445) is helpful and consistently attended for flight arrivals, but their town office at Egéou 36 (☎22710 26115) can be awkward about the return of cars prior to early-morning ferry departures.

Ferry/travel agents Whether for the short hop over to Turkey or long-haul ferries, these cluster to either side of the customs building towards the north end of Egéou, and along its continuation Neórion. Triaina, Neoríon 19 (☎22710 29292), handles the *Nissos Limnos* to various north Aegean destinations, and the *Panayia Psariani* to Psará. NEL (☎22710 25848) is a few paces south of customs, at the corner of Kanári and Egéou, while Sunrise Tours at Kanári 28 (☎22710 41390) is the central agent for GA and the fastest morning boat to Çeşme (the other is handled by Miniotis at Egeou 11, ☎22710 21463). The Turkish evening ferry to Çeşme, as well as the most regular boat to Inoússes (see p.395), is represented by Faros Travel at Egéou 18 (☎22710 27240).

Olympic Airways On Leoforos Egéou, as shown on map ☎22710 24515.

Opening hours A Hian idiosyncrasy is restriction, during summer, of afternoon shopping hours to Mon & Thurs only; on other days, make sure you buy what you need before 2pm.

The southeast coast: Karfás to Grídhia

The locals swim at tiny pebble coves near Vrondádhos, north of Híos Town, or from the somewhat grubby town beach in Bella Vista district, but for most visitors the closest decent beach to Híos Town is at **KARFÁS**, 7km south past the airport and served by frequent blue buses. Since 1988, most of the growth in the Hiot tourist industry has occurred here, to the considerable detriment of the 500-metre-long, minimally shaded beach: massive hotel construction has interfered with natural sand deposition, so that the once gently sloping shore is now steep, rock-studded and seaweedy, except at its far southern end where it broadens out and various watersports are offered.

Karfás practicalities

The main bright spot is a unique and popular **pension**, *Markos' Place* (☎22710 31 990 or 697 32 39 706, ⓦwww.marcos-place.gr; ❷; April–Nov), installed in the disestablished **monastery of Áyios Yeóryios and Áyios Pandelímon**, on the hillside south of the bay. Markos Kostalas, who leases the premises from Thymianá municipality, has created a uniquely peaceful, leafy environment much loved by special-activity groups. Guests are lodged in the former pilgrims' cells, with a kitchen available or superior breakfasts laid on by arrangement; individuals are more than welcome (there are several single "cells") as are families (two "tower" rooms sleep four), though reservations are advisable and the minimum stay is four days. Virtually the only other establishment shunning package-company contracts is the long-established seaview D-class **hotel**, *Karatzas* (☎22710 31180; ❸), midway along the beach, with its own ground-floor terrace-restaurant. Speaking of which, shoreline restaurants aren't brilliant, though *Karatzas* and *Giamos* (south end of beach) are striving valiantly to regain credibility after late 1990s bad patches; *Giamos* has the edge in food quality, with good *mayireftá* and fair prices. *Oasis*, between these two on the sand, is a popular breakfast, juice, snack and drinks café-bar; *La Notte*, with taped music, up on the slope near *Markos' Place*, acquits itself well for **nightlife** (especially amongst young Greeks) into the autumn.

Generally, it's better to strike inland for eating opportunities. *Ouzeri To Apomero* (open daily), in the hillside Spiládhia district west of the airport (go around the runway and follow the many luminous green signs) has lovely terrace seating, live music a few nights weekly in summer, and such delights as cumin pancetta, *garídhes saganáki*, and *sheftalyés* (Cypriot-style meat rissoles). Inland, between Thymianá and Neohóri, *Fakiris Taverna* (open all year but weekends only in winter) offers marinated aubergine and artichokes, *pastourmás*, goat baked in tomato sauce and excellent wood-fired pizzas along with well-executed seafood and pork-based *bekrí mezé* in big portions. Large groups (ten can eat well for about €100) should reserve on ☎22710 32780. Until a sign is put up, the easiest way to find it is to head south from Kondári on the road to Kalimassiá and then turn west onto the Áyios Trýfon–Ayía Vássa road, just before Neohóri, and continue about a kilometre, past the filling station.

Karfás is well sown with places to rent two- and four-wheelers: just uphill from the beachside bus stop and **bank** ATM, MG (☎22710 31432; also a branch in Híos Town, ☎22710 23377) is reliable for **cars**, while Kovas (☎22710 31461), a bit further along, is the biggest outlet for **scooters**.

Ayía Ermióni, Mégas Limniónas and Thymianá

Some 2km along the coast from Karfás, **AYÍA ERMIÓNI** is not a beach but a fishing anchorage surrounded by a handful of tavernas and rooms to rent. The nearest beach is a few hundred metres further on at **MÉGAS LIMNIÓNAS**, smaller than Kárfas, shingly and beset by road noise, but more scenic at its south end, where cliffs provide a backdrop. Both Ayía Ermióni and Mégas Limniónas are served by extensions of the blue-bus route to either Karfás or **THYMIANÁ**, the nearest inland village. This can offer, at its summit, the atmospheric, untenanted **monastery of Áyii Anáryiri**, with enormous pebble mosaics and thankfully unrestored vernacular architecture. **Taverna** options in Ayía Ermióni and Mégas Limniónas aren't brilliant; *Anamnisis*, visible on the hillside right above Mégas Limniónas beach, is probably the best of the lot.

Ayía Fotiní, Katarráktis and Grídhia

Beyond Mégas Limniónas, the coast road loops up briefly to Thymianá, from where you can (with your own transport only) continue 3km south towards Kalimassiá to the turning for **Ayía Fotiní**, a 600-metre pebble beach with exceptionally clean water. There's no shade, however, unless you count afternoon shadows from the various blocks of rooms, less monopolized than before by Scandinavian tour companies. A few tavernas cluster around the pedestrianized esplanade where the side road meets the sea, or try the basic, traditional, cheap **restaurant** operating (June–Sept 15) in the grounds of disused **Áyios Emilianós monastery**, a long (1.5km) walk south or more easily accessed by a separate road. Even out of peak season, parking at Ayía Fotiní is mayhem – you'll have to use one of two car parks (one of them free), considerably back from the water. The best place to **stay** (no packages) here is the central *Apartments Iro* (☎22710 51166 or 22710 32826; ❹), large self-catering studios with sea views, air conditioning and dedicated parking.

The last settlement on this coast, 5km beyond Kalimassiá and served by long-distance bus, is **KATARRÁKTIS**, remarkable mainly for its fishing port, pleasant waterfront of balconied houses and handful of **tavernas**. The best of these is near the south end of the quay opposite the boats, where *O Tsambos* is hard to fault for inexpensive fish, grilled or fried. Just beyond, on the far side of the dry ravine-mouth, *Iy Dhrosia* (better known as *Kyria Dhafní*) is a popular *ouzerí*, though table space is limited. If you're seized by an urge to stay, there's a small, fairly attractive **hotel**, the *Canadian/Kanadhas*, on the front (℡22710 61890, ℻22710 61149; ❸), while for a higher standard go for the *Ostria Studios*, a bit inland from the extreme south end of the bay (℡22710 62095, Ⓦwww.ostria.com; ❹), with a pool.

There are no beaches of any note in the vicinity, all the way down to the southeastern tip of the island, which is reached via the narrow-alleyed hill villages of **Nénita** (same bus service) and **Vounós**. You emerge on the coast again at **GRÍDHIA**, a decidedly scruffy place with one noteworthy **taverna** just past the little monastery of Panayía Agridhiótissa: *Snack Bar Iy Agridhi-oditssa*, where you can feast on three *mezédhes*, fresh sardines and a beer for under €13, sitting under the tamarisks of the sea-view terrace. It's open all year, best at night when the grill-coals are lit.

Southern Híos

Besides its olive groves, the gently rolling countryside in the south of the island is also home to the **mastic bush** (*Pistacia lentisca*). This rather unexceptional plant grows across much of Aegean Greece, but only here – pruned to an umbrella shape to facilitate harvesting – does it produce an aromatic resin of marketable quantity and quality, scraped from incisions made on the trunk during summer. For centuries Hiot mastic was used as a base for paints, cosmetics and the chewable jellybeans that became a somewhat addictive staple in Ottoman harems. Indeed, the interruption of the flow of mastic from Híos to Istanbul by the revolt of spring 1822 was one of the root causes of the brutal Ottoman reaction.

The wealth engendered by the mastic trade supported twenty *mastihohoriá* (**mastic villages**) from the time the Genoese set up a monopoly (the *maona*) in the substance during the fourteenth and fifteenth centuries. However, the demise of imperial Turkey, and the industrial revolution with its petroleum-based products, knocked the bottom out of the mastic market. Now it's just a curiosity, to be chewed – try the sweetened Elma-brand gum – drunk as a liqueur called *mastíha*, or rubbed over yourself as a soap or shampoo. Since ancient times it has also been used for medicinal purposes; contemporary advocates claim that mastic boosts the immune system and thins the blood. Whatever the truth about mastic, the *mastihohoriá* today live mainly off their tangerines, apricots and olives.

The villages themselves were the only settlements on Híos spared by the Ottomans when they put down the local uprising in 1822. Architecturally unique, they were laid out by the Genoese with anti-pirate defence foremost in mind, but retain a distinctly Middle Eastern air. The basic plan consists of a rectangular or pentagonal warren of tall stone houses, with the outer row doubling as the town's perimeter fortification and breached by just a few arched gateways. More recent additions, whether in traditional architectural style or not, straggle outside the original defences. All of the *mastihohoriá* lie on the same trunk route, and more or less share a bus service (see "Travel details" on p.395). However, if you're relying solely on public transport, you'll be hard pushed to see the most interesting villages and have a dip at one of the nearby beaches in a single day.

Armólia and Pyrgí

ARMÓLIA, 20km from town, is the smallest and least imposing of the mastic villages. Its main virtue is a **pottery industry**; the best workshop, selling useful kitchenware as well as the usual kitsch souvenirs, is Yeoryios Sfikakis, the third

△ Xistá technique on walls, Pyrgí, Híos

outfit on the right as you head southwest. **PYRGÍ**, 5km further south, is perhaps the liveliest and certainly the most colourful of the communities, with many of its houses elaborately embossed with *xystá*, geometric patterns cut into whitewash, revealing the layer of black volcanic sand underneath; strings of sun-drying tomatoes add a further splash of colour in autumn, when folk also sit at their doorsteps sifting mastic crystals. On the northeast corner of the central square, the twelfth-century Byzantine church of **Áyii Apóstoli** (Tues–Thurs & Sat 10am–1pm) is tucked under an arcade and embellished with seventeenth-century frescoes, with such interesting iconographic deviations as soldiers awake, rather than asleep, in front of the Empty Tomb. The giant cathedral of the Assumption on the square itself boasts a *témblon* in an odd folk style dating from 1642, and an equally bizarre carved figure peeking out from the base of the pulpit. All this sits a bit incongruously with the vast number of postcard racks and boutiques that have sprung up lately on every thoroughfare, detracting somewhat from the atmosphere. In Pyrgí's medieval core you'll find a **bank** (with ATM), a **post office**, and an assortment of cafés and *souvláki* stalls.

Emboriós old and new, Kómi and beaches

Pyrgí is actually closest to the two major **beach** resorts in this corner of the island. The nearest of these, 6km southeast, is **EMBORIÓS**, an almost land-locked harbour with several decent **tavernas** (*Porto Emborios* has the edge by virtue of such things as *atherína*-and-onion fry-up, local bulk wine and some-times homemade dessert).

The only clue to its former importance as a trading post for the ancient Hiots is well-signposted **ancient Emboreios** on the hill just northeast, excavated by John Boardman of the British Archeological School (1952–55). All the finds are in Híos Town's archeological museum, but the **site** itself (daily 9am–7pm summer, closes at sunset in winter; free) has been rehabilitated as a circular-walk-through archeological park, where you can admire waist-high house foundations of the eighth and seventh centuries BC, a few small megara, and (the best bit) the foundations and altar of an Athena temple up at the acropolis. Emboreios continued to be inhabited in later times, as evinced by a cruciform **early Christian baptistry**, signposted in a field just in from the modern waterfront; it's protected by a later, round structure (locked, but you can see everything through the grating).

For swimming, follow the same road past the baptistry to its end at an over-subscribed car park and obvious beach of **Mávros Yialós** (sometimes called Mávra Vótsala or Mávra Vólia), then continue southwest along a flagstoned walkway over the headland to the more dramatic pebble strand of **Fóki**, partly nudist, twice as long and backed by impressive cliffs. The purply-grey volcanic stones (with the odd orange one thrown in) absorb the sun, reducing reflective sunburn but becoming quite toasty to lie upon.

If you want pure (tan) sand, you'll have to go to **KÓMI**, 3km northeast of Emboriós, also accessible from Armólia via Kalamotí. It's bidding to become a sort of Greek-pitched Karfás, though so far there are just a few **tavernas** (most reliably open out of summer being *Nostalgia* and *Bella Mare*), drinks cafés and summer apartments along the largely pedestrianized, 1300-metre-long beachfront. The *Bella Mare* has some short-term rooms upstairs (⊤22710 71226; ❷), if you fancy **staying**. The bus service is fairly good in season, with extra local links to Pyrgí and Emboriós. If Kómi's not to your taste, you can head just 2km east to the quieter, pebbly coves of **Lilikás** or **Výri**, though these have no facilities – for a **taverna**, carry on a bit further east to **Áyios**

Ioánnis, where *To Mouragio* is well regarded for fish meals in an atmospheric setting by the church.

The road from Pyrgí forks just before Emboriós: the turning right leads for 5km past the ruined Genoese tower of **Dhótia**, ending in some hair-raising zigzags down to the 150-metre, pea-gravel beach of **Vroulídhia** (sometimes Vourlídhia). The dramatically sculptured volcanic bay, 5km from Emboriós, has views south to the very tip of Híos and Ikaría beyond, but gets packed in summer and has no facilities except for a cistern-spring.

Olýmbi and Mestá

Seven kilometres west of Pyrgí is **OLÝMBI**, the least visited of the mastic villages but by no means devoid of interest. The characteristic defensive tower-keep, which at Pyrgí stands half-inhabited away from the modernized main square, here looms bang in the middle, its ground floor occupied by the community *kafenío* on one side, and a taverna-bar on the other. However, the best **eating** here is found at *Ayioryítiko* by the Káto Pórta, where the menu can encompass game and mushrooms in the right season, though portions are on the small side. The only short-term **accommodation** is the superbly restored *Chrysanthi Apartments* (℡22710 76196, ®www.chrysanthi.gr), consisting of three units suitable for families and available only by the week.

The finest example of the *mastihohoriá* is sombre, monochrome **MESTÁ**, just 4km further along the road from Olýmbi; despite more snack-bars and trinket shops than strictly necessary on the outskirts, Mestá remains just the right side of twee as many people here still work the land. From its main square, dominated by the **church of Taxiárhis** (the largest on the island), a bewildering maze of cool, shady lanes, with anti-seismic buttresses and tunnels, leads off in all directions. Most streets end in blind alleys, except those leading directly to the six gates; the northeast one still has its original iron grate.

If you'd like to stay, there are half a dozen **rooms** in restored traditional dwellings managed by Dhimitris Pipidhis (℡22710 76029; ❸) and Dhespina Karambela (℡22710 76400 or 22710 22068, or ask at *O Morias sta Mesta* taverna; ❹). Alternatively, three separate premises managed by Anna Floradhi (℡ & ℻22710 76455; ❸) are somewhat more modernized, and like the other two outfits are open year-round, with heating. Of the two **tavernas** on the main *platía*, *O Morias sta Mesta* is renowned for tasty rural specialities like pickled *krítamo* (rock samphire) and locally produced raisin wine: heavy, semi-sweet and sherry-like. However, portions have shrunk of late, wine production is reduced, and *Mesaionas* – whose tables share the square – is better value and has perhaps the more helpful proprietress, Dhespina Syrimis (she also has a couple of studios, ℡22710 76494; ❸). One or other of these tavernas is open most of the year.

The mastic coast – and the Spíleo Sykiás Olýmbon

One drawback to staying in the mastic villages is a dearth of good local beaches. A recently regraded but still unpaved seven-kilometre side road beginning just near Pyrgí leads to the little beach of **Káto Faná**, home to a semi-permanent hamlet of Greek-owned caravans, despite signs forbidding the practice, the stunning averageness of the beach and the lack of any facilities. By the roadside, some 400m above the shore, are the remains of a temple to Apollo, which thus far amount to little more than scattered masonry around a medieval chapel – however, you can see ancient floor paving in the ruins of the baptistry, just below the apse of a larger Byzantine shrine.

From Olýmbi, a paved, six-kilometre road heads to the well-signed **Spíleo** (cave of) **Sykiás Olýmbon** (Easter–Oct Tues–Sun 10am–6pm; admission in groups of up to 25 every 30min; €3), only opened to the public in 2003. For years it was just a small hole in the ground where villagers disposed of their dead animals, but from 1985 on speleologists explored it properly. The cave, with a constant temperature of 18°C, evolved in two phases between 150 million and 50 million years ago, and has a maximum depth of 57m (though tours only visit the top 30m or so). The stalagmite and stalactite formations, with fanciful names like Chinese Forest, Medusa and Organ Pipes, are among the most beautiful in the Mediterranean. Before or after your subterranean tour, you can continue another 1500m on a dirt track to the little cape-top monastery of **Ayía Dhýnami** and two sheltered coves adjacent for a swim: the nearer sandy, the remoter gravel and sand.

The closest good beaches to Mestá lie just east of its port, Liménas Mestón, which has come down considerably in the world since ferry boats ceased calling here: **Dhídhyma** (4km away), a double cove with an islet protecting it; **Potámi**, with the namesake stream feeding it; and the least scenic **Ayía Iríni** (8km), which does have a reliable taverna. All of these little bays will catch surf and flotsam when the north wind is up.

Central Híos

The portion of Híos extending west and southwest from Híos Town matches the south in terms of interesting monuments, and good roads (being improved still further with EU funding) make touring under your own power an easy matter. There are also several beaches on the far shore of the island, which, though not necessarily the best on Híos (see "Northern Híos", p.386), are fine for a dip in the course of a day's touring.

The Kámbos

The **Kámbos**, a vast, fertile plain carpeted with citrus groves, extends southwest from Híos Town almost as far as the village of Halkío. This district was originally settled (and planted with orchards) by the Genoese during the fourteenth century, and remained a preserve of the local aristocracy until 1822. Exploring it with a bicycle or motorbike is apt to be less frustrating than going by car, since the web of narrow, poorly marked lanes sandwiched between high walls guarantee disorientation and frequent backtracking. Behind the walls you catch fleeting glimpses of ornate old mansions built from locally quarried sandstone, masoned so that blocks with varying shades alternate. Courtyards are paved either in pebbles or a checkerboard pattern of tiles, most still dominated by a pergola-shaded irrigation pond and a *mánganos* or water wheel used to draw the water from wells up to 30m deep, once donkey-powered but now electrically propelled.

Practicalities

Many of Kámbos' sumptuous three-storey dwellings, constructed in a hybrid Italo-Turko-Greek style unique in the country, have languished in ruins since 1881, but an increasing number are being converted for use as private estates or unique **accommodation**. The best and most consistently attended of these is *Mavrokordatiko* (☎22710 32900, ⓦwww.mavrokordatiko.com; ❺), about 1.5km south of the airport on Mitaráki, with enormous heated, wood-panelled rooms and breakfast (included) served by the *mánganos* courtyard. Runner-up is the well-signposted *Perivoli* at Aryéndi 11 (☎22710 31513, ⓕ22710 32042; ❹), supposedly open year-round, though with a significant package presence in season. The rooms, no two alike, are mostly en suite and equipped with fireplaces and sofas.

Panayía Krína and Panayía Sikelliá

Not strictly speaking in Kámbos, but most easily reached from it en route from Híos Town to the *mastihohoriá*, are two outstanding rural Byzantine monuments. The eleventh-century Byzantine church of **Panayía Krína**, isolated amidst orchards and woods, is well worth negotiating a maze of paved but poorly marked lanes from the village of Vavýli, 9km out of town. It's closed indefinitely for snail's-pace restoration, but a peek through the apse window will give you a fair idea of the finely frescoed interior, sufficiently lit by a twelve-windowed drum. Works to date consist largely of removing at least two layers of post-Byzantine images – which can be seen in Híos Town's Giustiniani and Byzantine museums (see pp.374–375) – to expose the original thirteenth- and fourteenth-century work. Specialists and art students can make arrangements for a full visit by contacting the Third Ephorate of Byzantine Antiquities (☎22710 44238; Mon–Fri 9am–1.30pm), or make initial enquiries at the Giustiniani Museum if your Greek isn't up to it. The *cloisonné* (alternating brick- and stonework) of the exterior alone justifies the trip here, though architectural harmony is marred by the later addition of a clumsy secondary cupola over the narthex, and the visibly unsound structure is kept from collapse by cable-binding at the roofline.

The monastic church of **Panayía Sikelliá** is much easier to find, visible from afar in its dramatic clifftop setting south of Tholopotámi, beyond which the three-kilometre dirt access road leading to it is well signposted. Roughly contemporaneous with Panayía Krína, Sikelliá is best visited near sunset, when the *cloisonné* surface of its blind arches acquires a golden tone. There's nothing much to see inside other than a fine, carved *témblon* and a peculiar, late fresco of John the Divine, so it's not essential to time your visit to coincide with that of the key-keeper, who may appear at dusk. Except for the festival on September 7–8, you're likely to have the atmospheric premises to yourself; the monastery outbuildings, save for a perimeter wall and a few fortifications above, have long since vanished, but it's worth climbing the latter for views over the adjacent ravine and the entire south of the island.

Néa Moní

Almost exactly in the middle of the island, the monastery of **Néa Moní** was founded in 1042 by the Byzantine emperor Constantine IX Monomahos on the spot where a wonder-working icon had been discovered. It ranks as one of the most beautiful and important monuments on any of the Greek islands; the mosaics, together with those of Dháfni and Ósios Loukás on the mainland, are among the finest surviving art of their age to be found in Greece, and the setting – high up in still partly forested mountains 15km west of the port – is no less memorable.

Once a powerful and independent community of six hundred monks, Néa Moní was pillaged during 1822 and most of its residents put to the sword; many of its outbuildings have languished in ruins since then, though a recent

EU grant has prompted massive restoration work. The 1881 tremor caused comprehensive damage, while exactly a century later a forest fire threatened to engulf the place until the resident icon was paraded around the perimeter wall, miraculously repelling the flames. Today the monastery, with its giant refectory and vaulted water cisterns, is inhabited by just a couple of lay workers, and one frail, elderly nun; when she goes, Néa Moní will reportedly be taken over by monks.

Visiting the monastery

Bus excursions formerly provided by the KTEL have been suspended since the *katholikón*, the main point of interest, closed until further notice for restoration work; neither is it worth shelling out specially for a taxi trip under the circumstances. Stopping in briefly under your own power is really all that's called for at the moment.

Just inside the main gate (daily 8am–1pm & 4–8pm) stands a **chapel–ossuary** containing some of the bones of those who met their death here in 1822; axe-clefts in children's skulls attest to the savagery of the attackers. Further along on the right, upstairs, is a small **museum** (Tues–Sun 8am–1pm; €2) devoted to ecclesiastical articles and the history of the monastery.

If and when it ever reopens, head straight for the *katholikón*, whose cupola, resting on an octagonal drum, is of a design seen elsewhere only in Cyprus; the frescoes in the exonarthex are comprehensively damaged by holes allegedly made by Turkish bullets, but the **mosaics** further inside are well preserved. The narthex contains portrayals of the various saints of Híos sandwiched between the *Niptir* (Christ Washing the Disciples' Feet) and *Judas' Betrayal*, in which the critical kiss has unfortunately been smudged out, but Peter is clearly visible lopping off the ear of the high priest's servant. In the dome of the sanctuary, which once contained a complete life cycle of Christ, only the *Baptism*, a partial *Crucifixion*, the *Descent from the Cross*, the *Resurrection* and the evangelists *Mark* and *John* survived the earthquake. But the *Baptism* and *Resurrection* in particular are exceptionally expressive and go a considerable way to justifying Néa Moní's claim to high rank among works of Byzantine art.

Avgónyma and Anávatos

With your own transport, you can proceed 5km west of Néa Moní to **AVGÓNYMA**, a cluster of dwellings on a knoll above the coast; the name means "Clutch of Eggs", an apt description when it's viewed from the ridge above. Since the 1980s, the place has been almost totally restored as a summer haven by descendants of the original villagers, though the permanent population is just seven. A returned Greek-American family runs a reasonable, consistent **taverna**/*kafenío*, O Pyrgos, in an arcaded mansion on the main square, serving fare such as *pantsétta*, *mastéllo* and *hortokefiédhes*; co-mananged *To Arhondiko* and *To Asteria* at the outskirts have far less reliable opening hours and uneven quality. The classiest accommodation option here is *Spitakia*, a cluster of small restored houses for up to five people (☎22710 20513 or 22710 81200, ⓦwww.spitakia.gr; ❹), though O Pyrgos restaurant also keeps more modernized units in the village (☎22710 42175; ❸).

A paved side road continues another 4km north to **ANÁVATOS**, whose empty, dun-coloured dwellings, soaring above pistachio orchards, are almost indistinguishable from the 300-metre-high bluff on which they're built. During the 1822 insurrection, some four hundred inhabitants and refugees threw themselves over this cliff rather than surrender to the besieging

Ottomans, and it's still a preferred suicide leap. Anávatos can now only muster two permanent inhabitants and, given a lack of accommodation, plus an eerie, traumatized atmosphere, it's no place to be stranded at dusk, with just a rather listless "snack-bar" at the village entrance. The ground is too hard to pass pipes through, and the archeological service administers the place, factors which together ensure there will be no renaissance here à la Avgónyma – though for some obscure reason archeologists *are* restoring the summit *kástro* (Tues–Sun 8.30am–2pm; free).

The west coast

West of Avgónyma, the main road descends 6km to the coast in well-graded loops. Turning right (north) at the junction leads first to the much-advertised beach at **Elínda**, which, though alluring from afar, has a rocky shore and murky waters. You're better off continuing towards the more secluded sand-and-gravel coves of **Tigáni** and **Makriá Ámmos** slightly northwest, probably the best this coast has to offer; there's some reef at the latter, but this drops away as you continue east along the beach. Just north of here, **Metóhi** bay has an OK beach and a seasonal eponymous fish **taverna**; below **SIDHIROÚNDA**, the only village hereabouts (another **taverna**) with views over the entire west Hian shore thanks to the spectacular hilltop setting, there are more beaches, the best being **Prastiá** and the most sheltered **Yeríta**.

All along this coast, as far southwest as Limáni Mestón, loom round **watch-towers** erected by the Genoese to look out for pirates; one of these has lent its name to **Kastélla** (officially Trahíli), the second sand-and-gravel cove you reach by turning left from the junction. This is attractive enough, with clean water offshore, but the short side road down is rough. The first beach left of the junction, reached by another rugged, 500-metre track, is popular **Xeropóta-mos**, more protected and consisting of mixed sand and pebbles.

Lithí and Véssa

Sparse, weekday-only bus service resumes 9km south of the coastal junction at **LITHÍ**, a friendly village perched on a forested ledge overlooking the sea; a mostly old core belies its rather unsightly outskirts. There are central snack-bars and *kafenía*, but most visitors head 2km downhill to the hard-packed, often windswept beach of **Paralía Lithioú**, despite its shortcomings a favourite weekend target of Hiot townees. They come mainly for the sake of two adja-cent, pricey fish **tavernas** at the far end, the better of these *Ta Tria Adherfia*; the other (*Kyra Despina*) has a few **rooms** (☎22710 73373; ③).

Some 5km south of Lithí, the valley-bottom village of **VÉSSA** is an unsung gem, more open and less kasbah-like than Mestá or Pyrgí, but still homoge-neous. Its honey-coloured buildings are arrayed in a vast grid punctuated by numerous belfries; there's a nameless *kafenío* installed on the ground floor of the tower-mansion on the main through-road, while its neighbour *Kostas* (aka *Froso's*) does excellent *yíros, loukániko* and *souvláki*.

Northern Híos

Northern Híos never really recovered from the Turkish massacre, and the still-perceptible desolation left by fires in 1981 and 1987 will further dampen inquisitive spirits. Since the early 1900s, its villages have been all but deserted for much of the year, which means correspondingly sparse bus services. About one third of the former population now lives in Híos Town, venturing out here only at major festivals or to tend grapes and olives for at most four months of the year. Others, based in Athens or North America, return to their ancestral homes for just a few intense weeks in midsummer, when marriages are arranged between local families and heritable properties thus consolidated.

The road to Kardhámyla

Blue city buses (labelled "ΔΑΣΚΑΛΟΠΕΤΡΑ" or "Teacher's Rock") run north from Híos Town only up to **VRONDÁDHOS**, an elongated coastal suburb that's a favourite residence of the island's many seafarers. Homer legendarily lived and taught here (thus the bus-front signs), and in terraced parkland just above the little fishing port and pebble beach (mostly local bathers) you can visit what is traditionally claimed to be his lectern, but is more probably an ancient altar of Cybele and is now signposted as such. An adjacent modern amphitheatre amidst the greenery serves as a pleasant venue for summer evening concerts.

If you have your own transport, you can make a stop 2km further along at the monastery of **Panayía Mersinidhíou** (Myrtidhiótissis) – of little intrinsic interest but notable for its photogenic setting overlooking the sea, best at first light. After another 5km, the route swoops down to the tiny bayside hamlet of **PANDOUKIÓS**, with several offshore fish nurseries and an excellent if pricey waterside **taverna**, *Lefteris Kourtesis*, where lobster can sometimes be had.

Langádha and Pityós

LANGÁDHA, just beyond, is probably the first point on the eastern coast road where you'd be tempted to stop. Set at the mouth of a deep valley, this attractive little harbour looks across its bay to a pine grove, and beyond to Turkey. Night-time visitors come for the sustaining seafood at two adjacent **tavernas** at the start of the quay, *Tou Kopelou* (aka *Stelios'*), whose good cooking belies the rather dreary inside decor, and second-choice *Paradhisos*. The rest of the esplanade supports a pair each of bars and fancy cafés, but there is no proper beach anywhere nearby; the bay of Dhelfini, just north, is an off-limits naval base. An ad hoc taxi-boat service from here to Inoússes island (20min journey) is provided by either Mr Tiniakos (☎694 41 68 104) or Mr Boundoulas (☎694 45 14 604) – expect to pay €45 each way per boatload.

Just beyond Langádha, an important side road leads 5km up and inland to **PITYÓS** (formerly Pityoús), an oasis in a mountain pass presided over by a Byzantine tower-keep; people come here from some distance to **dine** at *Makellos* on the west edge of the village, a shrine of local cuisine (mid-June to mid-Sept daily; rest of year Fri–Sun eves only). Continuing 4km further will bring you to a junction allowing quick access to the west of the island and the Volissós area.

Kardhámyla and around

From Langádha most traffic proceeds to **ÁNO KARDHÁMYLA** and **KÁTO KARDHÁMYLA**, the latter 37km out of Híos Town. Positioned at opposite edges of a fertile plain rimmed by mountains, they initially come as welcome relief from Homer's crags. Káto, better known as **MÁRMARO**, is larger, indeed the island's second town, with a bank (no ATM), post office and a filling station (one of just three in the north of Híos).

However, there is little to attract a casual visitor other than pastel-painted Neoclassical architecture in the hillside neighbourhoods of Ráhi and Perivoláki:

the quay and port, mercilessly exposed to the *meltémi*, is strictly businesslike, and there are few tourist facilities worth mentioning. A sterling exception is *Hotel Kardamyla* (☎22720 23353, ☏22720 23354; ❸), co-managed with Híos Town's *Hotel Kyma*, offering spacious, fan-equipped **rooms** and a few suites. It has the bay's only pebble beach, and the in-house restaurant is a reliable source of lunch (July & Aug) if you're touring. Worthwhile independent tavernas include *Ouzeri Barba Yiannis* (run by Irini Tsirigou; all year), beside the port authority, or *Iy Vlyhadha* (summer only), facing the eponymous bay west over the headland, with locally produced suckling pig and squid.

Nagós

For better swimming head west – by car from the signposted junction by the church, on foot past the harbour-mouth windmill for an hour along a cemented coastal driveway – to **NAGÓS**, a gravel-shore bay at the foot of an oasis. Lush greenery is nourished by active springs up at a bend in the road, enclosed in a sort of grotto and flanked by a *psistariá*, all overhung by tall cliffs. The place name is a corruption of *naós*, after a large Poseidon temple that once stood near the springs, but centuries of pilfering and orchard-tending, plus organized excavations after 1912, mean that nothing remains visible. Down at the shore the swimming is good, if a bit chilly courtesy of the spring water; here you'll also find two rather mediocre tavernas (there's a better one inland, by the spring), plus a few rooms. Your only chance of relative solitude in July or August lies fifteen minutes' walk west at **Yióssonas**, a much longer beach, but less sheltered, rockier and with no facilities.

Northwestern villages

Few outsiders venture beyond Yióssonas, and no buses cover the distance between Mármaro and Kambiá village, 20km west. Along the way, Amádhes and Víki are attractive enough villages at the base of 1297-metre **Pelinéo**, the island's summit, most easily climbed from Amádhes – a five-hour round trip. **KAMBIÁ**, overlooking a ravine strewn with the remains of a chapel, has very much an end-of-the-line feel, although a partly paved road heads 5km south towards Spartoúnda, and far worse tracks (jeeps only) venture west through lush valleys to the villages of Kéramos and Afrodhísia. The track heading west from just south of Spartoúnda towards Hálandhra is also pretty horrid, but from Spartoúnda a paved road resumes for the remaining 15km to the intersection with the main trans-island road bound for Volissós. About halfway, well signposted outside the village of **KIPOURIÉS**, there's a superb **psistariá** ideally placed for a meal stop while touring: *Iy Petrini Platia*, set in a fountain-nourished oasis. It's open daily June to mid-September, but weekends only otherwise; ring ☎22740 21672 to make sure, as it's a long trip out.

The monastery of Moundhón

About 5km south of Kipouriés, near the turning for the village of Dhievhá, you can make a detour to the engagingly set sixteenth-century **monastery of Moundhón**, second in rank to Néa Moní before its partial destruction in 1822. The gate to the grounds is kept open, but for admittance to the locked church seek out the warden, Yiorgos Fokas, in Dhievhá itself (☎22740 22011). The highlight is the *katholikón* with its naïve interior frescoes, the best one depicting the *Ouranódhromos Klímax* (Stairway to Heaven, not to be confused with Led Zeppelin's): a trial-by-ascent, in which ungodly priests are beset by demons hurling them into the mouth of a great serpent symbolizing the Devil, while the righteous clergy are assisted upwards by angels. In an era when illiteracy was the norm, such panels were intended quite literally to scare the hell out of simple parishioners.

Ayiásmata and around

If you're on foot in Kambiá, ask at one of the *kafenía* by the main church for directions to the start of a one-hour path across the canyon to the abandoned hamlet of Agrelopó; from the church here, a system of Jeep tracks leads in another ninety minutes to the tumbledown pier and seaweed-strewn beach at **Ayiásmata**. This is one of the strangest spots on Híos, consisting of perhaps twenty buildings: four of them are churches, the rest part of a rather soulless, jail-like **spa** which has ceased functioning in recent years.

Paved roads south from Ayiásmata pass through strikingly beautiful countryside up to the villages of Kéramos and **AFRODHÍSIA**, the latter the more attractive. Here the surfaced road splits: the southerly turning passes through Hálandhra and **NÉA POTAMIÁ**, the latter an ugly prefab village built to replace an older one destroyed by landslide. From here it's another 20km to Volissós.

The northwest coast

More worthwhile is the northwesterly turning from Afrodhísia which takes you along a corniche route, running parallel to but high above the coast, with views out to Lésvos (weather permitting) and Psará. **KOUROÚNIA**, 6km along, is beautifully arranged in two separate neighbourhoods, and set amid thick forest.

After 10km more, you reach **ÁYIO GÁLA**, whose claim to fame is a **grotto-church** complex, built into a stream-lapped palisade at the bottom of the village. Approaching the village from the south, signs ("Panayía Ayiogaloúsena") point to a lane crossing the water, but for access, except at the festival on August 22–23, you'll need to find the key-keeper (ask in the village) and descend to the complex from a flight of stairs leading down from a eucalyptus tree. Of the two churches inside the cave, the larger, at the mouth of the complex, dates from the fifteenth century but seems rather newer externally since a 1993 renovation. Inside, a fantastically intricate *témblon* vies for your attention with a tinier, older, freestanding chapel, built entirely within the rear of the cavern. Its fifteenth-century frescoes are badly smudged, except for one in the apse depicting a wonderfully mysterious and mournful Virgin, surely the saddest in Christendom, holding a knowing Child.

Beyond Áyio Gála, bleak scenery is redeemed mostly by fantastic sunset views across to Psará, but overshadowed by a huge, unaesthetic wind farm at **MELANIÓS**, typical of the four scrappy, impoverished villages along the 25-kilometre road to Volissós. At **PARPARIÁ**, roughly halfway between Melaniós and Volissós, there's a single **taverna** on the *platía*.

Volissós and around

VOLISSÓS, 42km from Híos Town by the most direct route (but just 44km via the much easier way through Avgónyma), was once the market town for the northwestern villages. Its old stone houses still curl appealingly beneath the crumbling hilltop Byzantine fort, whose towers were improved by the Genoese. Volissós can seem depressing at first, with the bulk of its 250 mostly elderly (permanent) inhabitants living in newer buildings around the square, but opinions improve with longer acquaintance. This backwater ethos may not last; the upper quarters are in the grip of a restoration mania, most of it done in admirable taste, with ruins changing hands for stratospheric prices.

Volissós practicalities

Grouped around the square you'll find a **post office**, a freestanding ATM, two well-stocked shops and three mediocre **tavernas**. A pair of **filling stations**, the only ones hereabouts, operate 2.5km out of town; the **bus** comes out here only on Sundays on a day-trip basis, or on Monday and Tuesday in the early afternoon (unless you care to travel at 4.30am). **Taxis** from Híos Town cost roughly €32 per car, versus about €3 per person for the bus (both fares one way).

You should therefore plan on overnighting – which should cause no dismay, since the area has the best beaches and some of the most interesting **accommodation** on Híos. The most reliably available and staffed of a few restoration projects are sixteen old houses restored in the early 1990s, mostly in Pýrgos district, available through Volissos Travel (☎22740 21413, ℱ22740 21521, ₩www.volissostravel.gr; ❸). Units accommodate two to four people – all have terraces, fully equipped kitchens, air conditioning and original features such as tree trunks upholding sleeping lofts. Alternatively, lower down by the old school stands the *Arhondiko Zorbas* (☎22740 21436, ₩www.chioszorbas.gr; ❸), more modern but still tasteful, by the post office. The final entry in the restoration sweepstakes is Sevasmia Kapiri's *Key to the Castle* (☎22740 21463; ❸), a house divided into four studios.

Limniá and local beaches

LIMNIÁ (sometimes Limiá), the port of Volissós, lies 2km south; it's an important fishing anchorage, though there are no longer any small ferries or *kaïkia* from here to Psará. There is also nowhere to stay on the harbour, though there are a few **tavernas** and cafés, including *O Zikos* on the jetty, where the emphasis is on *mayireftá*, and summer-only *To Limanaki* at the rear of the cove, which is better for fish.

From Limniá it's not far to the fabled **beaches**. A 1.5-kilometre walk southeast over the headland brings you to **Mánagros**, a seemingly endless, undeveloped sand-and-pebble beach (nudism goes unremarked on at the remote south end). More intimate, sandy **Lefkáthia** lies just a ten-minute stroll along the cement drive threading over the headland north of the harbour; amenities at this cove are limited to a seasonal snack-shack on the sand, and Ioannis Zorbas' apartments (❸), co-run with the *Arhondiko* (see above) and beautifully set in a garden just before the concrete track joins the asphalt road down from Volissós. This is bound for **Límnos** (not to be confused with Limniá), the next sheltered bay 400m east of Lefkáthia, where both *Taverna Akroyiali* and *Iy Limnos* provide good food and professional service; the latter perhaps has the edge for its setting on the sand, with excellent *mayirefta* (eg *kokorós krasáto*) and fish grills. Just inland, the spruce *Latini Apartments* (☎22740 21461, ℱ22740 21871; ❹) are graced with multiple stone terraces.

Ayía Markélla: beach and monastery

Ayía Markélla, 5km further northwest of Límnos, stars in many local postcards: a long, stunning beach fronting a monastery dedicated to the patron saint of Híos. The latter is not especially interesting or useful to outsiders, since its cells are reserved for Greek Orthodox pilgrims. In an interesting variation on the expulsion of the moneychangers from the temple, only religious souvenirs are allowed to be sold within the holy precincts, while all manner of plastic junk is on offer just outside. There's a single, rather indifferent taverna to hand as well, and around July 22 – the local saint's festival and biggest island celebration – "NO CAMPING" signs doubtless go unenforced.

Some maps show hot springs at one end of the beach; these, actually twenty minutes' walk north around the headland, turn out to be tepid dribbles into pot-sized cavities, not worth the bother and indicative only of the geological unity of this part of Híos with volcanic Lésvos. Potentially more useful is the dirt track heading north from the monastery grounds, passable (with care) to any vehicle and emerging in Parpariá village on the paved road between Melaniós and Volissós.

Satellite islets: Psará and Inoússes

There's a single settlement, with beaches and an isolated rural monastery, on both of Híos' satellite islands, but each is surprisingly different from the other, and of course from their large neighbour. Inoússes, the nearer and smaller (3km by 10km) islet, has a daily *kaïki* service from Híos Town in season; Psará (11km by 6km) has slightly less regular services subject to weather conditions (in theory, several weekly from Híos Town), with both schedules and its remoteness conspiring against a day-trip (see "Travel details", p.395).

Psará

The birthplace of the Greek revolutionary war hero Admiral Kanaris, **Psará** devoted its merchant fleets – the third largest in 1820s Greece after those of Ídhra and Spétses – to the cause of independence, and paid dearly for it. Vexed beyond endurance, the Turks landed overwhelming forces in 1824 to stamp out this nest of resistance. Perhaps three thousand of the thirty thousand inhabitants escaped in small boats and were rescued by a French fleet, but the majority retreated to a hilltop powder magazine and blew it (and themselves) up rather than surrender. The nineteenth-century poet Dionysios Solomos immortalized the incident in famous stanzas:

On the Black Ridge of Psará,
Glory walks alone.
She meditates on her heroes,
And wears in her hair a wreath
Made from a few dry weeds
Left on the barren ground.

Today, Psará is a sad, stark place fully living up to its name ("the grey things" in Greek), and it's never really recovered from this holocaust. The Turks burnt whatever houses and vegetation the blast had missed, and the permanent population barely exceeds four hundred. The only positive recent development was a 1980s revitalization project instigated by a French-Greek descendant of Kanaris and a Greek team. The port was improved, mains electricity and pure water provided, a secondary school opened, and cultural links between France and the island established, though this has not resulted in increased tourist numbers.

Since few buildings in the east-facing harbour community predate the twentieth century, it's a strange hotchpotch of ecclesiastical and domestic architecture

Greek script table

Híos	Χίος	ΧΙΟΣ
Afrodhísia	Αφροδίσια	ΑΦΡΟΔΙΣΑ
Amádhes	Αμάδες	ΑΜΑΔΕΣ
Anávatos	Ανάβατος	ΑΝΑΒΑΤΟΣ
Áno Kardhámyla	Άνω Καρδάμυλα	ΑΝΩ ΚΑΡΔΑΜΥΛΑ
Apothíkas	Αποθήκας	ΑΠΟΘΗΚΑΣ
Armólia	Αρμόλια	ΑΡΜΟΛΙΑ
Avgónyma	Αυγώνυμα	ΑΥΓΩΝΥΜΑ
Ayía Dhýnami	Αγια Δ‡ναμη	ΑΓΙΑ Δ ΝΑΜΗ
Ayía Ermióni	Αγία Ερμιόνη	ΑΓΙΑ ΕΡΜΙΟΝΗ
Ayía Fotiní	Αγία Φωτεινή	ΑΓΙΑ ΦΩΤΕΙΝΗ
Ayía Iríni	Αγία Ειρήνη	ΑΓΙΑ ΕΙΡΗΝΗ
Ayía Markélla	Αγία Μαρκέλλα	ΑΓΙΑ ΜΑΡΚΕΛΛΑ
Ayiásmata	Αγιάσματα	ΑΓΙΑΣΜΑΤΑ
Áyii Anáryiri	Άγιοι Ανάργυροι	ΑΓΙΟΙ ΑΝΑΡΓΥΡΟΙ
Áyio Gála	Άγιο Γάλα	ΑΓΙΟ ΓΑΛΑ
Áyios Emilianós	Άγιος Αιμιλιανός	ΑΓΙΟΣ ΑΙΜΙΛΙΑΝΟΣ
Áyios Ioánnis	Άγιος Ιοννης	ΑΓΙΟΣ ΙΟΑΝΝΗΣ
Áyios Yeóryios Sikoússis	Άγιος Γεώργιος Συκούσης	ΑΓΙΟΣ ΓΕΩΡΓΙΟΣ ΣΥΚΟΥΣΗΣ
Dhaskalópetra	Δασκαλόπετρα	ΔΑΣΚΑΛΟΠΕΤΡΑ
Dhídhyma	Δίδυμα	ΔΙΔΥΜΑ
Dhievhá	Διευχά	ΔΙΕΥΧΑ
Elínda	Ελίντα	ΕΛΙΝΤΑ
Emboriós	Εμπορειός	ΕΜΠΟΡΕΙΟΣ
Evangelismoú	Ευαγγελισμού	ΕΥΑΓΓΕΛΙΣΜΟΥ
Fourkeró	Φουρκερό	ΦΟΥΡΚΕΡΟ
Inoússes	Οινούσσες	ΟΙΝΟΥΣΣΕΣ
Kalamotí	Καλαμωτή	ΚΑΛΑΜΩΤΗ
Grídhia	Γρίδια	ΓΡΙΔΙΑ
Kambiá	Καμπιά	ΚΑΜΠΙΑ
Kámbos	Κάμπος	ΚΑΜΠΟΣ
Karfás	Καρφάς	ΚΑΡΦΑΣ
Karyés	Καρυές	ΚΑΡΥΕΣ
Katarráktis	Καταρράκτης	ΚΑΤΑΡΡΑΚΤΗΣ
Káto Faná	Κάτω Φανά	ΚΑΤΩ ΦΑΝΑ
Kéramos	Κέραμος	ΚΕΡΑΜΟΣ
Kómi	Κώμη	ΚΩΜΗ
Kondári	Κοντάρι	ΚΟΝΤΑΡΙ
Kouroúnia	Κουρούνια	ΚΟΥΡΟΥΝΙΑ
Langádha	Λαγκάδα	ΛΑΓΚΑΔΑ
Lefkáthia	Λευκάθια	ΛΕΥΚΑΘΙΑ
Lilikás	Λιλικάς	ΛΙΛΙΚΑΣ
Liménas Mestón	Λιμένας Μεστών	ΛΙΜΕΝΑΣ ΜΕΣΤΩΝ

that greets the eye on disembarking. There's a distinct southerly feel, more like the Dodecanese or Cyclades, and some peculiar churches, no two alike in style.

Practicalities

Arrival can be something of an ordeal: the regular small ferry from Híos Town can take over four hours (as against a nominal 3hr) to cover the 57 nautical miles of habitually rough sea. Once a week, large, main-line ferries appear from

Limniá	Λιμνιά	ΛΙΜΝΙΑ
Límnos	Λήμνος	ΛΗΜΝΟΣ
Lithí	Λιθί	ΛΙΘΙ
Makriá Ámmos	Μακριά Άμμος	ΜΑΚΡΙΑ ΑΜΜΟΣ
Mánagros	Μάναγρος	ΜΑΝΑΓΡΟΣ
Mármaro	Μάρμαρο	ΜΑΡΜΑΡΟ
Mávros Yialós	Μάυρος Γιαλός	ΜΑΥΡΟΣ ΓΙΑΛΟΣ
Mégas Limniónas	Μέγας Λιμνιοώας	ΜΕΓΑΣ ΛΙΜΝΙΩΝΑΣ
Melaniós	Μελανιός	ΜΕΛΑΝΙΟΣ
Mestá	Μεστά	ΜΕΣΤΑ
Metóhi	Μετόχι	ΜΕΤΟΧΙ
Moundhón	Μουνδών	ΜΟΥΝΔΩΝ
Nagós	Ναγός	ΝΑΓΟΣ
Néa Moní	Νέα Μονή	ΝΕΑ ΜΟΝΗ
Nénita	Νένητα	ΝΕΝΗΤΑ
Olýmbi	Ολύμποι	ΟΛΥΜΠΟΙ
Panayía Krína	Παναγία Κρήνα	ΠΑΝΑΓΙΑ ΚΡΗΝΑ
Panayía	Παναγία	ΠΑΝΑΓΙΑ
Mersindhíou	Μερσινιδιου	ΜΕΡΣΙΝΙΔΙΟΥ
Panayía Sikelliá	Παναγία Σικελιά	ΠΑΝΑΓΙΑ ΣΙΚΕΛΙΑ
Pandoukiós	Παντουκιός	ΠΑΝΤΟΥΚΙΟΣ
Parpariá	Παρπαριά	ΠΑΡΠΑΡΙΑ
Pelinéo(n)	Πελvναίο(v)	ΠΕΛΙΝΑΙΟ(Ν)
Pyrgí	Πυργοί	ΠΥΡΓΟΙ
Pityós	Πιτυός	ΠΙΤΥΟΣ
Potámi	Ποτάμι	ΠΟΤΑΜΙ
Prastiá	Πραστιά	ΠΡΑΣΔΙΑ
Psará	Ψαρά	ΨΑΡΑ
Sidhroúnda	Σιδηρούντα	ΣΙΔΗΡΟΥΝΤΑ
Spartoúnda	Σπαρτούντα	ΣΠΑΡΤΟΥΝΤΑ
Spíleo Tykiás	Σπιλαιο Τηκιάς	ΣΠΗΛΑΙΟ ΤΥΚΙΑΣ
Olýmbon	Ολύμπον	ΟΛΥΜΠΩΝ
Tigáni	Τηγάνι	ΤΗΓΑΝΙ
Vavýli	Βαβύλοι	ΒΑΒΥΛΟΙ
Véssa	Βέσσα	ΒΕΣΣΑ
Víki	Βίκι	ΒΙΚΙ
Volissós	Βολισσός	ΒΟΛΙΣΣΟΣ
Vounós	Βουνός	ΒΟΥΝΟΣ
Vrondádhos	Βροντάδος	ΒΡΟΝΤΑΔΟΣ
Vroulídhia	Βρουλίδια	ΒΡΟΥΛΙΔΙΑ
Výri	Βύρη	ΒΥΡΗ
Xeropótamos	Ξερόποταμος	ΞΕΡΟΠΟΔΑΜΟΣ
Yeríta	Γερίτα	ΓΕΡΙΤΑ
Yióssonas	Γιόσωνας	ΓΙΟΣΩΝΑΣ

Sígri (Lésvos) and Lávrio (Attica), though regular *kaïki* service from Limniá has been suspended as of writing.

You'll need to **stay** overnight, as most boats arrive in the evening. There's a choice between a handful of fairly basic rooms and three more professional outfits: *Psara Studios* (☎22740 61233, ⒻF22740 61195; ❹) and *Apartments Restalia* (☎22740 61000, ⒻF22740 61201; ❹), both a bit starkly modern but with balconies and kitchens, or the EOT inn (☎22740 61293; ❸) in a restored prison. A taverna or two, a **post office**, bakery and shop complete the tally of amenities; there's a bank agent, but no full-service bank.

Around the island

Psará's **beaches** are decent, improving the further northeast you walk from the port. You quickly pass **Káto Yialós**, **Katsoúni** and **Lazarétta** with its off-putting power station, before reaching **Lákka** ("narrow ravine"), fifteen minutes' walk from the port, apparently named after its grooved rock formations in which you may have to shelter; much of this coast is windswept, with a heavy swell offshore. **Límnos**, 25 minutes away from the port along the coastal path, is big and pretty, but there's no reliable taverna here, or indeed at any of the other beaches. The one other thing to do on Psará is to walk north across the island – the old track has now been paved – to the **Monastery of the Assumption**; uninhabited since the 1970s, this comes to life only during the first week of August, when its revered icon is carried in ceremonial procession to town and back on the eve of August 6.

Inoússes

Inoússes has a permanent population of about three hundred – less than half its prewar figure – and a very different history from Psará. For generations this medium-sized islet, originally settled by Hiot shepherds around 1750, has provided the Aegean with many of her wealthiest shipping families: various members of the Livanos, Lemos and Pateras clans (with every street or square named after the last-cited family) were born here. This helps explain the large villas and visiting summer yachts on an otherwise sleepy Greek backwater – as well as a **Maritime Museum** (daily 10am–1pm) near the quay, endowed by various shipping magnates. At the west end of the quay, the bigwigs have also funded a large nautical academy, engaged in training future members of the merchant navy.

Two church-tipped islets, each privately owned, guard the unusually well-protected harbour; the **town** itself is surprisingly large, draped over hillsides enclosing a ravine. Despite the wealthy reputation, its appearance is unpretentious and similar to İzmir across the water in Turkey, with the houses displaying a mix of vernacular and modest Neoclassical style.

Practicalities

On Sundays in summer can you make an inexpensive **day-trip** to Inoússes from Híos with the locals' ferry *Oinoussai II*; on most other days of the week this arrives from the big island at 3pm, returning early the next morning (☎22710 25074 for current info). During the tourist season there are also excursions from Híos, though these are pricier, with return tickets running at more than double the cost of the regular ferry. All that's really possible on a typical six-hour excursion is a look around the single town, a swim at one of Inoússes' attractive beaches and a meal.

Since most seasonal visitors stay in their ancestral or holiday homes, there is just one, fairly comfortable **hotel**, the *Thalassoporos* (☎22720 55475, ⊕22720 55476; ❸), on the main easterly hillside lane. **Eating out** is similarly limited; the most reliable option is the simple, good-value *Taverna Pateronissia*, conspicuous at the base of the disembarkation jetty. Otherwise, be prepared to patronize one of the three shops (one on the waterfront, two up the hill), but you may be better off bringing your own picnic food, especially out of season. Nightlife comprises such bars as *Navtikos Omilos* and *Karnayio*. Beside the museum is a **post office** and a **bank**.

Around the island

The rest of this tranquil island, at least the southern slope, is surprisingly green and well tended; there are no springs, so water comes from a mix of fresh and brackish wells, as well as a reservoir. The sea is extremely clean and calm on the sheltered southerly shore; among its **beaches**, choose from **Zepága**, **Biláli** or **Kástro**, respectively five, twenty and thirty minutes' walk west of the port. More secluded **Fourkeró** lies a 25-minute walk east, first along a cement drive to a seaside chapel, then by path past pine groves and over a ridge. As on Psará, there are no reliable facilities at any of the beaches.

At the end of the westerly road, beyond Kástro, stands the somewhat macabre convent of **Evangelismoú**, endowed by the Pateras family. Inside reposes the mummified body of the lately canonized Irini, whose prayers to die of cancer in place of her terminally ill father Panagos were answered early in the 1960s; he's entombed here also, having outlived Irini by some years. The abbess, presiding over around twenty novices, is none other than the widowed Mrs Pateras. Only modestly attired women are allowed admission, and even then casual visits are not encouraged.

Híos travel details

Island transport

NB All frequencies given are for the period June to September.

Buses – Blue City Lines

Híos Town to: Kondári (Airport), Karfás, Mégas Limniónas, Ayía Ermióni, Thymianá (19–27 daily 6.30am–9pm, Sun 8am–8.30pm, often with the order juggled); Vrondádhos, Dhaskalópetra (2 hourly 6.30am–8.30pm 1 hourly Mon–Sat, Sun).

Buses – Green long-distance KTEL

Híos Town to: Anávatos* & Avgónyma* (Thurs at 9am); Armólia (6 daily Mon–Fri, 3 Sat, 1 Sun); Ayía Fotiní (7 daily Mon–Fri, 4 Sat, 2 Sun); Ayía Markélla* (Sun at 8.30am); Emboriós (5 daily Mon–Fri, 3 Sat, 1 Sun); Katarráktis (7 daily Mon–Fri, 3 Sat, 1 Sun); Komí (4 daily Mon–Fri, 3 Sat, 1 Sun); Langádha (5 daily Mon–Fri, 3 Sat); Mármaro (5 daily Mon–Fri, 3 Sat); Mestá (5 daily Mon–Fri, 3 Sat, 1 Sun); Paralía Lithioú (3 daily Mon–Fri only); Pyrgí (7 daily Mon–Fri, 3 Sat, 1 Sun); Spíleo Sykiás Olýmbon* (Wed 9am); Volissós (Mon & Tues at 4.30am & 1.30pm, Sun* at 8.30am).
NB * indicates that this destination is part of a set-price KTEL tour taking in other destinations.

Buses – KTEL loop routes and local shuttles

Emboriós–Pyrgí (3 daily Mon–Sat, 1 Sun); Kómi–Pyrgí (3 daily Mon–Sat, 1 Sun); Pyrgí–Emboriós (4 daily Mon–Fri, 3 Sat, 1 Sun); Mármaro–Nagós (3 daily Mon–Fri, 2 Sat).

Inter-island transport

NB To simplify matters, the once-weekly sailing offered by LANE, northbound from Híos to Lésvos, Límnos and Alexandhroúpoli, and southbound to Sámos, Kálymnos, Kós, Rhodes, Hálki, Kárpathos, Kássos and Crete, has been omitted from the following schedules.

Large ferries

Híos to: Ikaría (3 weekly on GA; 5–8hr); Kavála (2 weekly on GA; 15hr); Lésvos (at least daily on NEL, 3 weekly on GA, 1 weekly on SF; 3hr 30min); Límnos (1 weekly on NEL, 3 weekly on GA, 1 weekly on SF; 10hr–11hr); Pireás (at least daily on NEL, 2 weekly on GA; 9hr–16hr); Sámos, usually both ports (3 weekly on GA; 3hr–5hr), Thessaloníki (1 weekly on NEL; 13hr).
Psará to: Áyios Efstrátios (1 weekly on SF; 6hr 30min); Lávrio (1 weekly on SF; 5hr 30min); Límnos (1 weekly on SF; 8hr 30min); Sígri, Lésvos (1 weekly on SF; 3hr).

Catamaran

NEL's *Aeolos Kenteris* plies 3–5 times weekly most of the year to Lésvos (1hr 30min), and Pireás (4hr); also twice weekly to Límnos (5hr) and either Kavála (7hr 30min) or Thessaloníki (9hr). Typical northbound departure time is around 10pm, towards Athens 10.30am or 6pm.

Small ferries

Híos Town to: Psará (5–6 weekly, currently on the *Panayia Psariani*; usually departs 3pm, returns from Psará 7am next day, but day-trips theoretically possible with 7am departure and 5pm return on Fri/Sat. Journey time nominally 3hr, but best to allow 4hr.

Kaïkia

Híos Town to: Inoússes (minimum 1 daily Mon–Sat 2pm, not Tues Oct–May, Sun 9am & 5pm; returns 8am Tues–Sat, 4pm Sun; 1hr). Other excursion boats according to demand.

Flights

Híos to: Athens (3–4 daily on Olympic, 2 daily on Aegean; 45–50min); Lésvos (3 weekly; 30min); Límnos (3 weekly; 1hr 35min); Rhodes (2 weekly; 55min–1hr 45min); Sámos (1 weekly; 35min); Thessaloníki (4 weekly; 1hr 10min–2hr 45min).

Ferries

Híos to: Turkey (Çeşme); 2–13 boats weekly, depending on season; Thurs evening (Turkish boat) and Sat morning (Greek boat) services tend to run year-round. Passenger fares on Greek boats (Miniotis Lines *Kapetan Stamatis* or similar, Sunrise Tours *San Nicholas*) or Turkish boat (*Ertürk II*) are officially about €40 return, including Greek taxes; no Turkish taxes, but "special offers" at €30–35 abound, particularly with Sunrise Tours, which also quotes one-ways at €25. Small cars €65–70 one way, €110 return, plus small Greek tax, taken on either morning (8.30am) or evening (6.30pm) boats. It is possible to leave with a Greek boat and come back on a Turkish boat, or vice versa. Journey time 30min (on *San Nicholas*) to 45min (others).

Lésvos

Lésvos (Mytilíni), the third-largest Greek island after Crete and Évvia, is not only the birthplace of Sappho, but also of Aesop, Arion and – more recently – the "naïve" artist Theophilos, the poet Odysseus Elytis and the novelist Stratis Myrivilis. Despite these artistic associations, Lésvos may not at first strike the visitor as particularly beautiful or interesting; much of the landscape is rocky, volcanic terrain, dotted with thermal springs and varying between vast grain fields, saltpans or even near-desert. But there are also oak and pine forests as well as vast olive groves, some of these over five hundred years old. With its balmy climate – even winter rain obliges by usually falling before dawn – and suggestive contours, the island tends to grow on you with prolonged acquaintance.

Historically, olive plantations, *oúzo* distilleries, animal husbandry and a fishing industry supported those inhabitants who chose not to emigrate; but with most of these enterprises stagnating since World War II, mass-market **tourism** has made considerable inroads. However, there are still few large hotels outside the capital or Mólyvos, villa-type accommodation just barely outstrips standard rooms, and the first of two official campsites opened only in 1990. While Lésvos is far more developed touristically than Híos, it is rather less so than Sámos, a happy medium that will accord with many people's tastes. Tourist numbers have in fact levelled off in recent years, the result of a fudged airport expansion, unrealistic hotel pricing and the dropping of the island from several tour operators' programmes. So, while a few disused olive-mill grindstones have found a new lease of life as hotel decor, tourism still makes up less than five percent of the local economy, and a healthy surplus in olive oil is sent annually to Spain and Italy for rebottling.

Some history

Lovers of medieval and Ottoman **architecture** certainly won't be disappointed on Lésvos. Byzantine/Genoese castles, many built on earlier

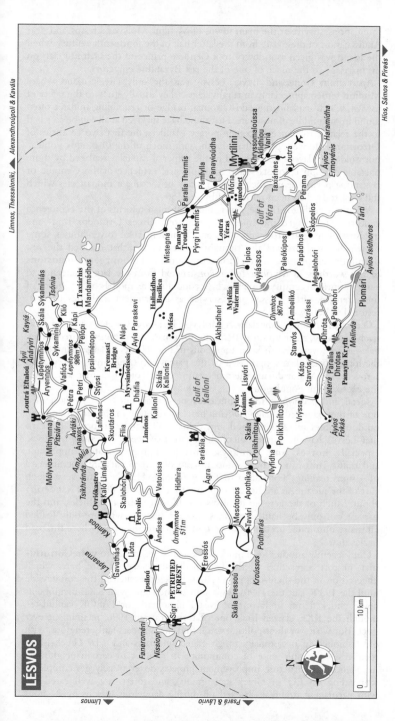

LÉSVOS

Límnos, Thessaloníki, Alexandhroúpoli & Kavála

Híos, Sámos & Pireás

Límnos

Psará & Lávrio

Faneroméni
Nissíopi

N

0   10 km

Mólyvos (Míthymna)
Pitsiára
Loutrá Eftaloú Áyii
Anáryiri
Avlági   Kayiá
Arvenoús   Skála Sykaminiás
Lepétymnos   Sykaminiá   Tsónia
Pétra   Vafiós   Klió
Avláki   Petrí   Kápi
Ambélia   Anaxos   968m   Pelópi
Tsikhránda   Ipsilométopo
Ovriókastro   Stypsi
Kaló Limáni   Lafíonas   Taxiárhis
Skalohóri   Skoútaros   Mandamádhos
Perivolís   Fília
Vatoússa   Limónos   Dháfia   Kremastí
Skalohóri   Bridge
Lióta   Myrsiniótissis
Gavathás   Ándissa   Hídhira   Kalloní   Ávios
Ipsiloú   Órdhymnos   Ágra   Skála   Parákila   Skála   Ioánnis
511m   Kalloní   Polikhnítou   Polikhnítos
PETRIFIED   Parákila
FOREST   Mesótopos   Vrýssa
Sígri   Apothíka   Nyfídha
Taváni   Ávios
Eressós   Podharás   Fokás
Skála Eressoú
Kroússos

Lepétymnos
Halinádhou
Basilica
Mésa
Ayía Paraskeví
Nápi

Mistegná
Panayía
Troulotí
Pýrgi Thermís
Loutrá
Yéras
Ípios
Ayiássos
Akhladhéri
Mytiléne
Waterwill
Olýmbos
967m
Ambelikó
Akrássi
Stavrós   Dhróta   Paleohóri
Káto
Stavrós   Dhróta   Melínda
Vaterá   Paralía
Panayía Kryftí

Paralía Thermís
Pámfylla
Panayioúdha
Mória
Aqueduct   Varriá
Mytilíni
Khryssomaloússa
Aklidhíou
Loutrá
Ayios
Ermoyénis
Pémma
Perama
Skópelos   Tárti
Paleókipos
Papádhos
Megalohóri   Ávios Isidhóros
Plomári

Gulf of Yéras

Gulf of Kalloní

Kámbos

Lápsarna

Haramídha
Taxiárhes

foundations, survive at the main towns of Mytilíni, Mólyvos, Eressós, and near Ándissa; most of these date from the latter half of the fourteenth century, when the island was given as a dowry to a Genoese prince of the Gattilusi clan on his marriage to the niece of one of the last Byzantine emperors.

Apart from Crete and Évvia, Lésvos was the only Greek island where Muslims settled appreciably in rural villages (they usually stuck to the safety of towns), which explains the odd Ottoman bridge or crumbling minaret often found in the middle of nowhere. That these have survived at all can be ascribed to the relative tolerance of contemporary islanders; the first two centuries of **Ottoman rule** were particularly harsh, with much of the Orthodox population sold into slavery or deported to the imperial capital – replaced by more tractable Muslim colonists – and most physical evidence of the Genoese or Byzantine period demolished, though many of the major monasteries which still exist today had been refounded by the 1500s.

Again unusually for the Aegean islands, Ottoman reforms of the eighteenth centuries encouraged the emergence here of a Greek Orthodox land- and industry-owning **aristocracy**, who built rambling, rural tower-houses, some of which have survived the thoughtless destruction that claimed the rest during the twentieth century. More common are the **bourgeois mansions** of the worthies in Mytilíni Town, constructed from the late nineteenth to early twentieth century on French Second Empire models; many more of these remain, often pressed into service as government buildings or even restored as hotels.

Out in the country, especially at Mólyvos, Turks and Greeks got along, relatively speaking, right up until 1923; the Ottoman authorities favoured Greek *kahayiádhes* (overseers) to keep the peons in line. However, large numbers of the lower social classes, oppressed by the pashas and their Greek lackeys, fled across to Asia Minor during the nineteenth century, only to return again after the exchange of populations.

Social and economic **idiosyncrasies** persist: anyone who has attended one of the extended village *paniyíria* here, with music for hours on end and outdoor tables piled with food and drink, will not be surprised to learn that Lésvos has the highest alcoholism rate in Greece. Breeding livestock, especially **horses and donkeys**, remains disproportionately important, and traffic jams caused by mounts instead of parked cars are not unheard of – signs reading "Forbidden to Tether Animals Here" are still very much part of the picture, as are herds of apparently unattended donkeys wandering about. Much of the acreage in olives is still inaccessible to vehicles, and the harvest can only be hauled away by those donkeys – who are duly loaded en masse onto pick-up trucks to be transported to the point where the road fizzles out.

Until recently, another local quirk was a marked tendency to **vote Communist**, in part a reaction to the late medieval quasi-feudalism here, which lingered on in the share-cropping system which prevailed in the countryside until the 1930s. But the 1990s saw a shift to the right, with KKE incumbents being chucked out in favour of Néa Dhimokratía or PASOK candidates, though the KKE clawed back one of three seats in 1996, retaining it ever since. But whatever their politics, you'll find the islanders fairly religious, with old-fashioned (if occasionally rough-edged) manners and – by Greek-island standards – a strong sense of community. In contrast to certain neighbouring islands, infrastructure improvement projects do eventually get completed (depending on EU or Greek-state grants), and forests are well cared for, with permanent firebreaks backed up during dangerous seasons by 24-hour surveillance crews. As a result, Lésvos has in recent years had only one devastating blaze (above Plomári).

Getting around the island

Public **buses** tend to be scheduled for the benefit of locals attending school or running errands in the capital, not day-tripping tourists. Carrying out such excursions is next to impossible anyway, owing to the size of Lésvos – about 70km by 45km at its widest points – and the last few appalling roads (most others have been improved, along with their signposting). Moreover, island topography is complicated by the two deeply indented gulfs of Kallóní and Yéra, which means that going on public transport usually involves an obligatory change of bus at either Mytilíni, on the east shore, or at the town of Kallóní, in the middle of Lésvos. In short, it's best to decide on a base and stay there for at least a few days, exploring its immediate surroundings on foot or by rented vehicle. Scooters or even proper motorbikes make little impact on this huge island, and will certainly go for a spill on some of the rougher dirt roads.

A special word of warning: **road rage** is a conspicuous feature of Lésvos life – there were two driving-related killings in 1998 – so avoid provoking locals by impeding them in any fashion.

Mytilíni Town

MYTILÍNI, the port and capital, home to nearly 30,000, sprawls between and around two broad bays divided by a fortified promontory, and in Greek fashion often doubles as the name of the island itself. Many visitors are put off by the combination of urban bustle and (in the traditionally humbler northern districts) slight seediness, and contrive to leave as soon as possible; the town returns the compliment by in fact being a fairly impractical and occasionally expensive place to base yourself. However, there are several diversions to occupy you for a few hours, particularly the marketplace and a few museums, all located within a few minutes' walk of the waterfront.

Arrival, orientation and information

The airport has a single ATM in arrivals as well as three car rental booths (Europcar, Hertz, and one shared by Budget and Payless). There's no bus link, so a **taxi** for the 7km into Mytilíni Town is the usual shuttle method; most of the drivers have lived in Australia, and thus speak English (of a sort). As on Híos, there are two **bus stations**: the *iperastykó* (standard KTEL) buses leaving from a small station near Platía Konstandinopóleos at the southern end of the harbour, plus the *astykó* (blue bus) service departing from one corner of the enormous free public **car park** nearby (which you should use if driving, as there are no other easily available spaces in the centre). Elsewhere, the best single parking spot is the currently unrestricted loop-street next to the new archeological museum. Most of the facilities you'll need are located on the waterfront along **Pávlou Koundouriótou**, which wraps itself around the entire south harbour. **Ermoú** begins one block west of this and threads north through the heart of the marketplace. If you're driving, **8-Noemvríou** – starting just behind the ferry quay and passing both archeological galleries – is the quickest way to the northern harbour of Epáno Skála and beyond to the Mandamádhos road.

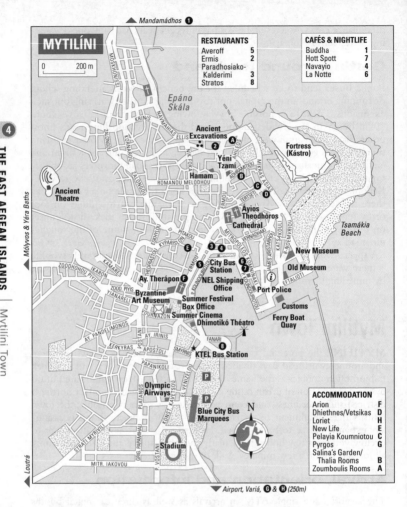

▲ *Mandamádhos* ❶

MYTILÍNI

0 — 200 m

RESTAURANTS
Averoff 5
Ermis 2
Paradhosiako-
  Kalderimi 3
Stratos 8

CAFÉS & NIGHTLIFE
Buddha 1
Hott Spott 7
Navayio 4
La Notte 6

Epáno Skála

Ancient Excavations

Fortress (Kástro)

Yéni Tzamí

Hamam

Ancient Theatre

Áyios Theodhóros Cathedral

Tsamákia Beach

New Museum

City Bus Station

Old Museum

Ay. Therápon

NEL Shipping Office

Port Police

Byzantine Art Museum

Summer Festival Box Office

Summer Cinema

Dhimotikó Théatro

Customs

Ferry Boat Quay

KTEL Bus Station

Olympic Airways

Blue City Bus Marquees

N

Stadium

ACCOMMODATION
Arion .... F
Dhiethnes/Vetsikas .... D
Loriet .... H
New Life .... E
Pelayia Koumniotou C
Pyrgos .... G
Salina's Garden/
  Thalia Rooms .... B
Zoumboulis Rooms .... A

▼ *Airport, Variá,* ❻ *&* ❽ *(250m)*

Before leaving town, you might visit the **EOT** regional headquarters at James Aristárhou 6 (Mon–Fri 8am–2.30pm; ☎22510 42511) to get hold of their excellent town and island maps, plus other brochures. However, the best island **map**, sometimes available locally, is Road Edition's no. 212 1:70,000 title "Lesbos", though road-surface ratings have not kept pace with ongoing works.

Accommodation

Finding **accommodation** can be initially daunting: the obvious waterfront hotels are noisy and exorbitantly priced. If you need to stay, it's preferable to hunt down budget rooms in the backstreets, especially between the castle and Ermoú, with supply usually exceeding demand. For better-value luxury, head towards the south of the town or even beyond the city limits, to Variá.

Centre and north of town

Dhiethnes/Vetsikas Yeoryíou Tertséti 1 ☏ 22510 24968. Relatively comfortable en-suite rooms in a side street off Mikrás Asías. ❷
New Life Rear of Olýmbou, cul-de-sac off Ermoú ☏ 22510 42650 or 693 22 79 057. Polished-wood-floored, en-suite rooms (some air con) in an old mansion with a garden, or similarly priced ones, but with bizarre modern murals, in the co-managed **Arion** down the street at Aríonos 4, Áyios Therápon church. ❸, also by the month
Pelayia Koumniotou Yeoryíou Tertséti 6 ☏ 22510 20643. Friendly, basic, non-en-suite rooms establishment. ❷
Salina's Garden Rooms Fokéas 7 ☏ 22510 42073. En-suite and very quiet rooms located near the Yéni Tzamí; kitchen facilities available. ❷
Thalia Rooms ☏ 22510 24640. Located across the street from *Salina's Garden Rooms* and under the same management – essentially its overflow. ❷
Zoumboulis Rooms Navmahías Ellís 11 ☏ 22510 29081, ☏ 22510 44204. En-suite, air-conditioned rooms in a modern building facing the water, but you may get some noise from traffic and the *kafenío* below. ❸

South of town

Loriet/Laureate At Variá shore, 4km south of town ☏ 22510 43111, ⓦ www.loriet-hotel.com. Lésvos' most sophisticated accommodation comprises a nineteenth-century mansion and modern wings, bracketing gardens and a 25m saltwater pool with a bar area. There's a wide variety of rooms, from blandly modern, marble-trimmed studios (less grim than they seem from outside) to massive suites in the "Big House" with retro decor and big bathrooms (plus three smaller ones under the roofline). Booking advisable year-round; on-site restaurant. Studios ❺, suites ❽
Pyrgos Eleftheríou Venizélou 49 ☏ 22510 25069, ⓦ www.pyrgoshotel.gr. The town's premier restoration accommodation, with utterly over-the-top kitsch decor in the common areas: Second Empire salon furniture, painted ceilings, the lot. However, the rooms are perfectly acceptable: most have a balcony, all differ in colour scheme, some have tubs in the baths and there are three round units in the tower. Also offers "American" breakfast and secure parking at the rear. ❼

The Town

The main street, **Ermoú**, links the town centre with the little-used north harbour and crumbled breakwater of Epáno Skála, following the course of a canal that used to join the two ports until the Byzantine era. Beginning at one of the more vivid **fish markets** in the Aegean, with flying fish, scorpion fish and other rarely seen species on sale, Ermoú forges north past several antique shops – now well picked over, so no longer the "Portobello Road" of the islands – and the roofless **Yéni Tzamí** (New Mosque), once heart of the Muslim quarter but now shut and derelict. Just a few steps east stands a superb Turkish **hamam**, restored in 2001 to its former glory but securely locked unless it's hosting a function. Between Ermoú and the castle lies a maze of atmospheric lanes lined with grandiose Belle Époque mansions and elderly vernacular houses, though most of the ornate town houses are to be found in the southerly districts of Sourádha and Kióski, on the way to the airport.

The town's skyline is dominated by two churches standing at opposite ends of the marketplace: the Germanic-Gothic spire of **Áyios Theodhóros** and the Sacré-Coeur-ish dome of **Áyios Therápon** are imposing if contrasting expressions of the nineteenth-century Ottoman–Greek bourgeoisie's post-Baroque taste. The interior decor of Áyios Therápon in particular seems more appropriate to an opera house than a church, with gilt aplenty in the vaulting and ornate column capitals.

The well-lit and well-laid-out **Byzantine Art Museum** (Mon–Sat 10am–1pm; €2), just opposite the entrance to Áyios Therápon, contains various icons rescued from rural island churches. The most noteworthy exhibit, and the oldest, is a fourteenth-century icon of Christ *Pandokrátor*; other highlights include a sultanic *firmáni* or grant of privileges to a local bishop, a rare sixteenth-century three-dimensional icon of *The Crucifixion* and a canvas of the *Kímisis (Assumption)* by Theophilos.

On the promontory between the bays sits the Byzantine-Genoese-Ottoman **fortress** (May–Sept Tues–Sun 8.30am–7pm; Oct–April Tues–Sun 8.30am–3pm; €2), its mixed pedigree reflected in the Ottoman-Turkish inscription immediately above the Byzantine double eagle at the southern outer gate. Inside you can make out the ruins, variously preserved, of the Gattilusi palace, a Turkish *medresse* (Koranic academy), a dervish cell and a Byzantine cistern. Just below the fortress, at **Tsamákia**, is the mediocre, fee-entry town "beach".

Tucked away on the westerly hill, and assiduously signposted, the **Hellenistic theatre** (unrestricted access) proves resoundingly anticlimactic on arrival; most of its masonry was pilfered for use in the castle, or reduced to plaster in Ottoman lime kilns.

The Archeological Museums

Mytilíni's excellent **archeological collection**, and the only real must-see in town, is housed in **two separate galleries** a few hundred metres apart. The newer, upper museum (Tues–Sun 8.30am–3pm; €3), about 200m up 8-Noemvríou, is devoted to finds from wealthy Roman Mytilene, in particular three rooms of well-displayed mosaics from second/third-century AD villas – highlights are a crude but engaging scene of Orpheus charming all manner of beasts, and two fishermen surrounded by clearly recognizable (and edible) sea creatures. Earlier eras are represented in the older wing (same hours, shared ticket with Roman wing), housed in a former mansion just behind the ferry dock. On the ground floor are Neolithic finds from Áyios Vartholoméos cave and Bronze Age Thermí, but the star exhibits, all from the late Classical period, are upstairs: a pair of acrobats, two *kourotrophoi* figures (goddesses suckling infants, predecessors of all Byzantine Galaktotrofoússa icons), children playing with a ball or dogs, and Aphrodite riding a dolphin. A specially built annexe at the rear contains stone-cut inscriptions of various edicts and treaties, plus a Roman sculpture of a drunken satyr asleep on a wineskin.

Eating and drinking

Dining options in Mytilíni have improved since a late 1990s nadir, when several of the more characterful old-style *ouzerís* and tavernas shut down in favour of fast-food joints, and there was hardly a sit-down meal to be had.

Averoff West quay, or back entrance at Ermoú 52. Run by the Kakambouras family since 1925, this is the town's classic *mayireftá* venue, doling out early-morning *patsás* (tripe soup) for those straight off a boat, and also where all and sundry have lunch before a late afternoon ferry departure. **Ermis** Kornárou 2, cnr Ermoú. Much the best of a cluster of *ouzerís* up at Páno Skála; a 1999 refit hasn't much affected its century-old decor (panelled ceiling, giant mirrors, faded oil paintings), or its claimed two centuries of purveying titbits to a jolly, mixed crowd in the pleasant courtyard. Better service than *Paradhosiako-Kalderimi* at comparable prices, and open daily (though restricted menu Sun). **Navayio** Arhipélagous 23 (the blue-bus square). The handiest place for a proper breakfast straight off the ferry; you can get omelettes, baked goodies and decent coffees. **La Notte** Koundouriótou 59. Strong on coffees, crêpes and pricey smoothies, plus a magnificent interior atrium occasionally hosting exhibits. **Paradhosiako-Kalderimi** Two adjacent premises in the bazaar at Thássou 2. The market characters' *ouzerí*, with the big plus its seating under the shade of vines. Large-portioned if plainly presented meals feature white beans, sardines and (in autumn) stuffed squash flowers. Closed Sun. **Stratos** Fanári quay, south end of port. The last, and marginally the best, in a series of touristy fish tavernas, and the only one that doesn't tout aggressively; also does grills and *mayireftá*.

Nightlife and entertainment

With an important university in residence, Mytilíni can offer decent **nightlife and entertainment**, especially along the northeast quay, which the student contingent have claimed as their own. Here, all in a row between Just Rent-a-Car and the NEL agency, you'll find *La Notte* (as described above) and the durable *Hott Spott* (with good music), plus a couple of others. The closest live music club is *Buddha*, in Karatepe district to the north. Formal live events constitute the Lesviakó Kalokéri **festival**, held in the castle or other venues from mid-July to late August. The summer **cinema** Pallas lies in between the post office and the park on Vournázon, plus there's a winter venue as well as a weekly cinema club of art films pitched at the university crowd.

Listings

Airlines Olympic offices are southwest of the bay and central park, at Kavétsou 44 (☎22510 28660); Aegean is only at the airport (☎22510 61120), but their tickets are sold through any travel agent.

Banks and exchange At least six banks along Koundouriótou have ATMs, plus there's a stand-alone one on the quay.

Car rental Most reputable agents cluster at the northeast corner of the harbour, on or just off Koundouriótou. Especially recommended is Payless at Koundouriótou 49 (also at the airport; ☎22510 43555, ☎automoto@otenet.gr), for good-condition cars and no surcharges on credit-card use. Alternatively, try Budget at no. 51 (☎22510 29600), Egeon at Híou 2 (☎22510 29 820), and Just at no. 53 (☎22510 43080). Further afield, there's Alpha in the alley off Koundouriótou 83 (☎22510 26113),

and Hertz at Koudourióti 87 (☎22510 37355), also at the airport (☎22510 61589) Off-peak rates for a B-category car should be maximum €33 day for four days or more. You may well find it cheaper to rent at the resort of your choice, but then you may not have the invaluable option of airport or ferry-dock drop-off upon departure.

Ferry/travel agencies All ferry and travel agencies are found along Koundouriótou. NEL has its own outlet at no. 47 (☎22510 28480), though their tickets (including the catamaran) can also be obtained from Dimakis Tours at no. 73 (☎22510 27865). Dimakis and Pan Tours at no. 89 (☎22510 46595) are the most reliable venues for any ferries running to Turkey, the latter also handling the *Nissos Limnos*, while Picolo Travel at no. 73a (☎22510 27000) handles GA Ferries.

Around Mytilíni

If you are based in Mytilíni, a few diversions lie within easy reach; of these, the Variá **museums** and the Loutrá Yéras **spa** are the most worthwhile.

North: Panayioúdha, Mória, Pýrgi Thermís

The coast road heading **north** from Mytilíni towards Mandamádhos (see p.428) follows a rather nondescript coastline, but offers startling views across the straits to Turkey. The most appealing spot en route is **PANAYIOÚDHA**, 8km away, with a church resembling a miniature Áyios Therápon, and waterside **tavernas** buzzing at weekends. The best, most popular and priciest of these is *Kostaras*, one of the first establishments you encounter coming from Mytilíni. At the far end of the flagstoned pedestrian quay, the simple *Akroyiali* is homier and also excellent value.

Just past Panayioúdha you can make a detour to **MÓRIA**, and thence to a valley 1km south, the site of a second-century-AD Roman **aqueduct** that used to bring water from the foothills of Mount Ólymbos; the eleven remaining spans of its 26-kilometre extent are intact to varying degrees, lofty and impressive. A little further along the coastal road at **PÁMFYLLA** and

PÝRGI THERMÍS you may glimpse various *pýrgi* (tower-mansions), relics of the nineteenth-century gentry. Also near Pýrgi Thermís stands the well-preserved, well-signposted Byzantine church of **Panayía Trouloti**, one of the few Byzantine monuments to escape Ottoman ravages. A small, domed, cross-in-square structure, built in stages from the ninth to fourteenth centuries, this may only have the narthex open, but through the door you glimpse extensive fresco fragments on the piers. Just 500m further at **PARALÍA THERMÍS**, the Roman/Byzantine **hamam** has been allowed to decay in favour of an ugly, sterile modern facility adjacent, though it still supplies the hot water, and you can stick your head in to admire the vaulted brickwork. You're a bit far (13km) from town here, but if you fancy a quiet stay there's a decent seafront B-class **hotel** back at Pyrgí, the *Votsala* (☎22510 71231, ⓦwww.votsalahotel.com; ➍), with watersports off the somewhat scrappy beach.

South: the Variá museums

Just south of town, on the road to the airport, you glimpse more tower-mansions at Khryssomaloússa and Aklidhíou. But the most rewarding targets in this direction are a pair of unlikely museums in the formerly elegant (and now overbuilt) village of **VARIÁ**, 5km from town; blue urban buses cover the distance every half an hour.

The Theophilos Museum

The **Theophilos Museum** (May–Sept Tues–Sun 9am–2.30pm & 5–8pm; Oct & April 9am–1pm & 4–6pm; Nov–March 9am–2pm; €2 admission includes key-catalogue), well signposted on the southern edge of Variá, honours this regional painter with five rooms of wonderful, little-known canvases specifically commissioned by his patron Thériade (see box opposite) during the years leading up to the artist's death. Theophilos' personal experience of pastoral Lésvos is evident in the wealth of accurate sartorial detail found in such elegiac scenes as fishing, reaping, olive-picking and baking. There are droll touches too, such as a cat slinking off with a fish in *The Fishmongers* (Room 2). The *Sheikh-ul-Islam* with his hubble-bubble (Room 2) seems drawn from life, as does a highly secular Madonna merely titled *Mother with Child* (also Room 2). As an ethnographic document, *The Albanian Dancer* (Room 5) is of most value. However, in classical scenes – such as *Sappho and Alkaeos* (Room 5), a landscape series of Egypt, Asia Minor and the Holy Land, and episodes from wars historical and contemporary – Theophilos was clearly on shakier ground; in the painting *Abyssinians Hunting an Italian Horseman* (Room 3), for instance, the subject has been conflated with New World Indians chasing down a conquistador. The sole concessions to modernity are the aeroplanes sketched in as an afterthought over various island landscapes.

The Thériade Museum

The **Thériade Museum** (Tues–Sun 9am–2pm & 5–8pm; €2), its palatial extent contrasting with the adjacent, cottage-like Theophilos Museum, is the brainchild of native son Stratis Eleftheriades (1897–1983). Leaving Mytilíni for Paris at the age of 18, he Gallicized his name to Thériade and went on to become a renowned avant-garde art publisher, persuading some of the leading artists of the twentieth century to participate in his ventures. The displays here comprise two floors worth of lithographs, engravings, wood-block prints and watercolours by the likes of Miró, Chagall, Picasso, Gris, Giacometti, Matisse, Le Corbusier, Léger, Rouault and Villon, either

> ## Theophilos Hadzimihaïl (1873–1934): the Rousseau of Greece?
>
> The "naïve" painter **Theophilos** Hadzimihaïl was born and died in Mytilíni Town, and both his eccentricities and talents were remarkable from an early age. After a failed apprenticeship as a shoemaker, he ran away to Smyrna, then to Mount Pílio on the Greek mainland in 1894 after allegedly killing a Turk. Wandering across the country from Pílio to Athens and the Peloponnese, Theophilos became one of the prize eccentrics of turn-of-the-century Greece, dressing up as Alexander the Great or various revolutionary war heroes, complete with *tsaroúhia* (pompommed shoes) and *fustanélla* (pleated skirt). A recluse who (it is claimed) neither drank, swore, smoked nor attended church, Theophilos was ill and living in severely reduced circumstances back on Lésvos when he was introduced to Thériade in 1919; the latter, virtually alone among critics of the time, recognized his peculiar genius and ensured that Theophilos was supported both morally and materially for the rest of his life.
>
> With their childlike perspective, vivid colour scheme and idealized mythical and rural subjects, Theophilos' works are unmistakable. Relatively few of his works survive today, because he executed commissions for a pittance on ephemeral surfaces such as *kafenío* counters, horsecarts, or the walls of long-vanished houses. Facile comparisons are often made between Theophilos and Henri Rousseau, the roughly contemporaneous French "primitive" painter. Unlike "Le Douanier", however, Theophilos followed no other profession, eking out a precarious living from his art alone. And, while Rousseau revelled in exoticism, Theophilos' work was principally and profoundly rooted in Greek mythology, history and daily life.

annotated by the painters themselves or commissioned as illustrations for the works of prominent poets and authors – an astonishing collection for a relatively remote Aegean island (albeit slightly depleted by a 1999 burglary), and one which deserves a leisurely perusal. Highlights include Miró's cheerfully lurid lithos for Alfred Jarry's *Ubu Roi* and *L'Enfance d'Ubu*, Matisse's *Jazz* series from 1947, Léger's uncompleted 1958 homage to Paris, *La Ville*, Chagall's surprisingly coarse, sometimes Brueghel-esque *Biblical Cycle* watercolours, and reproductions of illuminated medieval manuscripts from issues of *Verve*, the art quarterly which Thériade published from 1937 to 1971. There is also more by Theophilos, most notably *The Lion Wrestler* and *The Outdoor Barbers*.

Beaches: Haramídha and Áyios Ermoyénis

Beyond the airport and Krátigos village, a paved road loops around 9km more to the pebbly double beach of **Haramídha** (16km in total from town). The eastern bay has several **tavernas** – the best of these being *Theodhora Klava*, aka *Grioules*, with excellent home-style cooking encompassing onion *keftédhes* and smooth *khtipití* – and a medium-sized hotel. The western strand is marginally superior, but has no shade or facilities.

Remote as it seems, the more scenic double beach at **Áyios Ermoyénis**, 3km due west of Haramídha, can get very crowded at weekends with townees. The patron saint's chapel perches on the cliff separating two small, sandy coves from a larger, less usable easterly bay accessed by a separate track; there's a popular taverna by the parking area. If you're driving from Mytilíni, the most direct (13km) paved road is via Loutrá village, or you can brave a bit of scenic dirt track between Taxiárhes village above Variá, emerging just south of Loutrá.

Loutrá Yéras

For other pleasant immersions near Mytilíni, it's worth heading for **Loutrá Yéras**, 8km west along the main road to Kallóni. Just the thing after a sleepless night on a malodorous ferry, these **public hot springs** (daily: June–Sept 8am–7pm; Oct & April–May 8am–6pm; Nov–March 9am–5pm; €2.50) – the best appointed on the island – feature three marble spouts feeding 38°C water into a marble pool in a vaulted chamber; there are separate facilities for each sex (ladies have only two spouts, but pool size is comparable), and skinny-dipping is, unexpectedly in prudish Greece, obligatory. A seasonal café (weekends only off season) on the roof of the bathhouse overlooks the gulf.

Southern Lésvos

The southernmost portion of Lésvos is indented by two great inlets, the gulfs of **Kallóni** and **Yéra**. The former curves in a northeasterly direction, the latter northwesterly, creating a fan-shaped peninsula at the heart of which is pine-cloaked, 967-metre-high **Mount Ólymbos**. Both shallow gulfs are in turn almost landlocked by virtue of very narrow outlets to the open sea, which don't have – and probably never will have – bridges spanning them. This is some of the most verdant and productive territory on Lésvos; the best oil-bearing olives are grown here, and the stacks of pressing mills, many still functioning, are a familiar sight on the skyline.

Pérama

With its mostly abandoned industrial structures dedicated to the olive-oil and tanning trade, **PÉRAMA** is still one of the larger places on the Gulf of Yéra, and has a regular daytime **kaïki-ferry** service (no cars but two-wheelers OK; €1 per foot passenger) linking it with Koundouroudhiá and blue city buses to and from Mytilíni on the far side.

A more likely reason to show up is to patronize one of the better **taverna-ouzerís** (open all year) in the region: *Balouhanas*, northernmost of a line of eateries on the front, with a wooden, cane-roofed balcony jutting out over the water. The name's a corruption of *ballkhane* or "fish-market" in Turkish, and seafood is a strong point, whether grilled or made into croquettes, as are regional starters like *giouzlemés* (cheese-stuffed fried crêpe) and homemade desserts.

Plomári

Due south of Mount Ólymbos and perched on the edge of the "fan", **PLOMÁRI** is the only sizeable coastal settlement in the south, and indeed the second largest town on Lésvos. It presents an unlikely juxtaposition of scenic appeal and its famous *oúzo* distilling industry; among several local brands, Varvayianni is the most famous, but Yiannatsi and Arvanitou are reckoned nearly as good. They can all be sampled at the phenomenal number of **traditional kafenía** – especially the vine-shrouded one on central Platía Beniamín – interspersed with a few more contemporary bars, which crowd the old marketplace around the central plane tree.

The local *paniyíri* season kicks off in mid-July with an **oúzo festival**, and culminates towards the end of the month in celebrations honouring Áyios Harálambos and including such rural activities as horse races (but no longer, apparently, a bull sacrifice).

Oúzo!

Oúzo is the Greek version of a grape-mash spirit found across the Mediterranean from Lebanon to France. The fermented residue of grape skins, pips and stalks left after wine-pressing, called *stémfyla* in Greek, is boiled in a copper still. *Oúzo* was unknown until late medieval times, since before the perfection of copper-sheet technology such spirits could not be mass-produced. The resulting distillate was known under the Ottomans as *rakí*; its popularity grew during the nineteenth century, when shortages at distilleries in Smyrna, Constantinople and Lésvos tempted the unscrupulous to concoct pseudo-*rakí* by simply dumping pure grain alcohol into flavoured water. This was countered by the official, compulsory addition of dye to incoming alcohol shipments, necessitating distillation to remove it.

The modern term *oúzo* probably derives from the Italian *uso Massalia*, used to tag early shipments leaving the Ottoman empire for Marseille. Today it means a *rakí* base flavoured with various aromatic spices, usually star anise or fennel; exact flavourings and proportions are closely guarded secrets of each distiller. Bottled *oúzo*'s alcohol content varies from 38 percent to 48 percent, with 44 percent strength considered the minimum for any quality. It is illegal to bottle *oúzo* at more than 50 percent strength – the risk of explosion is too great – though you may find homemade *oúzo* in wooden barrels at such strengths. Mediocre commercial *oúzo* is often fortified with molasses, or even alcohol, as in Ottoman days. *Oúzo* has the harmless property of turning milky white when water or ice cubes are added; this results from the binding of anethole, an aromatic compound found in both fennel and anise.

Practicalities

Plomári is linked to Mytilíni by a direct **bus** route, which runs past the pretty villages of Paleókipos, Papádhos and Skópelos (as well as Áyios Isídhoros resort); if you have your own two-wheeler, you can cut the journey time slightly by using the *kaḯki*-ferry between Koundouroudhiá and Pérama.

Despite a resounding lack of good beaches in the immediate vicinity, Plomári is besieged in summer, but you can usually find a **room** (they are prominently signposted) at the edge of the charmingly dilapidated old town, which fills both sides of the Sidhoúndas ravine. Your best bet for an on-spec vacancy, above the inland Platía Beniamín, is the welcoming *Pension Lida* (T & F 22520 32507, E ledabiotravel@hotmail.com; ❷), a fine restoration inn occupying adjacent old mansions, with sea-view balconies for most units. Another quiet, attractive area for budget lodging is the western suburb of **Ammoudhélli**, 1km along the road to Melínda, poised above a church and little fine-gravel **beach**; examples here include *Irini Rooms* (T 22520 32875; ❷) and *Marcia Rooms* (T 22520 32755; ❸).

Prospects for a decent **meal** in or around Plomári are somewhat limited; a string of several waterfront tavernas are uniformly mediocre, with the honourable exception of *Berdema*, at the east end of the harbour square, a reliable and long-established venue for fairly elaborate *mezédhes* and casserole dishes. Ammoudhélli can offer the shambolic but friendly *Tò Ammoudhelli* (summer only), perched over the beach; skip the touristy printed menu and ask for the dishes of the day (eg *ambelofásola*, sardines) and *orektiká* such as *tyrokafterí* and grilled octopus. Rounding out the list of Plomári's vital amenities are two **bank** ATMs and a **post office** on the shoreline road.

Most tourists actually stay in **ÁYIOS ISÍDHOROS**, 3km east, essentially a cluster of hotels at the west end of a long, fine-pebble beach. Pick of the **hotels** here is the C-class *Pebble Beach* (T 22520 31651, F 22520 31566; ❹), managed by Evangelia Saropoulou, who grew up in Connecticut. Most of the large rooms (avoid those near the bar if you crave sleep) overlook the beach, where a boardwalk crosses a bit of reef; there's also a ground-floor restaurant, on-site **car rental**, a saltwater pool and a few sports facilities (including the municipal footie grounds next door). **Eating** out locally, the clear winner is *Taverna tou Panaï* (all year) at the rear of an olive grove just by the northerly "Áyios Isídhoros" town limits sign; here you'll find big, no-nonsense portions of meat, seafood and *mayireftá* dishes, and mostly Greeks in attendance.

Melínda, Panayía Kryftí and Tárti

Given the dearth of good beaches within walking distance, tourism supremos in Plomári promote **boat trips** to various better ones along the southwest coast. But of course there's nothing stopping you getting there under your own steam. The closest is **MELÍNDA**, 6km west of Plomári by paved road, a 700-metre sand-and-pebble **beach** at the mouth of a canyon choked with olive trees. The only real backpackers' resort on Lésvos, it's an alluring place, with sweeping views west towards the Vaterá coast and the cape of Áyios Fokás, and south (in clear conditions) to northern Híos, Psará and the Turkish Karaburun peninsula.

One of the best local excursions is to the **hot springs** at **Panayía Kryftí**. From the first curve of the paved road up to Paleohóri, a dirt track goes 2.2km to a dead end with parking space, with the final 300m on a downhill path to the little chapel just above a protected inlet. On the far side of this you'll see a rectangular cement tank, just big enough for two people, containing water at a pleasant 37–38° C.

Development at Melínda hamlet just behind the beach consists of several **taverna/rooms** outfits, of which easternmost *Maria's* (☎22520 93239; ❶) is an endearingly ramshackle place with simple but reasonably priced food and non-en-suite lodging; for more comfort try *Melinda* (aka Dhimitris Psaros; ☎22520 93234; ❷), at the west end of the strand by the monolith, offering a more elaborate menu and en-suite rooms (some with fridge and air con), or *Melinda Studios* towards mid-beach (☎22520 93282; ❷), a mix of gaily painted sea- and garden-view units with good-standard bathrooms.

Even more unspoilt (thanks to a formerly dreadful 10km side road in, now paved except for the last 3km), **TÁRTI**, some 22km in total from Plomári, is a 400-metre-wide cove where Lésvos hoteliers and restaurant owners take *their* holidays. Rocky capes gird it to either side, and for once the bay here deserves its blue-flag rating. Of the three beachfront **tavernas** here, two work late into September; **rooms** (eg those of Vangellis Asmanis, ☎22510 83577; ❷) flank the final approach road.

Ayiássos

AYIÁSSOS, nestled in a remote, wooded valley under the crest of Mount Ólymbos, is the most beautiful hill town on Lésvos, its narrow cobbled streets lined by ranks of tiled-roof houses. Its Shangri-la quality is heightened on the more usual northerly approach from Mytilíni Town, 26km away, which gives no clue of the enormous village until you see huge knots of parked cars at the southern edge of town (where the bus drops you).

Don't be put off by the endless ranks of kitsch wooden and ceramic souvenirs or carved "Byzantine" furniture, aimed mostly at Greeks, but continue uphill to the old marketplace, with its *kafenía*, yogurt shops and butcher stalls. Regrettably, multiple video-game arcades have marred the traditional ambience, but in certain cafés, bands of *sandoúri*, with clarinet, lap-drum and violin, may still play on weekend afternoons, accompanying spontaneous, inebriated dance performances on the cobbles outside.

The central church of the **Panayía Vrefokratoússa**, whose interior is lit by an improbable number of hanging *kandília* (oil lamps) – now electrified for safety reasons – was built in the twelfth century to house a wonder-working icon supposedly painted by the Evangelist Luke. With such a venerable icon as a focus, the local **festival** on August 15 is one of the liveliest in Greece (let alone Lésvos), and vividly illustrates the country-fair element in a traditional *paniyíri*, where pilgrims come to buy and sell as well as perform devotions. Stalls in the foundations of the sanctuary are leased year-round to small busi-nesses – a practice with age-old Greek antecedents, though currently far more common in Turkey. Ayiássos also takes **Carnival** very seriously; there's a club dedicated to organizing it, opposite the post office.

The Mylélia water mill

If you're headed for Ayiássos with your own car, you might consider a stop at the **Mylélia water mill**, whose inconspicuously signposted access track takes off 1km west of the turning for Ípios village. The name means "place of the mills", and there were once several hereabouts, powered by water brought by aqueduct from the same spring at Karíni up-valley that fed the Roman aque-duct at Mória (see p.403). The last survivor (open daily 9am–6pm), restored to working order in the mid-1990s, has thankfully not been twee-ified in the least; the keeper will show you the millrace and paddle wheel, as well as the flour making its spasmodic exit, after which you're free to buy gourmet pastas (pricey; consider the mark-up a donation), at the adjacent shop.

Practicalities

To reach Ayiássos from Mytilíni you have a choice of several daily **buses**. Access from Plomári is slightly more complicated; there's asphalt road and public transport only as far as Megalohóri, good dirt surface and your own conveyance thereafter up to some air-force radar balls where pavement resumes. The area between Megalohóri and the summit ridge was severely charred by a forest fire in 1994 and, though the road was unaffected, the countryside's appeal has been dented – until you cross the watershed with its military installations, and dense woods of unscathed oak and chestnut take over from scorched pine.

Ayiássos' best **restaurants** are *Dhouladhelli*, on your left as you enter the village from the extreme south (bus-terminal) end, or the idiosyncratic, after-dark *Ouzerí To Stavrí*, at the extreme north end of main thoroughfare 28-Oktovríou 1944 in Stavrí district, its walls bedaubed with maxims in local dialect.

Polikhnítos and around

A different bus route from Mytilíni leads to the inland village of **POLIKHNÍ-TOS**, also accessible from Kallóni by a paved short-cut road via Akhladherí. There are a few cafés and *barákia* around the central junction, but these are largely monopolized by conscripts from the huge nearby army camp. The main potential point of interest for outsiders is a restored **spa** 1.5km east of Políkhnitos (daily: July & Aug 9am–1pm & 5–8pm; spring & autumn 9am–1pm & 4–6pm; €2), with separate, pink-tinted domed bath chambers of iron-laced water for each sex. More attractive are the **hot springs** of **Áyios Ioánnis**, fairly well signposted 3km below the village of **LISVÓRI**, in turn

4km east of Políkhnitos, but also more directly accessible via an unmarked, 1.7-kilometre dirt road taking off from the main highway 500m east of an emergency military runway which crosses it. Flanking the eponymous chapel beside the stream here are two pools housed in unlocked, whitewashed, vaulted chambers (the left–hand, easterly one's nicer), with 40° C water and no dress code once inside. Bring candles or a torch at night, though a keeper is usually on hand to switch on the lights (€2 fee).

Skála Polikhnítou and Nyfídha

From Políkhnitos, a paved road leads 4km northwest to **SKÁLA POLIKHNÍ- TOU**, a pleasantly scruffy place with an uninspiring beach but an embarrass- ment of choice in **tavernas** located behind its prettified quay and open most of the year. At the north end of things, on the way to the saltworks, *T'Asteria* purveys *mayireftá*, while *Akroyiali* and *Iliovasilema* do fish. Skála has one unusual **accommodation** option: *Soft Tourism*, run by Lefteris and Erika (☎22520 42678 or 693 79 25 435; ❷). They generally host special–interest groups April to June, and in September, but especially welcome independent travellers during July and August.

Veering left on the approach road to Skála takes you after 5km to **NYFÍDHA**, which has a better, kilometre-long beach (though periodically beset by north winds) and just a few of **tavernas**, of which *Ouzeri Yiotis* at mid-beach and nearby *Exohiko Kendro O Grigoris* are the most reliable.

Vaterá and Vrýssa

The actual end of the Polikhnítos bus route, 9km south via the attractive village of Vrýssa, and 55km in total from the port, is **VATERÁ**. The seven-kilometre- long, sandy **beach** here, backed by vegetated hills and looking out to Turkey, Híos and Psará, offers some of the warmest, cleanest swimming on Lésvos. There's no direct coastal road between Vaterá and Melínda, and never will be, though you can follow an indirect inland route as described on opposite.

The Vaterá area hit the Greek news in 1997 when an Athenian paleontolo- gist, Michael Dermitzakis, confirmed what farmers unearthing bones had long suspected when he announced that the area was a treasure trove of **fossils**, including the bones of two-million-year-old gigantic horses, mastodons, monkeys and tortoises, the latter the size of a Volkswagen Beetle. Until 20,000 years ago, Lésvos (like all other east Aegean islands) was joined to the Asian mainland, and the gulf of Vaterá was a subtropical freshwater lake; the animals in question came to drink, died nearby and were trapped and preserved by successive volcanic flows. In **VRÝSSA**, the University of Athens has set up a **Natural History Collection** in the former girl's school (daily 9.30am–5pm; €1) dedicated to the paleontological finds – it's not exactly required viewing as presently organized, but a new, more extensive gallery is promised.

Practicalities

Development at Vaterá straggles for several kilometres to either side of the central T-junction; near the west end of the strip is one of the very few consistently attended and professionally run **hotels**, C-class *Vatera Beach Hotel* (☎22520 61212, ❻www.our-lesvos.com; ❺, but ❹ if booked on website; open Easter to early Oct), whose well-appointed rooms have fridges and air condi- tioning. It also has a good attached restaurant with home-grown produce and shoreline tables from which you can gaze out to the cape of **Áyios Fokás**, 3km west, where only foundations and broken column stubs remain of a temple of Dionysos with a superimposed early Christian basilica. The little tamarisk-shaded anchorage here has an acceptable **fish taverna**, *Akrotiri/Angelerou*, better than any of the several independent eateries at Vaterá proper, but not quite so good as those at Skála Polikhnítou.

The local **campsite** *Dionysos Club* (☎22520 61151; June–Sept), a walled compound with chalets as well as a pool, lies some way inland from the portion of Vaterá beach east of the main T-junction, where seasonal villas and apartments for locals predominate. In any season a handful of beach bars attempt to provide a semblance of **nightlife**.

If you intend to stay anywhere in Vaterá you'll certainly want your own transport, since the closest fully stocked shops are at Polikhnítos (there are a few "mini-markets" at Vaterá) and the bus appears rarely. You can **rent cars** from Alfa (☎22520 61132), near the T-junction.

East from Vaterá

Once past the *Hotel Irini* at the extreme east end of the strip, the beach ends and the seafront road veers inland up a river valley to Káto Stavrós, where the paved road ends. Ambelikó, the next village east on the hillside, can be reached via a paved road from the north, but the way in from Káto Stavrós is along a rough dirt track. The onward route to Akrássi, Megalohóri and Melínda is now paved (barring one short patch), allowing you to reach Melínda from Vaterá in about an hour in an ordinary car.

From Akrássi, a seven-plus-kilometre dirt track descends to the island's remotest coastal settlement, **Paralía Dhrótas**, a collection of shacks behind a coarse-pebble shore. Electric power arrived here (and in the inland village of Dhróta, 1km before) only in 1996, and it's the sort of place, with its near-Third World squalor, that makes you understand how the northeast Aegean got its poverty rating (see p.323) from the EU. Though the scenery is grand enough, there's no joy here except for a seasonal snack-bar that charges what it likes; given the state of the road, it wouldn't be much slower (one and a half hours) to walk in from Vaterá along the coast.

Western Lésvos

The main road **west of Loutrá Yéras** is surprisingly devoid of settlement, with little of interest before you glimpse the Gulf of Kalloní. The nondescript, eponymous town at its head is the gateway to a mostly treeless, craggy region whose fertile valleys offer a sharp contrast to the bare ridges. River mouths form little oases behind a handful of beaches which account for the existence of **resorts** like Skála Kallonís, Sígri and Skála Eressoú. A group of **monasteries** lining the road west of Kalloní, in addition to occasionally striking inland villages, provide architectural interest.

Kalloní and Skála Kallonís

KALLONÍ itself is an unembellished agricultural and market town more or less in the middle of the island, 41km from Mytilíni. You may pause here since it's the intersection of most bus routes, and has plenty of shops, including pharmacies and several **banks** with ATMs.

With time to spare, you might make the three-kilometre detour south to **SKÁLA KALLONÍS**, Lésvos' fifth-ranking package resort. Besides a long, coarse-sand beach on the lakelike gulf, there are a half-dozen **hotels** here, more comfortable than most at Vaterá, Skála Eressoú or Plomári. They're located west of town to the edge of the salt marsh, which attracts hundreds of **bird-watchers** during the March-to-May nesting season. Pick of the **accommodation** here is the human-scale bungalow complex *Malemi* (☎22530 22594, ☏22530 22838, ✉malemi@otenet.gr; ⑨), with a variety of units from doubles to family suites, attractive grounds, tennis court and a large pool. **Tavernas** lining the quay with its fishing fleet are generally indistinguishable – though the locals themselves tend to favour *Mimi's*, on the square just inland. Most offer the gulf's celebrated *sardhélles pastés*, sardines marinated in lemon and salt crystals for a day; an annual festival the first week of August celebrates this delicacy. From late summer through early autumn, you'll also find the sardines deliciously grilled fresh; high levels of plankton in the gulf are claimed to be the reason for their extraordinary tastiness. Local **sports facilities** include pedal-bike rental – ideal for the flat terrain hereabouts – and kayak rental near the hotel cluster.

Mésa temple, Kremastí bridge and Halinádhou basilica

Signposted about 1km east of the Akhladherí short cut (see p.409), some 14km east of Kallóni, are the traces of an ancient **Aphrodite temple** (currently closed for excavations) at **MÉSA** (aka Méson). At the site, marked by two great oaks and ringed by grain fields on a gentle slope, just the original eleventh-century BC foundations and a few later column stumps remain, plus the ruins of a fourteenth-century Genoese basilica built within; it was once virtually on the sea but a nearby stream has silted things up in the intervening millennia.

Some 7km west of Mésa, back towards Kallóni, lies the turning for **AYÍA PARASKEVÍ**, an appealing tableau of nineteenth-century bourgeois architecture, with its central crossroads flanked by an inordinate number of *kafenía* and shops – plus a Muslim structure of uncertain function opposite the town hall. The place is famed for its **bull-sacrifice rite** on Pentecost Saturday (seven weeks after Orthodox Easter, usually late May/early June), a festival also accompanied by less sanguinary horse-racing.

Another, perhaps more compelling, reason to pass through is to visit the Genoese-built **Kremastí bridge**, the largest and best preserved medieval bridge in the east Aegean. This stands 3km west of Ayía Paraskeví, beside a dirt road that branches off from the main paved onward road to Nápi (head straight through the central junction). This is slightly easier to find from the Kallóni–Mólyvos road; 3.7km south from the turn-off to Stýpsi, bear left (east) onto the dirt track signposted "Ayía Paraskeví 7km", then continue 4.3km – the bridge is obvious just to the north.

An equally worthwhile monument, the early Christian **Halinádhou basilica**, lies just over 5km east of Ayía Paraskeví on a dirt road, patchily signposted from the central crossroads (turn right, coming from the Kallóni road). Nearly a dozen columns of this three-aisled basilica remain standing, some with their capitals – a peaceful spot amidst a wilderness of pines and olives, which prompts speculation as to why it was built just here, as it was clearly never the *katholikón* of a monastery. Naturally the masonry is of a piece with the surrounding basalt boulders on the adjacent, pine-tufted ridge.

Limónos and Myrsiniotíssis monasteries

West of Kallóni, the road winds 4km uphill to the **monastery of Limónos**, (re)founded in 1527 by the monk Ignatios. Just a handful of monks and lay workers maintain this huge, rambling complex, comprising three storeys of cells around a vast, plant-filled courtyard; the north wing, where Ignatios' cell is preserved as a shrine, is the oldest section. The eighteenth-century *katholikón*, with contemporary frescoes, an elaborately painted carved-wood ceiling and archways, is built in Asia Minor style and is traditionally off limits to women. A sacred spring flows from the church's south foundation wall; men can request a look at the church interior when they visit the ecclesiastical collection.

A former abbot established a **museum** (daily 9.30am–6pm, may close 3pm low season; €1.50) on two floors of the west wing. The ground-floor ecclesiastical collection is, alas, the only wing open as of writing, with the more interesting upstairs ethnographic gallery off limits indefinitely. Content yourself with an overflow of farm implements stashed in a corner storeroom below at the northwest corner of the compound, next to a chamber where giant *pithária* (urns) for grain and olive oil are embedded in the floor. Just west, through a gateway, the pilgrims' inn and an old-age home share space with peacocks and an aviary.

Crowds of Greeks at Limónos can get overwhelming in season; for a contrasting experience, stop in at the nearby **monastery of Myrsiniotíssis** (8am–1pm & 3pm–sunset) just down the road, with its own access drive from the Kalloní–Mólyvos highway leading up a pine-fringed hillside site. There's nothing in particular to see – the *katholikón* was rebuilt in 1912 – just well-kept buildings and carefully tended gardens; the resident nuns do embroidery and distill rosewater.

Hill villages of the west

Beyond Limónos, the road heading west passes through **FÍLIA**, with its truncated minaret and pre-1923 mosque, where you can turn off for a broad, paved short cut to Skoutáros and the north of Lésvos. Most traffic continues through to the unusually neat village of **SKALOHÓRI**, with another battered minaret and houses stacked in tiers at the head of a valley facing the sea and the sunset. You can get up close to the water by following a dirt track from the north edge of the village about 3km to **Kálo Limáni**, meaning "Good Harbour", precisely that to the east side of an isthmus-hamlet; to the west, there's a somewhat exposed, limited sandy beach and a cult **taverna-bar**, *Ta Kokkina*, with a good menu of Greek music.

From Skalohóri you can alternatively head on to **VATOÚSSA**, the most landlocked but also the most beautiful of the western settlements. Its upper quarter – away from the through-road, with a few *kafenía* for refreshment – can offer a **folk museum** (no set hours) in the ancestral mansion of Grigorios Gogos, with exhibits ranging from old books and archival photos to ethnographic items.

From the edge of Vatoússa a paved, narrow road continues 7km to **HÍDHIRA**, remarkable mainly for its **Methymneos Winery** (daily July–Sept 9am–6pm, otherwise by appointment on ☎22530 51518; ⓦwww .methymneos.gr). Lesvian wines were highly esteemed in antiquity, but the local *krassostáfylo* grape succumbed to phylloxera between the world wars and was only revived by the Lambou family in 1985. Because of the altitude (300m) and sulphur-rich soil (you're in the caldera of Órdhymnos volcano), their velvety, high-alcohol, oak-aged red can be produced organically. Proprietor Ioannis Lambou gives a highly worthwhile twenty-minute tour of the state-of-the-art premises, in English.

Perivolís monastery

Some 8km beyond Vatoússa, a short track leads down to the sixteenth-century **monastery of Perivolís** (daily 8am–1hr before sunset; donation, no photos; pull on the bell-rope in the tree for admission if necessary), built in the midst of a riverside orchard (*perivóli*). Feeble electric light is available to view fine if damp-damaged frescoes in the narthex, which an elderly caretaker may explain to you. On the south wall, in an apocalyptic panel worthy of Bosch (*The Earth and Sea Yield Up Their Dead*), the Whore of Babylon rides her chimera, and assorted sea monsters disgorge their victims; just to the right, towards the main door, the Magi approach the Virgin Enthroned with the Christ Child. On the north side you see a highly unusual iconography of *Abraham, the Virgin, and the Penitent Thief of Calvary in Paradise*, with the mythical Four Rivers of Paradise gushing forth under their feet; just right of this are assembled the Hebrew kings of the Old Testament.

Ándissa and around

ÁNDISSA, 3km beyond Perivolís, nestles attractively under the only pine grove in the west of the island. At the edge of the village a sign implores you to "Come Visit our (Central) Square", not a bad idea for the sake of several *kafenía* and tavernas sheltering under three sizeable plane trees.

Directly below Ándissa, a paved road leads 6km north towards the fishing village of **GAVATHÁS**, with a shortish, partly sheltered beach and a bare handful of places to eat and stay – principally the friendly *Pension Restaurant Paradise* (℡22530 56376; ❷; May to early Oct), serving good fish and locally grown vegetables, or the *Tsolias Taverna* behind the beach. A side road leads one headland east to the huge, duney, surf-battered beach of **Kámbos**. You can keep going in the same direction, following signs pointing to "Ancient Antissa", though they actually lead you through fields of irrigated vetch and clover to **Ovriókastro**, the most derelict of the island's Genoese castles, evocatively placed on a promontory in plain sight of Mólyvos and with a good stretch of coast to either side. In legend the head of Orpheus, torn off by Thracian Maenads, was washed ashore here with his lyre, still singing – and imparting lyric gifts to the first islanders. The exposed, part-pebble, often dirty beaches here are decidedly unlyrical, though a nearby fish **taverna** works seasonally.

In the opposite direction from behind Gavathás beach, an inconspicuous but initially paved road leads up to the hillside oasis village of **LIÓTA** (officially Lygerí on some maps), with a small Byzantine chapel and two simple summertime **tavernas** nearby. From near the chapel, the road (now dirt) continues to the vastly sandy, but lonely (no facilities) and seaweed-littered beach of **Lápsarna**, from where it's 9km back to Ándissa.

Ipsiloú monastery

Just west of modern Ándissa there's an important junction. Keeping straight leads you past the turning for the monastery of **Ipsiloú**, founded in 1101 atop an outrider of the extinct volcano of Órdhymnos to the east, and still home to four monks. The *katholikón*, tucked in one corner of a large, irregular courtyard, has a fine wood-lattice ceiling, but its frescoes were repainted to detrimental effect in 1992. More intriguing are the bits of Iznik tiles stuck into the facade, and the exquisite double gateway. Upstairs you can visit a fairly rich **museum** of ecclesiastical treasure (sporadically open mornings only; donation in exchange for a postcard). Ipsiloú's patron saint is St John the Theologian, a frequent dedication for monasteries overlooking apocalyptic landscapes like the surrounding parched, boulder-strewn hills, some of the most desolate terrain in Greece.

The petrified "forest"

Signposted some 4km west of the monastery is the paved, five-kilometre side road to the main concentration of Lésvos' rather overrated **petrified "forest"** (daily: June–Sept 8am–sunset; rest of year closes 3pm; €2), indicated by placards which also warn of severe penalties for pilfering souvenir chunks. On an east-facing slope, this fenced-in reserve of the best specimens can be toured by a total of 3km in walkways. For once, contemporary Greek arsonists cannot be blamed for the state of the trees, created by the combined action of volcanic ash from Órdhymnos and hot springs between 15 and 20 million years ago. The mostly horizontal sequoia trunks average a metre or less in length, though there are a few two- to three-metre-long behemoths as featured in promotional posters.

Sígri

SÍGRI, near the western tip of Lésvos, has an appropriately end-of-the-line feel, accentuated by the general stagnation of tourism throughout the island. The town, a somewhat drab mix of traditional and modern cement dwellings, has limited prospects as a resort owing to its remoteness, though Sígri's role as a NATO naval base has been scaled down considerably from the early 1990s, when battleships could be seen moored in the superb harbour. The bay is guarded by a small castle and the long island of **Nissiopí**, which stretches across its mouth and acts as a buffer to the prevailing winds.

The eighteenth-century Ottoman **castle** sports a *tuğra* (the sultan's monogram) over its entrance; rarely seen outside Istanbul, this was a token of the high regard in which productive Lésvos (and specifically strategic Sígri) was held. The vaguely Turkish-looking **church of Ayía Triádha** overlooking the quay is in fact a converted **mosque**, with a huge water cistern taking up the ground floor by the belfry; this supplied, among other things, the half-ruined *hamam* just south.

In 2004, the **Natural History Museum of the Lesvos Petrified Forest** (daily: May 15–Oct 14 8am–8pm; Oct 15–May 14 8am–4pm; €2; ⓦwww .petrifiedforest.gr) opened at the edge of Sígri, encompassing a "geopark" of outdoor specimens, as well as worthy exhibits on the formation and paleobotany of the forest.

The nearest of several **beaches**, south of the castle headland, is somewhat narrow and backed by a little-used road to Eressós; the far superior one of **Faneroméni** lies 3.5km north by a coastal dirt track from the northern outskirts of town. This beach is long and scenic, but there are no facilities to hand, and non-4WD vehicles will founder in the sand of the frontage "road". A shorter but equally good strand, **Liména**, can be found 2km south of Sígri at another creek mouth, just off the rough one-lane, fifteen-kilometre track to Eressós (passable with care in an ordinary car most years, in 35min).

Practicalities

Most people staying at Sígri are British clients of Direct Greece and Sunvil, two small, specialist operators who have tried to make a go of selling holidays here. **Accommodation** likely to have on-spec vacancies include *Nelly's Rooms and Apartments* (☎22530 54230; ❸), overlooking the castle, and the nearby *Rainbow Studios* (℡ 22530 54310; ❸). Among several tavernas, the best all-rounder, just inland, is Italian-run, ultra-hygienic *Una Faccia Una Razza* (April to mid-Oct), with lovely grilled garlicky vegetables, creative salads, pizza, pasta, grilled seafood and an Italian wine list. The *Australia*, a bit seaward, has the Greek standards and an enviable position under the tamarisks. For **night-life**, look no further than *Notia* (June–Sept), a congenial jazz bar with a loyal following since 1993.

❹ Eressós and Skála Eressoú

The southerly option of the T-junction between Ándissa and Ipsiloú leads in just under 10km to the inland town of **ERESSÓS**. This is home to a large colony of expatriates who have bought or rented property, and a stroll along lanes flanked by the vernacular houses is rewarding during the cooler hours of the day.

During summer, half the population is down at the idyllic beach resort of **SKÁLA ERESSOÚ**, 4km further south, only resettled halfway through the nineteenth century after medieval piracy prompted the settlement of Eressós. Behind Skála stretches the largest and most attractive agricultural plain on Lésvos, a welcome green contrast to the volcanic ridges above. The three-kilometre beach here, given additional character by an islet within easy swimming distance, can match Vaterá's for quality; despite this, seasons either side of the millennium saw a sharp decline in Skála's fortunes, with few tour operators staying for successive years. Attempts to boost the place as a family resort have been stymied by its enduring reputation as the premier **lesbian watering hole** of Europe, engendered by a purported connection with Sappho and helped along by some sensational documentaries on UK television. Lesbians remain the most consistent and loyal customers, so locals are reluctant to bite the hand that feeds, though there was considerable annoyance about an autumn 2000 tour organized by London gay venue *Candy Bar*, whose salacious publicity, not exactly intended for island consumption, got "leaked" to the villagers. All that said, high summer still sees an odd mix of north European neo-hippies and Greek families putting in an appearance alongside those of the Sapphic persuasion.

Accommodation

Skála has countless **rooms** and **apartments**, but those near the sea fill early in the day or are block-booked by tour companies. Other vacancies – like those touted at the bus stop – can be attributed to the fairly appalling standard of some units. In peak season, the best and quietest rooms tend to be inland, overlooking a garden or fields. Since 2001, all but one package company have dropped the resort, citing a lack of commitment to "family values" – that's to say, the radical lesbian contingent was a bit hard for other tourists to handle – so vacancies are now fairly easy to come by. Still, it's wise to entrust the search to Sappho Travel (℡ 22530 52140, ℻ 22530 52000). Jo and Joanna are switched on and helpful, also serving as the local car rental station, ferry agent and air-ticket source; they are happy to place walk-ins in accommodation (❷–❹), but suggest you consult their UK-based website, ⓦ www.lesvos.co.uk, in advance.

Otherwise, there are just three bona fide **hotels** in Skála itself, plus the A-class *Aeolian Village* off to the west (℡ 22530 53585, ℻ 22530 53795; ❻, also pricier bungalows), 500m inland from the beach, western Lésvos' only luxury digs and large enough to have walk-in vacancies even in summer. Two establishments – the remote *Antiopi* (℡ 22530 53311; ❶ rooms, ❸ studios), off by itself in the fields behind town, and the seafront *Sappho the Eressia* (T 22530 53495, W www.sapphohotel.com; ❹), where a cheerful, trendy ground-floor café offsets basic rooms – are run exclusively by and for lesbians. Others have to make do with the central, air-conditioned *Galini* (T 22530 53138, F 22530 53137; ❹), slightly inland.

The Town

There's not much to Skála: just a roughly rectangular grid of perhaps five streets by eight, angling up to the oldest cottages on the slope of **Vígla** hill, and including the waterfront pedestrian lane (officially Papanikoli). The café-lined **square** at mid-waterfront is dominated by a bust of Theophrastos (372–287 BC), a renowned philosopher and botanist who hailed from **ancient Eressos**. This was not, as you might suppose, on the site of the modern village, but atop Vígla hill at the east end of the beach; crumbled bits of the remaining citadel wall are still visible from a distance. Once on top, the ruins prove even scantier, but it's worth the scramble up for the views – you can discern the ancient jetty submerged beyond the modern fishing anchorage.

Another famous reputed native of ancient Eressos was **Sappho**, the ancient poetess (ca.615–562 BC) and reputed lesbian. There are usually appreciable numbers of gay women paying homage to her – at the special-interest hotels noted above, certain of the waterfront *kafenía*, and at the clothing-optional zone of the beach west of the river mouth.

Ancient Eressos lingered on into the Byzantine era, whose main legacy is the basilica of **Áyios Andhréas**, behind the modern church. The surviving foundations are oddly aligned southwest-to-northeast rather than the usual west-to-east; a notable floor mosaic is currently hidden under sand and plastic until a permanent sunshade is built. A one-room archeological museum (Tues–Sun 8am–2.30pm; free), immediately behind the basilica, is of minimal interest.

Other practicalities

Most tavernas, with elevated wooden dining platforms, crowd the beach; in the wake of the recent tourism crash, they've been subjected to a harsh winnowing, with more closures or changeovers likely. The *Blue Sardine* at the far west end of the front is an excellent seafood *ouzerí* with good bread, clearly identified frozen items, unusual salads and extra touches to the fish. At the extreme east end of the esplanade, *Jay's* has an all-Asian or gourmet-Western menu most years, at premium prices. The best Greek cuisine is found at *Eressos Palace*, a few paces inland at the west edge of town, and accordingly well attended by Greek coach tours. Old favourite *Yamas* has lost its lease and now operates part-time out of the *Fuego Bar,* purveying its famous veggie burgers, wholemeal bread and decadent chocolate desserts. Popular with lesbians is *Dhekati Mousa/Tenth Muse*, on the Theophrastos *platía*; a summer cinema further inland and west rounds out the **nightlife**, as does the music club *Primitive*, in a suitably wild setting west of the river, going since 1990. Other amenities include a **post office**, a coin-op **laundry** near the church, a bank ATM outside the premises of Sappho Travel (there's another up in Eressós village should this one fail) and a small **Internet café**, *Cybersurf*, just east of *Dhekati Mousa*.

Beaches near Skála: Kroússos, Tavári and Podharás

Excursion boatmen at Skála Eressoú have a hard time convincing customers to leave the beautiful beach here, but if you get restless there are some potential targets a little further east; both are also accessible by road from Mesótopos (see overleaf).

Kroússos, the first attractive bay along, is 1km long and sandy, if shadeless aside from a few tamarisks; in springtime there's good bird-watching in the reedbeds of the river mouth. The rough road in discourages casual visitors, but the reward for braving it – aside from one of the finest beaches on the island – is the deceptively simple **kantína** of Kyra-Maria, installed partly in a derelict KTEL bus behind the east end of the beach. To reach it, *don't* follow signs to the "taverna-rooms", but bear left into the river bed and then up onto the left bank. From the *kantína* issues forth a steady, daily-changing stream of home-style food (snails, *dolmádhes*, beans, maybe sea urchin roe) and salad ingredients grown in the adjacent field, which have made this a cult favourite and required meal stop amongst Greek beach-goers.

Tavári, the next cove along, is by contrast emphatically not worth the extra effort, although it has a paved road in: apart from the stones and sea urchins in shallow water, the frontage road runs right along the beach, and the *Tavari Beach Hotel* does not inspire. You can head either west to Kroússos or east to much more worthwhile **Podharás** beach along coastal tracks.

East to Kalloní

If you're returning to the main island crossroads at Kalloní, you can complete a loop from Eressós along the western shore of the Gulf of Kalloní via the hill villages of Mesótopos and Ágra; this route is entirely paved, despite obsolete maps showing it as a track.

The only settlement of any consequence on the Gulf of Kalloní's west shore is **PARÁKILA**, which boasts a ruined mosque (whose minaret non-acrophobes can easily climb in 5min – but take care of crumbled plaster on the steps), an Ottoman bridge and the majority of Lésvos' limited citrus groves. Nearby beaches are not really worth stopping for, but back towards the mouth of the gulf lies dozy **APOTHÍKA**, reached by a short paved side road. Of three **tavernas**, best is *Tou Hondhrou* on the old harbour and what passes for a beach here; there's a better one at the end of the dirt road south to the open sea.

Northern Lésvos

The main road north of Kalloní winds up a pine-flecked ridge and then down the other side into increasingly attractive country stippled with poplars and blanketed by olive groves. Long before you can discern any other architectural detail, the cockscomb silhouette of Mólyvos castle indicates your approach to the oldest established tourist spot on Lésvos, and still the island's fourth most populous settlement.

Mólyvos

MÓLYVOS (officially **MÍTHYMNA**), 61km from Mytilíni, is arguably the most beautiful village on Lésvos. Tiers of sturdy, red-tiled houses mount the slopes between the picturesque harbour and the castle, some standing defensively with their rear walls to the sea. Concrete dwellings and hotels have been banned from the preserved municipal core, with a two-storey height limit imposed – a powerful watchdog group, "Friends of Molyvos", has seen to that – but this has, not surprisingly, promoted tweeness and steadily drained all the authentic life from the vine-canopied market lanes. Just one lonely tailor still plies his trade amongst souvenir shops far in excess of requirements, and the last

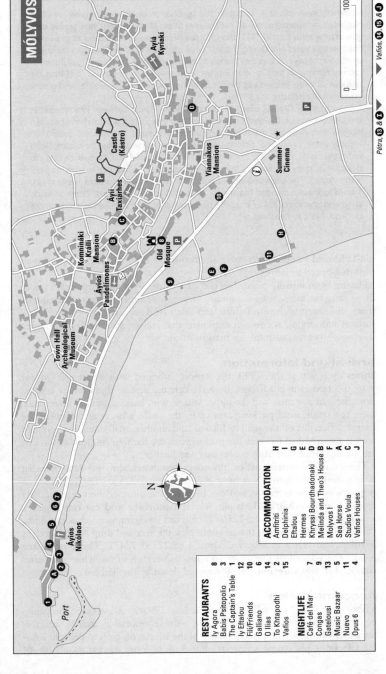

MÓLYVOS

▲ *Eftaloú*, **12** & **G**

▼ *Vafiós*, **14**, **15** & **J**

▶ *Pétra*, **13** & **I**

▶ *Vafiós*, **14**, **15** & **J**

Ayiá Kyriaki

Castle (Kástro)

P

Ayii Taxiárhes

Kominnáki Králli Mansion

Ayios Pandelímonas

Town Hall
Archeological Museum

Old Mosque

Yiannakos Mansion

Summer Cinema

P

D

C

B

A

E

F

H

8

9

10

11

Ayios Nikólaos

1 2 3 4 5 6 7

Port

N

4

0   100m

RESTAURANTS

Iy Agora	8
Babis Psitopolio	3
The Captain's Table	1
Iy Eftalou	12
Fili/Friends	10
Galliano	6
O Ilias	14
To Khtapodhi	2
Vafios	15

NIGHTLIFE

Café del Mar	7
Congas	9
Gatelousi	13
Music Bazaar	5
Nuevo	11
Opus 6	4

ACCOMMODATION

Amfitriti	H
Delphinia	I
Eftalou	G
Hermes	D
Khryssi Bourdhadonaki	B
Melinda and Theo's House	F
Molyvos I	A
Sea Horse	C
Studios Voula	J
Vafios Houses	J

The olives of Lésvos

No other Greek island is as dominated by olive production as Lésvos, which is blanketed by approximately 11 million olive trees. Most of these vast groves date from after a lethal frost in 1851, though a few hardy survivors are thought to be over five hundred years old. During the first three centuries after the Ottoman conquest, production of olive oil was a monopoly of the ruling pasha, but following eighteenth-century reforms in the Ottoman Empire, extensive tracts of Lésvos (and thus the lucrative oil trade) passed into the hands of the new Greek bourgeoisie, who greatly expanded the industry.

As in most of Greece, olives are harvested on Lésvos between late November and late December, the best ones coming from steep hillside plantations between Plomári and Ayiássos. Each grower's batch is brought to the local *trivío* (mill) – ideally within 24 hours of picking – pressed separately and tested for quality. Good first-pressing oil, some forty percent of that available in the fruit, is greenish and low in linoleic acid (by EU law, less than one-percent acidity is required to earn the label "extra virgin"). The remaining oil, much of it from the kernels and other waste mash, is used for inferior blended oils and for soap production. In general, Greek oil tends to exceed Spanish or Italian in quality, owing to hotter, drier summers which promote low acid levels in the olives.

old-fashioned locals' *kafenío-ouzerí* shut down in 1989 (though a replacement of sorts opened in 2004).

Having been initially pitched in the 1970s and 1980s as an upmarket resort, there were for many years no smutty postcards or other tacky accoutrements; that's all history, with silly T-shirts and other trinkets carpeting every vertical surface, and serving as constant reminders that you are still strolling through a stage set, however beautiful, for mass tourism.

Arrival and information

Buses drop you at the KTEL bus station, indicated with an asterisk on our map; the **taxi** rank is adjacent. If you're driving, beware that cars are banned from the harbour quay and the upper village, with parking limited in any case; there is a single, small **parking** area up by the castle, a larger one opposite the tourist office, just off the road to Eftaloú, and another small one a few hundred metres along Mihaïl Goútou, the road towards the harbour (in peak season cars are usually prohibited from proceeding any further).

The municipal **tourist office** (theoretically summer Mon–Fri 8am–9pm, Sat & Sun 9am–7pm; spring & autumn 8.30am–3pm; ℡22530 71347), by the bus stop, stocks some literature, and can help with accommodation. Immediately around it are two **bank ATMs** plus several **motorbike and car rental** places; among the latter, Kosmos (℡22530 71650) can be recommended, as can Alpha (℡22530 71942), offering the ability to pick up here and drop off in Vaterá or Mytilíni, and Hertz at Mihaïl Goútou 4 (℡22530 72471). The **post office** is near the bottom of the upper commercial street, Kástrou, while the better equipped of two **Internet** cafés is *Centraal*, down by the harbour.

Accommodation

Visitor numbers have fallen since the late 1990s, yet package companies continue to monopolize much of the more comfortable and/or desirable **accommodation**. The principal duty of the tourist office is to provide a no-fee telephone placement service for hundreds of more modest rooms (❷–❸) in the village. It's worth taking advantage of this, as staff appear to be relatively unbiased, and it will save you a fair bit of trudging around.

If you don't coincide with their opening hours, try ringing ahead the selected listings below, or hunting on the spot – just look for placards with the blue-on-white official EOT logo of a face in profile. Mólyvos **hotels** are all lower down, along or just off the main sea-level thoroughfare, which heads straight past the tourist office towards the harbour; the more modest of these are not yet completely taken over by package allotments. If all else fails, the official **campsite**, *Camping Methymna* (☎22540 71169; late June to early Sept), lies 2km northeast of town, on the way to Eftalóu.

Amfitriti Immediately inland from the *Olive Press* ☎22530 71741, ℱ22530 71744. This B-class hotel has its own pool in a peaceful garden setting, but it's monopolized by packages except during spring or autumn. ④

Delphinia 1km south of town ☎22530 71315, ⓦwww.hoteldelfinia.com. Mólyvos' first proper hotel is still an excellent choice, comprising stand-ard-room wings (insist on sea-view units) and larger, more private bungalow units scattered in 70 acres of thick vegetation. Huge pool with terrace view of the castle, plus direct access to Pitsiára beach; decent breakfasts (taken outdoors), well-trained, friendly staff, year-round operation. ④ rooms, ⑥ bungalows

Eftalou 1.5km along the Eftalóu road ☎22530 71584, ⓔparmakel@otenet.gr. A well-managed C-class hotel, with a loyal independent clientele amongst the package groups. Lush gardens, pool, balconied, tan-tiled rooms with subdued wallpaper, air con and double glazing. ④

Hermes Shore road ☎22530 71250, ℱ22530 72050. Variable, marble-floored, en-suite rooms at this C-class hotel, some with sea views; opens late April, closes late Oct, and far enough from bars that noise shouldn't be a problem; some packages. ④

Khryssi Bourdhadonaki Southeast hillside, towards Ayía Kyriakí district ☎22530 72193. Modern, plain self-catering rooms in an old house, with partial sea views. ③

Melinda and Theo's House Hillside, just under Krallis mansion ☎22530 71241 or 694 41 21 297, ⓦwww.lesvosvacations.com. Three-level stone house with great views, restored to very high standard, thus popular and needing advance book-ing; sleeps 4–6, rates for whole house vary from €90 to €140 by season.

Molyvos I Next door to the *Hermes* ☎22530 71496, ⓦwww.molyvos-hotels.com. Nominally B-class outfit nicely located on the shore, behind the tamarisks and its own stone-paved front terrace where breakfast is served under the palms. Large, tile-floored, balconied rooms, half with sea view. No special amenities (other than a quasi-private pebble beach), though you do get use of (and shuttle to) the pool and sports facilities at sister, out-of-town hotel *Molyvos II*. ④

Sea Horse Overlooking the port ☎22530 71320, ℱ22530 71374. Acceptable C-class hotel if you're not interested in making an early night of it, and somewhat overpriced, but superb location. ④

Studios Voula Below castle car park ☎22530 71305, 22530 72017 or 22530 71567 – ask for Theoktisti on last two numbers. Pleasant studios (③) with stunning views, while the adjacent four-person suite in a restored house is a good spot for families.

Vafios Houses Vafiós village ☎22530 71752, ⓦwww.taverna-vafios.gr. One-bedroom houses, built in 2003, with fully equipped kitchens and fire-places; air con/heating, available all year. ⑤

The Town

The perimeter walls and highest bastions of the Byzantine–Genoese **castle** (Tues–Sun: summer 8am–7pm; winter 8am–2.30pm; €2) provide interesting rambles and views of Turkey across the straits. Closer examination reveals a dozen weathered Turkish-inscribed fountains along flower-fragrant, cobble-stoned alleyways, a reflection of the fact that before 1923 Muslims constituted over a third of the population here and owned most of the finest dwellings. The **Komnináki Králli** mansion, high up in the town, is particularly worth getting into (daily 9am–5pm; free); the lower floor houses an art school, but the wall- and ceiling-paintings on the upper storey (dated 1833) rival those of the Vareltzídena mansion in Pétra (see p.423). A panel in the smallest room portrays some dervish musicians, while other murals depict stylized versions of Constantinople and Mytilíni Town; you can tell the men's and women's quarters apart by the wider recessed "throne" provided for the latter.

The contents of the small archeological museum, formerly in the basement of the town hall, have been transferred to Mytilíni while the building undergoes renovation. Barely excavated ancient Mithymna to the northwest is of essentially specialist interest, though a necropolis has been unearthed next to the bus stop and main car park; it's mainly the use of the Classical name that has been revived. The motivation for this, as so often in the Balkans, is nationalistic; *Mólyvos* ("Graphite", of which there is none locally) is an attempted Hellenization of the Turkish name *Molova*.

Beaches

Despite a plethora of organized activities and sunbeds to rent, the shingly **town beach** is mediocre, with rocks and sea urchins in the shallows, though it improves as you head towards the southerly beach of **Pitsiára**, with its clothing-optional zone. Advertised boat excursions to bays as remote as Ánaxos and Tsónia seem a frank admission of this failing; there are also seven to eight daily minibus shuttles in season, linking all points between Ánaxos and Eftaloú – schedules are posted locally.

Eating and drinking

Choose carefully when **eating out**; the obvious sea-view tavernas on 17-Noemvríou climbing up from near the tourist office are all much of a muchness, where you pay primarily for the view. Instead, you should head either to Eftaloú, Vafiós village, or down towards picturesque Mólyvos harbour, to where the centre of the village's nocturnal gravity has shifted since the mid-1990s. Note that even tavernas designated "open all day" may shut at lunch during spring or autumn.

Babis Psitopolio Just above the harbour car park. The favourite autumn-through-spring hangout for carnivores who pile inside; only three balcony tables make this an uncomfortable summer choice. Mainly supper.

The Captain's Table Harbour quay, towards the boatyard – look for the green chairs. Theo and Melinda offer reasonable and very fresh seafood, vegetarian *mezédhes* and meat grills, washed down by their very palatable own-label wine. Consistent quality since they opened in 1995; supper only.

Iy Eftalou 4km northeast, just before the eponymous spa. Splendid food, mostly meat/fish grills, served in the almond- and fig-shaded courtyard at this much-loved *exohikó kéndro* (rural taverna); open most of the year for supper, with a fireplace indoors for the cooler months. Open all day in season.

Fili/Friends Mihaíl Goútou, near tourist office. An excellent *psistariá*, open until the wee hours (and much of the year), where fishermen and Mólyvos restaurateurs go after *they* close up. Chicken nuggets in pitta a speciality.

Galliano Just before the harbour. Great wood-oven pizzas, open for supper only until the small hours.

O Ilias Vafiós, 5km east, bottom of village. Excel-lent bread, good bulk wine and genuine atmosphere; fried *mezédhes* are filling, so go hungry. Open all day.

To Khtapodhi By the entrance to the port. Perched in an unbeatable location, this is the oldest (1978) outfit here, housed in the former customs house; atmospheric and popular with locals, who treat it as an *ouzerí*, ordering such dishes as *piyázo* (white-bean soup), zucchini pie without fyllo, and *sardhélles pastés*. Supper only, early April to end Oct.

Municipal Cáfe/Dhimotiko Kafenio Just downhill from old mosque. Lovely, restored wood-floor premises with the full range of *oúzo* in *karafákia* and some traditional sweets. Their *oúzo-mezés* combo is such good value at under €2 that you can't see it lasting as a menu item.

Vafios Vafiós village, 5km east. More extensive menu than its rival *Ilias*, with slicker presentation (including 2004-revamped interior), better wine list and less undrained deep-frying. Best in the cooler months, when elaborate, hearty *mayireftá* are offered; in summer, go for their *pikilíes* (medleys) with *oúzo*. Still popular with Greeks despite inconsistent quality and rising prices; open all day Easter–Oct.

Nightlife

In terms of formal events, midsummer sees a short **festival** of music and theatre up in the castle; there's also a well-regarded summer **cinema** next to the taxi rank, with first-run fare. When out **tippling**, be advised that Mólyvos is as expensive in this regard as in everything else, though there are some happy hours.

Café del Mar Mihaíl Goútou. Popular hangout for drinking and watching the world go by, with variable taped music.

Congas Just above the shore road. Tropical-themed youth hangout; July & Aug only.

Gatelousi 3km out on the Pétra road. State-of-the-art outdoor techno-dub-trance disco on a cantilevered platform like a ship's deck. Open late June to Aug only.

Music Bazaar Just before the harbour. Long-lived indoor dance bar; only works high season.

Nuevo Behind the *Olive Press Hotel*. A more genteel hangout for older folk, with live or taped music. Open all season.

Opus 6 Just up from the harbour. The best thing to happen to Mólyvos nightlife for a while; competent live Greek, jazz or Western pop music nightly. Limited table space, so arrive early.

Pétra

Since there are both practical and political limits to the expansion of Mólyvos, many package companies have shifted their emphasis to **PÉTRA**, 5km south. Accordingly the place has sprawled untidily behind its broad, sandy beach and seafront square, but this has been partly pedestrianized to exclude idling buses, and the core of old stone houses, many with Levantine-style balconies overhanging the streets, remains.

Pétra takes its name from the giant volcanic monolith located some distance inland and capped by the eighteenth-century church of **Panayía Glykofiloússa**, reached via 103 rock-hewn steps on the northeast side. The walled compound at the top is of little intrinsic interest, but you should climb up at dawn or dusk for superb views of the surrounding agricultural plain. More intriguing local sights include the sixteenth-century church of **Áyios Nikólaos** (daily 9am–7pm), at the foot of the rock, sporting three phases of well-preserved frescoes up to 1721, and the intricately decorated **Vareltzídhena mansion** (Tues–Sun 8am–7pm; closes 3pm off season; free), some of whose rooms sport exquisite naïve, late eighteenth-century murals: courting couples, a bear being trained, sailing ships, and a stylized skyline of Constantinople complete with cannons booming in a naval engagement.

Practicalities

For **accommodation**, there are various small hotels and studio complexes, most block-booked by tour companies; one that's not is *Studios Ippokratis* on the shore road at the south edge of town (☎22530 41195; ❸), plain but large units mostly facing a pleasant front garden; the management will refer overflow to their in-laws next door. With more money to spend, head for the B-class *Clara Hotel-Bungalows* at Avláki, 2km south (☎22530 41532, Ⓕ22530 41535, Ⓦwww .clarahotel.gr; ❼), the first and still one of the best luxury complexes near Pétra, with a pool and tennis court. All of the large, tastefully furnished rooms face the sea and Mólyvos; some have bathtubs, all have heating/air con.

Plenty of inexpensive **rooms** are available through the Women's Agricultural Tourism Cooperative (☎22530 41238, Ⓔwomes@otenet.gr), formed by Pétra's women in 1984 to provide a more unusual option for visitors. In addition to operating an excellent, inexpensive, all-day **restaurant** on the square, with both grills and *mayireftá* served indoors or on a sea-view roof terrace, they arrange rooms or studios (❶–❷) in a number of scattered premises.

Aside from the cooperative's eatery, most tavernas lack distinction, with the exception of *O Rigas* buried in the backstreets behind the monolith. Further afield at tiny **Avláki** beach, 1500m southwest on the way to Ánaxos and accessible by a marked coastal path or its own signposted driveway, *Estiatorio Avlaki*, really more of an *ouzerí*, has been going since 1975 and, while quality has dipped and prices climbed since the late 1990s, it's still better than most nearby alternatives.

With the *Gatelousi* disco looming on the hillside to the north, organized **nightlife** in town is understandably very modest. The old olive press on the coast road has been converted into a "dance bar", *Machine*, with the industrial apparatus *in situ* – hence the name. During August, the municipality typically lays on a **festival**, with music and theatre events at various locales in Pétra and nearby Ánaxos.

In addition to a **bank ATM**, Pétra's amenities include a **post office**, next to Áyios Nikólaos, and a number of **scooter** or **car rental** places such as Homerus (☎22530 41577) on the north side of town, and Budget (c/o Nirvana Travel, ☎22530 41991). There's a tiny **Internet café** in the grid of market lanes, at 4-Dhekemvríou 1912.

Petrí and around

Inland from Pétra, a steep, partly paved road climbs 3km to soundalike **PETRÍ** village, unimprovably set on a natural, west-facing balcony. The main reason to come here is the excellent **taverna** *Tò Petri* (lunch & supper May–Oct 15) near the top of the village, with superb *mayireftá* and view-terrace seating. By day, Petrí is the trailhead for the partly waymarked **path to Vafiós**, though the start of this has been confused by bulldozing. It's forty minutes down to the Pigádhos ravine, with its ruined water mill and aqueduct, and thence a further twenty minutes' walk to an abandoned farm with an open irrigation tank among some poplars. From here you've another, tougher hour, sometimes through prickly shrubs, to reach Vafiós.

Drivers will also like to know that the unmarked but paved right turning at the edge of Petrí, by the army camp, emerges on the paved road just west of Stýpsi and knocks a good 8km off the drive there from Pétra on the main road.

Ánaxos and beyond

ÁNAXOS, 3km southwest of Pétra and also reachable via a coast-hugging path from Avláki, is a bit of a higgledy-piggledy mess, but it fringes by far the cleanest beach in the area, from where beautiful sunsets are framed by three offshore islets. The kilometre stretch of sand is dotted with pedalos, sunbeds, and a handful of **tavernas** that are an improvement (try *Khryssi Ammos*) on the unmemorable snack-bars of yore. Blocks of rooms inland are still apt to be monopolized by tour companies; there may also be mosquitoes from the river mouth.

For something utterly different, drive 1km south, then 3km west along a well-signposted side road (then right at the only fork) to **Ambélia**, a 700-metre sand-and-pebble beach. There are some large rocks in the shallows, and often washed-up seaweed, but generally the place is fairly clean, with an attractive, cultivated valley for a backdrop. Facilities are limited to a single **taverna** (*George's*), where decently prepared vegetables from the adjacent garden and fish in season belie the dubious appearance of the kitchen.

Just past Skoutáros village, you can ignore without regret a three-kilometre side road descending to the scrappy, exposed pebble beach of **Tsikhránda**, with two equally undistinguished summer snack-bars.

Loutrá Eftaloú

From Mólyvos, the shuttle-bus runs 5km northeast to the rustic, 2000-restored **thermal baths** at **Loutrá Eftaloú**. Patronize the hot pool under the Otto-man-era domed structure (Easter–Oct daily 10am–2pm & 4–8pm; winter hours uncertain; €3.50 for 45min), not the sterile modern tub-rooms in the adjacent annexe. The spa is currently well looked after, with the water changed twice daily and mixed to a comfortable 39–41° C (from the source which can reach 47° C). Still, you'll need to cool down regularly; outside stretches the long, good pebble beach of **Áyii Anáryiri**, broken up by little headlands, with the two easternmost coves nudist.

Around Mount Lepétymnos

East of Mólyvos, the villages of 968-metre **Mount Lepétymnos**, marked by tufts of poplars, provide a day or two of rewarding exploration. The main road around the mountain first heads 6km east to Vafiós before curl-ing north around the base of the peaks. **VAFIÓS** (for whose tavernas see p.422) is the starting point for the most direct **climb** up to the secondary 937-metre peak of **Profítis Ilías**, a three-hour walk there and back; begin in the obvious ravine with an aqueduct behind the village, and then, from a plane-shaded spring about half an hour along, angle steeply up to the chapel on the ridge here.

East of the village of Áryennos, and the landslip-ruined derelict village of Lepétymnos, stands the enchanting hill village of **SYKAMINIÁ** (Sykamiá). This is the birthplace of regional novelist Stratis Myrivilis, whose childhood home is identified among the imposing basalt-block houses below the "Plaza of the Workers' First of May", with its two traditional *kafenía* and sweeping views north to Turkey.

Skála Sykaminiás

A signposted trail from the roadside 800m west of Sykaminiá short-cuts the twisty 2.5-kilometre road down to **SKÁLA SYKAMINIÁS**, easily the most picturesque fishing port on Lésvos. Myrivilis used it as the setting for his best-known work, *The Mermaid Madonna*, and the tiny rock-top chapel at the end of the jetty will be instantly recognizable to anyone who has read the novel (see p.522).

On a practical level, Skála has a few **pensions**, such as the central, part air-conditioned *Gorgona* (☎ & ⓕ 22530 55301; ❷), with a shaded breakfast terrace, and the sea-view *Rooms Anna* (☎ 22530 55242; ❷), 200m west of the chapel. Several **tavernas** jostle for space around the fishing anchorage; most estab-lished of these is *Iy Skamnia* (aka *Iy Mouria tou Myrivili*), with seating under the mulberry tree in which Myrivilis used to sleep on hot summer nights. However, newer *Anemoessa* (closest to the chapel, open winter weekends also) has overtaken it qualitywise: in addition to good seafood – *gávros* (anchovy) in June or July, sardines in August or September – courtesy of the active local fleet, you can try sterling renditions of the island's late summer speciality of *kolokythóanthi yemistá* (stuffed squash blossoms).

The only local **beach** is the pebble-on-sand-base one of **Kayiá** just east. A fairly rough, roller-coaster track follows the shore west from Skála for 9km back to the baths at Eftaloú, its condition not deterring a steady stream of vehicles and the odd walker.

Klió and Tsónia

Continuing east from upper Sykaminiá, you soon come to **KLIÓ**, whose single main street (marked "*kentrikí agorá*") leads to a square with a plane tree, fountain, *kafenía* and views across to Turkey. The village is set attractively on a slope, down which a six-kilometre road, half paved, descends to the 600m of beautiful pink volcanic sand at **Tsónia** beach, with just a single taverna and another café at the fishing-anchorage end, and two modern rooms places plus another summer taverna at the beach end. The jerry-built prefab cottages just inland form the summer annexe of Klió, whose entire population migrates

Greek script table

Lésvos	Λέσβος	ΛΕΣΒΟΣ
Akhladherí	Αχλαδερή	ΑΧΛΑΔΕΡΗ
Ambélia	Αμπέλια	ΑΜΠΕΛΙΑ
Ambelikó	Αμπελικό	ΑΜΠΕΛΙΚΟ
Ánaxos	Άναξος	ΑΝΑΞΟΣ
Ándissa	Άντισσα	ΑΝΤΙΣΣΑ
Apothíka	Αποθήκα	ΑΠΟΘΗΚΑ
Ayía Marína	Αγία Μαρίνα	ΑΓΙΑ ΜΑΡΙΝΑ
Ayía Paraskeví	Αγία Παρασκευή	ΑΓΙΑ ΠΑΡΑΣΚΕΥΗ
Ayiássos	Αγιάσος	ΑΓΙΑΣΟΣ
Áyios Ermoyénis	Άγιος Ερμογένης	ΑΓΙΟΣ ΕΡΜΟΓΕΝΗΣ
Áyios Isídhoros	Άγιος Ισίδωρος	ΑΓΙΟΣ ΙΣΙΔΩΡΟΣ
Eressós	Ερεσός	ΕΡΕΣΟΣ
Fília	Φίλια	ΦΙΛΙΑ
Gavathás	Γαβαθάς	ΓΑΒΑΘΑΣ
Haramídha	Χαραμίδα	ΧΑΡΑΜΙΔΑ
Hídhira	Χίδηρα	ΧΙΔΗΡΑ
Ipsilométopo	Υψηλομέτωπο	ΥΨΗΛΟΜΕΤΩΠΟ
Kálo Limáni	Κάλο Λιμάνι	ΚΑΛΟ ΛΙΜΑΝΙ
Kalloní	Καλλονή	ΚΑΛΛΟΝΗ
Kápi	Κάπη	ΚΑΠΗ
Klió	Κλειώ	ΚΛΕΙΩ
Kroússos	Κρούσος	ΚΡΟΥΣΟΣ
Lápsarna	Λάπσαρνα	ΛΑΨΑΡΝΑ
Lepétymnos	Λεπέτυμνος	ΛΕΠΕΤΥΜΝΟΣ
Lióta	Λιωτα	ΛΙΩΔΑ
Lisvóri	Λισβόρι	ΛΙΣΒΟΡΙ
Loutrá Eftaloú	Λουτρά Εφταλού	ΛΟΥΤΡΑ ΕΦΤΑΛΟΥ
Loutrá Yéras	Λουτρά Γέρας	ΛΟΥΡΑ ΓΕΡΑΣ
Mandamádhos	Μανταμάδος	ΜΑΝΤΑΜΑΔΟΣ
Megalohóri	Μεγαλοχώρι	ΜΕΓΑΛΟΧΩΡΙ
Melínda	Μελίντα	ΜΕΛΙΝΤΑ
Mesótopos	Μεσότοπος	ΜΕΣΟΤΟΠΟΣ
Míthymna	Μήθυμνα	ΜΗΘΥΜΝΑ
Mytilíni	Μυτιλήνη	ΜΥΤΙΛΗΝΗ
Mólyvos	Μόλυβος	ΜΟΛΥΒΟΣ
Moní Ipsiloú	Μονή Υψιλού	ΜΟΝΗ ΥΨΙΛΟΥ
Moní Limónos	Μονί Λειμώνος	ΜΟΝΗ ΛΕΙΜΩΝΟΣ

here at weekends in season – a custom still observed to a diminishing degree at all shoreline colonies around the island.

South slope villages

Just south of Klió, the route forks at Kápi, from where you can complete a loop around the mountain by bearing west along a paved road tracing its southern flank. After 5km you reach **PELÓPI**, ancestral village of the unsuccessful 1988 US presidential candidate Michael Dukakis, who finally visited the island in 2000 – the main street has been renamed after him. Greenery-swathed **IPSI-LOMÉTOPO**, 5km further along, is punctuated by a minaret (but no intact mosque) and hosts revels on July 16–17, the feast of Ayía Marína. By the time you reach sprawling **STÝPSI**, 13km from Kápi, you're just 4km shy of the

Moní Perivolís	Μονή Περιβολής	ΜΟΝΗ ΠΕΡΙΒΟΛΗΣ
Moní	Μονή	ΜΟΝΗ
Mirsiniotísis	Μιρσινιωτις	ΜΙΡΣΙΝΙΩΤΙΣΙΣ
Mória	Μόρια	ΜΟΡΙΑ
Nyfídha	Νυφίδα	ΝΥΦΙΔΑ
Ovriókastro	Οβριόκαστρο	ΟΒΡΙΟΚΑΣΤΡΟ
Paleókipos	Παλαιόκαστρο	ΠΑΛΑΙΟΚΑΣΤΡΟ
Pámfylla	Πάμφυλλα	ΠΑΜΦΥΛΛΑ
Panayía Kryftí	Παναγία Κρυφτή	ΠΑΝΑΓΙΑ ΚΡΥΦΤΗ
Panayioúdha	Παναγιούδα	ΠΑΝΑΓΙΟΥΔΑ
Papádhos	Παπάδος	ΠΑΠΑΔΟΣ
Parákila	Παράκοιλα	ΠΑΡΑΚΟΙΛΑ
Paralía Thermís	Παραλία Θερμής	ΠΑΡΑΛΙΑ ΘΕΡΜΗΣ
Pelópi	Πελώπη	ΠΕΛΩΠΗ
Pérama	Πέραμα	ΠΕΡΑΜΑ
Pétra	Πέτρα	ΠΕΤΡΑ
Pýrgi Thermís	Πύργοι Θερμής	ΠΥΡΓΟΙ ΘΕΡΜΗΣ
Plomári	Πλωμάρι	ΠΛΩΜΑΡΙ
Podharás	Ποδαράς	ΠΟΔΑΡΑΣ
Polikhnítos	Πολιχνίτος	ΠΟΛΙΧΝΙΤΟΣ
Sígri	Σίγρι	ΣΙΓΡΙ
Skála Eresso	Σκάλα Ερεσού	ΣΚΑΛΑ ΕΡΕΣΟΥ
Skála Sykaminiás	Σκάλα Συκαμινιάς	ΣΚΑΛΑ ΣΥΚΑΜΙΝΙΑΣ
Skála Polikhnítou	Σκάλα Πολιώνιτοί	ΣΚΑΛΑ ΠΟΛΙΧΝΙΤΟ
Skalohóri	Σκαλοχώρι	ΣΚΑΛΟΧΩΡΙ
Skoutáros	Σκουτάρος	ΣΚΟΥΤΑΡΟΣ
Stavrós	Σταυρός	ΣΤΑΥΡΟΣ
Stýpsi	Στύψη	ΣΤΥΨΗ
Sykaminiá	Συκαμινιά	ΣΥΚΑΜΙΝΙΑ
Tárti	Τάρτι	ΤΑΡΤΙ
Tavári	Ταβάρι	ΤΑΒΑΡΙ
Tsikhránda	Τσιχράντα	ΤΣΙΧΡΑΝΤΑ
Tsónia	Τσόνια	ΤΣΟΝΙΑ
Vafiós	Βαφειός	ΒΑΦΕΙΟΣ
Variá	Βαρειά	ΒΑΡΕΙΑ
Vaterá	Βατερά	ΒΑΤΕΡΑ
Vatoússa	Βατούσσα	ΒΑΤΟΥΣΣΑ
Vríssa	Βρίσα	ΒΡΙΣΑ

main Kalloní–Mólyvos road; there's a large **taverna** at the edge of town to which coachloads of tourists descend in season for "Greek Nights".

Like Petrí, Stýpsi also makes a good jump-off point for rambles along Lepétymnos' steadily dwindling network of **trails**; throughout the north of the island you'll see advertisements for **donkey- or mule-trekking**, which in recent years has become more popular than walking. The Mytilíni EOT jumped into the fray during the mid-1990s, marking several long-distance routes across the island with yellow diamonds and documenting them in its brochure "Trekking Trails on Lesvos". However, these rely almost exclusively on vehicle tracks or roads, and are considered locally as something of a bad joke; the most worthwhile and pathlike of these are the coastal track from Pétra to Ambélia and the Kápi–Sykaminiá–Skála Sykaminiá traverse. A better printed **guide** is the locally sold, self-published one by Mike Maunder, *On Foot in North Lesvos*, which details some rambles on the hillsides.

Mandamádhos and Taxiárhis monastery

The main highway south from Klió to the capital runs through **MANDAMÁD-HOS**, 6km along. This attractive inland village is famous for its pottery, but more so for the "black" icon of the Archangel Michael, whose enormous **monastery of Taxiárhis** (daily: May–Sept 6am–9.30pm; Oct–April 6.30am–7pm), in a valley just northeast, is the powerful focus of a thriving cult, and a popular venue for baptisms. The image – supposedly made from a mixture of mud and the blood of monks slaughtered in a medieval massacre – is really more idol than icon, both in its lumpy three-dimensionality and in the former mode of veneration which seems a vestige of pagan times. First there was the custom of the coin-wish, whereby you pressed a coin to the Archangel's forehead; if it stuck, then your wish would be granted. Owing to wear and tear on the image, the practice is now forbidden; instead, supplicants leave enormous votive candles beside a substitute icon by the main entrance.

It's further believed that, while carrying out his various errands on behalf of the faithful, the Archangel gets through more footwear than Imelda Marcos. Accordingly the icon used to be surrounded not by the usual *támmata* (votive medallions) but by piles of miniature gold and silver shoes. The ecclesiastical authorities, embarrassed by such "primitive" practices, removed all the little shoes in 1986. Since then, a token substitute has reappeared: several pairs of tin slippers that can be filled with money and left before the icon. Just why his devotees should want to encourage these perpetual peripatetics is unclear, since in Greek folklore the Archangel Michael is also the one who fetches the souls of the dying, and modern Greek attitudes towards death are as bleak as those of their pagan ancestors.

Lésvos travel details

Island transport

Buses

Mytilíni to: Ayiássos (5 daily Mon–Fri, 4 Sat & Sun); Eressós (3 daily Mon–Sat, 2 Sun summer, 1 daily off season); Kalloní (4 daily Mon–Fri, 2 Sat, 1 Sun); Mandamádhos (4 daily Mon–Fri, 3 Sat & Sun); Mólyvos (4 daily Mon–Fri, 2 Sat, 1 Sun); Pétra (4 daily Mon–Fri, 2 Sat, 1 Sun); Plomári (4 daily Mon–Fri, 2 Sat & Sun); Sígri (2 daily Mon–Sat, 1 Sun summer only; 1 daily Mon–Sat off season); Vaterá (3 daily Mon–Fri, 2 Sat & Sun).

Inter-island transport

NB To simplify matters, the once-weekly sailing offered by LANE, northbound from Lésvos to Límnos and Alexandhroúpoli, and southbound to Híos, Sámos, Kálymnos, Kós, Rhodes, Hálki,

Kárpathos, Kássos and Crete, has been omitted from the following schedules.

Ferries

Lésvos (Mytilíni) to: Híos (daily on NEL, 3 weekly on GA, 1 weekly on SF; 3hr 30min); Kavála (2 weekly on GA; 11hr); Ikaría (3 weekly on GA; 8hr–11hr); Límnos (3 weekly on GA, 1 weekly on SF, 1 weekly on NEL; 5hr 30min–6hr); Pireás (daily on NEL, 3 weekly on GA; 13–19hr); Sámos, Vathý &/or Karlóvassi (3 weekly on GA; 7hr–9hr); Thessaloníki (1 weekly on NEL; 13hr 30min).

Lésvos (Sígri) to: Áyios Efstrátios (1 weekly on SF; 3hr 15min); Lávrio (1 weekly on SF; 11hr); Límnos (1 weekly on SF; 5hr); Psará (1 weekly on SF; 3hr).

Catamaran

NEL's *Aeolos Kenteris* sails to Híos (1hr 45min) and Pireás (5hr 45min) 3–5 times weekly, to Límnos (2 weekly), Kavála (1 weekly) and Thessaloníki (1 weekly).

Flights

Lésvos to: Athens (3–5 daily on Olympic, 4 daily on Aegean; 50min–1hr); Híos (2 weekly; 30min); Límnos (3–5 weekly; 40 min); Sámos (2 weekly; 45min–1hr 30min); Thessaloníki (5–8 weekly on Olympic, 1–2 daily on Aegean; 55min–1hr 10min–1hr 50min).

International transport

Ferries

Lésvos (Mytilíni) to: Turkey (Ayvalşk or Dikili); 4–9 weekly May–Oct, winter link unreliable). At least one of two craft, the Turkish *Jalehan* or Greek *Mytilini*, departs Mytilíni 8–8.30am most days; each carries a couple of cars. The *Jalehan* may also do an evening trip 3 days weekly. Passenger rates from €28 open return, all taxes inclusive. Small cars €60 one way, €90 return. Journey time 1hr 40min.

Límnos

Límnos is a sizeable agricultural and garrison island whose remoteness and peculiar ferry schedules protected it until the mid-1990s from the excesses of the holiday trade. Most summer visitors are Greek, particularly from Thessaloníki, though the locals have become increasingly used to northern European visitors flown in by ever more regular charter flights. Accommodation across the island tends to be comfortable if a bit overpriced, with a strong bias (near the capital at least) towards self-catering units. Having come late to the tourist trade, and saddled with a short tourist season owing to the northerly latitude, the Limnians have skipped the backpacker phase entirely – budget travellers are explicitly discouraged – and gone straight for the **high end of the market**. Indeed, this bucolic island has been getting trendy of late: there are upscale souvenir shops, village houses restored by Thessalonians as weekend retreats and some sort of noon-to-small-hours music bar at every beach.

At the nadir of Greco-Turkish relations in the late 1980s, the conspicuous **military presence** ran to 25,000 soldiers, though it is now down to about 7000; conventional tourism was slow in coming because the islanders made a reliable living off the soldiers and family members coming to visit them. Since the 1960s, the island has been the focus of periodic disputes between the Greek and Turkish governments; Turkey has a long-standing demand that Límnos should be demilitarized, and Turkish aircraft regularly intrude Greek airspace overhead, prompting immediate responses from the Greek Air Force squadron based here. Military security considerations also mean that there are no decent commercial maps of the island available.

The bays of **Bourniá** and **Moúdhros**, the latter one of the largest natural harbours in the Aegean, almost pinch H-shaped Límnos in two. The west of

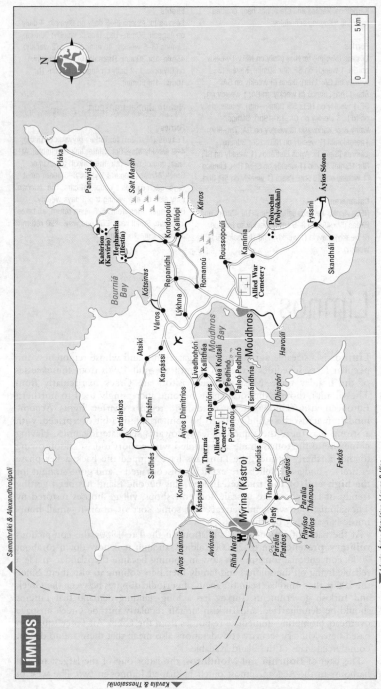

LÍMNOS

◀ Samothráki & Alexandhroúpoli

◀ Kavála & Thessaloníki

▶ Lávrio, Áyios Efstrátios, Lésvos & Híos

N

0   5 km

Pláka

Panayía

Salt Marsh

Kéros

Bourniá Bay

Kótsinas

Kabírion (Kavírio)
Hephaestia (Ifestía)

Kondopoúli

Kallópi

Repanídhi

Romanoú

Roussopoúli

Kamínia

Polyochni (Polyókhni)

Fyssíni

Áyios Sózon

Skandháli

Allied War Cemetery

Város

Lýkhna

Atsikí

Livadhohóri

Kallithéa

Néa Koútali

Moúdhros Bay

Moúdhros

Karpássi

Angariónes

Pedhinó

Tsimándhria

Dhiapóri

Havoúli

Fakós

Dháfni

Áyios Dhimítrios

Thermá

Paleo Pedhinó

Portianoú

Allied War Cemetery

Katálakos

Sardhés

Kornós

Kondiás

Thános

Evgátis

Paralía Thános

Káspakas

Áyios Ioánnis

Avlónas

Mýrina (Kástro)

Platý

Rihá Nerá

Playó Mólos

Paralía Platéos

the island is dramatically bare and hilly, with abundant basalt put to good use as street cobbles and house masonry. Like most volcanic islands, Límnos produces excellent **wine** from westerly vineyards – good dry whites and rosés, some of the best retsina in Greece (unfortunately none of this exported), plus *oúzo* from Kondiás. The low-lying eastern leg of the "H" is speckled with seasonal ponds or marshes popular with duck-hunters, while the intervening land is occupied by cattle, combine harvesters and vast cornfields.

The Limnians proudly tout an abundance of **natural food products**, including thyme honey and sheep's milk cheese, and indeed the population is almost self-sufficient in foodstuffs. Despite off-islander slander to that effect, Límnos is not flat, barren or treeless; much of the countryside consists of rolling hills or volcanic crags, the latter forming the backdrop for most of the west coast. There is plenty of **vegetation** except on the heights, with substantial, carefully nurtured clumps of almond, jujube, myrtle, oak, fig, poplar and mulberry trees. The island is, however, extremely dry, with irrigation water pumped from deep wells, and a limited number of potable springs. Yet various creeks bring sand to several long, **sandy beaches** around the coast, where it's easy to find a stretch to yourself – though in some years stingless but disgusting jellyfish pour out of the Dardanelles and die here in the shallows. On the plus side, beaches shelve gently, making them ideal for children and are quick to warm up early in summer, with no cool currents except near the river mouths.

Mýrina

MÝRINA (Kástro), the capital and port on the west coast, has the atmosphere of a provincial market town rather than a resort. With about five thousand inhabitants, it's pleasantly low-key, if not especially picturesque apart from a core neighbourhood of old stone houses dating from the Ottoman occupation, and the ornate Neoclassical mansions of Romeïkós Yialós. Few explicitly Turkish monuments have survived: a dilapidated octagonal structure with an inscription over the door, probably the *tekke* or lodge of a dervish order, hides behind the Co-op supermarket on the main harbour *platía* – though a fountain at the harbour end of Kydhá retains its calligraphic inscription and is still highly prized for its drinking water.

Arrival, transport and information

The sleek new civilian **airport** is 21km east of Mýrina, almost at the exact geographical centre of the island, sharing a runway with an enormous air-force base; the passenger terminal, equally enormous, contains nought but three car rental booths, a bank ATM, and a taxi rank outside – there's no shuttle bus into town. **Ferries** dock at the south end of the town, in the shadow of the castle and the modern clocktower; there are separate agencies for tickets with NEL (Khryssa Karaïskaki, ☎22540 22460), at the harbourfront junction; GA/LANE (Pravlis Travel, ☎22540 24617); and Saos Ferries (☎22540 29571), the latter two in the narrow, traffic-light-controlled street known as Perantzádha.

The **bus station**, for what little it's worth, is on Platía Eleftheríou Venizélou, near the north end of Kydhá. One look at the abysmally sparse schedules (only a single daily afternoon departure to most points, slightly more frequent buses to Kondiás and Moúdhros) will convince you of the need to **rent your own vehicle**. Cars and sometimes motorbikes or bicycles can be had from courteous and fair-priced Limnos Car Rental/Europcar at the north end of the market lane (℡ & ⒻⒻ22540 23777) and at the airport (℡694 54 95 104); Petrides Travel, Karatzá 118 (℡22540 22039) and the airport (℡22540 92700); or Holiday, on the port esplanade (℡22540 24357) or at the airport (℡693 24 81 056). Rates for bikes are only slightly above the island norm, but cars are expensive; a motorbike (most obviously from Moto Lemnos, ℡22540 25002, just in from the jetty clocktower) is generally enough to explore the nearby coast and the western interior, as there are few steep gradients but many perilously narrow village streets.

There are at least eight **bank ATMs**, some standalone, scattered across town; the **post office** and Olympic airlines terminal are adjacent to each other on Garoufalídhou, with a **laundry** across the way by the *Hotel Paris*. There are **Internet** facilities at *Excite Club*, just behind the port-plaza junction; at *Joy*, by the post office; and at *NetPoint* on Kydhá. The Maroula cinema, down the street near the intersection with Frýnis, now functions as a general indoor events venue.

Accommodation

Despite Límnos' steady gentrification, you may still be met off the boat with offers of a **room**. Romeïkós Yialós has a few **pensions** or **small hotels** in restored mansions, while just north of Romeïkós Yialós, the areas of Rihá Nerá and Áyios Pandelímon are good bets for **self-catering units**. There's **no official campsite** on Límnos; Greek caravanners and campers have been banished from their former haunt at the north end of Platý beach, though a few tents still sprout furtively at Paralía Thánous and Kéros.

Apollo Pavillion On Frýnis ℡22540 23712, ⓦwww.apollopavilion.com. Hidden away in a peaceful cul-de-sac about halfway along Garoufalídhou, this offers three-bed studios with air con, TV and mini-kitchen. Most units have balconies, with views of either the castle or the mountains. Open all year; the friendly owner's wine is excellent. ❹

Arhondiko Cnr Sakhtoúri & Filellínon, Romeïkós Yialós ℡22540 29800, ⓦwww.questinn.com. Briefly Límnos' first hotel in the nineteenth century, this 1851-built mansion was reopened in 2003 as three floors of restored, medium-sized, wood-trimmed rooms with all mod cons. There's a pleasant ground-floor bar/breakfast lounge. ❺

Ifestos Ethnikís Andístasis 17, Andhróni district, inland from Rihá Nerá ℡22540 24960, ⒻⒻ22540 23623. Quiet, professionally run C-class hotel, with pleasant common areas. Slightly small rooms have air con, fridges, balconies and again a mix of sea or hill views. Available through Sunvil; otherwise ❹

Lemnos Harbourfront ℡22540 22153, ⒻⒻ22540 23329. The more cheerful and better appointed quayside C-class hotel, with air con, fridges, balconies and limited parking out front offsetting small-hours ferry noise. ❸

Limnia Yi/Terra Limnia Romeïkós Yialós, lane off south end ℡22540 22254 or 694 66 74 274. Just

seven standard rooms with heating/air con, two with balconies. ❸

Porto Myrina Palace Avlónas beach, 1.5km north of Rihá Nerá ℡22540 24805, ⓦwww .portomyrina.com. The island's best beachfront lodging, though its five-star rating is probably one too many. A perimeter of standard rooms and freestanding bungalows closer to the water share the same cheerful decor of light furniture, fridges and full baths, with the majority having some sort of sea view; in the middle of it all is an Artemis temple found during construction (see p.434). Breakfast and other meals are good, though service is shaky. Vast common areas include tennis courts, a footie pitch, one of the largest (saltwater) pools in Greece, and summer watersports on the beach. Open May–Oct 15; through Sunvil/ Greek Sun, or ❼ standard rooms, ❽ bungalows

Romeïkos Yíalos Sakhtoúri 7 ℡22540 23787. A venerable B-class pension in a Romeïkós Yialós mansion with just eight good-sized if plain rooms, some with air con; quieter than waterfront outfits. ❸

Sotiris Studios Rihá Nerá ℡22540 25416. Good-sized units on a slope facing landscaped grounds, private parking, and the castle beyond. Open April–Oct, with heating available, but has a considerable package allotment, and Sotiris speaks no English, so best book through his brother Panayiotis (see *Villa Afroditi* listing, p.435). ❹

The Town

Mýrina is fairly large for an island town, but most things of interest face the main shopping street **Kydhá** and its continuation **Karatzá** – stretching from the harbour to **Romeïkós Yialós**, the beach and esplanade to the north of the castle – or on its perpendicular, **Garoufalídhou**, roughly halfway along. As town beaches go, Romeïkós Yialós is not at all bad, but **Rihá Nerá** to the north is rather better: well protected, popular with families and offering a non-motorized watersports facility. Southerly **Toúrkikos Yialós**, beyond the fishing port, provides a decent alternative, though without special amenities.

On the headland between Romeïkós Yialós and the south-facing ferry dock stands a **castle** (access unrestricted), dating from the Byzantine era and quite ruined despite later additions by the Genoese and Ottomans. It's worth climbing at sunset for views over the town, the entire west coast and – in clear conditions – over to Mount Áthos, 35 nautical miles west (also to be glimpsed from any suitable height east of town). Around its approaches live a herd of skittish, Rhodes-type (see p.126) **deer**, kept, fed and watered by the municipality.

The Archeological Museum

The **Archeological Museum** (Tues–Sun 8.30am–3pm; €2) occupies an Ottoman mansion behind Romeïkós Yialós, not far from the site of Bronze Age Myrina, currently being excavated in the suburb of Rihá Nerá. Finds are assiduously labelled in Greek, Italian and English, and the entire premises are exemplary in terms of presentation – the obvious drawback being that the best items have been spirited away to Athens, leaving a collection that's essentially of specialist interest. Because of Límnos' fertility and proximity to the Dardanelles, it was occupied in prehistoric times; exhibits belong predominantly to the Archaic period and before, since the island became a backwater satellite of Athens during Classical times.

In broad terms, the south ground-floor gallery is devoted to pottery from Polyókhni (Polyochni); the north wing contains more of the same, plus items from ancient Myrina; while upstairs are galleries of post-Bronze Age artefacts from Kavírio (Kabireio) and Ifestía (Hephaestia). The star upper-storey exhibits, much imitated in local modern jewellery, are votive lamps in the shape of sirens, found in an Archaic sanctuary at Hephaestia. Rather less vicious than the harpy-like creatures described by Homer, they are identified more invitingly as "muses of the underworld, creatures of superhuman wisdom, incarnations of nostalgia for paradise".

There are also numerous representations of the goddess Cybele/Artemis, who was revered throughout the island; her shrine was typically situated near a fauna-rich river mouth – on Límnos at Avlónas, now in the grounds of the *Porto Myrina* resort. Also noteworthy is an entire room devoted to metal objects, including gold jewellery and bronze objects both practical (cheese graters, door knockers) and whimsical (a vulture and a snail).

Eating and drinking

Mýrina's **tavernas** are usually better value than its lodgings. Abutting a little square off Karatzá, hemmed in by old houses and two plane trees, *O Platanos* serves well-executed traditional *mayireftá* to big crowds (particularly at lunchtime), with locals in conspicuous attendance.

Seafood on Límnos is generally excellent (if not exactly cheap), thanks to the island's position near the Dardanelles and seasonal migrations of fish through it; accordingly there are several tavernas arrayed around the little fishing port. There's little to distinguish their prices or menus, and all the proprietors are related by blood or marriage, though *O Glaros* at the far end is considered the best – and works out slightly more expensive.

Not too surprisingly given the twee setting, the few restaurants and many bars along Romeïkós Yialós are poor value, except perhaps for a drink with views of the castle, illuminated at night. The tree-shaded tables of *Iy Tzitzífies* on Rihá Nerá beach, the next bay north, are a far better option for a meal; most of the extensive menu is likely to be available on any given day. For a beach-front snack-bar, look no further than *Argo*, by the watersports facility. Other than the venues at Romeïkós Yialós, **nightspots** are not conspicuous; *Aelos*, a music bar-*ouzerí* right on the ferry dock, is as good as any.

Western Límnos

For more deserted beaches than those at Rihá Nerá and Toúrkikos Yialós, you should strike out 3km north from town to the beach at **Avlónas**. This is unencroached upon except for the *Porto Myrina* luxury complex to the south and the local power plant at the north end, the latter oddly juxtaposed with a fine old bridge over the stream, which may still contain a few terrapins. In between the two, a lively, yurt-like beach-bar (late June to early Sept) offers sunbeds to youthful punters. In the grounds of *Porto Myrina*, there's an extensive **sanctuary** dating from the seventh century BC through Hellenistic times, dedicated to both Artemis Tavropolio and her avatar of Selene, the moon goddess.

Some 3km further on from Avlónas, the non-bypass road works its way through **KÁSPAKAS**, its north-facing houses arranged in pretty, tiled tiers and acting as an irresistible magnet for those after a weekend retreat. Attractive as well is the central, terraced *platía* with a delicious, potable spring, near which is a **taverna**, *To Lykhnari* (all year), with an excellent chef (Kyriakos) and a range of *mezédhes*, meat and seafood in big portions. Compared to this, a trio of uneven, summer-only tavernas down at **Áyios Ioánnis beach** finish a distant second, though the middle one with seating in the shade of piled-up volcanic boulders is certainly worth stopping at for a drink. The beach between this, and *Taverna Iliovasilemata* to the south, is uncharacteristically rocky for Límnos and unattractive; the beach north of the boulders, beyond the fishing anchorage, is sandier and more popular, but this whole coast is often buffeted by southwest winds.

Platý: village and beach

PLATÝ village, 2km southeast of Mýrina, has had its profile spoilt by the kind of modern villa construction that is blighting many Limnian villages lately, but it does have two **tavernas** popular in the evening. By far the better of these is *O Sozos*, just off the main *platía*, where you'll have to show up early for a table (groups should reserve on ☎22540 25085). Fine *orektiká*, lamb chops, steamed mussels, grilled *biftéki*, *tsípouro* (the north-mainland answer to *oúzo*) and local bulk wine are strong points. The nocturnal activity here makes the handful of **rooms** a noisy proposition; it's better to head west beyond the village limits, to Nikos and Soula's *Panorama Studios* (☎22540 22487, ℗22540 24118; ❹; May–Sept), well-kept units fitting two to four persons, with sea views and easy parking.

The long, sandy **beach** (officially Paralía Platéos), 700m below, is popular and usually clean, with watersports on offer at the north end, and crags on the horizon. Except for the unsightly Mark Warner compound at the south end, the area is still rural, with sheep parading to and fro at dawn and dusk. The single hotel, low-rise *Plati Beach* (℡ 22540 23635, ℉ 22540 23583; ❹), has an enviable position in the middle of the beach; avoid the small ground-floor rooms in favour of upper storey linking units or the attic suites with their views. All have air conditioning and (most years) a substantial package presence. The ground-floor bar/restaurant shares trade with reliable *Grigoris* near the south end of the beach, though both lose out in the evenings to the village-centre tavernas.

The highest standard of **studios** in the area, if not the island, is the tastefully landscaped, well-appointed *Villa Afroditi* (℡ 22540 23141 or 694 53 90 320, ℉ 22540 25031; winter ℡ 210 96 33 488; ❺ or through Sunvil; open mid-May to end Sept), with a pleasant pool bar and one of the best buffet breakfasts in this book. Hospitable, multilingual Panayiotis and Afroditi Papasotiriou lay on reasonable-value Wednesday-night barbecues, with lobster or king prawns on request.

If Platý beach gets too crowded – likely in August – there's another cove, **Playíso Mólos**, less than 2km away, south past the Mark Warner complex on a dirt track. The water shelves sharply with rocks in the shallows (so it's not great for kids), but the bay is very scenic, with a little islet to give it definition.

Thános and Evgátis beach

THÁNOS, 2km further southeast, seems a bigger, more architecturally characterful version of Platý village, with high-standard mock-trad **bungalows** at the east edge (℡ 22540 23162 or 22540 25284; ❹). Above Thános, lodged in a volcanic cave, hides **Panayía Kakaviótissa**, the iconic postcard image of the isle.

A 1.5-kilometre paved but unsigned road leads down from the east edge of the village (or a marked one from the centre) to **Paralía Thánous**, perhaps the most scenic of the southwestern beaches, with Áyios Efstrátios island showing clearly on the horizon in the later afternoon. Of the two **tavernas**, *Nikos Yiannakaros* (lunch only except Aug) is more reliable.

Beyond Thános, the road curls over to the enormous beach at **Evgátis**, flanked by standard-issue volcanic crags to the west and reckoned the island's best, though it can get windy. A little river (currently devoid of turtles) meets the sea at mid-strand; facilities comprise a few unobtrusive umbrellas and wooden shade-pavilions, two summertime music bar-*kantínas* on the sand and equally seasonal watersports facilities, plus a full-service **taverna** across the road with a few comfortable **rooms** (℡ 22540 51700; ❸).

Kondiás

Some 3km further along (11km from Mýrina), **KONDIÁS** is the island's third-largest settlement, cradled between two hills tufted with Límnos' only natural pine forest. Stone-built, red-tiled houses combine with the setting to make Kondiás the most attractive inland village, a fact not lost on the urban Greeks restoring old houses with varying degrees of taste. Short-term facilities are limited, and aren't much better at the shore annexe of **Dhiapóri**, 2km east. The beach – backed by a huge, fenced-off minefield – is unappealing, the taverna listless and unreliable, with the main interest lent by the signposted wildlife refuge on the **Fakó** peninsula beyond (best take a jeep).

Portianoú War Cemetery, Pedhinó and hill villages

From Kondiás it's 11km northeast to the junction with the main trans-island road at Livadhohóri. En route, the first, brief detour worth making is a visit to one of Límnos' two **World War I cemeteries** (see opposite for the other) at **PORTIANOÚ** village, 5km along. Turn left (west) onto a lane marked by a blue-on-white sign reading "ANZAC ST", which passes below a large hilltop church. Keep left on a rough lane, avoiding the gated way up to the church, and behind it you'll discover the meticulously tended cemetery, edged by pines. Amongst the 348 graves here are those of two Canadian nurses, three Egyptian labourers, three Maori troops and one of the "enemy", a Levantine or Jewish Ottoman officer.

The next potential deviation is right of the road, to **PALEÓ PEDHINÓ**, mostly abandoned since a 1960s earthquake, but like Kondiás a magnet for those hunting out weekend houses. The main amenity for short-term visits is an excellent **psistariá**, *To Petrino Horio* (supper July & Aug), with all manner of roast beast served at tables on the fieldstoned, shaded *platía*.

Rather than using the fast but dull main highway west, you can vary the return to Mýrina by continuing northeast to Karpássi, and then bearing northwest towards Atsíki for the entirely paved "high" road back to the port. The villages and scenery en route give a good impression of rural Limnian life, though be prepared to reverse when confronted by giant grain combines or large flocks of sheep.

DHÁFNI, the first village you'll encounter, challenges stereotypical images of the island's flatness with a hillside setting above a wooded ravine. **SARDHÉS**, 2.5km further on, is the highest community on Límnos, providing wonderful views of broody sunsets, clusters of handsome houses, and one of the best **tavernas** on Límnos, *Mantella* (all year). Portions are huge, so go hungry; you'll need to book (☏22540 61349) in summer for either the pleasant courtyard or the interior, renovated in late 2004 but still doubling as the local *kafenío*.

Just past Kornós, you rejoin the main road and shortly afterwards pass the easterly turning for **Thermá (Thermés Piyés)**, a nineteenth-century Ottoman spa complete with calligraphic plaques. Restored in the mid-1990s, it only reopened again in summer 2004 (daily 9am–2pm & 5–9pm; €3) under energetic new management, who intend to run a snack-bar on site and carry out extensive improvements; for now you bathe in modern bathtubs in odd-sized rooms under the original domes. Unusually for a hot spring, the water is non-sulphurous and the tastiest on the island, so there is always a knot of cars parked nearby under the trees while their owners are filling jerry cans with warm water from a **public fountain** – again with a bilingual Greek/Ottoman inscription.

Eastern Límnos

The shores of sumpy **Moúdhros Bay**, glimpsed south of the trans-island trunk road, are muddy and best avoided. The bay itself enjoyed considerable importance during World War I, when it served throughout 1915 as the staging area for the unsuccessful Allied landings on the Gallipoli peninsula, and later saw Allied acceptance of the Ottoman surrender aboard the British warship HMS *Agamemnon* on October 30, 1918.

Moúdhros and the main Allied Cemetery

MOÚDHROS port, the second-largest town on Límnos, was (until recently) quite literally a God-forsaken place, owing to an incident late in Ottoman rule. Certain villagers killed some Muslims and threw them down a well on property belonging to the Athonite monastery of Koutloumousioú; the Ottoman authorities, holding the monks responsible, slaughtered any Koutloumousiot brethren they found on the island and set the local monastery alight. Two monks managed to escape to Áthos, where every August 23 a curse was chanted, condemning Moúdhros' inhabitants to "never sleep again"; the Athonite brothers finally relented in July 2001.

Moúdhros is an indisputably dreary place visually, and only a wonderfully kitsch church – looking like a Baroque Iberian shrine with its two belfries – redeems it. Despite this, there are two **hotels** here, including the frankly overpriced *To Kyma* (☎22540 71333, ⓕ22540 71484; ❹), though its **taverna** makes a more reasonable, if run-of-the-mill, lunch halt while touring. There is, however, little to prompt an overnight stay; the closest local beach, 4km south by dirt track, is **Havoúli**, mud-sandy and too close to the confines of the bay to be really attractive.

A kilometre or so northwest, on the paved road towards Roussopoúli, you pass the island's main Allied **military cemetery** (unlocked), maintained by the Commonwealth War Graves Commission, its neat lawns and rows of white headstones incongruous in such parched surroundings. Of the 36,000 Allied dead resulting from the disastrous Gallipoli campaign, 887 are buried here (plus the 348 noted at Portianoú) – mainly battle casualties, who died after having been evacuated to the base hospital at Moúdhros. Though the deceased are mostly British, there is also a French cenotaph, and – speaking volumes about imperial sociology – a mass "Musalman" grave for Egyptian and Indian troops in one corner, with a Koranic inscription.

Polyókhni

Indications of the most advanced Neolithic civilization in the Aegean have been unearthed at **Polyókhni** (Polyochni), 3km by paved road from the gully-hidden village of **KAMÍNIA**, 7km east of Moúdhros. Since the 1930s, ongoing Italian excavations have uncovered four layers of settlement, the oldest from late in the fourth millennium BC, predating Troy on the Turkish coast opposite; the town met a sudden, violent end from war or earthquake in about 2100 BC. Very little of Homeric or Mycenaean vintage has been found yet, though a gold hoard similar to the so-called "Priam's Treasure", rediscovered in Russia in the early 1990s, was uncovered in 1956 inside a clay vase where it had been hurriedly secreted.

The actual ruins (daily 8.30am–3.30pm, may open later in summer; free) are well labelled but of essentially specialist interest, though a *bouleuterion* (assembly hall) with bench seating, a mansion and the landward fortifications are impressive. The site occupies a bluff overlooking a long, narrow rock-and-sand beach flanked by stream valleys, the mouth of one of these being the old port; two wells within the fortifications suggest that reliable fresh water or sieges were major preoccupations. A small but well-presented museum behind the entrance kiosk brings the whole place to life and explains its historic significance; moreover, during August and September the Italian excavators are normally about, and may be free to show you around.

Ifestía and Kavírio

Ifestía and Kavírio, the other significant ancient sites on Límnos besides Avlóna's Artemis temple, are most easily reached via the village of **Kondopoúli**, 7km northeast of Moúdhros. Both sites are rather remote and only accessible by private transport.

Ifestía

Ifestía (or Hephaestia), in Classical times the most important city on the island, took its name from Hephaistos, god of fire and metalworking. According to legend, he attempted to intercede in a quarrel between his parents Hera and Zeus, and for his troubles was hurled from Mount Olympus by his father. A hard landing on Límnos left Hephaistos permanently lame, but he was adopted by the Limnians and held in high esteem thereafter.

A rough four-kilometre dirt track, well marked from Kondopoúli, leads to the edge of the **site** (unrestricted access), most of which remains unexcavated. Leave vehicles at the edge of the sumpy bay here, and walk ten minutes uphill to view the scant remains of a theatre, a temple dedicated to the god and a cluster of house foundations. All told, it's the most unevocative of the island's three major sites and can be skipped without regret by non-specialists.

Kavírio

Somewhat more rewarding is **Kavírio** (Kabirion), on the opposite shore of Tigáni inlet from Ifestía, and accessed by the same road built to serve the derelict Kaviria Palace luxury complex. The **ruins** (daily 8.30am–3pm; free) are of a sanctuary connected with the cult of the Kabiroi on the island of Samothráki just to the north, although the site on Límnos is probably older. Little survives other than the ground plan – aligned unusually southeast-to-northwest, an orientation dictated by the topography of the headland – but the setting is undeniably impressive. Eleven column stumps stake out a *stoa*, behind eight spots marked as column bases in the main *telestirio* or shrine where the cult mysteries took place.

More engaging, perhaps, is a nearby **sea-grotto** identified as the Homeric *Spiliá toú Filoktíti*, where the Trojan war hero Philoctetes was abandoned by his comrades-in-arms until his stinking, gangrenous leg had healed. Landward access to the cave is via steps leading down from the caretaker's shelter, though final access (from a little passage on the right as you face the sea) involves some wading.

Kótsinas

Besides these two sites, the only other attraction on the shores of Bourniá Bay, reached via Repanídhi village on the other side of Kondopoúli, is the often dirty, hard-packed beach of **Kótsinas**. The nearby anchorage (follow signs to "Kótsinas Fortress") offers a trio of **tavernas**; the most popular of these, *To Korali* by the water, is reliably open at lunch, with a wide range of *mezédhes* and fish; portions are on the small side but so are prices. Up on a knoll overlooking the jetty looms an oxidized-green, sword-brandishing statue of Maroula, a Genoese-era heroine who delayed the Ottoman conquest by a few years. Also on this hill stands the large church of Zoödhóhou Piyís (the Lifegiving Spring); this itself is nothing extraordinary, but from out front 63 steps lead down through an illuminated tunnel cut into the rock to the potable (if slightly minerally) spring in question, oozing into a cool, vaulted **subterranean chamber**.

Eastern beaches

Certainly the best beach on this part of Límnos is at **Kéros**, 2.5km by dirt road below **KALLIÓPI** (two snack-bar/**tavernas**, smart rooms at the edge of town – ⓣ22540 41730, ❹), in turn 1km from Kondopoúli. A 1.5-kilometre stretch of sand with dunes and a small pine plantation, shallow water and a certain amount of seaweed, Kéros attracts Greek tourists and Germans with camper vans and windsurfing equipment, but is large enough to absorb most weekend crowds. Near the parking area, a small *kantína*/snack-bar operates in July and August. By contrast, the beaches near the village of **PLÁKA**, at the northeastern tip of the island, are not worth the extra effort; the adjacent hot springs appearing on some maps are actually warm mud baths.

Áyios Efstrátios (Aï Strátis)

ÁYIOS EFSTRÁTIOS ("Aï Strátis" for short) is without doubt one of the quietest and loneliest islands in the Aegean. Historically, the only outsiders to stay here were compelled to do so – it served as a place of exile for political prisoners under both the Metaxas dictatorship of the 1930s and the various right-wing governments that followed the Civil War: up to six thousand of them during the 1950s. Before that, it was only permanently settled in the sixteenth century, after a long period of desertion since ancient times, and its land is still largely owned by three monasteries on nearby Mount Áthos. Despite increasing numbers of summer visitors, it's still unusual for foreign travellers to show up on the island.

Arrival

Large **ferries** between Límnos and Lávrio call also at Áyios Efstrátios regularly throughout the year; in summer, there's a small ferry too, the *Aiolis*, based on Límnos, which appears thrice weekly. The harbour was improved in 1993 to allow large ferries to dock, replacing the lighters which perilously transferred goods and passengers, but it is still a very exposed anchorage, and in bad weather you could end up stranded here longer than you bargained for. Unfortunately, the day-trips which used to be offered from Límnos seem to be a thing of the past, so there's no way to get just a brief taste of the islet.

The port

Áyios Efstrátios port – the sole settlement on the island – must be one of the ugliest habitations in Greece. Devastation caused by an earthquake in February 1968, which also killed half the population, was compounded by the rebuilding plan: the contract went to a company with connections to the colonels' junta, who prevented the survivors from returning to their old homes and used army bulldozers to raze even those structures that could have been repaired. From the northern hillside, some two dozen remaining houses of the old village overlook its replacement, whose grim rows of prefabs, complete with concrete church and underused shopping centre, constitute a sad monument to the corruption of the junta years. For comparison, check out a pre-earthquake photograph of the village in the *kafenío* by the port.

Architecture apart, Áyios Efstrátios still functions as a fishing and farming community of about three hundred, with the prefabs set at the mouth of a wooded stream valley draining to the sandy harbour beach. Tourist amenities

Greek script table

Límnos	Λήμνος	ΛΗΜΝΟΣ
Atsikí	Ατσική	ΑΤΣΙΚΗ
Avlónas	Αυλώνας	ΑΥΛΩΝΑΣ
Áyios Efstrátios	Άγιος Ευστράτιος	ΑΓΙΟΣ ΕΥΣΤΡΑΤΙΟΣ
Áyios Ioánnis	Άγιος Ιοάννης	ΑΓΙΟΣ ΙΟΑΝΝΗΣ
Dháfni	Δάφνη	ΔΑΦΝΗ
Dhiapóri	Διαπόρι	ΔΙΑΠΟΡΙ
Evgátis	Ευγάτης	ΕΥΓΑΤΗΣ
Fakós	Φακός	ΦΑΚΟΣ
Havoúli	Χαβούλι	ΧΑΒΟΥΛΙ
Ifestía	Ηφαιστεία	ΗΦΑΙΣΤΕΙΑ
Kalliópi	Καλλιόπη	ΚΑΛΛΙΟΠΗ
Kamínia	Καμίνια	ΚΑΜΙΝΙΑ
Karpássi	Καρπάσι	ΚΑΡΠΑΣΙ
Káspakas	Κάσπακας	ΚΑΣΠΑΚΑΣ
Kavírio	Καβείριο	ΚΑΒΕΙΡΙΟ
Kéros	Κέρος	ΚΕΡΟΣ
Kondiás	Κοντιάς	ΚΟΝΤΙΑΣ
Kondopoúli	Κοντοπούλι	ΚΟΝΤΟΠΟΥΛΙ
Kornós	Κορνός	ΚΟΡΝΟΣ
Kótsinas	Κότσινας	ΚΟΤΣΙΝΑΣ
Livadhohóri	Λιβαδοχώρι	ΛΙΒΑΔΟΧΩΡΙ
Lýkhna	Λύχνα	ΛΥΧΝΑ
Moúdhros	Μούδρος	ΜΟΥΔΡΟΣ
Mýrina	Μύρινα	ΜΥΡΙΝΑ
Paralía Platéos	Παραλία Πλατέος	ΠΑΡΑΛΙΑ ΠΛΑΤΕΟΣ
Paralía Thánous	Παραλία Θάνούς	ΠΑΡΑΛΙΑ ΘΑΝΟΣ
Pedhinó	Πεδινό	ΠΕΔΙΝΟ
Pláka	Πλάκα	ΠΛΑΚΑ
Platý	Πλατύ	ΠΛΑΤΥ
Polyókhni	Πολυόχνη	ΠΟΛΥΟΧΝΗ
Portiano	Πορτιανού	ΠΟΡΤΙΑΝΟΥ
Repanídhi	Ρεπανίδι	ΡΕΠΑΝΙΔΙ
Romanoú	Ρομανού	ΡΟΜΑΝΟΥ
Roussopoúli	Ρουσσοπούλι	ΡΟΥΣΣΟΠΟΥΛΙ
Sardhés	Σαρδές	ΣΑΡΔΕΣ
Thános	Θάνος	ΘΑΝΟΣ
Város	Βάρος	ΒΑΡΟΣ

consist of just three **tavernas** (*Thanassis, Andonis* and *Tassos*), plus a like number of **pensions**. Best of these, in one of the surviving old houses, is the *Xenonas Aï-Stratis* (☎ 22540 93329; ❸); Andonis Paneras (☎ 22540 93209; ❸) and Apostolos Paneras (☎ 22540 93343; ❸) have more conventional rooms out in the prefabs. These relatively stiff prices for such an out-of-the-way place reflect Aï Stratis' increasing popularity with Greeks, and you may have to ring all three spots for a vacancy in season.

The rest of the island

As you walk away from the village – there are few cars and no paved roads – things improve rapidly. The landscape, dry hills and valleys scattered with a surprising number of oak trees, is deserted apart from wild rabbits, sheep, an occasional shepherd, and some good beaches where you can camp in desert-island isolation – perhaps the main reason you're likely to visit Áyios Efstrátios. **Alonítsi**, on the north coast, a ninety-minute walk from the village along a track up the north side of the valley (bear right at the only junction), is a two-kilometre stretch of sand with rolling breakers and views across to Límnos.

South of the village, there's a series of greyish sand beaches, most with wells and drinkable water, although with few real paths in this part of the island, getting to them can be quite a scramble. **Lidharió**, at the end of an attractive wooded valley, is the first worthwhile beach but, again, it's a fairly strenuous ninety-minute walk from town, unless you can persuade a fisherman to take you by boat.

Límnos travel details

Inter-island transport

Kaïkia/small ferries
Límnos to: Áyios Efstrátios (from Mýrina Mon, Wed, Fri at 3pm, from Áyios Efstrátios 6.30am Mon, Wed, Fri; journey time 2hr).

NB To simplify the following schedules, the once-weekly sailing offered by LANE, northbound to Alexandhroúpoli and south to Lésvos, Híos, Sámos, Kálymnos, Kós and Rhodes, has been omitted.

Large ferries
Áyios Efstrátios to: Kavála; (1 weekly on SF; 7hr); Lávrio (1–3 weekly on SF; 8–10hr); Límnos (2–3 weekly on SF; 1hr 30min); Psará (1 weekly on SF; 6hr 30min); Sígri, Lésvos (1 weekly on SF; 3hr 15min).
Límnos to: Híos (3 weekly on GA, 1 weekly on SF, 1 weekly on NEL; 9hr 30min–12hr); Ikaría (2 weekly on GA; 16–20 hr); Kavála (3 weekly on SF, 2 weekly on GA; 4hr 30min–6hr 45min); Lávrio

(1–3 weekly on SF; 9hr 30min–10hr); Mytilíni, Lésvos (3 weekly on GA, 1 weekly on SF, 1 weekly on NEL; 6hr); Sígri, Lésvos (1 weekly on SF; 5hr 30min); Pireás (2 weekly on GA, 1 weekly on NEL; 18–27hr); Sámos (3 weekly on GA; 14hr); Thessaloníki (1 weekly on NEL; 9hr 30min).

Catamaran
The *Aeolos Kenteris* serves Lésvos, Híos and Pireás twice weekly from Límnos, Kavála and Thessaloníki once each weekly.

Flights
Límnos to: Athens (3 daily; 1hr); Híos (2 weekly; 1hr 30min); Lésvos (3–5 weekly; 35min); Rhodes (3–5 weekly; 2hr 5min–3hr 40min); Sámos (2 weekly; 1hr 45min–2hr 30min); Thessaloníki (1 daily; 45min).
NB Because of heavy use by the Greek armed forces, these flights need to be booked well in advance throughout the year.

Contexts

Contexts

History

This section serves merely to lend some perspective to travels in the Dodecanese and east Aegean, and is heavily weighted towards more recent centuries. Although these two island groups are the most recent additions to the modern Greek state, their Hellenic identity has been fairly consistent since ancient times.

Neolithic, Minoan and Mycenean ages: c.5500–1150 BC

It seems that people originally came to the Dodecanese and east Aegean in fits and starts, predominantly from the **Anatolian mainland** just opposite. Settlement of the islands after the sixth millennium BC is fairly well documented by archeological finds, particularly at present-day Thermí, Lésvos; Emboriós, Híos; Líndhos, Rhodes; various sites on Límnos; and in several caves on Kálymnos. In contrast to the exclusively farming communities on the mainland, these were trading posts founded at or near excellent natural harbours.

The years between about **2000 and 1100 BC** were a period of fluctuating regional dominance, based at first upon **sea power**; the Phoenicians in particular lingered briefly at Rhodes en route to Crete from the Middle East. Minoan Crete, which monopolized the eastern Mediterranean trade routes during an era subsequently called the **Minoan Age**, in turn dispatched more permanent colonists during the sixteenth century BC, establishing trading posts at Ialyssos and Kameiros on Rhodes' west-facing Aegean coast.

When the Minoan cities finally succumbed to disaster, natural or otherwise, around 1500–1450 BC, it was the flourishing mainland centre of **Mycenae** that assumed the leading role in these islands, until it in turn collapsed during the twelfth century BC. On Rhodes, the Mycenean invaders left traces of their distinctive **pottery** (which dominates the town's archeological museum), and re-established the cities of Ialyssos, Kameiros and Lindos. By now the island and some of its neighbours (including Kós and Sými) were prominent enough to participate in the semi-legendary **Trojan War**, with their ships included in Homer's roster of those who sailed to Troy.

The Dorian and Archaic eras: c.1150–500 BC

The collapse of the Mycenean (or more properly, Late Bronze Age) civilization has traditionally been attributed to the invasion from the north of a fair-skinned "barbarian" people, the **Dorians**, who devastated the existing culture and initiated the first "**Dark Ages**". Revisionist archeologists now see the influx more in terms of shifting **trade patterns**, though undoubtedly there was major disruption during the **twelfth century BC**.

Out in the islands, this era saw Lemnos apparently retain its indigenous, non-Mycenean population, and Lesbos play host to **Aeolians** displaced from mainland Thessaly. Meanwhile, the so-called Dorians took over most islands to the south, including Rhodes, where Ialyssos and Kameiros began to grow. Together with Lindos, Astypalia (on Kos), Knidos and Halikarnassos (the latter two on the Anatolian mainland opposite), these six settlements formed the confederacy known as the **Dorian Hexapolis**.

Two cultural trends are salient in this period: the almost total supplanting of earlier mother goddesses by **male deities** (a process begun under the Myceneans), and the appearance of an **alphabet** still recognizable by modern Greeks, which replaced the so-called "Linear A" and "Linear B" Minoan/Mycenean scripts.

Archaic Period

By around **800 BC**, the initially rigorous rule of the Dorians had relaxed on the islands as elsewhere in Greece, perhaps accelerated by the influx from Asia Minor of the so-called Ionians, particularly on Khios, Ikaria and Samos. The twelve-town **Ionian League**, centred at the Panionion shrine on Mount Mycale opposite Sámos, included these islands as members.

Here as elsewhere in the Hellenic world, the ninth century BC ushered in the beginnings of the more democratic Greek **city-state** (*polis*). Citizens – rather than just kings or aristocrats – became involved in government and took part in community activities organizing industry, worship and leisure. Colonial ventures by the wealthier cities (including Lindos) increased, as did commercial dealings, and the consequent rise in the import–export trade gradually gave rise to a new class of manufacturers.

Each city-state retained both its independence and a distinctive style, with the result that the sporadic attempts to unite against any external enemy were always pragmatic and temporary. The two most powerful states to emerge on the mainland were **Athens** and **Sparta**, who were to engage in fierce rivalry for the next five centuries. In the Dodecanese and east Aegean, the most important city-states were Lindos on Rhodes, Astypalia on Kos, Mithymna and Mytilene on Lesbos, and the eponymous island capitals, Khios and Samos. Their heyday was the sixth century BC, when Mytilene, Lindos and Samos were ruled by **tyrants** of distinction – Pittakos, Kleoboulos and Polykrates respectively, with the word "tyrant" yet to acquire all of its modern pejorative connotations.

Each city-state had its **acropolis**, or high town, where religious activity was focused. Worship at this stage was **polytheistic**, grouping the Olympic pantheon under Zeus. The proliferation of references to names and of sanctuary finds on the islands suggests a preference for the divine twins Apollo and Artemis, the latter often merely a thinly Hellenized version of the Anatolian goddess Cybele; Aphrodite and Hera were also well represented – only to be expected, bearing in mind the proximity to Asia with its cults of love goddesses such as Astarte.

The Classical and Hellenistic eras: c.500–166 BC

Of the outside threats faced by the various city-states, none was greater than that of the **Persians**, who under successive kings Darius and Xerxes made repeated attempts to subjugate both islands and mainland. By virtue of their position, as well as innate sympathies, many of the east Aegean and Dodecanesian city-states took the side of the invaders; though Rhodes successfully resisted Darius' first attack in 491 BC, in the year 480 it contributed nearly forty ships to Xerxes' fleet at the **Battle of Salamis**. It was the decisive Greek naval victory (479 BC) in the Mycale straits off Samos that finally ended the Persian threat. Shortly thereafter, the **Delian Confederacy**, an alliance dominated by Athens, was established, in which many island city-states (including those of Rhodes) were enlisted voluntarily or otherwise.

Athens again was the first to elaborate the concept of **democracy** (*demokratia*), literally "control by the people" – but at this stage "the people" did not include women or slaves. In Athens there were three organs of government. The **Areopagus**, composed of the city elders, had a steadily decreasing authority and ended up dealing solely with murder cases. Then there was the **Council of Five Hundred**, elected annually by ballot to prepare the business of the Assembly and attend to matters of urgency. Finally, the **Assembly** gave every free man a political voice; it had sole responsibility for law-making and provided an arena for the discussion of important issues. Other "democratic" city-states adopted variations of these institutions, but they were slow to catch on in the eastern islands, where in most cases oligarchies of some sort remained in power.

The power struggles between Athens and Sparta, each allied with various networks of city-states, eventually culminated in the Peloponnesian **Wars** of 431–404 BC. The Dodecanese and east Aegean saw little military action, but because of a Dorian heritage shared with Sparta, city-states there tended to defect to the Spartan side when given the opportunity; Mytilene for example revolted in 428 (partly to spite pro-Athenian neighbour Mithymna), and Rhodes, Kos and Khios changed sides in 412. Only Samos remained a more or less constant Athenian ally to the end of the war. These conflicts (superbly recorded by Thucydides) were nominally won by Sparta, and thereafter the small city-state ceased to function so effectively.

On Rhodes, decline was hastened by the founding in 408 BC of a single city intended to replace the three original centres of Ialyssos, Kameiros and Lindos. The result of this act of union (*synoekismos*) was **Rodos**, at the northeastern tip of the island, endowed with three natural harbours still in use today. The original trio slowly suffered a loss of status over the next few centuries, until only Lindos retained any importance or independence. Quickly growing wealthy from **trade** – particularly the export of wine to Egypt in exchange for grain – Rodos minted its own currency, which gradually replaced earlier coinage from Lindos, Ialyssos and Kameiros.

During this period, the islands of Samos and Khios were at their nadirs, intermittently occupied by the resurgent Persians taking advantage of disorder following the Peloponnesian Wars; Kos effected a *synoekismos* of its own in 366 BC, founding the present-day port and capital. Only the largest of a half-dozen original city-states on Lesbos remained important during the fourth century BC.

The most important factor in the decline of the city-states was emerging on the northern mainland, in the kingdom of **Macedonia**. Based at the Macedonian capital of Pella, Philip II (359–336 BC) was forging a strong military and unitary force, extending his territories into Thrace and establishing control over the southern mainland. His son, **Alexander the Great**, in an extraordinarily brief but dynamic thirteen-year reign, extended these gains into Persia and Egypt as well as parts of modern India and Afghanistan. The east Aegean and Dodecanese islands quickly sided with Alexander, especially mercenarily minded Rhodes, which was granted generous commercial concessions in the conqueror's new Levantine territories.

This unwieldy empire splintered almost immediately upon Alexander's death in 323 BC, and was divided into the three Macedonian dynasties of **Hellenistic Greece**. It was not long before the Antigonids in Macedonia, the Seleucids in Syria and Persia, and the Ptolemies in Egypt fell to fighting among themselves. Their conflicts involved Rhodes, whose islanders had understandably refused an "offer" by Antigonus to join him in attacking Egypt, their long-standing ally and trade partner. Enraged at this defiance, in 305 BC Antigonus sent his son Demetrios to bring the Rhodians to heel; the result was a year-long **siege**, one of the great battles of antiquity (see box on p.106). Having fought each other to a standstill, attackers and defenders agreed to a truce, and Demetrios' abandoned war machinery was sold to defray the costs of the **Colossus of Rhodes** (see box on p.124).

Hellenistic Rodos emerged from the war with redoubled prestige and wealth; poets, philosophers, rhetoricians and artists, both native-born and immigrant, made the city their home during a "**golden age**" that was to last until the middle of the second century BC. During this time Rhodes' seagoing power was such that her **maritime and trading law** became standard across the Mediterranean, and was adapted by Augustus three centuries later for application throughout the Roman Empire.

The Roman and Byzantine eras: 166 BC–15th century AD

Until now, **Rhodes** had proved adroit at avoiding political alliances and keeping commercial criteria paramount, but as the second century BC progressed, she became entangled with an expanding **Rome**. The mainland had been subdued by the Romans in a series of campaigns beginning in 215 BC, and by 190 BC their operations extended to the islands, Anatolia and the Middle East. Rome repaid Rhodes for its military assistance with a grant of authority over lands in Lycia and Caria, but the latter complained repeatedly to the Senate. Matters came to a head in 166 BC, when Rome withdrew the Rhodian concession in these two Anatolian realms, and declared the central Aegean islet of Delos a free port, sending Rhodian prosperity into free fall. Rhodes compounded her error by siding against the assassins of Julius Caesar in 42 BC; in retaliation, Cassius plundered and burnt Rodos city, massacring the citizens and forwarding enormous booty to Rome.

Kos' turn had come in 88 BC, at the hands of the brigand-king **Mithridates of Pontus**, who sacked the port town, relieving it of £1 million equivalent in bank deposits; the island was otherwise known for its wine and silk, both now long since disappeared. **Samos** had taken Mithridates' part and was punished accordingly, though later it was chosen to host the honeymoon of Antony and Cleopatra. Of all these islands, **Lesbos** was the Romans' favourite for its lively town life and gentle scenery, with money spent on lavish public works, and imperial visits to its academies and theatres. Following a decree by Emperor Augustus, these four cities were designated **venues of banishment** for disgraced notables – not too onerous a punishment given the creature comforts they afforded.

Christianity and Byzantium

Christianity came early to the east Aegean and Dodecanese. The apostle Paul stopped here in the first century to evangelize Rhodes, Kós, Sámos, Híos and Lésvos, and these, plus virtually every smaller island (particularly Kálymnos) have at least two ruined basilicas with mosaic floors, invariably from the fifth or sixth century, often built atop pagan shrines; these early churches were mostly levelled by Arab raids in the seventh century.

The **decline of the Roman Empire** involved its apportioning into eastern and western empires. In 330 AD Emperor Constantine moved his capital to the Greek city of **Byzantium**, and here emerged Constantinople (modern Istanbul), the "new Rome" and spiritual and political capital of the Byzantine Empire. While the last Western Roman emperor was deposed by barbarian Goths in 476, this eastern portion was to be the dominant Mediterranean power for some seven centuries; only in 1453 did it collapse completely.

Christianity had an influential advocate in Constantine (who, however, for reasons of state converted personally only on his deathbed), and by the end of the fourth century it was the **official state religion**; its liturgies (still in use in the Greek Orthodox Church), creed and New Testament were all written in the **koine**, a form of Greek evolved from the ancient dialect. A distinction was drawn, though, between perceptions of Greek as a language and as a cultural concept. The Byzantine Empire styled itself Roman, or *Romios*, rather than Hellenic, and moved to eradicate all remaining symbols of pagan Greece, for instance by dismantling ancient temples for use as masonry in building churches.

The seventh century saw **Constantinople** besieged by Persians, and later by Arabs, but the Byzantine Empire survived, losing only Egypt, the least "Greek" of its territories. During the ninth to the early eleventh centuries, culture, confidence and security flourished in the core Byzantine domains. Linked to the Orthodox Byzantine faith was a sense of spiritual superiority, and the emperors saw Constantinople as a "new Jerusalem" for their "chosen people". This was the beginning of a diplomatic and ecclesiastical conflict with the Catholic West that was to have disastrous consequences over the next five centuries.

From the seventh through to the eleventh centuries the Dodecanese and east Aegean became something of a provincial backwater, making little mark in the historical record, with islands such as Ikaría and Lésvos used mostly (as under the Romans) to house banished troublemakers; most illustrious of these was the disgraced **Empress Irene**, exiled to Políkhnitos – some say the village of Vassiliká, just east – in 802.

All the islands were ravaged repeatedly by piratical **Saracen raids**, and from these years date numerous castles and watchtowers. Only at the close of this period did two great Byzantine monuments appear: the imperially founded monasteries of **Néa Moní**, on Híos, and **Ayíou Ioánnou Theológou**, on Pátmos. The latter foundation involved an imperial grant of the entire, previously insignificant island to the abbot Khristodhoulos, with the sanctity of the place curiously respected by most subsequent rulers and invaders.

The coming of the Crusaders

Early in the eleventh century, **Latin Crusaders** began to appear in the region. In 1095 the Normans landed on the Dodecanese, with papal sanction, on their way to liberate Jerusalem. However, these were only a precursor to the rerouted **Fourth Crusade** of 1204, when Venetians, Franks and Germans diverted their armies from the Holy Land to Byzantium, sacking and occupying Constantinople. These Latin princes and their followers, intent on new lands and kingdoms, settled in to divide up the best part of the Empire. All that remained of Byzantium were four small peripheral kingdoms or **despotates**; none of these was based in the islands, though Rhodes was ruled by Leon Gavalas, a wealthy Byzantine governor, for three decades (a street in Ródhos Old Town bears his name).

There followed two centuries of manipulation by and struggle between Franks, Venetians, Genoese, Catalans and Turks. In 1261, the **Paleologos** dynasty, provisionally based at Nicaea, recovered the city of Constantinople but little of its former territory and power. Virtually their only Latin Catholic allies were the **Genoese**, whose support came at a heavy price: extensive commercial privileges in the capital itself, and the effective cession, at various moments during the thirteenth and fourteenth centuries, of virtually all the east Aegean and Dodecanese islands to assorted Genoese families.

Within a generation of driving out the Franks the Byzantine Greeks faced a much stronger threat in the expanding empire of the **Ottoman Turks**. Torn apart by internal struggles between two competing Byzantine dynasties, the Paleologi and Kantakuzenes, and unassisted except by the Genoese, they were to prove no match for the Turks. On Tuesday, May 29, 1453, a date still solemnly commemorated by the Orthodox church, Constantinople fell to the forces of **Sultan Mehmet II** after a seven-week siege.

Genoese and Crusader rule: 1248–1478

From the thirteenth century onwards the histories of the Dodecanese and east Aegean islands began to diverge slightly, with often widely varying dates of handover between one conqueror and another, even for neighbouring islands.

Genoese adventurers seized Rhodes from Venetian rivals in 1248, but in 1306 the chivalric order of the **Knights Hospitallers of St John** (see box on pp.116–117), expelled from Palestine and discontent on Cyprus, landed at Feraklós castle on the east coast of Rhodes. After a three-year war they evicted the Genoese from the island; Genoese-held Kós fell to the Knights in 1314, after which their possession – and prominent fortification – of most of the Dodecanese was a foregone conclusion. The main exceptions were Astypálea, Kárpathos and Kássos, which remained under Venetian rule, and the ecclesiastical idiosyncrasy of Pátmos.

From their main bases on Rhodes and Kós, the Knights engaged in both legitimate trade and piracy, constituting a major thorn in the side of the expanding Ottoman Empire, and – in the final century of their toehold – the only effective opposition to Ottoman authority in the Aegean. Attempts to dislodge them from these two islands during the fifteenth century were unsuccessful, and it took the Ottomans' acquisition of Kastellórizo as a base in 1512, and then a protracted siege of Rhodes by Sultan Süleyman the Magnificent in 1522 (see box on pp116–117), to send them packing off to Malta, and for all of the Dodecanese to fall into Turkish hands.

Remote Sámos and Ikaría supported garrisons of Venetians plus sundry other adventurers and pirates from the twelfth century onwards, but the **Genoese** gained undisputed possession of all islands from here north to the Thracian mainland during the fourteenth century. The marriage in 1355 of a Byzantine emperor to the daughter of the **Gattilusi family** resulted in Lésvos passing into the hands of the latter. By all accounts they ran a civilized and enlightened principality, except for the unsavoury last of their line, Nicolò, who was defeated and killed by the Ottomans in 1462. Límnos, briefly taken over by the Venetians, followed in 1478.

Híos was allotted to the **Giustiniani clan** in 1344, who instituted harsh government through a *maona* or holding company, monopolizing the lucrative gum mastic trade until the Ottoman conquest in 1566. Sámos, essentially deserted since the fifteenth century, and adjacent Ikaría were acquired by the sultan or his representatives in the same decade, making these three islands the last to fall under Ottoman suzerainty.

Ottoman occupation: 1478–1912

Under what Greeks refer to as the **Turkokratía** or years of Ottoman rule, the Dodecanese and east Aegean lapsed into rural provincialism, taking refuge in a self-protective mode of village life that endured undisrupted until the 1920s. Only those larger islands with plenty of flat, arable land, such as Rhodes, Kós and Lésvos, attracted extensive Turkish colonization and garrisoning, and then (except for Lésvos) only in the largest towns, where non-Muslims were forbidden residence in the strategic central citadels. Taxes and discipline from Istanbul were imposed locally through resident judges, tax collectors and military personnel, but large enterprises or estates could remain in the hands of local notables – civilian or military – who often enjoyed considerable independence.

By and large, provincial Ottoman government was lethargic if not downright lackadaisical; travellers reported extensive neglect and deterioration on Rhodes in the eighteenth and nineteenth centuries, with discarded weapons and unrepaired damage both still dating from the 1522 siege.

Greek identity, meanwhile, was preserved through the offices of the **Orthodox Church**, which, despite occasional instances of enforced conversion and intermarriage, and the transformation of some churches into mosques, suffered little interference from the Ottomans. All Orthodox people, Greek or otherwise, were officially grouped as one *millet* or **subject nation**, with the patriarch responsible for the behaviour of his flock, collecting taxes and for administering communal and inheritance law. **Monasteries** organized schools and became the trustees of Byzantine culture; this had gone into stagnation after the fall of the empire, whose scholars and artists emigrated west, adding impetus to the Renaissance.

As Ottoman administration became increasingly decentralized and inefficient, individual Greeks rose to local positions of considerable influence, and a number of communities achieved a significant degree of **autonomy**. Even on strictly governed Lésvos, much of the lucrative olive-oil trade had passed into Greek Orthodox hands by the eighteenth century; Híos enjoyed special privileges by virtue of its continued monopoly on gum mastic; Sámos produced fine tobacco and rope hemp; while the barren, maritime islets of the Dodecanese, such as Hálki, Kálymnos, Sými and Kastellórizo, made fortunes either by diving for sponges, transporting Anatolian goods on their own fleets, or building boats on Turkish commission. The Ottomans, until relatively late in their history, never bothered to acquire much seamanship, preferring to rely on island crews and shipyards.

A typical anecdote relates how the Symiots, on hearing of the fall of Rhodes, sought to allay imperial wrath by presenting Süleyman the Magnificent with a load of their finest sponges. Duly impressed, the sultan declared Sými a duty-free port, and gave the islanders a monopoly on sponge-diving anywhere in the Aegean, in return for a yearly tribute similar to their introductory gift. These and similar indulgences were mostly honoured until after the establishment of a Greek state in 1830 (see below), with incremental withdrawal of privileges occurring between 1874 and 1908 in response to continued warfare between the Ottomans and "free" Greece.

The struggle for Independence

By the eighteenth century, opposition to Turkish rule on the Greek mainland was becoming widespread, exemplified most obviously by the *klephts* (brigands) of the mountains. It was not until the nineteenth century, however, that a **resistance movement** could muster sufficient support and firepower to mount a real challenge to the Ottomans. In 1770 a Russian-backed uprising enjoyed considerable success out in the islands, with Sámos and Pátmos in particular occupied by Catherine the Great's favourite, Admiral Orlof, for three years. On the mainland, however, it was easily and brutally suppressed.

Fifty years later, however, the situation had changed. In Epirus, on the mainland, the Ottomans were overextended, subduing the expansionist campaigns of local ruler Ali Pasha. The French Revolution and its propagandists had provided impetus, rationale and confidence to national freedom movements; the Greek fighters were given financial and ideological underpinning by the **Filikí Etería**, or "Friendly Society", a secret group recruited among the exiled Greek merchants and intellectuals of central Europe. Accordingly, a somewhat motley coalition of *klephts* and theorists launched their insurrection in several places in the **Peloponnese** during the latter half of March 1821.

The Dodecanese and east Aegean islands participated to varying, often limited degrees in the insurrection; the Aegean was usually not a primary theatre of operations. Pátmos and Sámos had virtually liberated themselves by 1824, though an uprising on Sými was easily quelled and its historic privileges rescinded. At Eressós, on Lésvos, a Turkish frigate was blown up by a kamikaze fire boat, prompting widespread massacre on the island; appalling reprisals were also visited on Híos for rebelling at Samian instigation. Kássos and Psará both harassed Ottoman shipping with their own large fleets, and suffered overwhelming revenge in consequence.

However, even where entire populations (such as on Kós and Rhodes) were restrained en masse by Ottoman garrisons, it was impossible to prevent individual volunteers from slipping away on boats to join the fracas on the mainland – the start of a tradition that was to gather momentum over the next century and a quarter in various struggles involving mainland Greece, commemorated by the Rhodian street Ethelondón Dhodhekanisíon (Dodecanesian Volunteers).

In 1830, the Western powers confirmed **Greek independence**, and borders were drawn up at a supplementary conference of 1832, with a foreign king, the Bavarian **Otto**, imposed on Greece. Within these borders resided just 800,000 of the six million Greeks living in the Ottoman Empire, and the "free" territories were for the most part the poorest of the Classical and Byzantine lands, comprising Attica, the Peloponnese, the Argo-Saronic islands, the Sporades islands and the Cyclades. The rich agricultural belt of Thessaly, Epirus in the west, and Macedonia in the north, remained for the moment in Ottoman hands, as did all of the east Aegean islands and the Dodecanese. Alone among the east Aegean islands, Sámos, in recognition of its war efforts, was accorded special status by the 1832 **Treaty of London**; it ranked as a semi-autonomous Ottoman province overseen by a suitably compliant Christian "prince", who was appointed by the sultan.

The emerging state

From the outset, irredentism was to be the main engine of Greek foreign policy for the next century. The **Megáli Idhéa** (Great Ideal), as it was termed, enshrined the liberation of all ethnic Greek populations residing outside the initially limited Greek state, by expanding its borders to incorporate as much as possible of former Byzantine territories. Among other regions, the east Aegean and Dodecanese were prime targets and beneficiaries of such sentiments.

In 1862, the new king, a Danish prince who would rule Greece as George I, requested that Britain give up their "protectorate" of the Ionian islands as a condition of his accession to the Greek throne. In 1881, Thessaly, along with southern Epirus, was ceded to Greece by the Ottomans; less gloriously, the Greeks failed in 1897 to achieve *énosis* (union) with **Crete** by attacking Turkish forces on the mainland, and in the process nearly bankrupted the state. The island was, however, granted a status similar to Sámos' (here the prince was appointed by France, England and Russia), eventually becoming a de jure part of Greece in 1913.

It was also from Crete that the most distinguished Greek statesman of the twentieth century emerged. **Eleftherios Venizelos**, having led a civilian campaign for his island's redemption, was in 1910 elected prime minister of Greece. Two years later he organized an alliance with Serbia, Romania and Bulgaria to fight the two **Balkan Wars** (1912–13), campaigns that saw the Ottomans all but driven out of Europe and the Aegean islands.

In the east Aegean, the first island to revolt was Ikaría, in July 1912, which in typically idiosyncratic fashion declared itself independent, issuing its own stamps and flying its own flag. This mini-state lasted a mere five months, until the Greek fleet showed up in November, en route to landings on Híos, Lésvos and Límnos, where Ottoman troops resisted for only a few weeks. Already by September, members of the tiny Turkish garrison on Sámos had been bundled into *kaïkia* and sent to Asia Minor after the last prince, deemed collaborationist, had been assassinated. With Greek frontiers extended to include central Epirus and western Macedonia (with its capital, Thessaloníki), the *Megáli Idhéa* was approaching reality.

One area, however, that remained outside its scope was the Dodecanese, which had been seized by the Italians in a brief campaign during spring 1912, part of a larger war begun in autumn 1911 to push the Ottomans out of Libya. At first the Italians were acclaimed as Christian liberators by the overwhelmingly Greek Orthodox population, and the invaders in turn undertook not to outstay their welcome. At the outset of **World War I**, however, Italy elected to remain neutral, and was only persuaded to join the Allies by being promised, among other things, that its sovereignty over the Dodecanese would be recognized – duly codified after the war in the 1920 **Treaty of Sèvres** signed by the last sultan; it's this treaty (as well as others) that some Turkish diplomats repudiate today.

Since the Balkan Wars, Venizelos had proved himself a shrewd manipulator of domestic public opinion by revising the constitution and introducing a series of liberal social reforms. Division, however – the fabled *Ethnikós Dhíhasmos* or "**National Schism**" – was to appear with the outbreak of World War I. Venizelos urged Greek entry on the Allied side, seeing in the conflict possibilities for the "liberation" of Greeks in Thrace and Asia Minor. However, the new king, **Constantine (Konstantinos) I**, married to a sister of the German Kaiser, imposed a policy of neutrality. Eventually Venizelos and his adherents set up a revolutionary government in Thessaloníki, provoking a brief civil war which saw royalist Pireás also menaced by Allied battleships; all of the recently liberated east Aegean islands declared for the Venizelists. In 1917, Greek troops entered the war to join the French, British and Serbian armies in the Macedonian campaign. Upon the capitulation of Bulgaria and Ottoman Turkey, the Greeks occupied Thrace, and Venizelos presented at **Versailles** demands for the predominantly Greek region around Smyrna (now Izmir) on the Asia Minor coast.

The Katastrofí and its aftermath

This marked the beginning of one of the most disastrous episodes in modern Greek history, still referred to in Greece as the **Katastrofí** ("Catastrophe"). Venizelos was authorized to move forces into Smyrna in May 1919, but soon afterwards Allied support, except for Lloyd George's Britain, began to evaporate; in particular the Italians, now consolidating their hold on the Dodecanese, had no wish to be hemmed in on three sides by Greek territory. Within Turkey itself, a new nationalist movement – surreptitiously assisted by the French and Italians – was taking power under Mustafa Kemal, or **Atatürk** as he came to be known.

When Venizelos unexpectedly lost the 1920 elections, the Royalist party, along with the recently returned King Constantine, took over. They not only forfeited most support (including financial) from the British, but showed relatively little enthusiasm or competence in pursuing what they considered to be a rash imperialist venture inherited from the Venezelists, and little of the Cretan's skill in foreign diplomacy. Greek forces, now led for the most part by incompetent and corrupt Royalist generals, were ordered to advance upon Ankara in an attempt to crush Atatürk and the Turkish nationalist armies. Greece's Anatolian mandate ignominiously collapsed in late August 1922, when Turkish troops launched a massive attack at Afyon, forcing the Greeks back to the Aegean coast and into a hurried evacuation from Smyrna. After triumphantly entering Smyrna, the Turks systematically massacred a significant fraction of the remaining Armenian and Greek population before burning most of the city to the ground.

Although an entire Greek army remained intact in eastern Thrace, and was prepared to fight on, Britain, hitherto Greece's only backer, let it be known that Greece would be wisest to accept Atatürk's own terms, formalized by the **Treaty of Lausanne** in 1923, with Venizelos called back from retirement to salvage what he could from the loser's side of the negotiating table. Among other provisions, the treaty ordered the exchange of religious minorities in each country – in effect, the first regulated ethnic cleansing. Turkey was to accept 390,000 Muslims resident on Greek soil. Greece, mobilized almost continuously for the last decade and with a population of under five million, was faced with the resettlement of over 1,300,000 Christian refugees, some tens of thousands of whom were lodged on the east Aegean islands. Many of these had already read the writing on the wall after 1918 and arrived of their own accord, from Bulgaria and revolutionary Russia as well as Asia Minor. The *Megáli Idhéa* had ceased to be a viable blueprint for action.

Changes were immediate and far-reaching. The bulk of the **agricultural estates** on mainland Thessaly, as well as Crete, Évvia and Lésvos, were redistributed – completing a programme begun in 1909 – both to native Greek tenants and refugee farmers, and huge **shantytowns** grew into new quarters around Athens, Pireás and other cities, a spur to the country's then almost nonexistent industry.

Political reaction was even swifter. By late September 1922, a group of army officers under **Colonel Plastiras** assembled on Híos after the retreat from Smyrna, "invited" King Constantine I to abdicate and, after a November show trial, executed six of his ministers held most responsible for the *Katastrofí*. Democracy was nominally restored with the proclamation of a **republic**, but for much of the following decade changes in government were brought about by factions within the armed forces. Meanwhile, among the urban refugee population, unions were being formed and the **Greek Communist Party (KKE)** was established.

Venizelos' last gasp – and the rise of Metaxas

Elections in 1928 had returned **Venizelos** to power, but his freedom to manoeuvre was severely restricted by the Great Crash the following year. He had also borrowed heavily abroad and was unable to renegotiate loan terms in 1931. Late 1932 saw another, local crash brought on by England's abandonment of the gold standard, with Greek currency devalued sixty percent and Venizelos forced from office. His supporters attempted to forcibly reinstate him in March 1933, and again in March 1935, but both coups were quashed and Venizelos – personally implicated in the second attempt – fled into exile in Paris, where he died in 1936.

By 1936 the Communist Party had enough electoral support to hold the balance of power in an otherwise deadlocked parliament, and would have done so had not the army and the by then restored king decided otherwise. **King George II** had been returned by a plebiscite held – and almost certainly manipulated – the previous year, and so presided over an increasingly factionalized political scene. In April 1936, George II appointed as prime minister the Royalist officer **General John Metaxas**, despite the latter's support from only six parliamentary deputies. Immediately a series of KKE-organized strikes broke out, and the king, ignoring attempts to form a "national unity" coalition, dissolved parliament without setting a date for new elections. It was a blatantly unconstitutional move, and opened the way for five years of ruthless and at times absurdist **dictatorship**.

Metaxas averted a general strike with military force and proceeded to set up a state based on fascist models of the age. Left-wing and trade union opponents were imprisoned or forced into exile, a state youth movement and secret police set up, and rigid censorship, extending even to passages of Thucydides, imposed. It was, however, at least a Greek dictatorship and, while Metaxas admired Nazi organizational methods, he completely opposed German or Italian domination.

Italian rule in the Dodecanese: 1912–43

The **Italian tenure** in the Dodecanese always rested on a flimsy legalistic tissue, which contemporary Turkey has not been slow to criticize in its ongoing dispute with Greece over sovereignty in the Aegean. Briefly, the first **Treaty of Lausanne** (October 1912) stipulated that the Dodecanese were to be returned to the Ottomans when they had evacuated Libya. When Italy and the Ottomans entered World War I on opposite sides, the Italians claimed that this treaty was nullified, to be replaced by the 1915 **Treaty of London** formally acknowledging their possession of the Dodecanese (except for Kastellórizo, occupied by the French for military reasons). Between 1918 and 1923, various conferences agreed that the Dodecanese were to be handed over to Greece, with the exception of Rhodes, but after the beginning of Fascist rule in Italy, and the Greek collapse in Asia Minor, this became progressively more unlikely.

With the rise of **Mussolini and the Fascists**, Italy dropped all altruistic pretences in the Dodecanese, annexing them officially in 1923 as the "**Isole Italiane del'Egeo**" and embarking upon a gradual, forced **Latinization** campaign. Under the tenure (1922–36) of the first governor general, **Mario Lago**, land was expropriated for use by Italian colonists, and intermarriage with local Greeks encouraged, though only Catholic ceremonies were recognized. An attempt was made to set up a puppet **Orthodox bishopric**, and when this failed (except for three collaborationist bishops on Kálymnos, Rhodes and Kárpathos), the Orthodox rite, in all local secular institutions, was suppressed completely. Italian was introduced as the compulsory language of education and public life in December 1936, when the ardently Fascist governor **Cesare Maria de Vecchi** replaced Lago and accelerated all assimilationist measures; as a result anyone in the Dodecanese born before 1928 is probably bilingual in Italian and Greek. In response to these incremental strictures there were riots on Kastellórizo during 1934, and on Kálymnos in 1935 (with stone-throwing women in the front line in both instances), resulting in some loss of civilian life.

The Dodecanese were never considered a fully fledged part of metropolitan Italy, and had a status somewhat like Gibraltar vis-à-vis the UK, or as Puerto Rico is to the US. The islanders were awarded en masse the so-called "**lesser" Italian nationality**, with no obligation for military service (and no civic rights), while "major" or **full Italian citizenship** was reserved as a reward for those who collaborated with the Fascist administration in some conspicuous way. Emigration was possible with a "minor" passport, acting as a social safety valve like elsewhere in the Greek world, and indeed the Greek population of many islands dropped by nearly half even before World War II, which could only have pleased the Fascists. However, exit to the USA in particular became progressively more difficult throughout the 1930s – the result of racist anti-immigration laws, the onset of the Great Depression and worsening relations with Italy even before America entered World War II. Pressure groups of expatriated Dodecanesians were formed, especially in New York, Egypt, Australia and England, to lobby anyone who would listen about the Hellenic cause in the Dodecanese.

On the larger islands, massive public works were undertaken from the mid-1920s onwards to make them the showcases of the "**Italian Aegean Empire**" as Mussolini styled the archipelago; roads, monumental buildings and waterworks were constructed (sometimes with forced Greek labour), sound and not-so-sound archeology engaged in, and the islands accurately mapped for the first time. The first hotels were built on Rhodes and Kós, and the first tourists arrived by boat or seaplane for stays averaging months rather than weeks. However, smaller islands, except for militarily strategic Léros, were neglected and left punitively undeveloped once the requisite Art Deco or Rationalist municipal "palace" had been erected.

World War II and the Greek Civil War

Using a submarine dispatched from a naval base on Léros, the Italians tried to provoke the Greeks into prematurely entering **World War II** by surreptitiously torpedoing the Greek cruiser *Elli* in Tínos harbour on August 15, 1940. This outrage went unanswered, as Greece was ill equipped to fight; however, when Mussolini occupied Albania, and on October 28, 1940, sent an ultimatum demanding passage for his troops through Greece, Metaxas responded to the Italian ambassador in Athens with the apocryphal "*óhi*" (no). (In fact, his wording, in the mutually understood French, was "*Alors, c'est la guerre*".) This marked the entry of Greece into the war, and the gesture is still celebrated as a national holiday.

Galvanized into brief unity by the crisis, the Greeks drove Italian forces from the country, and in doing so took control of the long-coveted and predominantly Greek-populated northern Epirus (southern Albania). However, the Greek army subsequently frittered away its strength in the snowy mountains there rather than consolidate its gains or effectively defend the Macedonian frontier, and proposed coordination with the British never materialized.

Occupation and resistance

In April of the following year Nazi columns swept through Yugoslavia and across the Greek mainland, effectively reversing the only Axis defeat to date. By late May 1941, airborne and seaborne **German invasion** forces had completed the occupation of all the other islands, including those of the east Aegean (with the exception of Sámos, Ikaría and Foúrni, which were granted to the Italians). Metaxas died before their arrival, while King George and his new self-appointed ministers fled into exile in Cairo; few Greeks, of any political persuasion, were sad to see them go.

The joint Italian-German-Bulgarian **occupation** of Greece was among the bitterest experiences of the European war. Nearly half a million Greek civilians starved to death over the winter of 1941–42, as all food was requisitioned, principally by the Germans, to feed occupying armies. In addition, entire villages on the mainland and Crete were burnt and nearly 130,000 civilian residents slaughtered at the least hint of resistance activity.

With a puppet regime in Athens – and an unpopular, discredited Royalist government in Cairo – the focus of Greek resistance between 1942 and 1945 passed largely to **EAM**, or National Liberation Front. By 1943 it had assumed virtual control of most rural areas of the mainland and several islands (including Sámos and Lésvos), working with the British on tactical operations. Initially it commanded widespread popular support, and appeared to offer an obvious framework for a postwar government.

However, most of its highest-ranking members were Communists, and British Prime Minister **Winston Churchill** was determined to reinstate the monarchy. Even with two years of war remaining, it became obvious that there could be no stable post-liberation regime other than a republic. Accordingly, in August 1943 representatives from each of the main resistance movements – including two non-Communist groups – flew clandestinely to Cairo to request that the king not return unless a plebiscite had first voted in his favour. Both Greek and British authorities demurred, and the best possibility of averting civil war was lost.

The EAM contingent returned divided, as perhaps the British had intended, and a conflict broke out between those who favoured taking peaceful control of any government imposed after liberation, and hardline Stalinist ideologues who forbade participation in any "bourgeois" regime.

In October 1943, with fears of an imminent British occupation following the Italian capitulation of September, **ELAS** (the armed wing of EAM) launched full-scale attacks upon its Greek rivals; by the following February, when a ceasefire was arranged, they had wiped out all rivals except EDES, a rival right-wing grouping who had negotiated a truce with the Germans.

The **Italian-occupied** areas of the Aegean fared slightly better, though scenarios on neighbouring islands varied widely. In the Dodecanese it was business as usual, only more so owing to the exigencies of war; Governor De Vecchi – loathed even by many Italians, some of whom executed him in October 1943 – was replaced by two successive nonentities, Hector Bastico (December 1940 to July 1941) and Admiral Inigo Campioni (July 1941 to September 1943). On Foúrni, the Italian garrison and the islanders reached an understanding ensuring as calm and amicable an occupation as possible, while on adjacent Sámos an active resistance contingent on Mount Kérkis prompted a mass reprisal execution in one village.

German-occupied Híos was relatively quiet, though Lésvos – in keeping with its Communist sympathies – had, like Sámos, an active resistance contingent. Kaïkia and other small boats were requisitioned for German use – thus also nullifying their potential for smuggling people and goods between the islands and Turkey – while such fishing boats that continued to work often had a Wehrmacht officer posted on board to expropriate the entire catch. They also, it is claimed, encouraged the practice of dynamite-fishing, which has been a social nuisance ever since. Such measures caused fish to disappear from the civilian diet, and guaranteed widespread malnutrition. Both here and in the Dodecanese, thousands of civilians still managed to escape by kaïki to the Turkish coast, where they spent most of the war years avoiding starvation.

When Italy capitulated on September 8–11, 1943 (the date varied by locale), a brief free-for-all ensued on the islands it had controlled. As elsewhere in Greece, German troops attacked, disarmed and executed their erstwhile allies, particularly on Rhodes. The British quickly occupied Kós, Kastellórizo, Sámos and Léros, but in insufficient strength to repel German attacks; within two months they had to abandon these positions, with considerable losses. Churchill considered the Dodecanese easy pickings, but in the end was denied adequate resources for the job by the Americans, who refused to risk the already precarious advance through Italy proper. The British were compelled to reconquer the Dodecanese gradually from September 1944 onwards, picking off vulnerable islands one by one, though Rhodes, Kós and Léros were too strongly defended and only evacuated by the Germans after their surrender of May 1945 to the Allies, signed on Sými. With western Crete, these were the last Greek territories to be abandoned by the Axis.

Civil war

As the Germans began to leave in October 1944, most of the EAM leadership agreed to join a British-sponsored "official" **interim government**. This arguably proved a tactical error, however. With almost ninety percent of the countryside under their control, the Communists were given only one-third representation, and a new regular army began to form, based on the extreme-right-wing Mountain Brigade, the Sacred Band and even the fascist Security Battalions, rather than the ELAS officer corps. The king showed no sign of renouncing his claims and, in November, British forces ordered ELAS to disarm. On December 3 all pretences of civility or neutrality were dropped; the police opened fire on an EAM demonstration in Athens, killing at least sixteen; within days fighting broke out between ELAS and British troops, in the so-called **Dhekemvrianá** battle. Though ELAS quickly quashed all opposition in the countryside, they failed to drive the British and right-wing Greeks from Athens, thus losing their best chance of seizing power. In their fury at being thwarted, ELAS rounded up their most influential and wealthiest opponents in the largest towns, and marched them out to rural areas in conditions that guaranteed their death.

A truce of sorts was negotiated at Várkiza in February 1945, but this agreement was never fully implemented. The army, police and civil service remained in right-wing hands and, while collaborationists were often allowed to retain their positions, left-wing sympathizers, many of whom were merely Venizelist republicans and not Communists, were systematically excluded, the mildest aspect of what developed into a veritable "**White Terror**". The elections of 1946 were won by the right-wing parties (the Left boycotted them), followed by another, possibly rigged, plebiscite in favour of the king's return. By 1947 guerrilla activity had again reached the scale of a full **civil war**, with most of ELAS resurrected as the Democratic Army of Greece (**DSE** in Greek).

In the interim, King George had died and been succeeded by his brother Paul (with his consort Frederika), while the **Americans** had taken over the British role and begun implementing the cold-war **Truman** doctrine. In March 1947 they took virtual control of Greece, their first significant postwar experiment in anti-communist intervention. Massive economic and military aid was given to a client Greek government, while official decrees had to be countersigned by the American Mission chief in order to become valid.

In the mainland mountains, US military advisers trained the Nationalist army for **campaigns against the DSE**, and in the cities there were mass arrests, court martials and imprisonments – an extension of the White Terror – lasting until 1951. Over three thousand executions were recorded, including (for their pacifist stance and refusal to swear loyalty oaths) a number of Jehovah's Witnesses, "a sect proved to be under Communist domination", according to US Ambassador Grady. To deny the DSE local support, over 700,000 civilians were forcibly evacuated from mountain villages and dumped in squalid internment camps near towns, a move which helped destroy any hope of postwar rural existence. In the east Aegean, Ikaría, Foúrni and Áyios Efstrátios became – as they had been under Metaxas – venues of internal exile for thousands of "dangerous" leftists, who arrived off the boat manacled hand and foot.

In the autumn of 1949, with the Yugoslav–Greek border closed after Tito's rift with Stalin, the last DSE guerrillas finally admitted defeat and retreated into Albania from their strongholds on Mount Grámmos. Atrocities had been committed on both sides, including, from the Left, considerably more than three thousand executions, widespread vandalization of monasteries and the dubious evacuation of children from "combat areas". Such errors, as well as the total withholding of Soviet support, the high percentage of openly separatist Slavophones amongst their ranks, and the hopelessness of lightly armed guerrillas fighting an American-backed army equipped with aircraft and heavy artillery, almost certainly doomed the DSE's efforts from the start.

The Dodecanese: Union with Greece

The British ruled as an occupation force for approximately 22 months from May 1945, to the considerable unease and resentment of the Greek government, who suspected that they intended to set up a Cyprus-style colonial regime or (worse) hand some or all of the islands back to Turkey. However, the British claim they had always intended to hand the Dodecanese over to Greece at the right moment, not least to present the Nationalists an unqualified success to point to in their propaganda battle with the DSE, and were only holding off pending the **Italian-Greek peace treaty** negotiations of September 1946 to February 1947. In the interim, considerable progress was made in reconstituting the much-depleted Dodecanesian shipping, and the two surviving collaborationist bishops were forced into retirement by the Ecumenical Patriarch in Istanbul.

The main sticking points of the treaty were the offsetting of Greek demands for war reparations against Italian claims of compensation for "improvements" to the Dodecanese (in the end these were held to cancel each other out) and, more seriously, the fate of native Italians, and Greek islanders who had opted for "major" Italian **nationality**. Metropolitan Italians, including those who had married islanders, were given a year from February 1947 to choose between Greek or Italian nationality; if they went for the latter, they were obliged to leave for Italy (a surprising number stayed). Native islanders who had enjoyed "major" Italian citizenship had their cases examined minutely prior to any "renaturalization", and those shown to have obtained this status voluntarily and with enthusiasm could expect to be deported to Italy.

Once the peace treaty was ratified, the Greek Army assumed control of the Dodecanese from the British, on March 31, 1947 – a date responsible for the frequent, half-true assertion that the islands were joined to the mainland in that year. However, military governor **Vice Admiral Periklis Ioannidis** presided over a strict, ten-month regime of lustration – whose primary purposes were sifting through the cases of suspect "major" Italian subjects, and an equally stringent filtering for communists and fellow travellers, either home-grown or arriving from the mainland. Once this was deemed complete, the Dodecanese were **officially annexed** to Greece on January 9, 1948, and the first civilian governor, **Nikolaos Mavris** of Kássos, was appointed to general rejoicing.

Reconstruction American-style: 1950–67

After a decade of war that had shattered much of Greece's infrastructure (supposedly not one bridge was left standing by 1948), and had killed twelve percent of the 1940 population, it was a demoralized country that emerged into the Western political orbit of the 1950s. Greece was also perforce American-dominated, enlisted into the Korean War in 1950 and NATO the following year. In domestic politics, the US Embassy – still giving the orders – foisted a winner-take-all electoral system, which was to ensure victory for the Right over the next twelve years. Overt leftist activity was banned (though a "cover" party for Communists was soon founded); those individuals who were not herded into political "re-education" camps on barren islands, or dispatched by firing squads, legal or vigilante, went into exile, to return only after 1974.

The American-backed, highly conservative **"Greek Rally"** party, led by General Papagos, won the first decisive post-civil-war elections in 1952.

After the general's death, the party's leadership was taken over – and to an extent liberalized – by **Constantine Karamanlis**. Under his rule, stability of a kind was established and some economic advances registered. Health and life expectancy improved dramatically, as the age-old scourges of tuberculosis and malaria were finally confronted with American-supplied food, medicine and pesticides. Less commendable was Karamanlis' encouragement of the law of **andiparohí**, whereby owners of small refugee shanties or Neoclassical mansions alike could offer the site of such properties to apartment-block developers in exchange for two flats (out of eight to ten) in the finished building. This effectively ripped the heart out of most larger island towns like Híos, Sámos and Ródhos, and explains their baleful aesthetics a half-century on.

The 1950s was also a decade that saw wholesale **depopulation** of villages, as migrants sought work in Australia, America and western Europe, or the larger Greek cities. In the east Aegean and the Dodecanese this was especially pronounced – ironically in the case of Rhodes and its neighbours, where the long-sought union with Greece provided merely unhindered freedom to **emigrate**.

By 1961, unemployment, the Cyprus issue and the installation of US nuclear bases on Greek soil were changing the political climate, and when Karamanlis was again elected prime minister there was strong suspicion of a fraud arranged by the king and army. **Strikes** became frequent in industry and even agriculture, and both King Paul and the autocratic, fascist-inclined Queen Frederika, were openly attacked in parliament and at protest demonstrations. The far Right grew uneasy about "communist resurgence" and, losing confidence in their own electoral influence, arranged the **assassination** of left-wing deputy **Grigoris Lambrakis** in Thessaloníki in May 1963. (The murder, and its subsequent cover-up, was the subject of Vassilis Vassilikos's thriller *Z*, filmed by Costa-Gavras.) It was against this volatile background that Karamanlis dissolved parliament, lost the subsequent elections and left the country.

The new government – the first controlled from outside the traditional Greek Right since 1935 – was formed by **George Papandreou's Centre Union Party**, and had a decisive majority of nearly fifty seats. It was to last, however, for under two years as conservative forces conspired to thwart its progress. In this the chief protagonists were the army officers and their constitutional commander in chief, the new king, 23-year-old **Constantine II**.

Since power in Greece depended on a pliant military as well as a network of political appointees, Papandreou's most urgent task in order to govern securely and effectively was to reform the armed forces. His first minister of defence proved incapable of the task and, while he was investigating the right-wing plot suspected of rigging the 1961 election, "evidence" was produced of a leftist conspiracy connected with Papandreou's son Andreas (also a government minister). When the allegations grew to a crisis, George Papandreou assumed the defence portfolio himself, a move which the king refused to sanction. Papandreou then resigned to gain a fresh mandate at the polls, but the king would not order new elections, instead persuading members of the Centre Union – chief among them **Constantine Mitsotakis** – to defect and organize a coalition government. Punctuated by strikes, resignations and street demonstrations, this lasted for a year and a half until new elections were eventually set for May 28, 1967. They failed to take place.

The colonels' junta: 1967–74

It was a foregone conclusion that Papandreou's Centre Union would win the polls against the discredited coalition partners. And it was equally certain that there would be some anti-democratic action to prevent it from reassuming power. Disturbed by the party's leftward shift, King Constantine was said to have briefed senior generals for a coup d'état, to take place ten days before the elections. However, he was caught by surprise, as was nearly everyone else, by the **coup of April 21, 1967**, staged by a group of "unknown" colonels. It was, to quote Andreas Papandreou, "the first successful CIA military putsch on the European continent".

The colonels' **junta**, having dissolved all civilian poles of authority, was sworn in by the king and survived the half-hearted counter-coup that he attempted to mount a few months later. It was an ostensibly **fascist regime**, absurdly styling itself as the true "Revival of Greek Orthodoxy" against Western "corrupting influences", though in reality its ideology was nothing more than reheated dogma from the Metaxas era mixed with ultranationalism.

All **political activity** was **banned**, independent trade unions were forbidden to recruit or meet, the press was so heavily censored that many papers stopped printing or published blank pages in protest, and thousands of "communists" were arrested, imprisoned, and often tortured. Among the persecuted were both Papandreou, the composer Mikis Theodorakis (deemed "unfit to stand trial" after three months in custody), and Amalia Fleming (widow of Alexander). While relatively few people were killed outright – one, dissident lawyer Nikiforos Mandilaras, found mutilated in the sea off Rhodes, has a street named after him on the island – thousands were permanently maimed physically and psychologically in the junta's torture chambers. The best-known Greek actress, Melina Mercouri, was stripped of her citizenship *in absentia*, and thousands of prominent Greeks joined her in exile.

Culturally, the colonels put an end to genuine popular music (banning, for example, bagpipes on Mýkonos lest visitors think Greece too "primitive", and closing many Athens clubs), while inflicting ludicrous censorship on literature and theatre, including (as under Metaxas) a ban on production of the Classical tragedies. By contrast, chief colonel Papadopoulos's rambling, illiterate speeches became a byword for bad grammar, obfuscation and Orwellian Newspeak.

The junta lasted for seven years, opposed (especially after the first two years) by the majority of the Greek people, officially excluded from the Council of Europe, but propped up and given massive **aid by US presidents** Lyndon Johnson and Richard Nixon. To them and the CIA, the junta's Greece was an ideal client state: human rights considerations were then thought trivial, orders were placed for sophisticated military technology, and foreign investment on terms highly unfavourable to Greece was made available to multinational corporations – for the era, a fairly routine scenario of exploitation of an underdeveloped nation.

Opposition was from the beginning voiced by exiled Greeks in western Europe, Australia and the United States, but only in late 1973 did demonstrations break out openly in Greece – the colonels' secret police had done too thorough a job of infiltrating domestic resistance groups and terrifying everyone else into docility. On November 17 the students of the **Polytekhnío** (Polytechnic) in **Athens** began an occupation of their buildings. The ruling clique lost its nerve; armoured vehicles stormed the Polytechnic gates and a still-undetermined number of students (estimates range from tens to hundreds) were killed. (Today they are commemorated throughout the east Aegean and the Dodecanese, in leftist municipalities, by streets called Iróön Polytekhníon – "Heroes of the Polytechnic"). Martial law was tightened, and junta chief George Papadopoulos was replaced by the even more noxious and reactionary General Ioannides, until then head of the secret police.

Return to civilian rule: 1974–81

The end of the ordeal, however, came within a year as the dictatorship embarked on a disastrous political adventure in **Cyprus**, essentially the last playing of the *Megáli Idhéa* card. By attempting to topple the Makarios government and impose *énosis* (union with Greece) on the island, the junta provoked a Turkish invasion and occupation of nearly forty percent of the Cypriot territory. The army finally mutinied, and Constantine Karamanlis was invited to return from Paris to again take office. He swiftly helped negotiate a ceasefire (but no durable solution) in Cyprus, withdrew Greece temporarily from NATO, and warned that US bases in Greece would have to be removed except where they specifically served Greek interests.

In November 1974 Karamanlis and his **Néa Dhimokratía (New Democracy) party** was rewarded by a sizeable majority in **elections**, with a centrist and socialist opposition. The latter was the **Panhellenic Socialist Movement (PASOK)**, a new party led by Andreas Papandreou.

The election of Néa Dhimokratía was in every sense a safe conservative option, but to Karamanlis's enduring credit it oversaw an effective and firm return to democratic stability, even legalizing the KKE (Communist Party) for the first time in its history. Karamanlis also held a **referendum on the monarchy**; seventy percent of Greeks rejected the return of Constantine II, so Karamanlis instituted in its place a French-style presidency, a post he himself occupied from 1980 to 1985, and again from 1990 to 1995. Economically there were limited advances, although these were more than offset by inflationary defence spending (the result of renewed tension with Turkey), hastily negotiated entrance into the EC, and the decision to let the drachma float after decades of being artificially fixed at thirty to the US dollar.

Most crucially, Karamanlis failed to deliver vital reforms in bureaucracy, social welfare and education; while the worst figures of the junta were brought to trial and jailed for life, the ordinary faces of Greek political life and administration changed little. By 1981 inflation was hovering around 25 percent, and it was estimated that tax evasion was depriving the state of one third of its expected annual revenue. On the foreign policy front, the US bases remained, and it was felt that Greece, back in NATO, was still acting as little more than an American satellite. The traditional right had proved demonstrably unequal to the task at hand.

PASOK 1981–89

"Change" (*Allayí*) and "Out with the Right" (*Ná Fíyi íy Dhexí*) were the watchwords of the election campaign that swept **PASOK** and Andreas

Papandreou to power on October 18, 1981. This victory meant a chance for Papandreou to form the first socialist government in Greek history and break a half-century monopoly of authoritarian right-wing rule. With so much at stake, the campaign had been passionate even by Greek standards, and PASOK's victory was greeted with euphoria both by the generation whose political voice had been silenced after the civil war, and by a large proportion of the young. Their hopes ran naïvely and perhaps dangerously high.

The electoral margin, at least, was conclusive. PASOK won 174 of the 300 parliamentary seats and the KKE (Communists) – though not a part of the new government – returned another thirteen deputies, one of them composer Mikis Theodorakis. Néa Dhimokratía moved into unaccustomed opposition. There appeared to be no obstacle to the implementation of a **radical programme**: devolution of power to local authorities, the effective nationalization of heavy industry, improvement of the woefully skeletal social services, a purge of bureaucratic inefficiency and malpractice, the end of bribery and corruption as a way of life, an independent and dignified foreign policy following expulsion of US bases, and finally withdrawal from NATO and the European Community.

A change of style was promised, too, replacing the country's long traditions of authoritarianism and bureaucracy with openness and dialogue. Even more radically, given that Greek political parties had long been the personal followings of charismatic leaders, PASOK was to be a party of ideology and principle, dependent on no single individual member. Or so, at least, thought some of the youthful PASOK cadres.

The new era started with a bang. ELAS was officially recognized; hitherto they hadn't been allowed to take part in any celebrations, wreath-layings or other ceremonies commemorating the wartime Resistance. Peasant women were granted pensions for the first time – 3000 drachmas a month (about US$55 in 1982), the same as their outraged husbands – and wages were indexed to the cost of living. In addition, civil marriage was introduced, family law reformed in favour of wives and mothers, and equal rights legislation was put on the statute book.

These quick, low-cost and popular reformist moves seemed to mark a break with the past, and the atmosphere had indeed changed. Greeks no longer lowered their voices to discuss politics in public places or wrapped their opposition newspaper in the respectably conservative *Kathimerini*. At first there were real fears that the climate would be too much for the military, who would once again intervene to choke a dangerous experiment in democracy, especially when Andreas Papandreou, imitating his father, briefly assumed the defence portfolio himself. But he went out of his way to soothe military susceptibilities: increasing their salaries, buying new weaponry, and being fastidious in his attendance at military functions. Moreover, the resistance of the Polytekhnío students to the 1967–74 junta was constantly mythologized, and PASOK activists could be counted on to form human cordons around party headquarters at the least sign of unrest in the armed forces.

The end of the honeymoon

Papandreou promised a populist bonanza which he must have known, as an academically trained economist, he could not deliver; as a result he pleased nobody. He could not fairly be blamed for the inherited lack of investment, low productivity, deficiency in managerial and labour skills and other chronic problems besetting the Greek economy. However, he certainly aggravated the situation early in his first term by allowing his supporters to indulge in violently anti-capitalist rhetoric – which frightened off potential overseas investors – and by the prosecution and humiliation of the Tsatsos family, owners of one of Greece's few competitive businesses (Hercules Cement) for the illegal export of capital, something of which every Greek with any savings was guilty. These were cheap victories, not backed by any rational public investment programme, and the only nationalizations were of hopelessly lame-duck companies.

Faced with a sluggish economy and burdened with the additional expense of (marginally) improved social benefits and wage-indexing, Papandreou's government had also to cope with the effects of **world recession**, which back then always hit Greece with a delayed effect compared with northern Europe. **Shipping**, the country's main foreign-currency earner, was devastated. Remittances from émigré workers fell off as they became unemployed in their host countries, and tourism diminished under the dual impact of recession and US President Ronald Reagan's warning to Americans to stay away from the allegedly terrorist-vulnerable Athens airport.

With huge quantities of imported goods continuing to be sucked into the country in the absence of significant domestic production, the **foreign** debt topped £10 billion by the mid-1980s, with inflation still at 25 percent and the balance of payments deficit approaching £1 billion. Greece also began to experience the social strains of unemployment for the first time. Not that it did not exist before, but it had always been concealed as underemployment because of numerous family-run businesses and the rural/seasonal nature of the economy – as well as by the absence of reliable statistics.

The second term

A modest spending spree transparently intended to buy votes, continued satisfaction at the discomfiture of the Right and the popularity of his Greece-for-the-Greeks foreign policy gave Papandreou a second term with a **June 1985** electoral victory scarcely less decisive than the first; his complacent and dishonest slogan was "Vote PASOK for Even Better Days". By October PASOK had imposed a two-year wage freeze and import restrictions, abolished the wage-indexing scheme and devalued the drachma by fifteen percent. Papandreou's fat was pulled out of the fire by none other than his *bête noire*, the European Community, which offered a huge two-phase loan on condition that an IMF-style **austerity programme** was maintained.

The political price of such classic monetarist strategies, accompanied by shameless soliciting for foreign investment, was the alienation of the KKE and most of PASOK's own core constituency. Increasingly autocratic (ironic, given his earlier pledges of openness), Papandreou's response to **dissent** was to fire recalcitrant trade union leaders and expel some three hundred members of his own party. Assailed by strikes, the government stumbled badly, losing ample ground in the municipal elections of October 1986 to Néa Dhimokratía, including the mayoralties of the three major cities – Athens, Thessaloníki and Pátra – the first two retained by them ever since. Papandreou assured the nation that he had taken the message to heart, but all that followed were two successive cabinet reshuffles, which saw the departure of most remaining PASOK veterans; the new cabinet was so unsocialist that even the right-wing press called it "centrist".

Similar about-faces took place in foreign policy. The first-term anti-US, anti-NATO and anti-EC rhetoric had been immensely popular, and understandable for a people shamelessly bullied by bigger powers since 1830. The "realistic" policies that Papandreou increasingly pursued during his second term were far more conciliatory towards his big Western brothers. Not least was the fact that **US bases** remained in Greece until 1994, largely due to the fear that snubbing

NATO would lead to Greece being exposed to Turkish aggression, still the only issue that united the main parties to any degree. As for the once-reviled **European Community** (soon to be the European Union), Greece had by now become an established beneficiary, and its leader was hardly about to bite the hand that feeds.

Scandal

Even as late as **mid-1988**, despite the many betrayals and failings of Papandreou, it seemed unlikely that PASOK would be toppled in the 1989 elections. This was due mainly to the lack of a credible alternative. Constantine Mitsotakis, a bitter personal enemy of Papandreou's since 1965, when his defection had brought down his father's government and set in motion the events that culminated in the junta, was an unconvincing and unlikeable character at the helm of Néa Dhimokratía. Meanwhile, the liberal centrist parties had disappeared, and the KKE seemed trapped in a Stalinist time warp under the leadership of Harilaos Florakis. Only the **Ellenikí Aristerá (Greek Left)** or Euro-Communist party spun off from the KKE, seemed to offer any sensible alternative, but they had a precariously small following.

However, a combination of spectacular blunders, plus perhaps a general shift to the Right influenced by the cataclysmic events in eastern Europe, conspired against PASOK. First came the extraordinary **cavortings of the prime minister** himself. Late in 1988, 70-year-old Papandreou was flown to Britain for open-heart surgery. He took the occasion, with fear of death presumably rocking his judgement, to make public a year-long liaison with a 34-year-old Olympic Airways hostess, **Dimitra "Mimi" Liani**. Widespread media images of an old man shuffling about after a young, large-chested blonde, to the public humiliation of Margaret, his American-born wife, were not helpful (Papandreou soon divorced Margaret and married Mimi). His integrity was further dented when he missed important public engagements in order to relive his youth in flashy nightspots with Mimi.

The real damage, however, was done by a series of **economic scandals**, ranging from illegal arms deals to fraudulent farm-produce sales by assorted ministers. The most serious of these involved a self-made, Greek-American con man, **Yiorgos Koskotas**, director of the Bank of Crete, who embezzled £120 million (US$190 million) in deposits, distributed it lavishly amongst numerous Greek public figures, and worse still slipped through the authorities' fingers on a private jet back to the US, where he had begun his career as a house-painter. Certain PASOK ministers and even Papandreou himself were implicated in the scandal.

United in disgust at this corruption, the other left-wing parties – KKE and Elliniki Aristerá – formed a coalition, the **Synaspismós**, siphoning off still more support from PASOK.

Three bites at the cherry

In this climate, an inconclusive result to the **June 1989 election** was unsurprising. Less predictable, however, was the formation of a bizarre "**kathársis**" **(purgative) coalition** of conservatives and communists, expressly to cleanse PASOK's Augean stables.

Synaspismós would have formed a government with PASOK but set an impossible condition for doing so – that Papandreou step down as prime minister. In the deal finally cobbled together between the Left and Néa Dhimokratía, Mitsotakis was denied the premiership, too, in favour of

Ioannis Tzanetakis, a popular former naval officer who had led an unsuccessful mutiny against the junta.

During the three months that the coalition lasted, *kathársis* turned out to be largely a matter of burying the knife as deeply as possible into the ailing body of PASOK. Andreas Papandreou and three other ministers were officially indicted of involvement in the Koskotas affair – though there was no time to try them before Greece returned again to the polls. In any case, the chief witness and protagonist, Koskotas himself, was still imprisoned in America, awaiting extradition proceedings.

Contrary to the Right's hope that publicly accusing Papandreou and his cohorts of criminal behaviour would pave the way for a Néa Dhimokratía victory, PASOK actually recovered slightly in the **November 1989 elections**, though the result was again inconclusive. This time the Left refused to do deals with anyone, resulting in a caretaker government under the neutral aegis of Xenophon Zolotas, reluctantly dragged into the prime minister's office from the rectorship of Athens University. His only mandate was to keep the country on the rails while preparations were made for yet another election.

These took place in **April 1990** with the same party leaders *in situ*, and with Synaspismós having completed its about-turn to the extent that in the five single-seat constituencies (the other 295 seats were drawn from multiple-seat constituencies in a complex system of reinforced proportional representation), they supported independent candidates jointly with PASOK. Greek communists are good at about-turns, though; after all, composer Mikis Theodorakis, musical torchbearer of the Left during the dark junta years, and formerly a KKE MP, was now standing for Néa Dhimokratía, prior to his resignation from politics altogether.

On the night, Néa Dhimokratía scraped home with a majority of one, later doubled with the defection of a centrist, and Mitsotakis finally realized his long-cherished dream of becoming prime minister. The only other memorable feature of the election was the first parliamentary representation for an independent member of the **Turkish minority** in Thrace, Ahmet Sadiq, and in Attica for the Greens – a focus for many disaffected PASOK voters.

A return to the Right: Mitsotakis' tenure

On assuming power, Mitsotakis prescribed a course of **austerity measures** to revive the chronically ill economy. Little headway was made, though given the world recession that was hardly surprising. Greek inflation was still approaching twenty percent annually, and at nearly ten percent, unemployment remained chronic. Other measures introduced by Mitsotakis included laws to combat strikes and **terrorism**. This had been a perennial source of worry for Greeks since the appearance in 1974 of a group called **Dhekaeftá Novemvríou** ("November 17", the date of the colonels' attack on the Polytechnic in 1973). Before their unmasking in 2002 (see p.474), they (and spin-off group ELA) managed to kill 26 industrialists, politicians, judges, police and NATO military personnel, rob numerous banks and inflict massive damage to the property of foreign corporations in Athens. It hardly seemed likely that Mitsotakis' laws, however, were the solution. They stipulated that the long-winded, ideologically contorted statements of the group could no longer be published, which led to one or two newspaper editors being jailed for a few days for defiance – much to everyone's embarrassment. The **anti-strike laws** threatened severe penalties but were equally ineffectual, as frequent breakdowns in public transport, electricity and rubbish collection illustrated.

As for the Koskotas scandal, the man himself was eventually extradited and gave evidence for the prosecution against Papandreou and various of his ministers. The trial was televised and proved as popular as any soap opera, given its twists of high drama – which included one of the defendants, Agamemnon "Menios" Koutsoyiorgas, dying in court of a heart attack in front of the cameras. The case against Papandreou gradually ran out of steam and he was officially acquitted (by a margin of one vote on the tribunal panel) in early 1992. The two other surviving ex-ministers, Tsovolas and Petsos, were convicted, given jail sentences (bought off with a heavy fine) and barred from public office for a time.

The great showcase trial thus went out with a whimper and did nothing to enhance Mitsotakis' position. If anything, it served to increase sympathy for Papandreou, who was felt to have been unfairly victimized. The indisputable villain of the piece, Koskotas, was eventually convicted of major fraud and is serving a lengthy sentence at the high-security Korýdhallos prison.

The Macedonian question

The last thing the increasingly unpopular Mitsotakis needed was a major foreign policy headache. That is exactly what he got when, in 1991, one of the breakaway republics of the former Yugoslavia named itself **Macedonia**, thereby injuring Greek national pride and sparking off vehement protests at home and abroad. Diplomatically, the Greeks fought tooth and nail against anyone's recognizing the breakaway state, let alone its use of the name "Macedonia", but their position became increasingly isolated, and by 1993 the new country had gained official recognition from both the EU and the UN – albeit under the provisional title of the Former Yugoslav Republic of Macedonia (FYROM).

Salt was rubbed into Greek wounds when the FYROM started using the "Star of Vergina" (and of the ancient Macedonian kings) as a national symbol on their new flag, allegedly printed a banknote portraying the White Tower of Thessaloníki (Solun in Macedonian) and retained passages in its constitution referring to "unredeemed" Aegean territories. Greece still refuses to call its neighbour Macedonia, instead referring to it as *Proín Yugoslavikí Dhimokratía Makedhonás*, or *Tá Skópia* after the capital – and for quite some time you couldn't go anywhere in Greece without coming across officially placed stickers proclaiming that "Macedonia was, is, and always will be Greek and only Greek!"

The ongoing argument for legitimacy hinges mostly on whether the ancient Macedonian kings were pure-bred Hellenes (the Greek position), Hellenized barbarians (the neutral conclusion) or proto-Slavs (the Macedonian claim).

The pendulum swings back

The Macedonian problem effectively led to Mitsotakis' political **demise**. Mitsotakis had also been plagued for months by accusations of phone-tapping and theft of antiquities to stock his large private collection in Crete, plus links with a complicated contracts scandal focused around the national cement company. In the early summer of 1993 his ambitious and disaffected foreign minister, **Andonis Samaras**, jumped on the bandwagon of resurgent Greek nationalism to set up his own party, **Politikí Ánixi (Political Spring)**. His platform, still right-wing, was largely based on action over Macedonia, and during the summer of 1993 more **Néa Dhimokratía (ND)** MPs defected, making Politikí

Ánixi a force to be reckoned with. When parliament reconvened in September to approve austere new budget proposals, it became clear that the government lacked sufficient support, and early **elections** were called for **October 1993**.

On October 11, Papandreou romped to election victory with 169 parliamentary deputies; in an exact reversal of the 1990 results, Néa Dhimokratía lost in 85 percent of the constituencies (including the entire east Aegean and Dodecanese), though the Synaspismós disappeared temporarily from the electoral map, replaced as the third party in parliament by Samaras' Politikí Ánixi and the unreconstructed Communists, now under Aleka Papariga, with nine deputies each. The youthful Miltiades Evert, ex-mayor of Athens, replaced Mitsotakis as head of Néa Dhimokratía, so that – along with ex-KKE head Florakis – two of the "dinosaurs" of post-junta politics had passed from the scene.

The morning after

And so a frail-looking Papandreou, now 74, became prime minister for the third time. He soon realized that he was not going to have nearly so easy a ride as in the 1980s.

PASOK immediately fulfilled two of its pre-election promises by removing restrictions on the reporting of terrorists' communiqués and deprivatizing the Athens city bus company. The new government also began proceedings for Mitsotakis to be tried for his purported misdemeanours, though all charges were mysteriously dropped in January 1995, prompting allegations of an under-the-table deal between Papandreou and his old nemesis.

The root of popular dissatisfaction remained **the economy**, still in dire straits. Nor could PASOK claim to win any diplomatic battles over Macedonia, despite a lot of tough posturing. The only concrete move was the imposition in October 1993 of a **trade embargo** on the FYROM, which merely landed the Greeks in trouble with the European Court of Justice – and succeeded in virtually shutting down the port of Thessaloníki. By contrast, alone among NATO members, Greece was conspicuous for its open **support of Serbia** in the wars wracking ex-Yugoslavia, ostentatiously breaking that particular embargo with supply trucks to Belgrade via Bulgaria.

In **October 1994**, for the first time ever in a PASOK-sponsored reform, provincial governors were directly elected in regional elections, rather than appointed from Athens. In **March 1995**, **presidential elections** were held in parliament to designate a successor to the 88-year-old Karamanlis, who enjoyed just three years of retirement before his death in spring 1998. The winner (and completing his final term in office as of writing), supported by Politikí Ánixi and PASOK, was **Kostis Stefanopoulos**, ex-head of the dissolved party DIANA (Democratic Renewal), like Politikí Ánixi a breakaway movement from ND. Untainted by scandal if a bit of a nonentity, he had been nominated by Samaras and accepted by Papandreou in a deal that would allow PASOK to see out its term without ructions.

In November 1995, Greece **lifted its embargo** on "Macedonia", opening its mutual borders to tourism and trade in return for the Macedonians suitably editing their constitution and removing the offending emblem from their flag. Relations, in fact, were instantly almost normalized, with only The Name still moot; perennial possibilities include "New Macedonia" or "Upper Macedonia", though as of writing the place is still being referred to as FYROM (the Former Yugoslav Republic of Macedonia) by most outsiders, with the conspicuous exception of the United States, who "rewarded" "Macedonia" with recognition as such in November 2004, for its support in Iraq.

The end of an era

An increasingly critical issue was the 76-year-old Papandreou's obstinate cling-ing to power despite obvious signs of dotage. Numerous senior members of PASOK became increasingly bold and vocal in their criticism, no longer fear-ing expulsion or the sack.

By late 1995, Papandreou was in intensive care, dependent on life-support machinery. As there was no constitutional provision for replacing an infirm

Islets and the Ímia crisis

The Dodecanese and to a lesser extent the east Aegean are dotted with scores of tiny, uninhabited islets, frequented only by fishermen and yacht passengers. They are, however, cherished and minutely classified by the Greeks themselves, despite their resounding lack of natural endowments. The twin islets of Ímia were, in early 1996, the focus of a major international incident.

A **nisídha** (plural *nisídhes*) is defined as any islet of between four and sixteen square kilometres, which might at some point in the past have supported a small permanent population. Waterless specks smaller than four square kilometres are further subdivided into **vrahonisídhes**, which have enough soil to support a thin covering of thorny vegetation, and **vráhi**, essentially gull-roosts with no soil at all.

As far as the Greeks are concerned, the **sovereignty** of these islets is an open-and-shut case; they were ceded by Italy to Greece in 1947 as part of the same treaty that included the larger Dodecanese. Previously, in December 1932, Italy and Turkey had drawn up a complicated maritime frontier in the straits between the Dodecanese and Anatolia, which assigned most of the islets clearly to one country or another. As the successor state to Italy, Greece feels that she has clearly "inher-ited" all the islets so allotted at that time. Turkish threats to *vrahonisídhes* are seen as merely the thin end of the wedge, with the Turks deemed intent on graduating to attempted annexation of larger, inhabited islands unless firmly opposed. Memories of Turkey's 1974 intervention in Cyprus, where over one third of that island was over-run, remain vivid in Greece, and regarded – along with several recent islet incidents – as incontrovertible proof that an inherently expansionist Turkey harbours designs on more of the Aegean.

For their part, some Turks claim lately that the Dodecanese were strictly speaking not Italy's to keep or give away, as their seizure by the Italians in 1912 had never been assented to by Turkey. Moreover, Turkey has never ratified the Geneva Convention of 1958, nor the more recent **Law of the Sea**, whereby a country can claim territorial waters of up to twelve nautical miles around its islands. Various Turkish pronounce-ments have made it clear that any attempt by Greece to do so, effectively turning the Aegean into a Greek lake, would be considered by Turkey an act of war. Fishing rights and, further north, access to oil deposits are at stake, adding an economic dimen-sion to what is ostensibly a matter of national honour and the reputation of domestic politicians.

In July 1995, the Greek Defence Ministry announced that the **colonization** of numerous uninhabited islets across Greece was to be officially encouraged; appli-cations from "responsible" persons (ie no hippies or dope fiends), both foreign and Greek, were invited, with promised provision of basic shelter, desalinated water, solar electricity and satellite telephones, as well as a long lease. Several of the islets fell within the limits of the Dodecanese, precariously poised between larger islands and the Anatolian mainland. Overseas Greek consulates and embassies were immedi-ately deluged by eager calls from prospective applicants, to the extent that phones had to be put off the hook. As ever in the Balkans, there was an ulterior motive behind

(but alive) prime minister, the country was essentially rudderless for two months, until the barely conscious old demagogue finally faced up to his own mortality and signed a letter **resigning** as prime minister (though not as party leader) in January 1996. The "palace clique" of Mimi Liani and cohorts was beaten off in the parliamentary replacement vote in favour of the allegedly colourless but widely respected technocrat **Kostas Simitis**, who seemed to be just what the country needed after years of incompetent flamboyance.

Upon assuming office, Simitis indicated that he wouldn't necessarily play to the gallery as Papandreou had with (for a Greek politician) a remarkable

the Defence Ministry's altruism; by subsidizing resettlement of these long-neglected outposts, it hoped to emphasize their essential Greekness.

The first step in strengthening Greece's territorial claims was to plant Greek flags on these islets, done by Greek navy patrol boats during the latter half of 1995. This was bound sooner or later to provoke a Turkish reaction. In the event, an initial flare-up occurred on January 25, 1996, when a Turkish vessel ran aground in stormy weather on one of two islets, each less than three square kilometres, poised between Kalólimnos (near Kálymnos) and the Bodrum peninsula – if you look carefully you can see the two low-lying islets from any hydrofoil going between Kós and Léros. The skipper refused assistance from a Greek coastguard boat, claiming that the islet was Turkish territory, despite the presence of a Greek flag (planted in this case by the mayor of Kálymnos) and its description as **Ímia** on international nautical charts. For the Turks, this pair of islets was and always had been Kardak, and two days later some Turkish journalists landed by helicopter and replaced the Greek flag with a Turkish one. On January 28, the Greek navy appeared, restoring the Greek colours and leaving a permanent guard.

By January 30, more than twenty heavily armed naval vessels from each side were manoeuvring around each other in the vicinity of the goat-inhabited *vrahonisídhes*, and journalists the world over were rummaging about for large-scale maps – the Ímia duo is simply too minute to show up on conventional atlases. Then a Greek helicopter apparently developed a fault and went down, with three airmen drowned; if it was actually spooked by Turkish aircraft, or even shot down, the fact was concealed so as not to further inflame public opinion. For days the Greek and Turkish media focused almost exclusively on the developing crisis; war fever gripped each country, and provocative statements were issued by both political leaderships. Turkey in particular had just emerged from an inconclusive general election, and the consensus even there was that caretaker Prime Minister Çiller was indulging in a Falklands-style diversionary ploy to rally national opinion behind her.

In the end, open warfare was only averted by intensive, round-the-clock **diplomatic pressure** on both sides; as of January 31, both Greece and Turkey were required to remove their flags and commandos from the islets, and their fleets from the general area, pending mediation. To date, this has not transpired; the proposed civilian resettlement programme has been quietly scrapped, and instead more incontrovertibly Greek islets such as Farmakoníssi have been vigorously garrisoned to counter periodic Turkish claims that "the Greek state is not there to rule over all of the 132 Aegean rock islets which are really ours" (Turkish President Demirel, August 1998).

The Ímia episode was the worst such scare since a 1987 oil-prospecting dispute in the north Aegean, and hopefully will be the last. Many outside observers still have difficulty believing the earnestness of the conflict, dismissing it as scarcely more than a storm in a teacup that escalated out of control. Unfortunately for the parties involved, it was a deadly serious issue, with long historical antecedents and assorted potential implications.

471

statement: "Greece's intransigent nationalism is an expression of the wretchedness that exists in our society. It is the root cause of the problems we have had with our Balkan neighbours and our difficult relations with Europe."

These beliefs were immediately put to the test by a tense armed face-off with Turkey over the uninhabited Dodecanese double-islet of Ímia (see box on p.470), which very nearly escalated into a shooting war. Simitis eventually bowed to US and UN pressure and ordered a withdrawal of Greek naval forces, conceding "disputed" status to the tiny goat-grazed outcrops – in hindsight a wise decision, but one for which at the time he was roundly criticized in parliament by fire-eating ND MPs and the media.

Andreas finally succumbed to his illness on June 22, 1996, prompting a moving display of national mourning; it was genuinely the end of an era, with only Karamanlis (who died less than two years later) and junta colonel Papadopoulos (who died, still incarcerated, in June 1999) as the last remaining "dinosaurs" of postwar Greek politics. Papandreou's canonization process commenced promptly, with a spate of streets renamed to honour him in provincial towns where he was always revered, but the long-term **verdict of history** is likely to be harsher. Papandreou the Younger valued sycophancy over ability, and in his declining years was completely manipulated by the clique around Mimi. Alleged Bank of Crete transactions aside, he also enjoyed indubitable success as a "common cheat" (as described by Karamanlis in his tart memoirs), dying with a huge fortune which he could not possibly have amassed on a public servant's salary.

Simitis: 2, Néa Dhimokratía: 0

Papandreou's death was promptly followed by PASOK's summer conference, where Simitis ensured his survival as party leader by co-opting his main internal foe, Papandreou's former head of staff, Akis Tsohadzopoulos (subsequently defence and development minister), with a promise of future high office. Following the summer congress, Simitis cleverly rode the wave of pro-PASOK sympathy caused by Papandreou's death and called **general elections** a year early in **September 1996**.

The **results** were as hoped for: 162 seats for PASOK versus 108 for Néa Dhimokratía despite a margin of only three percentage points, the winner's strength artificially inflated by a convoluted electoral law. Given that the two main parties' agendas were virtually indistinguishable, the core issues boiled down to which was better poised to deliver results – and whether voters would be swayed by ND chief Evert's strident Slav- and Turk-baiting nationalism (they weren't). The biggest surprise was the collapse of Samaras' Politikí Ánixi, which failed to clear the three percent nationwide hurdle for parliamentary representation, but three leftist splinter parties did well: eleven seats and just over five percent for Papariga's KKE, ten seats (including a new Thracian Muslim deputy) with about the same tally for the Synaspismós under new chief Nikos Konstantopoulos, and nine seats at just under five percent for the Democratic Social Movement (DIKKI), founded early in the year by rehabilitated ex-minister Tsovolas to push for 1980s-vintage leftist policies. Evert resigned as ND leader, being succeeded by Karamanlis's nephew Kostas. Néa Dhimokratía was down but by no means out: in the **June 1999** Euroelections the party finished first nationwide and sent forty percent of Greece's Euro MPs to Strasbourg.

Simitis' first-term problems arose mainly from the continued imposition of **austerity measures**. In December 1996, protesting farmers closed off the country's main road and rail arteries for several weeks, before dismantling the blockades in time for people to travel for the Christmas holidays. Teachers or students (or both) spent much of 1997 on strike over proposed educational reforms – essentially about imposing some discipline on the notoriously lax school regimens. But September 1997 saw a timely boost to national morale with the awarding of the 2004 Olympic Games to Athens.

Simitis, far more pro-European than his maverick predecessor, devoted himself to the unenviable task of getting the Greek economy in sufficiently good shape to meet the criteria for **monetary union**. The *Eforía* or Greek Inland Revenue made some highly publicized headway in curbing the largest **black economy** in the EU, by requiring meticulous documentation of transactions and by publicly "outing" the more flagrant tax dodgers.

After some initial success with his "hard drachma" policy (often propping it up by dumping foreign currency reserves), Simitis was obliged to devalue it upon Greece's **entry to the ERM** in March 1998; however, with other internationally traded currencies badly exposed in the Far East economic crises, the drachma regained prior levels by October 1998. The fact that inflation stayed consistently down into single figures for the first time in decades was testament to Simitis' ability as a manager; indeed his nickname, amongst both foes and supporters, was *o loyistís*, "the accountant". Simitis also had the sense to delegate to the capable and refrain from meddling, so that his Finance Minister Yannos Papantoniou had an unprecedented six years on the job before taking up the defence portfolio.

Increasingly amicable relations with its Balkan neighbours – Greece is one of the largest foreign investors in Bulgaria and FYROM, for example – has the potential to trim unemployment, typically just over nine percent officially (though among recent graduates it is more like twenty percent). But the most dramatic **improvement in international relations** occurred with old nemesis Turkey, since the severe **earthquake** which struck northern Athens on September 7, 1999, killing scores and rendering almost one hundred thousand homeless. It came less than a month after the devastating tremor in northwest Turkey, and ironically spurred a thaw between the two historical rivals. Greeks donated massive amounts of blood and foodstuffs to the Turkish victims, as well as being the earliest foreign rescue teams on hand in Turkey, and in turn they saw Turkish disaster-relief squads among the first on the scene in Athens. Soon afterwards, **Foreign Minister George Papandreou** (son of Andreas) announced that Greece had dropped its long time opposition to EU financial aid to Turkey in the absence of a solution to outstanding Cyprus and Aegean disputes, and further indicated that Greece would no longer oppose Turkish candidacy for accession to the EU.

With his handling of the Turkish détente and progress towards EMU the main campaign issues, Simitis called **elections** five months earlier than required, on **April 9, 2000**. In the event, PASOK squeaked into office for an unprecedented third consecutive term by a single percentage point, 43.7 to ND's 42.7, with 158 seats against 125. The crucial factor that swung the cliff-hanger – not decided until 1am the day after – was voters' mistrust of Karamanlis the Younger's manifest inexperience. The KKE held steady at just over five percent and eleven seats, but Synaspismós barely cleared the three percent hurdle for its six seats, while DIKKI didn't.

Simitis capped his narrow victory by announcing Greece's official **entry into the euro-currency zone** on June 20, at an EU summit in Portugal.

He needed this bit of good news, as the country's reputation had again taken a battering on June 8, when the terror group November 17 emerged from two years' quiescence by assassinating **Brigadier Stephen Saunders**, the UK military attaché, while his car was stalled in Athens traffic. There were mutterings abroad (again, especially in the US) that adequate security could not be guaranteed for the forthcoming, Greece-hosted Olympics. In July, the Orthodox Church mounted a last-ditch attack on the **new-style national identity cards**, which omitted to state the bearer's religion; the government proclaimed that the old-style cards were illegal under EU regulations, and an ND-sponsored bill to allow for optional citation of religious faith was defeated in parliament.

The end of November 17 – and the eclipse of PASOK

Though Scotland Yard operatives had been helping their Greek opposite numbers in investigating the Saunders murder (see above), in the end a stroke of luck led to the **dissolution of November 17**. On June 29, 2002, a bomb prematurely exploded in the hands of one Stavros Xeros, ostensibly a 40-year-old icon painter but in reality a principal operative of the group. Severely wounded on a Pireás street, Xeros was picked up by police, who in hospital extracted from him the location of two arms- and explosives-laden safe houses in central Athens, along with the names of numerous other group members. By mid-July, November 17's intellectual godfather, Alexandros Giotopoulos, had been arrested in the act of attempting to leave his hideout on Lipsí island. After a nine-month trial before a tribunal of three judges, in a purpose-built court-room inside Korýdhallos high-security prison, guilty verdicts – and multiple life sentences – were handed down to fifteen out of the nineteen accused, thus bringing the curtain down on Europe's longest-lived "Red Terrorist" saga.

Notwithstanding the unravelling of November 17 and the kudos which pre-sumably should have accrued to the ruling party, the October 2002 **munici-pal and prefectural elections** saw PASOK slip badly, with opposition Néa Dhimokratía gaining a plurality of mayoral offices and doing nearly as well on the provincial level. Reaction within PASOK, delayed by Greece's six-month stint in the revolving presidency of the EU during early 2003, consisted of a minimal reshuffle in July of deputy cabinet ministers and the appointment of a new general secretary. On January 7, 2004, Simitis did what he'd long prom-ised to do, a first for a sitting Greek prime minister – effectively resign, nam-ing Foreign Minister George Papandreou to lead PASOK into the impending election. Simitis was thus signalling that one of his main reforms had been completed: the end of personality-based politics, and the completed evolution of an issue-based, centrist, technocratic party.

But anti-incumbent sentiment was rife in the run-up to the **parliamentary elections of March 7, 2004**. While no hint of scandal attached to Simitis personally, 19 out of the past 23 years in the saddle had undeniably made PASOK complacent, and corruption scandals were an almost monthly occur-rence; Papandreou, in appearing to be virtuous by deselecting ten candidates who had tabled a bill favouring an unauthorized tourist development in Halki-dhikí, merely confirmed this image for the electorate. Also confirmed – if any onlooker were still in doubt – was the dynastic nature of Greek politics, as "Yiorgaki" ("Georgie", son and grandson of prime ministers) squared off against "Kostaki" ("Chucky", nephew of a prime minister and then president). The results were hardly surprising: 45.36 percent and 165 seats for ND, 40.73

percent and 117 seats for PASOK, 5.9 percent and twelve seats for the KKE, with the Synaspismós just squeezing into Parliament with 3.26 percent and six seats. Karamanlis appointed a relatively young cabinet of little-knowns (the latter not too surprising after two decades in the wilderness), and reserved for himself the Ministry of Culture, thus taking on personal responsibility for the successful outcome of Olympic preparations, still then in the balance.

The standard PASOK taunt of "inexperience" at the ND team, and the failure of the Cyprus reunification referendum in late April, had little effect on the outcome of the **June 13 Euro elections**. At 43 to 34 percent, ND increased its margin over PASOK, taking eleven of 24 seats; the KKE at 9.47 percent also did well at the expense of both PASOK and Synaspismós, while an ominous note was provided by the first representation for LAOS (Laïkós Orthódhox Synayermós or Popular Orthodox Rally), a rabidly nationalist, Christian party.

Aside from the Olympics (see below), most of 2004 was taken up with ND demonstrating that the budget deficit and public debt had been systematically underreported by its predecessors for every single year since 2000, that PASOK had cooked the books to allow the country to enter the ERM in that year, and that Greece was in chronic danger of breaching the three percent EU-allowable ceiling for deficits. In October, four members of urban terrorist group **ELA** were convicted and sentenced to 25 years in jail, while in December Greece strongly backed giving Turkey a definite date to begin negotiations to join the EU.

The Olympic Games

As the Olympics approached ever closer, Greece mounted an increasingly sophisticated public relations campaign for the return of the **Elgin marbles** from the British Museum. 2003 opinion polls showed a 3:1 majority amongst the British public in favour of some sort of return scheme. Greece proposed "permanent loan" of the relics in a British Museum "annexe" in Athens (rather than "ownership"), reciprocated by loans of equally significant artefacts from Greece to the London galleries. Designs for a new three-level museum south of the Acropolis pointedly reserve the highest wing for the return of the Parthenon relics. Another potential quid pro quo for a gracious "return" could be vigorous Greek support for the London 2012 Olympic bid.

In terms of Athens' own Olympics, many foreign and domestic commentators had made a career of telling the doom of the preparations, predicting that the Greeks couldn't organize a piss-up in a brewery, much less an entire Games. On the night, everyone was compelled to eat large quanties of humble pie, as the **2004 Olympics** went off pretty much without a hitch, aside from numbers of disqualifications (including two star Greek sprinters) for failing, or not taking, banned-substances tests – "*tó dhóping*" is now standard Greek vocabulary. Despite the heavy security, most attendees had a great time, and the opening and closing ceremonies were (potentially) worth a decade's worth of tourist-board advertising.

The downside was the massive cost of the Games – at $7 billion, over three times what Sydney's cost, and it will take nearly three decades to pay off. Part of this was due to mandatory security precautions, but part also to massive overtime pay to hordes of foreign labourers hurriedly recruited to finish all the necessary venues. The haste resulted in thirteen fatalities (as against none for the Río–Andírrio bridge). Many have found a way to stay in the country, adding to the huge immigrant population (see p.478).

The tourism scene

Tourism, the most important foreign-exchange earner for the country, had a pretty good year in 1999 despite a slow start occasioned by the Kosovo war, but a well-publicized spate of forest fires during an unusually hot summer, plus the Express *Samina* shipwreck (see box, p.56) conspired to make 2000 an *annus horribilis* for tourist arrival numbers. 2001 was another bad season, even before the September 11 terror incidents (which meant no significant American arrivals for many months); 2002 saw the wettest summer in memory, while 2003 was blighted by murmurings of unwarranted euro-price inflation and an unsavoury sun, sand and sex image for the country in the wake of the Faliráki incidents (see p.135). After so many lean years, the Greek hospitality industry was positively salivating at its prospects for the Olympic summer of 2004. In the event, the fear of terrorism, scare stories about stratospheric hotel rates and the continued malaise of the euro effect meant that 2004 was even worse for the islands than previous seasons.

Through all this, government efforts to improve infrastructure proceed at a glacial pace, or not at all. A few yacht marinas and wide roads have been completed with EU assistance, while spas, casinos and golf courses (Rhodes has all three of these) have been or are being renovated. On the aesthetic front, in late May 2001 then-Minister of the Aegean Nikos Sifounakis announced a strict new building code for the smaller islands of the Cyclades, Dodecanese and east Aegean, to check the spread of concrete monstrosities completely at odds with their surroundings. Larger islands like Lésvos and Rhodes were, however, left unregulated – too many voters would be antagonized otherwise.

Fluctuating visitor numbers have been particularly evident in the Dodecanese and east Aegean, where stable tourism depends on consistently good **Greek relations with Turkey**. Basic geographical realities dictate that the islands, the last territories incorporated into the Greek state, are those least securely clasped to the mother country. If push comes to shove, all of these islands are fundamentally indefensible; a Turkish bomb lobbed onto island airport runways every few hours will suffice to keep them from being resupplied and guarantee their capture by Turkey within a matter of days. Common sense also suggests that Greece has much to gain by encouraging weekend (or longer) tourism from Turkey to these islands, by abolishing or easing visa requirements, though admittedly as a member of the Schengen Group Greece no longer has total discretion in this.

The biggest development on this front, however, and one with potentially the most permanent implication for island landscapes, is the phenomenal upsurge in what has been called "**residential tourism**" – the purchase of either old village houses or purpose-built modern structures as **holiday homes** for foreigners. Especially on Sými, Kálymnos, Pátmos, Léros, Astypálea and in Rhodes Old Town, there's a thriving real estate trade, though a finite number of properties and land mean that (except perhaps in southern Rhodes) it will never assume quite the dimensions of development on Cyprus or Crete.

Greek society today

The following summary can only give a flavour of the massive, ground-level changes which have occurred in Greece since the late 1980s. First and foremost, it's a conspicuously wealthier, more **consumerist society** than before, with sharp disparities in income, imbued with the prevailing neoliberal mania for privatization. Consuming interests in the most literal sense – essentially an overreaction to wartime privation – have given rise to a nationwide explosion in **slimming centres**, mostly pushing fad diets or amphetamines rather than exercise, and exploiting Greeks' guilt at their record-breaking obesity (see p.7). Athens, Thessaloníki and most large island capitals have their legions of **yuppies**, addicted to gourmet wines, properly made cappuccinos, designer trinkets, fast cars and **travel**; even small-town agencies promote junkets to Thailand, Tunisia, Cuba and European city breaks (the current trendy favourites). Greek domestic tourism is also heavily marketed, in particular weekend breaks to "name" islands like Corfu, Santoríni, Kós and Rhodes, or adventure expeditions to the mountains; there are numerous Greek-language travel magazines, Sunday supplements and bound guides, advising Greeks where to spend their surplus cash.

Mobile phones are ubiquitous – along with Italy and Cyprus, Greece has the highest per-capita use in Europe – and the success of the three private networks has forced OTE to offer its own mobile network at reasonable prices, and in general sharpen up. You can walk into an OTE phone shop and get any high-tech device or network service more or less instantly, unlike the bad old days – as recently as 1994 – when OTE was a national disgrace and provision of a simple analogue line could take years.

In tandem with this increased materialism, the **Orthodox Church** has, under the reactionary, publicity-seeking Archbishop Khristodhoulos of Athens, declined from "guardian of the nation" to national embarrassment. Rather than address the pressing social problems occasioned by Greece's immigrant crisis (see overleaf), its version of moral leadership has been to organize demos against the new secularized ID cards, and (more understandably) to extract from Pope John Paul II a grovelling apology for the 1204 sacking of Constantinople during his May 2001 visit to Athens. But the Church's medieval mindset is best exemplified in its continuing **ban on cremation**, and near-hysteria on the subject of bar codes. Greece is the only EU country where cremation is forbidden; every summer there's a malodorous backlog of corpses to be interred at the overcrowded cemeteries, whilst other remains are surreptitiously sent (under threat of excommunication) to be burnt in more accommodating Bulgaria or Romania. Orthodox doctrine is adamant that immolation would compromise the Resurrection, and that the bones of a saint (still revered as relics) might inadvertently be destroyed. But it's **bar codes** on ID cards, and hand- or forehead-stamping for casino patrons or bank employees, that have really exercised the clergy, in particular Athonite monks. They, and a considerable number of the lay believers, see this as a Jewish-Masonic conspiracy fulfilling Revelations 13:16–17 and 14:9, verses which relate to the mark of the Beast.

The clergy's rantings notwithstanding, bar-coded Greece is now firmly locked into the **global economy**, and not just in the matter of cross-border shipment of the dead. International franchises such as McDonald's, Next, Häagen-Dazs, TGIF and The Body Shop proliferate in most larger towns;

consumer interest rates have plunged while credit cards are aggressively marketed, the Athens stock exchange burgeoned (before crashing spectacularly, prompting a wave of suicides by those who lost their savings), and foreign or multinational companies have flocked to invest. It is they who in the main funded and executed massive infrastructure improvements designed to long outlast the 2004 Olympics: the airport at Spáta, the Athens metro and tramway, the Río–Andírrio bridge over the Gulf of Corinth, the Via Egnatia expressway across Epirus, Macedonia and Thrace. **Overseas companies** are also quietly **acquiring** more (or less) productive elements of the Greek economy; Britain's Blue Circle, for example, in 1998 purchased Hercules Cement from Italian interests, though after years of trying there are still no takers for red-ink-submerged Olympic Airways. The repeatedly postponed end of cabotage – whereby only Greek companies have been allowed to provide ferry services within Greece – is now set for 2007, and should weed out the flakier shipping companies and have the others pulling their socks up, under threat of potential challenges by P&O or Fred Olsen. There's been nowhere to go but up since the *Express Samina* sinking, which fully exposed the weaknesses in safety, pricing and personnel training of Greek Aegean transport – and most of all the oligopolies which have resulted from domestic companies following overseas examples and engaging in extensive **corporate takeovers**. Hellas Flying Dolphins, the responsible party in the shipwreck, had acquired Ceres Hydrofoils, several smaller steamship outfits, and a majority interest in an airline, to become the largest domestic transport company; Alpha Bank absorbed the troubled Ionian Bank in early 1999 and instantly became the second largest banking/insurance group in the country.

It used to be that a lifetime sinecure with the civil service was the goal for most graduates, but no longer – now young people crave a **career** in the private sector, with unlimited salary prospects. They're also willing to work for low rates of pay, which older, less qualified professionals with families – who often must cobble together part-time jobs – simply can't live on. Yet most Greeks have now become too grand for menial jobs; the late Andreas once grumbled that Greece shouldn't remain "a nation of waiters" – it seems he needn't have worried.

Greece may continue to occupy the EU's economic cellar with Portugal, but it's still infinitely wealthier (and usually more stable) than any of its neighbours, and this has acted as a magnet for a permanent **underclass of immigrants**. Since 1990 they have arrived in numbers estimated variously as 800,000 to well over a million, a huge burden for a not especially rich country of just over ten million native citizens (imagine Britain with six million refugees rather than a few hundred thousand). These days your waiter, hotel desk clerk or cleaning lady is most likely to be Albanian, Bulgarian or Romanian, to cite the largest groups of arrivals. There are also significant communities of Pakistanis, Egyptians, Poles, Bangladeshis, Syrians, Filipinos, Ukrainians, Russians, equatorial Africans, Kurds and Georgians (not to mention ethnic Greeks from the Caucasus) – a striking change in what had hitherto been a homogeneous, parochial culture.

The **Greek response** to this has been decidedly mixed: the Albanians, making up roughly half the influx and found living on all the larger islands, are almost universally detested (except for the ethnic-Greek northern Epirots), and blamed for all manner of social ills. For the first time, crime – especially burglaries – is a significant issue, with a brisk trade in alarms, armoured doors and "beware of guard dog" notices. The newcomers have also prompted the first anti-immigration measures in a country whose population is more used to being on the other side of such laws – Greece lies within the Schengen Zone and sees itself, as in past ages, as the first line of defence against the "barbarians" from the Orient. All of the east Aegean islands regularly receive boatloads of people fleeing from every country in Asia, and the country's single refugee camp (near Athens) is grossly inadequate. In June 2001, legal residence was offered to the estimated half a million illegals who could demonstrate two years' presence in Greece, and pay a hefty amount for retroactive social security contributions. But when this initial **amnesty period** ended in early September, fewer than 350,000 of these individuals had applied to be "regularized", and the arduous red tape involved meant that subsequent amnesties netted hardly any more successful applicants.

That said, the "illegals" are unlikely to be deported en masse any time soon; besides staffing hotels as noted, they do the difficult, dirty and dangerous work that Greeks now disdain, especially farm labour, restaurant prep work, construction and rubbish collection. From an employer's point of view, they are cheap – thirty to forty percent less costly than natives – and **net contributors** to the social welfare system, especially in respect of pensions where Greece, like much of southern Europe, has a shrinking and ageing population. The Albanians in particular are also buoying up much of the banking system by their phenomenal saving habits and wiring of funds home, so much so that the National Bank has installed ATMs with Albanian-language instructions.

On a positive note, these diverse groups, travel abroad by the Greeks themselves, touring bands or dance companies and programmes on private television channels have created a taste for **non-Greek music and foods**. One doesn't always have to wait for the summer festivals to see name jazz, blues or soul acts in the biggest towns, and there are now decent foreign-cuisine restaurants here, as well as in many of the major island resorts. All of these factors, however, have had the effect of making Greece less identifiably Greek and, it must be said, of making many native Greeks themselves rather less welcoming and more self-absorbed than before.

Wildlife

D
odecanese and east Aegean wildlife – in particular the flora – can prove an unexpected source of fascination. In spring, the colour, scent and variety of wild flowers, with the resulting wealth of insect and bird life, are astonishing. Islands cut off from continental landmasses have had many thousands of years to evolve their own individual species. Overall, there are some two thousand species of flowering plants on the islands (over half of which exist on Sámos alone), many of them unique to Greece.

Some background

In early antiquity Greece, including the islands, was thickly forested; Aleppo (*Pinus halepensis*) and Calabrian (*Pinus brutia*) pines grew in coastal regions, giving way to fir or black pine up in the hills and low mountains. But this **native woodland** contracted rapidly as human activities expanded. As early as Classical times, an artificial mosaic of habitats had been created through forest clearance, followed by agriculture (including the planting of olive groves), abandonment to scrub, and then a resumption of cultivation or grazing. Huge quantities of timber were consumed in the production of charcoal, pottery and smelted metal, and in shipbuilding or construction work. Small patches of old-growth woodland have remained on the largest islands, but even these are under threat from loggers and arsonists (see box overleaf).

Contemporary Greek **farming** often lacks the rigid efficiency of northern European agriculture. Many peasant farmers still cultivate little patches of land, without systematic use of pesticides and herbicides, while town-dwellers travel at weekends to collect food plants from the countryside. Wild greens under the generic term *hórta* are gathered to be cooked like spinach, while grape hyacinth bulbs are boiled as a vegetable. The buds and young shoots of capers are harvested, along with wild figs, carobs, plums, cherries, sweet chestnuts and the fruit of the strawberry tree. Emergent snails and mushrooms are collected after the first rains. The more resilient forms of wildlife can coexist with these uses, but for many Greeks only those species that have practical applications are regarded as having any value.

However, increased access to heavier earth-moving machinery means farmers can sweep away an ancient meadow full of orchids in an easy morning's work – often to clear a field that is used for forage for a year or two and then abandoned to coarse thistles. Increasingly, the pale scars of dirt tracks crisscross once-intact hill- and mountainsides, allowing short-termist agricultural destruction of previously undisturbed upland habitats. During the 1950s a policy of draining **wetlands** was instituted in order to increase agriculture, and many important areas were lost to wildlife completely. Those lakes, lagoons and deltas that remain on the larger islands are, in theory, now protected for their fragile biodiversity and their environmental and scientific value – but industrial and sewage pollution, disturbance and misuse are common. Local 4WD vehicles and noisy motorbikes race through dunes, destroying the surface stability and decimating nesting species; Greek military planes practice low-altitude flight over flocks of flamingos; rows of illegally overnighting camper vans disfigure the beaches; and locals drive to the nearest ravine to dump unwanted televisions and fridges. On Lésvos, one of the island's main tourist attractions, the Kallóni saltpans, once beloved by rare birds, are being poisoned by sewage. The terrapin population of Kós, Lésvos and Límnos has fallen to almost zero since the millennium; the prime suspected cause is pesticide runoff from mosquito spraying in adjacent resorts.

Since the 1970s, **tourist development** has ribboned out along coastlines, sweeping away both agricultural plots and wildlife havens as it does so. These expanding resorts increase local employment, often attracting inland workers to the coast; the generation that would have been shepherds on remote hillsides now work in tourist bars and tavernas. Consequently, the pressure of domestic animal-grazing, particularly goat-grazing on the larger islands, has been significantly reduced and allows the regeneration of tree seedlings.

Despite an often negative attitude to wildlife, Greece was probably the first place in the world where it was an object of study. Theophrastus of Lésvos (372–287 BC) was the first recorded **botanist** and a systematic collector of general information on plants, while his contemporary Aristotle studied the animal world. During the first century AD the distinguished physician Dioscorides compiled a herbal that remained a standard work for over a thousand years.

Flowers

Greek-island plants cease flowering (or even living, in the case of annuals) when it is too hot and dry – midsummer in Greece plays the same role for plants as winter does in northern Europe. Perennials survive in coastal Greece either by producing leathery or hairy leaves with a minimum surface area, or by dying back to giant tuberous rootstalks – both strategies for conserving moisture.

The arid Greek summers thus confine the main **flowering period** to spring, a climatic window when the days are bright, temperatures not too high and the ground water supply still adequate. Spring comes to the southern Dodecanese in late February or early March, with the east Aegean lagging behind until mid- or late April. The delicate flowers of early spring – orchids, fritillaries, anemones, cyclamen, tulips and small bulbs – are replaced as the season progresses by more robust shrubs, tall perennials and abundant annuals. May, marked by the yellow flowers of broom (*Spartium junceum*) or gorse (*Calycotome villosa*), signals the onset of **summer** at lower elevations; many plants close down completely now, though a few tough ones, like shrubby thyme and savory, continue to flower through July and August, acting as magnets for butterflies. Once the worst heat is over, and the first rain-showers have arrived (usually by late September), there's another burst of activity on the part of **autumn** flowering species – on a much smaller scale than in springtime, but no less welcome after the brown drabness of summer. Mid- to late October will usually bring more rain, germinating seeds for the following year's crop of annuals, but **winter** flowers only get underway after Christmas, continuing into late February.

Seashore and watercourses

Plants on the **beach** tend to be hardy, salt-tolerant species growing in a difficult environment where fresh water is limited and dehydrating winds often very strong. Feathery tamarisk trees are adept at surviving in this habitat, and consequently are often planted to provide shade. On hot days or nights you may see or feel them "sweating" away surplus salt water from their foliage.

Sand dunes on the southerly Dodecanese often support low gnarled trees of the prickly juniper. These provide shelter for a variety of colourful small plants like pink campions, yellow restharrow, white stocks, blue alkanet and violet sea lavender. The sandy depressions or "slacks" behind the dunes – where they have not been illegally ploughed for cultivation – serve as home to a variety of plants. Open stretches of beach sand usually have fewer plants, particularly nowadays in resort areas, where the bulldozed "spring-cleaning" of the beach removes all the local flora along with the winter's rubbish.

The spectacular yellow-horned poppy (*Glaucium flavum*) can be found growing on shingled banks, and sea stocks or Virginia stocks amongst rocks behind beaches. The small pink campion (*Silene colorata*) is often colourfully present before June. Between August and October, look for the enormous, fragrant, white flowers of the sea daffodil (*Pancratium maritimum*) at the inland edge of sandy beaches, for example, at Éristos on Tílos.

Forest fires – and other pests

Since 1928, **fires** have reduced Greece's proportion of forested land from just under one third to just under one fifth, with the most rapid loss since 1974. Huge infernos have raged almost annually on at least one among Rhodes, Kárpathos, Sámos, Ikaría and Híos from 1981 until 2004; of the larger islands of the east Aegean and Dodecanese, so far only Kós and Lésvos have escaped comprehensive damage.

A tiny fraction of these summer disasters occur naturally or accidentally, through a lightning strike during an electrical storm, sunlight refracted through a glass shard, or sparks from a badly insulated power pylon – any of these providing the necessary ignition to the highly volatile, resinous maquis shrubbery and pine which cover the middle altitudes of these islands. As for the other fires, conspiracy theories – ever popular in Greece – variously blame the CIA, KGB or its successors, the Freemasons, Mossad, the PLO, Turks, Albanians, etc, but the stark truth is that the vast majority are the result of arson perpetrated by the islanders themselves. Motives are simple and sordid: clearing land for grazing or building, tourist developers forcing stubborn farmers to sell up at depressed prices, or hampering tourism on a rival island or beach. There is often an upsurge prior to elections, the result of surreptitious promises by candidates to reclassify burnt forest land as suitable for development should they attain office. The Orthodox Church and the Forest Service own and administer vast tracts of land in a quasi-feudal system, implementing erratic methods and rates of taxation in addition to promulgating policies that enrage private owners and encourage firebugs. The arsonists themselves are usually locals with a grievance, but increasingly rent-a-thugs from elsewhere who are provided with sophisticated equipment (light planes and time-delay devices) by their employers.

The recurrence of blazes is often used as a justification by the Forest Service for the bulldozing of numerous dirt tracks through woods, presumably to allow fire engines easier access. Unfortunately this creates as many problems as it solves, since arsonists take advantage of the opportunity to drive their jerry cans full of petrol or time-bombs to the scene of operations. Experience has shown that only Canadian-made Bombardier prop-planes, modified for dumping seawater on the flames, and (for more difficult terrain) Russian-built Skorpion helicopters with five-tonne water slings, make a decisive difference in fire control. However, neither of these fly at night, when only desperate crews digging trenches with hand tools can attempt to encircle the burn zone. Accordingly the arsonists generally do their dirty work just before dusk, on a windy day, setting blazes at several points simultaneously, so that by the time morning arrives the fire is far out of control. Once a conflagration is underway, pine trees are their own worst enemies, since pine cones

Many **watercourses** dry up completely in the hot season, only filling periodically after torrential rains during December to April. Consequently, there are few true aquatic plants compared with much of Europe. However, species that can survive the regular drying-out flourish – for example, the giant reed or **calamus**, a bamboo-like grass reaching up to 6m in height and often cut for use as canes. It frequently grows in company with the shrubby, pink- or white-flowered and very poisonous oleander. Near the river mouths and in the damp ravines of Lésvos grows the yellow azalea (*Rhododendron luteum*), found nowhere else in Greece.

Cultivated land

Arable fields can be rich with colourful weeds in late spring: scarlet poppies, blue bugloss, yellow or white daisies, wild peas, gladioli, daisies, tulips

explode grenade-like when set alight, firing off blazing particles for up to 100m into unburnt tracts.

Since the mid-1990s the authorities have begun stationing red-and-yellow **fire-fighting planes** at major east Aegean and Dodecanese airports (in theory two on each runway), but there are rarely enough to go around, with planes sometimes off combating fire on an adjacent island when disaster strikes closer to home. **Ground surveillance** can also be inadequate; thus far only Lésvos and Sámos have comprehensive, 24-hour summertime watches maintained on strategic ridges, and only Rhodes has installed anything resembling a network of rural standpipes (conspicuous in and around Petaloúdhes).

As if the fire threat wasn't bad enough, island forests have another, more insidious but nearly as destructive natural adversary: the **pine processionary caterpillar**. This is the larval form of a moth which lays its eggs near the apical bunches of pine needles; when they hatch, the caterpillars form densely webbed trapezoidal nests, inside of which they steadily munch away at the tender young shoots, denuding the growing ends of the tree and severely stunting it. Forest service employees are supposed to conduct springtime patrols in years of heavy infestation, collecting and destroying the nests, but they rarely if ever do – not too surprising in light of the caterpillars' highly irritant qualities.

The underlying basis for both the blazes and the nonexistent pest control is social: there's little consensus in Greece that woodlands have any intrinsic value, now that few trees are tapped for resin or used in boat-building, so goats or villas will win hands down in any comparative assessment in rural minds. Only slowly is a connection being made between fire damage and subsequent winter flashfloods or steadily dropping water tables; tentative anti-erosion terracing on Sámos hillsides following its July 2000 blaze was inadequate to prevent massive soil loss and flooding in December 2001, as unusually heavy rains simply failed to sink into the denuded, hard-baked soil. Only when tourist receipts begin to fall as a partial result of denuded scenery – as has happened on Sámos since 2000 – is there likely to be a belated conversion to "Green consciousness". The saddest element of the story is that most of the lost vegetation was a mature crop of Aleppo, Calabrian and (on Sámos) black pines, which will be replaced haphazardly if at all. Carob, the most fire-resistent species (often resprouting from scorched trunks within two months of a blaze), is seldom used in replanting schemes. In typical Mediterranean climatic conditions, native conifers grow so slowly – fifty to seventy years to attain any appreciable size – that few of the readers of this book will live to see a mature, regenerated forest on many islands.

and grape hyacinths. Small **meadows** may be equally colourful, with slower-growing plants such as orchids in extraordinary quantities. The rather dull violet flowers of the mandrake belie its celebrated history as a narcotic and surgical anesthetic. In the absence of herbicides, **olive groves** can host extensive underflora. Where herbicides are used, there is instead usually a yellow carpet of the introduced, weedkiller-resistant *Oxalis pescaprae*, which now occurs in sufficient quantity to show up in satellite photographs.

Fallow farmland is good for bulbous perennials, in particular a gorgeous, multicoloured variety of anemone (*Anemone coronaria*) that blooms early in the year throughout most of the islands. The scarlet turban buttercup (*Ranunculus asiaticus*) on Rhodes, and Sámos' sweet-smelling blue hyacinths (*zoumboúlia* in Greek), ancestor of the cultivated variety, also emerge during late February and March.

Appearing between March and July – or even later – is the wild snapdragon (*Antirrhinum majus*), which loves chinks in low **rock walls**. Here too, from May to August, blaze forth the white-to-pinkish flowers of the spiny caper; the unopened flower bud is not the only edible bit, since on many islands the thorny shoots are also pickled and eaten whole.

Among **exotics**, the century plant (*Agave americana*), naturalized around the Mediterranean since the eighteenth century, is a familiar sight on the islands; the plant flowers once in its ten- to fifteen-year (not 100-year!) lifetime during June, after which the formidably spiky leaf-rosette withers away. It's commonly used as a fence substitute, like another import, the yellow-flowered prickly pear (*Opuntia indica*), supposedly brought back by Columbus from the New World. Its scarlet fruit, ripening in September, tastes like watermelon but requires peeling and putting through a blender to get rid of spines and seeds respectively.

Lower hillsides

The rocky earth makes terracing for cultivation on some hillsides difficult and impractical. Agriculture is often abandoned and such areas revert to a mixture of low shrubs and perennials – the **garigue** biome. With time, a decade of wet winters, and the absence of grazing, some shrubs such as juniper and kermes or holly oak develop into small trees – the much denser **maquis** vegetation. The colour yellow often predominates in early spring, with brooms, gorse, Jerusalem sage and the three-metre-tall giant fennel, followed by the magenta or white of bushy rockroses (*Cistus* ssp). An abundance of rockroses is often indicative of an earlier fire, since they flourish in the cleared areas. Strawberry trees (*Arbutus unedo*) are also fire-resistant; they flower in winter or early spring, producing an orange-red, edible (though disappointingly insipid) fruit in the autumn, fermented to make a more exciting if illicit liqueur. The Judas tree (*Cercis siliquastrum*) flowers on bare wood in spring, making a blaze of pink against green hillsides. From late October until the New Year, heather (*Erica manipuliflora*) provides a blaze of pink on slopes with acidic soil.

A third habitat is **phrygana**, smaller, frequently aromatic or spiny shrubs, often with a narrow strip of bare ground between each hedgehog-like bush. Many **aromatic herbs** such as lavender, rosemary, savory, sage and thyme are native to these areas, intermixed with other less tasty plants such as the toxic euphorbias and the spiny burnet or wire-netting bush.

Orchids in Greece are much smaller and altogether more dignified than the tropical varieties in florists' shops. On both Rhodes and Sámos there are nearly fifty species, mostly of the genera *Orchis* and *Ophrys*, blooming from March until May, according to altitude. Their complexity blurs species boundaries and keeps botanists in a state of taxonomic flux. In particular, the *Ophrys* bee and spider orchids have adapted, through their subtleties of lip colour and false scents, to seduce small male wasps. These insects mistake the flowers for a potential mate, and unintentionally assist the plant's pollination. Other orchids mimic the colours and scents of honey-producing plants, to lure bees. Though all species are officially protected, many are still picked for decoration – in particular the giant *Barlia* orchid – and fill vases in homes, cafés, tavernas and even on graves.

Irises have a particular elegance and charm, appearing between February and June according to species and island. The blue-to-violet winter iris, as its name suggests, is the first to appear, followed by the small blue *Iris gynandriris*. The flowers of the latter open after midday and into the night, only to wither by the following morning. The widow iris is sombre-coloured in funereal shades of black and green, while the taller, white *Iris albicans*, the holy flower of Islam, is a relic of the Ottoman occupation. In the limestone peaks of Sámos, *Iris suavolens* has short stems, but huge yellow-and-brown flowers.

You can often find deserted, shady terraces full of **cyclamen**, either *Cyclamen persicum* (ancestor of the domestic variety) or *Cyclamen repandum*, sprouting from small tubers or corms. Both exhibit white-to-pink blooms in early spring; the Rhodes form has white blossoms with a pinkish throat. By contrast, the pink autumn *Cyclamen graecum* flowers in September.

Once the heat of the summer is over, **autumn bulbs** come into their own. The sea squill (*Drimia maritima*) occurs inland as well as near the sea, with tall spikes of white flowers rising from huge bulbs. Smaller bulbs or corms, including various crocus species and their relatives, the pink-to-purple colchicums and the yellow sternbergias, bloom from September until November.

Mountains and gorges

The higher **mountains** of Rhodes and Kós, and the east Aegean islands of Sámos, Ikaría, Híos and Lésvos, have transient winter snow cover varying with altitude, and cooler weather for much of the year, so flowering is consequently later than at lower altitudes. Their limestone or schist peaks hold rich collections of attractive flowering rock plants whose nearest relatives may be from the Balkan Alps or from the Turkish Toros ranges. Gorges are another spectacular habitat, particularly rich on Sámos and Ikaría. Their inaccessible cliffs act as refuges for plants that cannot survive the grazing, competition, or the more extreme climates of open areas.

Much of the surviving Dodecanese and east Aegean **island forest** is found in the mountainous areas of Rhodes, Kós, Sými, Sámos and Lésvos, with tree cover on Sámos and Rhodes much reduced in the wake of the aforementioned fires. Depending on the island, the woodland can comprise cypress (widespread at low altitudes) or a few species of pine: Calabrian or Aleppo at lower altitudes, and a few surviving black pine on Sámos' Mount Ámbelos and Mount Ólymbos of Lésvos. Oaks are a reliable indicator of volcanic soil – they don't like limestone – and are found on Lésvos, southwest Sámos, northwestern Híos, northern Límnos plus Áyios Efstrátios. The cypress is native to the south and east Aegean, but in its columnar form it has been planted everywhere that has a Mediterranean climate. Some claim that the slim trees are male and the broader, spreading form are female, but female cones on the thin trees prove this wrong. On Kárpathos and Sými there are extensive stands of juniper in two species (as well as a few Aleppo pines), while shady stream canyons of the larger islands shelter plane, Oriental sweetgum and sweet chestnut (Sámos and

Lésvos). Clusters of introduced poplars indicate past, as well as current, human habitation, as do isolated mulberries, their leaves formerly fed to silkworms. The cooler shade of woodland provides a haven for plants which cannot survive full exposure to the Greek summer – for example, spectacular peonies, blooming during May on shaded slopes above 400m on several islands. Those on Kárpathos are white subspecies of *Paeonia clusii*, while those of Sámos and Rhodes are the more common, usually pink *Paeonia mascula*.

With altitude, the forest thins out to scattered individual hardy conifers and oaks, before finally reaching a limit ranging from 1000m to 1200m, depending on the island's latitude and rainfall. Above this treeline are limited summer meadows, and then bare rock. If not severely grazed, these habitats are home to many low-growing, gnarled, but often splendidly floriferous plants.

Birds

The Dodecanese and east Aegean host a large range of resident Mediterranean birds, with an additional bonus in the seasonal presence of **migratory species** that winter in East Africa but breed in Greece or northern Europe. Between January and mid-May – sometimes later, depending on the weather – they migrate up the Nile valley before moving across the eastern Mediterranean. These islands can be the first landfall after a long sea crossing, and smaller birds recuperate and feed for a few days before continuing north. Larger birds such as storks and ibis often fly very high, and binoculars are needed to spot them as they pass over. In autumn the birds return heading the other way, but usually in more scattered flocks. Although some species such as quail and turtle dove are shot, there is nothing like the wholesale slaughter that takes place in some other Mediterranean countries.

Seasonal **salt marshes** and **coastal lagoons** on Kós, Sámos, Límnos and Lésvos are excellent territories for bird-watching, especially during the spring migrations. Herons, egrets, glossy ibis, spoonbills, ducks, white pelicans and storks mingle with smaller waders such as the avocet and the black-winged stilt with its ridiculously long, pink legs. Greater flamingos arrive in January, lingering until April; upwards of two hundred of them can be counted at the salt marsh near the easterly Psilí Ámmos (Sámos) on a given winter's day.

In and just outside of **towns**, swallows (which prefer to nest under bridges and culverts), and their relatives the martins (which build mud nests on building exteriors), are constantly swooping through the air to catch insects, as are the larger and noisier swifts. In **lowland fields and olive groves**, especially on Lésvos, Sámos and Rhodes, hoopoes are a startling combination of pink, black and white, particularly obvious when they fly; they're about the only natural predator of the processionary caterpillar (see box overleaf). The much shyer golden oriole has an attractive song but is rarely seen for more than a few moments before hiding its brilliant colours among its favourite poplar tree. Rollers, which like to roost on wires, are bright blue and golden-brown, while multicoloured flocks of slim and elegant bee-eaters fill the air with their soft calls as they hunt insects. Tílos in particular, after many hunting-free years, has seen an explosion in the population of these last three species (especially in May), as well as rock-partridges. Other small insect-eaters include stonechats, flycatchers and woodchat shrikes.

Hillside maquis, with its junipers and other dense, prickly scrub, is also a good bird habitat. Warblers are numerous, with the Sardinian warbler often conspicuous on rough scrubby slopes because of its black head, bright-red eye and bold habits; the Rüppell's warbler is considerably rarer, and confined to thicker woodland. Lésvos plays host to two species of nuthatch native to Asia Minor: Krüper's nuthatch in the pine forests around Ayiássos, and rock nuthatch on the barer slopes throughout the west of the island. Also to be seen in the **mountains** are smaller birds such as black and white wheatears, and the blue rock thrush.

Larger raptors are relatively rare in the islands, but can occur around remoter gorges, cliffs and islets, for example on Rhodes west of Monólithos, or on neighbouring Hálki; on Télendhos and Tílos; and on Lésvos in the east Aegean, all locales which are famous for Eleonora's falcons, especially during late spring and summer. Buzzards are perhaps the most abundant type of raptor, mistaken by optimistic bird-watchers for the much rarer, shyer eagles, which do however appear in winter, when they're driven over from the mountains of Anatolia. Lesser kestrels are brighter, noisier versions of the common kestrel, and often appear undisturbed by the presence of humans, nesting communally and noisily in many small towns and villages. Equally bold red-footed falcons can often be seen perched on telegraph wires.

Seashore birds are also notable; the southern Dodecanese are home to a small population of Audouin's gulls, endangered by both human activity and the more versatile yellow-legged gull. Cormorants roost on and dive from cliffs, particularly on Sámos but also on certain Dodecanese, from autumn through until spring. Brightest of all is the kingfisher, more commonly seen saltwater-fishing than in northern Europe.

At **night**, the tiny Scops owl (*Otus scops*, in Greek *gióni*s) has a very distinctive, repeated, single-note call, very like the sonar beep of a submarine, but is rarely seen; the equally diminutive little owl (*Athena noctua*, in Greek *koukouváyia*) is by contrast more easily visible, and active by day, particularly on ruined houses or on power cables, and has a strange repertoire of cries, chortles and a throaty hiss. Certainly the most evocative nocturnal bird is the nightingale, which requires wooded stream valleys and is most audible on Sámos around midnight in May, its mating season.

Mammals

The variety of **mammals** is fairly limited, owing to long isolation from both the Anatolian and Balkan mainlands, and ruthless hunting. Most of the Dodecanese and east Aegean islands have the usual range of rodents such as rats, mice (many field varieties), hares and rabbits; the local hedgehog has a distinctive white underbelly. On the larger, more forested islands, particularly Sámos, which is separated from Anatolia by the narrowest of straits, there are fast-moving, ferret-like stone martens, weasels and even the odd jackal, but no foxes, badgers or larger predators, such as bears or wolves. In 1999, however, wild boar were (re)introduced to Sámos, where they colonized the remoter stream canyons; producing two septutlet litters annually, the creatures quickly became major pests, destroying terraces and crops, and

Flora and fauna field guides

In case of difficulty obtaining titles listed below from conventional booksellers, there is a reliable mail-order outlet for wildlife field guides within the UK. **Summerfield Books**, Main Street, Brough, Kirkby Stephen, Cumbria CA17 4AX ☎017683/41577, ⓦwww.summerfieldbooks.com, not only has new botanical titles, but also rare or out-of-print natural history books on all topics. Postage is extra, but they often have special offers on select products. The shop is open Mon–Sat 9.30am–4.30pm.

Wildlife, general
A.C. Campbell (o/p) *The Hamlyn Guide to the Flora and Fauna of the Mediterranean*. Very useful, so worth finding a secondhand copy; also published as *The Larousse Guide to the Flora and Fauna of the Mediterranean*.

Flowers
Hellmut Baumann *Greek Wild Flowers and Plant Lore in Ancient Greece*. Lots of interesting ethnobotanical snippets about the age-old Greek relationship with plants, plus good colour photographs.

Marjorie Blamey and Christopher Grey-Wilson *Mediterranean Wild Flowers*. Comprehensive field guide, with coloured drawings; recent and taxonomically up to date.

K. P. Buttler *Field Guide to the Orchids of Britain and Europe*. A wealth of colour plates and up-to-date taxonomy.

Lance Chilton *Plant check-lists*. Small pamphlets which also include birds, reptiles and butterflies, available for Kárpathos; Kós; Kokkári (Sámos); Sámos; Sými; Líndhos/Pefkos (Rhodes); and Rhodes. Contact the author directly at ☎01485/532710 or ⓦwww.marengowalks.com.

Pierre Delforge *Orchids of Britain & Europe*. A comprehensive guide, with recent taxonomy, though beware small inaccuracies in this translation. An updated version (Delachaux & Niestlé) is available in French.

Anthony Huxley and William Taylor *Flowers of Greece and the Aegean* (o/p). The only volume dedicated to the islands (and mainland), with colour photographs, but now slightly dated for taxonomy.

Oleg Polunin *Flowers of Greece and the Balkans*. Classic, older field guide (reprinted 1997), also with colour photographs, useful if Huxley and Taylor proves unfindable.

Oleg Polunin and Anthony Huxley *Flowers of the Mediterranean*. The larger scope means that many Greek endemics are missed out, but recent printings have a table of taxonomic changes.

---

are now being culled enthusiastically by local hunters. Lésvos, alone of the islands, has a conspicuous population of red squirrels, a subspecies of those native to Turkey and Iran.

Dolphins and **porpoises** are a less common sight than previously in the Dodecanese, but they still occasionally shadow ferries to feed on fish stirred up in their wake. The extremely rare **Mediterranean monk seal** is still sometimes seen near Sámos (see box, p.350) and increasingly around Tílos and northern Karpathós; on Kastellórizo, members of the clan resident in the island's sea-cave (see p.199) have been glimpsed playing in the harbour. Despite these encouraging recent developments, this species remains highly endangered since losing many individuals – and most of its main breeding ground – to a toxic algal bloom off Morocco; on present trends it's unlikely to survive much into this millennium.

Birds

Richard Brooks *Birding in Lesbos*. Superb little guide with colour photos, a list of bird-watching sites, and detailed maps, plus an annotated species-by-species bird list with much useful information. Revised periodically; contact the author directly at © email@richard-brooks.co.uk.

George Handrinos and T. Akriotis *Birds of Greece*. A comprehensive guide that includes island bird life.

Lars Jonsson *Birds of Europe with North Africa and the Middle East*. The ornithologist's choice for the best coverage of Greek birds, with excellent descriptions and illustrations.

Heinzel, Fitter and Parslow *Collins Guide to the Birds of Britain and Europe*; **Petersen, Mountfort and Hollom** *Field Guide to the Birds of Britain and Europe*. Though not specific to Greece, these two field guides have good coverage of Greek birds outside of Lésvos.

Mammals

Corbet and Ovenden *Collins Guide to the Mammals of Europe*. The best field guide on the subject.

Reptiles and amphibians

Arnold, Burton and Ovenden *Collins Guide to the Reptiles and Amphibians of Britain and Europe*. A useful guide, though it excludes the Dodecanese and east Aegean islands.

Jiri Cihar *Amphibians and Reptiles* (o/p). Selective coverage, but includes most endemic species of the Dodecanese and east Aegean isles.

Insects

Michael Chinery *Collins Guide to the Insects of Britain and Western Europe*. Although Greece is outside the geographical scope of the guide, it will provide generic identifications for most insects seen.

Lionel Higgins and Norman Riley *A Field Guide to the Butterflies of Britain and Europe*. A thorough and detailed field guide that illustrates nearly all species seen in Greece.

Marine life

B. Luther and K. Fiedler *A Field Guide to the Mediterranean* (o/p). Very thorough and includes most Greek shallow-water species.

Reptiles and amphibians

Reptiles flourish in the hot dry summers and rocky terrain of the islands, and there are many species, the commonest being **lizards**. Most of these are small, slim, agile and wary, rarely staying around for closer inspection. They're usually brown to grey, with subtle patterns of spots, streaks and stripes, though in adult males the undersides are sometimes brilliant orange, yellow, green or blue.

On most of the Dodecanese and east Aegean islands, you may see the angular, iguana-like *agama* or Rhodes dragon (*Agama stelio*). Attaining up to 30cm in length, these do look like miniature, spiny-backed dragons, their rough, grey-to-brown skin being vaguely patterned. Unlike other lizards, they will often stop to study you, before finally disappearing into a wall or under a rock.

Amongst the bushes of the maquis and garigue habitats you may see the Balkan green lizard, a brightly hued creature up to half a metre long, much of which is tail. You can often spot it running on its hind legs, as if possessed, from one bush to another; again they are shy unless distracted by territorial disputes with each other.

Geckos are large-eyed nocturnal lizards, up to 15cm long, with short, detachable tails and often rough skins. Their spreading toes have claws and ingenious adhesive pads – the inspiration for Velcro – allowing them to walk up house walls and upside down onto ceilings in their search for insects. Groups of them lie in wait near bright lights that attract their prey, and small ones living indoors can have very pale, almost transparent skins. Not always popular locally – the Kós dialect word for them, *miaró*, means "defiler", after their outsized faeces – they should be left alone to eat mosquitoes and other bugs. The **chameleon** is a rare, slow-moving and swivel-eyed inhabitant of some eastern Aegean islands, particularly Sámos. Although essentially green, it has the ability to adjust its coloration to match the surroundings. It prefers bushes and low trees, hunting by day.

Greek land **tortoises** (*Testudo graeca*) occur in the Dodecanese and east Aegean. They have suffered to varying extents from (now illegal) collecting for the pet trade, but they are still commonly found basking on sunny or wooded hillsides. Usually it is their noisy progress through vegetation that signals their presence; they spend their often long lives grazing the vegetation and can reach diameters of 30cm. Closely related stripe-necked **terrapins** (*Mauremys caspica*) are more streamlined, freshwater tortoises which love to bask on waterside mud; they used to be a guaranteed presence at river mouths on Límnos, Ikaría, Lésvos, Kós and Rhodes, but are severely reduced of late. Shy and nervous, they're often only seen as they disappear underwater, with just the tops of their heads protruding like submarine periscopes. They are scavengers and will eat anything, including your fingers if handled or offered food.

Snakes are abundant on many islands (though Astypálea has none); most, such as assorted racers and grass snakes, are shy and non-venomous. Several species, including the Ottoman and nose-horned vipers, do have a poisonous bite, though they are not usually aggressive. These are adder-like, often with a very distinct, dark zigzag stripe down the back. They are only likely to bite if a hand is put in the crevice of a wall or a rock face where one of them is resting, or if they are attacked. Unfortunately, most locals attempt to kill any snake they see, and thus greatly enhance their chances of being bitten. Leave them alone, and they will do the same for you (but if worst comes to worst, see the advice on p.44). Most snakes are not only completely harmless to humans, but beneficial in that they keep down populations of rodent pests. There are also three species of legless lizards – slowworm, glass lizard and legless skink – all equally harmless, which suffer because they are mistaken for snakes.

On those islands with permanent streams, you can't miss **frogs** and **toads**, especially during the spring breeding season. The green toad has green marbling over a pinkish or mud-coloured background, and a cricket-like trill. The common toad can often be found some distance from open water, especially on Sámos in May; even arid Kastellórizo is periodically and mysteriously overrun with them. Frogs prefer the wettest places, and the robust marsh frog particularly revels in artificial water storage ponds, where the concrete sides magnify their croaking impressively. Tiny, jewel-like tree frogs (*Rana arborea*) have a stripe down their flank and vary in colour from bright green to golden brown, depending on where they are sitting – they can change colour like a chameleon. Making their presence known through strident voices at night, they rest by day in trees and shrubs, and can sometimes be found in quantity plastered onto the leaves of waterside oleanders.

Insects and invertebrates

Greece teems with **insects**. Flies, wasps (especially on Ikaría and Kálymnos) and mosquitoes can be nuisances, but most other species are harmless to humans. The huge, slow-flying, glossy-black carpenter bee may cause alarm by its size and noise, but is rarely a problem; by contrast almost invisible gnats emerge on late summer nights and pack a mighty bite. Also harmless are the enormous, tarantula-sized hairy spiders found basking in spring on Sými stairways and balconies.

Grasshoppers and **crickets** swarm through open areas of grass and vegetation in summer, with several larger species that are carnivorous on the smaller and which can bite strongly if handled. Bigger still is the grey-brown **locust**, which flies noisily before crash-landing into trees and shrubs. Grasshoppers produce their chirping noise by rubbing a wing against a leg, while house crickets do it by rubbing both wings together.

Cicadas are not related to the locust or grasshopper, but giant relatives of the aphids that cluster on roses. Their continuous whirring call is one of the characteristic sounds of the Mediterranean summer, from mid-morning until sunset, and is produced by the rapid vibration of two membranes called tymbals on either side of the body. If you look closely at the tree trunk from which the racket is emanating, you may detect this well-camouflaged, salt-and-pepper-hued insect. The high-pitched and endlessly repeated chirp of house crickets can drive one to distraction on autumn nights when temperatures fall to a range of their liking – they are silent by day, and usually all through midsummer.

From spring through to autumn the larger islands are full of **butterflies**, particularly in late spring and early summer. There are three swallowtail species, so named for the drawn-out corners of their hind wings, in shades of cream and yellow, with black and blue markings. Their smaller relatives in the Dodecanese, the festoons, lack these spurs, but add red spots to the palette, or red and black zigzags. The rarer, robust brown-and-orange pasha is unrelated but is Europe's largest butterfly. Cleopatras are brilliant-yellow butterflies, related to the brimstone of northern Europe, but larger and more colourful. Look out for green hairstreaks – a small gem of a butterfly attracted to the springtime flowers of the asphodel, a widespread plant of overgrazed pastures and hillsides. In autumn the black-and-orange plain tiger or African monarch may appear, sometimes in large quantities. In areas of deciduous woodland, look high up and you may see fast-flying large tortoiseshells, while lower down, southern white admirals skim and glide through clearings between the trees. Some of the smallest but most beautiful butterflies are the blues. Their subtle, camouflaging grey and black undersides make them vanish from view when they land and fold their wings.

Many of the Greek **moths** are equally spectacular, particularly the green-and-pink oleander hawkmoth; their large caterpillars can be recognized by their tail horn. The hummingbird hawkmoth, like its namesake, hovers at flowers to feed, supported by a blur of fast-moving wings. Tiger moths, with their black-and-white forewings and startlingly bright-orange hindwings, are the "butterflies" that occur in huge numbers at Rhodes' "Butterfly Valley". The giant peacock moth is Europe's largest, up to 15cm across. A mixture of grey, black and brown, with big eye-spots, it is usually only seen during the day while resting on tree trunks.

Other insects include the well-camouflaged **praying mantis**, holding their powerful forelegs in a position of supplication until another insect comes within reach. The females are voracious, and notorious for eating the males during mating. Adult **ant-lions** resemble a fluttery dragonfly, but their young are huge-jawed and build pits in the sand to trap ants, while rhinoceros-horned beetles also dig holes in sand dunes. Hemispherical carob beetles collect balls of animal dung and push them around with their back legs. Cockroaches of varying species live in buildings, particularly hotels, restaurants and bakeries, attracted by warmth and food scraps. Glow-worms are occasionally found on hedges of Sámos. Centipedes are not often seen, but the fast-moving, twenty-centimetre *skolópendra* should be treated with respect since they can inflict very painful bites. Black millipedes or *vromoússes* ("stinkpots") are often found curled up on walls at night, their vernacular name a tribute to their pungent odour if disturbed.

Other invertebrates of interest include scorpions, which the islanders are terrified of but which, like snakes, are exceedingly shy and only active by night. Distantly related land crabs are found on most islands with running streams; they need fresh water to breed, but can cause surprise when found walking on remote hillsides. There are plenty of genuine **marine creatures** to be seen, particularly in shallow seawater sheltered by rocks – sea cucumbers, sea butterflies, octopus, cuttlefish, starfish and sea urchins. Octopus are bottom-dwellers, often hiding under rock overhangs or in the discarded tyres which litter many coves; squid move in large shoals near the surface, generally far from land. More solitary cuttlefish live in deeper water, but are often found close to shore; they typically swim with an undulating motion of their mantle, but if startled jet off at tremendous speed, leaving behind a cloud of their trademark ink. An abundance of sea urchins is indicative of clean seawater; as filter-feeders, they are extraordinarily sensitive to pollution and are in fact disappearing from many locales.

Lance Chilton, with Marc Dubin

Music

M usic is central to the culture of the Dodecanese and east Aegean, and it's difficult to exaggerate its significance for those who have grown up with it. Even the most tone-deaf visitor will become aware of music's ubiquitous presence in vehicles, tavernas, ferry boats and other public spaces. Music and dance form an integral part of weddings, betrothals, baptisms, saints' days observed at local churches or monasteries, name days observed at private homes or tavernas (for those who share the name of the saint), Easter and pre-Lenten Carnival.

Many songs and melodies, which vary from island to island, are specifically associated with **weddings**. Some of them are processional songs/tunes (*patinádhes*), sung or played while going to fetch the bride from her home, or as the wedding couple leave the church, and there are specific dances associated with different stages of a wedding ritual. It was common in the past (and in some places even today) for the music and dancing that followed a wedding feast to last for up to three days.

There are songs sung only at pre-Lenten **Carnival** (*Apókries* in Greek), accompanied by such rituals as shaking of large goat-bells roped together, or (as on Lésvos) lascivious dances and mummery. Such rituals (once widespread in Europe) date back to pre-Christian times.

Music also accompanies informal, unpublicized **private gatherings** in homes, *kafenía* or tavernas where music occurs. Ask people where you can hear *paradhosiakí mousikí* (traditional music). A few words of Greek (including names of instruments) go a long way towards inclining locals to help foreign travellers. Once it's clear that you're a budding *meraklís* (roughly, "aficionado") and past the Zorba-soundtrack stage, people will be flattered by the respect paid to "real" music, and doors will open for you.

Questionable innovations

Be forewarned that *paníyíria* (**saints'-day festivals**), though often well-advertised occasions for live music, may feature ear-splitting, over-amplified music, with the inclusion of instruments from other genres of Greek music – notably the **bouzoúki** (which belongs to urban *rebétika* music and its offshoots). Electric bass has also been added in places, and is present in all too many recordings of *nisiótika* (island music). Even where more traditional instrumentation such as **violí** (violin) and **laoúto** is used, their tone may be distorted by the use of excessive reverb and/or electric pick-ups linked to poor sound systems. Many island-born musicians live and work mostly in Athens and only tour the islands in the summer, and most have rejected the older sound for the modern one as described above. All of the above is less true for **Kárpathos** and **Lésvos**, two of the more musically traditional islands.

This vulgarization of *nisiótika* (and indeed most Greek folk music) began during the mid-1960s, a trend accelerated by the values of the 1967–74 junta. During this period many musicians were deprived of (or actively scorned) the oral-aural transmission of technique from older master players, though fortunately such attitudes have now changed. Also, recent CD rereleases of archival studio material, and high-quality field **recordings** of the last of the old-time players, are proving equally valuable to a new generation attempting to recapture traditional musicianship.

The older tradition

The music of the Dodecanese and east Aegean is wonderfully diverse, so only a general overview will be attempted here. Both archipelagos have their dances, songs and customs which vary between islands and even between towns on the same island. Different dances (or variants of the same dance) go by the same name (eg *syrtós*) from place to place, while different lyrics are set to many of the same melodies (or vice versa). The same tune can be played so idiosyncratically between neighbouring island groups (or between islands in the same group) as to be barely recognizable to an outsider. Compared to Western styles, Greek music in general is far less linear and more circuitous, as would be expected from its Byzantine origins and later Ottoman influences. As in all "folk music", pieces are learned primarily by ear, though transcriptions exist and there are some who teach with written notes.

Given the intimate contact between Asia Minor and present-day Greece during the thousand years of the Byzantine empire and the four subsequent centuries of Ottoman rule, culminating in the mass eviction of Greek Orthodox from Asia Minor in 1923, Byzantine, Anatolian (especially Turkish) and Balkan influences on Greek music were inevitable. Many older songs have direct antecedents in **Byzantine religious chant**, and the **modal system** used in most Greek music (related to the Arabic-Turkish modal system) also has correlates in the Byzantine ecclesiastical modal system. From the seventeenth century onwards, European instruments like the clarinet, violin and accordion appeared in Greece, played with techniques developed for use with (and mimicking techniques of) earlier indigenous instruments. **Lyrics**, especially on the smaller islands, commonly touch on the perils of the sea, exile and – in a society where long periods of separation and arranged marriage were the norm – thwarted or forbidden love. More playful love songs; songs for before, during or after weddings; and historical ballads also appear. Lyrics are sprinkled with references to local landmarks (straits, islets, rural monasteries and their saints) with which their audience will be well familiar.

Dances and rhythms

Most island pieces, whether sung or instrumental, are in **dance rhythms**, with a vital interaction between dancers and the musicians or singers. Dancers and listeners may also join in a song (solo or as a chorus), or even initiate verses of commonly known pieces. It is customary for a lead dancer to tip the musicians, often requesting a particular tune and/or rhythm for his party to dance to. A dance is defined not only by its rhythmic count, but often as well by a certain characteristic lilt (way of swinging the rhythm) or by certain kinds of melodic phrases (as in the **bállos**, which has a repeating line that descends at the end of each part).

A dance common to most of the Dodecanese is the **soústa**, which may vary in details, but is consistently "springy" (*soústa* means "spring") with an up-and-down movement. Also danced widely in the archipelago is the **siganós**, called **íssio** or **íssos** on Kálymnos, **melakhrinó** on Kós, and other names as well. This is a slower form of the *soústa*, and in some islands (eg, Kós, Kálymnos) leads directly into it, with just a couple of bars of the faster dance rhythm played to signal the dancers that the *soústa* proper is beginning.

A version of the Cretan dance called **Haniótikos** (after the city of Haniá, Crete) is known variously in the Dodecanese as **Krítikos**, **Rodhítikos** ("of Rhodes") or **Pidikhtós** ("the jumping dance"). The **east Aegean islands** also share common dances such as the **syrtós**, the quintessential Greek circle dance; **bállos**, an uptempo couples' dance; and the **hasápiko**, especially on Lésvos. The *hasápiko*, like the *kalamatianós* and *hasaposérvikos* which are also popular in the Dodecanese, are not indigenous to the islands or specific to any one Greek region, but "borrowed" from the mainland and old Constantinople.

On both Kárpathos and Sými, there are **fixed dance sequences** in which one dance leads into another without a break in the music. Yvonne Hunt (see below) notes that in northern Kárpathos "it is still not uncommon for the *káto horós*, which is danced to the singing of *mandinádhes . . .* to last for as long as six or seven hours. The music then 'shifts gears' so to speak from that segment to the next without any break or interruption; likewise the dance." More information on dances particular to specific islands or regions is given below, under the appropriate geographical region.

Yvonne Hunt's **Traditional Dance in Greek Culture** (published in Athens by the Centre for Asia Minor Studies, 1996) is an excellent introduction to the subject and, though primarily about dance, it also covers important festivals and customs, as well as the social role of music and musicians. A fine bibliography lists works of significant Greek musicological researchers, anthropologists and travellers. This book can be found most easily, and most reasonably priced (c. €12), at the Centre for Asia Minor Studies (Kydhathinéon 11) as well at the Folk Art Museum (Kydhathinéon 17) Plaka neighbourhood of Athens. Otherwise, contact Yvonne Hunt at 4837 38th NE, Seattle, WA 98105, USA, or ℗bg901@scn.org (North American price $25).

The Dodecanese

Of all the island groups in Greece, the **Dodecanese** arguably have the most vital musical tradition, owing to their isolation from the mainland, mutual separation and (until 1943) the political and emotional charge associated with preserving age-old customs in the face of Italian persecution.

In particular, the southerly arc of islands comprising Kássos, Kárpathos and Hálki is still one of the most promising areas for hearing live music at any season of the year. The dominant instrument here is the **lýra**, a pear-shaped, three-stringed fiddle played upright balanced on the thigh, with strings facing out; these are stopped with lateral action of the fingernails, and the bow held with the hand palm up. The Dodecanisian *lýra* is one variant of four similarly shaped instruments played in Greece. In Kárpathos, small bells are attached to the bow, providing rhythmic accompaniment as the bow moves. Three metal strings are tuned in fifths (G, D, A); melody is played on the outer two, while the middle one serves as a drone. The G-string is tuned one whole step below the A (rather than a fifth below the D).

At **Ólymbos**, north **Kárpathos** (see box overleaf), this instrument commonly accompanies *mandinádhes*. Similar to the ones sung in Crete, in alternation with instrumental interludes, these **rhymed couplets** about local personalities and incidents are often improvised on the spot, and may satirize, eulogize, commemorate, tease and wish well, fresh verses being thought up during the instrumental interludes. (In Kálymnos, such couplets are called *pismatiká*.) There are also set phrases, as well as entire couplets, which have entered the traditional canon. **Kássos** is a rich repository for melodies and lyrics, which find favour even on neighbouring Kárpathos; many are based on the events of the 1824 Kassian holocaust.

Usually the *llýra* is backed up by one or more *laoúta*, a member of the long-necked lute family, its name derived from the Arabic *al'ud* (known as the oud in the West). The *llaoúto* shares the large rounded back of the oud (traditionally made with many wood-staves curled and joined over a mould), but, unlike the short-necked, fretless, gut-strung oud, more resembles the old Byzantine *tambourás* in having a long neck with moveable frets and metal courses (pairs of strings each tuned in octaves. Interestingly, older *llaoúta* had the peg-head bent back from the neck as does the oud. The *laoúto* fulfils a strongly rhythmic role in most music from the Dodecanese, with few chord changes.

At several places in the Dodecanese, particularly northern Kárpathos, Kálymnos and Pátmos, a primitive (yet difficult to play, like many folk instruments) goatskin **bagpipe** with a double chanter – the *tsamboúna* – is heard, on its own or with the *llýra* and *laoúto*. The *tsamboúna* has no drone and two parallel chanters made of calamus reed. The left chanter does not vary between island groups, having five holes which allow an incomplete diatonic scale from "do" to "fa". The right chanter is of three types, with anywhere from two to five holes depending on the island. Some form of this instrument probably reached Greece from Asia Minor during late Roman times, though bagpipes have evolved independently (and more or less simultaneously) in most pastoral societies across Eurasia. During the colonels' dictatorship the playing of bagpipes was banned on some of the more accessible islands, lest foreigners think the Greeks too "primitive". The *lýra's* tonal range matches that of the *tsamboúna* played in the Dodecanese and can be played alone; with *laoúto*; with *tsamboúna*; or both of these together, often accompanying vocalists.

On most of the other Dodecanese, you'll find the *lýra* replaced by a more familiar-looking **violí**, essentially a Western violin, which reached Greece during the seventeenth century. The violin bridge may be sanded in Greece to a less highly arched form than that used for Western classical music (something done as well in some Western folk traditions). An alternate **tuning** known as *álla Toúrka*, more widespread in the past, is still used by some musicians on certain islands (eg, Kós). From high to low, its string values are D, A, D and G, with a fourth between the two higher-pitched strings instead of the typical all-fifths arrangement. The lowered high string is slacker and "sweeter", and the violin's tonality altered by the modified tuning. Some violinists have reported being pressured to tune *álla Fránga*; that's to say, the standard European tuning with E on top. It is claimed that violin techniques on these islands mimic *lýra* techniques (past and present).

In some locales, music for **unaccompanied voices** exists: Arhángelos on **Rhodes**, generally conceded to be the musical capital of the island, is known for *kanákia* or wedding songs, based on Byzantine hymns and (supposedly) imperial palace music. Peculiar to **Hálki** are *helidhonísmata* or "**swallow songs**", chanted since Roman times in early March to welcome these birds, heralds of spring.

Kálymnos preserves a vibrant musicality, heavily reliant on *tsamboúna* and *violí*; the distinctive Kalymniot violin style features a fairly aggressive bow "attack", dubbed *khtipitó* or "beaten" by some players on neighbouring **Kós**. This is just one of many examples of audibly different violin styles between contiguous islands (though the difference may not be apparent unless one hears consecutive recordings of the same pieces from the two islands). One of Kós' older violinists, **Gavrilis Yiallizis** (d. 2001), made three recordings during the 1990s (see discography) with **Manolis Poyias**, who plays accordion, *sandoúri* (see below) and sings. Poyias still performs on Kós with **Manolis Kefalianos**, a violinist in his fifties who may well be the island's finest living violinist. Look for a planned CD sometime in the near future with this violinist, joined by Poyias on accordion, and Yiorgos Skarpathiotakis on Cretan *laoúto* (or ask where you might hear them should you visit Kós).

Despite its modest size, even on Kálymnos music shows regional characteristics; for instance, melodies and rhythms from Árgos, Aryinónda and Skália supposedly differ from those of the rest of the island. A legend claims that these villagers are descendants of Argive stragglers from the Trojan War; the village name of Árgos, and the fact that their *syrtós* exists only in one other, Peloponnesian Argolid village, are cited in support of this hypothesis.

The Kalymnian *mihanikós*, danced only by men, consists of two alternating melodies, one fast and one slow. During the slow melody, the dancers mimic the movements of sponge-divers crippled by the "bends" (see box p.272) – an occupational hazard which afflicted many men in the Dodecanese for generations – then break into a faster dance, only to return to miming their affliction.

The *thymariótikos*, another dance found on Kálymnos, originally comes from Epirus on the northwest Greek mainland, where it is known as the *himariótikos* (after its village of origin, Heimara, now in Albania). This begins as a men's dance with an unusual clockwise *syrtós* (instead of the usual anticlockwise movement elsewhere in Greece). Then the melody changes, an anticlockwise *kalamatianós* takes over and the dancers launch into a song with lyrics from Asia Minor about a dark-haired girl (dark eyes, hair and even eyebrows being commonly praised features in many Greek songs).

If you remember Nikos Kazantzakis's classic novel (or the movie) *Zorba the Greek*, his hero played a *sandoúri* (**hammer dulcimer**) – though, according to one *sandoúri* player who saw the film, Zorba (Anthony Quinn) was playing his upside down(!). Today, accomplished players of this difficult instrument are few, and it's usually relegated to a supporting role in *nisiótika*; in actual fact it was hardly known in the Dodecanese until well into the twentieth century, when Anatolian refugee musicians introduced it. The *sandoúri* is scarcely used on Kálymnos, as the local melodic intervals are unsuited to its chromatic tuning; by contrast, on neighbouring Léros, Pátmos and Lipsí it's one of the favourite instruments at festival times.

East Aegean islands

There's more obvious Anatolian and Constantinopolitan influence in both the music and instrumentation of these islands. Largely because of the refugee background of its population, there has never been much of an indigenous musical tradition on **Sámos**. Matters are rather better on adjacent **Ikaría**,

Almost every island described in this book is represented in the following discography; that said, coverage is thin and much has been lost by the failure to record worthy vernacular musicians. All the titles below are pressed in Greece, and fairly easily obtainable at any of the stores listed in the box on p.501.

Uniform series

The **Songs of . . .** releases issued by the Society for the Dissemination of National Music (Greece) is an older, inexpensive series collected from the 1950s through the 1970s under the supervision of Simon Karas. There are more than thirty discs, each covering one geographical area or type of traditional music. All (except the cassettes) include notes in English, and are available as cassettes or CDs.

Songs of Kassos and Karpathos (SDNM 103) The Kárpathos side is unremittingly poignant (or monotonous, depending on your tastes), enlivened by interesting passages on the *tsamboúna*. You'll still hear material like this at Ólymbos festivals. The Kássos side is more sweetly melodic, closer to Crete both musically and geographically.

Songs of Rhodes, Chalki and Symi (SDNM 104) The pieces from Sými are the most accessible, while those from Rhodes and Hálki show considerable Cretan influence. All material was recorded in the early 1970s; you're fairly unlikely to hear similar pieces live today, though Sými retains the instrumentation (*violí, sandoúri*) heard here.

Songs of Mytilene and Chios (SDNM 110) **Songs of Mytilene and Asia Minor** (SDNM 125) The Mytilene (Lésvos) sides are the highlight of each of these discs. Sublime instrumental and vocal pieces, again from the mid-1970s. Most selections are from the south of the island, particularly Ayiássos, where a tradition of live festival music was – and still is – strong.

Songs of Ikaria and Samos (SDNM 128) Much older material, from the 1950s; even then it was obvious that indigenous styles here were dying out, as there is extensive reliance on "cover versions" of songs common to all the east Aegean and Anatolian refugee communities, and the music – mostly choral with string accompaniment – is executed by the SDNM "house band" of the time. The Ikarian side is the more distinctive, though marred by irritating voice-over narration.

Songs of the North and East Aegean (SDNM CD7) Features music of Límnos, Thássos, Samothráki, Lésvos and Híos including local dances (*pyrgoúsikos, kehayiádhikos)* using local musicians recorded during the early 1970s.

Island-wide/archipelago anthologies

Paradosiaki Skopi kai Tragoudia tis Dodekanisiou: Mousika Taxidhia (CD E2–205 by the Kinotita Asfendhiou Ko) The final, 1996 recording of violinist Gavrilis Yiallizis of Kós island, with Manolis Poyias on accordion, *sandoúri* and some vocals. Their instrumental version of the wedding song *Tou gambrou* (Of The Groom) is a wonderful example of Kós violin style. Poyias also appears on other 1990s recordings not on CD: 1994 **Omorfa Dodekanisa** (LP produced by Dimitris Kasiotis Bonapartis) and **Ta Dika Mas** (1995 LP and cassette) with Anna Karabessini.

Seryiani sta Nisia Mas, Vol I (MBI 10371.2) Excellent CD compilation of various *nisiótika* artists and hits from the 1950s and 1960s, with Emilia Hatzidhaki (from Léros) and sisters Anna Karabessini and Efi Sarri (from Kós) all well represented. The high point is arguably Emilia Hadzidhaki's rendition of *Bratsera*, a song particular to Léros and Kálymnos.

Anatolika tou Egeou/East of the Aegean (Verso CD101) Nikos Ikonomidhis, though born in the islet of Skhinoússa near Náxos, has become an adopted son of Híos. One of the more traditional violinists under 50 years of age, he leads this set of lively dance tunes, with a few songs thrown in (he is a fine singer, as well) all from the east Aegean islands. There's more genuinely Samian material here than on the SDNM disc, but the recording is marred by a persistently heavy electric bassline.

Ellines Akrites/The Guardians of Hellenism (FM Records) Vol.1 of this series, "Chios, Mytilene, Samos, Ikaria" (FM 801) is a solid, if rather studio-ish, acoustic session of standards from each of the islands cited; vocalist Stratis Rallis, who also appears on the *Lesvos Aiolis* disc, is featured here on most of the Mytilíni (Lésvos) tracks, which make up nearly half the disc. Vol.2 (FM 802), "Lemnos, Samothrace, Imbros, Tenedos", features excellent local *violí/lýra* players, plus top violinist Kyriakos Gouvendas from Thessaloníki. Volumes 9–11 cover the entire Dodecanese; Volume 9 at least, featuring Pátmos, Kálymnos, Léros, Kós and Astypálea, is excellent, with the late violinist Gavrilis Yiallizis on one track.

Individual artists

Anna Karabessini & Effi Sarri Two singing sisters born at Andimáhia on the island of Kós during the 1930s. The fact that they performed only for private gatherings added to their status. *To Yialo Yialo Piyeno* from 1975 was one of their first big recording hits, reissued on CD (Lyra 0102067.2). Two other available CDs are *Tis Thalassas* (Lyra 10777) and *Ena Glendi* (Lyra 10717).

Emilia Hatzidhaki *Thalassina Tragoudhia* (LP: Panvox 16311, reissued as CD by Lyra-MBI) The sole easily available collection dedicated to this artist, who otherwise appears only on *nisiótika* anthologies.

Individual islands

Kassos: Skopi tis Lyras/Lyra Melodies of Kassos (Lyra-Papingo CD0113) Recordings of three generations of musicians from the Perselis clan caught live at a 1993 festival.

Tragoudhia keh Skopi tis Kalymnou/Songs and Melodies of Kalymnos (Syrtos 564) Harsh but haunting songs reminiscent of Kálymnos itself. No longer part of the island's repertoire but revived in this 1993 production by native musicologist Manolis Karpathios, featuring *tsamboúna*, *laoúto* and *violí*.

Skopi tis Kalymnou/Kalymnian Folk Music (Lykio ton Ellinidhon E2-276-97) Double CD with excellent notes and song translations. Traditional Kalymnian repertoire and native musicians features septagenarian Mikes Tsounias on violin, his young grandson playing unison violin on some pieces, plus good *tsamboúna* accompaniment.

Tis Leros ta Tragoudhia/The Songs of Leros (Politistikos ke Morfotikos Syllogos Neon Lerou/Instructive & Cultural Lerian Youth Society) Double CD produced by Music Folklore Archive. Live field recordings from 1996 and 1998 of island musicians and singers; *violí*, *sandoúri*, *laoúto* and *tsamboúna* in various combinations, plus unaccompanied singing. Each disc finishes with an archival track of bygone greats Emilia Hatzidhaki and Manolis Skoumbouridhis, both Lerian.

Kastellorizo (Syrtos 561) Another Manolis Karpathios production, but the material, while worthy, is somewhat marred by studio-introduced echo.

Tragoudhia keh Skopi tis Patmou/Songs and Melodies of Patmos (Politistikon Idhryma Dhodhekanisou, Athens, CD 201) Yet another Karpathios project, but certainly the best of the three: live 1995 field recordings of well-edited pieces as raw but compelling as you'd hear them at a good festival. Local working singers and instrumentalists on *violí*, *tsamboúna* and (unlike Kálymnos) *sandoúri*.

Lesvos Aiolis: Tragoudhia keh Khori tis Lesvou/Songs & Dances of Lesvos (University Press of Crete/Panepistimiakes Ekdhoseis Kritis 9–10, 2 CDs) A decade's (1986–1996) worth of field recordings of the last traditional music extant on the island, a labour of love supervised by musicologist Nikos Dhionysopoulos. Fairly pricey, but the quality and uniqueness of the instrumental pieces especially, and the monstrous, well-written and well-illustrated booklet, merit the expense.

Lesvos: Mousika Stavrodhromia sto Egeo/Musical Crossroads of the Aegean (University of the Aegean/Panepistimiou tou Egeou) A five-CD set with an enormous book accompanying it: wonderful photos of many ensembles, seated and in street processions. Everything from Asia Minor music played in Lésvos (including some wonderful unaccompanied solo *taxímia* – unmetered solos in a particular mode) to carols, bawdy songs for *Apókries* and wedding songs. Again very pricey but worth it.

Thalassa Thymisou/Sea of Memories: Tragoudhia ke Skopi apo tis Inousses (Navtiko Mousio Inousson-En Khordais CD 1801/1802) The result of a "field trip" by the En Khordais traditional music school of Thessaloníki to Inoússes, a small islet northeast of Híos, to rescue vanishing traditional material with the help of the islanders' long memories; the result's superb, a mix of live sessions in Inoussan tavernas and some studio recordings. Thorough and intelligent notes, but no translations of the lyrics.

where skilled musicians still perform in the west of the island at spring and summer monastery-festivals, when goatskins, in no short supply on Ikaría, appear in the form of *tsamboúnes*. On his recording *Anatolika tou Egeou* (see discography) **Nikos Ikonomidhis** plays an outstanding *kariótikos*, the most popular dance from this island, a fiddler's delight made up of set melodic fragments joined in spontaneous sequence. This is the real article, not to be confused with the eponymous, much more commercial song written by Yiorgos Konitopoulos of Náxos.

On **Híos**, the more typical Aegean **violí**, **laoúto**, **and sandoúri** are played, as well as the **tsamboúna** accompanied by the smaller two-headed drum called a **toumbáki**. The latter is suspended to one side of the player's torso by a strap, and only one of the two heads is struck with two wooden (or bone) drumsticks. Of Hiot dances Yvonne Hunt writes: "Here the *syrtós* and *bállos* are frequently danced to lovely, lilting tunes. A form of the *syrtós* here is commonly referred to as *hiótikos*. It is done by couples moving counter-clockwise, each man leading his partner through his own series of variations . . . Though based on the same step found on so many of the Aegean islands, it is performed by crossing in front of the opposite foot on the slow count, which creates a definitive style that is not found on other islands." She also writes of the *Pyrgoúsikos* (from the village of Pyrgí): "a dance for groups of three, two men and one woman. A handkerchief links the first man and the woman while she and the second man are in a *klistó* (closed) handhold with fingers intertwined. The lines are directed wherever the leader desires, moving forward and backwards. The leader is free to improvise, performing squats, turning, forming a 'bridge', etc. After a while the two men change positions and the new leader will then do his variations . . . traditionally performed to the music of the *tsamboúna* . . . and the *toumbáki,* although these instruments are being rapidly replaced by . . . electrified instruments."

The island of **Límnos** also has its own dances, such as the *kehayiádikos*, a shepherd's dance "performed in a circle without the dancers holding on to each other…" (Yvonne Hunt). This dance is in a 7/8 rhythm (3+2+2) and the dancers do squats and leg-slaps at certain moments. Says Hunt: "Límnos is one of the few [east Aegean] islands on which the *lýra* can still be found . . .

Unfortunately it will disappear from here also as younger members of the society have not learned to play it. The only hope is that someone will learn before the last generation of *lýra*-playing musicians is lost."

Lésvos (Mytilíni) occupies a special place in terms of island music; even before the turbulent decade of 1912–1922 (followed by the influx of thousands of Asia Minor refugees), its "mainland" was Asia Minor rather than Greece,

Greek recording sources

UK

Trehantiri 367 Green Lanes, London N4 1DY ℡020/8802 6530, ⊛www.trehantiri .com. Has caches of rare/out-of-print discs, and also a worldwide mail-order service.

USA

Down Home Music 10341 San Pablo Ave, El Cerrito, CA 94530 ℡510/525-2129, ⊛www.downhomemusic.com. Respectable Greek section in this Aladdin's cave for world music enthusiasts.

Greece: Athens

Except for the first listing, the following shops lie within a few hundred yards of each other in central Athens, making it feasible to pop into all of them if you have half a day in Athens between connecting flights. All except the musical instrument museum and Okh Aman (both metro Monastiráki) are a few steps from the Panepistimíou metro station.

Museum of Greek Popular Musical Instruments Dhioyénous 1–3, Pláka (Tues & Thurs–Sun 10am–2pm, Wed noon–8pm). The gift shop of this highly worthwhile museum is a reliable if pricey spot to snag a range of folk recordings, including a few SDNM titles.

Xylouris Panepistimíou 39, in arcade. Run by the gregarious widow of Cretan musician Nikos Xylouris, this is usually the best spot for Greek folk recordings; despite the tiny space, stocks items unavailable elsewhere, in various formats.

Metropolis Multibranch chain, with outlets at Panepistimíou 54 and 64, as well as two branches in the airport.

Music Corner Panepistimíou 56. Modest-sized but very well-selected stock includes some of the better island recordings.

Tzina Panepistimíou 57. Reasonable if somewhat chaotically organized stock, including its own label (Venus-Tzina) of *nisiótika* recordings.

Okh Aman! Market Iféstou 24, Monastiráki. The best outlet for secondhand Greek music, all genres. Mostly vinyl, in good condition and well organized; some CDs as well.

Greece: Thessaloníki

In case you find yourself here between planes en route to Límnos, Lésvos, Híos, Sámos or Rhodes, there are two good possibilities:

En Khordais Margaríti 1, Platía Ippodhromíou. Lower-ground-floor shop devoted to traditional musical instruments and a careful selection of folk recordings. An affiliate of the traditional music school across the road.

Studio 52 Dhimitríou Goúnari 46. Cavernous basement premises, the oldest store in town, with rare vinyl and cassettes, plus well-sorted CDs.

In addition, the main towns of Rhodes, Kós, Kálymnos, Sámos, Híos and Lésvos all have passably stocked (if expensive) record shops where you can be fairly sure of finding at least a couple of the titles listed above.

its urban poles Smyrna and Constantinople instead of Athens. Accordingly its musical tradition is far more varied and sophisticated than the Aegean norm, having absorbed melodies and instrumentation from the various groups who lived in neighbouring Anatolia; for example, Lésvos is the only island with a vital tradition of both brass bands and clarinet-playing, and virtually every pan-Hellenic dance rhythm is represented in local music. Favourite local dances are the **karsilamás** and the **zeïbékiko**, both from Asia Minor. The latter, though it became famous as a solo dance with the *rebétika* music of the 1920s through the 1950s, is often danced in Lésvos by men in a circular formation, each doing his own movements.

Violin, *sandoúri* and guitar tuned like a *laoúto* – which itself is uniquely absent from the extraordinarily rich Mytilinian instrumental panoply – accompany *zeïbékika*; the violin is oddly often included in the **brass bands** which traditionally accompanied wedding marches or marked the start of horse-racing or bull-sacrificing festivals, part of the still-vital *paniyíri* tradition here. The keyed, single-reed European **clarinet** or *klaríno* – as opposed to the simpler, double-reed *zournás* – was unknown in Greece before 1830, and (depending on whom you believe) was introduced either by gypsies or Bavarians attached to the first royal court. As on the Anatolian mainland opposite, the lap drum (*toumbeléki*) or shoulder drum (*daoúli*) are preferred rhythm accompaniments to the clarinet. Other imports include the *gáïda* or bagpipe-with-drone of the northern mainland, instead of the *tsamboúna* known elsewhere in the Aegean; the accordion (also played on Kós), and of course the *bouzoúki*, which has in recent decades swept across most of the islands.

Susan Raphael, with Marc Dubin

The islands in literature

Secrets of Sými

William Travis and his wife Caroline came to live on Sými during the mid-1960s when it was still well off the tourist route, much less home to an expatriate community. Having set aside a bit of money in the yacht charter business, Travis was able to stay for three years, putting his boating skills to use along an island coast tailor-made for small craft. *Bus Stop Symi*, originally published in 1970 by Rap & Whiting, and unfortunately long out of print, is the chronicle of their time there. This extract is reproduced with the kind permission of Watson, Little Ltd.

C

The German forces finally abandoned Sými in December of 1944. When orders for their withdrawal were received they contained the instruction that the considerable stocks of explosives and munitions held on the island were to be destroyed rather than shipped elsewhere. At that time the major portion of these stores were held in numerous warehouses scattered about the town and, lacking time perhaps to move the explosives up into the hills and wishing to destroy them in one operation, German working parties set about the task of consolidating the various caches into one central dump. The final site selected for the operation was an unfortunate one.

The physical and spiritual centre of Symi's township is the old acropolis, a rocky outcrop atop the hillock separating the Upper and Lower Towns. This natural eminence bears upon it a complete record of the islet's human history, for Neolithic, Pelasgian, Classical, Roman, Byzantine, Crusader, Frankish, Venetian, Turkish and Italian remains can be traced there, often tiered one upon another within its one-acre extent. In 1944 the acropolis was topped by one of the island's finest churches, the Church of the Ascension of the Virgin, whilst around the base of the low cliffs on which it was perched clustered a whole complex of houses, storerooms and buildings belonging to the wealthier merchants of the Upper Town. It was here that the retiring German troops decided to consolidate their munitions and destroy them. A regrettable necessity of war made infinitely more regrettable owing to two grim factors. Firstly, the chosen method of destruction was by blowing up the whole dump and, secondly, and far more serious, the civilians living in and about the area were not consulted nor warned of the operation. In fact, some unknown officer had given precise instructions to the soldiers taking part that the whole scheme was to be carried out with the strictest military secrecy. Luckily for Symi, these orders were not obeyed.

Rudi – big, blond and Bavarian – Symi has no record of your surname, only of your religion which was Catholic, and your rank which was corporal. You, toiling day-long with your men, carrying ammunition boxes up the cobbled streets to their final destination beneath the walls of Our Lady of the Ascension, continually asked those of the villagers you met with and knew by sight: "Hey, Symiot – when is the celebration of the Ascent of the Virgin?" and when they replied, saying "August 15th of course, but why do you ask?" – you gave the cryptic reply: "Wrong, quite wrong. Ask me tomorrow and I'll tell you…".

And the next day you said the same and the day following as well. But by then your conundrum was well known, with people openly discussing the riddle, seeking to see within it some present application and, consequently, when on the fourth day you gave your version of the date of the Virgin's Ascension as… "tonight at eight you will see Her rise. Tonight at eight, mark you!" – it did not take the townsfolk long to tumble to your meaning. All that day, as unseen as mice behind the wainscot, the people of the Upper Town moved bed and baggage and what valuables they could from door to door and balcony to balcony, down a long corridor of neighbourly hands, to relatives and friends in other areas. Old people were carried piggy-back and small children in baskets. Caged birds went too, and so did those few cats that had remained uneaten. By dusk all was quiet and all was deserted with no sign of life about the citadel other than those few German soldiers detailed to guard the hidden mine. At eight o'clock an observer on a distant campanile saw two blobs of yellow light moving down the hill away from the doomed area and at exactly ten past eight the Church of the Virgin did ascend in a sheet of flame and with a roar that shattered windows throughout the town, besides totally demolishing over 260 houses adjacent to the acropolis. Had not a Bavarian corporal muttered his riddle to those he passed, how many Symiots might have died in that explosion? Five hundred perhaps – maybe more. As it was, the only fatality was an octogenarian known as Maria who, when told of what was going on, said: "I was born in this house. I have knelt in this one church all my life. I shall die here in my house along with my church" – and did.

And Rudi, what of Rudi, I asked?

Did anyone in the town ever hear from him afterwards? Did he write to those he had saved or did anyone seek to contact him?

"Hah! Rudi – no, he never wrote," I was told. "And you know why not, Vassili? The Germans left here the following day on board a ship that had called to collect them. Within an hour of leaving it struck a mine or was torpedoed. Out of the four-hundred-odd people on board some seventeen were saved. But not Rudi…"

The Church of the Virgin of the Ascension went up and within hours Rudi – surname unrecorded, Bavarian, a Catholic, serving as a corporal in the German Army occupying Greece – went down.

Thus war's see-saw.

[NB Travis, relying largely on hearsay, considerably romanticized actual history here. The real-life model for "Bavarian Rudi" was a lieutenant from the Sudetenland, Franz Friedrichs, who was on friendly terms with a number of prominent Symiots, who themselves contrived to discreetly notify the acropolis-dwellers. The blast described actually took place at 10pm on 25 September 1944, and in fact the Germans had left that afternoon, not "the following day". But Lieutenant Friedrich's ship was in fact sunk after leaving Sými, so it's unlikely that he survived the war; all attempts to trace him have come to nought.]

One morning, shopping in Yalou, I came across a unique scene. There, clustered around a long table in the little square known as Pallas Athene – on account of the plaster statue of that Britannia-like deity which surmounts the gable of a house overlooking it – was a strange mixture of Symiots. At one end sat the mayor, Dr Nikitiades, flanked by his secretary and the Town Clerk. At the other sprawled the curly-bearded, piratical figure of Papas Anastasius with, in turn, two of his acolytes. Plumb in the middle of the table stood an ornate silver candlestick and in it a standard yellow offertory candle. Between the two groups and standing, not sitting, were a line of Symiot shepherds – lanky, sun-blackened creatures, characterized by their beautiful and uniform soft boots and divergent crooks.

"What goes on?" I asked.

"It's the auction of the grazing on Nimos [the islet just north of Symi], Vassili. It happens every four years."

"But what happens?" I insisted.

"Wait and see," I was told.

After a mumbled prayer Papas Anastasius lit the taper and silence fell. For five minutes nothing happened till the mayor, out of the blue said "Twenty thousand…" – thus setting, so I was told in a whisper, the arbitrary minimum price acceptable by the community as rent for that particular auction. Again silence, till a puff of wind caused the candle-flame to gutter. "Twenty-two", "Twenty-four", "Twenty-eight…" – the shouts came tumbling one upon the other for, as I now learnt the winner of the auction was he whose bid was uttered last before the candle went out – whether blown out by wind or burnt out by time. The sudden breeze dropped, the flame steadied and the bidding lapsed. Another five minutes passed, with random bids made partly in jest and partly by way of testing out the opposition, and the grazing rights stood at an even thirty thousand. The bidders grew silent, with eyes on the candle, for the day was calm and further wind-eddies seemed unlikely. There remained but a quarter-inch of wax before the offers started up once more, and then the cries flew thick and fast across the table: "Thirty-five, thirty-seven, thirty-seven fifty, thirty-eight two…" – the stump dissolved into a pool of dark wax overflowing the holder and still the little flame lived on. "Forty-one, forty-one and a half, forty-two, forty-two and two, forty-two and four…" – but it was too late, the flame had gone out in a little puff of oily smoke and the bidder of forty-two thousand and two hundred drachma had won the right to graze five hundred sheep on Nimos islet for the next four years. Making a quick calculation in my head I said to my companion: "But surely nearly eighty-five drachma per head is expensive grazing, when sheep and goats can free-range here on Symi? And which poor shepherd can afford to put down six hundred pounds in hard cash for the privilege, anyway?"

"Ssh, Vassili – it's not just the grazing, you ignorant foreigner! He who has the right to graze his sheep on Nimos has the right to go there anytime, right? Without causing comment or arousing suspicion. And the far side of Nimos faces Anatolia and can't be seen from Yalou or Horio, right? What better place to use as a starting point for a little trip to Turkey, eh – or at which to unload ships coming back… Nimos is uninhabited, remember? Now do you understand why some people give the shepherds money with which to bid? And what does it matter? The community chest gains ten thousand drachma a year it would not otherwise see and, if it were not Nimos, there would be some other place used for this night-traffic across to Turkey . . ."

Crooked captains

A diaspora Greek two generations removed from Kássos, bleakest of the Dodecanese, Elias Kulukundis visited his ancestral island for the first time in 1964. The result of a lengthy stay was *Journey to a Greek Island*, first published by Cassell, London in 1968, and reissued in 2004. This extract is reprinted with the permission of Simon & Schuster. Often reading like nonfiction García Márquez, it is unsurpassed as an introductory exploration to local history, anthropology and genealogy, not just Kassian but Dodecanesian.

Like a number of other relatively barren Greek isles, Kássos has long made its living from the sea. At the time of the 1821 uprising, it possessed the fourth-largest island fleet after Ídhra, Spétses and Psará. Of these, only Kássos remained a maritime power after independence, and Kassiots are still disproportionately represented in the contemporary Greek shipping industry. In his discussion of the history of Kassiot seafaring, Kulukundis does not shy away from the subject of piracy – occasionally indulged in by the islanders during the first half of the last century. What follows, however, details the other, less well-known practice of barratry.

It was customary at that time, as it is today, for the cargo owner to charter a captain's ship at a given rate. After the agreement had been reached, the captain would simply load the cargo on his ship and sail away with it, and unless the charterer posted a representative or supercargo to accompany the ship and protect his interests, he would have to trust the captain for the duration of the voyage. The voyages of sailing ships lasted several weeks, and during that time, anything might happen. The captain might encounter heavy weather and find himself in danger of foundering unless he lightened his ship by jettisoning all his extra masts and rigging and even a portion of the cargo if necessary. In that event, under the laws of general average, the captain would not be responsible for the loss of cargo, and it would have to be sustained solely by the charterer. This was where certain captains were cunning enough to see a special opportunity. A captain might not encounter heavy weather at all, only *claim* to have encountered it.

The coasts of the Aegean Islands and mainland Greece are full of tiny coves, secret places where a ship might put in unnoticed, under the cover of a moonless night. There, by prearrangement, a caique might come out to meet the ship, and as it drew alongside, the captain might strike a stealthy bargain with the caique's owner to *sell* him a portion of the cargo. After the agreement had been concluded, a portion of the cargo would be lowered into the caique. The captain would sail out onto the high seas again, then to the island of Zante where there were certain legal experts. They could doctor the log of the voyage to show that on such and such a day, under the stress of heavy weather, the captain had found it necessary to jettison his extra masts and spars and sails (items which might never have existed) as well as that portion of the cargo he had actually sold. At the conclusion of the voyage, the captain would enjoy a double profit: the rate of hire agreed upon with the charterer, plus the proceeds of the sale. Then, his winter's work done in a single voyage, he could return to his native island and roister in the café.

The practice was widespread in the Aegean after the [Greek] Revolution, taking the place of piracy of old. The island of Zante, which had probably begun as a natural haven for mariners after a storm, became a nest of log-doctorers. Gradually, it became so common for captains to put into Zante after the sale of cargo, that underwriters refused to pay a claim if the ship had stopped there for any reason. Meanwhile, the Greek Government, anxious to protect the reputation of its growing merchant marine, ran down offenders and imposed heavy penalties on them. And wherever Greek captains were suspected of barratry, the Greek Government posted a consul to report any illegal sales.

Barratry became very popular among certain Kasiots. It appealed to their naturally wily nature, as much for its own sake as for any profit it would yield. They would sail home to Kasos, anchor outside the Bucca [the port] and sell a portion of the cargo to the island merchants. Then, sending the ship on to Zante to its doctors, they would ascend victorious to the café.

But no Kassiot ever got rich on barratry, and the names of the barrators have dropped long ago from the shipping history of the island. After the captain had sold the cargo, he would be open to blackmail at the hands of his very accomplices; and often in the years ahead, he would have to pay out much more than he had made by the original transaction.

Sometime in the latter half of the nineteenth century, a Kasiot captain whom we can call Captain Nikos put into Salonika to find a cargo. It was a very slack season, and cargoes were difficult to find, so for lack of anything better he contracted with two Jewish rabbis to carry a cargo of flagstones at a very unprofitable rate. But the rabbis rubbed salt into his wounds.

"You're a Kasiot, aren't you?" they said.

Captain Nikos said he was.

"Well, in that case we shall have to post supercargoes to keep watch over our flagstones."

"Very well," said Captain Nikos, taking no offense at this discrimination. "Who will be your supercargoes?"

"We will," said the rabbis. "Both of us."

"You will?" said Captain Nikos, smiling. "Very well."

So the rabbis packed their belongings and prepared to sail with Captain Nikos to keep watch over their flagstones. And in the meantime, Captain Nikos was thinking: "Two supercargoes to watch over flagstones? What must they think of me? If I sold all their stones at twice their value, I still would not make enough to pay for my expenses. But very well. Let them come if they wish. I will see they have an exciting voyage."

In the meantime, an idea had grown on him. The rabbis had heard so much about the mischief of certain Kasiots, Captain Nikos thought he could not very well disappoint them. Since they distrusted him so openly, even with a cargo of flagstones, he would not be one to let them down. He would sell their cargo anyway, worthless as it was, under their very noses.

So Captain Nikos set sail from Salonika, already smirking over what he planned; and the two rabbis sailed with him. Standing stiffly on either side of the tiller in their black robes and beards and broad brimmed black hats, they watched Captain Nikos with eagle eyes. When the ship sailed out beyond the harbour, a strong wind came up. And although the rabbis did not realize it, Captain Nikos did what any seaman knows not to do. He steered the ship broadside to the wind, so that immediately it began to roll.

"What's that?" said the rabbis, taken by surprise.

"The wind," said Captain Nikos.

"Ah, the wind," said the rabbis solemnly, composing themselves once again on either side of Captain Nikos. But now the ship was rolling so fiercely they had trouble keeping their balance. Though neither of them said a word and did not even look at each other, very soon they were both pale as ghosts.

"Is this normal?" said one rabbi at last, in a voice weak with nausea and with fear.

"As normal as the wind," said Captain Nikos.

"But what will happen?"

"I don't know. If you wish, you may go below where you can lie down and be more comfortable."

The rabbis looked at each other. For one longing moment they looked in the direction of their cabin. But at last, bravely, they decided against it.

"No, we must stay here to keep watch over our flagstones," they said.

"Very well," said Captain Nikos, raising his voice above the wind and water. "But if you must stand here, at least take hold of something. I'm afraid you may be thrown into the sea."

At that moment, appearing to be steering carefully in the face of danger, Captain Nikos turned the wheel violently one way and then the other, so that the ship plunged down towards the menacing white water, reprieving itself from catastrophe at the last moment, only to plunge down toward it again on the other side.

"But what is happening?" cried the rabbis. "Is this a storm?"

"Yes," said Captain Nikos, "a storm."

"Is it a bad one? Is it dangerous?"

"Any storm is a bad one, but this is the most dangerous storm I have ever seen."

"God of Moses. But what will happen? Will we drown?"

"We may," said Captain Nikos. "We are so heavy and the wind is so strong that at any moment we may go over."

"Go over? You mean into the sea?"

"Into the sea."

"God of Aaron, and is there nothing we can do?"

"Do? What should we do?"

"Is there nothing we can do to save ourselves?"

"Of course."

"What?"

"Pray. Pray to your God."

"Pray to our God? Is there nothing else?"

"Is that not enough?"

"God of Moses, is there nothing we can do to save ourselves? If we are so heavy, can't we lighten?"

"Lighten? How lighten?"

"If a ship is too heavy, they say the captain can throw some of the cargo overboard."

"Throw some of the cargo overboard?" said Captain Nikos. "You are asking me to throw some of the cargo overboard?"

"Why not?" cried the rabbis. "That would save us, wouldn't it? We would be lighter then, and we would be able to make it through this storm."

"Of course we would. We would be lighter in an instant, and the ship would right itself and be out of danger, and then there would be an end to this terrible sickness and dizziness and rolling first one way and then the other."

"Oh, dear God of Isaac, then let us lighten! God of Jacob, let us throw some of the cargo overboard."

"No," said Captain Nikos. "Upon my honour, as a captain and as a Kasiot, no."

"But why? Why in the name of God?"

"Because later, when we reached our destination, you would say we did not meet bad weather at all, that I didn't really throw the cargo overboard but sold it for my own profit. And as a Kasiot captain, I would rather drown than hear such accusations."

"Say you sold the cargo? Captain Nikos, put it out of your mind! We trust you completely!"

"Then why did you sail with me to watch over your cargo? That is the reason you find yourselves in this needless danger when you could be safe in your homes this very moment."

By now, the rabbis were close to tears.

"Oh why, Captain Nikos? We do not know why! We wish we had never sailed with you. But that is all forgotten. We promise you, on the bones of all the prophets, we shall never sail with you again. Only please, Captain Nikos, throw some of our flagstones overboard. You can trust us, Captain Nikos. We will sign a paper. We will do anything you say. Only please, Captain Nikos, before it is too late."

Captain Nikos deliberated for one unendurable moment.

"Very well," he said, "if you insist, I agree. But one of you must begin. That one." He pointed to one rabbi. "Let it be him. Let him cast the first stone."

"I will, I will," said the rabbi. "Only hurry, for the love of God, hurry before all is lost."

Captain Nikos directed his crew to open the cargo hatch and lift out one of the stones for the rabbi to throw overboard. As agreed, the rabbi awkwardly cast the first stone. Afterwards, at a signal from Captain Nikos, the seamen began to lift out a few of the stones, one by one, and throw them overboard. At that moment, Captain Nikos manipulated the wheel in such a way that a huge wave curled over the side and almost broke upon the rabbis.

"For the love of God," cried captain Nikos, "go below now, or the next wave will carry you away."

Without a word, the rabbis scurried below out of the menacing sea and wind. As soon as they disappeared, Captain Nikos ordered his men to stop what they were doing.

"What are you doing there, my lads?" he said. "Throwing stones into the sea? Have you lost your minds?"

Laughing, the crew stopped throwing stones into the sea, closed the hatch, and went about their business. After a discreet interval, Captain Nikos steered out of the wind, as even any landlubber knows he should. The ship righted itself, and the storm subsided into a placid Aegean afternoon.

The rabbis, by that time, were sound asleep. Delivered from the jaws of death and the terrible nausea which had menaced them far worse, they slept through the dinner hour and far into the night. And they were still asleep, near midnight, when Captain Nikos sailed into a deserted cove, and beckoning the owner of a caique to draw alongside, sold him the remaining flagstones. The next day, sailing toward their destination on an empty ship, the rabbis signed a paper Captain Nikos had prepared, attesting to the fact that the ship had met heavy weather a few miles out of Salonika, and at their insistence, the captain agreed to jettison the cargo. One of the rabbis, they admitted, had cast the first stone.

Captain Nikos' story became proverbial on Kasos. He was such a notorious barrator, he would sell flagstones for the sport of it, and he became the first Kasiot in history to get his supercargoes to doctor the log.

Lured from Léros

The British took over the administration of most of the Dodecanese, including Léros, in mid-September 1943, after the Italian capitulation. They had, as it turned out, barely two months in which to reinforce facilities inherited from the Italians against the massive German attack of November 12. Extra supplies could be landed by ship or submarine, but only under increasingly regular German air raids and via comprehensively laid minefields. The following self-contained interlude, narrated by a Maltese serviceman, is from a longer section devoted to Léros in *War in the Islands*, compiled by Adrian Seligman and reproduced by kind permission of Alan Sutton Publishing Ltd.

October [1943] was a disastrous month for the [British] Navy. Four cruisers, five more destroyers, an MTB, three MLs and numerous other smaller craft were lost or put out of action. The sowing of mines in the Kós and Kálymnos channels, and the arrival in the Aegean of the glider bomb, had completely altered the balance of power in the war at sea. The glider bomb in particular, launched and radio-controlled from an aircraft, and power-driven to its target with a warhead carrying well over 500lb of explosives, was a weapon against which there was no immediate defence....

From Navy House [a villa at Álinda used as British HQ] we had a clear view down the bay and out to sea. One night, early in November, we saw a glider bomb, easily recognizable by its red tail-light, pounce on a Brooklyn Yard Mine Sweeper (BYMS) passing the entrance to the bay. "Pounce" is an exact description of the way the bomb came cruising along, then suddenly tipped up and fell upon its wretched victim. The funnel and deck clutter aft took the full force of the explosion, thus saving the lives of the people in the great palace of a wheelhouse further forward. They now called us up to report the damage and request instructions. We signalled back telling the captain to make for Port Laki (Lakkí) round the northern end of the island. He would be met at the harbour entrance and piloted in.

I drove at top speed in my jeep down to the seaplane base [at Teménia on Lakkí Bay] to find our motor boat and, if possible, her crew. It was a moonlit night with a clear sky and [German] bombers overhead, which seemed to be concentrating on gun positions in the mountains and round the coast. I found our two boat-men turned fishermen, landing their evening's catch on the quay. We motored out to the harbour mouth and a mile or so beyond. In the bright moonlight, I remember, the sea looked black and bottomless. Then slowly round the northern cliffs and down past the Skrophes shoals came the BYMS which, we could see as she approached, had been badly damaged. And she was low in the water aft, where bomb splinters must have holed her. There was an air of silence about her above the slow, laboured beat of her screw turning at half speed.

I called her up with the recognition signal of the day, and when the correct reply came back I signalled "Follow me" and turned back towards the harbour mouth. Slowly she swung round after me, and we had almost reached the entrance, when all at once a loud voice speaking urgently in English rang out. I thought at first it must be the skipper of the BYMS calling us on his loud-hailer, but couldn't quite catch what he was saying. It sounded like a warning – certain the word "trap" came into it. Then to my horror, the BYMS began to alter course away down the coast toward German-held Kálymnos. I flashed and flashed, but there was no reply, and I realized that the voice on the loud-hailer was coming from somewhere to seaward.

There was nothing we could do but watch, appalled. The BYMS had increased to full speed, and it wasn't long before she rounded the southern headland of the bay and disappeared.

By a remarkable coincidence, I heard the rest of the story in 1953, several years after the end of the war, from the captain of a "Hansa" cargo vessel on her maiden voyage out east. She was celebrating her first call at Chittagong with a party on board, and I, as manager of a firm of jute exporters, and therefore a major shipper, was received by the master personally. It wasn't long before we discovered that we had both been involved in the battle for Léros. And after we'd well-I-nevered and slapped each other on the back for a bit, Captain Loetzmann said, "I remember one night in particular, because it gave me my first chance of a decoration... I was just twenty, in command of an E-boat patrolling to the east of the island – and pretty pleased with myself, I've no doubt – when we saw what must have been one of the first glider-bomb attacks on a ship in the Mediterranean area. Poor creature, I felt sorry for her. She was a small and most unwarlike-looking craft with a tall and strangely palatial design of wheelhouse."

"Sure, she was a BYMS," I couldn't help butting in. "We were watching her from Navy House at the head of the bay."

The captain looked astonished. "Then it was you we saw signalling?"

"Not me personally, but never mind."

"Anyhow, that was when my four years at an English public school came in handy. I was able to read your signal."

"So you knew that she was bound for Port Laki north-about?"

"Indeed… and that gave me a better idea than wasting a torpedo on such an unimportant target. Instead I turned away to round the southern end of the island and be ready to meet and board her at my convenience." Loetzmann chuckled. "One gets a bit caried away when one's young. On the way round I called up Kálymnos, where we had two batteries of eighty-eights covered Léros strait, asking them . . . no, I expect I told them . . . on no account to fire on a small vessel which I proposed to board and capture. After that it was easy. When she was about to enter harbour I called her up from seaward by loud-hailer. I was down moon, so she couldn't see me properly. There was a small boat in the harbour entrance signalling her."

"That was me," I had to tell him, "and we could hear you shouting, but with your loud-hailer aimed at him, we could only make out odd words."

"I'm glad of that."

"Why?"

"Well, I hope you will forgive me, but what I said was: 'Take no notice of that fool flashing . . . it's an Italian trap . . . follow me'."

"And he did, poor fellow… kind of wolf and Red Riding Hood stuff."

We had a drink on that. Then he said, "I suppose it was, but if you'd seen the relief on the poor chap's face when we boarded him and he knew it was all over, you'd have felt, as I did, that it had all been worth while."

I met Captain Loetzmann again on several occasions, when we happened to be in Chittagong at the same time. But I never did remember to ask him which public school he'd been to.

Ikarian idiosyncrasies

Joseph Georgirenes was Archbishop of the diocese of Sámos from 1666 until 1671, when – weary of Turkish interference – he voluntarily retired to the monastery of the Apocalypse on nearby Pátmos. Originally from Mílos, he had an involved outsider's view of his pastoral flock, if an occasionally jaundiced one. Following his residence on Pátmos, Georgirenes emigrated for unspecified reasons to London, where in 1677 he wrote *A Description of the Present State of Samos, Nicaria, Patmos, and Mount Athos*, which was translated into English by an unidentified acquaintance; its hundred-plus pages are packed with a wealth of detail – some of it doubtless exaggerated for effect – concerning Ottoman rule, religious observance, agriculture and ethnography. The good bishop was wrong in at least one particular, however: until the 1950s sleeping on the floor rather than in a bed was a widespread practice throughout village Greece.

The most commendable thing of this Island [Ikaría] is their Air and Water, both so healthful, that the People are very long liv'd, it being an ordinary thing to see persons in it of an hundred years of Age, which is a great wonder, considering how hardily they live. There is not a Bed in the Island, the Ground is their Tick, and the cold Stone their Pillow, and the Cloaths they wear is all the Coverlet they use. They provide no more Apparel than what they wear all at once, when that is past wearing any longer, then think of a new Suit. Betwixt their ordinary times of Eating, there is not a piece of Bread to be found in the Isle. A little before Dinner, they take as much Corn as will serve that Meal, grind it with a Hand-Mill, and bake it upon a flat Stone; when 'tis Bak'd, the Master of the Family divides it equally among the Family; but a Woman with child has two shares. If any Stranger comes in, every one parts with a Piece of his own share to accommodate the Stranger. Their Wine is always made with a third part Water, and so very weak and small. When they drink it, so much as is thought sufficient is put into one large Bowl, and so passes round. The Nicarians [Nicaria was the medieval name for Ikaría] are the only Islanders of all the Archipelago, that neither keep Wine to sell, nor lay it up in Wooden Vessels, but in long Jars, cover'd all over in the Ground. When they have a mind to Tap it, they make a Bung-hole in the top, and draw it out with Canes. Their Houses are so plain, that all the Furniture you can see is an Hand-Mill, besides this, there is nothing but bare Walls: That little they have besides is all hid under Ground; not so much for fear of the Corsairs (from whom their Poverty is a sure guard) as out of Custome. Nor are they all so poor, as not to be able to buy Beds, but custome has brought them into a contempt of Beds, as meerly superfluous; insomuch, that when they Travel into other Islands, they refuse the offer of a Bed. A Priest of Nicaria coming into Samos, was courteously entertain'd by those of his Order, and at Night was offer'd a Bed to lye in; he thank'd them, but refus'd, nor could by any importunity be prevail'd upon, but told them the Earth was his Mother, from whence he would not keep a distance; besides he was afraid of being Sick, if he should lye in a Bed; and therefore if they had a kindness for him, they must give him the liberty of sleeping after his own Country way.

When I went to visit them as Arch-Bishop, and ignorant of the custom of the Country, carry'd no Bed. At Night, where I first lodg'd, asking for a Chamber, they told me they had not other than that where I first came; then asking for a Bed, they told me it was not the Custom of the Country; then desiring to borrow some Bed Cloaths for Love or Money, all they brought me was one Smock made of course Dimity.

They have no great communication one with another, any farther than the publick times of Sacred Solemnities, or Civil Business doth cause them to come together. At other times they keep strictly within the narrow Sphere of their own affairs. Formal Visits, Treats, and Entertainments are things unknown. If any business do put them upon a Visit to their Neighbour, they come not close to his Door, but stand off at a great distance, and call aloud to him; If he make them answer, they discourse the Business they came about, standing off at the same distance; except they be earnestly invited to come in. And this way of discoursing at a distance they practise more in the Fields and Mountains; their Voices being so strong, that 'tis ordinary to talk at a Miles distance; sometimes at four or five, where the Valleys interpos'd between two hills, give advantage to the Voice. Sometimes they can discourse at that distance, that the carriage of the Sound through the Winding of the Valleys, shall require half a Quarter of an Hours time; and yet they make distinct, and proper Answers, both audible and intelligible, without the help of a Stentorophonical Trumpet.

Their Habit for the Men, is a Shirt, and over it a short cassock, down to the Knees, to which, in Winter they add only a short Vest, that reaches a little below the middle. Stockings they never wear. Their Shoes are only a piece of thin Copper, bow'd to the shape of their Feet, and every one is his own Shoemaker. The Women have nothing but one Smock, but so large, that they wrap it double, or treble down to the Girdle, but below the Girdle single. The Priests, for greater reverence in the Church, tye two Towels about their Legs, the one is their usual Bonnet, and the other their Girdle: so that they perfom sacred Offices ungirt, as well as uncover'd.

Of all the Isles of the Archipelago, this only admits of no mixture with Strangers in Marriage, nor admits any Stranger to settle with them: They being, as they pretend, all descended of the Imperial Blood of the Porphyrogenneti, must not stain their noble Blood with inferiour Matches, or mixtures with Choriats, or Peasants, for so they term all the other islanders.

Porphyrogenneti, were those of the Blood Royal, in the Days of the Greek Emperours, so call'd, from their wearing of Purple, which was a Badge of Royalty, and allow'd only to Princes of the Blood; and not from an house call'd Porphyra, where the Empresses were wont to lie in. But Purple was throughout the East, the known Badge of Royalty. Hence came that unsanctify'd Wit, and learned'st Writer that ever oppos'd the Christian Religion with his Pen, to be call'd Porphyrius: For his true name in the Language of Syria, his native Country, was Malchus, or King; but the Greeks did paraphrase it Porphyrius, or Purple-robed; that being a Colour peculiar to Kings.

They have a great Happiness, by reason of their poverty, in not being molested by the Turks, who think it not worth their while to come among them, nor if they should, were they likely to enjoy any quiet, without keeping a stronger Guard than the Revenues of the Isle would maintain. Once they slew a Caddee [judge] sent by the Grand Signior [ie the Sultan], and being summon'd to Answer for their Crime, they by common consent own'd the Fact, but would name no particular Man. So that the Turkish Officers looking upon their beggarly Cloaths, thought there was neither gain nor glory in punishing such Miscreants, and that in Justice, they must punish all, or none, dismiss'd them untouch'd. From that time no Turk ever troubled them: For they take all courses imaginable to seem poor; and wheresoe'er they come abroad, they count it no shame to beg Alms: Yet they make a shift every year to levy three hundred Crowns for the Arch-Bishop. They are govern'd by a Proesti [council of village elders] of their own chusing, who also levys their Haratch or Tribute to the Grand Signior, and takes care to carry it to the Aga [local Turkish chieftain] of Scio [Híos]. As for their Religion, it is the same with that of Samos; but their Priests are more ignorant.

Thus you have an account of a small Island, the Poorest, and yet the Happiest of the whole Aegean Sea. The Soil is Barren, but the Air is Healthful; their Wealth is but small, but their Liberty and Security is great. They are not molested withe the Tyrannous Insolence of a Turkish Officer, nor with the frightful Incursions of barbarous and merciless Pirates. Their Diet and Apparel is below the Rate of Beggars in other Countrys, and their Lodging is a thying of no more care, or cost, than that of the Beasts of the Field, yet their Bodies are strong and hardy, and the People generally long liv'd. They live with as little forecast, as if they expected not to survive a day, being contented to satisfy the present necessities of Nature. They do properly in diem vivere, or as we say, From Hand to Mouth. They have but little, yet they never Want. Their Ignorance is equal to their Poverty, and contributes much to their content. And how well they esteem of their own condition, their contempt of their Neighbouring Islands, and scorning to mix with them in Alliance by Marriage, is a manifest sign. Whence we may learn, that they approach the nearest to Contentedness in this Life; whose desires are contracted into the narrowest compass.

Books

For each recommended title in this section we only list imprint details when a book is not easily available online or at retailers, for example small presses in Greece. An out-of-print but still highly recommended book is indicated by the abbreviation "o/p"; most of these are easily and affordably found on the excellent used-book dealers' websites ⓦwww.abebooks.co.uk/.com, or ⓦwww.bookfinder.com. Books marked ⊡ are particularly recommended. One British publisher with a consistent record of publishing or re-issuing excellent social and historical studies of Greece is C. Hurst and Company (ⓦwww.hurstpub.co.uk).

Travel and memoirs

Howard Baker *Persephone's Cave* (o/p). Intimations of ancient worship on a reverential Aegean tour taking in Sámos, with good period detail (1960s) from before the advent of tourism.

Joseph Braddock *Sappho's Island: A Paean for Lesbos* (o/p). Precious little on the modern island, but good background on ancient Mytilene and on the "primitive" painter Theophilos.

Charmian Clift *Mermaid Singing* (o/p). Clift couldn't render a Greek word or personal name properly to save her life (which ended, sadly, in suicide) but hats off to her and her family for being effectively the first expats on Kálymnos during the mid-1950s, an island then still deeply traditional, primitive, innocent of tourism and in the thrall of the yearly sponge cycle.

Lawrence Durrell *Reflections on a Marine Venus*. Durrell spent 1945 to 1947 as a press officer on British-administered Rhodes; this was the result, rich in period detail but purple in the prose, alcohol-fogged as always, and faintly patronizing towards the "natives".

John Ebdon *Ebdon's Iliad* (o/p). Rhodes, Kós and Kárpathos as they (and their package trade) were in the early 1980s. No claims to profundity, but fun as light beach reading.

⊡ **Joseph Georgirenes** *A Description of the Present State of Samos, Nicaria, Patmos and Mount Athos* (Noti Karavia, Athens; limited facsimile edition – originals are worth £2000). An occasionally hilarious account of these spots as they were in the mid-seventeenth century, showing if nothing else that regional character was already well developed in medieval times. A choice morsel is excerpted on pp.511–513.

⊡ **William Johnson** *The Monk Seal Conspiracy* (o/p, but available as online version). Johnson spent almost three years on Sámos (1979–82), employed by various conservation organizations, lobbying to establish marine reserves for the endangered monk seal. The alleged "conspiracy" he uncovered was that the seals were to become victims of Greco-Turkish tensions, the complacency of his employers and the ultimate supremacy of the Greek military and secret services. Johnson was clearly a prickly fanatic (and is still conspicuously eloquent on ⓦwww.monachus.org), but even if half of what he says is true, you'll never donate to the WWF or Greenpeace again. Excellent on Sámos in pre-tourism days, and the mythology and life-cycle of the seals in question.

Katherine Kizilos *The Olive Grove: Travels in Greece* (o/p). Returned, ambivalent Greek-Australian's musings on the country and Constantinople, which include vignettes of Pátmos, Ikaría and Lésvos.

★ **Elias Kulukundis** *The Feasts of Memory: Stories of a Greek Family.* A journey back through time and genealogy by a diaspora Greek two generations removed from Kássos, poorest of the Dodecanese. This is a 2004 re-release, with an extra chapter, of his 1968 literary classic *Journey to a Greek Island*, a passage from which is excerpted on pp.505–509.

★ **Willard Manus** *This Way to Paradise: Dancing on the Tables* (Lycabettus Press, Athens). An American expatriate's memoir of four decades in Líndhos, Rhodes, beginning long before its sad descent into mass-tourist tattiness – he and wife Mavis were among the first foreigners to settle there in 1961. Wonderful period detail, including hippie excesses and hilarious appearances by the likes of S. J. Perelman, Germaine Greer and Martha Gelhorn.

★ **Tom Stone** *The Summer of My Greek Taverna.* An excellent cautionary tale, especially for those entertaining fantasies of a new life in the sun, set in northern Pátmos of the early 1980s; a rather trusting Stone mixes friendship and business at Kámbos beach, with predictable (to everyone else, anyway) results.

★ **Patricia Storace** *Dinner with Persephone.* A New York poet, resident a year in Greece, puts the country's psyche on the couch, while avoiding the same position with various predatory males. Storace has a sly sense of humour, and in showing how permeated – and imprisoned – Greece is by its imagined past, gets it right ninety percent of the time.

★ **William Travis** *Bus Stop Symi* (o/p). Chronicles three years' residence there in the mid-1960s; fairly insightful (if rather resented on the island itself for its liberties with the truth), though Travis erroneously prophesied that the place would never see tourism. Two passages are reproduced on pp.503–505.

Faith Warn *Bitter Sea: The Real Story of Greek Sponge Diving.* Short, photo-illustrated potted history of the traditional Kálymnos livelihood, as seen some four decades after Clift's experience (see opposite).

★ **Sofka Zinovieff** *Eurydice Street.* An anthropologist and journalist by training, Zinovieff first came to Greece in the early 1980s, then returned in 2001 with her diplomat husband. Zinovieff writes undeniably well; the book is already being hailed as a superb narrative of acculturation and adaptation (and has quickly gone into a Greek edition).

The classics

Many of the classics make excellent companion reading for a trip around Greece – especially the historians Thucydides and Herodotus. Reading Homer's *Odyssey* when you're battling with or resigning yourself to the vagaries of island ferries puts your own plight into perspective. Most of the standard undergraduate staples are part of the Penguin Classics paperback series. Routledge and Duckworth both also have a huge, steadily expanding backlist of Classical Studies, though many titles are expensive and quite specialized.

Herodotus *The Histories* (trans. A. D. Godley). Revered as the father of systematic history and anthropology,

this fifth-century BC Anatolian writer chronicled both the causes and campaigns of the Persian Wars, as well as the contemporary, assorted tribes and nations inhabiting Asia Minor.

Homer *The Iliad; The Odyssey*. The first concerns itself, semi-factually, with the late Bronze Age war of the Achaeans against Troy in Asia Minor; the second recounts the delayed return home of the hero Odysseus, via seemingly every corner of the Mediterranean. For a verse rendition, ✷ Richmond Lattimore's translations of each have yet to be bettered. For a prose rendition, ✷ Martin Hammond's *Iliad* and *Odyssey* currently edge out second-best choices by the father-and-son team of E.V. Rieu (*Iliad*) and D. C. H. Rieu (*Odyssey*).

Ovid *Metamorphoses* (trans. A. D. Melville). Though collected by a first-century AD Roman writer, this remains one of the most accessible renditions of the more piquant Greek myths, involving transformations as divine blessing or curse. Ted Hughes' more recent rendition has also been widely praised.

★ **Thucydides** *History of the Peloponnesian War*. Bleak month-by-month account of the conflict, which involved most of the larger islands, by a cashiered Athenian officer who remains remarkably objective despite his affiliation and dim view of human nature; see George Cawkwell's book (review below) for a revisionist interpretation.

Xenophon *The History of My Times*. Thucydides ended his coverage of the Peloponnesian War in 411 BC; this work continues events until 362 BC and the dawn of the Macedonian dynasty.

Ancient history and interpretation of the classics

★ **Mary Beard and John Henderson** *The Classics: A Very Short Introduction*. As it says; an excellent overview.

★ **A. R. Burn** *History of Greece*. Probably the best general introduction to ancient Greece, though for fuller and more interesting analysis you'd do better with one or other of the following, more specialized titles.

★ **Paul Cartledge** *Cambridge Illustrated History of Ancient Greece*. Large-format, pricey volume packed with information useful for both novices and experts. His more recent work, *The Spartans: The World of the Warrior-Heroes of Ancient Greece*, is the first thorough study of this much-maligned and secretive city-state, a source of speculation from outside even in its own time.

George Cawkwell *Thucydides and the Peloponnesian War*. Recent, revisionist overview of Thucydides' work and relations with prominent personalities of the war, challenging previous assumptions of his infallibility.

★ **M. I. Finley** *The World of Odysseus*. Latest reprint of a 1954 warhorse, pioneering in its investigation of the historicity (or otherwise) of the events and society related by Homer. Breezily readable and stimulating, with prejudices apparent rather than subtle.

Michael Grant and John Hazel *Who's Who in Classical Mythology*. Gazetteer of over 1200 mythological personalities, together with historical and geographical background.

★ **Pierre Grimal (ed)** *Dictionary of Classical Mythology*. Translated from the French and still considered to have the edge on the more recent Grant/Hazel title (see above).

Simon Hornblower *The Greek World 479–323 BC*. An erudite survey of ancient Greece at its zenith, from the end of the Persian Wars to the death of Alexander; now a standard university paperback text.

John Kenyon Davies *Democracy and Classical Greece*. Established and accessible account of the Classical period and its political developments.

Robin Lane Fox *Alexander the Great*. An absorbing study, which combines historical scholarship with imaginative psychological detail; the author, as part of the deal for serving as a consultant for Oliver Stone's less-than-great epic bio-pic, got a bit part as a cavalryman.

Robin Osborne *Greece in the Making 1200–479 BC*. Well-illustrated paperback on the rise of the city-state.

Graham Shipley *A History of Samos, 800–188 BC*. Somewhat dry treatment of Archaic-to-Hellenistic Sámos, though not without its moments of wit; most interesting for its catalogue of sites from all eras, and other unique appendices.

Tony Spawforth *Greece, an Oxford Archaeological Guide*. An interpretive guide, by the co-author, with Simon Hornblower, of the also-recommended *Oxford Classical Dictionary*.

F. W. Walbank *The Hellenistic World*. Greece under the sway of the Macedonian and Roman empires.

Ancient religion and culture

★ **Walter Burkert** *Greek Religion: Archaic and Classical*. Superb overview of ancient deities and their attributes and antecedents, rites, the protocol of sacrifice and the symbolism of major festivals; especially good on relating Greek worship to its predecessors in the Middle East.

Matthew Dillon *Pilgrims and Pilgrimage in Ancient Greece*. Pricey hardback exploring not only the main sanctuaries, but also minor oracles, the role of women and children, and secular festivities attending the rites.

Mary Lefkowitz *Greek Gods, Human Lives: What We Can Learn from Myths*. Rather than being frivolous, immoral or irrelevant, ancient religion and its supporting myths, portraying the gods' bleak indifference to human suffering, are shown as being more "grown up" than the later creeds of salvation and comfort.

Nano Marinatos and Robin Hagg *Greek Sanctuaries: New Approaches*. Form and function of the temples, in the light of recent scholarship.

Archeology and art

John Beckwith *Early Christian and Byzantine Art*. Illustrated, pricey study placing Byzantine art within a wider context.

William R. Biers *Archeology of Greece: An Introduction*. A 1990s-revised and excellent standard text.

★ **John Boardman** *Greek Art*. A very good concise introduction: part of the Thames and Hudson "World of Art" series.

Reynold Higgins *Minoan and Mycenaean Art*. A clear, well-illustrated summary.

Sinclair Hood *The Arts in Prehistoric Greece*. Sound introduction to the subject.

Roger Ling *Classical Greece*. Another useful illustrated introduction.

Gisela Richter *A Handbook of Greek Art*. Exhaustive survey of the visual arts of ancient Greece.

R. R. R. Smith *Hellenistic Sculpture*. Modern reappraisal of the art of Greece under Alexander and his successors.

★ **David Talbot Rice** *Art of the Byzantine Era*. Talbot Rice was,

Bookshops

The islands covered in this guide are, with the exceptions of Rhodes, Kós and Híos, bereft of decent bookshops with any foreign-language stock. If you're stopping over in Athens, however, the capital has a number of excellent ones, at which many of the recommendations above should be available (albeit at a fifty percent mark-up for foreign-published titles); all are centrally located. Try Eleftheroudhakis, Níkis 22–24; Compendium, Níkis 28; Iy Folia tou Vivliou, Panepistimíou 25; and Pantelidhes, Amerikís 11. In London, the Hellenic Bookservice, 91 Fortess Road, Kentish Town, London NW5 1AG ⊕020/7267 9499, ⊕7267 9498, ⊛www.hellenicbookservice .com, is the UK's premier walk-in Greek bookshop: knowledgeable and well-stocked specialist dealers in new and out-of-print books on all aspects of Greece, especially classics and educational texts. Rivals Zeno's are at 57a Nether Street, North Finchley, London N12 7NP ⊕020/8446 1985, ⊛8446 1986, ⊛www.thegreekbookstore .com and have more of an antiquarian stress, with their own line of reprints.

in Greece", this analysis of Classical and Byzantine texts demonstrates just how little Greek cuisine has changed in three millennia; also excellent on the introduction and etymology of common vegetables and herbs.

★ **Alan Davidson** *Mediterranean Seafood*. A 1972 classic, reprinted in 1992 and revised in 2003, this amazingly erudite and witty book catalogues (almost) all known edible species, complete with legends, anecdotes, habits, local names and a suggested recipe or two for each.

★ **James Davidson** *Courtesans and Fishcakes*. The politics, class characteristics and etiquette of consumption and consummation – with wine, women, boys and seafood – in ancient Athens, with their bearing on both historical events and modern attitudes. Highly recommended.

★ **Nico Manessis** *The Illustrated Greek Wine Book* (Olive Press Publications, Corfu; available at select retailers in Greece or through ⊛www.greekwineguide.gr). Covers almost all the wineries, including the islands, from mass-market to micro, with very reliable ratings (though coverage is only up to 2000); also fascinating features on grape varieties, traditional retsina-making, and even how Greeks were instrumental in introducing vines to the New World. Pricey but worth it.

Language

Dictionary (UK only) is palm-sized but exactly the same in contents – the best purse or day-pack choice.

Oxford Greek–English, English–Greek Learner's Dictionary. If you're planning a prolonged stay, this pricey, hard-bound, two-volume set is unbeatable for usage and vocabulary. There's also a more portable one-volume *Learner's Pocket Dictionary*.

Dialects and minority languages

If the lack of any standard Greek were not enough, Greece still offers a rich field of linguistic diversity, both in its regional dialects and minority languages. Island **dialects** are alive and well in many a remote area, and some of them are quite incomprehensible to outsiders (which can mean inhabitants of the next island). The dialect of Lésvos is a particularly strong Aegean dialect, which owes much to migration from more southerly islands and influences from Asia Minor respectively. The dialect of Sámos and that of adjacent Híos are completely different from one another, Híos being considered a more pure "Ionian" (and this thousands of years after the Ionians arrived from the mainland), while the rough "Samian" variant owes much to the diverse origins of its settlers. On Rhodes and Kós there is a dwindling Turkish-speaking population, probably not in excess of 3500 persons as of writing.

The Greek alphabet: transliteration and accentuation

On top of the usual difficulties of learning a new language, Greek presents the additional problem of an entirely separate **alphabet**. Despite initial appearances, this is in practice fairly easily mastered – a skill that will help enormously if you are going to get around independently. In addition, certain combinations of letters have unexpected results. This book's transliteration system should help you make intelligible noises, but you have to remember that the correct **stress** (marked throughout the book with an acute accent or sometimes dieresis) is crucial. With the right sounds but the wrong stress people will either fail to understand you, or else understand something quite different from what you intended – there are numerous pairs of words with the same spelling and phonemes, distinguished only by their stress.

The **dieresis** is used in Greek over the second of two adjacent vowels to change the pronunciation that you would expect from the table on opposite; often in this book it can function as the primary stress. In the word *kaïki* (caïque), the presence of the dieresis changes the pronunciation from "cake-key" to "ka-ee-key" and additionally the middle "i" carries the primary stress. In the word *païdhákia* (lamb chops), the dieresis again changes the sound of the first syllable from "pay" to "pah-ee", but in this case the primary stress is on the third syllable. It is also, uniquely among Greek accents, used on capital letters in signs and personal-name spellings in Greece, and we have followed this practice on our maps.

Set out opposite is the Greek alphabet, the system of transliteration used in this book, and a brief aid to pronunciation.

Greek	Transliteration	Pronounced
Α, α	a	a as in father
Β, β	v	v as in vet
Γ, γ	y/g	y as in yes except before consonants or a, o or ou when it's a breathy g, approximately as in gap
Δ, δ	dh	th as in then
Ε, ε	e	e as in get
Ζ, ζ	z	z sound
Η, η	i	i as in ski
Θ, θ	th	th as in theme
Ι, ι	i	i as in ski
Κ, κ	k	k sound
Λ, λ	l	l sound
Μ, μ	m	m sound
Ν, ν	n	n sound
Ξ, ξ	x	x sound, never z
Ο, ο	o	o as in toad
Π, π	p	p sound
Ρ, ρ	r	r sound
Σ, σ, ς	s	s sound, except z before m or g; single sigma has the same phonic value as double sigma
Τ, τ	t	t sound
Υ, υ	y	y as in barely
Φ, φ	f	f sound
Χ, χ	h before vowels, kh before consonants	harsh h sound, like ch in loch
Ψ, ψ	ps	ps as in lips
Ω, ω	o	o as in toad, indistinguishable from o

Combinations and diphthongs

Greek	Transliteration	Pronounced
ΑΙ, αι	e	e as in hey
ΑΥ, αυ	av/af	av or af depending on following consonant
ΕΙ, ει	i	long i, exactly like ι or η
ΕΥ, ευ	ev/ef	ev or ef, depending on following consonant
ΟΙ, οι	i	long i, exactly like ι or η
ΟΥ, ου	ou	ou as in tourist
ΓΓ, γγ	ng	ng as in angle; always medial
ΓΚ, γκ	g/ng	g as in goat at the beginning of a word, ng in the middle
ΜΠ, μπ	b/mb	b at the beginning of a word, mb in the middle
ΝΤ, ντ	d/nd	d at the beginning of a word, nd in the middle
ΤΣ, τσ	ts	ts as in hits
ΤΖ, τζ	tz	dg as in judge, j as in jam in some dialects

Greek words and phrases

Essentials

Né	Yes	Edhó	Here
Málista	Certainly	Ekí	There
Óhi	No	Aftó	This one
Parakaló	Please	Ekíno	That one
Endáxi	OK, agreed	Kaló	Good
Efharistó (polý)	Thank you (very much)	Kakó	Bad
(Dhén) Katalavéno	I (don't) understand	Megálo	Big
Parakaló, mípos	Excuse me	Mikró	Small
Miláte angliká?	Do you speak English?	Perisótero	More
Signómi	Sorry/excuse me	Ligótero	Less
Símera	Today	Lígo	A little
Ávrio	Tomorrow	Polý	A lot
Khthés	Yesterday	Ftinó	Cheap
Tóra	Now	Akrivó	Expensive
Argótera	Later	Zestó	Hot
Anikhtó	Open	Krýo	Cold
Klistó	Closed	Mazí (mé)	With (together)
Méra	Day	Horís	Without
Níkhta	Night	Grígora	Quickly
Tó proï	In the morning	Sigá	Slowly
Tó apóyevma	In the afternoon	Kýrios/Kyría	Mr/Mrs
Tó vrádhi	In the evening	Dhespinís	Miss

Other needs

Trógo/píno	To eat/drink	Trápeza	Bank
Foúrnos/ psomádhiko	Bakery	Leftá/Khrímata	Money
Farmakío	Pharmacy	Toualéta	Toilet
Tahydhromío	Post office	Astynomía	Police
Gramatósima	Stamps	Yiatrós	Doctor
Venzinádhiko	Petrol station	Nosokomío	Hospital

Requests and questions

To ask a question, it's simplest – though hardly elegant – to start with *parakaló*, then name the thing you want in an interrogative tone.

Parakaló, o foúrnos? - Where is the bakery?

Parakaló, ó dhrómos yiá . . . ? - Can you show me the road to . . . ?

Parakaló, éna dhomátio yiá dhýo átoma - We'd like a room for two people

Parakaló, éna kiló portokália? - May I have a kilo of oranges?

Poú? - Where?

Pós? - How?

Póssi, Pósses? or Póssa? - How many?

Póso? - How much?

Póte? - When?

Yiatí? - Why?

Sé tí óra . . . ? - At what time . . . ?

Tí íne/Pió íne ... ? - What is/Which is . . . ?
Póso káni? - How much (does it cost)?

Tí óra aníyi? - What time does it open?
Tí óra klíni? - What time does it close?

Talking to people

Greek makes the distinction between the informal (*essý*) and formal (*essís*) second person, as French does with *tu* and *vous*. Young people, older people and country people often use *essý* even with total strangers, though if you greet someone familiarly and they respond formally, it's best to adopt their usage as the conversation continues, to avoid offence. By far the most common greeting, on meeting and parting, is *yiá sou/yiá sas* – literally "health to you". Incidentally, as across most of the Mediterranean, the approaching party utters the first greeting, not those seated at sidewalk *kafenío* tables or doorsteps – thus the silent staring as you enter a village.

Hérete - Hello

Kalí méra - Good morning

Kalí spéra - Good evening

Kalí níkhta - Good night

Adío - Goodbye

Kaló taxídhi - Bon voyage

Tí kánis/Tí kánete? - How are you?

Kalá íme - I'm fine

Ké essís? - And you?

Pós se léne? - What's your name?

Mé léne . . . - My name is . . .

Parakaló, miláte pió sigá - Speak slower, please

Pós léyete stá Elliniká? - How do you say it in Greek?

Dhén xéro - I don't know

Thá sé dhó ávrio - See you tomorrow

Kalí andhámosi - See you soon

Páme - Let's go

Parakaló, ná mé voithíste - Please help me

Greeks' Greek

There are numerous words and phrases which you will hear constantly, even if you rarely have the chance to use them. These are a few of the most common.

Éla! - Come! (literally) but also Speak to me! You don't say!, etc.

Oríste! - Literally, "Indicate!"; in effect, "What can I do for you?"

Embrós! or Léyete! - Standard phone responses

Tí néa? - What's new?

Tí yínete? - What's going on (here)?

Étsi k'étsi - So-so

Ópa! - Whoops! Watch it!

Po-po-po! - Expression of dismay or concern, like French "*O là là!*"

Pedhí moú - My boy/girl, sonny, friend, etc.

Maláka(s) - Literally "wanker", but often used (don't try it!) as an informal term of address

Sigá sigá - Take your time, slow down

Accommodation

Xenodhohío - Hotel

Xenón(as) - Inn

Éna dhomátio . . . - A room . . .

yiá éna/dhýo/tría átoma - for one/two/three people

yiá mía/dhýo/trís vradhiés - for one/two/three nights

mé dhipló kreváti - with a double bed

mé loutró - with en-suite bath

Zestó neró - Hot water

Krýo neró - Cold water

Klimatismós - Air conditioning

Anamistíra - Fan

Boró ná tó dhó? - Can I see it?

Boroúme na váloume ti skiní edhó? - Can we camp here?

Kámping/Kataskínosi - Campsite

Skiní - Tent

Aeropláno	Aeroplane	Póssa hiliómetra?	How many kilometres?
Leoforío, púlman	Bus, coach		
Aftokínito, amáxi	Car	Pósses óres?	How many hours?
Mihanáki, papáki	Motorbike, scooter	Poú pás?	Where are you going?
Taxí	Taxi	Páo stó . . .	I'm going to . . .
Plío/vapóri/karávi	Ship	Thélo ná katévo stó . . .	I want to get off at . . .
Tahýplio	High-speed ferry, catamaran	O dhrómos yiá . . .	The road to . . .
Dhelfíni	Hydrofoil	Kondá	Near
Podhílato	Bicycle	Makriá	Far
Otostóp	Hitching	Aristerá	Left
Mé tá pódhia	On foot	Dhexiá	Right
Monopáti	Trail	Katefthía, ísia	Straight ahead
Praktorío leoforíon, KTEL	Bus station	Éna isitírio yiá . . .	A ticket to . . .
Stássi	Bus stop	Éna isitírio mé epistrofí	A return ticket
Limáni	Harbour	Paralía	Beach
Ti óra févyi?	What time does it leave?	Spiliá	Cave
Ti óra ftháni?	What time does it arrive?	Kéndro	Centre (of town)
		Eklissía	Church
		Thálassa	Sea

Numbers

énas/éna/mía	1	triánda	30
dhýo	2	saránda	40
trís/tría	3	penínda	50
tésseres/téssera	4	exínda	60
pénde	5	evdhomínda	70
éxi	6	ogdhónda	80
eftá	7	enenínda	90
okhtó	8	ekató	100
ennéa (or more demotic, enyá)	9	ekatón penínda	150
dhéka	10	dhiakóssies/ dhiakóssia	200
éndheka	11	pendakóssies/ pendakóssia	500
dhódheka	12		
dhekatrís	13	hílies/hília	1000
dhekatésseres	14	dhýo hiliádhes	2000
íkossi	20	éna ekatomírio	1,000,000
íkossi éna (all compounds written separately thus)	21	próto	first
		dhéftero	second
		tríto	third

Days of the week and the time

Kyriakí	Sunday	Tésseres pará íkossi	Twenty minutes to four
Dheftéra	Monday		
Tríti	Tuesday	Eftá ké pénde	Five minutes past seven
Tetárti	Wednesday		
Pémpti	Thursday	Éndheka ké misí	Half past eleven
Paraskeví	Friday		
Sávato	Saturday	Sé misí óra	In half an hour
Tí óra íne?	What time is it?		
Mía íy óra, dhýo íy óra/trís íy óra	One/two/three o'clock	S'éna tétarto	In a quarter-hour
		Sé dhýo óres	In two hours

Months and seasons

NB You may see *katharévoussa*, or hybrid, forms of the months written on schedules or street signs; these are the spoken demotic forms.

Yennáris	January	Ávgoustos	August
Fleváris	February	Septémvris	September
Mártis	March	Októvrios	October
Aprílis	April	Noémvris	November
Maïos	May	Dhekémvris	December
Ioúnios	June	Therinó dhromolóyio	Summer schedule
Ioúlios	July	Himerinó dhromolóyio	Winter schedule

A food and drink glossary

Basics

Aláti	Salt	Záhari	Sugar
Avgá	Eggs	Neró	Water
(Horís) ládhi	(Without) oil	Psári(a)	Fish
Hortofágos	Vegetarian	Psomí	Bread
Katálogos/Lísta	Menu	Olikís	Wholemeal bread
O logariasmós	The bill	Sikalísio	Rye bread
Kréas	Meat	Thalassiná	Seafood (non-fish)
Lahaniká	Vegetables		
Froúta	Fruit	Tyrí	Cheese
Méli	Honey	Yiaoúrti	Yoghurt

Cooking terms

Akhnistó	Steamed	Kondosoúvli	Any spit-roasted beast, whole or in chunks
Frikasé	A stew, either lamb, goat or pork, made with celery		
		Kourkoúti	Egg-and-flour batter
Iliókafto	Sun-dried	Makaronádha	Any spaghetti/ pasta-based dish

537

Pastó	Marinated in salt	Stó foúrno	Baked
Psitó	Roasted	Tiganitó	Pan-fried
Saganáki	Cheese-based red sauce; also any fried cheese	Tís óras	Grilled/fried to order
		Yakhní	Stewed in oil and tomato sauce
Skáras	Grilled	Yemistá	Stuffed (squid, vegetables, etc)
Sti soúvla	Spit-roasted		

Soups and starters

Avgolémono	Egg and lemon soup	Melitzanosaláta	Aubergine/eggplant dip
Bouréki, bourekákia	Courgette/zucchini, potato and cheese pie	Pipéria florínis	Marinated red sweet Macedonian peppers
Dolmádhes, yaprákia	Vine leaves stuffed with rice, sometimes mince too		
		Pittaroúdhia	Egg, flour, courgette and herb frittata
Fasoládha	Bean soup	Rengosaláta	Herring salad
Giouzlemés	Fried, cheese-stuffed crêpe; Lésvos only	Revythokeftédhes	Chickpea (garbanzo) patties
Hortópita	Turnover or pie stuffed with wild greens	Skordhaliá	Garlic dip, for certain fish/fried vegetables
Kápari	Pickled caper leaves	Taramosaláta	Cod roe pâté
Kopanistí khtypití	Pungent, fermented cheese purée	Tyrokafterí	Cheese dip with chilli added, different from kopanistí
Krítamo	Rock samphire	Tzatzíki	Yogurt, garlic and cucumber dip
Lahanodolmádhes	Rice-and-meat-stuffed cabbage leaves	Tzirosaláta	Cured and flaked mackerel dip
Mavromátika	Black-eyed peas		

Vegetables and vegetable-based dishes

Ambelofásola	Crimp-pod runner beans, late summer	Fasolákia	French (green) beans
		Fasóles	Small white beans, usually in sauce
Angin
áres	Artichokes	Fáva	Purée of yellow peas, served with onion and lemon
Angináres ala políta	Artichokes cooked with carrots and potatoes		
		Frésko kremýdhi	Spring onions
Angoúri	Cucumber	Horiátiki (saláta)	Greek salad (with olives, fétta etc)
Ánitho	Dill		
Bámies	Okra, ladies' fingers	Hórta	Greens (usually wild), steamed
Bouréki, bourekákia	Courgette/zucchini, potato and cheese pie	Kolokythákia	Courgette/zucchini
		Koukiá	Broad fava beans; fresh in spring, dried otherwise
Briám	Ratatouille		
Domátes	Tomatoes		
Fakés	Lentils	Maroúli	Lettuce

Melitzána	Aubergine/eggplant	Rýzi/Piláfi	Rice (usually with *sáltsa* – sauce)
Melitzánes imám	Aubergines baked with oil, onions, garlic, tomatoes, abundant olive oil	Rókka	Rocket greens
		Saláta	Salad
		Spanáki	Spinach
Patátes	Potatoes	Vlíta	Notchweed – another common *hórta*
Pipéria	Peppers		
Pligoúri/pinigoúri	Bulgur wheat	Yígandes	White haricot beans, large
Radhíkia	Wild chicory – a common *hórta*		

Fish and seafood

Varieties recommended for taste, value or dependable freshness are marked with an ★ in the lists that follow. This cites the most commonly offered fish species, in Greek alphabetical order, with English translation, their preferred method of preparation (this depends greatly on typical fish size and fat content), seasonal/local particularities, and other warnings. For more on individual species and what can be done with them, look no further than Alan Davidson's *Mediterranean Seafood* (see p.526).

Scaly fish

*Atherína (Sand smelt) Fried whole with flour and onions as *begotó*, a favourite *ouzerí* snack; east Aegean speciality

Bakaliáros (Hake, also cod) Fried in slices, served with *skordhaliá*; fresh specimens rare, usually dried Icelandic

*Ballás (Large-eyed dentex) Reddish, medium-sized; grilled

*Barboúni (Red mullet) Fried, sometimes grilled; famous smoky flavour, but fiddly to clean

Galéos (Hound shark, dogfish) Fried in slices, served with *skordhaliá*; fatty

Yermanós (Leatherback) Bony and tough-skinned, bland but pleasant white flesh; fried only. Found on Rhodes and surrounding islands, spring

*Gávros (Anchovy) Fried whole, late summer, suprisingly mild-flavoured; east Aegean speciality

*Glóssa (Sole) Lightly sautéed; mild flavour, springtime

Gópa (Bogue) Fried whole; very common

*Zargána (Garfish, saury) Small ones fried, big ones baked in sauce; east Aegean, autumn

*Kefalás (Axillary bream) Grilled, late summer to autumn, often on Ikaría

Kéfalos (Grey mullet) Grilled; rich, but a scavenger, thus rarely offered

Koliós (Chub mackerel) Baked in tomato sauce, also grilled; rich

*Koutsomoúra (Goatfish) Fried; same taste as *barboúni* but far cheaper

*Lakérdha (White-fleshed bonito) Marinated; expensive treat, meant as an *ouzerí* starter, not a main

*Lavráki (Sea bass) Baked or grilled; gourmet fare, but usually farmed

Lithríni (Red bream, pandora) Large bones, but tasty grilled

Loútsos, sfinoúra (Barracuda) Baked or grilled; usually caught May; heavy, mackerel-like flesh

Mayátiko (Amberjack) Bony, so best in soup, or baked; southern Dodecanese; spring to early summer

*Melanoúri (Saddled bream) Grilled; springtime; good value

Ménoula (Sprat) Larger than *marídha*; often fried, but also marinated on Kárpathos

*Mourmoúra (Striped bream) Grilled; not really a true bream, but quite tasty

Marídha (Picarel) Fried whole; common snack fish

Xifías (Swordfish) Baked, grilled; main season Feb–June

Palamídha (Bonito) Grilled; autumn fish

*Pandelís, sykiós (Corvina) Grilled; east Aegean native; flavour similar to *lavráki*

Pérka (Painted comber) Fried in batter; often frozen and rubbery, not esteemed

Peskandrítsa, spehandrítsa in some dialects (Monkfish) Usually fried, to its detriment; grilled by those who know; autumn

Rofós (Grouper) Unmistakably huge; cut into slices for grilling; texture like shark, but much tastier – like monkfish

*Salouvárdhos Similar to *pandelís*; small, sweet, white-fleshed fish

Sálpa (Salema) Explicitly not recommended; insipid, only for catfood

*Sardhélles (Sardines) Grilled, wonderful east Aegean speciality

Sargós (White bream) Grilled; good value

*Sfirídha, stýra (White grouper) Better than *rofós*, less bony, though richly fatty

*Skáros (Parrotfish) Fried or (less good) grilled; rather bony but exquisitely flavoured white flesh; needs to be cooked uncleaned; available much of the year but especially Aug/Sept

*Skathári (Black bream) Grilled; the succulent king of the breams, most frequent in spring and on Foúrni; males are dark black; females larger, grey and preferable

*Skorpína (Scorpion fish) Excellent for grills, as well as a classic *kakaviá* (bouillabaisse) ingredient; meaty white flesh, the equal of monkfish

Skoumbrí (Atlantic mackerel) Baked in sauce; *estiatório* staple

Spáros (Annular or two-banded bream) Grilled or in soup

Savrídhi (Horse mackerel) Fried whole; *ouzerí* food

*Synagrídha (Dentex) Baked in sauce; delicious

Tónnos (Tuna) Grilled or baked; light-fleshed variety much more satisfactory; autumn season

*Tsipoúra (Gilt-head bream) Grilled; gourmet fare when wild, but usually farmed

*Fangrí (Common bream, red porgy) Grilled; white, firm flesh

Hánnos (Comber) Fried or in soup; bony but flavourful

*Hióna (Kind of white bream) Excellent grilled, smoky flavour; may be the same as *psilomýtis* and *mytáki*

*Khristópsaro (John Dory) Baked, or in soup; rich white flesh, small bones

Other seafood

NB Species indicated with ** must be eaten alive to avoid poisoning. If they flinch when you drizzle lemon juice on them, they're alive.

Ahiní (Sea urchin) Raw; only the very briny orange roe eaten as *ahinosaláta*; increasingly scarce and expensive

*Astakós (Aegean lobster) Steamed, baked or flaked into pasta as *astakomakaraonádha*; gourmet fare; closed season Sept 1–Jan 1

Vátos, platý, seláhi (Ray, skate) Wings fried in slices, or steamed and shredded to be served with *skordhaliá*, or as soup

Garidhákia (Miniature shrimps) Steamed whole, served in oil/lemon dressing; found on Rhodes, Hálki, Sými, Kastellórizo; unmistakably sweet when fresh

*Garídhes (Shrimp, prawns) Preparation as for *garidhákia*, or stewed in sauce if big enough

**Yialisterés (Smooth Venus) Similar to *kydhónia*; typical seafood *ouzerí* fare

*Thrápsalo (Giant squid) Excellent grilled

Kalamária, kalamarákia (Small squid) Lightly fried; overcooking toughens

Kalógnomes (Noah's-Ark shell) Larger than *mýdhia*; steamed, served on Kálymnos

Karavídhes (Crayfish) Steamed or grilled; mostly carapace

**Kydhónia (Cockles, also Warty Venus) Raw or lightly steamed whilst alive; a delicacy despite the bizarre alternate name

Mýdhia (Mussels) Steamed, or in *saganáki* sauce

*(O)khtapódhi (Octopus) Grilled, stewed in wine; only tentacles used

**Petalídhes (Limpets) Served live; *ouzerí* snack in spring or autumn

**Pínna (Fan-shell flesh) Served raw; another *ouzerí* snack, especially on Sými

*Soupiés (Cuttlefish) Grilled, or stuffed and baked; also cut up and cooked with their ink in rice and greens

Spiniálo, spinóalo (Pickled *foúskes* – see below)

*Strídhia (Oysters) Raised in beds near Kálymnos, also wild-gathered near Rhodes; served raw; round, not lady's-slipper shape as elsewhere

*Hokhlí (Sea snails) On Kastellórizo, served steamed in the shell; discard membrane and extract flesh with a pin (provided)

*Hokhlióalo (Sea snails) Extracted from shells, blanched, salted, served in oil and vinegar on Sými

*Foúskes (*Violet* in French, *uovo de mare* in Italian) Scooped fresh out of unprepossessing husk, these are lovely and far superior to those marinated in own liquor; most common on Rhodes and Kálymnos, Sept/Oct; locals recommend that you eat no more than five at a time

Meat and meat-based dishes

Arní	Lamb
Bekrí mezé	Pork chunks in spicy red sauce, like Cypriot *afélia*
Biftéki	Mince patty
Brizóla	Pork or veal chop
Hirinó	Pork (meat)
Keftédhes	Meatballs, with egg and breadcrumbs as binder
Kokorétsi	Liver/offal roulade, spit-roasted
Kopsídha	(Lamb) shoulder chops
Kotópoulo	Chicken
Kounélli	Rabbit
Loukánika	Spicy homemade sausages
Moskhári	Veal
Moussakás	Aubergine, potato and lamb-mince casserole with bechamel topping
Ortíkia	Quail
Païdhákia	Rib chops, lamb or goat
Pansétta	Much thicker than Italian kind – more like spare rib
Papoutsákia	Meat-stuffed aubergine/eggplant "shoes"; like *moussakás* without bechamel
Pastítsio	Macaroni "pie" baked with minced meat
Pastourmás	Cured, highly spiced meat; traditionally camel, nowadays beef
Patsás	Tripe soup
Psaronéfri	Medallion of pork fillet
Salingária	Garden snails
Soutzoukákia	Minced meat rissoles/beef patties
Spetzofáï	Sausage and pepper red-sauce stew
Stifádho	Meat stew with tomato and boiling onions
Sykóti	Liver
T: Tiganiá	Pork chunks fried with onions in oil or butter
Tziyéro sarmás	Lamb's liver in cabbage leaves
Youvétsi	Baked clay casserole of meat and *kritharáki* (short pasta, same as *orzo*)

Sweets and desserts

Baklavás	Honey and nut pastry
Bougátsa	Salt or sweet cream pie served warm with sugar and cinnamon
Galaktobóureko	Custard pie
Halvás	Sweetmeat of sesame or semolina
Karydhópita	Walnut cake
Kréma	Custard
Loukoumádhes	Dough fritters in honey syrup, cinnamon and sesame seeds

Moustalevriá	Grape-must pudding	Ravaní	Spongecake, lightly syruped
Pagotó	Ice cream		
Pastélli	Sesame and honey bar	Ryzógalo	Rice pudding

Fruit and nuts

Akhládhia	Big pears	Lemónia	Lemons
Aktinídha	Kiwis	Míla	Apples
Fistíkia	Pistachio nuts	Pepóni	Melon (honeydew/ Persian)
Fráoules	Strawberries		
Himoniátiko	Autumn (casava) melon	Portokália	Oranges
		Rodhákina	Summer peaches
Karpoúzi	Watermelon	Sýka	Figs
Kerásia	Cherries	Stafýlia	Grapes
Krystália	Miniature pears	Vanílies	Plums
Kydhóni	Quince	Yiarmádhes	Autumn peaches

Cheese

Ayeladhinó	Cow's-milk cheese	Krasotýri	Wine-marinated Kós cheese
Fétta	Salty, white cheese		
Graviéra	Gruyère-type hard cheese	Ladhotýri	Lésvos "oil" cheese – best grilled
Kalatháki	Cylindrical, semi-soft Límnos sheep's cheese	Mastéllo	Grilling cheese of Híos, similar to Cypriot halloúmi; cow/goat
Katsikísio	Goat cheese		
Kasséri	Medium-sharp cheese	Myzíthra	Sweet cream cheese
		Própvio	Sheep cheese

Drinks

Alisfakiá	Island sage tea	kókkino/mávro	red
Býra	Beer	rozé/kokkinélli	rosé
Boukáli	Bottle	Lemonádha	Lemonade
Gála	Milk	Metalikó neró	Mineral water
Galakakáo	Chocolate milk	Portokaládha	Orangeade
Gazóza	Generic fizzy drink	Potíri	Glass
Kafés	Coffee	Stinyássas!	Cheers!
Krasí	Wine	Tsáï	Tea
áspro	white		

Ancient architecture and history glossary

ACROPOLIS Ancient, fortified hilltop.

AGORA Market and meeting place of an ancient Greek city.

AMPHORA Tall, narrow-necked jar for oil or wine.

APSE Polygonal or curved recess at the altar end of a church.

ARCHAIC PERIOD Late Iron Age period, from around 750 BC to the start of the Classical period in the fifth century BC.

ARCHITRAVE Horizontal masonry atop temple columns; same as ENTABLATURE (cf).

ATRIUM Open, inner courtyard of a Roman-era house.

BASILICA Originally colonnaded, early Christian "hall"-type church adapted from Roman models, found at several sites in the Dodecanese and east Aegean.

BOULEUTERION Auditorium for meetings of an ancient town's deliberative council.

BYZANTINE EMPIRE The empire created by the division of the Roman Empire in 395 AD; this, the eastern half, was ruled from Constantinople (modern Istanbul). Sámos, Rhodes, Híos, Kós and Lésvos were all important members of the Aegean *theme* or province.

CAPITAL The flared top, often ornamented, of a column.

CAVEA Seating curve of an ancient theatre.

CELLA Sacred room of a temple, housing the cult image.

CLASSICAL PERIOD Essentially from the end of the Persian Wars in the fifth century BC until the unification of Greece under Philip II of Macedon (338 BC).

CONCH Concave semi-dome surmounting a church apse, often frescoed.

CORINTHIAN Decorative columns, festooned with acanthus florets; a temple built in this order.

DORIAN Northern (Balkan?) civilization that displaced and succeeded the Myceneans and Minoans through most of Greece around 1100 BC.

DORIC Minimalist columns with little ornament, dating from the Dorian period; a temple built in this order.

DRUM Cylindrical or faceted vertical section, usually pierced by an even number of narrow windows, upholding a church cupola.

ENTABLATURE The horizontal linking structure atop the columns of an ancient temple.

EXEDRA Display niche for statuary.

EXONARTHEX The outer west vestibule of a church, when a true NARTHEX (cf) is present.

FORUM Market and meeting place of a Roman-era city.

GEOMETRIC PERIOD Post-Mycenaean Iron Age era named for the style of its pottery; begins in the early eleventh century BC with the arrival of Dorian peoples. By the eighth century BC, with the development of representational styles, it becomes known as the ARCHAIC PERIOD (cf).

HELLENISTIC PERIOD The last and most unified "Greek empire", created in the wake of Alexander the Great's Macedonian empire and finally collapsing with the fall of Corinth to the Romans in 146 BC; thus, "Hellenistic" refers to the art and architecture of this era.

HEROÖN Shrine or sanctuary, usually of a demigod or mortal; war memorials in modern Greece.

IONIC Elaboration of the older Doric decorative order; Ionic temple columns are slimmer with deeper "fluted" edges, spiral-shaped capitals, and ornamental bases. Again, a temple built in this order.

KOUROS Nude Archaic statue of an idealized young man, usually portrayed with one foot slightly forward of the other.

MACEDONIAN EMPIRE Empire created by Philip II in the mid-fourth century BC.

MEGARON Principal hall or throne room of a Mycenean palace.

MINOAN Crete's great Bronze Age Civilization, which dominated the Aegean from about 2500 to 1400 BC.

NAOS The inner sanctum of an ancient temple; also, any Orthodox Christian shrine.

NARTHEX Western vestibule of a church, traditionally for catachumens and the unbaptized; typically frescoed with scenes of the Last Judgment.

NEOLITHIC Earliest era of settlement in Greece, characterized by the use of stone tools and weapons together with basic agriculture. Divided arbitrarily into Early (c.6000 BC), Middle (c.5000 BC) and Late (c.3000 BC).

ODEION Small theatre, used for musical performances, minor dramatic productions, or councils.

PAL(A)ESTRA Gymnasium for athletics and wrestling practice.

PEDIMENT Triangular, sculpted gable below the roof of a temple; *aetoma* in Greek.

PENDENTIVE Any of four triangular sections of vaulting with concave sides, positioned at a corner of a rectangular space to support a circular or polygonal dome; in churches, often adorned with frescoes of the four Evangelists.

PERISTYLE Gallery of columns around a temple or other building.

POLYGONAL MASONRY Wall-building technique of the Classical and Hellenistic period, which used unmortared, closely joined stones; often called "Lesbian polygonal" after the island where the method supposedly originated. The much-(ab)used term "CYCLOPEAN" refers only to Mycenean/Bronze Age mainland sites such as Tiryns and Mycenae.

PROPYLAION Monumental, columned gate-way of an ancient building; often used in the plural, *propylaia*.

SQUINCH Small concavity across a corner of a columnless interior space, supporting a superstructure such as a dome.

STELE Upright stone slab or column, usually inscribed with an edict; also an ancient tombstone, with a relief scene and dedication.

STOA Colonnaded walkway in Classical-era marketplace.

TEMENOS Sacred precinct, often used to refer to the sanctuary itself.

THOLOS Conical or beehive-shaped building, especially a Bronze Age tomb.

Medieval and modern Greek glossary

AGORÁ The commercial "high street" of any village or town.

ÁNO Upper; common prefix element of village names.

ARHONDIKÓ Elaborate mansions of the medieval upper classes, found for example at Hóra, Pátmos and Líndhos, Rhodes.

ASTYKÓ (Intra) city, municipal, local; adjective applied to phone calls and bus services.

ÁYIOS/AYÍA/ÁYII Saint or holy (m/f/plural). Common place-name prefix; abbreviated Ag. or Ay., often spelt AGIOS or AGHIOS.

DHIMARHÍO Town hall.

DHOMÁTIA Rooms for rent in purpose-built blocks.

EPARHÍA Greek Orthodox diocese, also a subdivision of a modern province analagous to an American county.

FROÚRIO Medieval castle; nowadays, usually means a modern military headquarters.

GARSONIÉRA/ES Studio villa/s, self-catering apartment/s.

HAMAM Turkish-style steam bath, dating from the Ottoman era; there is a functioning ones in Ródhos Old Town.

HOKHLÁKI Mosaic of coloured pebbles, found in church or house courtyards in Rhodes and the southern Dodecanese. See also VOTSALOTÓ.

HÓRA Main town of an island or region; literally it means "the place". An island *hóra* is often known by the same name as the island.

ICON Representation of a saint or sacred event painted on a board, an object of veneration and pilgrimage in the Orthodox Church.

IERÓN Literally, "sacred" – the sanctuary between the altar screen and the apse of a church, reserved for priestly activities.

IKONOSTÁSI Screen between the nave of a church and the *ierón*, supporting at least three icons.

IPERASTYKÓ Inter-city, long-distance – as in phone calls and bus services.

KAFENÍO Coffee house or café; in a small village the centre of communal life and possibly serving as the bus stop, too.

KAÏKI (plural KAÏKIA) Caique, or medium-sized boat, traditionally wooden and used for transporting cargo rather than passengers; now refers mainly to island excursion boats.

KALDERÍMI Cobbled mule-tracks and footpaths.

KÁMBOS Fertile agricultural plateau, usually near a river mouth.

KANTÍNA Shack, caravan or even a disused bus on the beach, usually serving just drinks and perhaps sandwiches or quick snacks.

KÁSTRO Any fortified hill (or a castle), but most usually the oldest, highest, walled-in part of an island *hóra*.

KATHOLIKÓN Central church of a monastery.

KÁTO Lower; common prefix element of village names.

KENDRIKÍ PLATÍA Central square.

MELTÉMI North wind that blows across the Aegean in summer, starting softly from near the mainland and hitting the Dodecanese and certain of the east Aegean islands full on.

MONASTIRÁKI "Little monastery": Small, rural church with an outbuilding or two, but uninhabited.

MONÍ Formal term for a monastery or convent.

NÉOS, NÉA, NÉO "New" – a common prefix to a town or village name.

NOMÓS Modern Greek province – there are more than fifty of them.

PALEÓS, PALEÁ, PALEÓ "Old" – again a common prefix in town and village names.

PANAYÍA Virgin Mary.

PANDOKRÁTOR Literally "The Ruler of All"; generally refers to the stern portrayal of Christ in Majesty frescoed or in mosaic in the dome of many Byzantine churches.

PANIYÍRI Festival or feast – the local celebration of a holy day.

PARALÍA Beach or seafront.

PERÍPTERO Street-corner kiosk.

PLATÍA Square, plaza.

PROSKYNITÁRI A roadside shrine (see feature on p.8).

PYLIÓNAS (plural **PYLIÓNES**) Ornate decorated doorways found in Rhodion villages.

PÝRGOS Tower-mansion found on Lésvos or Híos.

SKÁLA The port of an inland island settlement, nowadays often larger and more important than its namesake, but always younger, since built after the disappearance of piracy.

TÁVLI Backgammon; a favourite café pastime, especially among the young. There are two more difficult local variations (*févga* and *plakotó*) in addition to the standard international game (*pórtes*).

TÉMBLON Wooden altar screen of an Orthodox church, usually ornately carved and painted and studded with icons; more or less interchangeable with the IKONOSTÁSI.

VÓLTA Ritualized evening promenade on the seafront of a larger island town; akin to the Italian *corso*.

VOTSALOTÓ More or less synonymous with HOKHLÁKI, but more widely used, and can refer to any pebble-paved surface, whether patterned or not.

Acronyms and initials

DIKKI Democrat Social Movement, a more left-leaning spin-off from PASOK, now defunct.

EAM National Liberation Front, the political force behind ELAS.

ELAS Popular Liberation Army, the main resistance group during World War II and the basis of the Communist army (DSE or "Democratic Army of Greece") during the civil war.

ELTA The postal service.

EOT Ellinikós Organismós Tourismoú, the National Tourist Organization.

KKE Communist Party, unreconstructed.

KTEL National syndicate of bus companies. The term is also used to refer to individual bus stations.

LANE Lasithiakí Anónymi Navtiliakí Etería (Lasithian Shipping Company Ltd).

ND Conservative (Néa Dhimokratía) party.

NEL Navtiliakí Etería Lésvou (Lesvian Shipping Co), which runs many of the east Aegean ferries.

OA Standard abbreviation and international airline code for Olympic Airlines.

OTE Telephone company.

PASOK Socialist Party (Pan-Hellenic Socialist Movement).

Rough
Guides
advertiser

Rough Guides travel...

...music & reference

Rough Guide Maps, printed on waterproof and rip-proof Yupo™ paper, offer an unbeatable combination of practicality, clarity of design and amazing value.

CITY MAPS

Amsterdam · Barcelona · Berlin · Boston · Brussels · Du
Florence & Siena · Frankfurt · London · Los Angeles
Miami · New York · Paris · Prague · Rome
San Francisco · Venice · Washington DC and more...

COUNTRY & REGIONAL MAPS

Andalucía · Argentina · Australia · Baja California · Cu
Cyprus · Dominican Republic · Egypt · Greece
Guatemala & Belize · Ireland · Mexico · Morocco
New Zealand · South Africa · Sri Lanka · Tenerife · Thail
Trinidad & Tobago · Yucatán Peninsula · and more...

US$9.99   Can$13.99   £5.9

Algarve • Amsterdam •
ntigua & Barbuda • Athens • Barbados • Barcelona •
Bruges • Cancún & Cozumel • Costa Brava •
Edinburgh • Florence • Ibiza & Formentera •
isbon • London • Madrid • Mallorca • Malta & Gozo •
Marrakesh & Essaouira • New Orleans •
New York City • Paris • Prague • Rome •
San Francisco • Tenerife & La Gomera •
Venice • Washington DC

US$10.99 · CAN$15.99 · £6.99
www.roughguides.com

small print and

Index

A Rough Guide to Rough Guides

In the summer of 1981, Mark Ellingham, a recent graduate from Bristol University, was travelling round Greece and couldn't find a guidebook that really met his needs. On the one hand there were the student guides, insistent on saving every last cent, and on the other the heavyweight cultural tomes whose authors seemed to have spent more time in a research library than lounging away the afternoon at a taverna or on the beach.

In a bid to avoid getting a job, Mark and a small group of writers set about creating their own guidebook. It was a guide to Greece that aimed to combine a journalistic approach to description with a thoroughly practical approach to travellers' needs – a guide that would incorporate culture, history and contemporary insights with a critical edge, together with up-to-date, value-for-money listings. Back in London, Mark and the team finished their Rough Guide, as they called it, and talked Routledge into publishing the book.

That first *Rough Guide to Greece*, published in 1982, was a student scheme that became a publishing phenomenon. The immediate success of the book – with numerous reprints and a Thomas Cook prize shortlisting – spawned a series that rapidly covered dozens of destinations. Rough Guides had a ready market among low-budget backpackers, but soon also acquired a much broader and older readership that relished Rough Guides' wit and inquisitiveness as much as their enthusiastic, critical approach. Everyone wants value for money, but not at any price.

Rough Guides soon began supplementing the "rougher" information about hostels and low-budget listings with the kind of detail on restaurants and quality hotels that independent-minded visitors on any budget might expect, whether on business in New York or trekking in Thailand.

These days the guides – distributed worldwide by the Penguin group – offer recommendations from shoestring to luxury and cover more than 200 destinations around the globe, including almost every country in the Americas and Europe, more than half of Africa and most of Asia and Australasia. Our ever-growing team of authors and photographers is spread all over the world, particularly in Europe, the USA and Australia.

In 1994, we published the *Rough Guide to World Music* and *Rough Guide to Classical Music*; and a year later the *Rough Guide to the Internet*. All three books have become benchmark titles in their fields – which encouraged us to expand into other areas of publishing, mainly around popular culture. Rough Guides now publish:

- Travel guides to more than 200 worldwide destinations
- Dictionary phrasebooks to 22 major languages
- History guides ranging from Ireland to Islam
- Maps printed on rip-proof and waterproof Polyart™ paper
- Music guides running the gamut from Opera to Elvis
- Restaurant guides to London, New York and San Francisco
- Reference books on topics as diverse as the Weather and Shakespeare
- Sports guides from Formula 1 to Man Utd
- Pop culture books from *Lord of the Rings* to Cult TV
- World Music CDs in association with World Music Network

Visit **www.roughguides.com** to see our latest publications.

Rough Guide credits

Text editor: Fran Sandham, Melissa Graham and Ruth Blackmore
Layout: Ajay Verma
Cartography: Maxine Repath
Picture research: Jj Luck
Proofreader: Nikki Twyman
Editorial: London Martin Dunford, Kate Berens, Claire Saunders, Geoff Howard, Ruth Blackmore, Gavin Thomas, Polly Thomas, Richard Lim, Alison Murchie, Sally Schafer, Karoline Densley, Andy Turner, Ella O'Donnell, Keith Drew, Edward Aves, Andrew Lockett, Joe Staines, Duncan Clark, Peter Buckley, Matthew Milton, Daniel Crewe, Nikki Birrell, Chloë Thomson; **New York** Andrew Rosenberg, Richard Koss, Chris Barsanti, Steven Horak, AnneLise Sorensen, Amy Hegarty
Design & Pictures: London Simon Bracken, Dan May, Diana Jarvis, Mark Thomas, Jj Luck, Harriet Mills, Chloë Roberts; **Delhi** Madhulita Mohapatra, Umesh Aggarwal, Ajay Verma, Jessica Subramanian, Amit Verma
Production: Julia Bovis, Sophie Hewat, Katherine Owers

Cartography: London Maxine Repath, Ed Wright, Katie Lloyd-Jones
Delhi Manish Chandra, Rajesh Chhibber, Jai Prakash Mishra, Ashutosh Bharti, Rajesh Mishra, Animesh Pathak, Jasbir Sandhu, Karobi Gogoi
Online: New York Jennifer Gold, Suzanne Welles, Benjamin Ross; **Delhi** Manik Chauhan, Narender Kumar, Manish Shekhar Jha, Rakesh Kumar, Lalit K. Sharma
Marketing & Publicity: London Richard Trillo, Niki Hanmer, David Wearn, Demelza Dallow; **New York** Geoff Colquitt, Megan Kennedy, Milena Perez; **Delhi:** Reem Khokhar
Custom publishing and foreign rights: Philippa Hopkins
Finance: Gary Singh
Manager India: Punita Singh
Series editor: Mark Ellingham
PA to Managing Director: Megan McIntyre
Managing Director: Kevin Fitzgerald

SMALL PRINT

Publishing information

This fourth edition published July 2005 by
Rough Guides Ltd,
80 Strand, London WC2R 0RL.
345 Hudson St, 4th Floor,
New York, NY 10014, USA.
14 Local Shopping Centre, Panchsheel Park,
New Delhi 110017, India
Distributed by the Penguin Group
Penguin Books Ltd,
80 Strand, London WC2R 0RL
Penguin Putnam, Inc.
375 Hudson Street, NY 10014, USA
Penguin Group (Australia)
250 Camberwell Road, Camberwell
Victoria 3124, Australia
Penguin Books Canada Ltd,
10 Alcorn Avenue, Toronto, Ontario,
Canada M4V 1E4
Penguin Group (New Zealand)
Cnr Rosedale and Airborne Roads
Albany, Auckland, New Zealand

Typeset in Bembo and Helvetica to an original design by Henry Iles.

Printed and bound in China

Marc Dubin © 2005

568pp includes index
A catalogue record for this book is available from the British Library

ISBN 1-84353-472-X

1   3   5   7   9   8   6   4   2

Help us update

We've gone to a lot of effort to ensure that the fourth edition of **The Rough Guide to the Dodecanese and the east Aegean islands** is accurate and up-to-date. However, things change – places get "discovered", opening hours are notoriously fickle, restaurants and rooms raise prices or lower standards. If you feel we've got it wrong or left something out, we'd like to know, and if you can remember the address, the price, the time, the phone number, so much the better.

We'll credit all contributions, and send a copy of the next edition (or any other Rough Guide if you prefer) for the best letters. Everyone who writes to us and isn't already a subscriber will receive a copy of our full-colour thrice-yearly newsletter. Please mark letters: "**Rough Guide Dodecanese Update**" and send to: Rough Guides, 80 Strand, London WC2R 0RL, or Rough Guides, 4th Floor, 345 Hudson St, New York, NY 10014. Or send an email to **mail@roughguides.com**

Have your questions answered and tell others about your trip at
www.roughguides.atinfopop.com

Acknowledgements

The author would like to thank Efi and Spyros Dede, Gerald Brisch, Constance Rivemal and Patrick in Rhodes Town, plus Kim Sjögren and Isabella at Triton Travel; Mihalis Mavrikos in Líndhos; Christine and Alex Sakelaridhes on Hálki; Alf, Roberta, George Niotis and Minas Yiallizis on Kárpathos; Nikos Halkitis, Wendy Wilcox, Adriana Shum and Jean Manship on Sy*mi; David, Lynda, Iain and Lynn on Tílos; Alexis, Ippokratis and Dhionysia Zikas on Kós; Themelina and Andonis Andonoglou on Kálymnos, plus Eleni for the low-down on the museum; Elina Skoutari on Pátmos; Markos Kostalas, Stella Tsakiri, Theodhore and Güher Spordhilis on Híos; George & Barbara Ballis, Theo and Melinda Kosmetos, plus George and Jennifer Yiannakou on Lésvos; Panayiotis and Aphrodite Papasotiriou on Límnos; Dudley der Partogh at Sunvil Travel; the managements of *Marina's Studios* on Tílos, *Hotel Porphyris* on Níssyros, the *Maltezana Beach Hotel* on Astypálea, *Stafylia Beach Hotel* on Rhodes and *Krithoni Paradise* on Léros; editor Ruth Blackmore for creatively fitting in most important bits despite page constraints, plus her usual unflappable patience; and last but not least to my sister and brother-in-law Gail and Michael for safaris to the remotest corners of Ikaría, to Pamela for sharing summer trips to Sámos, Foúrni and Agathoníssi and to Zitsa for travels on Rhodes and Sámos.

Thanks also to Ajay Verma for typesetting, Maxine Repath for maps, Jj Luck for picture research and Nikki Twyman for proofreading.

Readers' letters

Our thanks to readers of the previous edition who sent in comments and suggestions. The roll of honour:

Neil Bailey, Carey Blanden, Judy Branson, Graham & Caroline Brown, Stefan Buczacki, Claire Cunningham, Paul Gardner, Claire Goedman and Jeroen Bottema, Alistair Grant, Mike & Ruth Hall, Kurt Jewkes, Debbie Marshall, Steve Pomeroy, Mabel Richmond, G. Smith, Mr & Mrs H. Sparling, Joe Swan, Ian M. Taylor, Debbie Marshall

Photo credits

SMALL PRINT

Index

Map entries are in colour.

INDEX

563

INDEX

Map symbols

maps are listed in the full index using coloured text

INDEX **I**

═══	Paved road	🦌	Waterfall
───	Dirt road	♛	Castle
-----	Footpath	∴	Archeological site
▓▓▓	Pedestrianized street	🕯	Lighthouse
─ ─	Ferry route	✝	Church (regional maps)
▬▬▬	National border	♙	Monastery
── ──	Chapter division boundary	♖	Mosque
───	River	✡	Synagogue
♦	Point of interest	ⓘ	Information office
✕	Airport	✉	Post office
Ⓗ	Heli-pad	Ⓣ	Taxi rank
★	Bus stop	▪▪▪▪	Wall
🅿	Parking	▬	Building
⚠	Campsite	⊞	Church (town maps)
▲	Mountain peak	⁺₊⁺	Cemetery
◔	Crater	▨	Park
✲	Viewpoint	≈	Marsh
⌒	Cave	∴∴	Beach
⩕	Hot spring, potable spring		